A
BIOGRAPHICAL DICTIONARY
OF THE SUDAN

A BIOGRAPHICAL DICTIONARY OF THE SUDAN

RICHARD HILL

THE SECOND EDITION
of
A Biographical Dictionary of the Anglo-Egyptian Sudan

FRANK CASS & CO. LTD.
1967

First published in 1951 by the Clarendon Press, Oxford
as '*A Biographical Dictionary of the Anglo-Egyptian Sudan*'

Published by
FRANK CASS AND COMPANY LIMITED
67 Great Russell Street, London W.C.1

First edition 1951
Second edition 1967

Printed in Great Britain by
Thomas Nelson (Printers) Ltd., London and Edinburgh

PREFACE
TO THE SECOND EDITION

Since the publication of the first edition of this book in 1951 two works, both outstanding, have added their small contribution to the biography of the Sudan: the second edition of Khair al-Dīn al-Zuruklī's great biographical dictionary, *al-A'lām* (10 vols, Cairo, 1954–59), and W. R. Dawson's laconic *Who was Who in Egyptology* (London, 1951). Other general biographies contain brief lives of Sudanese worthies, works such as Muḥammad Sulaimān, *Suwar min al-buṭūla* (Khartoum [?1956]), and Salāḥ al-Dīn Maḥjūb, *Lamaḥāt min ta'rīkh al-Sūdān* (Cairo [ ]). *Shakhṣiyāt min al-Sūdān*, by Yaḥyā Muḥammad 'Abd al-Qādir (3 vols, Khartoum, 1954–56), like all *Who's Whos* which record the living, is understandably wanting in critical comment. 'Abduh Badawī's *Shakhṣiyāt Ifrīqiyā* (Cairo [?1960]), published by the Ministry of Public Guidance of the United Arab Republic, includes a number of short biographies of selected Sudanese including personalities as disparate as Muḥammad Aḥmad b. 'Abd Allāh al-Mahdi and Rābiḥ Faḍl Allāh.

In specialized biography the emphasis is still on the literary and away from the technological. Poets take pride of place, politicians are almost, engineers are quite, unnoticed. Following on Muḥammad 'Abd al-Raḥīm's *Nafathāt al-yarā': al-adab, al-ta'rīkh wa'l-ijtima'*, vol. 1 (Khartoum, [?1944]) came a study of quality on Sudanese poetry and poets, Aḥmad abū Sa'd, *al-Sh'ir wa'l-shu'arā' fī'l-Sūdān, 1900–1958* (Beirut, 1959). The recent explosive entry of women into the public life of the Sudan has not gone unrecorded. *Adībāt al-Sūdān*, by Munīr Ṣāliḥ 'Abd al-Qādir (Cairo, 1960), is a modest pantheon of literary ladies and poetesses headed by Mihaira bint 'Abūd, the Shā'iqīya heroine in the Sudanese resistance to the Turk.

There have been all too few full-scale biographies of individual persons and families. Two, both of *'ulamā'*, are noteworthy: 'Abd al-Maḥmūd Nūr al-Dā'im's manuscript life of Shaikh Aḥmad al-Ṭaiyib wad al-Bashīr was printed as *Azāhir al-riyāḍ fī manāqib al-'ārif bi'llāh al-Shaikh Aḥmad al-Ṭaiyib* (Khartoum, 1954), and

Muḥammad b. 'Abd al-Majīd al-Sarrāj's lives of prominent members of the religious family, Āl'Īsā al-Anṣārī, *Irs͟hād al-sārī li tarājim Āl 'Īsā b. Bus͟hāra al-Anṣārī* (Khartoum, 1955). A patriot of 1924, 'Ali 'Abd al-Laṭīf, has been commemorated by Muḥammad Ḥasan 'Awaḍ's *Qiṣṣat kifāḥ al-baṭal 'Alī 'Abd al-Laṭīf* (Cairo, 1955) which adds little to what we already know from Muḥammad 'Abd al-Raḥīm's *al-Ṣirā' al-musallaḥ 'alā al-waḥida fī'l-Sūdān au al-ḥiqā'iq 'an hawādit͟h 1924* (Cairo [ ]). Recent autobiography includes the life of an educational reformer, Babikr Badrī, *Ta'rīk͟h ḥayātī* ed. Yūsuf Badrī (3 vols, Khartoum, 1959–61); of an elder statesman, al-Dardīrī Muḥammad 'Ut͟hmān, *Mud͟hakkirātī . . . 1914–1958* (Khartoum, 1961) and finally the diverting adventures of Aḥmad Ḥasan Maṭar, *Ṣad͟diq au lā tuṣaddiq wa lākin mud͟hakkirāt mug͟hamarāt awwal sā'iḥ sūdānī 'ālamī t͟halāt͟hūn 'āmān ḥawl al-'ālam* (Khartoum, [?1959]), jauntily englished as *Memoirs of a Sudanese* (Khartoum, [?1962]).

The record must remain defective while the Sudan, though she has printing presses, still lacks publishers in the sense understood in much of the world outside. Little books are born by the dozen without imprint, without date, even without title page. They circulate for a brief season and die without trace. Until this year the Sudan had no law compelling the deposit of copies of newly printed books in the national library, the University Library of Khartoum. In the writing of biography the Sudan is poised on the edge of change as the old annalists, invaluable in their day for the biographical material which they garnered, give way to young historians trained in the scientific examination of biographical evidence. Meanwhile, in the biographical half-light stands a sure beacon in the form of a classified list of works in Arabic (as far as they can be traced) over the whole field of Sudanese studies, published between 1874 and 1961, prepared by the University Library of Khartoum.

Some of the corrections and additions to the present edition of *A Biographical Dictionary of the Sudan* come not however from books but from the experience and memories of friends. These I thank with all my heart.

School of Oriental Studies,
University of Durham. 23rd June, 1966.

PREFACE
TO THE FIRST EDITION

This dictionary contains over 1,900 short notices of people who have died before 1948 and who have contributed, each after his fashion, to the story of the Sudan. The term Sudan, as used here, includes the present Anglo-Egyptian Sudan and the former Egyptian possessions in the region of the Great Lakes and on the Red Sea coast.

The telling of the deeds of ancestors comes naturally to a people nurtured in Islam and ever harking back to a heroic tribal and nomadic past. But the tribal story-teller had no leaning towards the cold precision of the shorter biographical collections of the modern West. He rarely descended to the bathos of dates or weakened his stories by too much objectivity. His prose and verse were to the glory of great men; his tales were for recitation, not for reading out of books.

The foundation of modern biography in the Sudan is the Arabic manuscript called *Ṭabaqāt wad Ḍaif Allāh*, written about 1805 by Muḥammad al-Nūr wad Ḍaif Allāh and consisting of an account of the lives of Islamic saints in the sultanate of Sennar. Two editions, one by Ibrāhīm Ṣādiq, the other by Sulaimān Dā'ūd Mandīl, were both published in Cairo in 1930. There is a partial translation into English, with introduction and notes, by Sir H. A. MacMichael in his *History of the Arabs in the Sudan* (1922). More recent biographical collections, mostly contemporary, are contained in a small book, *Muḥāḍara 'an al-'arūba fī'l-Sūdān* (Khartoum [1937]), by Muḥammad 'Abd al-Raḥīm, and in a larger volume, *al-Sūdān baina 'ahdain* (Cairo [1937]), by Sa'd Mīkhā'īl. The first author is a Sudanese, the second an Egyptian of long service in the Sudan. It is still a long road to a full, authoritative dictionary of Sudanese biography, and that will be a task for the Sudanese and for them alone.

The present dictionary is no more than a stop-gap, and its scope is different. It is not a dictionary of national biography in the accepted sense, for, while it mentions persons who would not be admitted to the usual national biography, it omits others who would assuredly have been included had there existed the necessary minimum of biographical information concerning them. It is, therefore, rather as a record of the human contribution to Sudan history that it must seek its justification.

There are omissions in plenty. The lack of interest of the older generations of Sudanese in chronology and the comparatively recent, and still haphazard, compulsory registration of births and deaths in the Sudan, account for the incomplete state of many notices. Nor had the other inhabitants of the Ottoman Empire represented in Sudan history either the means or the inclination to preserve biographical statistics, though here and there the piety of descendants has kept alive the memory, if not the dates, of a once-great name.

Foreign biography ignores all but the Worldly Great. Many of the Europeans who played a notable part in the exploration, commerce, and government of the Sudan were men of obscure origin who made their mark, then disappeared into the shades whence they came. Many British subjects noticed here were those whom the caprice of fortune excluded from the *Dictionary of National Biography*. Too often a deceased Sudan Government official has been relegated to a biographical limbo. For, after the finance department has struck him off the Pensions List and the public works department has provided him with a standard gravestone, little remains in his official dossier save controversy with the Auditor-General over the forage allowance for his donkey.

To have restricted this biography to persons domiciled in the Sudan would have necessitated the omission of a large number of those of foreign birth whose contribution to the history of the Sudan has been profound. References have been made to persons who, of little abiding importance in themselves, have nevertheless in their lifetime been the object of contemporary interest. Also included are some whose part in the work of the Sudan was small, but who went on to win fame in the world outside; and certain geographers and others who, although they may never have set foot in the Sudan, nevertheless advanced the world's knowledge of the country.

The length of a notice has been determined not so much by the relative importance of the person noticed as by the amount of information available. More than one 'life' has had to be excluded from sheer lack of ascertainable fact. Of others, particularly minor German and Austrian figures, the information exists but awaits the intellectual recovery of Europe to be made available.

Ancient Egyptian and Nubian names generally appear in their hitherto current spellings. Readers requiring more exact renderings are recommended to consult such sources as Dows Dunham and M. F. L. Macadam, 'Names and relationships of the Royal Family of Napata', *Journal of Egyptian Archaeology*, xxxv, 1949.

The transliteration of Arabic names into Roman characters presents some difficulty. The Sudan Government gives its official sanction to two variant systems and uses half a dozen deviations. I have, therefore, resorted to one of the more internationally accepted systems which is already standard for much historical work. I have used this system also for the transliteration of Turkish words on the ground that the modern Turkish script contains forms with which Western European and Sudanese readers are not familiar. Wherever local usage permits I have rendered Turkish personal names in their arabicized forms. At the same time most Ottoman court, military, and naval designations are given in their Turkish, not their arabicized, forms since the latter are less familiar to Western ears. Thus binbā<u>sh</u>ī, not bikbā<u>sh</u>ī; mīrālai, not amīr al-alai. Exceptionally the Arabic soldiers' slang liwā' for amīr al-liwā' has been preferred in the more recent notices. It is impossible to render these and other ranks in strict European equivalents since the value of ranks varies in different periods and in different places. To assist the reader in mastering these variations a glossary of designations is added below.

In the transliteration of Arabic place-names I have followed the somewhat fluid practice of the Sudan Surveys except where local versions do excessive violence to the original Arabic or depart too far from the general system of transliteration used for personal names.

No attempt has been made to standardize the use of the Arabic words walad, wad, and ibn (son [of]), and their inclusion or omission has been influenced by local usage in each case. In placing names in alphabetical order they, like abū (father [of]) and bint (daughter [of]), have been ignored unless they precede a name. Each name is alphabetically placed in its popular acceptation, thus the conventional Muḥammad al-Ḥājj Aḥmad will be found instead of the more correct Muḥammad Aḥmad, even though al-Ḥājj is no part of the name.

A question mark against the year of birth or of death indicates that the date given is insufficiently established.

The limitations of space have prevented any detailed citation of sources for statements made in the text. For the same reason only the briefest record has been made of works published by persons noticed in this dictionary.

As there are omissions so there are certainly errors. The frequent conflict of evidence as to dates and genealogies must inevitably have caused some inaccuracies. Readers would be doing me a kindness in bringing them to my notice.

I thank the Principal and Council of Gordon Memorial College, Khartoum, for leisure and funds for the travel which the study of Sudan biography compels, and the Sudan Government for allowing me the fullest access to its archives and for the grant of a subsidy for printing a dictionary which is not even remotely an official publication. And to those several hundred collaborators, Sudanese and foreign, official and private, whose help has gone into the making of this book, I record my gratitude.

A
BIOGRAPHICAL DICTIONARY
OF THE SUDAN

A star placed against a notice in the text indicates that an addition or correction to it will be found at the end of the book

GLOSSARY OF RANKS, TITLES, AND OTHER DESIGNATIONS

TERMS derived from or through the Arabic language are followed by the abbreviation (Arab.); those derived from or through the Turkish language are followed by the abbreviation (Turk.).

ABŪ (Arab.). Father [of], e.g. Muḥammad abū Aḥmad, i.e. Muḥammad, son of Aḥmad's father.

AGHĀ (Turk.). Honorary title for military and naval officers in general. In a narrower sense accorded to officers below those bearing the title of BEY, and occasionally to tribal notables during the Egyptian occupation of the Sudan. Its use declined after the creation of the regular army, *al-niẓām al-jadīd*, by Muḥammad 'Alī Pasha (1821–4) and the contemporary Tanẓīmāt reforms in the Ottoman army, and is now extinct in the Sudan except where it is retained as a hereditary family name.

'AJĪB (Arab.). Lit. wonderful. Title of honour used in the Funj sultanate of Sennar.

ALAI (Turk.). Infantry regiment. MĪRĀLAI, see MĪR.

'ĀLIM, plural 'ULAMĀ' (Arab.). One learned, especially in the Islamic religion. In the plural used of a bench or panel of Islamic religious notables.

* 'ĀMIL (Arab.). Term used by the Mahdists of an AMĪR charged with the governing of a territory or with a mission to collect taxes.

AMĪN (Arab.). One entrusted with a duty or office. AMĪN al-RUBA', commander of a division of the Mahdist army consisting of a variable number of men averaging 500. AMĪN (or AMĪR) al-RAIYA, commander of four RUBA'. AMĪN BAIT al-MĀL, official in charge of the central treasury and warehouse at Omdurman in the Mahdist Government; also used of the heads of the Mahdist provincial treasury-warehouses.

AMĪR (Arab.). See MĪR.

ARBĀB. Senior dignitary, high functionary, title conferred by the sultans of Sennar and used also in Abyssinia. Its derivation is uncertain and is possibly from the Arabic RABB, a lord.

ARNĀVŪṬ, ARNĀBŪṬ (Turk.), ARNĀ'ŪṬ (Arab.). Albanian, ALBĀNĪ (Arab.) also, but rarely, used.

BAIRĀQDĀR (Turk.). Ensign in Muḥammad 'Alī Pasha's regular army.

BĀSH-BŪGH (Turco-Bulgarian hybrid word). Commander-in-chief.

* BĀSHĪ (Turk.). Head, commander, thus: YŪZBĀSHĪ, lit. commander of a hundred [men], the equivalent of captain. See also BINBĀSHĪ, BULŪK. BĀSHĪ-BŪZUQ (or BUZŪQ, Turk.). Literally crack-brained. Irregular troops, mostly of Albanians, Circassians, and Kurds, though used loosely in the Sudan of the Mughārba and Shā'iqīya irregulars.

* Bey (Turk.), Bik (Arab.). Civil and military title immediately below that of Pasha. In the regular army from the time of Muḥammad 'Alī Pasha it was automatically bestowed on holders of the rank of Mīrālai (bey of the fifth grade) and later of Qā'immaqām (bey of the sixth grade). Beylerbeyi, lit. bey of beys, was used in the combination Rumeli-Beylerbeyisi, a grade of Pasha above that of Mīrmīrān, accorded rarely to governors-general of the Egyptian Sudan. The position of Bey in an Arabic name is movable, thus: Muḥammad Bey Aḥmad or Muḥammad Aḥmad Bey.

Binbāshī (Turk. from old Turkish Biñbāshī, colloquially rendered in Egypt and the Sudan as Bimbāshī), Bikbāshī (Arab.). Lit. commander of a thousand [men], i.e. battalion commander in the Egyptian regular army created by Muḥammad 'Alī Pasha. The responsibilities of the rank in the Sudan Defence Force are now approximately those of senior major.

Bulūk (Turk.). A company. Bulūk Amīn, quartermaster. Bulūk-Bāshī, troop-commander of Bāshī-Būzuq (irregular cavalry).

Caliph. See Khalīfa.

Daftardār (Arab.). Intendant of finance, keeper of the register of lands, the key to taxation.

Dalīl-Bāshī (Arab. + Bāshī). Lit. chief of guides. Officer of irregular military formations.

Dimlig (plural Dimālig). A word of uncertain origin widely used in Dār Fūr, among both Arab and non-Arab tribes, of a tribal shaikh.

Dīvān (Turk.), Dīwān (Arab.). A council. Dīvān Efendīsi (Turk.), Dīwān Effendī (Arab.), a secretary to a commander or governor.

Dragoman, correctly Tarjumān (Arab.). Lit. interpreter, properly used of an oriental secretary to an ambassador or consul. Popularly used (but not in this dictionary) of persons who, for gain, conduct tourists to antiquities, brothels, &c.

* Efendī (Turk.), Effendī (Arab.), from the Greek αὐθέντης. In general, Mister, Mr. Up to the time of the Khedive Ismā'īl Pasha, and even later, an honorary appellation given to members of learned professions (including religion and Islamic law) and sparingly accorded. Now used of, and by, all literate Arabic-speaking persons, other than tribal notables, the lowest-rated artisans, and those engaged in the profession of Islamic law and religion. The term, used vocatively, shows a tendency in Egypt and the Sudan to give place to Ustādh, lit. professor, in certain professional callings.

Faqī (Arab., commonly Fakī in the Sudan). One who teaches Islam, an Islamic holy man.

Farīq (Arab.). General of division, roughly equivalent to both lieutenant-general and major-general.

Firqa (Arab.). A division of the army. In the Sudan used also of the suite of a tribal chief.

Ḥājj (Arab.). One who has made the pilgrimage to the holy places of Arabia.

Ḥākim (Arab.). Governor, ruler. Khuṭṭ-Ḥākimi (Turk.), Ḥākim al-Khuṭṭ (Arab.), officer in charge of a subdivision of a province in the Egyptian Sudan. Ḥākimdār is now used in the Sudan of an officer in command of a garrison, police post, guard, &c., and of a ganger-foreman on the Sudan railways. See Nāẓir.

Ḥānim (Turk.). Lady, Mrs.

Ḥukumdār, Ḥikimdār (Arab.). Lit. commissioner. Applied to governors-general of the Sudan, 1835–85, though towards the end of this period they tended to be styled Ḥukumdār ʿUmūm. Since 1899 the designation has been Ḥākim ʿĀmm.

Ibn (Arab.). Son [of], thus: Muḥammad ibn Aḥmad, i.e. Muḥammad the son of Aḥmad; Muḥammad ibn Aḥmad ibn Mūsā, i.e. Muḥammad the son of Aḥmad and the grandson of Mūsā.

Idāra (Arab.). Lit. organization. Used in the Egyptian provinces of Dār Fūr and Equatoria of a territorial subdivision corresponding elsewhere in the Sudan to the qism. Used in the Eastern Camel Corps of the Sudan Defence Force for a composite company of camelry and infantry.

Imām (Arab.). Originally a leader. In Islamic theology the leader of the Muslims, e.g. the Caliph. For acceptance as Imām in this sense certain personal and hereditary qualifications are essential. Muḥammad Aḥmad al-Mahdī was, and is, accorded the title of Imām by his followers. The title is also used of the founders of the four orthodox schools of Islamic law, of certain mosque officials, and of Islamic chaplains to the forces.

Jarkas, Sharkas (Arab.), Charkas (Turk.). Circassian.

Kāshif (Arab.). Lit. uncoverer, revealer. General title of officers holding ranks roughly equivalent to the modern field rank who were engaged, or competent to be engaged, in administrative duties concerned with the collection of taxes. Used in Egypt and the Sudan in the time of Muḥammad ʿAlī Pasha of officers in charge of districts within a province. The use of the term in the Sudan in this sense has not been traced after 1862.

Khalīfa (Arab.), Caliph and variants in most European languages. Lit. successor, regent. Title of the supreme head of the Muslim community. In the Mahdist movement in the Sudan Muḥammad Aḥmad al-Mahdī, following the precedent of the Prophet, chose four caliphs of whom the Khalīfa ʿAbd Allāhi Muḥammad Tūrshain was appointed his successor. The title is also used in Islamic religious brotherhoods in the Sudan of the delegate or spiritual legatee of the founder of the brotherhood.

Khedive (from the Persian Khedīv through the Turkish), Khidīwī (Arab.). Title used informally by the Wālī of Egypt since about 1850, but officially recognized by the Porte and conferred on Ismāʿīl Pasha and his heirs by firman of 7 July 1867. The intention of the Porte was to confer a status higher than that of Wālī while avoiding any attribution of sovereign rights.

Khuṭṭ (Arab.). Administrative subdivision of a province. See also Ḥākim.

Kinj (Turk.). Lit. a youth, i.e. junior.

Kuchūk (Turk.). Lit. small, i.e. junior.

Kurdī (Arab.). Kurd.

KURJĪ (Arab.). Georgian.

LIVĀ (Turk.), LIWĀ' (Arab.). Lit. a flag, hence a brigade. MĪRLIVĀ, MĪRLIWĀ', see MĪR.

MAHDĪ (Arab.). Lit. the [divinely] guided one. A popular Muslim conception—not wholly sanctioned by orthodox Sunnite theologians—of an ultimate deliverer and restorer of Islam, who must be descended from the family of the Prophet and who will govern the temporal Muslim powers.

MALIK (Arab.). King, style assumed by the rulers of Egypt in place of SULṬĀN since 15 March 1922. MAK, which may be an abbreviation of MALIK or possibly a derivation from a Meroïtic word, is used in the Sudan of a tribal kinglet. In Western Dār Fūr MALIK is a small chieftain while in Northern Dār Fūr the title is reserved for a chieftain of importance.

MAMLŪK (Arab.). Mameluke; soldier, usually, but not necessarily, of some white race and of slave origin.

MA'MŪR (Arab.). Lit. ordered. Used in the Sudan of a governor of a province from the beginning of Egyptian rule till 1833. Now a civilian administrative assistant to a district commissioner. MA'MŪR BŪLĪS, police officer of equivalent rank to YŪZBĀSHĪ. See also MUDĪR.

MANJIL, MĀNJILAK, MĀNJILUK. Title conferred on, or used by, a limited number of chieftains subject to the sultans of Sennar, and still in use by the Hāmaj chieftains of Gulé in the valley of the Blue Nile. The word is said to be of Hāmaj origin.

MĪR (Persian), from AMĪR (Arab.). A commander, prince. MĪR occurs in the Egyptian regular army from the time of the creation of the *niẓām al-jadīd* (1821–4) in MĪRĀLAI (Turk.), AMĪR al-ALAI (Arab.), officer commanding a regiment, roughly equivalent to junior brigadier or senior colonel; and in MĪRLIVĀ (Turk.), AMĪR al-LIWĀ' (Arab.), latterly abbreviated to LIWĀ', officer commanding a brigade, roughly equivalent to junior major-general or brigadier. MĪRMĪRĀN, the lowest grade of pasha, was that usually, and afterwards automatically, conferred on a MĪRLIVĀ, and was rendered into Arabic as AMĪR al-UMARĀ'. A senior military commander under Muḥammad Aḥmad al-Mahdī, and subsequently under his temporal successor, the Khalīfa 'Abd Allāhi, was given the title of AMĪR, and the few most important that of AMĪR al-UMARĀ'. A senior Mahdist AMĪR holding an independent command was AMĪR [or AMĪN] al-RAIYA, lit. a flag amir. The Mahdist military vocabulary was adopted by 'Alī Dīnār Zakarīyā, sultan of Dār Fūr (1899–1916).

* MU'ALLIM (Arab.). Lit. a teacher. Accountant, usually in the Egyptian Sudan a Copt, exceptionally an Armenian or Jew. The term is no longer used in the financial sense.

MU'ĀWIN (Arab.). Assistant in general, civil or military. The military rank of MU'ĀWIN, which was immediately below that of BINBĀSHĪ, was suppressed in the Egyptian army in 1880 and merged with that of ṢĀGH QŌL AGHĀSI. In the earlier years of the present Sudan Government MU'ĀWIN 'ARAB denoted an official agent or intermediary between the Government and the local tribes, later superseded (except in the Red

Sea hills) by the MA'MŪR and local administration. The term MU'ĀWIN was used locally in Dār Fūr from 1917 to about 1930 for MA'MŪR. Otherwise the term survives in the Sudan only in the police in which it is the lowest commissioned rank and is equivalent to MULĀZIM II. MU'ĀWIN al-IDĀRA, administrative officer in the Egyptian régime, in charge of the administrative services at a province headquarters and virtually assistant governor.

MUDĪR (Arab.). Governor, manager, in general. Governor of a province of the Sudan since 1833 replacing the term MA'MŪR in this meaning; commissioner of the Sudan Police. MUDĪR 'UMŪM, title accorded to governors of the more important provinces of the Egyptian Sudan such as Dār Fūr and Equatoria, and of groups of provinces such as the Eastern Sudan.

MUFATTISH (Arab.). Inspector. Since 1899 used of a district commissioner as MUFATTISH MARKAZ.

MUFTĪ (Arab.). Islamic canon lawyer qualified to issue a fatwā, a formal legal opinion. Used in the Sudan of the official head of the Islamic religious notables who is also deputy grand qāḍī.

MUḤĀFIẒ (Arab.). Commissioner, officer commanding troops in a province, or a fortress town, e.g. Sawākin and Muṣawwa', or a territory not sufficiently important or established to be created a province, e.g. the muḥāfiẓate of the White Nile, under the Egyptian régime.

MULĀḤIẒ (Arab.). Superintendent in general. Superintendent of Sudan Police with equivalent rank of BINBĀSHĪ.

MULĀZIM (Arab.). Lieutenant. Used during the Mahdist rule of a member of the bodyguard of the Khalīfa 'Abd Allāhi.

MUNTADAB (Arab.). Representative, agent. Used of the agents in Egypt of the governors-general and provincial governors of the Egyptian Sudan.

MUQADDAM (Arab.). Used of a subordinate officer of the Mahdist army. MAQDŪM (perhaps a variant of MUQADDAM), used in Dār Fūr of a vizier or representative of the Fūr sultans.

MU'TAMAD (Arab.). Commissioner. Used of the commissioner of Port Sudan and of the resident of Dār Maṣālīṭ in Dār Fūr in the present Government.

NĀẒIR (Arab.). Director, manager of an industrial or commercial establishment, head of an Egyptian Government department before the establishment of responsible government. Used in local administration in the Sudan of the head of a tribe or section of a large or widely distributed tribe. NĀẒIR al-KHUṬṬ, notable in charge of a subdivision of an administrative district, usually on a tribal basis. NĀẒIR 'UMŪM in the Sudan is a title, sparingly recognized by the Government, of certain heads of tribal confederations, the title in this connexion being usually traditional and sometimes hereditary. NĀẒIR 'UMŪM has also a regional connotation as a subordinate salaried administrative official in the Jazīra.

PASHA (Turk., of disputed derivation), BĀSHĀ (Arab.). The highest title in the Ottoman and Egyptian court hierarchy. There were four military grades of Pasha: the first was conferred on those of the rank of MUSHĪR (marshal), the second on those of the rank of BIRINJĪ FARĪQ (senior general), the third, that of RUMELI-BEYLERBEYI, on those of the rank of FARĪQ, the fourth, that of MĪRMĪRĀN, on those of the rank of MĪRLIVĀ (AMĪR al-LIWĀ'). In the Egyptian Sudan the recipients were mostly of the fourth, exceptionally of the third, grade. There were also four corresponding civil grades. Muḥammad 'Alī was commonly known as the Pasha of Egypt. Since 1914, when the last vestiges of Ottoman sovereignty over Egypt disappeared, the grade of pasha has been conferred in the Sudan by the rulers of Egypt, although, since 1924, the year of the creation of the Sudan Defence Force, conferment by this source has been limited to the civil grades. The commandant of the Sudan Defence Force and his chief of staff derive their local, temporary, and courtesy titles of pasha from the governor-general of the Sudan by virtue of their military ranks. The position of the title in an Arabic name is movable, thus: Muḥammad Pasha Aḥmad or Muḥammad Aḥmad Pasha. The use of PASHA and BEY by the wives of recipients of these grades, or as a quasi-hereditary title, has no official sanction.

* QĀḌĪ (Arab.). Judge qualified to expound and interpret Islamic law. QĀḌĪ al-QUḌĀA, chief justice in Islamic law in the Sudan, Grand Qāḍī.

QĀ'ID al-'ĀMM (Arab.). Lit. general commanding officer. Used of the commandant of the Sudan Defence Force.

QĀ'IMMAQĀM (Arab.). Used in the Sudan of a junior administrative officer, of an assistant to the KĀSHIF, in the time of Muḥammad 'Alī Pasha, then dropped in this sense after the introduction of the regular army in which QĀ'IMMAQĀM was used of an officer second in command to a MĪRĀLAI with rank roughly the equivalent of a senior lieutenant-colonel or junior colonel. In the Sudan Defence Force the rank approximates more closely to that of lieutenant-colonel.

QAPŪDĀN (Turk.), QABŪDĀN (Arab.), from the Italian capitano, or, possibly, from Turk. qapū + Persian –dān. General term for sea captain. Naval ranks in Muḥammad 'Alī Pasha's European-organized fleet were approximated to existing military ranks as in the Ottoman navy, e.g. binbāshī for captain of a ship of the line, ṣāgh qōl aghāsi for frigate captain, followed by the word al-baḥr (sea) to distinguish the holders from military officers.

QISM (Arab.). Administrative subdivision of a province, branch of a department.

QŪMANDĀN (from the French commandant). Used in the Sudan of an officer (of rank equivalent to QĀ'IMMAQĀM) commanding police in a province.

RĀS MĪYA (Arab.). Lit. head of a hundred men, a minor leader in the Mahdist army.

RET, RETH. King of the Shilluk tribe of the White Nile valley.

ṢĀGH (Turk.). Abbreviation for ṢĀGH QŌL AGHĀSI. In the new regular army of Muḥammad 'Alī Pasha were created the ranks of ṢĀGH QŌL AGHĀSI, lit. commander of the right wing, a junior field officer roughly equivalent to adjutant-major, and SŌL QŌL AGHĀSI, lit. commander of the left wing, who ranked next above a YŪZBĀSHĪ but was junior to a ṢĀGH QŌL AGHĀSI. The general designation for an officer junior to BINBĀSHĪ and senior to YŪZBĀSHĪ was KŌL AGHĀSI. In the Sudan

Defence Force Ṣāgh Qōl Aghāsi (abbreviated to Ṣāgh) is the approximate equivalent of major, while Sōl Qōl Aghāsi (abbreviated to Sōl) is now used in the Sudan Defence Force and Sudan Police of a warrant officer.

* Saiyid (Arab.). Religious title indicating original or inherited sanctity.

Sanjaq (Turk.). Lit. a flag. Sanjaq Beyi, an old rank roughly corresponding to Mīrlivā, suffered a diminution of status; the Bey was dropped in popular usage and Sanjaq, after Muḥammad ʻAlī Pasha's military reforms, was the rank given to the commander of a squadron (or approximate equivalent) of irregular cavalry. The rank of Sanjaq was used in the Shā'iqīya cavalry until the Mahdist revolt and is now extinct.

Shaikh (Arab.). Tribal chief or notable, religious notable whether Muslim or Coptic Christian, member of the profession of Islamic law. Shaikh ʻĀmm, a synonym for Shaikh al-Mashāyikh. Shaikh al-Balad, head of a collection of villages making an administrative unit. Shaikh al-Islām, honorary title popularly and unofficially conferred on the most famous religious notables, e.g. by the hagiographer Wad Ḍaif Allāh on Shaikh Muḥammad ibn Dafaʻ Allāh ibn Muqbal al-ʻArakī. There is no trace in the Sudan of official conferment, the nearest approach to which was the appointment of Shaikh al-Amīn Muḥammad al-Ḍarīr as *ra'īs mumayiz ʻulamā' al-Sūdān* by firman of the Ottoman sultan during the governorship-general of Jaʻfar Pasha Maẓhar (1866–71). Shaikh al-Khuṭṭ, notable in charge of a subdivision of an administrative district, usually of lesser standing and responsibility than a Nāẓir al-Khuṭṭ. Shaikh al-Mashāyikh, senior Shaikh charged with the administration of a large tribe or federation of tribes. The term was introduced in the time of Muḥammad ʻAlī but was discontinued after the Mahdist revolt.

Sharīf (Arab., feminine Sharīfa). Lit. blessed. Title accorded to one descended from the family of the Prophet.

Sharkas. See Jarkas.

Shartai (Fūr language). The approximate equivalent of ʻUmda in the local administration of Dār Fūr and parts of Western Kordofan.

Sirʻaskar (Arab.). Commander-in-chief.

Sirdār (Arab.). Used of commander-in-chief of the Egyptian army.

Sirr Tujjār (Arab.). Senior merchant chosen to represent the merchants of a town or trade.

Sirsūwārī (Arab.). Commander of a regiment of irregular cavalry, roughly equivalent to colonel.

Sōl, Sōl Qōl Aghāsi. See Ṣāgh.

Sulṭān (Arab.). Muslim sovereign. Style assumed by the rulers of Egypt from 19 December 1914 to the assumption by Sultan Fū'ād of the style of Malik (king) on 15 March 1922. In the Sudan used by the rulers of the Funj and Fūr and by certain lesser chieftains as a traditional and, in general, hereditary title.

Tūm (Arab. from classical Taw'ām). A twin, e.g. Muḥammad Tūm Aḥmad, Muḥammad son of the twin Aḥmad. Tūm is also used in the Sudan as a proper name, generally from a distinguished ancestor who was a twin.

'ULAMĀ'. See 'ĀLIM.

'UMDA (Arab.). Head of an administrative unit comprising a collection of villages or, less commonly, a town not provided with a town council. Generally the equivalent of SHAIKH al-BALAD.

UMM (Arab.). Mother [of].

VĀLĪ (Turk.), WĀLĪ (Arab.). Governor-general of a province of the Ottoman Empire, the official designation of Muḥammad 'Alī Pasha as the ruler deputed by the Ottoman sultan with the governance of Egypt. The term is frequently rendered in this dictionary as viceroy in deference to European convention. The title of VĀLĪ was superseded by that of KHEDĪV by firman of 7 July 1867. The term was never (except by clerical error) used of the governors-general of the Sudan which was administratively a dependency of the VILĀYET (Turk.), WILĀYA (Arab.), of Egypt. Governors of provinces in the Mahdist régime were popularly accorded the title of WĀLĪ.

WALAD (Arab., plural AWLĀD, often abbreviated to WAD.). Son [of], e.g. Muḥammad wad Aḥmad, Muḥammad the son of Aḥmad.

WALĪ (Arab.). Saint, used of certain Islamic religious notables.

WAZĪR (Arab.). Minister of the Egyptian cabinet or head of an Egyptian public administration. Used in the Sudan of the chief minister of a sultan.

YŪZBĀSHĪ (Turk.). Lit. commander of one hundred [men], officer commanding a company of regular troops, of rank equivalent to captain.

A BIOGRAPHICAL DICTIONARY OF THE SUDAN

Abbakr. *See* ABŪ BAKR.

'Abbās I ('Abbās Ḥilmī Pasha, 1813–54), viceroy of Egypt, son of Prince Aḥmad Ṭūsūn Pasha and grandson of the viceroy Muḥammad 'Alī Pasha; he fought under the command of Ibrāhīm Pasha al-Wālī against the Ottoman Empire in the Syrian campaign; in 1848 he succeeded Ibrāhīm as regent on the latter's death and in 1849 was appointed viceroy on the death of Muḥammad 'Alī; a conservative by nature his reign was marked by a reversal of Muḥammad 'Alī's policy of encouraging the influx of Europeans into Egypt and by retrenchment in the expenditure of government which was applied with rigour to the Sudan; the gold mines of Fāzūghlī were closed down and a solitary primary school in Khartoum, founded by the celebrated man of letters, Rifā'a Bey Rāfi' al-Ṭahṭāwī, who had been banished to the Sudan in 1851, was allowed to languish for want of equipment; he began the practice of making frequent changes of governors-general, none of whom during his reign served more than two years each; nevertheless, he left the finances of Egypt in a sound condition; he died at Benha where he is said to have been murdered by two slaves.

'Abbās II ('Abbās Ḥilmī Pasha, 1874–1944), khedive of Egypt; the eldest son of Muḥammad Taufīq Pasha whom he succeeded to the khediviate in 1892, he received a European education and was devoted to the social and economic improvement of Egypt; he showed a lack of discretion at a parade of troops at Wādī Ḥalfā when, during a tour of Upper Egypt and Nubia, 1894, he outspokenly criticized the military efficiency of British officers serving in the Egyptian army; this so-called 'frontier incident' caused the downfall of the Riyāḍ ministry; in the winter of 1901–2 he visited Berber and Khartoum amid public acclamation; while in Khartoum he held a review and opened the new mosque; he again visited the Sudan when he came ashore at Port Sudan to open the port in 1909; while on a visit to Constantinople he was shot at and wounded by an Egyptian student in July 1914; he was deposed in December 1914 on the grounds of his avowed sympathy with the enemies of Britain, and was succeeded by his uncle, Ḥusain Pasha Kāmil; he died in exile in Geneva; for many years he unsuccessfully pressed claims against the British Government for the restitution of his properties sequestered when he was deposed.

'Abbās al-Bāzārlī, called **al-Jundī** (*c.* 1802–*c.* 1840), governor of Berber province, 1832–5 and 1836–8, the exact dates being uncertain; he was by race a Kurd; several foreigners visiting his province, including the Englishmen Captain W. Bourchier, R.N., and G. A. Hoskins, remarked upon his character and hospitality; early in his term of office he had the misfortune to run foul of the ʿAbbādī chieftain, Khalīfa wad al-Ḥājj Muḥammad, an old friend of the Egyptian régime, whose loyalty lessened as time passed; in the end the troops of ʿAbbās killed him for refusing to give up a brigand who had sought his protection; ʿAbbās lost the favour of his subjects who complained to the governor-general of his exactions; ʿAlī Khūrshīd Pasha, the retiring governor-general, seems to have taken no action, but his successor, Aḥmad Pasha abū Widān dismissed him from his governorship about 1838; he died shortly after at Berber; his brother Sulaimān who came from Egypt to take the dead man's family home was killed on the desert road by Baraka, brother of Khalīfa whom ʿAbbās's troops had slain; among ʿAbbās's descendants in the Sudan is Aḥmad Efendi ʿAbbās Aghā, a judge of the civil courts.

ʿAbbās Muḥammad Badr al-ʿUbaid (–1915), Mahdist tribal leader, son of the holy man, Shaikh Muḥammad Badr al-ʿUbaid of Umm Dibbān; he and his brother al-Ṭāhir fought on the Mahdist side in the war in the northern Jazīra, 1884, which culminated in the siege and capture of Khartoum; he afterwards served with the Mahdist forces in Dongola and was present at the battle of the Atbara under the command of the amīr Maḥmūd Aḥmad, 1898; later in the year he went over to the Anglo-Egyptian army on the eve of the battle of Omdurman; Kitchener made him ʿumda of Masallamīya, a post which he held till his death.

ʿAbbās Raḥmat Allāh (–1946), Sudanese notable of Omdurman; a Jaʿlī by tribe he was shaikh of the Jaʿlīyīn of Omdurman; in his youth he saw fighting in the Mahdist revolt and in later years enjoyed a wide reputation for his generosity.

* **ʿAbbās Bey Wahbī** (–1883), mīrālai of the Egyptian army; he commanded the cavalry and artillery in W. Hicks Pasha's army of Kordofan with rank of qā'imaqām and was promoted mīrālai on the field for his energy and zeal; he was killed a few days after in the disastrous battle of Shaikān (Kashgil); his diary (also attributed to ʿAbbās Ḥilmī, muʿāwin of ʿAlā' al-Dīn Pasha) fell into Mahdist hands and was recovered on the battlefield of Omdurman.

Abbate, Onofrio (1824–1915), Italian physician and scientist; born at Palermo he spent his youth in the Kingdom of the Two Sicilies where he became a friend of Francesco Crispi, later prime minister of Italy, and where he wrote a little of medicine and letters; in 1845 he came to Egypt and there entered the State medical service; he followed the Egyptian fleet as chief medical officer during the Crimean war, 1853–5; he was later appointed director of the government hospital, Alexandria, and was for many years doctor to the Khedivial family; in 1856–7 he accompanied the viceroy Muḥammad Saʿīd Pasha to the Sudan as medical attendant, and wrote an account of the journey published in 1858 and sponsored by his old friend Crispi, then a political exile in Paris; he was a founder and president of the Khedivial Geographical Society and the author of scientific treatises on the Sudan; he died at Como in Italy.

ʻAbd Allāh Aghā (*fl.* 1822–40), Sudanese soldier of the *niẓām al-jadīd*, the new regular army formed by the viceroy Muḥammad ʻAlī from Egyptian peasants and Sudanese slaves; he was perhaps the first of the few Sudanese to obtain commissions in this army; enrolled as a private in the 2nd infantry regiment of the line in 1822, he was transferred later to the 1st Guards, promoted sergeant, and, in 1838, commissioned as a mulāzim II; on the disbandment of his regiment after the Syrian war he joined the 1st infantry regiment with the rank of yūzbāshī, his subsequent career is at present unknown.

ʻAbd Allāh Aghā (*fl. c.* 1825–49), another Sudanese soldier, of the same name as the preceding, who served in the *niẓām al-jadīd*; officially described as from Berber (his origin may have been Negro), he was enrolled in the 10th infantry regiment of the line in 1825 or 1826; then, transferring to the 2nd Guards, he received his commission as a mulāzim II in 1838 and was promoted yūzbāshī in 1849.

ʻAbd Allāhi Aḥmad Dinkī (*c.* 1861–1941), commonly called ʻAbd Allāhi Aris; Tunjurāwī notable of Dār Fūr and president of the branch court of Kurma, some forty miles north-west of al-Fāshar.

ʻAbd Allāhi Aḥmad abū Jalaha wad Ibrāhīm (*c.* 1854–1939), Ḥazamī religious notable; born at Abū Ḥarāz, about twenty-seven miles south-west of al-Ubaiyaḍ, where immigrants from Dongola had built many water-wheels and cultivated with success, he studied under the religious shaikhs Muḥammad al-Ṣughaiyar wad al-Amīn in his native village and al-ʻĀlim Ṭaha wad Bashīr at al-Rāhad; the Egyptian Government then appointed him a qāḍī at the tribal seat of Ḥamad Asūsa, nāẓir of the ʻAbd al-ʻĀlī branch of the Ḥawāzma Arabs of Kordofan; he went over to the Mahdist cause on the arrival of the Mahdī from Jabal Qadīr to undertake the siege of al-Ubaiyaḍ in 1882 and was for some time a qāḍī in Dār Fūr under the amīr al-umarāʼ Maḥmūd Aḥmad; transferring his loyalty to the Sudan Government on the collapse of the Mahdist régime he helped in the pacification of the Nuba hills where he lived as qāḍī of Dilling for four years, retiring in 1907; he was later made ʻālim of the Ḥawāzma ʻAbd al-ʻĀlī court.

ʻAbd Allāh ibn Aḥmad ibn Sulaim (or **Salīm**) **al-Aswānī** (*fl.* 969), official and historian of Nubia at the time of the Saracen domination of Egypt; in 969 he headed a political mission to the Sudan on behalf of the Muslim Greek general, Jawhar, and wrote an account of Nubia between the years 975 and 996; in this account he expressed his amazement at the great herds and crops in the Christian kingdoms of ʻAlwa and Maqurra.

ʻAbd Allāh wad ʻAjīb al-Fīl (–1799), shaikh of the ʻAbdullāb tribe and local titular *manjil* or viceroy of the kings of Sennar; his seat was at Ḥalfaiya, having some time before transferred from Qarrī; his rule was distinguished for kindness and consideration for his people; his allegiance to Sennar was nominal for the Blue Sultanate was in a state of dissolution; he was killed in the course of an inter-tribal fight near Ḥalfaiya and was succeeded by Shaikh Nāṣir ibn al-Shaikh al-Amīn who submitted to the conqueror Ismā'īl Pasha who passed through his territory on his way to Sennar in 1821.

'Abd Allāh 'Awad al-Karīm abū Sin (–1923), notable of the Shukrīya Arabs, the son of Aḥmad Pasha 'Awad al-Karīm abū Sin; he was an early adherent to the Mahdist cause and later fought under the command of the amīr Maḥmūd Aḥmad in the battle of the Atbara, 1898; escaping from the defeat he went south and joined the amīr Aḥmad Faḍīl who was campaigning in the region of Gedaref; Aḥmad Faḍīl magnanimously released him from further allegiance to the cause of the Khalīfa 'Abd Allāhi; he thereupon submitted to the Anglo-Egyptian administration and in 1902 was appointed shaikh of the Shukrīya, a post which he held until his death.

'Abd Allāh abū Bakr Taimā' (–*c.* 1910), Mahdist amīr; by birth a member of the Kunjara branch of the Fūr tribe, he was brought up in the region of Gedaref; in the summer of 1885 the amīr al-umarā' 'Uthmān abū Bakr Diqna appointed him to command the assault on Kassala where the Egyptian garrison, though in sore straits, was still holding out; he fought under the command of the amīr Aḥmad Faḍīl Muḥammad during the campaign of 1898 round Gedaref and later at Dakhila on the Blue Nile, after which he surrendered to the Anglo-Egyptian forces; a son, 'Abd Allāh, formerly a yūzbāshī in the Sudan Defence Force, is nāẓir of the Fūr of Gedaref.

'Abd Allāh ibn Dafa' Allāh al-'Arakī (*fl.* 1570), Arab holy man and founder of the Arab tribe of the 'Arakīyīn of the Jazīra who began the tradition of a sound, moderate conservatism, basing mysticism on study and steering a middle course between the ascetics and the antinomians; in his youth he studied the Mālikite teaching under the Rikābī master, Shaikh 'Abd al-Raḥmān ibn Jābir, and later became one of the caliphs of Shaikh Tāj al-Dīn al-Baghdādī, called al-Bahārī, at Wad Sha'īr; he was buried at Abū Ḥarāz.

'Abd Allāh Dūd Banja (–1889), pretender to the throne of Dār Fūr and cousin of the former leader of the Fūr resistance movement, Muḥammad Hārūn al-Rashīd; he claimed the sultanship from 1880 after Hārūn al-Rashīd had been killed by an Egyptian force under al-Nūr Bey Muḥammad 'Anqara; on the collapse of the Egyptian administration in Dār Fūr he continued to resist the Mahdists who succeeded the Egyptians; finally in 1884 he was defeated, taken prisoner, and sent to the Khalīfa 'Abd Allāhi in Omdurman as a captive; the Khalīfa pardoned him and he embraced the Mahdist cause; he was killed while fighting under the amīr Zakī Ṭamal in the battle of Gallabat against the Abyssinians.

* **'Abd Allāh al-Dūma** (–1941), notable of al-Fāshar, shartai, and president of the Simiyāt subsidiary shaikhs' court of the town; he died in Khartoum.

'Abd Allāh wad Ibrāhīm (–1893), Mahdist amīr; by birth a Ja'lī Arab he is said to have attempted to murder Muḥammad Aḥmad al-

Mahdī by shooting him in his sleep during the siege of al-Ubaiyaḍ late in 1882; the story goes that his rifle failed to fire and that the Mahdī forgave him and appointed him an amīr; he subsequently fought under the amīr Ḥamdān abū 'Anja in the war against the Abyssinians in 1887; he was killed in battle against an Italian force near Agordat while fighting under the command of the amīr Aḥmad wad 'Alī wad Aḥmad who was also killed in the battle.

* **'Abd Allāh Jād Allāh** (1872–1922), Kāhlī notable, nāẓir of all the Kawāhla in Kordofan from which post he was dismissed in 1916; he married a daughter of Muḥammad Aḥmad al-Mahdī to whose cause he was devoted.

'Abd Allāh ibn Jahān (*fl.* 830), 'Abbāsid general; in 831 the Beja revolted and he marched against them, defeating them several times, finally making a treaty with Kanūn, their king, who lived at a place called Ḥajar; Kanūn promised to pay tribute, to respect the lives and goods of Muslims, and to refrain from speaking contemptuously of their religion.

'Abd Allāh Jawdat (–1937), Taqalāwī notable, 'umda of Taqalī in the Nuba hills.

'Abd Allāh wad Jammā' (*fl.* 1560), tribal leader of the Qawāsma branch of the Juḥaina Arabs who, in alliance with 'Umāra Dunqas, the first Funj sultan of his line, overran the Christian kingdoms of Soba and Qarrī and helped to found the sultanate of Sennar; he himself was the founder of a succession of hereditary viceroys, each known by the title of *manjil*, with their headquarters first at Qarrī and later, perhaps towards the end of the eighteenth century, at Ḥalfaiyat al-Mulūk; the lands under their guardianship extended from the Sabalūka, or Sixth, Cataract to Arbajī in the Jazīra; his tribal descendants became known as the 'Abdullāb.

'Abd Allāh Muḥammad (*c.* 1821–1911), Egyptian engineer; born in Cairo and educated there, he served for some years in the dockyard at Būlāq; in 1870 he came to the Sudan accompanying the fleet of steamers which navigated the Nile to Khartoum in connexion with the mission of Sir S. W. Baker Pasha to the equatorial regions; he was employed as a foreman in the Khartoum dockyard until the sack of Khartoum by the Mahdists in 1885; he survived the Mahdist revolt unscathed and was employed by the Khalīfa 'Abd Allāhi as chief engineer of steamers; in 1898, on the approach of the Anglo-Egyptian forces, he sabotaged an attempt by the Mahdists to plant a mine in the course of the attacking gunboats; on the setting up of the Condominium Government he was made supervisor in the steamers and boats department, a post which he held till his death.

* **'Abd Allāhi Muḥammad Tūrshain, Khalīfat al-Mahdī** (1846–99), commander of the Mahdist forces and ruler of the Mahdist dominions in the Sudan, 1885–98; he was one of the four sons of a holy man of the tribe of the Ta'ā'isha Baqqāra of Dār Fūr and was born at Turdat in the south-western part of that province; as a young man he is said to have hailed Zubair Bey (afterwards Pasha) as the Mahdī or Expected

One when Zubair conquered Dār Fūr in 1874; on learning of the fame of Muḥammad Aḥmad al-Mahdī he hastened eastwards to join him at Abā island on the White Nile near the site now occupied by Kosti and served him in a humble capacity; the Mahdī recognized his worth and made him his staff officer; in 1881 the Mahdī appointed him one of his four caliphs, naming him after Abū Bakr al-Ṣiddīq and handing him a black flag; along with his chief he retired to Kordofan and there organized a series of crushing victories over the government forces which gave to the Mahdist movement the reputation of invincibility; he fought in the Jazīra and superintended the siege of Khartoum which, after a long resistance, fell in January 1885; on the death of the Mahdī in the following June he assumed the temporal functions of government and from then on he was dictator of an empire which extended from Dār Maḥas to the Upper Nile and from the Red Sea to Dār Fūr; except at Omdurman in 1898, when his power was overthrown, he did not lead his armies in person but remained at Omdurman, his headquarters, and from there organized his forces, leaving operational details to his commanders in the field; his rule was harsh and arbitrary and he bled the country to maintain his large military establishments; nevertheless, his genius for organization showed itself in his system of taxation and in his attempts to maintain workshops and steamers and to manufacture ammunition and coins; he insisted on the strict observance of Islamic law and of the prescribed religious exercises; he was hostile to the religious brotherhoods, suppressing them where the Mahdī had only discountenanced them; but his merciless rule at length roused the opposition of most of the tribes under his sway, though his own Baqqāra whom he pampered remained loyal to him; after the advance of the Anglo-Egyptian army into Dongola in 1896 his prestige suffered in a number of military defeats later accentuated by the incompetent generalship displayed by the amīr al-umarā' Maḥmūd Aḥmad at the battle of the Atbara and culminating in the fateful battle of Omdurman in September 1898; fleeing with a few followers towards the south he, with several of his old companions in arms, was defeated and killed at Umm Dibaikarāt; he was buried on the battlefield which lies a few miles south-east of Tendelti on the Kordofan railway, where his tomb is venerated.

'Abd Allāh Musā'd (–1917), shaikh of the Ḥalāwīyīn, or Ḥalāwīn, Arabs; he was appointed in the early days of the Condominium Government at the request of the tribe in opposition to another claimant named Imām Muḥammad; he was succeeded on his death by his brother al-Amīn Musā'd.

'Abd Allāh Najjār Jalīl al-Dīn (–1935), religious notable, shaikh of the Majadhīb religious brotherhood of al-Dāmar.

'Abd Allāh Pasha Naṣrat (1852–1911), liwā' of the Egyptian army; born of Egyptian stock, he entered the Cairo military school in 1873 and received a commission in 1875; temporarily transferred to the artillery in 1877, he returned to the military school as an instructor; about 1897 he was appointed an engineer staff officer on the Soudan

Military Railway which at that time was extended by the Egyptian army engineers as far as Kerma; in the same capacity he served later on the Red Sea railway and at Khartoum; in 1903 he was promoted qā'imaqām and returned to Egypt in 1904 on appointment to a staff post; in Egypt he was engaged for some time in prospecting for minerals, being promoted liwā' in 1908 when he retired; he died in Cairo.

'Abd Allāhi wad al-Nūr (–1885), Mahdist amīr and tribal leader of the 'Arakīyīn Arabs; he fought in many of the earlier campaigns of Muḥammad Aḥmad al-Mahdī, including the sieges of al-Birka, then a fortified government post, 1882, and of al-Ubaiyaḍ, 1882–3; he was killed in action during the final stage of the siege of Khartoum; he was a brother of Makīn wad al-Nūr, also an amīr, who died of wounds received in the battle of Tushkī (Toski), 1889.

'Abd Allāh Sa'd (–1897), notable of the Ja'līyīn Arabs of Matamma; although the Mahdists appointed him an amīr, he and his brother 'Alī Sa'd and the Ja'līyīn tribesmen under their command were in continual friction with the Baqqārī amīr Ḥamūda Idrīs during the campaign on the northern frontier, 1887–9; finally, on the approach of the Anglo-Egyptian army in 1897, he rose in open revolt against the Mahdist power and was killed at Matamma by the amīr al-umarā' Maḥmūd Aḥmad whom the Khalīfa 'Abd Allāhi had ordered to destroy the rebel Ja'līyīn; in the general massacre most of the inhabitants of the town were killed.

* **'Abd Allāh ibn Sa'd ibn abū Sarḥ** (*c.* 600–*c.* 660), Arab leader of a Muslim army of 20,000 men which unsuccessfully invaded Nubia in 641; appointed governor of Upper Egypt, he again invaded Nubia about 651, destroying the Christian church at Dongola and afterwards making peace with the Nubians.

'Abd Allāh ibn Sanbū (*fl.* 1311), the first recorded Muslim king of Nubia; he succeeded the last Christian king Kerenbes who was captured by the Mamelukes of Egypt; though a nominee of the Mamelukes, he was presently overturned and killed by Kanz al-Dawla, chief of the Banī Kanz tribe settled round Aswān; Kerenbes and Kanz al-Dawla both subsequently ruled a second time.

'Abd Allāh al-Sihainī (–1921), holy man of Nyāla in Dār Fūr; in 1921 he announced himself to be Jesus and proclaimed a holy war; after serious fighting in which several lives were lost, he was captured and hanged.

'Abd Allāh Pasha al-Wānlī (–1865), Kurdish soldier in the Egyptian army; he was governor of the combined provinces of Berber and Dongola, 1859–62, with rank of mīrālai; he was promoted mīrlivā and given command of the irregular troops in the Sudan; he died at Kassala of illness contracted during the siege of the town by mutinous Sudanese soldiers.

'Abd al-'Aẓīm Bey Ḥusain Khalīfa (*c.* 1850–1928), 'Abbādī notable and guerrilla leader, born at Darāw in Upper Egypt the son of

Ḥusain Pasha Khalīfa, governor of Berber, 1869–73 and 1883–4; he commanded a *sanjaq* of ʿAbābda irregulars in the campaign of Lieutenant-General W. Hicks Pasha on the White Nile in 1883, and during the greater part of the Mahdist régime he was engaged in helping to guard the southern frontier of Egypt from Mahdist raids; he succeeded his elder brother Ṣāliḥ Ḥusain Khalīfa on the latter's death in action at Murrāt wells in 1893; seizing the wells he raided to the southward in wide sweeps; he was present at the battle of Abū Ḥamad, 1897, and under Major (afterwards Major-General) E. J. M. Stuart-Wortley commanded an irregular force which advanced up the Nile valley on the east bank to Omdurman; he retired from military service in 1899 and devoted himself to tribal government as nāẓir of the ʿAbābda in the Sudan; he visited England in 1927 and died in Cairo.

ʿAbd al-ʿAzīz Muḥammad Nūr (1882–1940), Maḥasī religious notable who lived during his later life at Wādī Ḥalfā where after 1912 he was chief khalīfa to the head of the Khatmīya brotherhood in the area; he spent his youth in Arqū in Dongola district where at the time of the battle of Omdurman he was studying the Qur'ān under Shaikh Muḥammad Muḥammad Khair; he was later for eight years a pupil of al-Saiyid Maḥjūb al-Mīrghanī at Omdurman; he spent a period in Egypt as guardian of al-Saiyid Ibrāhīm al-Mīrghanī who was studying under his uncle al-Saiyid Muḥammad Sirr al-Khātim al-Mīrghanī; he then settled at Wādī Ḥalfā where he became president of the bench of magistrates.

ʿAbd al-Bāqī ʿAbd al-Wakīl (–1918), Mahdist amīr, a Taʿā'ishī by tribe; he fought in the great battles of the time and, in the preparations made in 1898 to resist the Anglo-Egyptian advance from the north, showed considerable military skill in the building of forts in the Sabalūka gorge and on the river bank at Omdurman; after the battle of Omdurman he fled with the Khalīfa ʿAbd Allāhi and was wounded and taken prisoner in the battle of Umm Dibaikarāt in 1899; he died in Omdurman.

ʿAbd al-Bāqī Muḥammad al-Baḥar (–1946), notable of the Farajīyīn branch of the ʿArakīyīn Arabs of the Jazīra and a member of a distinguished tribal family; he was president of the local administration at Manāqil where he died.

ʿAbd al-Bāqī al-Naiyil, called **al-Walī** (–*c.* 1750), religious teacher whom the Walīya section of the Kawāhla Arabs claim as their ancestor; the hagiographer Muḥammad al-Nūr wad Ḍaif Allāh wrote that he was one of those by whose lives the world profited; he died at Jabal Moya and his tomb, much frequented, is at Umm Qarqūr.

ʿAbd al-Bārī Min Allāh Muḥammad (–*c.* 1830), ʿArakī notable, shaikh of al-Taqanīya where he or his fathers had been given land by the sultans of Sennar; his son, al-Amīn ʿAbd al-Bārī, who succeeded him, was an important man in the Jazīra during the Egyptian rule.

ʿAbd al-Dāfiʿ al-Qandīl ibn Muḥammad ibn Ḥammād al-

Jamū'ī (1689–1767), holy man; born at Ḥalfaiya he was a follower of Shaikh Khūjalī; he taught for fifty-eight years and performed the pilgrimage; he died at Sennar and was buried at Ḥalfaiya.

'Abd al-Ghaffār Ḥasan Khalīfa (1880–1945), son of Ḥasan Bey Khalīfa; he was born at Berber of the Milaikāb section of the 'Abābda tribe; after working as a camel contractor on the construction of the Haiyā–Kassala railway till 1923 he was 'umda of the 'Abābda of the Shendi district to 1930; in 1932 he was appointed superintendent of Sudan Railways dock labourers at Port Sudan, a post which he held till his death.

'Abd al-Ghanī 'Alī Mūsā (1889–1947), contractor; born at Shallāl of Kanzī stock he came to the Sudan as a youth and was employed as a waiter on the Sudan Government Railways; in 1916 he began work as a contractor in a small way at Wādī Ḥalfā; his elder brother, also a contractor at Wādī Ḥalfā, having died in 1921, he took over his brother's business; he built up substantial interests in labour and porterage contracts at Wādī Ḥalfā where he owned property and taxi-cabs; he controlled a road motor-haulage service linking Wādī Ḥalfā and the Dongola district and bought land near Kom Ombo and at Shallāl; he was appointed a magistrate at Wādī Ḥalfā in 1936.

'Abd al-Hādī (*fl.* 1821), shaikh of Jabal Ḥarāza in northern Kordofan on the desert road between al-Dabba and al-Ubaiyaḍ; in 1821 he attempted to ambush the invading Turkish army of Muḥammad Khusraw, the bey daftardār, on its way southward to the conquest of the plains of Kordofan; forewarned, the Turks took another route and the ambush miscarried; he fled to al-Ubaiyaḍ before the Turks arrived at Jabal Ḥarāza but was later captured and, for this and his support of the Maqdūm Musallam, commander of the forces opposed to the Turks, he was sentenced to perpetual slavery; his subsequent fate is unknown.

'Abd al-Hādī Faḍl Allāh (–1938), Shukrī notable, 'umda of Kaira't (Sadārna) near Rufā'a.

'Abd al-Hādī Ṣabr (–1882), Dūlābī notable who enjoyed under the Egyptian régime the title of nāẓir of Khursī, Ṭaiyāra and Sharq al-'Aqaba and mulāḥiẓ of Bāra; an able and influential leader he was, next to Faḍl Allāh wad Sālim Bey al-Kabbāshī, the chief man in northern Kordofan; on the outbreak of the Mahdist movement he adhered to the government and was killed fighting under Yūsuf Pasha Ḥasan al-Shallālī at the battle of Jabal Qadīr.

'Abd al-Ḥalīm Faḍl Muḥammad Faraḥ (1878–1944), Furāwī, born at Karmakol village in the district of al-Dabba; he was appointed 'umda of Jabrīya and in 1926 of Qūshābī.

* **'Abd al-Ḥalīm Musā'd wad al-Hāshimī** (–1889), Mahdist amīr; he fought and was wounded in the battle of Shaikān (Kashgil), 1883, when Lieutenant-General W. Hicks Pasha and his army were destroyed; in

the siege of Khartoum, 1884–5, he took an active part; in 1887 he accompanied his chief, the amīr ʿAbd al-Raḥmān wad al-Najūmī, to Dongola and there helped to organize what was intended to have been an invasion of Egypt; he was killed with wad al-Najūmī at the battle of Tūshkī (Toski); his reputation for bravery on the field stood high.

ʿAbd al-Ḥamīd Bey. *See* Du Couret, Louis.

ʿAbd al-Ḥamīd Bey (–1851), mīrālai of the Egyptian army; he died at al-Ubaiyaḍ while in command of the 1st regular infantry regiment and was replaced by Mīrālai Muqtadar Mudrik.

ʿAbd al-Ḥamīd Muḥammad al-Faḍl (1871–1931), amīr of Zalingei and a member of the former reigning house of Dār Fūr; he was a great-grandson of Muḥammad Faḍl, sultan of Dār Fūr, 1802–39, and the twenty-sixth son of Ibrāhīm Muḥammad, sultan 1873–4; his father was killed by Zubair Pasha Raḥma Manṣūr in 1874, whereupon Dār Fūr came under Egyptian rule; he was sent to Egypt together with his brothers and cousins and there treated with consideration; for some time he studied in the Palace school with the Khedive's sons; on the Anglo-Egyptian reoccupation of the Sudan after the end of the *Mahdīya* he returned and, according to some records, appears to have been a government candidate for the governorship of Dār Fūr; however, along with Ibrāhīm ʿAlī, third son of Sultan Ibrāhīm Muḥammad, another government candidate for the position, he was forestalled by ʿAlī Dīnār who seized power in 1899; he then settled down to farm on the White Nile near Kosti; in 1928 he was appointed Maqdūm of Zalingei and was later given the title of amīr; he proved to be popular and able, and a fully fledged local administration was being established when he died.

ʿAbd al-Jabbār Nūr al-Dā'im (1851–1937), religious notable, son of Shaikh Nūr al-Dā'im wad al-Shaikh al-Ṭaiyib and youngest brother of Shaikh Muḥammad Sharīf Nūr al-Dā'im, one of the teachers of Muḥammad Aḥmad al-Mahdī; by tribe a Jamūʿī he studied Arabic and theology under Shaikh al-Qurashī wad al-Zain; he was born at Wad Ramlī and lived at Tabat.

ʿAbd al-Jalīl Dafaʿ Allāh (1852–1939), Dilaiqābī notable from the central Jazīra near Ḥaṣṣa Ḥaiṣa; he led a retiring life during the Mahdist rule and in 1908 was made ʿumda of Ḥamad.

ʿAbd al-Laṭīf Pasha ʿAbd Allāh (*c.* 1805–1883), governor-general of the Sudan; a Rumelian Turk he was born at Nuṣratlī in the district of Drama and in the course of time entered the Egyptian navy in which he rose to frigate captain; in 1850 he was appointed governor-general of the Sudan in succession to Khālid Pasha Khusraw; he spent most of his period of office in Khartoum, where he fell foul of the European colony over matters of trade; he was recalled in 1852 and was succeeded by Rustum Pasha when the Egyptian Government declared that navigation and commerce on the White Nile would thenceforward be free of government restriction; J. Hamilton, the British traveller, alleged that he had been recalled for misconduct on the complaint of a European merchant whose money he was said to have misappropriated to his own use; he has on the contrary been called uncorrupt, if arbitrary and narrow-minded in his dealings; he suspected most Europeans of being liars and evil-doers; in 1862–3 we find him inspector of dockyards and boats in Būlāq, where he was concerned with the dispatch of four steamers to Khartoum for the use of the governor-general there; in person he was said to have been a handsome, well-mannered man, possessed of a little Italian and a short, brown beard; he is also said to have built a new palace for himself in Khartoum and to have attempted to clean up the capital; he died in Cairo where he had lived for many years in retirement.

'Abd al-Maḥmūd Muḥammad al-Sharīf Nūr al-Dā'im (–1915), religious teacher; he sprang from the Jamū'īya Arabs of Ṭābat in the Jazīra and was the son of Shaikh Muḥammad Sharīf Nūr al-Dā'im, one of the first teachers of Muḥammad Aḥmad al-Mahdī at his *khalwa* at the village called Nūr al-Dā'im on the White Nile near Abā island, the Mahdi's sanctuary; in 1883 he hastened to join the Mahdist cause, in spite of his father's adherence to the government, but grew into disfavour with the Khalīfa 'Abd Allāhi who had him flogged and imprisoned; he was eventually released by the Anglo-Egyptian army which entered Omdurman in 1898, and returned to Ṭābat where he built a mosque and where he died; he was a historian and the author of three histories in manuscript: of the Mahdī, of the Khalīfa 'Abd Allāhi, and of the famous pupils of al-Saiyid Aḥmad al-Ṭaiyib wad al-Bashīr; his memory is perpetuated by a large, unfinished tomb; he was succeeded as head of the Sammānīya brotherhood in the Sudan by his cousin, Shaikh Qarīb Allah abū Ṣāliḥ al-Ṭaiyib (d. 1936).

'Abd al-Maḥmūd al-Nūfalābī (*c.* 1650–*c.* 1710), holy man of 'Arakī Arab stock; born at al-Kūbya he attained great fame in his teaching; he was a contemporary of Shaikh Khūjalī ibn 'Abd al-Raḥman ibn Ibrāhīm whose daughter he married.

'Abd al-Mājid Naṣr al-Dīn abū' l-Kailak (–1885), Mahdist amīr; a Mīrafābī, son of the last mak of Berber he was a mu'āwin on the staff of Ḥusain Pasha Khalīfa, governor of Berber; in 1884 on the capitulation of Berber to the Mahdists he joined their cause and was made an amīr; he commanded a Mahdist force opposed to Major-General W. Earle's river column in the Nile campaign of 1885 and was killed in the battle of Jinnis (Giniss); Aiyūbé 'Abd al-Mājid, present head of Berber local administration, is his son.

'Abd al-Masīḥ Tādrus Nākhla (–1933), Coptic commercial notable of Omdurman and a magistrate, the son of Tādrus Bey Nākhla, a leading financial official under Gordon Pasha during the siege of Khartoum.

'Abd al-Mun'im Aḥmad Salāma (–1935), Egyptian holy man, a member of the Tījānīya religious brotherhood; he came to the Sudan during the Egyptian régime and in Khartoum concealed his membership of the brotherhood on account of its unpopularity with the government; he died, a very old man, at Umm Sa'dūn near Bāra.

'Abd al-Mun'im Muḥammad (1896–1946), Sudanese business man and benefactor; born in Omdurman he entered business in 1912 and later went into partnership with his cousin, Yūnus Aḥmad, under the name of Yūnus Aḥmad and 'Abd al-Mun'im Muḥammad, an important firm of importers and exporters of which he became manager; he was a founder and one-time manager of the Printing and Publishing Company, Limited, of Khartoum, publishers of *al-Nīl* newspaper, and was a large contractor to the Sudan Government and the proprietor of a glass factory in Omdurman; on the death of his partner Yūnus Aḥmad in 1923 he became associated with his relative Ḥasanain abū 'l-'Ilā; he was one of the first to join the Sudan Graduates' Congress and in one of its earlier sessions was a member of the Congress committee; he was a great benefactor and at his death left considerable sums to charity.

'Abd al-Mut'āl Aḥmad al-Idrīsī (*c.* 1790–1878), leader of the Aḥmadīya or Idrīsīya religious brotherhood in the Sudan, son of Aḥmad ibn Idrīs al-Fāsī (1760–1837), founder of the brotherhood; as a young man he followed al-Saiyid Muḥammad 'Uthmān al-Mīrghanī I from Dongola to Bāra in 1817 and at first joined the Mīrghanīya brotherhood, but later adhered to the tenets of the Idrīsīya; he died at Dongola where a conspicuous tomb was built over his grave; al-Saiyid Muḥammad 'Abd al-Mut'āl Aḥmad al-Idrīsī, the fighting saint of 'Asīr, was his son.

'Abd al-Qādir I (*c.* 1500–43), sultan of the Funj and the son of 'Umāra Dūnqas, founder of the sultanate of Sennar, whom he succeeded in 1534; little is known of him save that he was a pious Muslim and that he successfully besieged the people of Jabal Moya and Jabal Saqadī; on his death his brother Naiyil reigned in his stead.

'Abd al-Qādir II (–1604), sultan of the Funj; he followed Ūnsā and was succeeded by 'Adlān wad Aya, reigning from 1598 until his deposition in 1604, when he fled from Sennar to Chelga in Abyssinia; during his reign he sent an unsuccessful expedition into Abyssinia to fight 'Arzō, a pretender to the Abyssinian throne; the expedition was massacred.

'Abd al-Qādir abū Ajbar (–*c.* 1842), Baqqārī chieftain of the Zurruq section of the Missirīya of western Kordofan; he was killed in inter-tribal fighting with the Ḥumr.

'Abd al-Qādir wad Dalīl (–1898), Mahdist amīr; sent to govern western Dār Fūr under 'Uthman Adam, amīr of all Dār Fūr, he made Kābkābīya his headquarters, 1888, and in the same year was badly defeated by the holy man nicknamed 'Abū Jummaiza' who had revolted against the Mahdist rule; on the death of 'Uthmān Adam in 1890 he was recalled to al-Fāshar to await the arrival of 'Uthmān's successor, the amīr Maḥmūd Aḥmad; serving under the latter he was killed at the battle of the Atbara at which his commanding amīr himself was taken prisoner and the Mahdist army scattered by an Anglo-Egyptian force under Kitchener.

'Abd al-Qādir Pasha Ḥilmī (1837–1908), governor-general of the Sudan; he was born at Ḥoms in Syria, the son of 'Uthmān Sam'ī, an officer in the occupying Egyptian army of Ibrāhīm Pasha, and of a Syrian lady, a member of an old and respected local family; at the end of the Syrian campaign the child was taken to Egypt with his father and educated there; in 1851 he was sent to Vienna to study medicine but, although he completed the medical course, he preferred the profession of arms and, on his return to Egypt, was admitted to the engineer corps as a cadet; commissioned with the rank of mulāzim II in 1856 he was promoted rapidly and by 1864 was a mīrālai when he was appointed a member of a mission sent to France in connexion with Ismā'īl Pasha's scheme of military reform; in 1874 he was promoted liwā' and pasha; during the Egyptian-Abyssinian war of 1875–6 he was stationed at Zaila and Harar; he returned to Egypt and in 1876 was made chief civil engineer of the Sudan Railway then being constructed from Wādī Ḥalfā towards Dongola; his promotion to farīq in 1878 was the prelude to several years of service as governor of Port Said and of the Canal Zone; the Mahdist revolt having become a serious threat to the Sudan Government, and Muḥammad Ra'ūf Pasha having been unable to stem the tide of revolt, 'Abd al-Qādir was appointed governor-general and commander-in-chief in February 1882; returning to Cairo on a hurried mission to collect arms and ammunition, he unsuccessfully opposed the decision of the Egyptian Government to send General W. Hicks Pasha to Kordofan, favouring instead a defensive strategy on shorter lines of communication; as his views were not in accord with those of the government, he was recalled and succeeded by 'Alā' al-Dīn Pasha in February 1883, but not before he had performed a notable work for the defence of the Sudan; he provided Khartoum with fortifications round the perimeter of the town which would have served well for a large garrison but proved to be too extended for the small force available during the siege of 1884–5; it was, nevertheless, due to his foresight and energy in improving the defences of the capital that the garrison were able to resist so long; not content with defence alone, he led a column from Khartoum against the Mahdist forces in the Jazīra, defeating the Nifaidīya under the amīr Wad Karrif and another force under Aḥmad al-Makāshfī, finally hacking his way through to Sennar which he fortified; there he detached a force of Shā'iqīya irregulars under Ṣāliḥ Bey al-Mak to clear the Mahdists from Jabal Moya and Jabal Saqadī; on his return to Egypt he became minister for war and marine, and in 1883 sat on a commission to report on the future of railways in the Sudan; early in 1884 he declined an invitation to undertake a mission to the Sudan, afterwards accepted by Major-General C. G. Gordon Pasha, to effect the withdrawal of the Egyptian garrisons and civilian population, as he considered the proposed means insufficient for the task, which he estimated would take up to one year to complete; he was said to have recommended the evacuation of the Sudan in order that, in the ensuing chaos, the reoccupation might be facilitated; he left the government service in 1887 and lived in retirement on his estate until his death; his son, Isḥāq Bey Ḥilmī, a noted sportsman, swam the English Channel; Ilyās Zakhūra's *Kitāb mir'āt al-aṣr* (Cairo, 1897), and ʿAbd al-Raḥmān Zakī's *Aʿlām al-jaish* (Cairo, 1947), contain biographies.

ʿAbd al-Qādir al-Jīlānī (1077–1166), Islamic notable; a Persian, he studied at Baghdad and became the founder of the religious brotherhood of the Qādirīya, numerously represented in the Sudan, which includes among its virtues tolerance and charitableness, and among its practices an emphasis on rhythm and breathing; there are numerous biographies, some not free of fiction.

* **ʿAbd al-Qādir wad umm Maryam** (–1893), Mahdist amīr, by origin a Taʿā'ishī; he took part in the siege of Khartoum by the army of Muḥammad Aḥmad al-Mahdī in 1884–5; while in command of the Mahdist forces at Shaqqa in southern Dār Fūr, he and his men were destroyed in battle with the Dinka negroes in the south.

* **ʿAbd al-Qādir Muḥammad ʿAbd al-Raḥmān** (1823–86), Sudanese tribal leader; a member of the branch of the Maḥas of ʿĀilafūn, near Khartoum, he was a son of Shaikh Muḥammad ʿAbd al-Raḥmān and, like his father, was a follower of the cult of the saint, Shaikh Idrīs Muḥammad al-Arbāb (1607–50); he took an active part in tribal government during the Egyptian rule and was made nāẓir al-qism of an extensive territory reaching from ʿĀilafūn along the east bank of the Blue Nile as far as the region of Wad al-Ḥaddād near Sennar, under the authority of Aḥmad Bey abū Sin ʿAwad al-Karīm; on the fall of Khartoum to the Mahdists in 1885 he visited Muḥammad Aḥmad al-Mahdī in Omdurman and was by him appointed an amīr; although his own relations with the Mahdist movement were peaceful, his son, Shaikh Muḍāwī ʿAbd al-Raḥmān, later quarrelled with the Khalīfa ʿAbd Allāhi and fled to Egypt, returning after the Anglo-Egyptian occupation and becoming qāḍī of Dongola.

ʿAbd al-Qādir Muḥammad Imām wad Ḥabūba (–1908), Mahdist, of the Ḥalāwīyīn tribe; he served with the force of the amīr ʿAbd al-Raḥmān wad al-Najūmī in Dongola about 1887 and was later present at the battles of Akasha, Firka (Firket), and Ḥafīr, 1896, and at Omdurman, 1898; he survived all these fights and returned to his home in the Jazīra to find his brother possessed of his lands and, after raising unsuccessful lawsuits for the recovery of his property, grew hostile to the local Egyptian ma'mūr; in the ensuing excitement he and his sympathizers murdered the ma'mūr and the inspector C. C. Scott-Moncrieff at Tuqr village and incited the neighbouring people to revolt; the suppression of the rebellion cost the lives of two more Egyptian officers and fifteen Egyptian soldiers; he was finally brought in by villagers opposed to the rebellion and hanged.

ʿAbd al-Qādir wad Nimr wad Bishāra (–*c.* 1884), nāẓir of the Ḥasanīya of the White Nile; an early adherent of Muḥammad Aḥmad al-Mahdī he died of small-pox during the wars against the Egyptian Government and was succeeded by his brother Muḥammad.

ʿAbd al-Qādir wad al-Zain (–1857), Sudanese notable of the Yaʿqūbāb Arabs of the district of Sennar; in 1826 ʿAlī Khūrshīd Bey, Egyptian governor of Sennar, appointed him local shaikh al-mashāyikh, having been chosen by the notables of the province to be their representative with the government; his territory extended from Ḥajar al-ʿAsal, near the Sixth Cataract of the Nile, to the southern end of the Funj mountains on the borders of Abyssinia; he remained in office under successive governors until his death, when he was succeeded by his son Zubair ʿAbd al-Qādir.

ʿAbd al-Raḥīm Bey Sālim abū Daqal (*c.* 1850–1933), tribal leader of the Gharaisīya branch of the Ḥamar Arabs of Kordofan; at the outset of his career he was an unimportant shaikh; the third son of Sālim Naiyīl he steadily won his way by diplomacy and ability during the latter days of the Egyptian rule; C. G. Gordon Pasha (governor-general 1877–80) made him a binbāshī and ʿAbd al-Qādir Pasha Ḥilmī (governor-general 1882–3) a bey; in 1881, at the beginning of the Mahdist movement, he supported the government and in 1882 was wounded in battle with the Mahdist forces at Abū Ḥarāz near al-Ubaiyaḍ when he deserted to the cause of Muḥammad Aḥmad al-Mahdī; as a minor Mahdist amīr he fought in several campaigns under the amīrs Ḥamdān abū ʿAnja, Zakī Ṭamal, and Aḥmad Faḍīl, distinguishing himself in the war against the Abyssinians; in 1898, while on the Blue Nile with part of Aḥmad Faḍīl's retreating army, he received a letter of amnesty and a commission from the sirdār of the Anglo-Egyptian army which he promptly accepted; issued with rifles he and his men pursued a Mahdist column of Taʿā'isha tribesmen under Ṣāliḥ Ḥammād and defeated them near Fashashūya, capturing Ṣāliḥ and with him the Khalīfa Muḥammad al-Sharīf and the Mahdi's sons al-Fāḍil and al-Bushrā; he then chased another retreating party of Taʿā'isha to the borders of Dār Silā; on his return he resumed the office of chief of the Gharaisīya with the title of nāẓir; he married a daughter of Carlo Contarini, a Venetian trader in Khartoum before the Mahdist revolt; on his death he was succeeded by his youngest son Muḥammad.

ʿAbd al-Raḥmān Bey . . . (–*c.* 1861), officer of the Egyptian army; in 1859 he was sent on a mission to Theodore, emperor of Abyssinia; reaching Dambiya near Gondar in March 1859 he was at first welcomed but afterwards detained for two years at Magdala by the emperor; finally, after strongly worded protests from the Egyptian Government, he was allowed to depart; on his way to the Sudan frontier he was plundered of all he had by the *shum* of Chelga and arriving at Berber destitute and broken in health he is said to have poisoned himself there.

ʿAbd al-Raḥmān ʿAbd Allāh (–1941), trader of Dongolāwī origin; he lived in Wad Madanī where he was agent for al-Saiyid Sir ʿAbd al-Raḥmān al-Mahdī Pasha; noted for his hospitality he was a prominent figure in local government, a magistrate, and a member of the town bench; he died in Wad Madanī.

'Abd al-Raḥmān (abū Zaid) Walī al-Dīn ibn Khaldūn (1332–1406), Arab historian and statesman, the author of the celebrated sociological work, *al-Muqaddima*; he was born in Tunis and travelled widely, writing a history of the Arabs in Spain and Africa; in his *Kitāb al-'ibār* (Cairo, 1384) he briefly described the last days of Christian Nubia; he died in Cairo.

'Abd al-Raḥmān Aḥmad Bukr or **Bukkur** (–1799), sultan of Dār Fūr; a son of Sultan Aḥmad Bukr he was the successor in the sultanship to his brother Muḥammad Tīrāb, after a period of anarchy, and reigned from 1785 to 1799; an energetic ruler, he founded the present capital of al-Fāshar and built a mosque the ruins of which are still to be seen; in war with the Hāmaj rulers of Sennar he was successful, driving their partisans out of Kordofan and occupying al-Ubaiyaḍ in 1796; he corresponded with General Bonaparte during the latter's campaign in Egypt; estimates of his character vary; the British traveller, W. G. Browne, who was in Dār Fūr 1793–6, wrote that he was a misanthropic, licentious tyrant under the cloak of piety, and that he had some reputation for learning; on his death his son Muḥammad al-Faḍl succeeded him; he was buried in the ancestral cemetery of the Fūr sultans on Jabal Marra.

'Abd al-Raḥmān al-Amīn Muḥammad al-Ḍarīr (*c.* 1859–1939), Islamic notable; a son of Shaikh al-Amīn Muḥammad al-Ḍarīr, Shaikh al-Islām during the latter part of the Egyptian rule, he was born on Tūtī island near Khartoum and was educated by his father and afterwards at the University of al-Azhar; on his return to the Sudan the Mahdist revolt soon broke out; joining the Mahdist cause he was made qāḍī in Berber; his father, who was opposed to Mahdism, probably owed his life to his sons' adherence to the Mahdī; on the establishment of the Condominion Government he was at first qāḍī and finally inspector of Islamic courts of law; his brother 'Abd al-Raḥmān was an amīr under Maḥmūd wad Aḥmad.

'Abd al-Raḥmān Firtī (–1912), Sudanese tribal chief of western Dār Fūr and sultan of all the Zaghāwa tribe which has, since his time, been divided by the frontier, demarcated in 1924, between French and Anglo-Egyptian territory; in 1912 one Ḥajar, a distant relative with no title to the sultanate, obtained the favour of the French, led a force into Dār Tīnī, and attacked and killed him.

'Abd al-Raḥmān Ḥasan . . . al-Jabartī (1754–1822), Egyptian chronicler, of Abyssinian origin, who lived in Cairo during the French occupation and the first years of the viceroy Muḥammad 'Alī Pasha and who wrote a chronicle of what he saw and heard; there are references to Nubia in his *'Ajā'ib al-āthār fī tarājim wa'l-akhbār* (Cairo, 1879–80) which ends in 1805–6 and which was partly translated (with many errors) into French as 'Merveilles biographiques et historiques'

(Cairo, 1888–94); he was murdered near Cairo possibly, it was suggested at the time, because his independent spirit as a chronicler was inconvenient to the government.

'Abd al-Raḥmān ibn Jābir (*fl.* 1572), religious teacher of the Awlād Jābir whose descendants are called Jābirīya or Jawābra; three mosques at Kūrtī were devoted to his ministry; many famous names of saints occur among his pupils and he is noteworthy as having not only four sons famed for their learning but a daughter, Fāṭima, equally learned and pious.

'Abd al-Raḥmān al-Khōrasānī (–1885), Persian mystic; he entered the Sudan and about 1870 came to Berber where he founded a centre of the Qādirīya brotherhood which practised his peculiar rite; the members of the brotherhood in Berber say that he was divinely guided to the Sudan in order to teach Shaikh Aḥmad al-Ja'lī; his end is uncertain; he was in Khartoum during the siege of 1884–5 and was not heard of since; there is a tradition at Berber that he was killed in the sack of the city by the Mahdists and that his body was thrown down the same well as that of the Faqī Faiyid Muḥammad.

'Abd al-Raḥmān Bey al-Manfūkh (*fl.* 1813), Mameluke leader; he commanded the Mameluke refugees in Dongola after the death of Ibrāhīm Bey al-Kabīr in 1813; his subsequent fate is uncertain.

'Abd al-Raḥmān Muḥammad Ṣāliḥ (*c.* 1888–1944), teacher; born at Omdurman of Dongolāwī origin he was educated at Gordon Memorial College, Khartoum, and entered the Sudan civil service as a teacher of Arabic and Islamic religion in 1910; he was for long a local inspector of schools, Dongola province, and finally headmaster of the intermediate school at Khartoum North which under his guidance became the leading intermediate school in the country; he died in Khartoum.

* **'Abd al-Raḥmān wad al-Najūmī** (–1889), Mahdist 'amīr al-umarā' (principal amīr); by origin a Ja'lī of the 'Abd al-Dā'imāb branch, he joined the cause of Muḥammad Aḥmad al-Mahdī in 1881 and was counted among the Mahdī's earliest followers; he was made guardian of the youthful caliph, Muḥammad al Sharīf; in the siege and capture of Khartoum he took a principal part, leading the assault on the Masallamīya gate, 1885; in the same year, as temporary amīr of Berber and Dongola, he was defeated in the battle of Jinnis (Giniss) by a force under General F. C. A. Stephenson; he was later appointed commander of an army intended for the invasion of Egypt, but his army was destroyed and himself killed in battle at Tūshkī (Toski), near Abū Simbel, by an Anglo-Egyptian army under General F. W. Grenfell Pasha, the sirdār; among the Mahdist amīrs he was outstanding for bravery and military skill; al-liwā' 'Abd Allāh al-Najūmī Pasha is his son.

'Abd al-Raḥmān abū Qarn (–1870), trader in the Baḥr al-Ghazāl, an early associate of Zubair Raḥma Manṣūr (afterwards Pasha), and a companion of the British trader J. Petherick; establishing a trading station near Tonj he was probably the first trader from the

White Nile to penetrate the country of the Azande; in 1863 he rescued Zubair from starvation in the wilderness; he accompanied the Pethericks in their endeavours to enter the country of the Bongo; repulsed by the Monbuttu he was killed in battle with the Azande not far from the residence of Chief N'doruma.

'Abd al-Raḥmān Saiyid al-'Awad (*c.* 1891–1931), Dūlābī notable who was, like his father before him, 'umda of Omdurman.

'Abd al-Raḥmān ibn al-Shaikh Ṣāliḥ Bān al-Nuqā (1709–), a celebrated holy man of his day, somewhat overshadowed by the reputation of his father, Shaikh Ṣāliḥ ibn Bān al-Nuqā, the great saint of the Funj kingdom; little intimate is known of him save his various teachers and disciples recorded in the *Ṭabaqāt* of Muḥammad al-Nūr wad Ḍaif Allāh.

'Abd al-Rasūl Ḥamdān 'Abd al-Qādir (–1943), notable of the religious family of the Ya'qūbāb of the neighbourhood of Sennar; he was 'umda of Wad Nu'mān, a magistrate and a member of the court at Ḥājj 'Abd Allāh.

'Abd al-Rāziq 'Abd al-Qādir Bey (*c.* 1890–1945), Egyptian engineer; he joined the Egyptian irrigation service in 1917; in 1939 he entered the ministry of 'Alī Māhir Pasha as secretary-general to the minister of public works and in 1940–2 was inspector-general of the Egyptian irrigation service in the Sudan; he was director of public health in 1942.

'Abd al-Rāziq Ḥaqqī Pasha (*fl.* 1866–79), Turkish soldier; governor of Tāka, 1866–70; during his term of office he fell foul of Aḥmad Pasha Mumtāz for damping the latter's over-optimistic projects for growing cotton in the delta of the Gash; he had had a long experience of the Sudan, but the Khedive Ismā'īl Pasha removed him from the governorship in 1870 in deference to Mumtāz who, as governor of the Red Sea littoral, included Tāka in his territory; he was governor of Sennar about 1873–6 and was acting governor-general after the departure of Ismā'īl Aiyūb Pasha from the Sudan in 1876; he was then appointed acting governor-general of Dār Fūr in 1877 during the illness of Ḥasan Pasha Ḥilmī, going to Dār Fūr in command of a force to suppress the revolt of Muḥammad Hārūn al-Rashīd, claimant to the sultanate, whose followers had invested the principal towns; he quickly relieved al-Fāshar and quelled the revolt; promoted mīrlivā and elevated to the *pashalik* in the same year, he returned to Egypt on account of sickness in 1879.

'Abd al-Razzāq bey Naẓmī (–1884), mīrālai of the Egyptian army; he was deputy governor of Khartoum in 1876; while still a ṣāgh qōl aghāsi he helped to draw the great map of Africa prepared by the Egyptian general staff in 1877 and embodying the results of successive explorations of the Sudan up to that date; on the outbreak of the Mahdist revolt on the Red Sea coast we find him engaged in the campaign against the forces led by the Mahdist amīr 'Uthmān abū Bakr

Diqna (Osman Digna); he was in Sinkat in August 1883 under Muḥammad Tawfīq Bey, the gallant defender of the town; here he built fortifications and, returning to Suakin, later fought in the battle of Tamai; appointed chief of staff to General V. Baker Pasha he was killed at the battle of el-Teb, fighting bravely to the end.

'Abd al-Ṣamad abū Ṣafīya (*c.* 1825–1915), tribal leader of the Awlād Ṣafīya branch of the Bidairīya Arabs of Kordofan; in his youth he hunted slaves in the Nuba hills and later became a minor amīr in the Mahdist army; on the collapse of the Mahdist rule in 1898 he made peace with the government and was made nāẓir of the Bidairīya of Kordofan; among his near relatives Muḥammad abū Ṣafīya fought against the British column at Abū Ṭulaiḥ (Abu Klea), 1885, and Aḥmad Badawī abū Ṣafīya led part of the Mahdist army at the battle of Tokar, 1891.

'Abd al-Shakūr Pasha (*fl.* 1880–85), notable of Dār Fūr; the son of 'Abd al-Raḥmān Shatūt and the grandson of Sultan Muḥammad al-Faḍl, he was banished on his father's death in 1880 to Cairo; in 1884 he was invited by C. G. Gordon Pasha, then governor-general of the Sudan, to accompany him from Egypt and to return to Dār Fūr with the promise of the sultanship in return for his aid to the Egyptian Government; he set out from Cairo with his retinue and got as far as Dongola; the retreat of the Khartoum relief expedition in 1885, after having failed to accomplish its object, left him without support, so he returned to Cairo where he died and was buried in the Imām al-Shāfi'ī cemetery.

'Abd al-Wahhāb Ibrāhīm al-Kabbāshī. *See* AL-BASHĪR ṬAHA IBRĀHĪM AL-KABBĀSHĪ.

'Abd al-Wahhāb Muḥyī al-Dīn (*c.* 1868–1946), legal notable of eastern Dār Fūr; he was qāḍī of Jabal al-Ḥilla in the sultanate of 'Alī Dīnār and remained in office after the Anglo-Egyptian occupation of 1916; in 1917 he was confirmed in his functions as qāḍī of eastern Dār Fūr and for many years officiated at the Umm Kadāda court; a quiet, retiring man of considerable learning in the Islamic law, he was much respected.

Abeken, Heinrich (1809–72), Prussian diplomat and traveller; born at Osnabrück he studied theology at the University of Berlin; in 1842 he accompanied the expedition of Professor K. R. Lepsius to the Sudan, travelling over the Nubian desert from Korosko to Abū Ḥamad and publishing contributions to the geography of the country; after a diplomatic career he served on the Prussian general staff in the Prussian–Austrian war of 1866 and in the Franco–Prussian war of 1870–1.

'Ābidīn ('Ābdī) Bey al-Arnā'ūṭ (*c.* 1780–1827), Albanian officer, brother of Ḥasan Pasha al-Arnā'ūṭ and one of Muḥammad 'Alī Pasha's most trusted friends; in the Turkish correspondence of the time his name was sometimes written ʿĀbdī, an Albanian and Rumelian diminutive of ʿĀbidīn; he was governor of Mīnyā where he was known for his hospitality to travellers, and was then appointed second in command of the army being mobilized in 1820 under Ismāʿīl Pasha for the invasion of the Sudan; he commanded the Turkish cavalry in the fighting against the Shā'iqīya at the end of that year, distinguishing himself in the battle of Kūrtī; when the Egyptian army moved on towards Sennar he was left behind and charged with the government of the country between Wādī Ḥalfā and Merowe; he was relieved in 1825 by Qāsim Aghā and returned to Egypt where he was murdered at Manfalūṭ by mutinous Turkish soldiers; G. B. English, Ismāʿīl Pasha's commander of artillery, wrote of him as brave and respectable; G. Waddington recorded that he could neither read nor write.

Abū ʿAbd Allāh Muḥammad ibn Baṭṭūṭa (1304–68), Arab traveller and geographer; he was born at Tangiers and spent thirty years (1325–54) in journeys through the countries of Islam and the Far East; returning to Morocco he settled at Fez and wrote the history of his travels; his writings contain several references to the movements of the Arab tribes in the Sudan; about 1325, in the course of his travels, he sailed from Jidda to Rās Duwair, between ʿAidhāb and Sawākin, visiting the Beja people living along the coast, including Sawākin, and crossing the Nubian desert between ʿAidhāb and Qūṣ.

Abū ʿAbd Allāh Muḥammad al-Idrīsī (*c.* 1100–64), Arab geographer; born at Ceuta he was educated at Cordoba and travelled in Spain, Barbary, and Asia Minor; he afterwards attached himself to the half-Christian, half-Muslim court of King Roger II of Sicily where he constructed a map of the world and wrote a description of the earth; this great work, *al-nuzhat al-mushtāq* (*The Book of Roger*), was completed in 1154; the portion referring to Africa contains an account of Nubia.

Abū ʿAbd al-Raḥmān ibn ʿAbd Allāh . . . al-ʿAmrī (*fl.* 868), Arab general in the employ of the Mameluke ruler of Egypt, Abū 'l-ʿAbbās Aḥmad ibn Ṭūlūn; in 868, with an army composed chiefly of Rabīʿa and Juhaina Arabs, he invaded Nubia and, turning eastward, pacified the Beja.

Abū ʿAnja. *See* Ḥamdān abū ʿAnja.

Abū ʿĀqla Ḥamad al-Turābī (–1940), religious notable of the ʿArakīyīn, khalīfa of the great founder of the family, Shaikh Ḥamad wad al-Turābī (1639–1704).

Abū Badawī abū Bakr (Abbukr) Ismāʿīl (–1945), brother of Muḥammad Baḥr al-Dīn Ismāʿīl, sultan of Dār Maṣālīṭ in western Dār Fūr; he died at al-Jinaina.

Abū Bakr Dūdū (–1928), ʿumda of Dago (Mīrī) in southern Dār Fūr; he was a magistrate.

Abū Bakr Ismāʿīl (–1814), king of Taqalī in the Nuba hills of southern Kordofan who about 1773 succeeded his father, Ismā'īl Muḥammad; during his reign Taqalī, formerly tributary to the Funj kingdom of Sennar, regained its independence; his people remember him as a good and popular king; he was succeeded on his death by his son 'Umar.

Abū Bakr Ismā'īl (–1907), sultan of Dār Maṣālīṭ in Dār Fūr, 1889–1905; a son of Faqī Ismā'īl 'Abd al-Nabī, a nāẓir whom the people elected to succeed Hajjām Ḥasab Allāh as chief nāẓir in Dār Maṣālīṭ after the latter had been deposed by the Mahdists; in 1883 his father was captured by the Mahdists, but he escaped and maintained guerilla warfare against them; he later established his authority at Derjeil and proclaimed himself sultan of Dār Maṣālīṭ; the entire period of his sultanship was spent in continuous war; first against the Mahdists and then against 'Alī Dīnār, sultan of Dār Fūr, on the east, and against the Dājū on the west; about 1905 he was captured by the forces of 'Alī Dīnār and taken to al-Fāshar; Dār Maṣālīṭ was occupied by one of 'Alī Dīnār's generals; one of his sons, who had fled to Wadā'i on his father's defeat, returned and defeated the Fūr, killing their agent in charge of Dār Maṣālīṭ; in revenge 'Alī Dīnār had Abū Bakr Ismā'īl executed; his brother, Tāj al-Dīn Ismā'īl, was recognized as sultan of Dār Maṣālīṭ; the present sultan, Muḥammad Baḥr al-Dīn, another son of Abū Bakr Ismā'īl, succeeded to the sultanship when Tāj al-Dīn Ismā'īl was killed by a French column in the battle of Darūtī.

Abū Bakr Sambū (–1940), Fallātī negro of Tokar where he lived most of his life and where he died; he was 'umda of the Fallāta community in the town.

Abū Bakr abū Shaqqa (*c.* 1890–1943), chief of the Golo tribe of the Baḥr al-Ghazāl region between Wau and Raga; he was appointed chief in 1931 and was a magistrate and president of the Buṣailīya court.

Abū Dakka. *See* 'ALĪ ABŪ DAKKA; 'ALĪ ḤAMAD BEY FAṬĪN ABŪ DAKKA.

Abū Dakka Ḥamad Faṭīn (– 1925), nāẓir of the Daqāqīm branch of the Ḥamar of Kordofan and son of the preceding nāẓir, Abū Jilūf Ḥamad Faṭīn.

Abū Daqal. *See* 'ABD AL-RAḤĪM BEY SĀLIM ABŪ DAQAL; MUḤAMMAD 'ABD AL-RAḤĪM ABŪ DAQAL.

Abū Dilaiq. *See* 'ALĪ, called ABŪ DILAIQ.

Abū'l-Faraj. *See* GRIGORIOS ABŪ'L-FARAJ BAR 'EBHRĀYĀ (BAR HEBRÆUS).

Abū Fāṭima Ḥassāb (–1941), Shukrī notable; he was 'umda of the Nūrāb branch of the Shukrīya in the Kassala province.

Abū Fāṭima 'Umar (–1930), shaikh of the Artaiga Beja tribe in the delta of the Gash; he died at Kassala.

Abū'l-Fidā'. *See* ISMĀ'ĪL IBN 'ALĪ ABŪ'L-FIDĀ'.

Abū'l-Ḥasan 'Abd al-Maḥmūd (1876–1940), son of Shaikh 'Abd al-Maḥmūd Nūr al-Dā'im, head of the Sammanīya brotherhood in the Sudan; born at Umm Ṭarfaiya near Ṭābat between al-Ḥaṣṣa Ḥaiṣa and al-Qiṭaina of Surūrābī (Jamū'ī) stock he was appointed shaikh of Ṭābat village soon after the foundation of the present government and in 1914 shaikh of khuṭṭ; he was a magistrate and, from 1930 till his death, president of the Ṭābat shaikhs' court.

Abū'l-Ḥasan 'Alī al-Mas'ūdī (–956), Arab geographer and traveller; born in Baghdad he visited Nubia and described the country and its people in *Murūj al-dhahab wa ma'ādin al-jawāhir* (*Meadows of Gold and Mines of Gems*), an encyclopaedic work of historical geography which he wrote in Egypt; he died at al-Fusṭāṭ.

Abū'l-Ḥasan (Ḥusain) Jawhar ibn 'Abd Allāh . . . al-Rūmī (–992), Fāṭimid general; he was born within the boundaries of the Byzantine Empire and was believed to be of Greek origin; while governor of Egypt he sent Aḥmad ibn Sulaim al-Aswānī at the head of a mission to Gheorghios, king of Nubia, in 969, to receive the tribute and to invite the king to embrace Islam; the king paid the tribute.

Abū'l Ḥasan . . . ibn Sa'īd al-Maghribī (*c.* 1214–*c.* 1286), Arab philologist and historian; born and educated in Spain he lived in various countries of the Near East; he was one of the sources from whom al-Maqrīzī copied information; he described the tribes of the western and eastern Sudan including the Beja in the neighbourhood of Sawākin.

Abū-Ḥijil al-Ajaid Raḥma (*fl.* 1821), malik of the 'Ajībāb branch of the Rubāṭāb at the time of the Turkish invasion; in the last few years before the arrival of the Turks he had subjugated the entire southern half of the Rubāṭāb country; his administrative ability so impressed the Turks that they regarded him as chief of all the Rubāṭāb; his son Sulaimān later became hākim al-khuṭṭ of Abū Hashīm.

See also IBRĀHĪM MUḤAMMAD MUḤAMMAD ABŪ ḤIJIL; MUḤAMMAD ABŪ ḤIJIL; 'UMAR MUḤAMMAD ABŪ ḤIJIL.

Abū'l-Huṣain Muḥammad ibn Aḥmad ibn Jubair al-Kinānī (*c.* 1150–*c.* 1200), Arab traveller from Andalusia, author of *Rihla ibn Jubair*, containing references to Nubia and the Red Sea coast of the Sudan.

Abū Jārid. *See* BAKR. . . .

Abū Jilūf Ḥamad Faṭīn (–*c.* 1917), nāẓir of the Daqāqīm branch of the Ḥamar of Kordofan; on his death his son Abū Dakka Ḥamad Faṭīn (d. 1925) succeeded him.

Abū Jummaiza. *See* AḤMAD ABŪ JUMMAIZA.

Abū Kalām Ballāl abū Hūra (–*c.* 1871), nāẓir of the Jima'a Arab tribe of the White Nile and a member of the ruling family of

Sharak; he succeeded his father in the early days of the Egyptian Government and exercised authority over his own Jima'a tribesmen and also over the Sulaim, Aḥamda, and Shānkhāb in a loose federation called *al-niẓārat al-baqar* (the cattle nāẓirate); he first resisted the Turks but afterwards submitted to their rule, for his people lacked firearms; about 1870 he fell out with the Sulaim who appealed to the Government; the Government arrested him and sent him to Egypt where he died in captivity; he was succeeded in the nāẓirship by his son 'Asākir abū Kalām.

Abū Khairāt. *See* Yūsuf Ibrāhīm.

Abū Likailik (abū'l-Kailak). *See* 'Abd al-Mājid Naṣr al-Dīn abū'l-Kailak; Idrīs wad Muḥammad abū'l-Kailak; Muḥammad abū'l-Kailak (abū Likailik) Kamtūr; Naṣr al-Dīn abū'l-Kailak.

Abū Madyān. *See* Muḥammad abū Madyān.

Abū Makārim Hibat Allāh (*fl.* 1200), chief of the Rabī'a Arabs who settled in Nubia; as a reward for his services the Fāṭimid caliph conferred on him and his heirs the title of Kanz al-Dawla (Treasure of the State).

Abū'l-Qāsim Aḥmad Bukr or **Bukkur** (–1752), sultan of Dār Fūr; he ruled 1739–52 in succession to his nephew, 'Umar Laila (Lele) Muḥammad Dawra; during his reign the Fūr armies were defeated in wars with Silā and Bagirmi and the Fūr commander Khamīs was banished in disgrace; himself a son of a former sultan, Aḥmad Bukr or Bukkur, he was succeeded by his brother Muḥammad Tīrāb Aḥmad Bukr or Bukkur.

* **Abū'l-Qāsim Aḥmad Hāshim** (–1934), legal notable; of the Jawdalāb branch of the Ja'līyīn his family came from al-Kimair near Shendi but lived latterly in Berber; during the Mahdist régime he was confidential secretary to the Khalīfa 'Abd Allāhi and on the Anglo-Egyptian occupation was a judge in the Blue Nile province till 1911; he became president of the board of 'ulamā' of Omdurman in 1931 and in 1932 retired; among many duties he was the first president of the Ma'had al-'Ilmī institute at Omdurman; he visited England in 1919; Shaikh al-Ṭaiyib Aḥmad Hāshim, muftī of the Sudan, 1900–24, was his brother; no less than three of his sons are judges in the Islamic law of whom Shaikh Hāshim abū'l-Qāsim Aḥmad is the present muftī.

Abū Rūf. *See* Yūsuf al-Marḍī, called Yūsuf abū Rūf.

Abū Ṣāliḥ the Armenian (*fl.* 1200), supposed author of an Arabic manuscript written in the early thirteenth century and describing the churches and monuments of Egypt and Nubia; the author was possibly a member of the Armenian colony in Egypt and 'Abū Ṣāliḥ' possibly a corruption of his Armenian name; he visited Nubia and noted the religious houses he met with on his way; although he does not seem to have ascended the Nile farther than the great white monastery of Akhmīm, his descriptions extend to the region of the present Merowe.

* **Abū Sin.** *See* 'Abd Allāh 'Awad al-Karīm abū Sin; Aḥmad Bey abū Sin 'Awad al-Karīm; Aḥmad Ḥilmī abū Sin; 'Alī 'Awad al-Karīm abū Sin; 'Alī al-Karīm abū Sin; 'Awad al-Karīm 'Abd Allāh abū Sin; 'Awad al-Karīm abū Sin; 'Awad al-Karīm Pasha Aḥmad abū Sin; Ḥamad 'Awad al-Karīm abū Sin; Ḥamad Muḥammad 'Awad al-Karīm abū Sin; Ḥasan Aḥmad Bey abū Sin; Ibrāhīm 'Abd Illāh abū Sin; Muḥammad Aḥmad abū Sin; Muḥammad Aḥmad Bey abū Sin, called Ḥārdallū; Muḥammad 'Awad al-Karīm abū Sin; 'Umāra Muḥammad abū Sin; Yūsuf 'Abd Allāh abū Sin.

Abū Sinaina. *See* Muḥammad ibn Naṣr al-Tarjamī al-Ja'lī, called Abū Sinaina.

Abū Surūr al-Faḍlī (*fl.* 1670), holy man, a pupil of the celebrated Shaikh al-Zain ibn Sughaiyarūn he was born at Ḥalfaiya where he taught for some time before going to Dār Fūr to continue his mission; according to the hagiographer Muḥammad al-Nūr wad Ḍaif Allāh he was killed in Dār Fūr by his concubines who smashed his skull with stones while he was asleep.

Abū Su'ūd Bey. *See* Muḥammad abū Su'ūd Bey al-'Aqqād.

Abū Yazīd Shāwīsh (–1889), official of the Soudan Railway at Wādī Ḥalfā during the Mahdist war; deserting to the Mahdist cause he was made a minor amīr and in this capacity guided several Mahdist raids on riverain villages north of Wādī Ḥalfā; he was captured by the Egyptian army after the battle of Tūshkī (Toski) in 1889 and shot in the presence of the villagers of Dabarosa whom he had betrayed.

Abū Zaid Ismā'īl Sa'd (*c.* 1837–1934), notable of Sinja where he was a merchant of importance; he was born in Dongola of a family which came originally from Daraw in Upper Egypt; he died at Sinja.

'Abūdī Muḥammad Sulaimān (*fl.* 1710), holy man who traced his descent from the Kawāhla tribe and who came from the locality of al-Ḥaṣṣa Ḥaiṣa to the village of 'Abūd (called after him) where his tomb stands; he devoted his life to good works and left a succession of holy men who are still represented in the village; his son Muḥammad was given land near Manāqil by Rānfī, sultan of Sennar in 1803, but since the sultans of that period were puppets, the gift was disputed by other claimants.

Abukr, Abbukr. *See* Abū Bakr.

Acerbi, Giuseppe (1773–1846), Italian consul; born at Castelgoffredo near Mantua, he was a man of great learning; while serving as Austrian consul-general at Alexandria, 1826–35, he travelled much in Egypt and Nubia collecting antiquities for the museums of Vienna and Italy.

Adal, Takla Haymanot (–1899), Abyssinian chief, by origin of the Amhara; while governor of Gojjam King John charged him with guarding the frontier with the Sudan at Gallabat and placed a considerable force under his command; in 1887 the Mahdist amīr Ḥamdān

Abū ʿAnja invaded Abyssinia opposite Gallabat and defeated him after a fierce battle on the plain of Debra Sin, thirty miles west of Gondar; he himself escaped, but his son was captured by the Mahdists and, after the sack of Gondar, his wife and daughter also were taken; he died in mysterious circumstances, at the time it was alleged that he had been poisoned.

* **Adam Dabbalū** (–1884), king of Taqalī; about 1864 he seized the throne from his uncle Nāṣir ibn al-mak Abū Bukr who had alienated his people by his tyranny; he was a peace-loving ruler encouraging trade with al-Ubaiyaḍ and the west and generally promoting the prosperity of his kingdom; he did not pay tribute to the Egyptian Government but, on the other hand, did not openly defy it, while the Government left him in peace; it was said that the years 1870–80 were a golden age in Taqalī; in 1881 Muḥammad Aḥmad al-Mahdī came by Taqalī on his first flight to Jabal Qadīr; he refused at first to join the Mahdī in revolt against the Government but at length yielded; it was reported that, during the disastrous march of the Egyptian army into Kordofan in 1883, the commander, Hicks Pasha, wished to send a guide to Taqalī to ask his aid but that he was dissuaded by ʿAlāʾ al-Dīn Pasha who contended that the kings of Taqalī, consistently unfriendly ever since the Egyptian conquest, could not be relied on; in 1884, secure in his rising power, the Mahdī ordered him to come to al-Ubaiyaḍ, where he was made a prisoner, dying shortly after at Shabasha in Dār al-Jimaʿa during the Mahdi's advance on Khartoum; a son, ʿUmar, joined the Mahdist cause and later occupied a position under the Khalīfa ʿAbd Allāhi; Taqalī was ravaged and depopulated by the Mahdist leaders Ḥamdān Abū ʿAnja and al-Nūr Muḥammad ʿAnqara in 1885.

Adam Dalīl (–1941), a member of the Kunjara ruling branch of the Fūr tribe and ʿumda of Dōka between Gedaref and Gallabat; he died at Dōka.

Adam Dumo Ibrāhīm (–1932), ʿumda of the Zaiyādīya tribe of Dār Fūr and a magistrate; he died at Koma.

Adam Ḥasūba (–1934), ʿumda of the Kawāhla at Daiyāna near Ḥājj ʿAbd Allāh in the Jazīra; he died at Daiyāna.

Adam al-Nūr Jahī (*c.* 1870–1931), notable of Dār Fūr; he was born at Abū Ṭulaiḥ in southern Dār Fūr and as a boy met Muḥammad Aḥmad al-Mahdī at Shaṭṭ at the beginning of his revolt; he followed the Mahdī to Omdurman and lived there for several years; in 1894 he saw service with the Mahdist armies at Gallabat, Kassala, in Kordofan, and in the Nuba hills, rising to the rank of rās mīya; in 1895 he was sent to Rejaf in command of a detachment convoying prisoners and stores; ʿArabī Dafaʿ Allāh was then governor of Rejaf, and when a Belgian column under Colonel L. N. Chaltin defeated him at Bedden and Rejaf early in 1897, he retired with his command to Mongalla; Adam al-Nūr accompanied the defeated amīr as one of his lieutenants to Mandua and finally to Dār Fūr; when ʿArabī Dafaʿ Allāh surrendered to ʿAlī Dīnār he surrendered with him; he first enjoyed the sultan's confidence and was employed in the Fūr army first as a rās mīya and later as a commander of several hundred men at Kalaka in Dār Habbanīya; in 1914 he was reported to the sultan for having 'eaten' 1,500 head of cattle, but the sultan, who still placed great trust in him, was satisfied with his explanation; in 1917 he was made ʿumda of Nyāla town and in 1923 a magistrate.

Adam Rijāl (–1911), Takrūrī notable; he was a well-known soldier in the time of Ibrāhīm Muḥammad, sultan of Dār Fūr, and later commander-in-chief of the Fūr armies under Sultan ʿAlī Dīnār; he normally commanded a *rubaʿ*, a unit of the sultan's army numbering about 1,000 riflemen; though a Takrūrī by origin he became assimilated to the Fūr among whom he lived; ʿAbd al-Raḥmān abū Ḥabbū, head of the Banī Ḥalba tribe, was his cousin; he married a daughter of ʿAlī Dīnār who had confidence in him, giving him precedence over all other commanders and permitting him to stand next to him at parades; he acted as *wazīr* during the absence of the sultan from the capital; however, the sultan came to suspect him of tampering with the loyalty of the army and of plotting against his life, suspecting that he assisted the Banī Ḥalba, under ʿAbd al-Raḥmān Ḥabbū, to emigrate to Dār Sūla taking with them a large number of the sultan's horses; in 1911 he was thrown into prison; it is uncertain how he met his death; according to some ʿAlī Dīnār had him executed privately, a suspicion supported by present-day local opinion; according to another source he is held to have died of dysentery.

Adam Tamīm Bis͟hāra (–1933), s͟hartai of the Berti tribe of Dār Fūr; he was a magistrate and the president of the Mellīt court.

Adam Yaʿqūb (*c.* 1865–1939), s͟hartai of the Birgid Kajjar people of southern Dār Fūr; for four generations his family had held the headship of the tribe in direct descent, the line having been broken at the time of his father Yaʿqūb who died in 1879–80 when R. von Slatin Bey was governor of Dāra; Adam Yaʿqūb took no part in the Mahdist revolt, and when ʿAlī Dīnār returned from the east and seized power in 1899, he appointed him s͟hartai and placed him under the leadership of Adam Rijāl, his right-hand man, with whom he took part in expeditions against Dār Maṣālīṭ, Kabkabīya, and Dār Rizaiqāt; when Adam Rijāl fell from favour ʿAlī Dīnār had Adam Yaʿqūb's brother killed for his loyalty to the fallen wazīr, an act which Adam Yaʿqūb neither forgot nor forgave; when the Fūr sultanate came to an end in 1916 he fought in the battles against ʿAlī Dīnār and was confirmed in his position of s͟hartai by the Sudan Government; he was less helpful to the government during the attack on Nyāla by the rebel fanatic ʿAbd Allāh al-Sihainī in 1921 and was convicted of harbouring outlaws and of criminal appropriation; he was deposed but was later reinstated and remained an able ruler of his tribe until his death; he was known locally as Adam Taw.

Addà, Casimiro (*fl.* 1873), Italian postal official; born in Leghorn he was one of the collaborators of G. Muzzi Bey who from 1865 organized the Egyptian Government postal service in place of the former private postal agency called La Posta Europea; in 1873 the State postal service was extended to the Sudan when he established post offices at Aswān, Korosko, Wādī Ḥalfā, Dongola, Berber, and Khartoum.

* **Adham Pasha al-ʿĀrifī,** called **al-Taqalāwī** (*c.* 1815–   ), Sudanese soldier, liwā' of the Egyptian army, the first Sudanese to attain this rank; he received his military education in Egypt in the time of Muḥammad ʿAlī Pasha and as a junior officer fought under Ibrāhīm Pasha in the Syrian campaigns; he served as a qā'immaqām in the Egyptian contingent which formed part of the Ottoman army in the Crimean war of 1853–5, being second in command of the 9th regular infantry regiment; posted to the Sudan in 1862 to raise a new Sudanese regiment, he led 1,000 regular troops which accompanied Aḥmad Bey ʿAwad al-Karīm abū Sin, governor of Khartoum and Sennar, on a tax-collecting patrol in the mountains of Fāzūghlī in 1863; in 1865 he was ordered to bring a Sudanese battalion from Kassala to Egypt for service in Mexico as a reinforcement, or perhaps relief, to the Sudanese battalion already there; his battalion mutinied and the mutiny spread to the entire force of Sudanese troops in Kassala; for his masterly handling of the mutiny he was congratulated by Ismāʿīl Pasha, wālī of Egypt, promoted liwā', and placed in command of the 1st and 2nd Sudanese regiments serving in the Sudan; for a few months in 1872 he was acting governor-general of the Sudan before the arrival of Ismāʿīl Pasha Aiyūb.

* **ʿAdlān.** *See* IDRĪS RĀJAB WAD ʿADLĀN; MUḤAMMAD WAD ʿADLĀN; RĀJAB WAD ʿADLĀN.

ʿAdlān I wad Aya (–1611), sultan of the Funj dominions of Sennar; reigning from 1604 till 1611 he suppressed a revolt by Shaikh ʿAjīb wad ʿAbd Allāh, called ʿAjīb the Great, defeating and killing him in battle at Jaraif Karkōj near Khartoum; many holy men flourished during his reign; he succeeded ʿAbd al-Qādir II and was himself succeeded on his death by Bādī I Sīd al-Qūm.

ʿAdlān II ibn Ismāʿīl (–1788), puppet sultan of Sennar; about 1777 he ascended the throne vacated by his father Ismāʿīl ibn Bādī IV who had been exiled to Sawākin by the powerful vizier Shaikh Bādī wad Rājab; he attempted in vain to throw off the yoke of the Hāmaj viziers and died, it is said, of despair.

ʿAdlān Ḥasan (–1916), mak of the Funj of Sinja and a member of the royal line; he avoided the Mahdist régime by retiring to the village of Umm Binain near Sinja, later settling at Maina opposite Sinja, where his family is now established.

ʿAdlān Muḥammad Dafaʿ Allāh (–1879), Hāmaj notable, a son of the important Shaikh Muḥammad al-Arbāb Dafaʿ Allāh wad Aḥmad of Ṣūraiba in the Jazīra and grandson of the arbāb Dafaʿ Allāh wad Aḥmad wad Ḥasan; under him the family importance waned with the introduction of more closely controlled local administration by the Government; he succeeded his father on the latter's death in 1854 while he himself was followed by his son Idrīs wad ʿAdlān wad Muḥammad who was made ʿumda of Ṣūraiba.

ʿAdlān wad Muḥammad abū'l-Kailak (–1803), Hāmaj chieftain and for a few weeks vizier to the puppet king of Sennar; a son of the great king-maker and conqueror of Kordofan he spent his life in bloody civil war, killing several of his rivals until he was himself killed by a rival faction on the grounds that he had become weak and pleasure-loving.

Adol Anyuat (–1942), chief of the Atet section of the Bor Gok Dinka of the Upper Nile province.

Adye, Sir John (1857–1930), British major-general; entering the army in 1876 he took part in the Nile expedition of 1884–5 as a major and aide-de-camp to the commander-in-chief, Sir G. J. (afterwards Lord) Wolseley, and was present at the battle of Abū Ṭulaiḥ (Abu Klea); he later fought in the South African war and was promoted major-general in 1911; in the First World War he was with the British forces in Macedonia, Egypt, and Palestine; he was a colonel-commandant of the Royal Artillery, 1926–7; among other works of biography and fiction he published a biographical collection called *Soldiers I have known* (1925).

Aezanes (*fl.* 350), king of Axum in the highlands of what is now the Tigrai province of Abyssinia; about 350 he invaded the Meroïtic kingdom and defeated the Meroïtes near the confluence of the Nile and the Atbara.

* **Agati, Pietro** (1828–1918), Italian bricklayer, born in Pisa, who came to the Sudan with Bishop I. Knoblehar, 1853, as an artisan attached to the Roman Catholic mission in Khartoum; he took part in the building of the mission in Khartoum, the first structure in the capital to be built of kiln-baked bricks, a lost art since Meroïtic times; he later left the mission and during the Mahdist rule plied his trade, the house of the Khalīfa ʿAbd Allāhi at Omdurman being his handiwork; he married and had children by a Sudanese wife who is said to have saved his life during the famine of 1889; on the reoccupation of the Sudan he refused to be repatriated, having a family in the Sudan and having become habituated to native dress and ways of life; in his declining years 'Pietrino' was looked after by the Roman Catholic mission at Omdurman where he died.

Aḥmad Aghā (*c.* 1800–), one of the first Sudanese officers of the new regular army created by the viceroy Muḥammad ʿAlī Pasha in which he was enrolled as a private soldier in 1822 or 1823 in the 2nd infantry regiment; promoted shāwīsh in 1826 and transferring to the 6th infantry regiment he was commissioned as a mulāzim I in 1835; he later retransferred to the 1st infantry regiment; his subsequent career is unknown.

Aḥmad Ajaibar abū Shilūkh (1875–1944), Sudanese tribal leader; he commanded a force of Maṣālīṭ tribesmen who attacked a French column at Darūtī in 1910 and killed the commander, Colonel Moll; he subsequently led the forces of the Maṣālīṭ sultan against ʿAlī Dīnār, sultan of Dār Fūr, and suppressed various local rebellions; after 1919 he was the right-hand man of the sultan of Dār Maṣālīṭ, but his main work was done as the sultan's viceroy in the southern part of the sultanate.

Aḥmad al-ʿAjba (–1942), nāẓir of the Rufāʿa al-Hūī in the Blue Nile valley and himself of the Rufāʿa tribe.

Aḥmad ʿAjīlat al-Subkī Bey (–), qā'immaqām of the Egyptian army; educated in Egypt, finally at the School of Engineering, Cairo, he was sent to France to study military science, 1844; he was attached to the cavalry school at Saumur and later to the French army; on his return to Egypt he was variously employed including a period as assistant to Maḥmūd Aḥmad Ḥamdī al-Falakī Bey (afterwards Pasha) during the latter's mission to Dongola to observe the eclipse of the sun, 1860; for four months in 1867 he worked with Ismāʿīl Muṣṭafā al-Falakī, Maḥmūd's brother, who was surveying a trace for a projected railway from Sawākin to Shendi; he was afterwards an engineer in the Egyptian public works department.

Aḥmad wad ʿAlī (–1892), Islamic judge and Mahdist 'amīr al-'umarā; he was serving as a district judge at Shaqqa in Dār Fūr in 1882 when, hearing of the rising fame of Muḥammad Aḥmad al-Mahdī, he deserted his post to join the Mahdist cause; having taken a leading part in the storming of al-Ubaiyaḍ the Mahdī placed him at the head of the legal jurisdiction of the movement with the title of *qāḍī al-Islām*, though he was popularly known as *qāḍī al-azraq*; in this capacity he served the Mahdī and his temporal successor, the Khalīfa ʿAbd Allāhi, for ten years, acquiring an immense influence and some wealth; it has been said that jealousy of his influence caused the Khalīfa to listen to accusations made against him by Yaʿqūb, the Khalīfa's brother; by others he is said to have abused his position as chief judge; whatever the truth he was sentenced to imprisonment and died shortly after in unexplained circumstances.

* **Aḥmad wad ʿAlī wad Aḥmad** (–1893), Mahdist amīr; a Taʿā'ishī of the Jubārāt branch he was a cousin of the Khalīfa ʿAbd Allāhi; he informed against the amīr Zakī Ṭamal, producing a story that the Italians had made an agreement with Zakī whereby the latter was to hand over Kassala to them in return for his being made governor of the town; as a result of this accusation Zakī was put to death in Omdurman and he was appointed governor of Kassala in Zakī's stead; he fought against the Italians and was killed while commanding the Mahdist army in battle near Agordat.

Aḥmad Bey ʿAlī Jallāb (–1885), Egyptian official; by origin from Aswān, his father is said to have been qāḍī of the Sudan before the Mahdist revolt; when Khartoum was in danger of capture by the Mahdists, and Gordon Pasha arrived in the capital in February 1884, he appointed Aḥmad ʿAlī Jallāb governor of the city with rank of bey;

Gordon afterwards removed him from office on suspicion of treachery but soon reinstated him; he was killed by the Mahdists in the general massacre which followed the taking of Khartoum.

Aḥmad al-Amīn Aderob (–1945), shaikh of the Ebsher branch of the Hadendowa Beja tribe and a man of religion; he died at Erheib in the Red Sea hills.

Aḥmad Bey ʿAwad al-Karīm abū Sin (*c.* 1790–1870), Sudanese notable, nāẓir of the Shukrīya Arabs, a prominent official during the Egyptian rule, and a man possessed of great character; early in the Egyptian occupation, unlike his brother Muḥammad ʿAwad al-Karīm who held aloof from contact with the invaders, he made peace with the Egyptians and by them was appointed shaikh and finally bey and governor, being for ten years (1860–70) governor of Khartoum, in which capacity he had authority over the nomadic tribes between the White Nile and the frontier of Abyssinia; his rule was marked by the foundation of Rufāʿa, which became his headquarters, and of Gedaref, known after him as Sūq abū Sin; during his governorship he stayed at the Rās al-Tīn palace at Alexandria as the guest of the viceroy Ismāʿīl Pasha who presented him with a sword and jewelled belt; he died in Cairo during a subsequent visit; several foreign travellers, including J. Hamilton who met him at Rufāʿa in 1854, were struck by his personality.

* **Aḥmad al-ʿAwwām** (–1884), Egyptian clerk employed in the War Office, Cairo, by Aḥmad ʿUrābī Pasha, he took part in the nationalist revolt of 1882; on the suppression of the revolt he was tried and sentenced to banishment in the Sudan; in Khartoum during the siege he wrote a history of ʿUrābī's revolt entitled *al-nasīḥa al-ikhwān* which he sent through the defence lines to Muḥammad Aḥmad al-Mahdī; he was discovered, tried by court-martial as a traitor, and hanged; copies of his history were printed on a primitive lithograph press at Omdurman during the Mahdist rule.

Aḥmad al-Badawī ʿAsākir abū Kalām (*c.* 1877–1917), nāẓir of the Jimaʿa of the White Nile, a member of a ruling family of the naẓārat al-baqqar, the Cattle Nāẓirate; he was succeeded on his death by his son Makkī.

Aḥmad Badawī abū Ṣafīya. *See* ʿAbd al-Ṣamad abū Ṣafīya.

Aḥmad al-Baghlī (*fl.* 1821), religious notable from Upper Egypt; he was among a party of religious and legal dignitaries sent by the viceroy Muḥammad ʿAlī Pasha with the military expedition of 1820 to the Sudan to endeavour to effect the bloodless subjugation of the people by persuasion; he accompanied the army of Ismāʿīl Pasha to Sennar in 1821 in the capacity of muftī of the Shāfiʿites in the Sudan; he returned to Egypt in 1824 by order of ʿUthmān Bey Jarkas, his mission having been completed.

Aḥmad Bakr (or **Bukkur**) **Mūsā** (–1722), sultan of Dār Fūr, Sultan Mūsā Sulaimān's youngest son; he ruled from 1682 until his death and was succeeded by Muḥammad Dawra; he is said to have built the stone mosque near the Fūr sultans' ancestral cemetery on Jabal Marra.

Aḥmad al-Baṣīr (–1829), holy man of the Jazīra; he was born in Dulqa village and such was his reputation that Muḥammad ʿAdlān abū'l-Kailak, last of the Hāmaj king-makers of the decaying Funj Empire, exempted him from taxation; he was buried at al-Baṣīr, the village which was named after him, and here his tomb was built in 1839–40 by Shaikh al-Ḥusain wad al-Ṣubāḥī.

* **Aḥmad Bey Dafaʿ Allāh** (–1883), Jaʿlī notable, from al-Juwair near Shendi; he was in command of a force of Sudanese irregulars in the defence of al-Ubaiyaḍ against the Mahdists; on the surrender of the garrison the Mahdists sent him to Shaqqa where he was killed by Madibbū Bey ʿAlī, chief of the Rizaiqāt.

Aḥmad Faḍīl Muḥammad (–1899), Mahdist amīr; by tribe of the Jubārāt branch of the Taʿā'isha Baqqāra and a relative of the Khalīfa ʿAbd Allāhi whom he loyally served; he put himself at the head of a force of black troops at Omdurman during the threatened revolt of the *ashrāf*, the relatives of Muḥammad Aḥmad al-Mahdī led by the Khalīfa Muḥammad Sharīf, against the dictatorship of the Khalīfa ʿAbd Allāhi; in the declining days of the Mahdist power ʿAbd Allāhi, after the disastrous battle of the Atbara in 1898, sent him to bring men from Gedaref and Gallabat for the defence of Omdurman now threatened by the Anglo-Egyptian army advancing up the Nile valley; too late to fulfil his task he marched on Gedaref, but, before he arrived, the amīr Saʿd Allāh, who had been holding the town, was dislodged by a force under Liwā' C. S. B. Parsons Pasha and Liwā' H. M. L. Rundle Pasha; he thereupon retreated towards the Blue Nile; at Dākhila near Roseires he was defeated by Mīrālai D. F. Lewis Bey and fled with a few followers, crossing the White Nile at al-Renk, where most of his remaining force surrendered, and rejoining the Khalīfa ʿAbd Allāhi in Kordofan; after leading an audacious raid in the region of Abā island he was killed at the battle of Umm Dibaikarāt in which several of the great Mahdist amīrs, among them ʿAbd Allāhi himself, met their death.

Aḥmad Faḍlī Pasha (1852–1901), Egyptian soldier; born at Mīnyā he graduated from the Cairo military school and received a commission as mulāzim II in 1874 when he was posted as an instructor to the artillery school; promoted yūzbāshī in 1877 he was sent in 1881 to take command of the big guns at Kafr al-Duwwār covering Alexandria, a post which he held until the outbreak of the rebellion of Aḥmad ʿUrābī Pasha in 1882; in December 1882 he commanded a battery of coastal artillery and afterwards became an artillery staff officer; he served on the line of communication during the Nile campaign of 1884–5; he was in command of the Egyptian artillery on the southern frontier and at Sawākin from 1885 when he was promoted binbāshī; he fought at

Jummaiza in 1888 when he was made qā'immaqām; a mīrālai in 1890, he became president of the army council and in 1894 assistant adjutant-general with rank of liwā'; he was later director of quarantines.

Aḥmad al-Ḥājj Ḥamad Ḥasab Allāh (–1908), Mīrafābī religious notable of Berber where he studied Islamic law under Shaikh Muḥammad al-Khair ʿAbd Allāh; after the Mahdist occupation of Berber in 1884, he was appointed a judge; in this office he was chiefly concerned with legal business connected with the Berber treasury under the Mahdist régime; on the establishment of the present government he served as an Islamic judge at al-Kawa, al-Dāmar, and Sennar; while still in office he died at Makka on the pilgrimage.

Aḥmad al-Ḥājj al-Ṭāhir (–1942), notable of the Fādnīya branch of the Jaʿlīyīn Arabs and a descendant of Shaikh Naʿīm al-Fādnī, a prominent holy man who lived near ʿUmm ʿAlī; he was a magistrate and president of the Fādnīya East branch court.

Aḥmad Ḥamad Maḥmūd (1883–1947), Beja notable; nāẓir of the Amarar tribe of the Red Sea littoral.

Aḥmad Ḥamd al-Sīd (1862–1941), religious notable, by origin a Jaʿlī; he settled in Rufāʿa in 1870 and during the Mahdist régime (under which he lost seven sons in battle) he was recognized as an authority on law; in 1930 he was appointed a religious member of the Shukrīya shaikhs' court; he had a valuable library and frequently lectured in Wad Madanī.

Aḥmad Hāshim Bey (–1841), vice-governor-general of the Sudan; he died of fever in Khartoum.

Aḥmad Bey Hāshim Baghdādī (*c.* 1875–1933), merchant and benefactor; a Persian by birth he was brought up in Baghdad and in 1900 came to the Sudan a poor man; he steadily amassed a fortune which, on his death in Khartoum, he left in trust for maintaining poor students at the Kitchener School of Medicine; he was a man of culture and an enthusiastic student of the Persian poets.

Aḥmad Ḥilmī abū Sin (–1946), tribal notable of the Shukrīya Arabs and soldier; born at Rufāʿa he entered the Military School at Khartoum and received a commission in the Egyptian army; retiring in 1932 with the rank of ṣāgh he devoted himself to tribal administration and was counsellor to the nāẓir of the Shukrīya; he died after a long illness at Rufāʿa.

Aḥmad wad Ḥilū (*c.* 1860–1944), Mahdist amīr; of the Jubārāt branch of the Taʿā'isha Baqqāra to which belonged the Khalīfa ʿAbd Allāhi, he fought in the principal battles of the Mahdist régime and distinguished himself as a leader of the Mahdist forces covering Kassala against the Italians; he survived the collapse of the Khalīfa's power and died an old man in Omdurman; he was no relation to the brothers ʿAlī and Mūsā wad Ḥilū of the Daghaim, also amīrs in the Mahdist army.

* **Aḥmad al-Hūdai** (-1884), Mahdist amīr, of the Shā'iqīya Arabs; he fought unsuccessfully against Muṣṭafā Pasha Yawar, Egyptian governor of Dongola, in 1884, and was killed by a government force in a battle at Korti.

Aḥmad al-Ḥusain (-1944), Rubāṭābī notable of the 'Ajībāb branch; he was 'umda of Abū Hashīm near Berber.

Aḥmad Bey Ḥusain Khalīfa (1836–1901), 'Abbādī Arab leader, a son of Ḥusain Pasha Khalīfa, governor of Berber 1869–73 and 1883–4, he was born in Berber and became the head shaikh of the Fuqarā and Milaikāb branches of the 'Abābda Arabs; he commanded a force of Arab irregulars which fought at Tūshkī (Toski), 1889, and which accompanied the Anglo-Egyptian army during the Dongola and Nile campaigns of 1896–8; he was present at all the bigger battles from Firka (Ferket) to Omdurman, capturing Berber from the Mahdists in August 1897; he died at Darāw in Upper Egypt.

Aḥmad Ḥusain Malik (*c.* 1860–1945), notable of Nubian (Wālīyābī) origin; shaikh of Okma since the days of Gordon Pasha whom he saw in Khartoum, he was a refugee in Egypt during the Mahdist revolt and was appointed 'umda in 1898 on his return.

Aḥmad Ibrāhīm 'Alī Burr (1863–1946), 'umda of Tūtī island, Khartoum; a Maḥasī by birth he traded on the White Nile as a young man during the latter years of the Egyptian Government; he returned to Khartoum when Muḥammad Aḥmad al-Mahdī revealed his mission and, on the conquest of the Sudan by the Mahdists, worked in the treasury of the Khalīfa 'Abd Allāhi in Omdurman; at one period he was keeper of the Khalīfa's privy purse; during his long tenure of office under the present government he rendered great service as a mediator in tribal disputes; he was a magistrate and a member of Khartoum North Bench.

Aḥmad Ibrāhīm al-Nitaifa (-1946), notable of the 'Arakīyīn tribe and 'umda of Ma'tūq in the western Jazīra.

Aḥmad Idrīs (1865–1933), notable of the Bāqīya branch of the Kawāhla Arabs who live in the Jazīra; he was born and bred at Daiyāna of which he was 'umda under the nāẓirship of al-Faḍl Ḥasan; he was a magistrate.

Aḥmad Pasha 'Iffat (*c.* 1830–85), Egyptian governor of Kassala during the siege of 1884–5 when the Egyptian garrison was hemmed in by a Mahdist force; after a long siege which lasted until the summer of 1885 he surrendered the fortress only after food and ammunition had been exhausted; while a prisoner of war he was murdered by order of the amīr 'Uthmān abū Bakr Diqna (Osman Digna) who, having a few days previously been heavily defeated at Kufit by an Abyssinian force under Alula, ras of Tigrai, vented his anger upon the leading officers of the surrendered garrison.

Aḥmad al-Imām ʿAlī (1896–1942), by birth a member of the ʿAbūdāb branch of the Kawāhla tribe of the Jazīra; he was ʿumda of ʿAbūd from 1933 and a member of the Manāqil court.

* **Aḥmad Ismāʿīl al-Azharī**, called **al-Walī** (*c.* 1810–81), learned man of the Dahmashīya section of the Bidairīya Arab tribe claiming ultimate descent from al-ʿAbbās, uncle of the Prophet; born at al-Ubaiyaḍ he went to Egypt about 1830–40 and entered the University of al-Azhar in Cairo where he remained studying for twelve years, first as a student then as a teacher of the Malakite code; he returned to al-Ubaiyaḍ where he followed the profession of the Islamic law; in 1881 he proposed to return to Cairo, but, on reaching Khartoum, Muḥammad Raʾūf Pasha, then governor-general, asked him to accompany an expedition against the newly risen Mahdī, Muḥammad Aḥmad, and attempt conciliation through an appeal to religious argument; arriving at Abā island where the Mahdī lay with his followers the expedition was all but destroyed and he was among the slain; his son, Shaikh Ismāʿīl al-Azharī, was muftī of the Sudan, 1924–32.

Aḥmad al-Jaʿlī (–1902), holy man of the Saraiḥāb branch of the Jaʿlīyīn tribe and founder of the Qādirīya religious brotherhood in Berber; he was born at Kadabās, a village near by, and was taught a particular version of the Qādirīya rite by the Persian mystic, ʿAbd al-Raḥmān al-Khōrāsānī, who visited Berber about 1865–70; soon after the capture of Berber by the Mahdists in 1884 the Khalīfa ʿAbd Allāhi, always suspicious of *ṣūfīs*, summoned him to Omdurman where he lived under surveillance until the entry of the Anglo-Egyptian forces into the town in 1898; he now returned to his home at Kadabās where he died; he was succeeded as head of the Qādirīya brotherhood in Berber by his son Muḥammad al-Ḥājj Aḥmad who was followed by another son, al-Jaʿlī al-Ḥājj Aḥmad, present head of the local brotherhood.

Aḥmad Jubāra (–1882), Mahdist amīr and learned man; he was a member of the Jubāra family who came to the Sudan with the Turkish army in 1821 and settled there; he was an early adherent to the cause of Muḥammad Aḥmad al-Mahdī who appointed him *qāḍī al-Islām*; he was killed during the siege of al-Ubaiyaḍ.

Aḥmad abū Jummaiza (–1889), notable of the Maṣālīṭ tribe of Dār Fūr; he rose in revolt against the Mahdist power in Dār Fūr in 1888, proclaiming himself to be the Khalīfa ʿUthmān and obtaining the support of several Dār Fūr tribes; he destroyed a Mahdist army under ʿAbd al-Qādir Dalīl and a week later defeated another under Muḥammad Bishāra; his death from small-pox was the undoing of his movement, his adherents lost enthusiasm and were utterly defeated in battle near al-Fāshar by the amīr ʿUthmān Adam.

Aḥmad Khair al-Sīd (*c.* 1870–1940), tribal worthy of the Dubāsīyīn north of Ḥaṣṣa Ḥaiṣa in the Jazīra; born at Kāb al-Jadīd he was shaikh of the locality till 1930 when he was made ʿumda.

Aḥmad Maḥmūd Mūsā (–1941), shaikh al-mashāyikh of the residential suburbs southward of Khartoum and by origin a Mīrafābī from Berber; he died in Khartoum.

* **Aḥmad al-Makāshfī** (–1883), Mahdist leader; a descendant of Shaikh ʿAbd al-Bāqī al-Naiyīl, holy man of the Kawāhla Arabs, he claimed Sharīfī descent; one of the earliest supporters of Muḥammad Aḥmad al-Mahdī he collected a following in the Jazīra and made several attacks on Egyptian Government posts both in the Jazīra and on the White Nile to the west; in 1882 he invested Sennar until a force under Ṣāliḥ Bey al-Mak raised the siege for a time; he was killed in an engagement with Ṣāliḥ Bey's troops at Jabal Saqadī near Sennar.

* **Aḥmad Pasha Manliklī** (or **Maniklī**) (*c.* 1795–1862), farīq of the Egyptian army and governor-general of the Sudan; he has been called a Mingrelian from the Caucasus, but his name suggests that he was a Rumelian Turk from Manlik in the mudīrīya of Kavala, a suggestion strengthened by the occasional ascription to him of the name Kāvāla-li, a native of the town or region of Kavala; he may have got the name Maniklī from a birth-mark on his face; he was one of Ibrāhīm Pasha's generals in the Syrian campaigns; in 1829 he was in command of one of three brigades of regular cavalry raised by the viceroy of Egypt, Muḥammad ʿAlī Pasha, and was given the rank of mīrlivā'; while in command of the 4th regiment of cavalry he made a decisive charge at the battle of Konia in 1832; after holding the post of *wālī* of Adana he returned to Egypt and was in 1837 appointed minister of war; in the second Syrian campaign of 1839–40 he again took the field and was in command of a column of infantry of the line which retreated from Damascus through Gaza and al-ʿArīsh to Egypt in 1840; the sudden death in 1843 of Aḥmad Pasha abū Widān, governor-general of the Sudan, had thrown that country into some confusion and the provincial governors were doing much as they liked; in November 1843 he was appointed ma'mūr of a mission, backed by a military force, to seek mineral deposits in the Sudan, but in January 1844 he was charged, concurrently with his mineralogical mission, with the reorganization of the Sudanese provinces on a decentralized basis; decentralization proving unworkable the viceroy chose him as Aḥmad Pasha's successor; he assumed office and soon restored administrative order; in 1844 he carried out a punitive expedition against the Hadendowa Beja of Tāka, the brutal thoroughness with which he subjugated the revolting tribesmen earning him the local nickname of *al-jazzār*, the butcher; he had forty Beja notables hanged in the market-place of Khartoum; he was recalled to Egypt in 1845 and was succeeded by Khālid Pasha Khusraw; he commanded the 2nd Egyptian division in the Crimean war of 1853–5 from which he was invalided by rheumatism; he died at al-Amamīn in Egypt.

Aḥmad Muḥammad abū Diqn (1880–1940), Islamic legal notable; a member of the tribe of Inqarriyāb Arabs he was educated at Gordon

Memorial College, Khartoum, and, entering the service of the Sudan Government, he was appointed qāḍī of Dongola, 1908; of Nahūd, 1912; of Omdurman, 1914; and of al-Ubaiyaḍ, 1918; in 1924 he was inspector of the Islamic law courts and latterly president of the board of *'ulamā'* and a municipal councillor of Omdurman; he retired from his legal duties in 1936.

Aḥmad Muḥammad Ḥamad al-Nīl (–1930), 'Arakī notable, a descendant of al-Saiyid Muqbil and a kinsman of Shaikh Ḥammād Aḥmad al-Nājī, khalīfa of the Qādirīya religious brotherhood at Abū Ḥarāz at the confluence of the rivers Rāhad and Blue Nile; he himself was 'umda of the town.

Aḥmad Muḥammad Ḥasanain Pasha, Sir (1889–1946), Egyptian court official and explorer; after attachment in 1914–16 to the staff of General Sir John Maxwell, commander-in-chief of the allied forces in Egypt during the First World War, he was employed in the Egyptian civil service and, from 1925, was first chamberlain to King Fū'ād I and King Fārūq I, and chief of the royal cabinet; his explorations of the Libyan desert have contributed greatly to a fuller knowledge of that area; in 1920–1 he crossed the Libyan desert from Egypt to the oasis of Kufra; in 1922–3 he made a long desert journey from Sollum to Dār Fūr, discovering the oases of Arkanū and 'Uwaināt; he died in Cairo as the result of a motor accident.

Aḥmad Muḥammad Ḥusain abū Shōk (1864–1937), Bidairī notable, 'umda of the Bidairīya of Ganetti between al-Dabba and Kūrtī in the Northern Province from 1904 till his death and from 1936 president of the Bidairīya court; his ancestors were the Duffār *mulūk* of Ganetti and during the Mahdist rule he was 'āmil of his village and district.

Aḥmad Muḥammad Kinaish (–1932), shā'iqī notable; 'umda of Nūrī near Merowe, a magistrate and president of the Nūrī village court.

Aḥmad Muḥammad al-Majdhūb (–1930), member of the religious family of the Majādhīb which has its traditional centre at al-Dāmar and which is of Ja'lī origin; he was a teacher at the Ma'had al-'Ilmī institute at Omdurman, a magistrate, and a member of the board of 'ulamā' of Omdurman; he died while on retirement after a long life of public service.

Aḥmad Muḥammad Qadaḥ al-Dam (1872–1924), shaikh of the western Sudanese; his father, Muḥammad Kurenga, a man of religion, came from Katgum now included in northern Nigeria and was descended from one of the ruling families of the Burnu Fallāta who claimed sharīfī descent; while on the pilgrimage to Makka he settled in Dār Fūr where he married a daughter of Sultan Muḥammad al-Ḥusain; to this lady Aḥmad was born at al-Fāshar where as a young man he joined the Mahdist cause; he fought under the Mahdist flag in several battles including Omdurman, 1898; after the Anglo-Egyptian occupation he continued to live at Omdurman and became the spiritual leader of the western Sudanese there, while the large floating population of Westerners, passing through Omdurman on their way to and from the pilgrimage, recognized him as their leader; although he preached against Dervish excesses, he championed the use of the distinctive patchwork garments of Mahdism and the study of the *rātib* of Muḥammad Aḥmad al-Mahdī; by encouraging his Westerners to become good citizens he did much to lessen the contempt with which they were then regarded by the people of the Nile valley; he lent the weight of his influence in the pacification of the country still restive by reason of the abolition of slavery; he accompanied the Anglo-Egyptian expedition against Sultan 'Alī Dīnār of Dār Fūr as an adviser in West African affairs, 1916; he died at Omdurman.

Aḥmad Muḥammad 'Uthmān al-Mīrghanī (–1928), religious notable, son of al-Saiyid Muḥammad 'Uthmān al-Mīrghanī II and brother of al-Saiyid Sir 'Alī al-Mīrghanī Pasha, the present head of the Mīrghanīya, or Khatmīya, religious brotherhood; he lived at Khatmīya, the ancestral seat of the Mīrghanī family in the Sudan, where he died.

Aḥmad Muḥammad al-Zain (*c.* 1842–1942), Ja'lī notable, 'umda of Zainūba near Kosti since 1899 when he assisted in the pursuit of the Khalīfa 'Abd Allāhi in eastern Kordofan; he is said to have passed his hundredth year.

Aḥmad Mumtāz Pasha (*c.* 1825–74), liwā' of the Egyptian army and governor-general of the so-called southern Sudan in 1871–2; information as to his early life is obscure; by some he is dubiously said to have been born in Egypt of Turkish stock and to have been educated in Germany; he is variously stated to have entered the Egyptian cavalry and the corps of engineers; certainty comes only with his transfer to Sawākin mu'āwinate in 1864 and his appointment as the first Egyptian governor of Sawākin after its cession to Egypt, and his promotion to the rank of bey in 1865; he suppressed a military mutiny in the town, advised the Khedive Ismā'īl on a proposed railway from Sawākin to the Nile valley, drew up town-planning schemes for Sawākin, and made proposals to tap the mountain torrents in the Red Sea hills to supply water for consumption in the town and for cultivation in the hinterland; making use of local forced labour he built a great earth barrage at Shata near Sawākin while he established the systematic production of cotton at Tokar in the delta of the River Baraka; commended by the Khedive for his enterprise he was promoted pasha and appointed governor of the eastern Sudan including the province of Tāka, the ports of Sawākin and Muṣawwa', and the Somali coast, in 1870; he continued to encourage the culture of cotton in selected spots along the coast and by stern measures against thieves made safe the roads from Sawākin to Kassala and Berber; the arbitrary manner of his drive to increase the production of cotton roused hostility among other governors and led to a quarrel between him and Ja'far Pasha Maẓhar, the governor-general at Khartoum; the Khedive took Mumtāz' side, recalled Ja'far, suppressed the governorate-general, and, in November 1871, Mumtāz took over the combined governorates of Khartoum, Sennar, the White Nile, and Fāzūghlī; after less than a year in office, during which he combined sensible administrative acts with gross irregularities, he was dismissed by the Khedive and his property confiscated; in August 1872 Ismā'īl Pasha Aiyūb was appointed his successor and the governorate-general was restored; he remained in Khartoum until the beginning of 1874 when he died on the eve of his trial by a commission on charges of mal-administration and fraud.

Aḥmad Nāṣir al-Mak Ibrāhīm (1840–1928), Jamū'ī notable; born on the island of Islānj near Jailī of a leading tribal family he was caught up in the Mahdist revolt and was made an 'āmil responsible for collecting taxes from the riverain tribes from Omdurman to Ḥajar al-'Asal at the upstream approach to the Sixth Cataract; on the Anglo-Egyptian occupation he was appointed 'umda of Islanj.

Aḥmad al-Raiyaḥ ibn Yūsuf abū Shāra al-'Arakī (*fl.* 1821–30), leader of the 'Arakīyīn Arabs of the Jazīra; discontented with the harsh government of the Turks and their crippling taxation he led his people to the southern Buṭāna, out of reach of the government; when 'Alī Khūrshīd Pasha, then governor of Sennar, declared an amnesty in 1830 he returned with (it is said) 12,000 of his people to their ancestral home; his son Ṭīraifī ibn Aḥmad al-Raiyaḥ al-'Arakī, who succeeded him, died in the cholera epidemic of 1857.

Aḥmad Rāshid Ḥusnī Pasha (1834–1905), soldier of the Egyptian army; born in the Caucasus of Circassian parentage he was educated in Egypt for the army and in 1854 was sent to complete his studies in France; returning to Egypt he received a commission, rising to yūzbāshī in 1856 and to mīrālai in 1860; in 1863 he was in command of the newly raised 4th infantry regiment sent to Kassala; he then commanded the 1st infantry regiment in Khartoum and the 7th regiment in the Ḥijāz; from Arabia he returned to the Sudan as officer commanding the 9th regiment; in 1864 he commanded the Egyptian garrison at Berbera on the Somali coast; in 1867 he again commanded the 7th regiment which was now in Crete subduing the Greek insurrection there; his promotion to liwā' came in that year when he returned to Egypt as a brigade commander; before the year was out he had been further promoted to farīq and was appointed to command the Guards regiments; he served in the Egyptian contingent in the Serbian war of 1876 and in the Russo-Turkish war of 1877–8; in the revolt of Aḥmad 'Urābī Pasha in 1882 he was aide-de-camp to the Khedive Muḥammad Tawfīq.

Aḥmad Ṣādiq (1858–1923), notable of the Fuqarā branch of the 'Abābda Arab tribe; he helped in the defence of the Egyptian southern frontier against the Mahdist forces and was in charge of Fuqarā and Milaikāb tribesmen during the Dongola and Nile campaigns of 1896–8 under Aḥmad Bey Ḥusain Khalīfa with whom he at one time quarrelled; his work during the war was the maintenance of camel transport over the desert route between Korosko and Abū Ḥamad; the war over he emigrated to Wad Madanī where he died.

Aḥmad al-Salāwī al-Maghribī (–*c.* 1840), religious notable of North African ancestry who was sent with a party of religious colleagues to accompany the military expedition of Ismā'īl Pasha to the Sudan in 1820–1, the mission of the party being the peaceful subjugation of the Sudanese by means of an appeal to religion; on his arrival he was appointed muftī of the Mālikites of the Sudan; he returned to Egypt with the Bey Daftardār Muḥammad Khusraw in 1824; his son Muṣṭafā afterwards became a judge in the Sudan.

Aḥmad Shaṭṭa (–1874), Fūr general; Zubair Bey Raḥma Manṣūr having captured the town of Shaqqa in Dār Rizaiqāt the Fūr sultan Ibrāhīm sent Aḥmad Shaṭṭa with Sa'd al-Nūr in command of an army to recover the captured lands; he and Sa'd were killed and their army defeated by Zubair near Shaqqa.

Aḥmad abū Shutāl (*c.* 1860–1937), Hāmaj chieftain, head shaikh of the Hāmaj and 'umda of the *'umudīya* of the Hāmaj; during the Mahdist rule he played a minor part and with his tribesmen fought at the battle of Dākhila near Roseires where he had his seat.

* **Aḥmad Sulaimān** (–1889), Mahdist amīr; by birth a Maḥasī of the Rufā'a branch and one of the earliest followers of Muḥammad Aḥmad al-Mahdī; he served both the Mahdī and his temporal successor, the Khalīfa 'Abd Allāhi, as treasurer; for his participation in a plot to depose 'Abd Allāhi in favour of the Khalīfa Muḥammad Sharīf, the former had him arrested and sent to the amīr Zakī Ṭamal at Fashoda (Kodok) where he was killed.

Aḥmad wad al-Sulṭān (–1928), chief of the Fallāta settlements at Jalqānī and 'Abd al-Khāliq in the Blue Nile valley.

* **Aḥmad al-Sunnī** (–1928), tribal notable of the Madanīyīn family of Wad Madanī; under the Egyptian régime he was a merchant and, happening to be in al-Ubaiyaḍ trading in 1882, he met Muḥammad Aḥmad al-Mahdī; he at once joined the Mahdist cause in which his ability marked him for high office; he was in due course made a treasury official and later supply officer and tax collector for the Jazīra, a post in which he was assisted by a force of soldiers, amounting latterly to over 2,000 men, as the source of revenue began to run dry; on the collapse of the Mahdist rule he made his peace with the Anglo-Egyptian administration in 1898 and was made 'umda of Wad Madanī town.

Aḥmad Ṭaha (–1882), holy man and Mahdist leader; at the outbreak of the Mahdist revolt in the Blue Nile valley in 1882 Giegler Pasha, then vice-governor-general, suspected him of Mahdist sympathies and sent a force to arrest him; this force he ambushed and slew; Giegler thereupon called in the Shukrīya Arabs under 'Awad al-Karīm abū Sin (afterwards pasha) who defeated and killed him near Abū Ḥarāz and sent his head to Khartoum.

Aḥmad al-Ṭāhir ʿAbd al-Qādir (–1934), Beja notable of the Hadendowa tribe of the Red Sea hills, ʿumda of the Ḥamdāb Aslīya section of the tribe, and a magistrate; he died at Sinkat.

Aḥmad Ṭai al-Sīd (–1929), ʿumda of the ʿAwwāmra living in the locality of al-Qitaina on the White Nile.

* **Aḥmad al-Ṭaiyib wad al-Bashīr** (–1824), now popularly called Shaikh al-Ṭaiyib; Jamūʿī holy man; he introduced the Sammānīya (a branch of the Khalwatīya) religious brotherhood into the Sudan and first set up a *khalwa* at Umm Maraḥī, twenty-five miles north of Omdurman; he toured the Jazīra where he founded branches of the brotherhood among the Ḥalāwīyīn, Jamūʿīya, and Kawāhla, appointing as his *khalīfa* Shaikh al-Tūm Bān al-Naqā; he died at Umm Maraḥī where his tomb (built in 1906) is located; the poet Ibrāhīm ʿAbd al-Dāfiʿ composed an elegy to him; Muḥammad Sharīf Nūr al-Dā'im, his grandson, was one of the teachers of Muḥammad Aḥmad al-Mahdī; another grandson was ʿAbd al-Maḥmūd Nūr al-Dā'im who wrote a history in manuscript of his grandfather's more famous pupils.

Aḥmad ʿUmar Hawwār al-Shaikh (1862–1946), tribal notable, a member of one of the leading families of the Jawāmaʿa Arabs of Kordofan; he and his father (later killed at Gallabat fighting the Abyssinians) joined the Mahdī and fought in several wars during the Mahdist period; latterly he was an amīr al-raiya under Maḥmūd Aḥmad and was with his commander at the battle of the Atbara in 1898; he deserted the Mahdist cause before the battle of Omdurman and retired into Kordofan, but shortly returned to the Nile valley after the Anglo-Egyptian occupation and made his submission at al-Duwaim; raising a force of his own he accompanied a column commanded by Colonel F. W. Kitchener, the sirdār's brother, which failed to attack the Khalīfa ʿAbd Allāhi at Sharqaila in 1899; his prestige survived the change of régime and from 1916 he was nāẓir ʿumūm of the district of eastern Kordofan with a population of about 200,000; he resigned the nāẓirship in 1943 when he was succeeded by his son Hārūn.

* **Aḥmad ʿUrābī Pasha** (1840–1911), Egyptian nationalist leader; born near Zagazig in the delta of Lower Egypt of peasant stock, he served in the army and was commissioned in 1862; during an undistinguished military career, in which his promotion was perhaps retarded by reason of his Egyptian origin, he was serving in 1875–7 as a commissariat officer on the lines of communication between Muṣawwaʿ and the hinterland, a term of service which brought him into brief contact with the Egyptian Sudan; his commanding officer at the time was the Circassian ʿUthmān Pasha Rifqī, afterwards vice-governor-general of the Sudan and later Egyptian minister for war, for whom ʿUrābī had no love; after playing a subordinate part in the officers' revolt in Cairo in 1879, he began in 1881 to win great popularity among the national

elements of the Egyptian army as the embodiment of the resentment against foreign control whether European or Turkish; the military revolt which he led having been suppressed in 1882, he was sentenced to death, but the sentence was immediately, by previous arrangement, changed into one of banishment; he and his chief associates were exiled to Ceylon whence he returned to Egypt in 1901; during his trial there was talk of banishing him to the Sudan, but this proposal was abandoned; various attempts have been made to identify the movement named after him with that of Muḥammad Aḥmad al-Mahdī, though there seems to have been no connexion between them other than a common hostility to foreign domination; 'Urābī was said by his defending lawyer to have dissociated his movement from Mahdism on religious grounds (Broadley, *How we defended Arabi* (1884), p. 496).

* **Aḥmad 'Uthmān al-Mīrghanī** (–1926), religious notable, head of the Khatmīya Islamic brotherhood, the son of al-Saiyid Muḥammad al-Ḥasan 'Uthmān and the brother of al-Saiyid Sir 'Alī al-Mīrghanī Pasha, the present head of the brotherhood; he died at Khatmīya, the seat of the Mīrghanī family, situated at the foot of the great granite crag behind Kassala.

* **Aḥmad Pasha abū Widān** (–1843), governor-general of the Sudan, 1838–43; said originally to have been a Circassian slave he entered the army and rose rapidly fighting in the Egyptian army in Arabia against the Wahhābites, in the Morea against the Greeks, and in Syria against the Ottoman power; in the Sudan he commanded the 8th regiment of regular infantry and on one occasion deputized for the then governor-general, 'Alī Khūrshīd Pasha; a difference of opinion with 'Alī Khūrshīd Pasha caused his recall to Egypt where he was soon appointed minister of war; on his appointment to the governorship in succession to 'Alī Khūrshīd Pasha he at once displayed energy and ability; he introduced date palms from Dongola to Khartoum, completed the building of a mosque in the capital, established an indigo dye factory at Shambāt, developed at Kamlīn on the Blue Nile an estate having fifty water wheels, a sugar plantation, and factories for making soap, sugar, and arrack, and he admitted slaves into government service; in 1840, after a gruelling campaign against the Hadendowa, he occupied the delta of the River Gash, established the Egyptian province of Tāka and founded the town of Kassala; he had married a daughter of Muḥammad 'Alī Pasha, an informed and cultivated woman, who is alleged to have undermined her husband's position by her propensity for intrigue; relations between him and the viceroy became strained and, having disregarded an order of recall, a force was said to have been sent from Cairo to bring him back; on his return from a tour of the Nuba mountains he fell ill with fever and died in Khartoum, his end having been hastened, the story goes, by poison; the circumstances of his death have given rise to speculation; from one source it was said that he received a communication from 'Abd al-Majīd, the Ottoman sultan, containing a proposal that the Sudan be detached from Egypt and ruled directly by the Sublime Porte; doubting

the authenticity of the document Aḥmad Pasha was said to have returned it to Constantinople for verification and that, on its way, it was intercepted by Muḥammad ʿAlī Pasha who sent an Albanian detachment under the sanjaq Damus Aghā to the Sudan for the purpose of arresting the treasonable governor-general, who committed suicide before the detachment arrived; evidence is at present lacking to confirm or refute these speculations; his tomb stands on the north side of ʿAbbās avenue, Khartoum; he has been described as a handsome man of light complexion, energetic and brutal, and is remembered as a strong and capable ruler.

Aḥmad Zarrūq (*c.* 1884–1946), shartai of Dār Kubra and Dār Fongoro; he was born during the sultanship of ʿAbd Allāhi Dūd Banja and was a posthumous son of a former shartai; he went with Maḥmūd al-Dādinjāwī on an expedition against Dār Maṣālīṭ and about 1905 took part in the fight with, and capture of, Sultan Abū Bakr Ismāʿīl; he accompanied Salīm abū Hawā against the Banī Ḥalba and, after a hard-won battle at Sagargarri, drove them into Dār Silā; he had been made shartai about 1910, just before the latter campaign; war having broken out between Sultan ʿAlī Dinār and the Sudan Government, an Anglo-Egyptian force entered al-Fāshar in 1916; he went to Abū Jabra to drive off the Taʿalba who were molesting the retreating Fūr army as it fled from the captured capital; he was with ʿAlī Dīnār immediately before the latter was killed and then took refuge in flight; later he made his peace with the new government which confirmed him in his tribal leadership which he held till his death; in 1936 he was appointed vice-president of the amīr of Zalingei's court.

Aird, Sir John, 1st Baronet (1833–1911), British contractor; born in London of Scottish descent, his father was a stonemason and afterwards contractor for several large works, among them the Crystal Palace, London; in partnership with Lucas he undertook the construction of a railway from Sawākin to Berber in 1885, but the work was abandoned after about twenty miles of line had been laid, the British Government having decided to withdraw the military expedition which protected the construction; he was afterwards head of the contracting firm of John Aird and Company of Westminster which, among many gigantic engineering undertakings, built the Aswān dam in 1898–1902.

al-ʿAjamī Ḥamza (–1865), notable of the Raḥmāb section of the Mīrafāb branch of the Jaʿlīyīn tribe; he was the son of Shaikh Ḥamza who was mak of Rās al-Wādī slightly north of the mouth of the River Atbara and nominally subject to the sultanate of Sennar; J. Bruce, the Scottish traveller, mentions his grandfather Muḥammad Babikr Ḥamza, mak of the Raḥmāb when Bruce passed through his lands in 1772; he was appointed nāẓir of the qism of Berber and shaikh of Rās al-Wādī in the Turkish administration but was discharged in 1854 by order of the governor-general ʿAlī Pasha Sirrī al-Arnāʾūṭ; he later brought complaints against the governor-general but apparently declined to appear before a board assembled to inquire into the complaints; Maḥmūd al-

'Ajamī Ḥamza, his son (d. 1919), was a ḥākim al-khuṭṭ of Rās al-Wādī and afterwards a Mahdist amīr; the present 'umda of Dārmālī is his grandson, Muḥammad Maḥmūd al-'Ajamī.

'Ajīb wad 'Abd Allāh, called **al-Kāfūta,** or **al-Mānjilak** (*c.* 1540–*c.* 1610), Arab leader, son of Shaikh 'Abd Allāh Jammā' of the Qawāsma branch of the Rufā'a tribe and ancestor of the 'Abdullāb, who helped 'Umāra Dunqas to found the Funj kingdom of Sennar; Shaikh 'Ajīb the Great, as he was called, was appointed *manjil* or viceroy of Qarrī by King 'Umāra abū Sakaikīn on his father's death; he extended his authority, it has been said, as far as Dongola, and it is certain that he included the Shā'iqīya among his vassals; he was a chief supporter of the great religious Shaikh Tāj al-Dīn al-Bahārī; at the command of his sovereign, King Dakīn wad Naiyīl of Sennar, he appointed various judges in his territory; finally he overstepped himself, revolting against his own king, though dissuaded from this venture by the holy man Shaikh Idrīs Arbāb of al-'Āilafūn; he was slain by King 'Adlān wad Aya in battle at Kālkūl near Kamlīn; the title of *'ajīb* has been assumed by his successors both under the Funj dominations and after: thus 'Ajīb wad 'Iraibī (*fl.* 1669), 'Ajīb wad Muḥammad 'Ajail (*fl.* 1691), 'Ajīb wad 'Abd Allāh (*fl.* 1760), and others.

Akkalili Mayya (*c.* 1865–1944), Lotuxo chieftain, son of Mayya who was murdered in 1897; on the death of Lomoro in 1912 he became chief of his section of the Lotuxo people whose tribal centre was at Oronyo-Ilyeu; naturally pious he carried out his rain-making functions with thoroughness and was rewarded by abundant rain; his children attended the Roman Catholic mission school at Torit and he himself died a Christian, but was buried according to the pagan rite by his conservative subjects.

Akol Atiang (–1941), chief of the Ajak section and recognized leader of the Paliet group of the Aweil Dinka of the Upper White Nile; he was a magistrate.

'Akūd ibn Salfāb ibn al-Amīn (–1819), grand shaikh of the Ḥannakāb section of the Shā'iqīya Arabs and the official ancestor of the Suwārāb section of the tribe; he was born at Qarrī and lived most of his life at Qurair; a contemporary of the great Shā'iqī mak Ṣubair and of the kings Musā'd and Nimr of the Ja'līyīn, he died the year before the Turks defeated his people in battle; the conquerors appointed his son, Shaikh Aḥmad wad 'Akūd, a sanjaq of Shā'iqīya irregular troops.

'Alā' al-Dīn Pasha Ṣiddīq (–1883), farīq of the Egyptian army; of Circassian descent he was originally a cavalry officer; his first administrative post in the Sudan was the governorship of Muṣawwa' from which he was elevated in 1871 to the more senior governorship of Tāka which carried with it the vice-governorship of the eastern Sudan, a newly demarcated province then independent of Khartoum; he greatly assisted the passage of C. G. Gordon Pasha and his staff from Sawākin to the interior in 1874, and during the Egyptian-Abyssinian war of 1875–6 he rendered valuable service in supplying the Egyptian army with camels and cattle from the Sudan; in 1879 Gordon, now governor-general of the Sudan, recommended his promotion to farīq, for since 1877 he had been in sole control of the ports of Sawākin and Muṣawwaʿ with the designation of muḥāfiẓ; in 1882 he became governor of the eastern Sudan in place of ʿAlī Riḍā Pasha al-Ṭūbjī and in 1883 civil governor-general of the Sudan in succession to ʿAbd al-Qādir Pasha Ḥilmī, the former military functions of the post being assumed first by Sulaimān Pasha Niyāzī, afterwards by Lieutenant-General W. Hicks Pasha; after superintending the transport of Hicks's army from Sawākin to Berber he himself joined the fatal expedition and was killed with Hicks and the greater part of the Egyptian army at Shaikān (Kashgil) in November 1883; little is now preserved to recall his personal character; he spoke no European languages and undoubtedly had difficulties with Hicks (since Hicks spoke no Arabic) during the last days of the march to Shaikān.

Alessandro Molodiang Longono (–1945), Bari chieftain, a magistrate and a member of the Belinian court near Juba.

Alexander, Boyd (1873–1910), traveller and ornithologist; he entered the British army in 1893 and, after making a journey from the Niger to the Nile, entered the Sudan from the Congo Free State in 1905; he attempted to traverse the country between Lake Chad and Dār Fūr but was killed at Nyeri in Dār Tāma, possibly by the agents of Sultan ʿAlī Dīnār.

Alfieri, Raffaele (*c.* 1840–), Italian doctor of medicine; a Neapolitan according to R. Gessi Pasha, an Abruzzese according to others, he was a volunteer under Garibaldi; taken prisoner at the battle of Mentana, 1867, he was in 1868 expelled from the Papal States; he came to Egypt about 1870; in 1879 he was serving as government doctor at Dāra in Dār Fūr under G. B. Messedaglia Bey who had a poor opinion of him; C. G. Gordon Pasha thought him incapable; in 1880 he was at Fōja (Fogia) in western Kordofan when the Italian explorers P. Matteucci and A. M. Massari passed through on their way to the west coast; robbed by Egyptian soldiers he left the Sudan in disgust, and travelling by Gallabat to Abyssinia was welcomed by Takla Haymanot, king of Gojjam; he was taken prisoner in civil war by Menelik, king of Shoa, whom he served as doctor from 1882 to about 1885; he was present at the death of O. Antinori the explorer at Let Marefia, 1882; he was in Rome in 1888 when he went to South Africa in search of adventure, and here all trace of him is lost.

ʿAlī, called **Abū Dilaiq** (*fl.* 1550), Arab holy man, paternal uncle of Shaikh Badawī wad abū Dilaiq and a disciple of Shaikh Salmān al-Ṭawwālī; he devoted his life to religion and was called 'Abū Dilaiq' (Father of Rags) from his asceticism and, after his death, 'Dhanab al-ʿAqrab' (Scorpion's Tail) from the swiftness by which God struck down those who swore falsely on his tomb which is situated at al-Niqfa, near the present Abū Dilaiq, the tribal centre of the Baṭāḥīn Arabs, about ninety miles east of Khartoum; he is said to have been a Kahlī by tribe; his followers are called after him the Dilaiqāb.

'Alī 'Abd al-Wāhid al-'Abbādī (*fl.* 1851), 'Abbādī religious notable who was born at Berber and died at Shaṭba near Darāw; Captain W. Peel (son of the prime minister of Britain), who visited him in Khartoum in 1851, referred to his great age and scholarship.

'Alī wad 'Adlān (–1821), notable of the Hāmaj family of 'Adlān who played an important and disruptive part in the last years of the Funj sultanate of Sennar; he submitted to Ismā'īl Pasha on the Turkish occupation of Sennar in 1821 but was shortly after suspected by the Turks of disloyalty and was hanged at Sennar.

'Alī Aḥmad Ḥarīra (*c.* 1820–96), Baṭḥānī chieftain, nāẓir of the Baṭāḥīn during Egyptian and Mahdist times; his family, which had settled slightly east of Khartoum North since the Funj rule, had held the nāẓirship of the tribe for several generations; he died peacefully at Omdurman and his son Aḥmad succeeded him as 'umda.

* **'Alī 'Awad al-Karīm abū Sin** (–1874), nāẓir of the Shukrīya, 1872–4; the younger brother of Shaikh 'Awad al-Karīm abū Sin (d. 1802), he was chosen to be nāẓir not only because of his character but because his elder brother Aḥmad (d. 1870) was a prominent figure in the Egyptian administration.

'Alī Bashīr Kanbal (1891–1947), officer of the Egyptian army and afterwards of the Sudan Defence Force; a son of the great Shā'iqī soldier, Bashīr Bey Kanbal, he received a commission in 1912 and was promoted yūzbāshī in 1925 and binbāshī in 1938; on his retirement from the army he was ma'mūr of Abū Dilaiq and a member of the rural district council; he was stabbed to death by a madman at his home in Ḥalfaiyat al-Mulūk.

'Alī abū Dakka (–1942), nāẓir of the Daqāqīm branch of the Ḥamar Arabs of Kordofan and magistrate; he died at al-Uḍaiya.

* **'Alī Dīnār Zakarīyā Muḥammad al-Faḍl** (*c.* 1865–1916), sultan of Dār Fūr; a grandson of Sultan Muḥammad al-Faḍl who reigned from 1779 to 1839, he succeeded Abū Khairāt, son of Sultan Ibrāhīm, in 1889 during the years of the Mahdist supremacy in Dār Fūr; at first he held aloof from the Mahdists and it was said that he meditated an insurrection against the Mahdist amīr of Dār Fūr, Maḥmūd Aḥmad, who, suspecting his loyalty, sent him to the Khalīfa 'Abd Allāhi at Omdurman in 1897; the Khalīfa reproved him and gave him lowly employment in the Mahdist capital; he assisted in a Mahdist attack on the king of Taqalī in the Nuba hills in 1898 when, hearing of the Anglo-Egyptian victory at Omdurman, he deserted the Mahdist cause and, collecting followers and arms, made for Dār Fūr; there he captured al-Fāshar from the Mahdist garrison, defeated Ibrāhīm 'Alī, another

member of the Fūr royal house and the sirdār's dilatory candidate for the sultanship, and seized the throne; in 1900 he was officially recognized by the Sudan Government and paid a nominal tribute; he organized his sultanate in a fairly efficient, if barbarous, manner, crushing all opposition and ensuring the Fūr supremacy by a series of punitive raids against the dissident tribes in his dominions and on their borders; in one of these raids he killed Sanīn Ḥusain of Kabkabīya in 1907; his armies were not always successful as when in 1913 one was heavily defeated by the Rizaiqāt; the First World War was his undoing; persuaded by Turkish and Sanūsī intrigue he renounced his allegiance to the Anglo-Egyptian power in 1916 and prepared for war, forcing on his people a primitive, home-made, currency to raise money; after a short campaign his main army was totally defeated at Birinjiya near al-Fāshar by an Anglo-Egyptian force commanded by al-liwā' P. J. V. Kelly Pasha and fled only to be killed at Kulmé, south of Zalingei, by a chance bullet during the pursuit.

'Alī Ḥamad Bey Faṭīn abū Dakka (1872–1942), nāẓir of the Ḥamar Arab tribe of Kordofan; on the outbreak of the Mahdist revolt his father took to the wilderness but was afterwards captured and imprisoned by the Khalīfa 'Abd Allāhi; young 'Alī became a messenger in the Khalīfa's household and was so great a favourite that he succeeded in persuading the Khalīfa to order his father's release; the latter having died in 1931 he was appointed in his father's place in 1932.

'Alī ibn Ḥammūda al-Kahlī al-Aswadī, called **'Alī wad Baqādī** (–1803), man of religion; a Kahlī, born at al-Sharā'ana in the Jazīra, he was a famous and learned faqī; his son, al-Sanūsī wad Baqādī, was impaled in 1830 by the Turks for disaffection.

'Alī Bey Ḥasīb (*fl.* 1851–4), qā'immaqām of the Egyptian army; there is a certain obscurity surrounding his origin; by some he is stated to have been a Cairo water-carrier's son adopted by the widow of Ismā'īl Pasha Kāmil, son of the viceroy Muḥammad 'Alī, and to have been educated by her; by others he is said to have been a bastard son of Ismā'īl or of Ibrāhīm; whatever his beginnings he was brought up in the household of Muḥammad 'Alī Pasha and, joining the army, was governor of Berber in 1851–2; the Syrian traveller Yūsuf Khūrī, who met him at Berber in 1851, recorded that the governor read him a literary composition of his own consisting of a description of the Sudan and that, though ignorant, he was naturally talented; another informant, J. Hamilton, described him as handsome and the most intelligent official in the Sudan; his talents were not appreciated by the Government, for in 1852 he was removed from his post for malpractices and attached as an aide-de-camp to 'Abd al-Laṭīf Pasha, the governor-general, with whom he seems to have been on bad terms; in 1854, while 'Alī Pasha Sirrī al-Arnā'ūṭ was governor-general, he was ordered to build a prison at Qaissān between Fāzūghlī and the Abyssinian border, but fled while on the way there and took refuge in the Ḥijāz.

ʿAlī Ḥasīb al-Ṣiddīq (1858–1947), notable of the religious family of the Majādhīb, of Jaʿlī origin; his father was one of the teachers of Muḥammad Aḥmad al-Mahdī and on his mother's side he was descended from Muḥammad Ḥamza, mak of Rās al-Wādī (Dārmālī), a few miles north of the confluence of the Nile and Atbara; born at Qūz al-Funj near Berber he entered the legal department of the Sudan Government as an Islamic judge and served as qāḍī in Kordofan, the Red Sea province, and at Berber; in 1924 he retired and lived at Qūz al-Funj where he taught religion till his death.

* **ʿAlī wad Ḥilū Khalīfat al-Mahdī** (–1899), Mahdist leader of the Daghaim Baqqāra Arabs; immediately before the outbreak of the Mahdist revolt the tribe was living on the White Nile and, together with the Kināna, joined the Mahdī in 1881, first among the Baqqāra converts to the new cause; the Mahdī appointed him one of his four caliphs when he was chosen to represent the historic Caliph ʿUmar ibn al-Khaṭṭāb; he served the Mahdī and his temporal successor, the Khalīfa ʿAbd Allāhi, in many battles; at Omdurman in 1898 he had a force of 5,000, mostly Daghaim and Kināna, fighting under his green flag; he was killed at the battle of Umm Dibaikarāt along with ʿAbd Allāhi and several of the leaders of the Mahdist movement; the amīr Mūsā wad Ḥilū was his brother.

ʿAlī wad ʿIshaib (*fl.* 1580), religious man; born at Old Dongola he studied in Egypt under Shaikh Banūfarī, returned to the Sudan, and settled in the region of Sennar; Shaikh ʿAjīb the Great built him a mosque and the king of Sennar granted him land; he seems to have given himself rather to the hearing of cases and to the practical interpretation of the Islamic law than to religious teaching in its stricter sense; he was buried at al-ʿAidai and a tomb built over his grave.

* **ʿAlī Jaifūn** (*c.* 1836), soldier, a member of the Shilluk tribe of the Upper White Nile; born at Fashoda in the time of the Shilluk *reth* Niadok wad Yor he was captured while a young man by raiding Ḥawāzma Arabs near Fungor and by them handed over to the government in part payment of taxes; he was pressed into the regular army; he first served in the Sudan and took part in one of the many assaults made by the Egyptian army on Jabal Taqalī in the Nuba hills; he was next with the Sudanese battalion in Mexico under the command of Marshal Bazaine, 1863–7; on his return he joined the Sudan garrisons on the eastern frontier; during the Mahdist revolt he fought in the defence of Kassala and later of Amideb on whose fall he escaped to Muṣawwaʿ and was taken to Egypt; receiving his commission he was posted to the 10th Sudanese battalion and in 1889 was promoted yūzbāshī; he fought the Mahdists at Ḥandūb, Tokar, and in the Nile valley, and was finally promoted sāgh qōl aghāsi.

ʿAlī Jarkas Pasha (*fl.* 1854–7), Turco-Egyptian governor-general of the Sudan between 1854 and 1855 following ʿAlī Sirrī Pasha al-Arnāʾūṭ; he appears to have returned to Egypt at the end of his term of office and to have re-entered the Sudan in the winter of 1856–7 in the suite of Muḥammad Saʿīd Pasha, the viceroy of Egypt, who was making a tour of inspection and ordering many administrative changes; it is known that ʿAlī Jarkas Pasha left for Egypt in 1857 carrying with him the archives of the governorate-general which Muḥammad Saʿīd Pasha had abolished; nothing is known of him save that he was, as his name signifies, of Circassian descent, and that he was known by the more intimate as Koko Pasha.

ʿAlī Jārūt (–1945), shaikh of the Awlād Jābir branch of the Zaiyādīya tribe of northern Dār Fūr; he died at Umm Ḥijīj.

* **ʿAlī Julla** (*c.* 1845–1944) notable of the Missīrīya Arabs of Kordofan and grandfather of the present nāẓir ʿumūm of the tribe, Shaikh Bābū Nimr; as a young man he acted as a guide to C. G. Gordon Pasha during one of the latter's whirlwind rides in his campaign against Sulaimān wad Zubair in 1877; attracted early to the cause of Muḥammad Aḥmad al-Mahdī his tribesmen afterwards became one of the most trustworthy sections in the army of the Khalīfa ʿAbd Allāhi; their bravery at the battle of Tūshkī (Toski) cost them serious losses; he himself was appointed an attendant of the Khalīfa and in this capacity met R. K. von Slatin Bey, formerly Egyptian governor of Dār Fūr, who was then similarly employed; he fought both at Omdurman in 1898 and at Umm Dibaikarāt in 1899 where he was captured, only to be released by his old friend Slatin; he then returned to Dār Ḥumr where he held sway from 1905 to 1920, when his reactionary methods of administration caused his removal from office in favour of his son Muḥammad Nimr.

ʿAlī Kanūna (*c.* 1830–*c.* 1875), shaikh of the Ghudīyāt Arabs who occupy the region south-west of al-Ubaiyaḍ in Kordofan; he was the seventh manjil of that tribe; little tangible information is available as to his life; he rebelled against the government or, more correctly, he was a party in an inter-tribal dispute in which he had the misfortune to have the government on the wrong side; he was attacked by a government force and killed in battle at Khōr ʿIfaināt.

ʿAlī al-Karīm abū Sin (–1802), son of Shaikh ʿAwad al-Karīm abū ʿAlī and leader of the Shukrīya Arabs; he combined with the ʿAbdullāb from the north to sack the town of Arbajī in 1784 and was later killed in a fight with the Baṭāḥīn.

ʿAlī Khūrshīd Pasha (*c.* 1786–1845), governor-general of the Sudan, the first among the Egyptian rulers to unite the full civil and military functions of a head of an established administration; after campaigning under Ibrāhīm Pasha against the Greek insurgents in the Morea he was in 1826 appointed governor of Sennar and its dependencies, including the territory between the Sixth Cataract and the Abyssinian foothills; in 1828 he sent an expedition against the Dinka living on the east bank of the White Nile, while in 1829 he raided the people of the Funj mountains; in 1831 he warred against the Shilluk; he conducted these campaigns chiefly for obtaining slaves for the army; during his term of office Khartoum developed from a military headquarters into an administrative capital. Here in 1830 he built brick buildings including a mosque; he raided Tāka in 1832 and again in 1834 when he met with a reverse; called to Egypt Muḥammad 'Alī Pasha discussed with him the affairs of the Sudan and obtained for him from the Sublime Porte the rank of pasha of the grade of mīrmīrān; in 1835 he returned to Khartoum as governor-general; he raided various Arab tribes which had fled to the borders of Abyssinia to escape taxation and the inconveniences of ordered government; on one occasion he is said to have met the king of Gondar on the border and to have asked him to prevent the emigration of Arabs from the Sudan; he is also said to have induced many of the escaping tribesmen to return to their former homes; finding conciliation did not produce the co-operation of the Abyssinians he marched on Gallabat and threatened Gondar; to placate the British Government, which took umbrage at this high-handed action, Muḥammad 'Alī Pasha recalled him in 1838 to inquire into the incident and appointed Aḥmad Pasha abū Widān as governor-general in his place while making him governor of Adana under his old commander Ibrāhīm Pasha who had won a series of victories over the Turks; at the time of his death he was governor of the province of Sharqīya in Egypt; one of his last acts as governor-general of the Sudan was to prepare, under the direction of Muḥammad 'Alī Pasha, an expedition to discover the source of the White Nile, a project which was afterwards attempted by a party under Salīm Qapūdān; he was undoubtedly an efficient administrator, making frequent inspections of his provinces and holding periodical conferences with his subordinate governors; by his good government he did much to efface the terrible memory of the massacres carried out by Muḥammad Khusraw, the Bey Daftardār, in 1822.

'Alī Bey Luṭfī (–1882), qā'immaqām of the Egyptian army; the towns of al-Ubaiyaḍ and Bāra having been surrounded by the Mahdist forces, he was sent from Khartoum with a considerable body of reinforcements, consisting of two battalions of regular infantry and 750 bāshī-būzuq irregulars, in September 1882; the Jawāma'a Arabs under Raḥma Manūfal fell upon them at Kawa; a remnant survived the engagement and forced their way into the besieged town of Bāra then being defended by al-Nūr Bey 'Anqara; 'Alī Bey, however, was among the slain.

'Alī al-Mahdī (1881–1944), religious notable, the fifth son of Muḥammad Aḥmad al-Mahdī; born at Omdurman he was arrested along with other members of the Mahdī's family after the revolt of political prisoners at Shukkāba in the southern Jazīra in 1899 and with his kinsmen was in exile at Rosetta where he received part of his education; on the release of his family in 1905 he entered the service of the Sudan Government, resigning in 1926 to become agent for his brother, al-Saiyid Sir 'Abd al-Raḥmān al-Mahdī Pasha, in Omdurman; he retired from active work in 1929 when he devoted himself to writing a history of the Mahdist movement (as yet unpublished); he died in Omdurman.

'Alī ibn Muḥammad al-Hamīm, called **al-Nīl** (*fl.* 1620), holy man, the third caliph of the great religious shaikh Tāj al-Dīn al-Bahārī of the Islamic brotherhood of the Qādirīya; he was called al-Nīl from the floods of knowledge that he poured into the dry wastes of people's minds; he lived during the time of King al-Rubāṭ of Sennar and was buried at Mundara.

'Alī Muḥammad Muṣṭafā (–1929), Ḥalāwī tribesman, shaikh of Ḥillat Mi'aijna near Ḥaṣṣa Ḥaiṣa.

'Alī Muḥammad Nūr (1881–1946), civil servant; born in Kassala, the son of an Afghan merchant from Kābul who came to the Sudan after making the pilgrimage to Makka, he made an adventurous escape with his family from Mahdist-controlled Kassala to Sawākin where he entered the newly established government school; in 1901 he joined the Sudan postal service as a clerk, ultimately retiring as a postmaster when he engaged in commerce; he held high office in the Mīrghanīya religious brotherhood.

'Alī Muḥammad abū Qiṣaisa (–1947), Rubāṭābī religious notable; he died at Berber.

'Alī Mūsā Bey Shawqī (–1885), liwā' of the Egyptian army; he had been governor of the Baḥr al-Ghazāl province during the last years of the Egyptian rule and, on the arrival of C. G. Gordon Pasha in Khartoum from Egypt in February 1884, he was provisionally appointed governor of the town in the absence of 'Awad al-Karīm Pasha abū Sin who, on account of the unsettled state of his district, was unable to come to Khartoum to take up his duties; in the sack of Khartoum, rather than fall into the hands of the Mahdists, he first shot his family then himself.

'Alī Qurānī al-Naqshabandī (–*c.* 1870), holy man; a relative by marriage of al-Saiyid Muḥammad 'Uthmān al-Mīrghanī, he lived first at Makka and later in Dongola whence he regularly revisited the Holy Places; in Sha'bān, 1278 (Feb.–March 1862), Muḥammad Ḥusain, sultan of Dār Fūr, persuaded the viceroy Muḥammad Sa'īd Pasha to grant him a pension.

'Alī Bey Riḍā al-Kurdī (*c.* 1814–), officer of Shā'iqīya irregular troops in the Egyptian army; of Kurdish origin he came as a boy with his father to the Sudan in Ismā'īl Pasha's army in 1820–1 and was at an early age appointed a bulūk-bāshī; for many years he was employed in tax-collecting in the country east of the Blue Nile; he was promoted sanjaq and in 1865 was commanding 200 Shā'iqīya troopers at the post of Asār near Sūq abū Sin, the modern Gedaref, taking part in frontier raids under Mūsā Pāshā Ḥamdī, governor-general of the Sudan; promoted qā'immaqām he was governor of the newly constituted White Nile province, 1866–71, when he suppressed a revolt of the Shilluk; in 1871 Aḥmad Pasha Mumtāz, then governor of the so-called South Sudan, a territory which included the White Nile, had him tried on a charge of abuse of power, a charge of which he was acquitted; he was without employment till 1875 when he returned to his former governorate of the White Nile and crushed a Shilluk rebellion; during the earlier years of the Mahdist revolt he was fighting in the Jazīra; locked up in Khartoum during the siege in 1884 he left the doomed city with the fleet of steamers under the command of Muḥammad Nuṣḥī Pasha which steamed down to Matamma to meet the British column which was attempting to relieve Khartoum; from 1885 he was employed as a leader of irregulars in the defence of the southern frontier of Egypt; in 1890 the Sudan bureau under which he was employed placed him on the retired list; he lived in Cairo till his death.

'Alī Riḍā al-Ṭūbjī Pasha (1828–1900 ?), liwā' of the Egyptian army; born at Retimo in Crete of Turkish descent, he served [with the Egyptian contingent] in the Russo-Turkish war, 1877; he was governor-general of the Red Sea littoral, 1880–1, and of Harar, 1883–4, and then held administrative posts in Egypt; his career is recorded in 'Abd al-Raḥmān Zakī's *A'lām al-jaish* (Cairo, 1947).

* **'Alī al-Rūbī Pasha** (–1891), liwā' of the Egyptian army; an Egyptian, born in the Fayyūm, he was commissioned in the army and as a binbāshī in the cavalry served in the Egyptian-Abyssinian war of 1875–6, being taken prisoner by the Abyssinians at the battle of Gura; promoted qā'immaqām he was sent on a mission to King John a few weeks after the battle to treat for peace, but the mission failed; on his return to Egypt he was employed in administrative duties in the ministry of the interior and in other civil service posts; he was under-secretary for the Sudan during the years 1881–2; joining the Nationalist cause he fought at Kassassin, and at Tel el Kebir commanded the Egyptian army; for his part in the rising he was condemned to twenty years imprisonment at Muṣawwa'; he was latterly blind.

'Alī Bey Sabastopoli (–1865), officer of the Egyptian army; while serving as qā'immaqām of the regular infantry regiment in Kordofan he was appointed mīrālai of the 10th regiment then on its way from Egypt to the eastern Sudan, but died before he could take over the command.

'Alī Pasha Ṣādiq (–1890), Egyptian official; educated at the School of Engineering in Cairo he was sent to England to study mechanical engineering and railway management, 1847–53; on his return he was employed on the Egyptian State railways, eventually becoming governor of Cairo, 1876; in that year he was appointed general manager of the Soudan railway and in 1877 director of the finance department of the Sudan Government; he was president of the commission which in 1882–3 investigated the revolt of Aḥmad 'Urābī Pasha.

'Alī Bey Sharīf (–1883), formerly governor of Kordofan he was appointed governor of Dār Fūr in 1880 in succession to G. B. Messedaglia Bey whom the governor-general of the Sudan, Muḥammad Ra'ūf Pasha, had discharged; he was present in al-Ubaiyaḍ in 1882 as assistant to the governor, Muḥammad Pasha Sa'īd, during the siege of the town by the Mahdists; on its surrender he was captured and beheaded by Nawai of the Ḥawāzma tribe at al-Birka near al-Rāhad; after his death the Mahdī looked after his family.

ʿAlī Pasha Sirrī al-Arnāʾūṭ (1814–66), governor-general of the Sudan from July to November 1854; an Albanian and a Mameluke by origin as his name indicates, he was originally known as ʿAli Ḥusain Qūlī Kahlī and later, at the time of his receiving his commission, ʿAlī Ḥusain; in 1831 he was a pupil at the Citadel school in Cairo from which he passed to join the militia in the training school at al-Khānkā, rising to sōl qōl aghāsi in the 3rd infantry regiment; promoted mulāzim I in 1832 and yūzbāshī in 1833, he served in the expedition to the Ḥijāz, and in 1838 was promoted binbāshī; in 1842 he was appointed to the personal staff of Prince Muḥammad Saʿīd Pasha and in 1847 was attached to the 1st Guards regiment; his rise was now meteoric, for he was promoted mīrālai in 1848 and liwāʾ in 1849; his short stay in the Sudan was without importance since he was appointed merely as a deputy to cover staff changes due to the Crimean war of 1853–5, to which Egypt sent a contingent, and to the illness of his predecessor, Salīm Pasha Ṣāʾib; except for a visit to Sennar he never left Khartoum; on his recall to Egypt he was succeeded by ʿAlī Pasha Jarkas; he was a member of the *majlis al-aḥkām*, a body combining the functions of privy council and court of appeal, from 1865 until his death.

ʿAlī al-Ṭai (–1943), notable of the Shukrīya Arabs of the Buṭāna, ʿumda of the Shukrīya khuṭṭ of Abū Dilaiq, and a magistrate; he spent his old age in retirement.

ʿAlī al-Tūm Faḍl Allāh Sālim, Sir (1874–1938), nāẓir ʿumūm of the Kabābīsh Arabs of northern Kordofan, a nephew of Ṣāliḥ Bey Faḍl Allāh killed by the Mahdists at Umm Badr in 1887; he was an enlightened, fine type of Arab, much respected by his people; his father was killed at al-Ubaiyaḍ by the Mahdists in 1883 and he himself, surviving the violence of the times, was appointed to the headship of the tribe on the Anglo-Egyptian occupation of the Sudan; from 1915 he was nāẓir ʿumūm; in 1919 he visited England and in 1925 he was knighted by King George V; on his death his son, Shaikh al-Tūm ʿAlī al-Tūm (1897–1945), assumed the office.

ʿAlī ʿUmar Barsī (1890–1947), Jaʿfarī notable, chief merchant of al-Dāmar; born in Khartoum he was the son of Shaikh ʿUmar Barsī, a well-known merchant, and the brother of Maḥmūd ʿUmar Barsī, formerly chief merchant of al-Dāmar.

ʿAlī Bey ʿŪwaiḍa (*fl.* 1868–74), soldier of the Egyptian army; in 1868 he was governor of Berber with rank of mīrālai when he was charged with negligence, theft, and malversation of public funds; he was acquitted of the other charges but convicted of negligence and dismissed from the governorship; in 1872 he was in command of the 1st Sudanese regiment when he was convicted with others of theft from the government treasury which it was the duty of his regiment to guard; a commission, of which Khālid Pasha Nadīm was president, was sent from Egypt in 1874; the commission found him innocent of the charges concerning his conduct while governor of Berber.

ʿAlī abū Zanait wad Adam (*c.* 1860–1922), titular king of Taqalī in the Nuba hills from 1885 to 1896; after the defeat and massacre of his people by the Mahdists during the years 1885–7 he continued the struggle for independence as the successor to his father, King Adam Daballū, who had died a captive of the Mahdists in 1884; for several years he carried on guerrilla warfare against the Mahdists who sought in vain to dislodge him from his hilly stronghold; finally he fell out with his brother Jailī and civil war ensued; defeated in 1896, when Jailī was reinforced by numerous well-armed deserters from the declining Mahdist cause, he fled to Jabal Daiyar, leaving his brother king of Taqalī; in 1900 the new Government allotted him a small (afterwards somewhat enlarged) territory including the hills of Tukam and Taishan which he administered until his death; in character he was a mixture of courage and brutality.

al-ʿĀlim, called **al-Sharīfī** (*fl.* 1650), holy man of the Ḥalāwīyīn Arab tribe of the Jazīra; he was born at al-Faḍlīn near Masallamīya of a family currently supposed to have been of the Prophet's stock; he became a disciple of the celebrated religious teacher, Dafaʿ Allāh Muḥammad abū Idrīs al-ʿArakī, and was credited with miraculous powers; his tomb at Qurashī is used for the binding of oaths.

Allenby, Sir Edmund Henry Hynman, 1st Viscount Allenby of Megiddo and of Felixstowe (1861–1936), British soldier who played a prominent part in the First World War; in 1915–17 he commanded the 3rd army in France and in 1917–19 achieved his greatest military fame as commander-in-chief of the Egyptian expeditionary force which destroyed the Turkish armies in Palestine and Syria; he was promoted field-marshal and raised to the Peerage; he was high commissioner for Egypt in 1919–25, a period of political activity which included the signing of the Nile Waters agreement in 1920 and the assassination of Sir Lee Stack, governor-general of the Sudan, in 1924; he visited the Sudan in 1920 and met many Sudanese notables.

Almkvist, Herman Napoleon (1839–1904), Swedish philologist; born at Stockholm he was professor of Semitic languages at the University of Upsala; he travelled in Turkey and Egypt; in 1877–8 he was in the Sudan studying the Nubian and Beja languages on which he wrote treatises; he died at Upsala.

Alūlā, Ras (1847–97), Abyssinian governor of Tigrai; in 1884–5 he assisted the evacuation of Egyptian garrisons from towns along the Sudan–Abyssinian frontier when their investment by the Mahdists was threatened; in 1885 he left Asmara with a force ostensibly to relieve Kassala, but he failed to do so, though later in the year he heavily defeated a Mahdist force under the command of ʿUthmān abū Bakr Diqna (Osman Digna) at Kufit near Agordat; in 1887, while leading the vanguard of an Abyssinian army advancing on Muṣawwaʿ against the Italians who had landed there in 1885, he destroyed an Italian column at Dogalī; he died at Adowa.

Alvarez, Francisco (*fl.* 1520), Portuguese priest, chaplain of Coimbra, and a member of a Portuguese embassy to the emperor of Abyssinia which travelled by way of Muṣawwaʿ to the interior in 1520; his account of the embassy, published at Coimbra in 1540, and afterwards translated into several languages, contains interesting remarks on Sawākin and the decaying kingdom of Alwa.

Amatore, Michele (1826–83), Sudanese soldier in the Piedmontese army; he was born in the Nuba hills and was captured as a boy by slave raiders from whose hands he at length found deliverance by his purchase in 1832 by Dr. Castagnone, personal medical attendant to the viceroy Muḥammad ʿAlī Pasha; the doctor gave him the name of Michele Amatore and becoming a Christian he accompanied a friend of Castagnone's to Italy, acquired Italian nationality, and joined the Bersaglieri regiment of the Piedmontese army in 1848; he served with his regiment in the campaign against Austria in 1848–9 and again in 1859; promoted corporal in 1859 his rise was then rapid, for by 1863 he had attained the rank of captain; he was decorated by King Victor Emmanuel II for his unselfish services in the Sicilian cholera outbreak of 1869; he died a pensioner at Rosigno Monferrato in Piedmont.

Ambron, Abramo (1851–1904), Cairo surgeon; born in Tripoli on the Barbary Coast of Tuscan forbears, he studied medicine in the universities of Pisa and Florence; after some years of practice in the medical service of the Egyptian army in the Sudan before the outbreak of the Mahdist revolt, he settled in private practice in Cairo where his talents brought recognition.

Amenemipt (*fl.* 1300 B.C.), Egyptian viceroy of Ethiopia (the northern Sudan) during the reigns of the nineteenth dynasty Egyptian kings Rameses I, Sethos I, and the joint reign of Sethos I and Rameses II; he held office from about 1315 B.C. to about 1290 B.C.

Amenophis, or **Amenhetep, I** (*fl.* 1550 B.C.), Egyptian king of the eighteenth dynasty who reigned between 1557 B.C. and 1540 B.C.; he led campaigns against the Ethiopians in the land of Kush (Upper Nubia) and completely conquered it; he appointed Thury as his viceroy of the conquered territories; this Thury was the first of a long line of Egyptian viceroys who ruled the northern Sudan during the eighteenth and nineteenth dynasties.

Amenophis, or **Amenhetep, III** (*fl.* 1500 B.C.), Egyptian king of the eighteenth dynasty; he built a temple at Napata near the present Merawe; on the island of Sai in Dār Sukkōt there is a small temple bearing his inscriptions.

* **Amery Bey, Harold François Saphir** (1877–1915), British major; commissioned in 1897 in the Royal Highlanders he was transferred to the Egyptian army in 1901, being promoted captain in 1902; he spent several years in the Sudan and was for some time assistant director of intelligence, Sudan Government; he died of wounds received in the First World War; he published *Aids to Arabic* (Khartoum, 1911).

Amīn Pasha. *See* SCHNITZER, EDUARD CARL OSCAR THEODOR.

al-Amīn ʻAbd al-Barī Min Allāh (*c.* 1809–92), notable of the ʻArakīyīn Arabs of the Blue Nile; a member of the Fawāḍla branch of the tribe he was a shaikh of great local influence; he fought a long but bloodless war against the ʻAbūdī tax-collector, Ibrāhīm al-Badawī, and eventually secured his dismissal by the government of Sennar; his son Bābikr al-Amīn ʻAbd al-Barī fought in the Mahdist wars under the amīr Ḥamdān abū ʻAnja.

al-Amīn Iḥaimir (–1935), ʻumda of Ḥaṣṣa Ḥaiṣa, and president of the Ḥaṣṣa Ḥaiṣa town bench of magistrates; he was by tribe a Dubāsī.

al-Amīn Akkām (1880–1943), Sudanese tribal leader, nāẓir of the Shanābla Arabs of Kordofan from 1928 until his death.

al-Amīn Bullād (–1946), Jaʻlī notable, ʻumda of the Jaʻlīyīn of northern Kordofan; he died at Umm Saiyāla between Bāra and Khartoum.

al-Amīn Ḥāmid Sulaimān (-1942), Beja notable; ʻumda of the Jamīlāb Taulīl section of the Hadendowa tribe.

al-Amīn Ijaibir abū Shilūkh (–1943), wazīr of Dār Maṣālīṭ; he died at al-Jinaina in western Dār Fūr.

* **al-Amīn Muḥammad al-Ḍarīr** (–1885), religious notable; he was a Maḥasī born on Tūtī island opposite Khartoum; he received a sound education under his father Shaikh Muḥammad al-Ḍarīr on the island and, arrived at manhood, he went to Rufāʻa and there built a mosque and taught; during the tenure of office of the governor-general Jaʻfar Pasha Maẓhar (1866–71) he was appointed *ra'īs mumayiz ʻulamā' al-Sūdān* by firman of the Ottoman sultan, the only traced instance of the official conferment of that title during the Egyptian régime; he was a poet of renown and a member of Jaʻfar Pasha's literary circle in Khartoum; his son Muḥammad al-Amīn al-Ḍarīr (d. 1933) was a religious shaikh of Omdurman.

al-Amīr Ghanī. *See* MĪRGHANĪ.

al-Amīr ʻUthmān (–1863), head shaikh of the Arteiga tribe, a branch of the Beja group of the Red Sea littoral; on his death he was succeeded by his son al-Jailānī (afterwards Bey).

Ampère, Jean-Jacques (1800–64), French man of letters and historian, son of A. M. Ampère, the pioneer of electrodynamics; in the winter of 1844–5 he visited Abū Simbel and the Second Cataract in the pursuit of antique remains, a journey described in his *Voyage en Égypte et en Nubie* (Paris, 1868).

ʻAmr ibn al-ʻĀṣ (al-ʻĀṣī) al-Sahmī (*c.* 570–*c.* 663), Arab conqueror of Egypt and a general of the caliph ʻUmar; the occupation of Egypt by the Arabs, begun in 641, brought Nubia within the influence of the Muslim power; about 642 ʻAmr sent an army into Nubia under the command of ʻAbd Allāh ibn Saʻd; the Arabs established themselves at

Aswān but, after ʿAbd Allāh had returned to Cairo, the Nubians took the offensive and invaded Upper Egypt, laying waste part of it; in 652 ʿAbd Allāh returned with a vengeance, sacked Old Dongola, the seat of the Christian kingdom of Nubia, and made the Nubians tributary to Egypt.

Anderson Bey, George Whitfield (1856–1915), British major; he joined the Seaforth Highlanders in the ranks and fought in the Afghan war of 1878–80, at Tel el Kebir, 1882, and in the Nile campaign of 1898 when he was present at the battles of the Atbara and Omdurman; an honorary captain and quarter-master in 1898 he entered the Egyptian army in 1901; promoted to honorary major in 1908 he rose to the rank of mīrālai in the Egyptian army, dying in Cairo.

Andreis, Amalia (1852–82), mother superior, of the Roman Catholic Church; born at S. Maria di Zevio near Verona she entered the religious order of the Pie Madri della Nigrizia in 1876, and after a period in Cairo she came to the Sudan at the end of 1880; in 1881 she went to the newly established mission station at Dilling in the Nuba hills as mother superior of the sisters there; the missionaries at Dilling were captured by the Mahdists in 1882 and brought to al-Ubaiyaḍ, where she died in captivity.

Anei Kur (*c.* 1900–45), Shilluk tribal dignitary, *reth* or ruler of the Shilluk from 1944 and president of the central court; he administered about 70,000 tribesmen; he was succeeded on his death by Dak (son of Fadiet Kwadker, a former *reth*) who was installed in 1946; an attempt to assassinate him was made in 1934 by a member of a disgruntled rival family.

Anley, Frederick Gore (1864–1936), British brigadier-general; commissioned to the Essex Regiment, 1884, he served with the mounted infantry in the Nile campaign, 1884–5; transferred to the Egyptian army, 1896–9, he was first posted to the 2nd battalion and was afterwards a staff officer at Sawākin; he fought in the South African war, 1899–1902, and in the First World War, 1914–18, retiring in 1919.

Annesley, George, 2nd Earl of Mountnorris, 9th Viscount Valentia (1770–1844), British traveller; accompanied by H. Salt as his secretary and draughtsman he was sent on a diplomatic mission to Abyssinia in 1805 to obtain a port on the Danakīl coast which might enable Britain to take Egypt in the rear if that country were again seized by the French; on the journey he visited Sawākin in 1806 and described the place.

Anson, William (1855–74), son of Admiral Anson and a member of the British civil service; he threw up a promising career in the Post Office to join his uncle, C. G. Gordon Pasha, then governor of the Equatorial province; he arrived at Sawākin early in 1874 and, travelling up the Nile, died shortly afterwards in the arms of R. Gessi Pasha in the Baḥr al-G͟hazāl.

Antinori, Orazio, Marchese (1811–82), Italian patriot and naturalist, born at Perugia of an old, aristocratic family; on the outbreak of the revolution of 1848 he enlisted in the Liberal army under Garibaldi; he fought in the Veneto against the Austrians and was wounded at Cornuda; elected a deputy of the Roman constituent assembly he assisted in the defence of Rome against the French until the fall of the city; the Liberal cause having been defeated he left Italy and travelled abroad; from Egypt he came to the Sudan in 1858; setting out from Khartoum he visited the country of the Rivers Rāhad and Dinder in 1859 and from Gedaref went by Gallabat to Roseires; with the French traveller G. Lejean he visited Kordofan in 1860 and the Baḥr al-Ghazāl in 1860–1; he then returned to Cairo and distributed his ornithological collections to various museums; a founder of the Italian geographical society in 1867 he was a member of the Italian delegation at the opening of the Suez Canal in 1869; with O. Beccari and A. Issel he travelled in Abyssinia in 1870–2 when C. Piaggia, another Italian explorer of the Sudan, helped him in making zoological collections; in 1871–2 he travelled from Muṣawwaʿ to Kassala; he died in Abyssinia while leading a scientific expedition; he was a self-reliant man of pioneering temperament and was a skilful mechanic and carpenter.

Antognoli, Adolfo (1826–68), Italian surveyor and trader; born at Lucca and educated as an engineer, he came to Egypt in 1855 and was employed as a schoolmaster; in 1857 he set up in Khartoum as a trader, entering into partnership with a fellow countryman A. Castelbolognesi and dealing in Abyssinian produce, a business which took him and his partner to Gallabat and Roseires, 1859–60; in 1861 he took part in an expedition to succour A. Peney who had gone exploring in the Equatorial regions and had got lost; he found Peney who shortly afterwards died of fatigue; in 1864 he married Peney's Abyssinian widow, Sarah; in 1868 he accompanied the British military expedition against Theodore II of Abyssinia and later carried out surveys for the Italian navy in the Red Sea; while so employed he died of yellow fever on board ship near Sawākin.

Anville, Jean-Baptiste Bourguignon d' (1697–1781), French geographer; he was the first geographer to trace with relative accuracy the map of the Nile valley up to Khartoum.

Anyonywe Auranomoi (–1946), Didinga chieftain, a magistrate and the president of the Didinga branch court; his tribe live eastwards of the Imatong mountains.

al-ʿĀqib al-Amīn (–1930), religious shaikh of Rubāṭābī origin; he studied at al-Azhar University, Cairo, and returned to the Sudan with Zubair Pasha Raḥma Manṣūr as a teacher; he afterwards became a member of the board of ʿulamāʾ of Omdurman.

al-ʿAqqād. *See* HAṢAN MŪSĀ AL-ʿAQQĀD; MUḤAMMAD AḤMAD AL-ʿAQQĀD; MUḤAMMAD ABŪ SUʿŪD BEY AL-ʿAQQĀD; MŪSĀ BEY AL-ʿAQQĀD.

Arabi Pasha. *See* AḤMAD 'URĀBĪ PASHA.

'Arabī Dafa' Allāh (–*c.* 1916), Mahdist amīr, a Ta'ā'ishī Baqqārī related to the Khalīfa 'Abd Allāhi; one of the first to join the cause of Muḥammad Aḥmad al-Mahdī, he was in Dongola during the earlier part of the *Mahdīya*; in 1890 he was appointed amīr of the Equatorial province with headquarters at Rejaf; he left Omdurman with two steamers and 300 men with orders to depose al-Ḥājj Muḥammad abū Qarja, the Mahdist governor of the province; he defended the southern approaches to the Sudan with ability; he ambushed and killed Faḍl al-Mūlā Bey Muḥammad, one of Emin Pasha's officers, near Rejaf, and held down the native tribes with a firm hand; the tide turned in 1897 when, after ambushing a Belgian detachment near Rejaf, he was beaten in battles at Bedden and Rejaf by another Belgian force commanded by Colonel L. N. Chaltin; after some attempt at a rearguard campaign his force disintegrated and, with the way north closed by the advancing Anglo-Egyptian army and the collapse of the Khalīfa 'Abd Allāhi's power, he fled with 3,000 men to Mandua near the present border of French Equatorial Africa in Dār Ta'ā'isha; from there he conducted an abortive parley by letter with the new Government, the failure of which may have been due to his resentment at the high-handed actions of 'Abd al-Raḥīm Bey Sālim abū Daqal whom the Government had sent in pursuit of him; after an unsuccessful attack on French outposts in the region he surrendered to Sultan 'Alī Dīnār with his men and their arms in 1902; his veterans were known in Dār Fūr as the 'Baḥāra'; he then lived in al-Fāshar but was continually under suspicion; in 1903 he was imprisoned for alleged intrigue and was periodically reported as having been executed; he continued, however, to take part in many of the sultan's military expeditions; he is said by some to have died in 1915, but more reliable evidence suggests that he was executed in the following year by 'Alī Dīnār on the news of the withdrawal of the Fūr forces from Jabal al-Ḥilla.

Arakīl Bey al-Armanī (1826–58), Armenian governor of Khartoum, Sennar, and other territories comprised in the newly created province of the south Sudan; a relation of Nubar Pasha Boghos, prime minister of Egypt, he was born in Smyrna and joined the viceregal service; he accompanied the viceroy Muḥammad Sa'īd Pasha on the latter's visit to the Sudan in the winter of 1856–7 and was appointed governor in 1856 in succession to 'Alī Pasha Jarkas, last of the governors-general until Mūsā Pasha Ḥamdī to rule the whole Sudan; a governor of enlightened ideas, though strict, according to local tradition, he commissioned L. Ori, his principal medical officer of health, to improve the sanitation of the river front at Khartoum and did much to make Khartoum a less unhealthy town, but his premature death in the capital cut short his projected reforms; he was buried without religious rites in the Christian cemetery at Khartoum, but his body was later re-buried in Egypt; he was followed by Ḥasan Bey Salāma who held the governorship from 1859 to 1861.

* **Arakīl Bey Nubar** (–1875), Armenian official, a nephew of Nubar

Pasha Boghos and a relation, through his mother, of Arakīl Bey al-Armanī, governor of the southern Sudan, 1856–8; a cultured man, speaking several European languages, he was educated at the Collège de Sorrèze in France; he entered the Egyptian ministry of foreign affairs and was in the suite of Muḥammad Sa'īd Pasha during the latter's visit to the Sudan in 1856–7; while in the Sudan he accompanied F. M. de Lesseps, the future creator of the Suez Canal, on a short expedition up the White Nile south of Khartoum; he was afterwards private secretary to the Khedive Ismā'īl and finally a chief of division in the Egyptian ministry of foreign affairs; in 1868 he was with the French man of letters, Edmund About, on a journey from Cairo to Upper Egypt; appointed governor of Muṣawwa' in 1873 he was active in pushing forward the construction of a telegraph line from Muṣawwa' to Kassala, completed in 1874; on the outbreak of the Egyptian-Abyssinian war in 1875 he took the field with S. A. Arendrup's force and was killed, or perhaps committed suicide to avoid capture, at the battle of Gundet.

al-Arbāb Dafa' Allāh wad Aḥmad Ḥasan (–1822), Hāmaj vizier of the sultans of Sennar during the anarchy which accompanied the last days of the sultanate; he came to power by violence and remained in authority till the coming of the Egyptian army of conquest in 1821 when he and Rājab wad 'Adlān went out from Sennar to meet Ismā'īl Pasha as the delegates of Bādī IV, the last sultan; later in the year he helped the Coptic accountant, Ḥanna al-Ṭawīl, to assess the taxes on the inhabitants of the Jazīra; in the course of the Sudanese revolt which followed the murder of Ismā'īl Pasha at Shendi in 1822 he fled from Wad Madanī and took refuge with Ḥasan Rājab; the two collected an army at Abū Shōka and gave battle to an Egyptian force under Muḥammad Sa'īd Efendi; the Egyptians won a crushing victory, Ḥasan Rājab was killed, and al-Arbāb is said to have made for Abyssinia and to have died there; his son Muḥammad returned later to Wad Madanī and submitted to 'Alī Khūrshīd Aghā, then governor of Sennar; by 1840 he had become a great man locally and married Naṣra, sister of Idrīs 'Adlān, shaikh of the Funj and grandson of Muḥammad abū'l-Kailak; he visited Cairo with 'Abd al-Qādir wad al-Zain in 1845 and was presented to the Wālī, Muḥammad 'Alī Pasha.

al-Arbāb wad Kāmil wad al-Faqī 'Alī (–1822), religious notable of the village on which Khartoum now stands; he was a descendant of the holy man al-Arbāb al-Ajaid who, about 1690, moved to the village from the nearby island of Tūtī; Arbāb wad Kāmil was living in the village at the time of the Egyptian occupation of Sennar in 1821 when, in the general massacre of Sudanese in revenge for the murder of Ismā'īl Pasha, son of the viceroy Muḥammad 'Alī Pasha, by mak Nimr of Shendi, the Daftardār Bey killed him by shooting him from a cannon; his nephew, 'Abd al-Raḥmān wad Muḥammad, buried at Khartoum North, was the last notable of the line.

Ardagh, Sir John Charles (1840–1907), British major-general of the Royal Engineers; he entered the Royal Military Academy at Woolwich in 1858 and during the years 1876–81 was employed in various capacities in the Ottoman Empire; after serving with the British army in the campaign against Aḥmad 'Urābī Pasha in 1882 he was engaged on the Red Sea coast of the Sudan in 1884 when he was present at the second battle of el-Teb as officer commanding the Royal Engineers, with rank of lieutenant-colonel; he was military commandant of Cairo during the campaign of 1884–5 to relieve Khartoum; among the posts he subsequently held was that of director of military intelligence in the War Office, London, 1896–1901; his 'life', by his wife, Lady Susan Harris, Countess of Malmesbury, was published in 1909.

* **Arendrup, Søren Adolph** (1834–1975), Danish officer in the Egyptian army; born at Frederikshavn he was commissioned in the Danish army in 1859 and in 1863 was promoted 1st lieutenant in the artillery; affected by consumption he went to Egypt where in 1874 he took service under al-farīq C. P. Stone Pasha, chief of the Egyptian general staff; in 1875, war between Abyssinia and Egypt having broken out, he was placed in command of an Egyptian force of 2,500 men with artillery which advanced from Muṣawwa' into the Abyssinian highlands and was heavily defeated at Gundet; surrounded by the enemy he fought, sword in hand, until he was killed.

Arimondi, Giuseppe Edoardo (1845–96), Italian major-general; born at Savigliano in Piedmont he was commissioned as a sub-lieutenant of Bersaglieri in 1865 and first saw active service against the Austrians in the Veneto in 1866; he began his service in Eritrea in 1887, becoming commandant of troops in the colony in 1892; in a battle near Agordat he defeated a Mahdist army and killed its commander, Aḥmad wad 'Alī, in 1893; in 1894 he directed the military operations which led to the Italian occupation of Kassala; he commanded a brigade at the disastrous battle of Adowa against the Abyssinians in 1896 and was left dead on the field.

Armstrong Bey, Edgar Hubert (*c.* 1868–1903), British soldier; he was commissioned in the Lancashire Fusiliers, 1889, and in 1900 was seconded to the Egyptian army; while holding the rank of qā'immaqām he was transferred to the Sudan Government and was appointed an inspector in the Baḥr al-Ghazāl; he was killed by an elephant.

Armstrong, Sir William George, Baron Armstrong of Cragside (1810–1900), British engineer and industrialist; he visited Aswān in 1872 to advise on a means of opening the First Cataract to continuous steam navigation, a work projected in connexion with the construction of the Soudan Railway southward from Wādī Ḥalfā; although he and his manager G. W. Rendel recommended the building of a hydraulically operated ship incline, the Egyptian Government could not afford the cost and the project was dropped.

Arnaud Bey, Joseph-Pons d' (1812–84), French engineer, known to his friends by the nickname 'Prince de la Lune' in allusion to his bald head; he came to Egypt as a disciple of the French social philosopher Saint-Simon and was for some time engineer of the port of Maḥmūdīya;

in 1838–9 he accompanied Muḥammad ʿAlī Pasha on a visit to the Sudan and with the viceroy ascended the Blue Nile to the mines in the region of Fāzūghlī; here Muḥammad ʿAlī entrusted him with the building of a palace, a project which was not realized; he made three voyages to the upper White Nile in search of its source, 1839–42; these expeditions, commanded by Salīm Qapūdān, succeeded in ascending the White Nile as far as the neighbourhood of Gondokoro; he published a map of the newly discovered regions in 1843 in the bulletin of the geographical society of Paris; Sir F. Galton, the great anthropologist, who met him at Korosko in 1845, has recorded that D'Arnaud stimulated his interest in scientific problems; he died at Chatou in France.

Arsenios (1879–1940), Greek Orthodox bishop of Nubia, 1931–6; born at Alassata in Asia Minor he was appointed bishop of Hermopolis (Ṭanṭā, in Lower Egypt) shortly before his death.

Arthur, Sir George (1860–1945), British soldier and biographer; entering the army in 1880 he served in the Nile campaign of 1884–5 as a lieutenant in the 2nd Life Guards; from 1914 to 1916 he was Lord Kitchener's private secretary; he was for many years a member of the executive committee of Gordon Memorial College; he published the official life of Kitchener (1920) and, with Sir F. Maurice, that of Lord Wolseley (1924), and edited the letters of Lord and Lady Wolseley (1922).

Artīn Arakīliān (1824–89), Armenian farmer; born in Constantinople he left Turkey as a youth and came by way of Egypt to the Sudan, arriving in Khartoum in 1854; here he set up in retail trade, later moving to Asār, near Gedaref, where he married an Egyptian lady, daughter of the Muʿallim Saʿd, in 1859; on his lands at Asār he introduced the culture of Turkish tobacco, a novelty in those days; the tobacco was sent to Khartoum for curing and packing by Armenian experts; he also exported the produce of Abyssinia and the crops of the district, importing groceries; at the beginning of the Mahdist revolt the rebels looted his property at Asār and Khartoum; he died, a ruined man, in Gedaref.

Asʿad Milḥam Rāshid (1860–1932), Syrian doctor; born at Marjaʿyūn in the Lebanon of a Christian family he graduated in medicine and surgery at the Syrian Protestant College (afterwards called the American University) of Beirut, and emigrated to Egypt where he joined the Egyptian Army Medical Corps; he served in the Dongola campaign, 1896, and was present at the battles of Firka and Ḥafīr; later medical officer commanding military hospitals at Wādī Ḥalfā and Dongola he was disappointed by his slow advancement in the Egyptian army and resigned his commission with the rank of ṣagh qōl aghāsi; deciding on taking up a career in agriculture he bought lands in Dongola and, in 1913, near Wādī Ḥalfā where he became a pioneer of scientific fruit-growing; he died suddenly at Arqū near Dongola.

Asʿad ibn al-Muḥadhdhab ibn abī al-Milīḥ Mammātī (1149–1209), Egyptian official, minister in the Aiyūbid Government, a Coptic

Christian from Asyūṭ, a distinguished man of letters, and a poet who perpetuated his versatility by turning the classic stories of Kalīla and Dimna into Arabic verse; he made reference to the Red Sea coast of the Sudan in his more serious *Kitāb qawānīn al-duwāwīn*, an edition of which, by Suryāl ʿAṭīya, was published by the Royal Agricultural Society of Egypt in Cairo, 1943; he died in Aleppo.

* **ʿAsākir wad abū Kalām** (–*c.* 1903), nāẓir of the Jimaʿa tribe of the White Nile; he succeeded his father Abū Kalām Ballāl abū Hūra who was deposed by the Egyptians about 1870 but, unlike his somewhat stern father, he was lenient towards his tribesmen; at the opening of his preaching crusade, Muḥammad Aḥmad al-Mahdī is said to have had no immediate success in converting his people, for he took no active part in the Mahdī's revolt until 1883 when he led a mixed force of Jimaʿāb and Jawāmaʿa to harry the army of al-farīq W. Hicks Pasha on its march through Kordofan; in 1885 the Khalīfa ʿAbd Allāhi ordered him to bring his tribe to Omdurman; when they hesitated he sent a force under Yūnus wad al-Dikaim who seized their cattle and broke up the tribe; he himself was first imprisoned at Omdurman and returned to Dār Jimaʿa only to collect taxes; he was later banished to Rejaf whence he escaped about 1897 and died in Dār Fūr while fighting under ʿArabī Dafaʿ Allāh.

Ashburnham, Sir Cromer (1831–1917), British major-general; he joined the King's Royal Rifle Corps as a cornet, 1855, and fought in India, Afghanistan, and South Africa; present at the battle of Tel el Kebir, 1882, in which year he was promoted colonel and knighted, he was posted with Sir G. Graham's field force at Sawākin, 1884; he fought in the second battle of El Teb and at Tamai, and was governor of Sawākin, 1884.

al-Aʿsir ibn ʿAbd al-Raḥman ibn Ḥammādtu (*fl.* 1670), holy man who was born and lived at Nūrī near the present Merowe; he combined the functions of prophet and Shā'iqī patriot in the struggle against the ʿAbdullāb viceroys of the sultanate of Sennar.

Asser Pasha, Sir Joseph John (1867–1944), British soldier; entering the Royal Artillery in 1887 he served in the Nile campaign in 1897–9 having joined the Egyptian army in 1892; he was brigade major in the 3rd Egyptian brigade at the battles of the Atbara and Omdurman, 1898; he was in command of the campaign in southern Kordofan in 1910 and for some years was a member of the governor-general's council with rank of liwā'; he served in the First World War and in 1926 was promoted general; he died in London.

Atherton, Walter Hyde (1855–85), British major; he received a commission in the 5th Dragoon Guards in 1874 and was promoted captain in 1879 and major in 1884; taking part in the Nile campaign of 1884–5 he was killed in the battle of Abū Ṭulaiḥ (Abu Klea).

Aubert-Roche, Louis-Rémy (1810–74), French doctor who was medical officer at the construction of the Suez Canal; he travelled in the Sudan; while passing through Dongola in 1857 the Belgian traveller, E. de Pruyssenaere, met him there; he was an authority on typhus on which he wrote two noteworthy papers; he also wrote *Essai sur l'acclimatation des européens dans les pays chauds* (Paris, 1854).

* **Aumont, Louis-Marie-Joseph**, Duke d'Aumont et de Villequier (1809–88), French traveller, born in Paris; in 1855–6 he made a remarkable journey by sailing-boat from Cairo to Rejaf; leaving Cairo in June 1855 he navigated the Nile cataracts on the flood, lightening ship between Merowe and Matamma by sending much of his cargo overland; at Abū Ḥamad he saw his first hippopotamus; arriving at Khartoum in January 1856 and at Rejaf in the following April, he regained Khartoum in May only to find the town in the grip of a cholera epidemic; after travelling by river to Berber he crossed the Nubian desert to Korosko, thence continued by river to Cairo; here he died during a later visit to Egypt.

Austin, Herbert Henry (1868–1937), British brigadier-general; he entered the Royal Engineers in 1887 and served on railway surveys in India and Uganda; in the course of two surveys on the western border of Abyssinia in 1899–1901, he, with lieutenants Bright and Garner, travelled from Omdurman overland to Mombasa, 1900–1, and determined the position of Omdurman and other places in the Nile valley; he later served in India and was in Mesopotamia during the First World War; he wrote several autobiographical works including *Among Swamps and Giants in Equatorial Africa* (1902).

'Awad Allāh, called **al-Malik 'Awad Allāh** (–*c.* 1835), Rubāṭābī notable of the Ḍaifāb sub-section of the Farānīb section of the tribe, ḥākim khuṭṭ of Baqīr, during the early part of the Turkish rule; the Mahdist amīr wad al-Malik 'Awad Allāh (d. 1895) was his son.

'Awad al-Karīm 'Abd Allāh abū Sin (1877–1943), nāẓir 'umūm of the Shukrīya Arabs from 1923 when he succeeded his father 'Abd Allāh 'Awad al-Karīm; caught up in the Mahdist revolt he went as a child with his family to Omdurman in 1886 and was educated in Koranic schools there; he and his people were opposed at heart to the rule of the Khalīfa 'Abd Allāhi and avoided fighting in the battle of Omdurman in 1898; on the Anglo-Egyptian occupation of the Sudan he was appointed 'umda in 1900 and shaikh of khuṭṭ in 1902; he visited England in 1919.

'Awad al-Karīm Pasha Aḥmad abū Sin (–1886), notable of the Shukrīya Arabs, eldest son of Aḥmad Bey abū Sin; appointed nāẓir of the Shukrīya in 1872 after the death of his father, he did not long hold the nāẓirship as he was transferred to a post in the central government in Khartoum, and his younger brother 'Alī was appointed nāẓir in his stead; during his tenure of the nāẓirship, with a government force in support, he fought the Kawāhla at Kūfa where his son Aḥmad was killed; on the eve of the Mahdist incursion into the Blue Nile valley he resumed the nāẓirship and came to the help of the government troops under Giegler Pasha in 1882, leading a body of his Shukrīya tribesmen; Major-General C. G. Gordon Pasha in 1884 appointed him governor of Khartoum but, when he saw the hopelessness of the government cause and his own tribal territory overrun by the Mahdists, he retired to the desert fastness of Raira while his son ʿAbd Allāh made his peace with the Mahdī; his own loyalty to the Egyptian cause cost him dear, for he fell into disfavour with the Khalīfa ʿAbd Allāhi and was imprisoned in Omdurman only to die a captive.

ʿAwad al-Karīm abū ʿAlī (–1779), notable of the Shukrīya Arabs and founder of the ruling house of Abū Sin; the Shukrīya were tributary to the Rikābīya Arabs until he defeated them in battle and established Shukrīya supremacy in the Buṭāna steppe between the Blue Nile and the Atbara rivers; over-confident of his power he presumed to offer battle to the Hāmaj lords of Sennar who defeated and killed him, after which his tribe resumed the payment of tribute to Sennar.

ʿAwad al-Karīm Ḥasab Rabbu (–1944), Shukrī notable, shaikh of the Shukrīya khuṭṭ of Abū Dilaiq in the Buṭāna and a magistrate; he died at Abū Dilaiq.

ʿAwad al-Karīm abū Sin (–1820), Shukrī Arab chieftain, grandson of Abū ʿAlī, hero of the battle of Mandara against the Hāmaj and Rikābīya; he is said to have spent his boyhood with his tribe on the banks of the Atbara river and to have been chosen shaikh of the Shukrīya while still a youth; he engaged in the customary inter-tribal fighting and died on the eve of the Turkish occupation of Sennar in 1821, leaving his sons Aḥmad and ʿAlī to deal with the conquerors.

ʿAwad al-Karīm Sulaimān Kāsir (*c.* 1849–1934), Ḥasānī notable, son of Sulaiman Kāsir, shaikh of khuṭṭ of the Ḥasanīya during Turkish times; he himself was ʿumda of the Ḥasanīya living in the district of Shendi.

ʿAwad al-Karīm wad Zaid (1860–1942), Ḍubbānī tribal notable, nāẓir of the eastern khuṭṭ of Gedaref district; he succeeded his brother soon after the Anglo-Egyptian occupation of 1898 and in 1901 was a representative on the Sudan–Abyssinian boundary commission; in 1928 he was appointed president of the local court; possessed of an encyclopaedic memory he was an authority on the tribal history of the Sudan.

ʿAwad ʿUqail (–1892), shaikh of the Ḥamrān of the eastern Sudan, who played an important part in the Mahdist wars; in 1884 Aḥmad ʿIffat Bey, governor of Kassala, entrusted him with the camel transport for evacuating the outlying Egyptian garrison of Jira (Gera) on the Setit river, but it was afterwards decided to hold Jira; after the fall of Kassala he carried a letter from the Egyptian Government to King Yōḥannes (John IV) which led to the evacuation of the garrison via Muṣawwaʿ with the protection of an Abyssinian force, 1886; the murder of Aḥmad ʿIffat Bey by the amīr ʿUthmān abū Bakr Diqna (Osman Digna) after the fall of Kassala so disgusted him that with his tribe he retired to Eritrea; while allied with the Italians he was killed in battle at Dugga; after the defeat of Mahdism his son and successor returned with a remnant of the tribe to their ancestral lands.

Aweit Chal (–1935), Dinka worthy; chief of the Ageir section of the Dinka of the Upper White Nile.

ʿAwūḍa ibn ʿUmar, called **S͟hakkāl al-Qāriḥ** (*fl.* 1659), Sudanese holy man, a disciple of S͟haik͟h Ḥasan wad Ḥasūna; several miracles were attributed to him.

Bābikr Aḥmad Faḍl al-Mūla (1894–1937), Jamūʿī notable; his father was ʿumda of the G͟hamarāb branch of the tribe, semi-nomads who live near Umm Indarāba, and during the Mahdist times was appointed the ʿāmil of his people; his son, born at G͟hamarāb village, followed in his father's steps and on the latter's death was made ʿumda.

Bābikr al-Amīn ʿAbd al-Bārī (–1921), son of the influential ʿArakī s͟haik͟h, al-Amīn ʿAbd al-Bārī Min Allāh of al-Taqanīya; he joined the Mahdist movement and fought under the amīr Ḥamdān abū ʿAnja in Abyssinia; on his death he was followed in the tribal office by his son Aḥmad Bābikr al-Amīn who became s͟haik͟h of the fourth k͟huṭṭ of Manāqil.

Bābikr ʿĀmir (–1920), Mahdist amīr, of the ʿAmārna tribe; he took a leading part in the Mahdist assault on Ḥalfaiya during the siege of Khartoum in 1884; banished from al-Duwaim for his alleged interest in the rebellion of ʿAbd al-Qādir Muḥammad Imām wad Ḥabūba, 1908, he lived latterly at Saqadī near Sennar.

Bābikr Jaʿfar (–1943), an important trader of Khartoum, a magistrate and a member of the town bench; by origin he was a Jaʿfarī; he died in Khartoum.

Badawī ʿAbd al-Karīm (*c.* 1744–*c.* 1840), tribal notable of the Abūdāb family in the neighbourhood of Manāqil in the Jazīra; he was the head of the tribe during the last days of the kingdom of Sennar; the Turks after their occupation of Sennar in 1821 confirmed him in his authority and Aḥmad Pasha abū Widān, the governor-general, who visited Wad Madani in 1839, in humorous mood nicknamed him *Fahl al-Jazīra* (Stallion, i.e. Stalwart of the Jazīra), a name which gave rise to several local songs in his honour; on his death he was succeeded by Ibrāhīm who was head of the family until 1878.

Badawī wad abū Dilaiq (–1706), religious teacher, by tribe a Kāhlī Arab; Wad Ḍaif Allāh the hagiographer records that wisdom and miracles were attributed to him.

Badawī abū Ṣafīya (–*c.* 1848), religious notable of the Bidairīya Arab tribe of Kordofan; it is said that some Negro raiders from the Nuba hills made their way into al-Ubaiyaḍ and killed his sister who refused to go with them; he thereupon preached a holy war and called upon the Muslims of Kordofan to attack the Nuba who are said to have submitted and consented to accept Islam; he took some children of Negro converts to al-Ubaiyaḍ where he had them instructed in Islam, and then sent them back to the Nuba hills to propagate the faith among the unconverted; of the various Muslim missionaries to the Nuba he is the best known; he died at al-Rāhad shortly after meeting K͟hālid Pasha K͟husraw, governor-general of the Sudan, who was on his way to the Nuba hills; his tomb, much visited, is at al-Ubaiyaḍ.

al-Badawī Zarrūq (–1940), notable of the Jawāmaʻa in Kordofan and a magistrate; he died at Umm Ruwāba.

Bādī I Sīd al-Qūm wad ʻAbd al-Qādir (–1614), sultan of the Funj; he ascended the throne of Sennar in 1612, succeeding ʻAdlān I wad Ayā; while raiding the frontier lands of Abyssinia his army was cut to pieces by the Abyssinians who penetrated the Funj kingdom and laid part of it waste; he was followed by his son Rubāṭ wad Bādī I.

Bādī II abū Diqn wad Rubāṭ I (–1677), sultan of Sennar; he came to the throne in 1642; a man of talent and bravery he raided the Shilluk on the White Nile and, crossing the river, invaded Taqalī and Kadarū in the Nuba hills; he built the royal palace and mosque at Sennar, structures which were still visible, though in ruins, when Ismāʻīl Pasha occupied Sennar with a Turkish army in 1821; in person continent and pious, his reign marked the highest power attained by the Funj kings, a period notable for religious learning and internal peace.

Bādī III al-Aḥmar wad Ūnsā (–1715), sultan of Sennar; ascending the throne in 1689 in succession to Ūnsā wad Nāṣir he suffered much from rebellions against his rule; his murder in 1705 of the members of the French diplomatic mission headed by Le Noir du Roule while on its way from Cairo to Abyssinia was a dark feature of a reign otherwise illuminated by the respect and honour in which he was held by his more loyal subjects; he was succeeded on his death by his son Ūnsā the Frivolous (Ūnsā III).

Bādī IV ibn Nūl, called **Abū S͟hilūk͟h** (c. 1700–61 ?), sultan of Sennar, last of the powerful Funj sultans who preceded the years of anarchy which lasted till the occupation of Sennar by the Turks in 1821; he succeeded his father Nūl about 1723; his authority was weakened by the pressure of the Abyssinians and the Fūrs without and by dissensions within; in 1738 (or perhaps 1744) his army was defeated on the Dinder river by the Abyssinians led by King Īyāsū II who was subsequently routed near Sennar by another Funj army under K͟hamīs, a refugee Fūr general, as the result of a stratagem; according to another source Īyāsū was defeated near ʻAjīb east of the Dinder; in 1747 his army, led by Muḥammad abū'l-Kailak assisted by K͟hamīs, drove the Musabaʻāt overlords out of Kordofan which passed temporarily under the rule of Sennar; his rule degenerated into tyranny and his arbitrary acts alienated the nobles; he was finally deposed in 1760 and banished by Muḥammad abū'l-Kailak who placed Bādī's son, the puppet sultan Nāṣir, on the throne; the year of his death is uncertain.

Bādī V wad Ṭabl II (–*c.* 1789), puppet sultan of Sennar; he was killed in civil war at Ḥalfaiyat al-Mulūk.

Bādī VI wad Ṭabl II (1797–), last of the sultans of Sennar; he is said to have been long confined to prison by his Hāmaj overlords when he was released by a revolution in which his predecessor was killed and himself restored on the eve of the arrival of the Egyptian invading force of Ismā'īl Pasha in 1821; he rode out to Wad Madanī to meet Ismā'īl and surrendered the decaying sultanate to the Ottoman sultan; Ismā'īl appointed him nominal shaikh al-mashāyikh of Sennar.

Bādī Aghā (*fl.* 1836), one of the few Sudanese officers in the *niẓām al-jadīd*, the new regular army created by the viceroy Muḥammad 'Alī Pasha from Egyptian serfs and Sudanese slaves; a private in the 3rd infantry regiment in 1822, he is next located as a sergeant in the 33rd infantry regiment in 1836; commissioned in the same year as mulāzim II in the militia battalions he was transferred to the 1st infantry regiment after the militia was disbanded in the general demobilization and retrenchment that followed the second Syrian war of 1839–40.

Bādī wad Rājab (–1780), Hāmaj vizier of the Funj sultanate of Sennar; he virtually ruled the sultanate from 1776 until 1780 when he was killed in battle against a party of rivals including Muḥammad al-Amīn, the shaikh of Qarrī, who killed him in single combat.

Badrī al-Amīn Faqīrī (–1933), Beja worthy who was 'umda of the Shara'āb section of the Hadendowa tribe.

Badrī al-Amīn Muḥammad Nūr (1855–1937), notable of the Surūrāb tribe of the Ja'lī group who live near Omdurman; he was born in Khartoum.

Baghdādī, Georges (1850–1913), Syrian merchant; born in Aleppo of a Christian family he came to Egypt when a young man and, shortly after the Anglo-Egyptian occupation of Omdurman in 1898, he went there as the Sudan agent for the firm of Georges Brahāmsha and Ilyās Ajūrī of Cairo; he was the first merchant in Omdurman, since the fall of the old Egyptian Government, to reintroduce Manchester goods; he later left his employers and traded in his own name; he died at Vichy while undergoing a cure.

Bagnold, Arthur Henry (1854–1943), British soldier; he entered the Royal Engineers in 1872 and was promoted captain in 1884; he was in charge of the telegraph line from Cairo to Dongola during the Nile campaign of 1884–5; a colonel in 1903 he served in the First World War; during his service in Egypt he assisted the Egyptologist, Sir E. A. T. W. Budge, with engineering work in connexion with archaeological excavation.

al-Bahārī. *See* MUḤAMMAD TĀJ AL-DĪN AL-BAGHDĀDĪ, called AL-BAHĀRĪ.

Baibars I, al-Malik al-Ẓāhir Rukn al-Dīn al-Ṣāliḥī (1223–77), fourth sultan of the Baḥrī Mamluks; he seized Egypt by murder and force; in 1260 his generals invaded Nubia and laid it waste, King Meshked becoming his vassal; in 1275 they drove David, the Christian king of Dongola, from his throne, and those of his former subjects who were unable to pay a head tax were forcibly converted to Islam.

Bainbridge Bey, Sir Edmond Guy Tulloch (1867–1943), British major-general; gazetted 2nd lieutenant in the Buffs in 1888 and promoted captain in 1897 he served in the Egyptian army in the Dongola and Nile campaigns of 1896–8; after fighting in the South African war, 1899–1900, he returned to the Egyptian army with the rank of qā'immaqām and in 1901–3 commanded the Khartoum military district; he was a divisional general in the First World War and retired from the army in 1923.

Baker, Augustus (–1891), British consul; after serving as vice-consul at Nish, Serbia, he was promoted consul for the Western and Central Sudan with residence at Khartoum, 1883, but owing to the Mahdist revolt he did not proceed to his post; he was acting consul at Sawākin from December 1883 to November 1884 when he was appointed consul for the Eastern Sudan with residence at Sawākin; he was transferred from Sawākin to Vera Cruz, Mexico, where he died.

Baker, Julian Alleyne (1845–1922), British sailor, nephew of Sir Samuel White Baker Pasha; entering the Royal Navy he was promoted to lieutenant in 1868; in 1869–73 he was a member of Baker Pasha's expedition to the Equatorial province; in the war against Muḥammad Aḥmad al-Mahdī he was in command of a small warship at Sawākin and in 1885 commanded a detachment of Sudanese troops at Kūrtī on the line of communication of the force which vainly attempted to relieve Khartoum; he was promoted to rear-admiral in 1903; his death occurred at Malvern, England.

* **Baker Pasha, Sir Samuel White** (1821–93), British administrator, traveller, and sportsman, farīq of the Egyptian army, and brother of V. Baker Pasha; he completed a desultory education at the University of Frankfurt-am-Main and then embarked on a varied career, visiting Mauritius in 1844, founding an English agricultural colony in Ceylon in 1846–55, and undertaking the management of the construction of a railway being built from the Danube river over the Dobruja to the Black Sea in 1859–60; he married Florence Ninian von Sass (d. 1916), a Hungarian lady, who accompanied him on his journeys through the Sudan and Equatoria; anxious to take part in the discovery of the source of the White Nile and to meet the explorers J. H. Speke and J. A. Grant who were believed to be on their way from the Lakes region to the Sudan, he arrived in Cairo with his wife in 1861 and, ascending the Nile and Atbara, spent five months in exploring the country of the Setit and hunting with the Ḥamrān tribesmen; the Bakers then went to Khartoum where they spent the last six months of 1862 preparing an expedition to the Upper White Nile; in December they started on the journey with three steamers and, arriving at Gondo-

koro, met Speke and Grant; while in the equatorial regions Baker explored the Latuka country in the face of opposition from the slave traders, then, starting southward, he reached the south-eastern shore of the great lake which he named Albert Nyanza; coasting along the eastern edge of the lake to the entrance of the Victoria Nile he returned to Gondokoro which he reached in March 1865; he then left the Sudan by way of Khartoum, Berber, and Sawākin; in 1869, while travelling in the suite of the Prince of Wales (afterwards King Edward VII) who was on a visit to the Nile, he met the khedive Ismāʿīl who appointed him governor-general of Equatoria for four years with rank of farīq and title of pasha; his instructions were to subject to Egyptian authority the countries lying to the south of Gondokoro, to suppress the slave trade, to open the Great Lakes of the equator to navigation, and to introduce regular commerce in the region; to carry out this programme he was given 1,200 Egyptian and Sudanese troops and supplies of all kinds including a fleet of small steamers which were sent up the Nile to Khartoum or dispatched in sections over the Nubian desert; he was accompanied by a staff of British engineers and artisans and, during 1869–70, by a French volunteer, Henri Comte de Bizemont; he was thus the first Englishman to serve in high office under the Egyptian Government, a task in which he was in no way supported by the British Foreign Office; assisted generously by the governor-general, Jaʿfar Pasha Maẓhar, he and Lady Baker reached Gondokoro in April 1870; having formally annexed the Bari country to Egypt he pressed on southward through Unyoro which he proclaimed at Masindi in May 1872 to be an Egyptian protectorate; after much fighting and hardship his expedition returned to Gondokoro in April 1873 after leaving garrisons at various key points in the newly acquired territory; he left Gondokoro in May 1873 on the completion of his term of office; the period of his administration was too short to be successful; the slave traders incited the Bari people to hostility against the Egyptian rule, and Baker has been the object of considerable criticism for his excessive use of force and prodigality of expenditure; at the same time he established the framework of an ordered government and struck the first blow against the slave trade; on his return to Britain he became a tireless advocate against the abandonment of the Sudan; an enormous figure of a man, he was a great hunter who used guns which would have shattered the shoulders of lesser men; besides his books on his service and sport in the Sudan and in the equatorial regions, he wrote a book of adventure for boys.

Baker Pasha, Valentine (1827–87), British soldier, younger brother of Sir S. W. Baker Pasha; after a brilliant military career in which he had been appointed assistant quartermaster-general at Aldershot, he was convicted of a criminal offence and dismissed from the army in 1875; the Ottoman sultan accepted his services on the outbreak of the Russo-Turkish war of 1877–8 in which he fought with great distinction, earning promotion to the rank of farīq; seconded to the Egyptian service he was in command of the Egyptian police from 1882 until his death; in 1884 he was sent with an indifferent Egyptian army to the Red Sea coast of the Sudan to assist in the defence against the rising menace of Mahdism; landing at Trinkitat his force was massacred at el-Teb while attempting to relieve the Egyptian garrison at Tokar; with the remnant of his shattered army he got back to Sawākin by sea; he died at Tel el-Kebir in the Delta of Egypt.

* **Bakhīt Bey Batrākī** (–1885), mīrālai of the Egyptian army; of Sudanese birth, he joined the army in the ranks and served as a quartermaster-sergeant with the Sudanese battalion in the Mexican campaign under Marshal Bazaine in 1863–7; on his return to Egypt he was promoted mulāzim II; transferred to the Sudan, he served in the Equatorial province where he was promoted qā'immaqām and made governor of Makraka in 1876; suspended in 1878, he was reinstated by Emin Pasha (E. C. O. T. Schnitzer) about 1880; in 1882 he went to Khartoum as second in command of the Sudanese regiment under Faraj Bey Muḥammad al-Zainī; on the promotion of the latter in the course of the siege of Khartoum he took command of the regiment with rank of mīrālai and was killed during the assault on Khartoum while defending the eastern entrenchments of the capital.

Bakr . . . (*fl.* 1610), religious leader, founder of the sect of Abū Jārid which took its name from Bakr's disciple; the sect, which is also known as al-Zabālla'a, inhabit the country between the Rāhad and the Dinder rivers; Abū Jārid's tomb is at Ḥillat Bunzuqa; as its practices are secretly performed the confraternity has been suspected of heresy and worse by orthodox Sunnite Muslims in the Sudan.

Bakrī al-Mīrghanī (–1887), religious notable of the Mīrghanīya brotherhood, son of al-Saiyid Ja'far, and cousin of al-Saiyid Muḥammad 'Uthmān al-Mīrghanī II; he lived for the greater part of his life at Khatmīya, the traditional seat of the family, near Kassala; on the investment of Kassala by the Mahdists in 1884 he took a leading part in the defence of the town, lending the weight of his name to the Egyptian cause; the garrison finally surrendered and he, having been severely wounded in the fighting, was carried by his men to Sawākin whence he travelled to Makka, dying there as a result of his sufferings; he left two prominent sons, al-Saiyid Muḥammad al-Ḥasan and al-Saiyid Ja'far (d. 1944).

Baldissera, Antonio (1838-1917), Italian general; born at Padua he was commissioned in the Austrian army, 1857; on the cession of his native city to Italy he transferred to the Italian army; in 1888 he was posted to Eritrea where he commanded a brigade which had desultory brushes with the Mahdist forces based on Kassala; he superseded General O. Baratieri after the Italian disaster at Adowa and in 1897 organized the relief of Kassala which was hemmed in by the amīr Aḥmad Faḍīl.

Balfour, Sir Andrew (1873–1931), British scientist; born in Edinburgh and educated at Edinburgh and Cambridge, he served in the South African war, 1900–1, and in 1902 was appointed director of the newly established Wellcome Tropical Research Laboratories in

Khartoum and the first medical officer of health to the city; here he inspired and directed fruitful research into tropical hygiene and pathology; he relinquished the directorship in 1913 and engaged in medical research in England; in the First World War he served in the Dardanelles and Mesopotamian campaigns first as a member, later as director, of the medical advisory committee in these theatres of war; then followed service as scientific adviser in East Africa; he was president of the public health commission in Egypt and finally, in 1918, he went to Palestine to initiate an anti-malarial campaign; after holding various important official and non-official posts in public health he was appointed director of the London school of hygiene and tropical medicine in 1923, a post which he held till 1930; he was present at the opening of the Sennar dam in 1926; he was a prolific writer of papers on tropical medicine and public health concerning the Sudan and else where; his interests extended to fiction and in his student days he was the author of five novels, including *Golden Kingdom* (1903).

Ball, John (1872–1941), British geographer, geologist, and engineer; after some years spent in engineering he joined the survey of Egypt in 1897 and devoted the rest of his life to the geographical and geological exploration of Egypt and the Sudan; during the First World War he was engaged in military reconnaissance and surveying in the Western Desert, Palestine, Arabia, and Somaliland; his contributions to the literature of geography and geology included notes on the journeys of Aḥmad Muḥammad Ḥasanain Pasha, D. Newbold, and W. B. K. Shaw in the south Libyan desert, and a study of the Semna Cataract; for many years he was technical adviser of desert surveys in the Egyptian Government.

Bālla Muḥammad ʿAlī (1867–1922), nāẓir of Dār Maḥārib when he was dismissed and succeeded by Ismāʿīl Aḥmad who in turn was replaced in 1909 by Bālla who returned to office; he was finally dismissed in 1913 and no successor has been appointed.

Balūl (*fl.* 1750), sultan of the Bidairīya Arabs of northern Kordofan; leading his people northward from the neighbourhood of al-Ubaiyaḍ he conquered the land round Kaja and Surrūj and made his seat at Jabal Bis͟hāra Ṭaiyib at a spot known later as Kāb Balūl (Balūl's fort): he was killed by Hās͟him, sultan of the Musabaʿāt.

Bamsaika al-Baṭḥānī (–*c.* 1890), romantic murderer; a tribesman belonging to the Baṭāḥīn Arabs living eastward of Khartoum he was taunted by his fellow tribesmen as being inferior to Naiyīl, one of the young bloods of the S͟hukrīya with whom the Baṭāḥīn were then at feud; stung by their taunts he killed Naiyīl and escaped to the west where he lived with the Kabābīs͟h in northern Kordofan; finally, about 1878, tired of being an outlaw, he resorted to Muḥammad Badr al-ʿUbaid, the famous religious man of Umm Dibbān, who prayed with him and blessed him, ordering him to go to Khartoum and present himself to the governor-general who was then C. G. Gordon Pasha; Gordon made him his orderly; he loyally served at the Palace until the sack of Khartoum and died in peace at Omdurman; the story is told in several versions and should be accepted with some caution.

Bān al-Nuqā. *See* MUḤAMMAD IBN ḤAMAD IBN AL-<u>SH</u>AI<u>KH</u> IDRĪS AL-FAḌLĪ, called BĀN AL-NUQĀ.

* **Bankes, William John** (c. 1790–1855), British traveller and minor politician, a man of learning and wealth; in 1821, accompanied by Giovanni Finati, an Italian soldier of fortune, he visited Sennar in the suite of Ibrāhīm Pasha who had been appointed commander of the Egyptian forces in the Sudan; he afterwards edited Finati's autobiographical *Life and Adventures* (1830).

Bar Hebræus. *See* GRIGORIOS ABŪ'L-FARAJ BAR 'EBHRĀYĀ (BAR HEBRÆUS).

Baraka wad al-Ḥājj Muḥammad al-'Abbādī (c. 1800–40), 'Abbādī chieftain, brother of <u>Sh</u>ai<u>kh</u> <u>Kh</u>alīfa wad al-Ḥājj Muḥammad who was killed at the order of the governor of Berber, 'Abbās A<u>gh</u>ā al-Bāzārlī; Baraka, thirsting for revenge, retired to Murrāt wells in the Nubian desert; here he waylaid the governor's brother Sulaimān, killing him and his retinue at a place since known as Tal'at al-Jundī near Murrāt; a rival 'Abbādī chief, Sulaimān abū Nimr, with government support, led a punitive expedition against Baraka who, with forty of his men, was captured and killed at Ḥajar al-Zarqā in the 'Atbāi.

Barakāt <u>Gh</u>uwainim (–1946), 'umda of the Barassa section of the Ra<u>sh</u>aida Arabs; he died at Kassala.

Baratier, Augustin (1864–1917), French general; born at Belfort he served as a captain in the Marchand expedition of 1896–8 on which he wrote several books and articles; he fought with distinction in the First World War.

Baratieri, Oreste (1841–1901), Italian soldier; born at Condino in the Trento he fought as a captain of volunteers under Garibaldi at the battle of Capua, 1860; entering the regular army in 1872 he was in Eritrea in 1887–8 with rank of colonel of Bersaglieri; in 1891 he was commander of Italian troops in Africa and in 1892 governor of Eritrea; in 1893 he was promoted major-general; in 1894, after a brilliant forced march from Keren with a mobile column, he captured Kassala from the Mahdists who defended the place with indifferent skill; his military reputation later suffered a tragic reverse when an army under his command was almost destroyed by the Abyssinians at Adowa in 1896; although acquitted by a court-martial he retired from the army, dying at Arco in the Trentino; he published his memoirs (Turin, 1898).

Baring, Evelyn, 1st Earl of Cromer (1841–1917), British administrator; after beginning his career as a soldier he went to Cairo in 1877 as first British commissioner of the *Caisse de la Dette*; he was British controller of the debt, with De Blignières as his French colleague, in 1879, a fateful year which saw the abdication of the Khedive Ismā'īl and the accession of Muḥammad Tawfīq Pasha to a Khediviate threatened by public bankruptcy and internal unrest; in 1883 he began his long term of office as British agent and consul-general; the peculiar circumstances in which he found himself by reason of the now dominant position of Britain in Egypt caused his advice to be given the force of commands; after the defeat of General W. Hicks Pasha in Kordofan in 1883 and the discomfiture of other Egyptian expeditions against the Mahdi's rising power—all draining the Egyptian treasury—he advised the Egyptian Government to withdraw temporarily from the Sudan; he reluctantly consented to Major-General C. G. Gordon Pasha's mission to the Sudan in 1884 but, when Khartoum was threatened, urged the sending of a military expedition to relieve the city; after the fall of Khartoum in January 1885 he recommended the evacuation of all the Sudan except Sawākin and Wādī Ḥalfā; in 1891 he was created Baron Cromer; the finances of Egypt having been strengthened he supported Kitchener, now the sirdār of the Egyptian army, in the war of 1896–8 to recover the Sudan; he devised the Anglo-Egyptian condominium rule for the Sudan excluding international interference; he visited the Sudan in 1898–9 during which he addressed Sudanese notables in Omdurman, promising religious freedom and local autonomy; he paid the country another visit in 1899–1900 and reported general progress in the setting up of a stable administration; in the winter of 1902–3 he made a third visit, ascending the Nile to Gondokoro; he made a last visit in 1905–6 when he opened the Nile–Red Sea railway; he resigned in 1907 and was created an earl; his books include *Modern Egypt* (1908), containing many references to the Sudan; though his policy has been the subject of praise and criticism, it has been generally conceded that he laid firmly the foundations of modern Egypt and the Sudan.

Barnett, Oliver (1830–85), British military surgeon; commissioned in 1854 as an assistant surgeon he was promoted to surgeon in 1867; during the Egyptian war of 1882 he was principal medical officer at Ismāʿīlīya and in 1885, being now a deputy surgeon-general, he was principal medical officer on the staff of Lieutenant-General Sir G. Graham's Sawākin Field Force against the Mahdists on the Red Sea coast, 1885.

Barnham, Henry Dudley (1854–1936), British consul; appointed a student-dragoman in the British Embassy at Constantinople in 1877 he occupied various consular posts in the Ottoman Empire, including that at Sawākin, 1888–94; he was later consul-general at Iṣfahān, 1906–8, and at Smyrna, 1908–14; he retired from the consular service in 1915.

Barnim, Adalbert von, Baron (1841–60), German nobleman and traveller, the son of Prince Adalbert of Prussia and great-nephew of King Frederick William III; accompanied by the German naturalist, R. Hartmann, he set out on a journey to the upper reaches of the Blue Nile in 1859; the pair entered the Sudan from Egypt, crossed the Bayūda desert from Old Dongola to Khartoum, and thence ascended the Blue Nile; he fell ill with fever and died at Roseires; Hartmann returned to Europe with his body.

Barry, Sir Charles (1795–1860), British architect; he designed many famous buildings in London including the Houses of Parliament; he visited Wādī Ḥalfā and Abū Ṣīr rock, 1819.

Barthélemy, Delphine (–1866), French trader; his activities were centred in Khartoum from about 1844; he had an estate at Burrī near Khartoum and a trading station on the White Nile at Ḥillat Ba<u>kh</u>īta which he leased from the government and was operating in 1859; with C. Piaggia, the Italian explorer, he ascended the White Nile to Gondokoro in 1857; in 1862 he and the Belgian explorer, E. de Pruyssenaere, left Khartoum for Gondokoro but were compelled to return after reaching the country of the Aliyāb Dinka; he died at Sawākin while on his way from Egypt to the Sudan with a consignment of goods belonging to the Maltese trader, A. Debono.

Bartolomeo da Tivoli (*fl.* 1330), Italian priest of the Dominican Order of the Roman Catholic Church; in 1316, with eight fellow Dominicans, he ascended the Nile from Egypt and founded a mission in Dongola where he is said to have built a monastery, which the missionaries called 'Alleluia', and to have been appointed bishop of Dongola by Pope John XXII in 1330; little is now known of these and other journeys of Dominican and Franciscan missionaries of the Latin Church in Nubia during the Middle Ages.

Barttelot, Edmund Musgrave (1859–88), major in the British army; he served in the Nile campaign of 1884–5; in 1887 he joined the expedition, led by H. M. Stanley, to relieve Emin Pasha who was beleaguered in Equatoria by Mahdists in the north and by mutineers within the province; the relief expedition moved up the Congo river and through the Ituri forest to Lake Albert; Barttelot remained in charge of the stores at Yambuya where he was shot by an Arab.

Ba<u>sh</u>īr ʿAbd Allāh Muḥammad Andarqī (–1908), Mahdist amīr of the famous fighting tribe of the Jubārāt Taʿāʾi<u>sh</u>a; born at Rāhad al-Birdī near Nyāla in southern Dār Fūr he saw service in the army of the amīr Maḥmūd Aḥmad under whom he fought in the battle of the Atbara, 1898; taken prisoner, he died in captivity at Wādī Ḥalfā, hostile to the end.

Ba<u>sh</u>īr A<u>gh</u>ā al-Izairiq (1883–1947), notable of the Suwārāb branch of the <u>Sh</u>āʾiqīya Arabs; a native of Qurair, of which he was ʿumda, he was the son of a noted chief of Turkish times; he presided over the northern <u>Sh</u>āʾiqīya court from 1936 and was a man of some wealth.

Ba<u>sh</u>īr wad Aḥmad ʿAqīd (*fl.* 1821–37), notable of the Mīrafāb branch of the Jaʿlīyīn of Berber; he did not oppose the occupation of his country by the Egyptians in 1821, and in 1823 he helped to ransom his fellow Jaʿlīyīn tribesmen from captivity when Muḥammad <u>Kh</u>usraw, the Bey Daftardār, was ravaging the Nile valley in the course of a punitive expedition following the killing of Ismāʿīl Pasha, Muḥammad ʿAlī's son, at Shendi by Mak Nimr; in 1835–6 his land disputes with members of his own tribe caused so much stir that <u>Kh</u>ūr<u>sh</u>īd Pasha, the governor-general, and the qāḍī ʿumūm of the Sudan, both went to Shendi to settle them; his son Aḥmad was acting governor of Dongola when C. Cuny, the French doctor and explorer, passed through the town in 1858; there is a portrait in G. A. Hoskins's *Travels in Ethiopia* (1835).

Bashīr Aḥmad Jalāl al-Dīn (1854–1937), religious notable, by birth a Jaʿlī, a member of the noted religious family of the Majādhīb of al-Dāmar where he was born and bred; a substantial landowner he was in 1933 appointed a member of the court of the local qism; in 1932 he became the head of the Majādhīb brotherhood in al-Dāmar.

Bashīr ʿAjab al-Faiya (–1899), Mahdist amīr of the Kināna tribe with rank of amīr al-rubaʿ; he was born at Taiqu near Sinja in the Kināna colony there; an early follower of Muḥammad Aḥmad al-Mahdī he was killed in the battle of Umm Dibaikarāt.

Bashīr Bey Jubrān (1833–1913), head shaikh of the ʿAshabāb branch of the ʿAbābda Arabs and a commander of irregular troops who patrolled the southern frontier of Egypt between the campaigns of 1885 and 1896; he had difficulties with Ṣāliḥ Bey Khalīfa, his fellow tribesman, on account of the brawls which broke out among the troops of both leaders, provoking some nasty incidents; he was born at al-Bihaira near Arqū where also he died.

* **Bashīr Bey Kanbal** (–1919), mīrālai of the Egyptian army, son of al-Malik Kanbal, and a member of one of the leading families of the Shā'iqīya Arabs; he served in the Egyptian-Abyssinian war, 1875, and in Dār Fūr, 1877; in the Mahdist wars he fought round Kassala; appointed by the Sudan Government as muʿāwin of the Arabs in Kordofan he took part in the conquest of Dār Fūr, 1916.

al-Bashīr Raḥma Baṭrān (–*c.* 1908), notable of the Bidairāb branch of the Rubāṭāb; he was head man and judge of the khuṭṭ of Abū Ḥamad during Turkish times; ʿUmar al-Bashīr Baṭrān, ʿumda of Muqrat (d. 1942), was his son.

Bashīr al-Shaib (–1938), ʿumda of the sedentary Banī Jarrār Arabs of Kordofan.

al-Bashīr Ṭaha Ibrāhīm al-Kabbāshī (1882–1936), grandson of the holy man, Shaikh Ibrāhīm al-Kabbāshī (d. 1865), and himself the khalīfa of his father, Shaikh Ṭaha Ibrāhīm al-Kabbāshī; he was born at Ḥillat al-Kabbāshī near Jaili; another noteworthy descendant of Shaikh Ibrāhīm was his son, ʿAbd al-Wahhāb Ibrāhīm al-Kabbāshī (*c.* 1860–1937); he was a prominent member of the Jailānīya brotherhood during the Mahdist régime and was khalīfa of Shaikh Ibrāhīm on the death of his brother Ṭaha.

Bāshirī Bey Muḥammad ʿAlī (1825–1910), head shaikh of the ʿAbūdīya and Shinātīr branches of the ʿAbābda Arabs from 1891; in 1896 he raised a force of irregulars for desert patrolling during the campaigns against the Mahdists; he was born, and died, at Sayāla between Aswān and Wādī Ḥalfā.

Basiyūnī. *See* Ben Zion Koshti.

Bates, Gilbert Laurence (1884–1918), British business man; he joined the firm of Gellatly, Hankey & Co. in London and in 1908 joined the firm's branch office at the newly created Port Sudan; later manager of this branch, he died at Port Sudan.

Bates, Oric (1883–1918), American archaeologist; he was educated in the Universities of Harvard and Berlin and in 1908–9 took part in the Nubian archaeological survey; he made archaeological explorations in the Libyan desert in 1910–11 and made excavations in the Sudan in 1911–12 and again in 1915; he was later curator of African archaeology and ethnology at the Peabody Museum in the University of Harvard; his publications include several contributions to the archaeology of the Sudan.

Bauer . . . (–1845), German peasant, born near Würzburg; he established a soap and brandy manufactury at Kamlīn on the Blue Nile in 1840 where he lived with an old German housekeeper in the simple style of his native country; he died in Khartoum; he was probably the first in the Sudan to manufacture soap after the European recipe; after his death his factory ceased soap production and the government was forced to recommence its importation from Egypt.

* **Baumgarten . . .** (–1839), Swiss mining engineer; educated in the Austrian School of Mines he joined the service of Muḥammad ʿAlī Pasha and was employed as a frigate captain; in 1839 he accompanied the first voyage commanded by Salīm Qapūdān in quest of the source of the White Nile; he died in Khartoum shortly after his return.

Bayard or **Bayart** (*fl.* 1705), French engraver of medallions; he accompanied the ill-fated diplomatic mission led by Le Noir du Roule which left Egypt in 1704 and which, with the exception of Bayard, was massacred at Sennar in 1705; employed to draw curiosities seen on the journey he fell sick and was left resting at ʿĀilafūn where, in order to save his life, he became a Muslim; De Maillet, the French consul in Egypt, sent him a sum of money and a letter for the Negus, but he was never heard of again.

Bazaine, François-Achille (1811–88), French soldier, a marshal of France; he was in command of a French military expedition to Mexico in support of the Archduke Maximilian of Austria who had accepted the Mexican throne; Bazaine's command included a battalion of Sudanese regular infantry, under their own officers, provided by the Khedive Ismāʿīl Pasha; these troops arrived in Vera Cruz in 1863 and, after continuous and successful fighting against the Mexican rebels, returned to Egypt by way of Paris in 1867; in 1873 Bazaine was court-martialled for surrendering the town of Metz to the Germans in the Franco-German war of 1870–1; he escaped from prison and died in Madrid.

Beam, William (1866–1919), American chemist; he joined the Wellcome Tropical Research Laboratories in Khartoum in 1904 as a research chemist; he died in Khartoum; he made valuable contributions to soil chemistry.

Beaman, Ardern George Hulme (1857–1929), British journalist; he began his career as a student-interpreter in the British consular service and served in the Ottoman Empire; he defended the leaders of the revolt of Aḥmad 'Urābī Pasha in the courts at Alexandria in 1882, and in 1883 joined the *Standard* newspaper of London which he represented as a war correspondent in the Dongola campaign of 1896; among other books he wrote *Twenty Years in the Near East* (1898).

Beatty, David, 1st Earl Beatty of the North Sea and of Brooksby (1871–1936), British admiral of the fleet; a native of County Wexford, Ireland, he entered the Royal Navy and as a lieutenant served in the Dongola and Nile campaigns of 1896–8 as second in command of the naval brigade; he attracted the notice of Kitchener by his skilful handling of the gunboat *Fateh* which he commanded in several actions; he was in command of the British fleet at the Dogger Bank in 1915 and of the battle-cruiser squadron in the battle of Jutland in 1916.

Beke, Charles Tilstone (1800–74), British explorer in Abyssinia, 1840–3; in 1848 he prepared an expedition under C. H. F. Bialloblotzky which was intended to go inland from Zanzibar, discover the source of the White Nile, and descend the river through the Sudan to Egypt; the expedition, much discussed at the time, was abandoned before it started; Beke was one of the first to hold the view that the great lake, afterwards called the Albert Nyanza, was within the drainage area of the Nile.

Békir-Bey. *See* MARI BEY.

Belkwai De Dop (–1934), head chief of the Kwil and Paweng sections of the Ruweng Dinka of the Upper White Nile.

Bellefonds. *See* LINANT DE BELLEFONDS.

Belmore, Earl of. *See* LOWRY-CORRY (SOMERSET), 2nd Earl of Belmore.

* **Beltrame, Giovanni** (1824–1906), Italian priest and linguist; born in Valeggio in the province of Verona, he came to the Sudan in 1853 and was one of the founders of the Roman Catholic mission station of Holy Cross, since abandoned, between Shambe and Bor on the Upper White Nile in 1854; in 1854–5 and again in 1857–8 he travelled in the country of the Banī Shanqūl, while in 1859 he ascended the River Sobat; he made important contributions on the Dinka language which he was one of the first to study; returning to Europe in 1862 he came back to Africa, living his later years in Asmara where he died.

Belzoni, Giovanni Battista (1778–1823), Italian excavator of antiquities; born in Padua, the son of a barber who spelt his name Belzon, he was educated for the priesthood but, abandoning his intention, married and went to England in 1803; an enormous man, six feet seven inches tall, he supported himself and his wife by performing feats of strength and exhibiting models of hydraulic engines in the streets and at Astley's circus; in 1815 he went to Egypt and was commissioned by the viceroy Muḥammad ʿAlī Pasha to build a hydraulic machine; finding no success as an engineer he was next employed by H. Salt, the British consul-general in Egypt, in the excavation of antiquities; he was digging in the temple of Abū Simbel in 1817, being the first European to go inside it; his rough methods of excavation have been criticized by later archaeologists; he died near Benin while on a journey of discovery to Timbuktu.

Ben Zion Koshti, known in the Sudan as **Basiyūnī** (1842–1917), Jewish business man; born in Hebron in Palestine, where his father (of Spanish and Russian Jewish descent) was grand rabbi, he was educated for the rabbinical life but instead entered the service of the Ottoman Government and was appointed to a financial post in his native town; with his wife he left for Egypt during the Russo-Turkish war of 1877–8 and shortly after came to the Sudan as agent for a commercial firm in Egypt, living chiefly at Khartoum and Masallamīya; he was shut up in Khartoum during the siege of 1884–5 when he lent money to Gordon Pasha for the defence of the city; after the fall of Khartoum he was compelled by the Mahdists to remain in Omdurman; he soon won the confidence of the Khalīfa ʿAbd Allāhi who entrusted him with various confidential missions including the bartering of Sudan produce for Egyptian luxury goods imported through Sawākin; after the Anglo-Egyptian occupation in 1898 he assumed the leadership of the local Jewish community, building a small synagogue at Omdurman and working to rehabilitate members of the community who had been ruined by the unsettled times.

Bennett, Sir Ernest Nathaniel (1865–1947), British scholar and minor politician; a Fellow of Hertford College, Oxford, 1891–1914, and vice-principal of St. Edmund Hall, 1893–5, he was war correspondent of the *Westminster Gazette* in the Nile campaign of 1897–8 and in 1911–12 served in the Ottoman army in Tripoli and Thrace; he was a member of Parliament, 1906–10 and 1929–45, and was assistant postmaster-general, 1932–5; he died at Chart Sutton, Maidstone; he wrote *The Downfall of the Dervishes* (1898).

Beresford, Charles William de la Poer, 1st Baron Beresford of Metemmeh and of Curraghmore (1846–1919), British sailor; the younger son of the Marquess of Waterford he entered the Royal Navy in 1859; he first became prominent in 1882 when he commanded the small ship of war *Condor* at the bombardment of Alexandria; he commanded the naval brigade in the Nile campaign of 1884–5; after fighting in the battle of Abū Ṭulaiḥ (Abu Klea) in January 1885 he went upstream from Matamma in Gordon's steamer *Ṣāfia* and rescued Sir C. Wilson who had been on a reconnaissance to Khartoum only to find that the city had fallen; in 1906 he was promoted full admiral and in 1916 was made a peer; he was at various times a member of the British Parliament in which he advocated a strong naval policy; he died at Berriedale in Caithness, Scotland.

Berghof, Carl (-1881), German official in the service of the Egyptian Government; he was formerly a photographer in Khartoum when Muḥammad Ra'ūf Pasha, governor-general of the Sudan 1880–2, appointed him an inspector for the repression of the slave trade; he accompanied Rā<u>sh</u>id Bey Aymān, governor of Fashoda, on his disastrous march against the Mahdists in the Nuba hills, and was killed in the battle of Jabal Qadīr.

Bernard Pasha, Sir Edgar Edwin (1866–1931), British soldier and official; born in Malta the son of Count Bernard, a count of the Holy Roman Empire, he entered the army in 1887 and served in the Nile campaign of 1898, and from 1899 was employed as deputy assistant adjutant-general in the Egyptian army; he transferred in 1901 to the Sudan with rank of qā'immaqām and in 1902 was appointed financial secretary to the Sudan Government; promoted liwā' and pasha in 1905 and knighted by King George V in 1918, he retired from the service of the Sudan Government in 1923 and lived in Malta.

Bertin, Edouard-François (1797–1871), French painter, a pupil of of the celebrated artist Baron Gros; he was a brother of Louise-Angélique Bertin, poet and musician; in the winter of 1828–9 he accompanied the archaeological expedition of J. F. Champollion to Abū Simbel and Wādī Ḥalfā; he was afterwards editor of the Parisian *Journal des Débats* founded by his father.

Bertrand, Georges (-1860), French trader; long resident in Syria he came to the Sudan where he set up in business; he died at Berber.

Beurmann, Karl Moritz von (1835–63), German explorer, of Potsdam, Prussia; in 1860–1 he visited the Sudan exploring the country between Sawākin, Muṣawwa', and Khartoum, when he travelled from Khartoum to Qūz Rājab on the Atbara; while engaged in an expedition to endeavour to find the lost explorer E. Vogel, he was killed at Kanem by order of the sultan of Wadā'i; the French explorer G. Lejean suggests that he was of an arrogant temperament and that he wrote uncritically, though Lejean's unfavourable comment may have been prompted by Beurmann's nationality.

Bialloblotzky, Christoph Heinrich Friedrich (1799–1868), Jewish scholar; born at Pattensen near Hanover he was converted from Judaism to Christianity and wrote on Christian theology and Hebrew studies; in 1848 the explorer C. T. Beke invited him to lead an expedition to discover the source of the White Nile; the expedition was to go inland from the coast opposite Zanzibar and to descend the Nile through the Sudan to Egypt; he was compelled to abandon the enterprise which was taken up fourteen years later by the British explorers J. H. Speke and J. A. Grant who, following approximately the same route, succeeded in discovering the origin of the White Nile.

Bilharz, Theodor (1825–62), German doctor, discoverer of the disease *bilharzia*; born at Sigmaringen he entered the service of the Egyptian

Government in 1850; in 1859 he observed the presence of the disease (called after his name) in members of a Sudanese regiment then in Cairo; in 1862 he travelled in the eastern Sudan with Ernst, Duke of Saxe-Coburg-Gotha, and died of exhaustion on his return to Cairo.

Billāl Ag͟hā (*fl.* 1849), the first Sudanese soldier, so far as is known, to receive a commission in the *niẓām al-jadīd*, the new regular army created by the viceroy Muḥammad ʿAlī Pasha, in which he was enrolled in 1824 or 1825 in the 9th infantry regiment; commissioned as mulāzim II in 1829 or 1830 and mulāzim I in 1834 or 1835, he transferred in 1842 to the 2nd guards infantry regiment and in 1849 to the 2nd infantry regiment; the subsequent career of Billāl Ag͟hā is not known.

Billāl Rizq (1888–1927), Sudanese officer in the Egyptian army; born in Idfū in Upper Egypt he was commissioned in 1907; he served in the Beir and Anuak patrols in the Southern Sudan in 1912 and was in 1917 promoted yūzbās͟hī; while in command of a detachment of mounted infantry he bravely conducted the defence of the government buildings at Nyāla in Dār Fūr during the insurrection led by the fanatical holy man, ʿAbd Allāh al-Sihainī, in 1921.

* Binder, Franz (*fl.* 1855–65), Austrian trader, said to have been of Transylvanian origin; he traded on the Upper White Nile and had a station at Shambe, having bought Rumbek station after the death of A. de Malzac in 1860; he was acting Sardinian vice-consul in Khartoum in 1859; in 1864 he was in the Sudan as a visitor from Cairo whither he had transferred his business; while in the Sudan he married a woman of the Beni S͟hanqūl; the register of the Roman Catholic mission in Khartoum records the baptism of a son, Eduard ('Edwardus Benisangolensis'), in 1855.

al-Birair wad al-Ḥasin (*c.* 1830–19), prominent religious s͟haik͟h of the Idrīsīya brotherhood; binding oaths are sworn on his tomb at S͟habas͟ha on the White Nile; his sons al-Nūr (d. 1923) and al-Sammānī (d. 1946) were both prominent in the Sammānīya brotherhood; he was a Jaʿlī by tribe.

Biselli. *See* Maḥjūb al-Buṣailī.

Bis͟hārī Bey wad Bakr (*fl. c.* 1880), tribal leader of the Banī Ḥalba tribe of south-western Dār Fūr; he was one of the tribal beys appointed by the Egyptian Government to administer that administratively difficult and remote region; he, with a force of Banī Ḥalba tribesmen, revolted and fought the loyal Misīrīya round Dāra.

Bis͟hārī Muḥammad Raida (–1898), Mahdist amīr, born of the Jubārāt branch of the Taʿāʾis͟ha Baqqāra; he killed Manāwir Habīla, a Ḥumr chieftain, at Ḥijaiwa in Kordofan in the course of subduing those of the Ḥumr who were opposed to the Mahdist rule; he was killed later in the battle of the Atbara.

Bizemont, Henri-Louis-Gabriel de, Count (1839–99), French naval officer and geographer; born at Nancy he entered the French navy in

1855, rising to commander in 1866 and capitaine de frégate in 1880; he saw active service in Italy and in Cochin China where he was in the judicial administration; he offered the Geographical Society of Paris to take the place of the explorer J.-F.-M. Le Saint who had died in the Baḥr al-Ghazāl in 1868; the society appointed him its representative with the expedition of Sir S. W. Baker Pasha in 1870; Baker at first resented his intrusion into the expedition but was soon conquered by his charm; he and his companion Le Blanc accompanied the sections of one of Baker's steamers from Korosko over the Nubian desert to Berber; on the outbreak of the Franco-Prussian war in 1870 he renounced the expedition and returned to assist in the defence of France; he was in 1882 promoted officier d'ordonnance to the minister of the navy and retired from the service in 1882; he was president of the Geographical Society of Paris; among his published works are a biography of Baker (1894), a summary of geographical discovery since 1877, and letters on his journey from Cairo to Khartoum (1870–1).

Blanc, Sir Henry Jules (1831–1911), British physician; he served as an army doctor in the Crimean war of 1853–5, and later, having entered the Bombay medical service, he was at his own request appointed medical officer to a British mission to enter into negotiations with King Theodore II, king of Abyssinia, for the release of prisoners; the mission, headed by H. Rassam, the Assyrian explorer, arrived in Muṣawwaʿ in 1864 and after much delay was ordered by Theodore to enter Abyssinia by way of Gallabat (Matamma); the party travelled through Keren, Kassala, and Gedaref, and from Gallabat ascended the Abyssinian highlands; on the arrival of the mission at Theodore's court he and the rest of the mission were thrown into chains, to be released on the arrival of the British invading force at Magdala in 1868; he returned to India, retiring in 1887 with the rank of deputy surgeon-general; he settled in Cannes and died in Paris.

Blewitt Bey, Arthur (1861–1917), British lieutenant-colonel; he was commissioned in 1883 to the King's Royal Rifle Corps and later transferred to the Egyptian army, serving in the Nile campaign of 1897–9; he was governor of Fashoda, 1900–1, and of the Jazīra province, 1902; promoted major in 1900 he retired from the British army in 1905 and lived in New Zealand; on the outbreak of the First World War he returned to the British army and was in command of a labour battalion in France when he was killed in an air-raid.

Blondeel van Cuelebroeck, Edouard (1809–72), Belgian diplomat and traveller; born in Ghent he entered the Belgian diplomatic service in 1832; while consul-general at Alexandria he was sent by his government on a commercial mission to Abyssinia in 1840; the state of insecurity in Abyssinia moved him to leave and he returned to Egypt through the Sudan; travelling from Gondar by way of Qalaʿa al-Naḥl and Abū Ḥarāz he reached Khartoum in May 1842 accompanied by a Lazarist priest, L. Montuori; Blondeel stayed two months in Khartoum where he arranged with the governor-general, Aḥmad Pasha abū Widān, for a small plot of land on the southern boundary of the town to be ceded to Belgium for use as a Christian cemetery; he also obtained Aḥmad Pasha's good offices for a church and school which Fr. Montuori established in Khartoum, and wrote a long memorandum to the Propaganda in Rome suggesting the foundation of a Roman Catholic missionary centre in Khartoum; in August and September 1842 he travelled towards the Upper White Nile, rescuing the French traveller, J. P. d'Arnaud, from shipwreck on the rocks of al-Zalait; in October he reached Cairo; he died in Madrid while Belgian minister there; for his services to the Roman Church he was made a Count of the Holy Roman Empire.

Bohndorff, Friedrich (1849–), German adventurer and naturalist; born at Plau in Mecklenburg he started life as a goldsmith's apprentice but soon took to wandering; the French arrested him in Savoy during the Franco-German war and deported him to Italy on suspicion of being a German spy; from Italy he wandered to Tunis and Egypt where after working some time at his trade in Cairo he came to the Sudan with the botanist Witt; finding that Witt was an impostor he left him and in 1874 entered the service of C. G. Gordon Pasha, governor of Equatoria, who employed him on odd jobs as he was penniless; returning to Egypt he set out thence in 1876 to Dongola, Khartoum, and Dār Fūr, and so to the western parts of the Azande country, arriving finally in the Nsakkara district west of the River Shinko at one of Zubair's remotest stations; he returned to Cairo in 1879 where W. Junker engaged him; he accompanied Junker to the Azande country, but ill health compelled him to leave Junker in 1882; delayed by a revolt of the Dinka in the Baḥr al-Ghazāl he did not leave the Upper White Nile till the end of 1883, arriving in Khartoum at the end of the year with the news of the murder of J. M. Schuver by the Dinka; he afterwards took service under the Congo Free State and subsequently with the German East African Company; his surveys of the Baḥr al-Ghazāl and Azande country, interesting though of limited scientific value, were published in *Petermann's Mitteilungen* (Gotha, 1885).

Bond Pasha, Edmund Edward (1865–1943), British sailor; he entered the Royal Navy in 1887 and, transferring to the Khedivial service, was appointed to the Nile flotilla of the Egyptian war department during the Nile campaign of 1898; in 1900 he was promoted chief engineer of the flotilla; his great work in laying the foundations of the inland water transport services operated by the Sudan Government began in 1899 when he was made director of steamers and boats; in 1907 he retired from the Royal Navy with the rank of engineer-commander; on the eve of the outbreak of the First World War he retired from the directorship of steamers and boats and rejoined the navy in which he saw active service with the East Coast and Dover patrols; in 1919 he finally retired from the navy with the rank of engineer captain.

Bonnel de Mézières, Albert Louis Marie Joseph (1870–), French colonial official and explorer; after being attached to several French Government missions in North Africa he was appointed head of an economic mission to the regions of the Rivers M'Bomu and Baḥr al-Ghazāl, a mission which originated the Société des sultanats du Haut-Oubanghi, 1898–1900; he was again sent to the Sudan on an economic mission, 1906; retiring from the French colonial service, 1907, he founded a commercial and finance company in the Sudan, 1908, but the project was abandoned for diplomatic reasons within a few months; he afterwards made important contributions to the history of the Sahara; an account of his work in the Sudan in 1906 appeared in *L'Afrique française* (Paris), xvi, 1906.

Bonomi, Joseph (1796–1878), British sculptor and draughtsman of Italian descent who was attached to the Prussian archaeological expedition under K. R. Lepsius which visited Nubia and Sennar in 1843–4; Bonomi had been a student at the Royal Academy of London and illustrated works on ancient Egypt.

* **Bonomi, Luigi** (1841–1927), Italian missionary priest; born in Verona he was educated in the college of missions there; coming to the Sudan in 1874 he was appointed superior of the newly founded mission at Dilling in the Nuba hills in 1875; in 1881 he and Bishop D. Comboni made a journey in the Nuba hills and the borders of Baḥr al-Ghazāl region; in September 1882 the mission station at Dilling was overrun by the Mahdists who led Bonomi and his fellow workers to al-Ubaiyaḍ and captivity; in June 1885 he, with Sisters C. Chincharini and E. Venturini, escaped from al-Ubaiyaḍ to Dongola; appointed a chaplain to the Italian navy in 1888 he was later in Eritrea as chaplain to the military hospital in Asmara where, after a long and active life, he died.

Bonus, Ernest M . . . (1869–1940), British lawyer and civil servant, a son of General Bonus of the Indian army; educated at the University of Oxford he was called to the Chancery Bar and was for a time a deputy judge-advocate-general in England; he was director of agriculture and lands, Sudan Government, 1905–9, when he resigned to practice law in London.

Boreani . . . (*fl.* 1838), Italian mining engineer of Piedmontese origin; it is thought that he came to Egypt before 1820; in 1822 he was prospecting for gold in the neighbourhood of Khartoum; in 1825 he succeeded Ḥusain Bey as director of the arsenal at Būlāq where he was described as a captain of engineers; his work at the arsenal included the establishment of a cannon foundry which produced some good guns among many of indifferent manufacture; during the years 1833–6 he was prospecting for minerals in the Taurus mountains at the request of Ibrāhīm Pasha, commander of the Egyptian forces in Syria; he was then recalled to look for gold in the region of Sennar; said now to have been given the rank of qā'immaqām (though the date of appointment is doubtful) he began work in the mines of Fāzūghlī in October 1837 and prospected for a short time in the Nuba hills; he returned to Egypt in the summer of 1838 when he lost favour with Muḥammad 'Alī Pasha owing to his pessimistic reports as to the presence of exploitable gold in the Sudan; though ill with fever the viceroy ordered him back to

Fāzūghlī and while on the way there he was shipwrecked at the Sixth Cataract, arriving in Khartoum a few days before the viceroy himself who had come from Egypt on a tour of inspection; after fruitless attempts to find gold in payable quantity Muḥammad ʿAlī was at last convinced of Boreani's good faith; contemporary descriptions of his character vary; Prince H. L. H. von Pückler-Muskau who met him in the Sudan wrote of him as a man of polished and agreeable manners.

Borghese, Giovanni Battista, Prince (1855–1918), Italian nobleman of a celebrated Roman family; he financed the geographical expedition of P. Matteucci and A. M. Massari which crossed Africa from Khartoum to the Niger in 1880–1; he accompanied the explorers as far as Nyeri in Dār Tāma on the borders of Wadā'i when he was recalled to his mother's bedside and returned by way of Kordofan to Italy.

Bōsh ibn Muḥammad al-Faḍl (–1875), titular sultan of Dār Fūr; he succeeded his nephew, Sultan Ibrāhīm Muḥammad, on the latter's death in the battle of Manawāshī against the forces of Zubair Pasha Raḥma Manṣūr in 1874; he reigned for only a few months during a period of anarchy; in attempting to prolong the resistance against Zubair's army he and Saif al-Dīn were killed and their followers dispersed; his son Muḥammad Hārūn al-Rashīd succeeded him as legitimate heir to the throne of Dār Fūr.

* **Botta, Paul-Émile** (1802–70), French assyriologist; of Italian origin he was born in Turin and studied medicine; he entered the medical service of Muḥammad ʿAlī Pasha in 1830 and spent the next four years in the province of Sennar in which he travelled extensively, collecting geological, botanical, and zoological specimens; he was later French consul at Alexandria; his love of travel carried him to the Yaman, Palestine, and the Barbary Coast; he died in retirement at Anchères in France.

Bòttego, Vittorio (1860–97), Italian explorer; born at San Lazzaro near Parma he joined the Italian artillery and reached the rank of captain; during the course of a second geographical expedition to western Abyssinia he visited the Akobo basin where he was ambushed and killed by the Galla at Gobo near the Sudan frontier.

Botzaris (Bozzari), Dimitrios (–1822), physician; said by some to have been a Hellenized Armenian, by others a Smyrniote Greek and the nephew of Yanni Botzaris, at one time physician to Muḥammad ʿAlī Pasha; he accompanied Ismāʿīl Pasha on the military expedition to Sennar in 1820–1 as his *protomedico*; during the campaign he fell out with other Europeans accompanying the army and was suspected by the American G. B. English and the British travellers Waddington and Hanbury of having poisoned the Italian doctor A. Gentili, a more gifted rival; he was said to have been cruel to the natives of the Sudan whom he is accused of torturing; he was with Ismāʿīl Pasha at Shendi on the night when the inhabitants, at the instigation of al-mak Nimr, burnt Ismāʿīl and his suite to death; for the *protomedico* they reserved another fate, for they killed him by the same manner of torture as he had used upon them.

Boulnois Bey, William Arthur (1867–1905), British major and mīrālai of the Egyptian army; commissioned to the Royal Artillery in 1886 he was promoted captain in 1896 and major in 1901; after serving in the Nile campaign of 1897 he joined the Egyptian army in 1898; he took part in the reoccupation of the Baḥr al-Ghazāl province in 1900–2 and in 1904 was appointed governor of that province; he died in the Baḥr al-Ghazāl shortly after taking up his post; a screen in the Anglican cathedral at Khartoum was erected in his memory.

Bourchier, William (–1844), captain of the Royal Navy; he was promoted lieutenant in 1810 and commander in 1815; in 1834 he was shipwrecked while a passenger in the armed brig *Nautilus* and with the ship's company was put ashore at Sawākin where they were hospitably entertained by the governor; with Lieutenants Lynch and Smith, and a Mr. Hill, formerly advocate-general at Bombay, he set out for Egypt by way of Obak, Berber, Abū Ḥamad, and Korosko, a route necessitated by the absence of shipping from Sawākin to Suez; Bourchier tells the story of the journey in a little-known and rare book called *Narrative of a passage from Bombay to England describing . . . journies across the Nubian desert* [*etc.*] (1834); later promoted captain, he died of scarlet fever at Georgina, Canada.

Bowra, Brook Hay (1853–1926), British business man; a Londoner by birth he joined the London office of the firm of Gellatly, Hankey, Sewell & Co. about 1871 and in 1886 was engaged in the company's business at Sawākin; he later returned to their London office where he worked till his death.

Brackenbury, Sir Henry (1837–1914), British general and military writer; he entered Woolwich Military Academy in 1854 and in 1856 joined the Royal Artillery; after active service in India, Ashanti, Cyprus, and Zululand he was appointed chief of staff to the river column in the Nile campaign of 1884–5 which had as its object the relief of Khartoum; on the death of General Earle in the battle of Kirbikān in 1885 he took over the command; he was director-general of ordnance during the South African war, 1899–1902; he published various works on military subjects including *The River Column* (1885).

Bramble Bey, James John (1883–1943), British soldier and administrator; commissioned to the Royal Marines he was seconded to the Egyptian army in 1913 and saw service in the First World War; transferred from the Egyptian army he was appointed an inspector and posted to the Upper Nile province; here he took part in the Lau Nuer patrol, 1917; he was promoted temporary qā'immaqām, 1920, and retired from the Royal Marines, 1922; in 1923 he was appointed a civilian district commissioner and from 1927 until his retirement in 1935 he was district commissioner, Omdurman, during a period of great municipal development; in 1935–8 he was a recruiting staff officer, Liverpool; on the outbreak of the Second World War he was recalled to the colours and died while serving in the Naval Intelligence division of the Admiralty.

Bray Pasha, Hubert Alaric (1867–1935), British doctor; joining the Royal Army Medical Corps he served on the north-west frontier of India, 1897–8, and in the Sudan from 1905, having been seconded to the Egyptian army; in 1912 he was appointed director-general of the Sudan medical department with the rank of liwā'; he relinquished the directorship-general in 1914 on the outbreak of the First World War in which he served from 1914 until 1918; he retired from the British army in 1921 with the rank of colonel.

Breasted, James Henry (1865–1935), American Egyptologist; born at Rockford, Illinois, he studied at the Universities of Yale and Berlin; he held several academical posts of distinction, notably in the University of Chicago where he was director of the Oriental Institute; in 1905–7 he was the leader of an archaeological expedition in Nubia for the University of Chicago; among his many works, devoted chiefly to Egyptology, he wrote *The Temples of Lower Nubia* (1906) and *The Monuments of Sudanese Nubia* (1908).

Brehm, Alfred Edmund (1829–84), German zoologist, son of the ornithologist C. L. Brehm; he was born, and died, in Renthendorf in Thuringia; as secretary to Baron J. W. von Müller he travelled in 1847–52 from Egypt to Dongola and thence over the Bayūda from Merowe to Matamma and Khartoum; from Khartoum the two travellers continued to Roseires and al-Ubaiyaḍ, making an excursion to Jabal Taqalī in the Nuba hills; they completed the return journey from Khartoum to Cairo in two boats provided by Khālid Khusraw Pasha, then governor-general; returning to Europe he studied at Jena and Vienna, becoming, in 1863, director of the Hamburg zoological garden; his account of his travels in the Sudan first appeared in Jena, 1855.

Breuvéry, J . . . de. *See* CADALVÈNE, E . . . DE.

Brévedent, Charles François Xavier de (1659–99), French priest of the Jesuit Order; born in Rouen of a good family he entered the Society of Jesus in 1674 and for some time taught philosophy and the humanities; he proved a competent linguist and occupied his leisure with the invention of a machine intended to be propelled by perpetual motion; in 1696–7 he was engaged in missionary work in Trebizond, Persia, Syria, and Egypt, having come to Cairo in the latter year with a certain Fr. Verzeau or Verseau in an attempt to penetrate into Ethiopia with missionary intent; without Verzeau he left Egypt under the assumed name of Yūsuf as interpreter and apothecary to the French doctor, C. J. Poncet, in 1698; the party travelled by way of the western oases, regaining the Nile near the present Dongola, and thence over the Bayūda to the junction of the two Niles and on to Sennar where they stayed from February to May 1699; on their way to Gondar by way of Gallabat Brévedent died of dysentery at Barko near Gondar in July; from Sennar he wrote two interesting letters, under the pseudonym of Joseph Duval, one to Fr. Fleuriau, the other to B. de Maillet, consul of France in Egypt.

Brewster Bey, Alfred Berry (1856–1928), British official in the Khedivial service; he was born in London and in 1877 entered the Egyptian customs administration and coastguard service; in 1879 C. G. Gordon Pasha, then governor-general of the Sudan, appointed him director of customs at Sawākin, a post which he held, with breaks of war service, till 1890; in the Egyptian campaign of 1882 he served on the commissariat staff and in 1883–4 was in General Valentine Baker's intelligence department in the campaigns against the Mahdists round Sawākin; he also acted during part of this period as sub-governor of the town; he was on the intelligence staff of General Sir G. Graham's Sawākin Field Force in 1885; in 1891 he became secretary and controller of the coastguard service at Alexandria and, a few months later, was appointed private secretary to the Khedive Muḥammad Tawfīq, a post which he also held under Tawfīq's successor, ʿAbbās II; at the age of sixty he volunteered for service with the British forces in the First World War.

Brindle, R . . . (1837–1916), Roman Catholic bishop; after ordination he was commissioned as an army chaplain, 1874, and served in the Nile campaign of 1884–5, in the Sawākin Field Force, 1885, and in the Dongola and Nile campaigns of 1896–8 when he retired from the army; in 1899 he was consecrated bishop-auxiliary for Westminster and from 1901 to 1916 was bishop of Nottingham.

Broadwood Bey, Robert George (1862–1917), British lieutenant-general; commissioned to the 12th Lancers in 1881 he was promoted captain in 1888, brevet-colonel in 1898, and major-general in 1906; between 1892 and 1899 he served in the Egyptian army, rising to the rank of mīrālai; he was in all the chief battles of the Dongola and Nile campaigns, 1896–8; in the battles of the Atbara and Omdurman he commanded the Egyptian cavalry; he led a British cavalry brigade in the South African war, 1899–1902; he died of wounds received while in command of the 57th division in the First World War.

Brocchi, Giovanni Battista (1772–1826), Italian geologist and naturalist; born of a patrician family in Bassano near Vicenza he was educated for the law in the University of Padua; in 1808 he was appointed an inspector of mines which involved his transfer to Milan where he became a member of various learned societies; he met G. Forni in 1821 and was inspired to come to Africa; he arrived in Egypt in 1822 and, after conducting scientific work there and in the Lebanon and Syria, left for Sennar in 1825; he died in Khartoum while engaged on a scientific survey of the dominions of Muḥammad ʿAlī Pasha; the Italian explorer O. Antinori erected to his memory an inscription (since lost) in the Christian cemetery in Khartoum; on the occasion of the centenary of his death the city of Bassano brought out a memorial volume; his written works are of high scientific value; his journal (Bassano, 1841–3) is an indispensable source of information for Berber and Sennar in 1825–6.

Brocklehurst, Henry Courtney (1888–1942), British soldier; he was commissioned to the 11th Hussars in 1908 and served in Palestine,

Tanganyika, and North Russia in the First World War, 1914–19; in 1919 he resigned from the British army and was in 1922 appointed game warden, Sudan Government, a post he held till his retirement in 1931; in the Second World War he returned to the active list with rank of lieutenant-colonel and, while leading a Commando detachment through the mountains and jungle in the Allied retreat from Burma to India, he was drowned; he wrote *Game Animals of the Sudan* (1931).

Browne, William George (1768–1813), British traveller; educated at the University of Oxford he went to Egypt in 1792 and in 1793 followed a caravan returning to Dār Fūr along the Darb al-Arbaʿīn, arriving in Dār Fūr in the reign of Sultan ʿAbd al-Raḥmān; he settled at Kobbé disguised as a North African Arab; there persecuted by fanaticism he returned to Egypt by the same route in 1796; the narrative of his travels, published in 1800, though in parts criticized for inaccuracy, remains an authority on Dār Fūr; after travelling in Turkey and the Levant in 1800–2 he set out for Tartary in 1812, passing through Anatolia and Armenia; he was murdered near Tabriz.

Brownell, Clarence Melville (1828–62), American doctor and explorer; born at East Hartford, Conn., the son of a local doctor, he studied at the medical schools of Pittsfield, Woodstock, and New York; after practising his profession first at Wawatosa, Wis., and then at East Hartford, and becoming an enthusiastic amateur botanist, he set out in 1859 on a series of travels which took him to Canada and the Amazon river; in 1861, on the outbreak of the American civil war, he was offered a commission in the medical corps of the Federal army, but he had already left for Cairo; from Cairo he travelled by way of Korosko and the Nubian desert to Khartoum where he joined John Petherick and his wife then starting on a trading expedition to the Upper White Nile; falling ill of fever contracted, according to Petherick, by negligent exposure, he died on the voyage and was buried on the east bank of the White Nile near Aliyāb, Bor, on 20 May 1862; his diary (up to Khartoum), with other unpublished papers, is preserved by his family.

Bruce of Kinnaird, James (1730–94), Scottish traveller; he spent part of his early life in the study of Arabic and Ethiopic, and as British consul at Algiers he made an archaeological tour of the Barbary Coast; determined to visit Abyssinia he reached Egypt in 1768 and from Aswān crossed the Nubian desert to the Red Sea and landed in Muṣawwaʿ in 1769; after reaching Gondar and exploring the sources of the Blue Nile he left Abyssinia in 1771 and travelled through Sennar and on through Berber to Aswān which he attained in 1772, and whence he continued to Egypt and Scotland; in 1790 he published an account of his journey, a work bitterly attacked at the time by ignorant critics but since vindicated; his description of the Sudan remains a valuable authority on the country in the last days of the Funj Empire of Sennar.

* **Brugsch Bey, Heinrich Karl** (1827–94), German Egyptologist, born in Berlin; he travelled in Nubia in 1853–4 and in 1857–8, and from

1870 was director of the School of Egyptology in Cairo; he died at Charlottenburg near Berlin; his autobiography was published in Berlin, 1894.

* **Brun-Rollet, Antoine** (1810–58), Savoyard trader and explorer; born at Saint-Jean-de-Maurienne he was originally destined for the church but changed his mind and sailed in 1831 to Alexandria where he was employed for a short time as a cook under the name of Yaʿqūb; he then became an employee of J. M. F. Vaissière and entered the Sudan in late 1831; here he rapidly amassed a fortune by trading on his own account; he accompanied the governor-general, Aḥmad Pasha abū Widān, on the latter's expedition to Tāka in 1840; in 1844 he ascended the White Nile and founded a trading post at Bilinian in the Bari country; meanwhile he married a talented young Frenchwoman of Marseilles who was born in 1831 and died in Khartoum in 1856 of a kind of homesickness, a tragedy which Brun-Rollet did not long survive; she accompanied her husband on many of his perilous journeys; he was the first European to explore the Baḥr al-Ghazāl as far as Mushraʿ al-Raq, 1856–7; revisiting Europe in 1855 he was welcomed by the Geographical Society of Paris and by the academy of his native Savoy; his work on the White Nile, published in Paris in 1855, shows him an intelligent observer and an advocate of steamers and railways, while his letters to learned societies are of geographical importance; in 1856–7 he was Sardinian vice-consul in Khartoum where he died.

Brunyate, Sir William Edward (1867–1943), British lawyer; he entered the Khedivial service, 1898, and held high appointments as a law officer of the Egyptian Government; in 1899 he was sent to the Sudan to assist Lord Kitchener in drafting fundamental laws for the newly occupied country; these included a code of criminal procedure, a penal code, and in 1900 with the help of E. Bonham Carter, a civil justice ordinance.

Buchta, Richard (1845–94), Austrian photographer; born at Radlow in Galicia he learnt photography and came to Egypt in 1870; R. Gessi Pasha enlisted him as a photographer and explorer in 1877, and in 1877–8 he took careful photographs on the Upper White Nile; he later accompanied Emin Pasha on journeys to Unyoro and Uganda; Buchta was the first serious photographer to practise his art in these regions; he was with Gessi at Daim Sulaimān in 1879 and afterwards went back to Emin with whom he was again working in 1879–80; he returned to Europe and died in Vienna.

Budge, Sir Ernest Alfred Thompson Wallis (1857–1934), British Egyptologist; he was keeper of the Egyptian and Assyrian antiquities at the British Museum, London, 1893–1924; during a long career devoted to ancient Egyptian, Coptic, and Assyrian studies, he excavated at Jabal Barkal, Meroë, Semna, and other ancient sites in the Sudan; he was a voluminous writer; his works on the Sudan concern archaeology, travel literature, and general history; his *Egyptian Sudan* (1907) is a compendious source of information on the early years of the Anglo-Egyptian administration.

Bull, René (1872–1942), British press artist and journalist; he was war artist of *Black and White*, a London journal, in the Nile campaign, 1898; born in Ireland he studied engineering in Paris but gave it up for art work in London, 1892; he followed his calling in many wars including the Turco-Greek war, 1896; in the First World War he served first in the Royal Navy and later in the Royal Air Force.

Bullen, Herbert Guy (1896–1937), assistant bishop of the Anglican Church in Egypt and the Sudan; born at Leyton near London he was commissioned in a territorial battalion in 1915 and fought in France, 1916–18, in the First World War; the war over he studied at Cambridge University and at Ridley Hall, Cambridge, 1919–24; after taking Orders he served as a priest in England and Nigeria; in 1935 he was consecrated assistant bishop of Egypt and the Sudan; his work in the southern Sudan was cut short by his death in a flying accident at Pap in the country of the Aliyāb Dinka on the Upper White Nile; a book of memoirs entitled *Guy Bullen* was published by his friends, 1938.

Buller, Sir Redvers Henry (1839–1908), British general; he received a commission in the army in 1858 and saw active service in many parts of the world, winning the Victoria Cross in the Kaffir war in South Africa in 1879; in the Egyptian campaign of 1882 he was chief of the intelligence staff; he was afterwards posted to the Sawākin Field Force under Lieutenant-General Sir G. Graham and commanded the 1st infantry brigade in battles at el-Teb and Tamai, 1884; he was chief of staff in the expedition which vainly attempted to relieve Khartoum, 1884–5; in February 1885 he led the British retreat from Matamma to Kūrtī after the fall of Khartoum had rendered the expedition fruitless; after service in Ireland he held important posts in the War Office, London; on the outbreak of the South African war he was appointed to command the British forces against the Boers; although he won successes in 1899 his leadership was much criticized; on his return to England in 1900 he received a warm, popular welcome; his reappointment to his former command in England was sharply criticized in the press and, having made an indiscreet statement in his own defence, he was removed from command, 1901.

Burckhardt, Johann Ludwig (1784–1817), Swiss explorer; born at Lausanne and educated at several European universities, he entered the employment of the African Society of London and was sent to explore inner Africa; after much travel in Asia Minor and Egypt he visited Cairo in 1812; prevented from going by Fezzan to the Niger river he traversed the Sudan in 1812–14 on his way to Makka; clothed in Arab dress and speaking Arabic with fluency he travelled as a Muslim merchant; first he ascended the Nile valley by land through Aswān and Wādī Ḥalfā to Dār Maḥas, then, retracing his steps, he returned to Aswān in 1813; at the end of 1813 he joined a caravan of slave traders and crossed the Nubian desert from Darrāw to Berber and Shendi where he arrived early in 1814; from Shendi he travelled eastward with another caravan by Kabushīya, Qūz Rājab, and the delta of the Gash to Sawākin; he died of dysentery in Cairo while waiting to join a caravan going to Fazzān.

Burges Pasha, Frank (1867–1943), British soldier; in 1889 he was commissioned to the Gloucestershire Regiment; later seconded to the Egyptian army he served in the Nile campaign in 1898–9 when he joined the Sudan Government as an inspector with the rank of binbāshī and was posted to Sawākin; while on the Red Sea coast he took a leading part in the capture of the Mahdist amīr, 'Uthmān abū Bakr Diqna (Osman Digna) in 1900; promoted captain in the British army in 1900 and qā'immaqām in the Egyptian army in 1903 he retired from both armies in 1908 when he accepted a legal appointment; he received the rank of liwā' in 1916 when serving in Egypt as assistant provost.

Burleigh, Bennet (*c.* 1840–1914), British journalist; he fought on the Confederate side in the American civil war and was twice condemned by the Federal authorities to be shot; as correspondent of the *Daily Telegraph* of London he was present in the campaign on the Red Sea coast in 1884 and was the first to report the news of the disastrous first battle of el-Teb; he next accompanied the expedition of 1884–5 for the relief of Khartoum and was wounded in the battle of Abū Ṭulaiḥ (Abu Klea) in which he was mentioned in dispatches, the first honour of its kind awarded to any English war correspondent; he next came to the Sudan in 1896 when he represented the *Daily Telegraph* in the Dongola and Nile campaigns, 1896–8; he served his newspaper in twenty-five campaigns.

Burnaby, Frederick Gustavus (1842–85), British soldier and traveller; he joined the Royal Horse Guards in 1859; a facile linguist and of enormous physical strength he won fame by his travels in Central Asia; he greatly admired C. G. Gordon Pasha whom he visited in Equatoria in 1875, first meeting him at the mouth of the River Sobat; in 1881 he was appointed colonel of the Royal Horse Guards; he was at Sawākin in 1884 with the army of V. Baker Pasha and fought in the battle of el-Teb armed with a double-barrelled gun; he attached himself to the expedition for the relief of Khartoum and was killed at the battle of Abū Ṭulaiḥ (Abu Klea).

Burrām Ḥāmid (–1944), Rizaiqī notable; 'umda of the Umm Saif al-Dīn section of the Maḥāmīd branch of the Rizaiqāt of southern Dār Fūr; he died at Sibdu.

Burt al-Masallamī (*fl.* 1620), Sudanese holy man, a disciple of Shaikh Salmān al-Ṭawwālī; according to the hagiographer Wad Ḍaif Allāh he possessed the power of prophecy; his grave lies between Wad Ḥasūna and Wad abū Dilaiq in the northern Buṭāna.

Burton, James. *See* HALIBURTON, JAMES.

Buṣātī Bey Madanī (1850–83), official in the Egyptian Government service; a Maḥasī, son of the Faqī Madanī, he was born in Khartoum; he is said when a youth to have been appointed a clerk in the governor-general's office and was afterwards employed first as under-secretary, then secretary, to C. G. Gordon Pasha during his first term of office as governor-general; about 1878 he was appointed governor of Khartoum, then governor of Sennar, then inspector of Sudan finances; he was killed during the Mahdist revolt while accompanying the army of Lieutenant-General W. Hicks Pasha on its fatal march through Kordofan; Gordon, who returned to Khartoum in February 1884, found his family in dire straits and helped them.

Butcher, Arthur Douglas Deane (1884–1944), director in charge of hydraulic research at the Nile Delta barrage, Egypt; he joined the Egyptian irrigation service in 1906; in 1924 he was appointed consulting engineer (hydraulics) to the Sudan Government and in 1929 he became director-general of irrigation for the Sudan and southern Nile; he was a leading authority on the hydraulics of the swamp region of the Upper White Nile and a brilliant practical mathematician.

Butler, Arthur Lennox (1873–1939), British zoologist and game warden; born in Karachi of an Anglo-Irish family, he served for two years in the Federated Malay States; in 1901 he was appointed superintendent of game preservation to the Sudan Government, a post which he held until 1915 when he proposed his own discharge as an economy to a branch of government activity hard hit by the First World War; he made valuable zoological collections for various museums, while he contributed occasional notes to *Ibis* and *Sudan Notes and Records* on Sudan ornithology on which he was an authority.

Butler Pasha, James Henry (1863–1928), British soldier and administrator; born at Bayle in the County of Roscommon, Ireland, he was appointed in 1887 a head constable in the Egyptian police; in 1892 he was promoted binbāshī and staff officer; he joined the Egyptian army in 1896 and served in the transport throughout the Dongola and Nile campaigns of 1896–8, being divisional transport officer in the advance on Omdurman, 1898; transferring to the Sudan Government in 1899 he was in 1901 promoted qā'immaqām; he was governor of the White Nile province, 1905–13, with rank of mīrālai from 1910; retiring in 1913 with rank of liwā' he died at Newtownbarry, County Wexford, Ireland.

Butler, Sir William Francis (1838–1910), British lieutenant-general; he was commissioned to the 69th foot in India in 1858 and saw service in India, the Channel Islands, Canada, Ashanti, and Zululand; he fought in the Egyptian war of 1882 against Aḥmad 'Urābī Pasha, and in 1884–5 was charged with the organization of small boats which carried the supplies of the column advancing up the Nile to attempt the relief of Khartoum; in the British victory at Kirbikān he played a prominent part; in the same year he was a brigadier-general under General F. C. A. Stephenson at the battle of Jinnis (Giniss); he afterwards served in the South African war, but his sympathy with the Boers caused his retirement from the war in 1899; he retired from the army in 1900; among his writings are *The Campaign of the Cataracts* (1887) and a life of Gordon (1889).

Cadalvène, Edouard de (*fl.* 1831), French business man; he came to Egypt in 1829 and was established in Cairo for some years as the representative of French banks; in company with J. de Breuvéry he ascended the Nile in 1831, visiting Dongola and the region as far upstream as Jabal Barkal; their account of the journey, published in Paris in 1841, is an uninspiring but well-informed work.

Cadeau, André (1793–1830), French soldier in the service of the Viceroy Muḥammad ʿAlī Pasha; in 1813 he enrolled in the French infantry and served under General Marulas in the siege of Besançon in 1814; in the Hundred Days he was a quartermaster-sergeant in the 6th Lancers, but after the Restoration he reverted to the infantry, accompanying the 89th legion to the Antilles where he served as a sergeant for five years; returning to France he was commissioned as a sub-lieutenant in 1821 when he resigned from the army, travelled leisurely through Germany and Italy whence he took ship to Alexandria where we find him entering the service of the viceroy as a military instructor; after service at the camps of the niẓām al-jadīd at Aswān and Banī ʿĀdī he joined the staff of ʿU͟thmān Bey Jarkas commanding the 1st regiment which was about to leave for the Sudan, travelling with it to Khartoum where he arrived in September 1824; hampered by ill health and failure to receive his back pay he deserted his post at al-Ubaiyaḍ and returned to Cairo in 1828; there he was sentenced by a court-martial to forfeit his pay for unauthorized absence from his post; he committed suicide in Alexandria.

Cailliaud, Frédéric (1787–1869), French traveller; born at Nantes the son of a jeweller and watchmaker of that town he went to Egypt as a geologist and mineralogist; there he was charged by Muḥammad ʿAlī Pasha in 1815 to rediscover the ancient emerald mines of Mount Zabora in the ʿAtbāi; with B. Drovetti, consul-general of France in Egypt, he ascended the Nile as far as Wādī Ḥalfā and tried without success to enter the temple of Abū Simbel, then choked with sand, 1816; returning from France to Egypt in 1819 with a companion, P. C. Letorzec, a young naval officer, he accompanied the military expedition of Ismāʿīl Pasha which the viceroy sent to the Sudan in 1820; with Letorzec he explored the Nile as far as Khartoum, and the Blue Nile to Fāzū͟ghlī, in 1820–3; he was the only scientific reporter of the expedition after the Italian, E. Frediani, one of the few other Europeans capable of recording scientific information, went mad at Sennar; Cailliaud has been accused by recent Italian writers of making unacknowledged borrowings from Frediani's notes, of which no trace survives; his monumental account of the journey, published in Paris 1823–7, contains the first serious survey of the ancient monuments of the Sudan and is an indispensable authority on the Egyptian expedition to Sennar; he was appointed keeper of the natural history museum at Nantes in 1827.

Caimi, Pietro (1830–86), Italian rear-admiral; born at Sondrio he died at Spezzia; he commanded the Italian forces which landed at Muṣawwaʿ and ousted the Egyptian garrison, 1885.

Caisson . . . (*c*. 1790–   ), French soldier; a deserter from the Greek insurrectionary cause he entered the service of Muḥammad ʿAlī Pasha, viceroy of Egypt, as a taʿlīmjī-bāshī or instructor to the new regular army which the viceroy was creating; in 1824 he left Egypt for the Sudan on the staff of Mīrālai ʿUthmān Bey Jarkas, officer commanding the 1st infantry regiment; in 1826 he was chief instructor to the regular troops in the Sudan.

Callot, Eduard Ferdinand von, Baron (1792–1855), Austrian soldier and traveller; of an old Austrian military family he fought in the Austrian army as a junior officer in the Napoleonic wars, 1809–15; in 1831 he travelled to Egypt and ascended the Nile, visiting the ruins of Meroë and travelling by Shendi, Nāqa, and Ḥalfaiya to Khartoum; there he reported that he had discovered on Tūtī island the remains of a Coptic church; from Khartoum he went up the Blue Nile valley through Sennar and Gallabat into northern Abyssinia, finally returning to Egypt by way of Muṣawwaʿ and the Red Sea; an account of his journey was published at Leipzig in 1855 in a collection of travels called *Der Orient und Europa, Erinnerungen und Reisebilder von Land und Meer*; L. Frobenius and F. J. Bieber mention his travels in *Zur Herrlichkeit des Sudans* (Stuttgart, 1923).

Cambyses (–521 B.C.), Persian king, son of Cyrus the Great; he conquered Egypt about 527 B.C. and is said to have invaded the northern Sudan in person in 525 B.C. in a campaign against the Nubians which cost his army dearly in lives.

Cameron, Charles Duncan (*c*. 1826–70), British captain and consul; in 1846 he was commissioned to the army from which he retired in 1851; he entered the British consular service in 1860 and was appointed consul in Abyssinia on the murder of Consul Plowden near Gondar; he reached Muṣawwaʿ in 1862 and Gondar shortly after, where he was received favourably by the Emperor Theodore; he later re-entered Abyssinia by way of Kassala and Gallabat, but this time he was cast into prison where he lay until his delivery by a British army in 1868; he retired in that year and died at Geneva.

Cameron, Donald Andreas (1856–1936), British consul; he entered the Levant consular service in 1879 as a student-interpreter; he was acting consul at Sawākin during the campaign of 1885 and was consul there from 1885 to 1888; he then filled various consular and legal posts in Egypt and Tangier until his retirement in 1919.

Cameron, John Alexander (–1885), British journalist; born at Inverness he was first employed as a bank clerk, and then in a business house in Bombay, where he began his journalistic career; he followed the Afghan war of 1878–80 for the *Standard* newspaper of London; in the South African war of 1881 he was taken prisoner by the Boers at Majuba hill; in 1884 he was at Sawākin, narrowly missing the massacre of el-Teb; he next joined the Khartoum relief expedition, still writing for the *Standard*, and was killed at the battle of Abū Kurū (Kru) near Matamma.

Campbell, William P . . . (–1875), American soldier from the State of Tennessee; he graduated from the Annapolis Naval Academy and fought as a naval officer with the Confederate forces in the American civil war of 1861–5; in 1870 he entered the Khedivial service as a binbāshī and was first employed along with A. McC. Mason in charge of the Egyptian Government steamers plying between Alexandria and Constantinople; in 1874 he was appointed on the staff of of C. G. Gordon Pasha on the Upper White Nile where he was in charge of military stores; at Gondokoro he was attacked by fever and was taken to Khartoum where he died.

Camperio, Manfredo (1825–99), Italian geographer; he fought in the Five Days' revolt of the Milanese against the Austrians in 1848; in 1877 he founded the geographical journal *L'Esploratore* which devoted much space to the geography of the Sudan, and was in close correspondence with Italian officials in the Sudan at the time of R. Gessi Pasha and G. B. Messedaglia Bey.

Caneva, Carlo (1845–1922), Italian general; he was in command of the Italian garrison at Kassala in 1897 when the sirdār of the Egyptian army, Sir H. H. (afterwards Earl) Kitchener, visited the town and arranged for the Italian withdrawal; the fort was transferred to the Egyptian army on Christmas Day 1897; he was later commander-in-chief of the Italian forces in the Libyan campaign in the Italo-Turkish war of 1911–12, and president of the inquiry into the Italian defeat at Caporetto in the First World War.

Capato, Angelo Helia (Angelos Helia Kapatos) (*c.* 1860–1937), Greek merchant; born on the island of Cephalonia he went abroad while still a boy and entered on an adventurous career which included service in the British Navy; in the Sawākin campaign of 1884–5 he managed a canteen and shop in the port where he was connected with the British Red Sea trading house of Ross; on the Anglo-Egyptian occupation of 1898 he set up in business in Khartoum and later founded branch shops at Wad Madanī and Ḥaṣṣa Ḥaiṣa; he specialized in fitting out big-game hunting parties and his name was a byword among sportsmen, officers, and officials to whom he rendered services; he spent the last few years of his life in Egypt where he died; he left an interesting account of his life in manuscript compiled in his old age.

Capellen, Adrienne van Steengracht (–1864), aunt of Miss A. P. F. Tinné and sister of the Baroness H. M. L. van S. Capellen whom she accompanied on an expedition to the White Nile in 1863–4; after returning from Gondokoro sickness kept her in Khartoum while the rest of the party set out on its tragic journey to the Baḥr al-Ghazāl; she herself did not long survive the news of the death of her sister and was buried in Khartoum.

* **Capellen, Henriette Marie Louise van Steengracht** (–1863), Dutch lady, daughter of Vice-Admiral Baron T. F. van Capellen and mother of Miss A. P. F. Tinné; she accompanied her daughter's expedi-

tion to the Baḥr al-Ghazāl in 1863 and died of fever in the camp of Maḥjūb al-Buṣailī near Wau with two of her Dutch women servants.

Capper, Sir Thomson (1863–1915), British major-general; commissioned to the East Lancashire Regiment in 1882 he was employed in the Egyptian army, 1897–9, with the rank of binbāshī and fought in the battles of the Atbara and Omdurman, 1898; he saw service in the South African war, 1899–1902, and in the First World War commanded the 7th British division in France where he was killed in action.

Carcereri, Stanislao (1840–99), Italian missionary priest of the Roman Catholic Church, a brother of Don G. B. Carcereri; he came to the Sudan in 1871 with Daniele (afterwards Bishop) Comboni; in 1875 he was elected superior of the Camillian mission at Berber and took part in the founding of missions in al-Ubaiyaḍ and Dilling; differing from Comboni in matters of missionary policy he left the Sudan with the rest of the Camillian missionaries in 1877; he was later superior of a religious house in Verona.

Carmichael, Ludovick Montefiore (1837–85), British soldier; he joined the 5th Lancers as a cornet in 1861 and was promoted captain in 1870; in 1877 he passed out of the Staff College and in 1884–5 served, with the rank of major, with the British army which attempted to relieve Khartoum; he was killed in the battle of Abū Ṭulaiḥ (Abu Klea).

Carr Bey, Frederick Ulysses (1872–1917), British veterinary officer; graduating as a veterinary surgeon in 1893 he joined the Army Veterinary Corps in 1895 and was promoted captain in 1902 and later lieutenant-colonel; after service in India, 1897–8, in the South African war, 1899–1901, and in West Africa, 1906, he was seconded to the Egyptian army and in 1908 was appointed principal veterinary officer, Sudan Government, the designation of the post being changed in 1910 to director, veterinary department; he retired from the Egyptian army with the rank of mīrālai and died in retirement in England.

* **Casanova, Lorenzo** (–1870), Italian game-hunter; in 1864, after one of his big-game expeditions to the Sudan, he went to Vienna and Dresden to sell a collection of wild animals which he had brought with him; the German wild animal dealer Carl Hagenbeck bought his collection and he thereafter regularly supplied Hagenbeck with animals which he caught in the Sudan; he died in Alexandria while convoying animals to Europe.

Casati, Gaetano (1838–1902), Italian explorer; born at Lesmo near Milan he enrolled at twenty-one years of age in the Bersaglieri and took part in the war of 1866 against the Austrians with the rank of captain; his aptitude for geography secured his transfer to the topographical detachment working on a military map of Italy; he retired from the army in 1879 and joined the staff of *L'Esploratore*, the Milanese geographical journal founded by M. Camperio; R. Gessi Pasha, then governor of the Baḥr al-Ghazāl, asked Camperio for the services of a young topographical officer; Casati accepted employment and arrived in the equatorial regions early in 1880; he explored the region of Wau where he met Gessi, then moved southward to the country of the Azande and Monbuttu; in March 1883 he traced the upper course of the River Uélé, but the advance of the Mahdist forces into Equatoria rendered his position dangerous, so he went to Lado to join Emin Pasha, the governor of the province; Emin sent him on a mission in May 1886 to Kabarega, king of Unyoro, by whom he was held prisoner for a time, but escaped; while escaping he was the first European to see the snow-topped Ruwenzori mountains, he and Emin were at length joined by an expedition under H. M. Stanley which had come to the Nile by way of the Congo river in 1888; the combined parties of Emin, Stanley, and Casati reached Bagamoyo in 1889; returning to Italy he retired to his native district to compile his record of this epic journey which was first published in 1891; he died at Monticello near Brianza.

* **Casolani, Annetto** (–1858?), Maltese priest of the Roman Catholic Church; a memorandum which he wrote in 1840 is said to have originated the proposal to establish a mission on the Sudan Nile; he was associated with Bishop I. Knoblehar (Knoblecher) during the formation of the mission and in 1846 was designated its first vicar apostolic; he disagreed with Knoblehar on matters of policy in 1847 and withdrew from participation, leaving M. Ryllo to be elected pro-vicar apostolic in his stead but volunteering to serve as a missionary under Ryllo; he came to Khartoum with Ryllo's party in 1848 but left for Europe in 1849 to seek aid for the mission; he died in Malta.

Castelbolognesi, Angelo (1836–75), Italian trader and explorer; a native of Ferrara, G. Lejean, who praised him, called him a Jew, he came as a boy to Egypt whence he made his way to the Sudan and became first an employee of the British trader, J. Petherick, then an ivory-buying agent for a Cairo house in which capacity he explored the Baḥr al-Ghazāl river to its upper limit, and the region of the Rivers Req, Ajak, and Jur, in 1854–7, publishing an account in the journal *Le Tour du Monde* of Paris (No. 1, June 1862); with A. Antognoli and F. L. Magrini he travelled from Khartoum to Gallabat in 1857–8; he accompanied O. Antinori on an exploration of the region of Sennar in 1859–60; he had now become a trader on his own account, trading in the produce of Abyssinia; he returned to Egypt about 1860 and later committed suicide in Alexandria.

Castro, Juan de. *See* GAMA, ESTEVAM DA.

Cavendish, Spencer Compton, Marquess of Hartington and 8th Duke of Devonshire (1833–1908), British statesman; he was secretary of state for war in the administration of Mr. W. E. Gladstone in 1882–5 and was partly responsible for sending C. G. Gordon Pasha to Khartoum in 1884 and for the failure to take prompt measures to rescue him and his garrison from the Mahdists; he carried out the Cabinet's decision to build a railway from Sawākin to Berber in 1885 and when, a few months later, this project was declared impracticable by Lord

Wolseley, the commander-in-chief, he ordered the stoppage of railway construction and the withdrawal of staff and equipment from Sawākin; his *Life*, by B. Holland, appeared in 1911.

Cecil, Lord Edward Herbert Gascoyne (1867–1918), British soldier and civil servant, son of the 3rd Marquess of Salisbury, prime minister of the United Kingdom; joining the Grenadier Guards in 1887 he was aide-de-camp to Sir H. H. (afterwards Earl) Kitchener, sirdār of the Egyptian army, in the Dongola and Nile campaigns, 1896–8; he was agent-general of the Sudan Government in Cairo and director of intelligence, 1904–5; appointed under-secretary of state in the Egyptian ministry of finance in 1905 he was financial adviser in 1912 and acted as high commissioner for Egypt in 1914–15; he died at Leysin, Switzerland; he was the author of an amusing satire, *The Leisure of an Egyptian Official* (1911).

Cecil, Robert Arthur Talbot Gascoyne, 3rd Marquess of Salisbury (1830–1903), British statesman; as leader of the Conservative opposition in the House of Lords he was a critic of the policy of the Gladstone administration in the Sudan in 1884–5; the failure of Mr. Gladstone to effect the relief of Khartoum and other beleaguered Egyptian garrisons in the Sudan deprived his Cabinet of the confidence of Parliament and on its resignation he became prime minister and foreign secretary in June 1885, but found himself unable to reverse Gladstone's decision to evacuate the Sudan; out of office for a few months in 1886 he was again prime minister and foreign secretary from 1886 to 1902; by granting a Royal Charter to the British East African company in 1888 he ensured British occupation of the upper waters of the White Nile; he carried through the policy which led to the Anglo-Egyptian occupation of the Sudan in 1896–8; following the Fashoda Incident of 1898 he caused the French to relinquish their claims in the Sudan after a period of tension which nearly brought Britain and France to war; in 1900 he resigned the foreign secretaryship and in 1902 the premiership; he was a close student of science and theology and in his political views a critic of democratic and radical fallacies; he was a master of satire.

Cecil, Lord William (1854–1943), British soldier and court official; he was commissioned in 1876 to the 2nd Foot and in 1877 was transferred to the Grenadier Guards; he served in the Sawākin campaign of 1885 with the rank of captain and retired from the army in that year; he was later groom-in-waiting to Queen Victoria, comptroller to Princess Henry of Battenberg, and extra gentleman to King George V.

Chaillé-Long Bey, Charles (1842–1917), American officer; born at Princess Anne in Maryland he fought on the Confederate side in the American civil war, 1861–5, then practised as a journalist; he joined the service of the Khedive Ismā'īl in 1870 and in 1874 accompanied Colonel C. G. Gordon Pasha, governor of Equatoria, from Egypt by way of Sawākin and Berber to the upper White Nile; Gordon sent him to report on the state of Uganda with a view to its annexation to the Egyptian dominions; he explored the regions of Lakes Victoria and

Kioga, the latter of which he discovered and named Lake Ibrāhīm after Ibrāhīm Pasha al-Wālī; after a brief period in Khartoum he returned to the equatorial province and explored the country of the Azande in 1875; he retired from the service of the Egyptian Government in 1877 and died at Virginia Beach, Norfolk, Va., in 1917; he wrote bombastically of his own exploits and was a reckless detractor of Gordon; he rendered some service to the American subjects of Alexandria during the bombardment and troubles of 1882.

Chalmers, Albert John (1870–1920), British doctor; qualifying for the medical profession in 1890 he was a Holt Fellow of University College, Liverpool, before entering the West African medical service in which he spent four years; he was registrar at Colombo Medical College, 1901–11, and, after a period of service with the pellagra field commission, he was appointed director of the Wellcome Tropical Research Foundation in 1913; he died in Calcutta after his departure from the Sudan on retirement from the directorship; among his works are: *A Manual of Tropical Medicine* (1913, jointly with A. Castellani) and various papers on the pathology and bacteriology of the Sudan.

Chaltin, Louis-Napoléon (1857–1933), Belgian soldier and administrator; born at Ixelles he entered the Belgian infantry as a lieutenant and in 1890 joined the service of the Congo Free State; there he fought under Van Kerckhoven and Lemarinel against the Arabs in the eastern Congo; at the end of 1896 he took command of a column which advanced against the Mahdist amīr ʿArabī Dafaʿ Allāh in the equatorial province; he beat the Mahdists in battles at Bedden and Rejaf, 1897, and forced the retirement of ʿArabī Dafaʿ Allāh towards the north; after further service in the Congo he retired with the rank of colonel; he died at Brussels.

Champollion, Jean-François (1790–1832), French Egyptologist, born at Figeac, Lot; he led a French archaeological expedition which joined forces with a similar Italian expedition led by I. Rosellini; in the winter of 1828–9 he and his party visited Abū Simbel and Wādī Ḥalfā; Champollion is best known as the discoverer of the key to Egyptian hieroglyphics and is thus reckoned the founder of Egyptology.

Chélu Pasha, Alfred (–1916?), French engineer employed by the Egyptian Government; he was posted to Khartoum in 1876 as chief engineer of the Sudan; his book on the hydrography of the Nile, *Le Nil, le Soudan, l'Égypte* (Paris, 1891), won a prize of the Geographical Society of Paris, 1892; this work contains a detailed charting of the Nile cataracts.

* **Chermside Bey, Sir Herbert Charles** (1850–1929), British lieutenant-general; after a brilliant career in the Royal Military Academy, Woolwich, he was commissioned to the Royal Engineers in 1870; he served on the Turkish side in the Russo-Turkish war of 1877–8 and, transferring to the Egyptian army, was governor of the Red Sea littoral, 1884–6, and afterwards commandant at Wādī Ḥalfā; after a period as British military attaché at Constantinople and British commissioner

in Crete, he left for the South African war in which he commanded a British division in 1900; he was governor of Queensland in 1902–4 and retired from the army in 1907.

Chiene, Walter Glass (*c.* 1850–83), British engineer from Helensburgh, Scotland; he was superintendent engineer of the arsenal at Khartoum in 1883 and was attached to al-farīq W. Hicks Pasha's field force in that year; the circumstances of his death are obscure, but he was possibly killed in the battle of Shaikān (Kashgil) along with Hicks and his staff.

* **Chippendall, William Harold** (1850–1942), British soldier and explorer; in 1871 he was commissioned to the Royal Engineers and in 1874 left England to take service under the Khedivial Government with Colonel C. G. Gordon Pasha, then governor of the equatorial province; with a fellow lieutenant, C. M. Watson, he mapped the course of the Nile from Khartoum to Gondokoro and traversed the country between Gondokoro and the neighbourhood of Lake Albert in 1874–5; his subsequent service included duty in India, 1878–85, Singapore, 1898–1901, and a professorship of fortifications at the Royal Military College, Sandhurst, 1892–8; he retired from the army with the rank of colonel in 1902.

Chown, Harry (1891–1921), British veterinary officer; after graduating as a veterinary surgeon in 1914 he was commissioned to the Army Veterinary Corps in 1915 when he was seconded to the Egyptian army with the rank of binbāshī; in 1918 he was transferred to the veterinary department of the Sudan Government and was killed at Nyāla in Dār Fūr during the revolt of the fanatic ʿAbd Allāh al-Sihainī Muḥammad Idrīs.

Christian Victor of Schleswig-Holstein, Prince (1867–1900), major in the British army to which he was commissioned in the 60th Rifles in 1888; he served in the Nile campaign of 1898 and narrowly escaped death when the gunboat *Ẓāfir* sank in the Sabalūka gorge a few days before the battle of Omdurman, 1898.

Christy, Cuthbert (1863–1932), British surgeon and explorer; he graduated in medicine from the University of Edinburgh and served in many parts of Africa and in India; he explored and mapped the region of the Nile-Congo watershed for the Sudan Government, making ornithological collections, 1915–16; after an interlude of service in the Royal Army Medical Corps and on the intelligence staff of the War Office, London, he returned to the Sudan where he explored the hinterland of the Baḥr al-Ghazāl; among his various writings were contributions to the geography of the Nile-Congo watershed.

Churi, Joseph. *See* KHŪRĪ, YŪSUF.

* **Clayton Pasha, Sir Gilbert Falkingham** (1875–1929), British soldier and administrator; joining the Egyptian army in 1900 he transferred to the Sudan civil service in 1906, and in 1908 was appointed private secretary to Major-General Sir F. R. Wingate Pasha, governor-general;

in 1914 he was director of military intelligence in Cairo; promoted brigadier-general in 1917 he served in the Egyptian expeditionary force and in 1919–22 was adviser to the Egyptian ministry of the interior; in 1922–5 he was chief secretary, Palestine; he negotiated the treaty of Jidda in 1927, disposing of differences between Saʿūdī Arabia and Great Britain; he died in Baghdad while British high commissioner for ʿIrāq, collapsing suddenly after playing polo.

* **Clot Bey, Antoine-Barthélemi** (1796–1868), French doctor; born at Grenoble he was practising his profession in Marseilles when F. Werne, a German later in the service of Muḥammad ʿAlī Pasha, met him there; he came to Egypt in 1825 and founded the hospital and medical school of Abū Zaʿbal, near Cairo; he was the organizer and then president of the Egyptian public health council; when ʿAbbās Ḥilmī I succeeded to the viceroyalty in 1849 Clot was discharged with many other Europeans in the Egyptian service and returned to France; on the accession of Muḥammad Saʿīd he was recalled to Egypt in 1854 to reorganize the School of Medicine which had fallen into decay under ʿAbbās; he established a hospital at Qasr al-ʿAinī in Cairo; by critics he has been called a conceited mountebank; by others the founder of modern medicine in Egypt; he trained many Egyptian doctors who served with the garrisons in the Sudan.

Cochrane, Basil Edward (1841–1922), British vice-admiral; he entered the Royal Navy in 1854 and served in the Crimean war of 1853–5; promoted commander in 1872 and captain in 1884 he was on duty at Sawākin and at other points on the Red Sea coast during the campaign of 1884 against the Mahdist forces of ʿUthmān abū Bakr Diqna (Osman Digna); he retired from the Royal Navy in 1904.

Colborne, Francis Lionel Lydstone (1855–1924), British soldier; educated at Oxford University and Sandhurst Military College, he entered the army and served in India; he took part in the Nile campaign of 1884–5 and in 1886 was in the Sudan Frontier Field Force; after further service in the South African war, 1900, and in the First World War, 1914–17, he retired from the army with the rank of colonel and entered the insurance business.

Colborne, John (1830–90), British colonel; formerly in the 11th Foot he joined the Egyptian army and was on the staff of al-fariq W. Hicks Pasha in 1883 and fought in the campaign on the White Nile against the Mahdists which culminated in the Egyptian victory at Jabalain; invalided from the front he was employed on rear-guard duties by which he escaped death at the massacre of Shaikān (Kashgil) in which Hicks and his army were destroyed; during the campaign he was war correspondent for the *Daily News* of London; he wrote *With Hicks Pasha in the Soudan* (1884).

Collinson Pasha, John (1859–1901), British soldier; he entered the army in 1879 and saw service in the Zulu war, 1879, and in the first Boer war, 1881; later transferring to the Egyptian army he fought in the Dongola campaign of 1896; he commanded the 4th Egyptian brigade in the Nile campaign of 1898 when he was appointed governor of the Kassala province; he died suddenly at Kassala; at the time of his death he held the British rank of lieutenant-colonel and the Egyptian rank of liwā'.

Colston Bey, Raleigh Edward (1825–96), American brigadier-general; born in Paris where he received his early education, he was sent to America in 1842; entering the Virginia Military Institute he graduated in 1846 and remained at the institute as an assistant professor, becoming professor in 1854; on the outbreak of the American civil war in 1861 he fought on the Confederate side, rising to brigadier-general; on the conclusion of peace he conducted a successful private military school; in 1874 he was appointed a mīrālai on the Egyptian general staff and served six years in Egypt and the Sudan; he conducted two exploring expeditions: one in the Nubian desert, the other in Kordofan during which he received a serious injury by a fall from a camel; after six months rest in al-Ubaiyaḍ he was able to return to Cairo by way of Khartoum in 1875; his surveys over the Nubian desert increased the existing knowledge of the route between Qinā and Berenice and that over the 'Atmūr southward to Abū Ḥamad and Berber which he covered in 1874; his work in Kordofan took him from Debba on the Nile to Bāra and al-Ubaiyaḍ where after his accident he handed over command of the expedition to his assistant, H. G. Prout Bey; he retired from the Khedivial service in 1878; on his return to the United States he lost all his savings through unwise investments and secured a clerkship in the war department which he held till complete disability, the result of his injury received in Kordofan, overcame him in 1894; he spent the last two years of his life in the Confederate soldiers' home in Richmond, suffering greatly but always cheerful.

Colvile, Sir Henry Edward (1852–1907), British lieutenant-general; joining the Grenadier Guards in 1870 he served in the campaign of 1884–5 to attempt the relief of Khartoum, and was the official historian of the campaign; he was British acting commissioner in the Uganda protectorate, 1893, commanding a force of Sudanese troops consisting of survivors of Emin Pasha's garrisons in the Egyptian equatorial province who elected to serve under the British flag; he fought in the South African war, 1899–1901, but ruined his military career by his failure to relieve beleaguered garrisons; he wrote *The History of the Sudan Campaigns* (1889).

Colville, Sir Stanley Cecil James (1861–1939), British admiral; he fought in the Nile campaign of 1884–5 in the naval brigade and was given command of the flotilla of river steamers which accompanied the Dongola campaign of 1896 in which he was severely wounded; promoted captain after the campaign he was made rear-admiral in 1906; he held senior naval commands in the First World War.

* **Combes, Edmond** (1812–), French traveller; born at Castelnaudary, Aude, he was vice-consul of France in Asia Minor and Morocco and a Saint-Simonian in his philosophical views; he later turned to

travel and journeyed from Cairo to Dongola and thence by Khartoum and Berber to Sawākin in 1833–4, leaving a purple-tinted account of his journey, published in Paris in 1846; Isambert (*Guide Jaune*, 1878) wrote untruthfully that he was the first European to follow the shortest route from Berber to the Red Sea; he was employed as the local agent of the Compagnie Nanto-Bordelaise which in 1840–1 attempted, without success, to open up trade with Abyssinia through the Red Sea; he acquired for the company the port of Edd between Muṣawwaʿ and Assāb in 1846.

Comboni, Daniele (1831–81), Italian missionary bishop of the Roman Catholic Church; he was born at Limone San Giovanni on the Lake of Garda near Brescia and received his theological education in the institute of Don Mazza at Verona; ordained priest in 1854 he came to the Sudan with G. Beltrame in 1857; he and Beltrame travelled on the White Nile, but sickness compelled Comboni's return to Italy in 1859; after teaching in Mazza's institute, 1861–4, he published a pamphlet entitled *Plan for the Regeneration of Africa* (Turin, 1864) in which he advocated the conversion of the pagan negroes of Africa to Christianity by means of an African priesthood and by African schools and institutes; encouraged to put his plan into practice he visited France, Spain, England, Germany, and Austria to collect funds; in 1867 he established in Verona his own Missionary Institute for Negroland, to educate priests and laymen for the mission, and another centre, the Institute of the Pious Mothers of Negroland, to supply female help; he also opened similar institutes in Cairo to acclimatize the missionaries; in 1872 the Pope appointed him pro-vicar apostolic of Central Africa; during the year before he had returned to the Sudan and was engaged in restoring the mission in Khartoum and in creating new missions, first at al-Ubaiyaḍ and later at Dilling, Malbès (near al-Ubaiyaḍ), and Berber; in 1877 he was made vicar apostolic of Central Africa and titular bishop of Claudiopolis; in 1881 he travelled in the country between the Nuba hills and the Baḥr al-Ghazāl basin; his map of Jebel Nuba, in the compilation of which he was assisted by his missionaries and by A. Roversi, was published by the Italian Geographical Society (Rome, 1882) and inaccurately reproduced in *L'Esploratore* (Milan, Nov., 1882); he died in Khartoum shortly after his return; Comboni roused the interest of people in Europe in religious missions to the negro peoples, and five times travelled from Africa to Europe to appeal for missionaries and funds; besides his summary of African exploration, *Quadro storico delle scoperte africane* (Verona, 1880), he contributed, mainly on geography, to various scientific journals; J. C. Mitterrützner's works on the Bari and Dinka languages (Brixen, 1866 and 1867) are based largely on Comboni's manuscripts; his institute in Verona, called since 1894 the Congregation of the Sons of the Sacred Heart, continues his work in the Sudan; several schools, colleges, and missionary establishments in Europe, the Sudan, and Eritrea bear his name.

Connolly Bey, William Edward Gunnell (1866–1946), British soldier of a family with a hereditary connexion with the Royal Marines; he was commissioned in the Royal Marine Light Infantry and in 1901 was seconded to the Egyptian army in which he commanded the 11th Sudanese battalion; promoted major in 1905 he retired from the Egyptian army in 1911 and from the Royal Marines a few months later owing to illness; he served in Macedonia in the First World War.

Conry Bey, James Lionel Joyce (1873–1914), British soldier; commissioned to the Connaught Rangers in 1893 he joined the Egyptian army in 1906 with the rank of binbās͟hī; promoted major in the British army in 1908 and holding the rank of qā'immaqām in the Egyptian army he was killed near Sofi on the River Setit in a revolt led by the Faqī Abbukr.

Contarini, Carlo Teofilo (*c.* 1820–*c.* 1865), Italian trader, born in Venice; the manner of his coming to the Sudan is obscure; he possibly fought under Daniele Manin in the Venetian insurrection of 1848–9, and on the failure of the insurrection became an exile and came to the Sudan about 1850; on the other hand, when Blondeel van Cuelebroeck, Belgian consul-general at Alexandria, came to the Sudan in 1842 from Abyssinia, he was accompanied by his servant named Contarini; he went with J. A. Vayssière on trading expeditions to the Upper White Nile as interpreter, 1855–7, while Mrs. Petherick in *Travels in Central Africa* (1869) refers to 'Signor Carlo' who accompanied her and her husband on a journey to the region of Gondokoro apparently as an employee; he and his wife, Cattarina (*née* Nobili) of Venice, both died in Khartoum; he was said to have been wealthy in slaves and to have had a fine house in Khartoum enriched by a good library; his son Luigi was killed in 1885 in the massacre of Khartoum, while the descendants of his many daughters are still living in Egypt and the Sudan.

Cook, John Mason (1834–99), British tourist agent, son of Thomas Cook, founder of the firm of Thos. Cook & Son; in 1870 the Khedive Ismā'īl appointed him government agent for passenger traffic by steamer and *d͟hahabīya* on the Nile; during the Nile campaign of 1884–5 he contracted with the British Government for the carriage of military personnel and stores from Asyūṭ to Wādī Ḥalfā; he performed a useful service, carrying 17,000 British and Egyptian troops, 40,000 tons of stores, 40,000 tons of coal, and 800 small boats, in 27 steamers and 650 sailing boats of from 70 to 200 tons capacity; he did much to develop the extensive tourist traffic of Europeans and Americans to Egypt and the Sudan which reached its peak during the last ten years preceding the First World War.

Cooper, Edward Joshua (1798–1863), Irish astronomer and traveller who travelled in Nubia in 1821 and fixed the latitude of Wādī Ḥalfā as 21° 52′ (present reckoning 21° 55′); he published *Views in Egypt* in 1824.

Corbett, Sir Julian Stafford (1854–1922), British author and journalist, correspondent of the *Pall Mall Gazette* of London in the Dongola campaign of 1896; he later turned from journalism and fiction-writing to military history and was a naval historian of the First World War.

Corkran, Charles Edward (1872–1939), British soldier; he received a commission in the Grenadier Guards in 1893 and in 1898 fought at the battle of Omdurman; after service in the South African war of 1899–1902 and in the First World War he was promoted major-general in 1921; in 1923 he was appointed commandant of the Royal Military College, Sandhurst.

Corner, Giulio Andrea (1787–*c.* 1840), Italian traveller; of noble stock from the Veneto, he served in the Austrian dragoons, rising to the rank of captain; in 1810 he married, his wife dying in 1880 aged eighty-nine; with E. Frediani and G. Segato he accompanied the expedition of Ismāʿīl Pasha, son of the viceroy, Muḥammad ʿAlī Pasha, to Sennar in 1820–1 but soon returned disgusted, it was said, by the intrigues of Ismāʿīl's chief doctor, D. Botzaris; an alternative name for the family is Cornaro.

Corrall, William Rousall (*c.* 1874–1922), British major; he enlisted in the ranks in the Buffs (East Kent Regiment), 1892, and was commissioned, 1914; seconded to the Egyptian army in 1919 he died at Soda in the Ingassana hills.

Coveny, Robert Charles (1842–85), British soldier; he entered the 23rd Foot as an ensign in 1862 and served in the Ashanti war, 1874; for gallantry in the battle of Tel el-Kebir, 1882, he was promoted brevet lieutenant-colonel; posted to the British army in the Nile campaign of 1884–5 he was killed at the battle of Kirbikan.

Cowdray, 1st Viscount (1857–1927). *See* PEARSON, WEETMAN DICKINSON, 1st Viscount Cowdray.

Crabitès, Pierre (1877–1943), American judge and author; born in the state of Louisiana and of French origin, he entered the profession of the law; while a judge of the Mixed Courts in Cairo he published *Gordon, the Sudan and Slavery* (1933), *The Winning of the Sudan* (1934), also biographies of Ibrāhīm Pasha al-Wālī, the Khedive Ismāʿīl, and of the Americans in the Egyptian army, all in a journalistic vein; he had retired from the Bench to take up a professorship in the University of Louisiana when, on the entry of the United States into the Second World War in 1941, he joined the United States diplomatic service and at the time of his death was in Baghdad as legal assistant to the American minister to ʿIrāq.

Cradock, Sir Christopher George Francis Maurice (1862–1914), British admiral; he served as a 1st lieutenant in the *Delphin* screw sloop in the Red Sea fleet in 1891 and took part in the fighting at Afafit against the Mahdists and in the reoccupation of el-Teb; promoted rear-admiral in 1910 he went down in his flagship, the *Good Hope*, in the battle of Coronel against a superior squadron under the German admiral, Count von Spee.

Crawford Pasha, Archibald (1861–1929), British soldier; commissioned to the Royal Garrison Artillery, 1881, he was made lieutenant-colonel, 1909, and colonel, 1915; he served for some years in the Egyptian army in which he was latterly commandant of the artillery with rank of liwā', 1911–14; he was acting governor-general of the Sudan, 1911 and 1913.

Cromer, Earl of. *See* BARING, EVELYN, 1st Earl of Cromer.

Cross, Henry (*c.* 1867–98), British journalist; graduating in 1888 from the University of Oxford where he had been a rowing 'blue', he was first an assistant master at Bedford Grammar School and in 1898 accompanied the Nile expedition of 1898 as war correspondent for the *Manchester Guardian* newspaper; he died of enteric fever in Atbara shortly after the battle of Omdurman.

Crossland, Cyril (1878–1943), British marine biologist; he was born in Sheffield and obtained a doctorate of philosophy; the Sudan Government engaged him to report on the possibilities of establishing a pearl-fishing industry on the Red Sea coast and in 1906 he was appointed director of a specially created pearl fisheries department; the fisheries proved a commercial failure and were closed in 1923 when the department was abolished; after his retirement from the Sudan he lived for some years at Copenhagen where he died during the German occupation of Denmark; he made several short contributions to the botany, zoology, and anthropology of the Sudan and wrote a longer work, *Desert and Water Gardens of the Red Sea* (1913).

Crowther, Frank (1906–46), British scientist; born in York he finished his education at the Royal College of Science, London, and from 1926 to 1928 was a ministry of agriculture research scholar; he came to the Sudan as plant physiologist at the Jazīra research farm in 1928; temporarily employed in Egypt by Imperial Chemical Industries, 1933–8, he then went on a scientific tour of India and Java; he returned to the Sudan in 1938 and continued important work as senior plant physiologist on the correlation between climatic conditions and cotton yields, and the introduction of fallow weed control as a means of improving cotton crops.

Cuny, Charles (1811–58), French doctor and traveller; born at Goin in Lorraine of peasant stock he entered the French army as a pupil-pharmacist and served in Algeria; dismissed from the army for indiscipline he entered the Egyptian service as a military surgeon and married a daughter of L. M. A. Linant de Bellefonds Bey (afterwards pasha); in 1853 he qualified as a civilian doctor with the medical authorities of Paris; in 1857 he set out on a journey of exploration to Dār Fūr, travelling by way of Dongola, the Bayūda, and al-Ubaiyaḍ; he died of dysentery in al-Fāshar; his biography, by H. Roy, was published in Paris in 1930, entitled *La Vie Héroïque et Romantique du Docteur Charles Cuny*.

Currie, Sir James (1868–1937), British educationist; he was educated at Edinburgh and Oxford Universities and joined the Sudan civil service in 1900 as the first director of education, a post which he held till 1914;

the post carried with it the principalship of Gordon Memorial College, opened in 1903; he was a member of the governor-general's council, 1911–14; to him fell the duty of organizing modern education in the Sudan from its beginning; resigning his appointment with the Sudan Government he occupied a senior post in the British ministry of munitions, 1916–18, during the First World War; from 1919 to 1921 he was in the ministry of labour; among his many voluntary duties he was a governor of the Imperial College of Science and Technology.

* **Cuzzi, Giuseppe** (1843–1923), Italian adventurer; born at Nava, Brianza, in Lombardy, he chose a life of action; he fought in the Ravelli legion in Garibaldi's volunteer force aiding the French in the Franco-Prussian war of 1870 and was later commissioned as a sub-lieutenant of foot chasseurs in the Maritime Alps; he is next found fighting in the Montenegrin army against the Turks in 1878; he then came to Egypt and about 1880 entered the Sudan as a clerk in the firm of A. Marquet; in 1884 General Gordon appointed him his personal agent at Berber as well as British consular agent there; on the eve of the capture of Berber by the Mahdists in April 1884 he, his Sudanese wife, and family fled from the town but were taken a few days later; he became a Muslim and took the name of Muḥammad Yūsuf; during the siege of Khartoum he corresponded with Gordon and tried to induce him to surrender; Gordon accused him of betraying Berber to the Mahdists, but proof is lacking; in 1887 he was sent to Omdurman in chains on suspicion of wanting to escape from the Sudan, and on his release made a bare living by selling dates in the Berber district; repatriated to Egypt in 1898 on the Anglo-Egyptian occupation, and now a broken man, he left Egypt for Italy; a daughter, Margherita, born in the Sudan in 1894, lives in Milan; see C. Zaghi, *Gordon, Gessi e la riconquista del Sudan.* Firenze, 1947; Zaghi is preparing a biography of him.

Cyriacus. *See* KYRIAKOS.

Dafaʿ Allāh wad Aḥmad Ḥasan. *See* AL-ARBĀB DAFAʿ ALLĀH WAD AḤMAD ḤASAN.

Dafaʿ Allāh ibn Muḥammad al-Kahlī al-Hadhalī (–1709), Sudanese holy man, born and bred in Ḥalfaiya; he was a disciple of Muḥammad al-Azraq ibn al-Shaikh al-Zain who taught him Islamic law.

Dafaʿ Allāh ibn Muqbal al-ʿArakī (*fl. c.* 1600), Sudanese holy man from Bīr Serrār about thirty miles north-east of Bāra in Kordofan; he lived at Jarf al-Jimīʿāb, a few miles north of Khartoum.

Dafaʿ Allāh ibn al-Shaikh Muḥammad abū Idrīs (1594–1683), Sudanese holy man, a follower of Shaikh Ṣughaiyarūn, he was born at Dubāb, about fifteen miles south-west of Rufāʿa, and settled at Abū Ḥarāz; he founded a number of mosques in the Jazīra and lived a life of meditation and asceticism; it was said of him that, so great was his independence, he never went to Sennar, the Funj capital, but that, if King Bādī wad Rubāṭ wished to speak to him, he would go to Abū

Ḥarāz on purpose; he was the nephew and successor of Shaikh 'Abd Allāh Dafa' Allah al-'Arakī, founder of the 'Arakīyīn tribe of the Jazīra; his death was followed by a terrible famine.

Daftardār. *See* MUḤAMMAD BEY KHUSRAW AL-DARAMĀLĪ.

Ḍaif Allāh ibn 'Alī ibn 'Abd al-Ghanī ibn Ḍaif Allāh al-Faḍlī (–1684), Sudanese holy man, born at Ḥalfaiya where he was a renowned teacher; he was a disciple of Shaikh al-Zain ibn al-Shaikh Ṣughaiyarūn who taught him Islamic law and apostleship, and of Shaikh abū Idrīs who taught him mysticism.

Ḍaif Allāh ibn Muḥammad ibn Ḍaif Allāh (–1768), Sudanese holy man, father of the hagiographer Muḥammad al-Nūr wad Ḍaif Allāh; he was instructed by a number of famous religious teachers of his day including the great Khūjalī ibn 'Abd al-Raḥmān ibn Ibrāhīm who taught him mysticism; he began to teach in 1718; among his disciples was 'Abd al-Raḥmān ibn al-Shaikh Ṣāliḥ Bān al-Nuqā.

Dakīn wad Naiyīl (–1577), Funj sultan of Sennar; he succeeded 'Umāra abū Sakaikīn in 1562 and was followed in the succession, on his death, by Ṭabl I; a man of exceptional power both in law and in rule, he organized his sultanate into governorates and drew up rules of precedence at court; his fair dealing with his people earned for him the title of The Just.

Dal Ayual (–1933), chief of the Beir section of the Dinka of Melūt on the White Nile; he was a magistrate.

Damien . . . (*fl.* 1704), French Franciscan priest who, with another priest of the same order, travelled through the Sudan, possibly on their way from Abyssinia, in 1704; at the oasis of Salīma, on their way to Egypt along the desert caravan route through the Kharja oasis, they met the ill-fated French diplomatic mission to Abyssinia, headed by Le Noir du Roule, on its way south to Sennar.

Dandolo, Emilio, Count (1831–57), Italian patriot and traveller; he took part in the Italian uprising in Milan in 1848 and in the defence of Rome against the French in 1849, and, on the collapse of the Italian insurrection, visited Egypt in 1850 as an exile in company with the Marquess B. L. Trotti, a fellow patriot from the barricades of Milan; together they visited Nubia and Khartoum, travelling over the desert from Korosko to Berber; they made an excursion by ship on the White Nile to the borders of the country of the Shilluk; Dandolo wrote a spirited account of the journey (Milan, 1854); he was a grandson of Vincenzo Dandolo, the agricultural scientist and Napoleonic governor of Dalmatia, whose father was a Jewish pharmacist converted to Christianity by a Venetian aristocrat who gave him the Venetian name of Dandolo.

Danels Bey, K . . . Leonard (1884–1932), British veterinary officer; he graduated from the Royal College of Veterinary Surgeons in 1905 and received his commission in the same year in the Army Veterinary Corps, being promoted captain in 1910 and major in 1920; in 1913 he was appointed a veterinary inspector, with rank of binbāshī, in the Egyptian army and in 1914 was recalled to the British army on the outbreak of the First World War; in 1915 he was re-engaged as a veterinary officer in the Egyptian army and in 1917 was promoted qā'immaqām; he held the post of assistant director of the veterinary service in the Sudan, 1918–22, and in 1922–4 he was principal veterinary officer in the Egyptian army and director of the Sudan veterinary service with rank of mīrālai; he reverted to the British army in 1924 and in 1930 was appointed assistant director-general of the Army Veterinary Service.

Dangala Dima (–1926), a Fulānī from Sokoto in Nigeria, son of the wazīr of Sultan Abbukr Atiqu of Sokoto; he migrated east across Africa to the Sudan and from 1910 till his death was wazīr to Sultan Muḥammad Bello Maiwurnu.

Dardīrī Muḥammad al-Khalīfa (*c.* 1849–1939), religious notable, khalīfa of the Tījānīya brotherhood in Kordofan; a member of the Duwālīb branch of the Rikābīya Ashrāf of Dongola, he lived at Khūrsī, where he was imām of the mosque.

Dā'ūd al-'Abbādī (1767–1827), 'Abbādī leader, born on the Atbai, the barren country between the Red Sea hills and the Nubian Nile, he became kāshif, or local semi-independent ruler, of al-Derr between Aswān and Wādī Ḥalfā; he commanded a portion of the 700 'Ābābda irregulars led by Shaikh Khalīfa wad al-Ḥājj Muḥammad al-'Abbādī who fought in Ismā'īl Pasha's battles against the Shā'iqīya in 1820; he died in Khartoum.

Dā'ūd 'Abd al-Jalīl (*fl. c.* 1550), religious teacher; Wad Ḍaif Allāh the hagiographer wrote that he came from the Ḥijāz and entered the Sudan with Tāj al-Dīn al-Baghdādī; he established himself at Arbajī and gave his name to the Jalīlāb of Wad Rawa on the Blue Nile, or so the Jalīlāb relate; he was succeeded by his son, al-Ḥājj Sa'īd whose descendants wore the ceremonial cap conferred by the sultans of Sennar upon their more important tributary chiefs and functionaries.

Dā'ūd Aḥmad Yūsuf (–1932), member of the religious family of the Ya'qūbāb living in the Jazīra near Sennar; he was a magistrate and succeeded al-Imām 'Alī as shaikh of the first khuṭṭ of Manāqil where he died.

Dā'ūd Kūkī (*c.* 1830–1941), shaikh of the cataract at Wādī Ḥalfā; he helped warp the ships of the Nile expedition of 1884–5 through the Second Cataract and again rendered great services in the more serious operation at the cataract in 1896–7 when the Nile flotilla of gunboats and transports was passed upstream on its way to support Kitchener's army; his father and uncle were shaikhs of the cataract before him; he lived to a great age and died at Wādī Ḥalfā.

Dā'ūd Mandīl (1830–1901), trader of Algerian Jewish descent; he was born in Alexandria and became a pioneer in the ginning of cotton lint by machinery in Egypt; he erected a ginnery at Kafr al-Zaiyāt about 1870; he next came to the Sudan and established himself in al-Ubaiyaḍ where he started a business for selling Manchester goods and buying gum arabic, ostrich feathers, and ivory in 1881; captured by the Mahdists in the fall of al-Ubaiyaḍ in 1883 he embraced Islam and was afterwards employed by the Khalīfa ʿAbd Allāhi as a translator and expert on precious stones; during the revolt he married a daughter of Muḥammad Aghā ʿAinṭāblī, a Turkish officer killed in the siege of Khartoum; on the Anglo-Egyptian occupation he continued in business; he died at al-Nahūd.

David, Christian king of Dongola. *See* BAIBARS I.

David Bey, Ernest Frederic (1862–98), British major; he was commissioned to the Royal Marine Light Infantry in 1881 and served at Sawākin during the campaign of 1884–5; in 1888 he was seconded to the Egyptian army and fought in the battles of Jummaiza (Gemaiza), 1888, and Tūshkī (Toski), 1889; in 1890 he was promoted major; he commanded the 4th Egyptian brigade in the Dongola campaign of 1896 with rank of mīrālai and was promoted lieutenant-colonel in the British army for his work in the campaign; in 1897 he was in charge of the operation of warping gunboats through the Fourth Cataract; he reverted to the Royal Marines and shortly afterwards died at Chatham.

Davis, Sir John (1832–1901), British general; as a junior officer he served in the Indian mutiny of 1857; as a major-general he commanded the 2nd infantry brigade at the second battle of el-Teb early in 1884 when a force of British troops under the command of Lieutenant-General Sir G. Graham beat a Mahdist army; he was made colonel of the Royal Sussex Regiment in 1900.

Debbas, Elias George (1846–1927), Syrian cotton ginner and merchant; born in Beyrout, he came to the Sudan in 1864; from Khartoum he went in 1865 to Sawākin and, following in the steps of his parents who were the proprietors of a cotton-ginning factory, he engaged in fostering the infant cotton production on the Red Sea coast in which he collaborated with Aḥmad Mumtāz Bey (afterwards pasha), the governor of Sawākin and an enthusiastic promoter of cotton-planting in the district of Tokar; he set up his first ginning plant at Sawākin in 1876, near the site of the present factory; in 1877 he engaged ʿUthmān abū Bakr Diqna, the future Mahdist amīr, as his contractor for the supply of fresh water; in 1880 he built the present factory with thirty-six gins; he was the first to gin cotton on the Red Sea coast of the Sudan and thus played an important part in the development of the cotton plantation in the delta of Baraka torrent; he also traded in Sudan produce for export; he retired to Egypt in 1917 and died in Cairo.

* **Debono, Andrea** (–1871), Maltese trader and explorer; he came to the Sudan in 1848, erecting a corn mill in Khartoum and manufacturing lime and kiln-dried bricks; his activities led him to enter the White Nile trade; he used the Islamic name of Laṭīf Efendi while,

being a British subject, his ships sailed under the Union Jack; in 1853 he crossed the cataracts upstream of Rejaf on the Upper White Nile; in 1855, with P. Terranova, he explored the lower reach of the River Sobat; in 1854–61 he was actively trading on the White Nile; the first European to explore the Lotuka country, he was with A. Peney when the latter died a few miles south of Rejaf in 1861; in 1862 J. Petherick, the British consul in Khartoum, surprised Debono's nephew Amabile Lanzon engaged in slave trading, but in the absence of sufficient proof Amabile was released; British consular records for 1863 show that he was then in partnership with ʻAqqād and Company, a trading concern with interests in ivory and other Sudan produce; he left the Sudan in 1865 and established himself in Cairo, leaving a trading agent, Maḥmūd Aḥmadānī, in Khartoum; he sold his original Sudan business to ʻAqqād & Co. who also traded on the White Nile; his Abyssinian wife Vittoria survived him and claimed his estate through the British consular court in Cairo.

De Coëtlogon Pasha, Henry Watts Russell (1839–1908), British soldier; born in Munich he joined the East Yorkshire Regiment as an ensign, 1858, and was selected for a captaincy, 1872, before the abolition of the purchase system, having been passed over thirteen times; he then transferred to the East Surrey Regiment, retiring, 1881, with rank of honorary major; after service with the Madras Light Infantry he entered the newly reconstituted Egyptian army, 1883, and was posted to the staff of al-farīq W. Hicks Pasha in the Sudan with rank of qā'immaqām; in Khartoum he commanded the troops under Ḥusain Pasha Wāṣif Sirrī and was promoted mīrālai; while Hicks was campaigning against the Mahdists on the White Nile and in Kordofan he patrolled the river as far south as the Shilluk country and engaged in brushes with the enemy; he was commanding the Khartoum garrison when news was brought of the disaster to Hicks's army at Shaikān (Kashgil), September 1883; he continued strengthening the city's defences, a work begun by ʻAbd al-Qādir Pasha Ḥilmī, 1882; he was appointed acting governor-general with rank of mīrlivā, February 1884; his telegrams to Cairo during January 1884 gave the impression of panic: on the 4th he asked for 12,000 men to defend Khartoum, on the 10th he asked for an order to retire from the city, on the 25th he telegraphed 'all well'; on the arrival of C. G. Gordon Pasha in Khartoum, 18 February, he left for Egypt where he was employed in the police force, serving as police commandant at Asyūṭ and Alexandria; he then entered the British consular service and occupied several posts in the Pacific and United States until his retirement, 1907; he died at Oxford.

De Cosson, Emilius Albert (1850–89), British soldier and traveller; he was commissioned to the 2nd Middlesex Militia, 1871, and transferring to the King's Royal Rifle Corps was promoted captain, 1876; in 1873 he and his brother travelled from Muṣawwaʻ via Adowa to Gondar and thence by Gallabat and Gedaref to Khartoum, Berber, and Sawākin, a journey which he described in *The Cradle of the Blue Nile*

(1877); he retired to the reserve, 1880, but returned to active service and was on the commissariat and transport staff of the British army at Sawākin, 1885, and for his services was promoted major in the reserve; he wrote of his war experiences in *Days and Nights of Service with Sir Gerald Graham's Field Force at Suakin* (1885).

Delanghe, Florimond (1861–95), Belgian soldier; born at Bruges he was commissioned in the engineers in the Belgian army; arriving in the Congo Free State in 1892 he took command of a column making for the White Nile, 1893; in March 1894 he repulsed a Mahdist attack on Mundu on the Nile in an engagement in which Captain Bonvalet and M. Devos were killed; he himself died at sea on his way to Europe on leave.

De Montmorency, Raymond Harvey, 3rd Viscount Frankfort de Montmorency (1835–1902), British major-general; he joined the army in 1854, serving in the Crimean war (1854–5), the Indian Mutiny (1857–8), and the Anglo-Abyssinian war of 1868; transferred to the Egyptian army he commanded the frontier force based on Wādī Ḥalfā, 1886–7, and directed a field column during the operations in the Nile valley against the Mahdists in 1887; in 1889 he succeeded to the peerage and was promoted to major-general.

Deng Malwal (–1946), noted Dinka chief, magistrate, and president of the Nyareweng court; he was buried at Terakeka on the Upper White Nile.

Denis de Rivoyre, Barthélemy Louis (1837–), French traveller; born at Villefranche-sur-Saône he fought in the Polish insurrection, 1863, and in 1865 set out for Africa, visiting Sawākin, Muṣawwaʿ, and the highlands of Keren, 1866; returning to France he fought in the Franco-German war, 1870–1, and later held various posts in the French civil service; he returned to the Red Sea, 1880, devoting himself to spreading French influence; his writings include *Mer Rouge et Abyssinie* (Paris, 1880) and *Aux pays du Soudan* (Paris, 1885).

Dennison, James Alfred (1846–1900), American soldier; born in Indiana, a lineal descendant of Commodore Perry, the famous American sailor, he was educated at the United States Military Academy at West Point and fought on the Federal side in the American civil war of 1861–5; he was admitted to the Bar in 1873; in 1874 he joined the Egyptian general staff and was appointed a staff officer in the ill-fated army led by Colonel S. A. Arendrup in the Egyptian-Abyssinian war of 1875; advancing from Muṣawwaʿ the main body of the force was destroyed at Gundet; Dennison with a brother-officer, ʿUmar Rushdī (afterwards bey), were with a small Egyptian detachment a few miles away from the battle and succeeded in regaining Muṣawwaʿ; he contributed to the great map of Africa completed by the Egyptian general staff in 1877; returning to the United States in 1876 he served as assistant attorney-general of the State of New York; he died in New York City.

Dentamaro, Emmanuele (1880–1935), Italian contractor; born in Bari in south Italy he was a self-educated man; apprenticed early to the masonry trade he was engaged in various engineering works in Egypt and the Sudan, including the quarrying and cutting of stone for the Jabal Awliyā dam, a work which he undertook in partnership with Sasso; among his constructions are the General Post Office and Comboni College in Khartoum; he died in Cairo.

Derrick, Clarence (1837–1907), American soldier; he was born at Washington, D.C., and graduated from the United States Military Academy, West Point, 1861; he resigned his commission in the Corps of Engineers to join the Confederate army at the outbreak of the civil war and was later taken prisoner by the Federal forces; in 1873 he joined the Egyptian general staff and was chief engineer to Muḥammad Rātib Pasha, commander-in-chief of the Egyptian army invading Abyssinia, 1876; he fought in the battle of Gura when the Egyptian army was routed; like several other American officers on the general staff he assisted in the compilation of the map of Africa which the general staff prepared in 1877; he retired from the Khedivial service in 1878 and was variously occupied in the United States as lawyer, professor, and cotton planter; he died at Greensboro, Alabama.

Devonshire, Duke of. *See* CAVENDISH, SPENCER COMPTON, Marquess of Hartington and 8th Duke of Devonshire.

Dhanis, François, Baron (1862–1909), Belgian soldier; born in London he entered the Belgian army and chose a career in the Congo Free State forces; he served in the Congo in 1884, taking part in several expeditions of a geographical and military nature; in 1895 he was appointed to command the troops of the Free State at Stanley Falls; in this capacity he was charged with the formation of a column which had as its object the attainment of the Nile in co-operation with a second column under Captain L. N. Chaltin; he occupied Lado in 1897 and made treaties with the neighbouring chiefs; after a term as vice-governor-general of the Congo Free State he returned to Europe in 1900.

* **Didier, Charles** (1805–64), French novelist, poet, and traveller; of Swiss origin he was born at Geneva and came to France as a young man; after a mediocre success in journalism and fiction-writing he undertook a series of journeys in Spain, Morocco, Egypt, and Arabia; crossing from Jidda in March 1854 he landed at Sawākin and travelled to Egypt by way of Kassala, Wad Madanī, Rufā'a, Soba, and Khartoum; he wrote two uninformative and sensational books on his journey through the Sudan, published in Paris in 1857 and 1858; he later became blind and died in Paris.

Diocletian (Valerius Diocletianus) (245–313), Roman emperor; marauding bands of Nubians called Blemmyes forced him to summon the Nobatae from al-Kharja to the Nile valley to assist in its defence as confederates of the Roman Empire.

Dixon, Sir Henry Grey (1850–1933), British general; he entered the army in 1868 and served in the Afghan war, 1878–80; he commanded at Sawākin in 1886 and was present at the battle of Jummaiza (Gemaiza), 1888; in 1889 he took a prominent part in the operations on the Nile against the army of the amīr ʻAbd al-Raḥmān wad al-Najūmī; he served in the South African war, 1901–2, and in the First World War in Egypt and Cyprus.

Domville, Sir William Cecil Henry (1849–1904), British sailor; he commanded the Naval Brigade in the Sawākin Field Force in 1885 with rank of commander, Royal Navy; promoted captain in 1886 he retired in 1893.

Dormer, Sir James Charlemagne (1834–93), British lieutenant-general; he received a commission in the 13th Foot in 1853 and fought in the Crimean war, 1885, and in the Indian mutiny, 1858; after serving in several campaigns including that of Egypt, in which he was present at the battle of Tel el-Kebir, 1882, he served in the Nile campaign of 1884–5; he had been promoted major-general in 1882; having completed his part in the evacuation of the British army after the fruitless attempt to relieve Khartoum, he returned to Cairo to resume his duties as chief of staff to General Sir F. C. A. Stephenson.

Douloghlu, Gheorghios Dimitrios (*c.* 1830–83), Greek physician, of a family long domiciled in Egypt; he studied at the school of medicine in Cairo and in 1850 was sent by the Egyptian Government to complete his medical studies in the University of Pisa on a stipend of 48 piastres and 13 paras a month; at Pisa he met his future wife, Laura (*née* Pancani), who died of fever in Khartoum in 1876; returning to Cairo in 1857 he was appointed to a post in the hospital at Qaṣr al-ʻAinī, and in 1863, in the capacity of doctor and translator, was posted to the staff of Mūsā Pasha Ḥamdī, governor-general of the Sudan, with rank of yūzbāshī; after serving for a short time with the garrison at Kassala he was appointed chief physician and surgeon-general to the forces in the Sudan; he was a popular figure in Khartoum and several contemporaries wrote well of him; Lieutenant-Colonel the Hon. J. Colborne, who met him in 1883 shortly before his death, respected his medical opinions; Emin Pasha knew him well; he was attached to the army of al-farīq W. Hicks Pasha and was killed by the Mahdists on the eve of the disastrous battle of Shaikān (Kashgil); six children survived him.

Doyle, Sir Arthur Conan (1859–1930), British author; although he qualified as a doctor he took to writing, achieving fame as the author of *The Adventures of Sherlock Holmes*, a series of detective stories begun in 1891; in 1895–6, during a visit to Egypt for the sake of his health, the Dongola campaign began and he was appointed honorary correspondent of the *Westminster Gazette* of London; he followed the expedition as far as Sārras in the opening months of 1896 and thence returned to England; a previous trip in a Cook's steamer to Wādī Ḥalfā, and a donkey-ride to Abū Ṣīr rock near by, in the winter of 1895–6, inspired his novel *The Tragedy of the Korosko* (1898); his service as a war correspondent gave him material for his short story, *The Three Correspondents*; he visited Port Sudan about 1920 while on a tour of Africa.

Drage Pasha, William Henry (1852–1915), British soldier; he joined the army in the ranks, 1872, and became a warrant officer, 1882; he served in the Nile expedition of 1884–5 and then entered the Commissariat and transport department; he was attached to the Frontier Field Force, 1885–6; his attachment to the Egyptian army, 1886, was the prelude to quick advancement; his conduct at the battle of Tūshkī (Toski), 1889, led to his promotion to honorary captain and quartermaster, while the Dongola campaign of 1896 saw him honorary major; he served throughout the campaigns of 1897–9 and emerged honorary lieutenant-colonel; he was later controller of stores in the Sudan Government and retired from the Egyptian and British armies, 1904, with the Egyptian rank of liwā'.

Driberg, Jack Herbert (1888–1946), British administrator and anthropologist, a leading authority on the tribes of the south-eastern Sudan; he entered the administrative service in Uganda in 1912 and spent the years 1912–21 mainly among the Lango, Lugbara, and Acholi people, then within the Uganda protectorate; after a punitive expedition had been sent to the Didinga he was lent as civil administrator to that tribe; in 1923 he was transferred to the Sudan political service; retiring in 1926 he became a lecturer in anthropology at the University of Cambridge; during the Second World War he returned to government service and was employed in the Near East and latterly was concerned with Arab affairs in the British ministry of information; he was a gifted writer on social anthropology and was a highly individual personality of unorthodox methods; he had a profound admiration for the religion of Islam; besides his books he contributed to *Sudan Notes and Records* and anthropological journals.

Drovetti, Bernardino (1776–1852), Italian in the French consular service; born at Barbania in the commune of Canavese, Piedmont, he graduated at the University of Turin and practised the profession of the law; this he early abandoned and in 1797 he was commissioned in the Cisalpine army under the French command; in 1803 he joined the French consular service and from that year till 1815 was consul in Cairo; during the years 1815–21 he lived in Egypt as a private resident until he returned to the service as consul-general of France in Egypt, a post which he held from 1821 till his retirement in 1830 when he returned to his native Piedmont and died in Turin; the ruling passion of his life was the collection of Egyptian antiquities, a passion shared by other European consuls whose antiquarian rivalries occasionally embarrassed their respective governments; he visited Nubia several times and made excavations at Abū Simbel; his son visited Khartoum in 1852 and was prostrated by fever there.

Drury Bey, William Byron (*c*. 1877–1917), British sailor; he entered the Royal Navy and was promoted lieutenant, 1898, when he saw service in the Nile flotilla; he was promoted acting commander, 1917; transferring to the service of the Sudan Government he assisted in 1902–3 in the marine development of Sawākin for the reception of material for the construction of the Red Sea railway which was to join the port with the Nile valley railway at Atbara in 1905; as controller of the harbours and lights administration, 1905–14, he helped to plan the new harbour and dockyard of Port Sudan, 1907–10; he was director of the steamers and boats department, 1914–17; he died in Cairo.

Du Bisson, Raoul, Comte (*fl.* 1863–5), French adventurer, a member of a Norman family ennobled by Louis XVIII and a relative of Dr. Cuneau, doctor to Napoleon III; recruiting a party of down-at-heel Europeans from the cafés of Egypt he left Cairo and arrived in Khartoum at the end of 1863, giving out that he had come to establish an agricultural colony for the culture of cotton; the Egyptian customs had discovered a large quantity of arms, including cannon, among his baggage, and it is possible that Ismāʿīl Pasha first intended to use him in connexion with a projected invasion of Abyssinia though, after making inquiries in Paris as to his credentials, Ismāʿīl quickly dropped him; Du Bisson outstayed his welcome in Khartoum and embarrassed Mūsā Pasha Ḥamdī, then governor-general, by his arrogant demands; early in 1864 he left Khartoum with his party and went to Kassala and thence eastwards towards the outposts of the Sudan where he established his party at Kufit and engaged in intrigue with the local tribesmen; exasperated by his conduct the Egyptian Government ordered his expulsion and the party retired by way of Kassala and Sawākin; during the military mutiny of 1864–5 his men gave proof of courage against the mutineers at Kassala; Du Bisson himself returned to France where his subsequent career is in doubt; according to one account he was killed while taking part in the defence of Paris against the Germans, 1870, according to another he was involved in the Paris Commune, 1871, and died in exile; he described his experiences in the Sudan in a highly coloured book, *Les femmes, les eunuques et les guerriers du Soudan* (Paris, 1868).

Du Bourg de Bozas, R . . . , Vicomte (–1903), French explorer; he attempted to cross Africa from east to west but died before reaching the Atlantic coast; starting from Addis Ababa in March 1901 on a mission from the French ministry of education to explore southern Abyssinia, he travelled by the northern end of Lake Rudolf and reached the Nile near Nimule; he wrote an account of this part of his journey in *La Géographie* (Paris, 1903), vii.

Du Camp, Maxime (1822–94), French journalist and photographer; born in Paris he and Gustave Flaubert came to Egypt and ascended the Nile as far as Wādī Ḥalfā in 1850; a magnificent album of photographs—probably the first taken in Nubia—was the fruit of his journey which extended also to Palestine and Syria; the album with explanatory text was published in Paris in two volumes in 1852–4.

Duchesne, Jean-Baptiste-Joseph (1777–1856), French painter, from Gisors in the department of Eure; he accompanied the archaeological expedition led by J. F. Champollion to Abū Simbel and Wādī Ḥalfā in 1828–9.

* **Du Couret, Louis-Laurent,** otherwise **Hadji Abd-el-Hamid Bey** (1812–67), French traveller and perhaps charlatan; born at Huningue, Alsace, the son of a colonel of the Napoleonic empire who was killed in action in Spain, he made his first journey to the East in 1836; joining the Egyptian army in Syria he fought in the battle of Nazīb wherein Sulaimān Pasha (Colonel Sève) won a resounding victory over the Turks; the Syrian war over he visited, among other places, Nubia, Sennar, Kordofan, and Dār Fūr, having embraced Islam and made the pilgrimage to Makka; his travels and indeed his identity are in doubt; Professor H. Kiepert of Berlin questioned the authenticity of many of his claims; there is a suspicion that the French writer, A. Dumas the Elder, who had a hand in the composition of at least two of his books, may have invented or coloured the story of this ambiguous person; the above notes on his life and travels have been taken from various works published under his name, and are offered with reserve.

Dufton, Henry (–1868), British traveller; in 1862–3 he travelled from Cairo over the Nubian desert through Berber to Khartoum; alone and on a donkey he left Khartoum, sauntering through Masallamīya, Wad Madanī, Abū Ḥarāz, Gedaref, and Gallabat on his way to Lake Tana; from Gallabat he accompanied G. Lejean, the consul of France at Muṣawwa'; he described the journey through the Sudan in *Narrative of a Journey through Abyssinia* . . . (1867); he joined the intelligence department of the British army in the Anglo-Abyssinian war of 1868 when he was murdered by Shosho bandits inland of Annesley Bay while superintending the building of roads.

Dumas, Alexandre, the Elder (1802–70), French writer, popularly known as the author of *The Three Musketeers* and other widely read novels; he wrote a preface to *Voyage au Pays des Niam-Niams* (Paris, 1854), ostensibly written by one Hadji Abd-el-Hamid Bey, otherwise Louis du Couret, and in 1856 published an account, by the same author, of a journey to Madina and Makka; the German geographer, H. Kiepert, cast doubt on the authenticity of Du Couret's travels in the Sudan and elsewhere, and it has been suggested that they were largely the result of Dumas's fertile imagination.

Dümichen, Johannes (1833–94), German Egyptologist, of Weissholz near Gross Glogau, professor at Strassburg University; his book *Die Flotte einer ägyptischen Königin* (Leipzig, 1868), translated into English as *The Fleet of an Egyptian Queen* (Leipzig, 1868), contains a report by the author of his archaeological journey of 1863–5 through Nubia and the Sudan; he died at Strasbourg.

Dumont, Agricola (–1843), French apothecary of Marseilles; he came to Egypt before the penetration of the Sudan by the sons of Muḥammad 'Alī and may have accompanied Ismā'īl's expedition to Sennar in 1820–1 as an army doctor; he visited the mountains of the Funj and about 1835 was established with the garrison at Wad Madanī; he followed a punitive expedition to Tāka in command of the governor-general, Aḥmad Pasha abū Widān, in 1840; F. Werne, who was also a member of the same expedition, recounted Dumont's cruelty to his slave; he had a son, Alexandre, born in 1843 and baptized in Khartoum in 1848.

Dupuis, Charles Edward (1864–1943), British engineer; he joined the Indian public works department in 1888 and in 1899 transferred to the service of the Egyptian ministry of public works; he was inspector-general of the Egyptian irrigation department, 1904–12, and later adviser to the Egyptian ministry of public works; as a result of studies initiated by Sir W. E. Garstin in 1905 he projected a low-level weir over the Blue Nile at Sennar in order to irrigate part of the Jazīra by dispensing with water storage; the project was abandoned in favour of the present dam and canal system, completed in 1925; in 1923 he planned the dam at Jabal Awliyā, completed in 1934.

Dupuis, Charles George (1886–1940), British official; he joined the Sudan political service in 1909, was governor of the Funj in 1927 and of Dār Fūr from 1928 to 1935 when he retired to devote his leisure to local government in England.

Dushain wad Ḥamad, called **al-Qāḍī al-ʿAdāla** (*fl.* 1570), holy man, a Buṣailābī originally from Upper Egypt he came to the sultanate of the Funj where he was known for his intimacy with God and for the fame of his pupils; a follower of the S̲h̲āfiʿite code he was one of the four judges appointed by S̲h̲aikh ʿAjīb wad ʿAbd Allāh by order of Sultan Dakīn wad Naiyīl; his responsibility was for the town of Arbajī and for the S̲h̲āfiʿites in general within the sultanate; he is said to have lived for 114 years and was buried at Arbajī; his grandson Muḥammad Madanī Dus̲h̲ain al-Sunnī was the founder of Wad Madanī.

Dye, William McEntyre (1831–99), American soldier; born in Pennsylvania, he graduated from the United States Military Academy as a brevet lieutenant in 1853; he fought on the Federal side in the American civil war of 1861–5, rising to temporary colonel of the regular army; disliking peace-time soldiering he resigned in 1870, married, and farmed; in 1873 he joined the Egyptian general staff as an assistant to General C. P. Stone Pasha, chief of staff; he was wounded at the battle of Gura in the disastrous Egyptian-Abyssinian war of 1875–6; after his retirement from the Khedivial service he wrote an account of the war, *Moslem Egypt and Christian Abyssinia* (New York, 1880).

Earle, William (1833–85), British soldier; he joined the army as an ensign in 1851 and was present at all the great battles of the Crimea, 1854–5; promoted major-general in 1880 he served in the campaign against Aḥmad ʿUrābī Pasha, 1882, and was officer commanding the garrison of Alexandria till 1884 when he was placed in command of the river column of the expedition to relieve Khartoum; his force had advanced up the Nile and was marching through the country of the Manāṣīr when it came into conflict with a Mahdist force at Kirbikān; the British force won, but he was killed in the battle.

Edrisi. *See* ABŪ ʿABD ALLĀH MUḤAMMAD . . . AL-IDRĪSĪ.

Egerton, Sir Charles Comyn (1848–1921), British field-marshal; in 1867 he joined the British army and in 1871 transferred to the Indian army in which he spent most of his career; he commanded the Indian contingent which arrived in Sawākin in 1896; this force, after garrisoning Sawākin, was so reduced by sickness during the hot summer that it was withdrawn and returned to India; he was a member of the council of India from 1907 to 1917 when he was promoted field-marshal.

* **Ehrenberg, Christian Gottfried** (1795–1876), German naturalist; he accompanied a scientific expedition led by Baron H. C. M. von Minutoli in 1821–3 to Nubia; with W. F. Hemprich he ascended the Nile valley to Ambuqōl and Dongola; a man of ingenuity he designed a fortress and dwelling at New Dongola for ʿĀbidīn Bey the governor; in collaboration with Hemprich he wrote *Symbolae Physicae* (Berlin, 1829–45) in which many birds inhabiting the Sudan were first described; he was born in Delitzsch in Prussian Saxony and from 1839 was professor of medicine at the University of Berlin; he is best known as the founder of the science of microscopic organisms and was the author of studies on the coralline formations of the Red Sea.

Eirpanomos (*fl. c.* 600), Ethiopian (Nobatæan) ruler who was converted to Monophysite Christianity.

Elgood Bey, Percival George (1863–1941), British soldier; he was commissioned to the Devon Regiment and was promoted major in 1903; he served for many years in the Egyptian army in Egypt and the Sudan and spent his retirement in Cairo where he died; he was the author of several books on the history of Egypt.

Elias Enoch (*fl.* 1705), Syrian Maronite Christian in the service of the consul of France in Egypt; he journeyed to Abyssinia by way of Muṣawwaʿ in 1704; the Negus entrusted him with a letter to Le Noir du Roule, head of a French diplomatic mission then on its way to Abyssinia via the Nile valley; he set out for Sennar to meet the mission but, hearing that most of its members, including its leader, had been murdered at Sennar by Sultan Bādī III wad Ūnsa, he went back to Abyssinia in 1705 and lived there till 1718 when he returned to Egypt.

* **Elliott Smith, Sir Grafton.** *See* SMITH, SIR GRAFTON ELLIOTT.

* **Emiliani dei Danziger Bey, Francesco** (1838–82), Italian soldier and cartographer; little is known of his early years beyond the probability that he was born at Udine; he entered the Khedivial service and in 1877 was attached to the geological mission, led by the American mining engineer, L. H. Mitchell, which was captured by the Abyssinians a few miles inland of Muṣawwaʿ; he was then transferred to Dār Fūr where in 1878 he assisted G. B. Messedaglia Bey; appointed ma'mūr of Kobbé in 1879 he fought successfully against the leader of the Fūr resistance, Muḥammad Hārūn al-Ras͟hīd, and was made sub-governor of Dāra; he died at S͟haqqa of heart failure aggravated by fatigue, and was buried at Dāra; he was a kindly man but, partly owing to his lack of Arabic, a weak disciplinarian.

Émily, Jules Michel Antoine (*c.* 1868–1944), French naval surgeon in the colonial service; graduating in 1892 he was sent to the French Sudan where he saw active service; he was then attached to the Marchand expedition as medical officer and was with Marchand at Fashoda, 1898; after a distinguished career in the French colonial forces and in the First World War he was promoted médecin-général and inspector of colonial troops, retiring 1928; he wrote *Mission Marchand* (Paris, 1913), the best eye-witness account of the mission.

Emin Pasha. *See* SCHNITZER, EDUARD CARL OSCAR THEODOR.

English, George Bethune (1787–1828), American adventurer; he was born in Cambridge, Massachusetts, and in 1807 graduated from Harvard University; after an unsuccessful start as a minister of religion and afterwards as an editor of a newspaper, he obtained a commission as a lieutenant of marines through the influence of John Quincy Adams, secretary of State; in 1820 the ship in which he was serving put into Alexandria where he resigned his commission, embraced Islam, and entered the service of Muḥammad ʿAlī Pasha who appointed him commander of artillery in the expedition of Ismāʿīl Pasha to Sennar, 1820–1; his account of the campaign, *A Narrative of the Expedition to Dongola and Sennaar* (London, 1822; Boston, Mass., 1823), is a straightforward description; after the conquest of Sennar he resigned from the Pasha's service as the expected financial reward was not forthcoming, and served the Government of the United States in several minor missions to the Porte; eccentric, handsome, and an accomplished linguist, he suffered from a weakness of character which hindered material recognition of his talents.

Eratosthenes (*c.* 276 B.C.–194 B.C.), Greek geographer, born at Cyrene in North Africa, and librarian at Alexandria; with the help of various accounts by travellers he sketched with fair accuracy the course of the Nile as far south as the junction of the Blue and White rivers, and suggested the existence of the lake sources in Central Africa.

Ernst, Duke of Saxe-Coburg-Gotha (1818–72), member of the German royal house of Saxe-Coburg-Gotha; he and his hunting party, including T. Bilharz the discoverer of bilharzia, travelled from Egypt to the region of Keren in 1862; the journey was not without scientific interest; see R. Kretschmer's *Reise des Hertzogs . . . in Aegypten*, &c. (Leipzig, 1864).

* **Escayrac de Lauture, Pierre-Henri-Stanislas d', Count** (1826–68), French explorer; born in Paris of an ancient family from Quercy, he lived in Egypt between 1847 and 1850; in 1849 he ascended the valley of the Nile, crossed the Bayūda, and visited Kordofan and later Sennar; he corresponded with the unfortunate French doctor, C. Cuny, and advised Cuny on the preparations for his fatal journey to Dār Fūr in 1858; in 1856 the viceroy, Muḥammad Saʿīd Pasha, appointed him leader of an expedition to discover the source of the White Nile, but the venture failed before he left Cairo; he later accompanied a French

scientific mission to China where he was imprisoned by the Chinese; he died at Fontainebleau; Cuny's biographer, H. Roy, wrote of him as a great explorer, while Sir H. H. Johnston in *The Nile Quest* (1905) dismissed him as a mountebank; he wrote several works on the Sudan.

Eugénie de Montijo de Teba, Countess de Guzman, Empress of the French (1826–1920), wife of Napoleon III, Emperor of the French; after formally opening the Suez Canal as the guest of the Khedive Ismāʿīl she paid a visit by steamer to Upper Egypt and Nubia, including Abū Simbel and Wādī Ḥalfā, in 1869; many years later, a tragic widow, the Second Empire gone, and her only son killed, she revisited the Nubian scene.

Evans, Edward Baldwin (1843–83), British trader and soldier; born at Rhuddlan, north Wales, he was in business in Egypt and afterwards at Jidda for some years when he joined the intelligence staff of the British force operating in the Suez Canal zone against the Egyptian Nationalist army and was present at the battle of Tel el-Kebir, 1882; he volunteered for service under al-farīq W. Hicks Pasha and was appointed chief of Hicks's intelligence department, 1883; he was the only British officer with Hicks who knew Arabic; appointed a binbāshī he accompanied the doomed army of Kordofan and was killed in the massacre of Shaikān (Kashgil); foreseeing his own death he left £20 for a memorial to himself in Rhuddlan church; his diary and papers, found in Khartoum, are preserved by a member of his family.

* **Evliyā Çelebī (Evliyā Muḥammad Dervīsh)** (1611–82), Turkish traveller; born in Istanbul he called himself *seyāḥ-i-ʿālem*, the globe-trotter; in the 10th and last volume of his *Seyāḥatnāmesi*, printed in Istanbul in 1938, he claimed to have visited Sawākin, Sennar and Muṣawwaʿ, 1672/1673; he was a credulous, and sometimes incredible, writer; J. von Hammer-Purgstall translated parts of his journal under the title *Narrative of travels in Europe, Asia and Africa by Evliya Efendi* (London, 1846–50); for an account of the man and his travels see art. Evliya Çelebî, by M. C. Baysun, in *Islâm Ansiklopedisi* (Istanbul, 1947).

Ewart, Charles Brisbane (1827–1903), British lieutenant-general; he joined the Royal Engineers in 1845 and served in the Crimean war of 1853–5; he was a brigadier-general in the Sawākin Field Force under the command of Lieutenant-General Sir G. Graham in 1885; lieutenant-governor of Jersey in 1887–92, he was appointed colonel-commandant of the Royal Engineers in 1902.

Eyre, Philip Homan (1832–85), British soldier; he joined the South Staffordshire Regiment in the ranks in 1851 and was promoted ensign in 1854; he served in the Crimean war, 1854–5, and in the Indian mutiny, 1857–9; in 1876 he was promoted major and in 1881 lieutenant-colonel; he was present at the battle of Tel el-Kebir, 1882, and later joined the expedition of 1884–5 for the relief of Khartoum; while serving with Major-General W. Earle's river column he was killed in the battle of Kirbikān.

* **Fabricius (Favrkios) Pasha, Dimitrios** (1848–1907), Greek architect; of German ancestry he was born on the Aegean island of Syra and emigrated to Egypt where he was appointed architect to the Khedive ʿAbbās II; among the many prominent buildings which he designed was Gordon Memorial College, Khartoum; he died at Būlāq and was buried in the Greek Orthodox cemetery in Old Cairo.

Fadia Turuk (–1935), mak of Jabal Mandal in the western Nuba hills.

Fadiet walad Kwadker (–1917), reth of the Shilluk tribe of the White Nile; his son Dak was installed as reth in 1946 after the death of Reth Anei Kur in 1945.

Faḍīlī Muḥammad (–1944), shaikh of the Jikhaisāt Arab nomads of Kordofan and a magistrate; his tribe ranges from al-Uḍaiya to Foja and Umm Bel; he died at al-Nahūd.

Faḍl Allāh, nicknamed **al-Labakh** (*c.* 1876–1916), criminal; born of the Jawāmaʿa tribe of Kordofan, he entered the Egyptian army and for a time was stationed at the barracks at Shambat north of Omdurman; while still a soldier he gambled with fellow soldiers and civilians in coffee houses picking quarrels with those who won and taking their money by force; in 1913 occurred a series of murders and robberies in Omdurman; he was dismissed from the army for misconduct in 1914 and thereafter became a professional gambler and thief; in Omdurman he created popular terror; finally he murdered two brothers, Hamza and Bushāra, one a judge, the other a schoolmaster, and disappeared; when arrested in 1915 he confessed to twenty-two crimes involving murder in Omdurman and in Kordofan; he escaped from custody while travelling by train from Khartoum to al-Ubaiyaḍ, but was later re-arrested, tried, and hanged at al-Ubaiyaḍ; he derived his nickname from the labakh tree, a symbol of strength.

Faḍl Allāh Aḥmad ʿAbd al-Qādir al-IʿAisir (–1929), nāẓir ʿumūm of the Kawāhla of Kordofan, a magistrate; he died in Khartoum.

Faḍl Allāh wad Ballāl Faḍl Allāh Bey Sālim (*c.* 1890–1941), Kabbāshī notable, first cousin of Sir ʿAlī al-Tūm Faḍl Allāh Sālim, nāẓir ʿumūm of the Kabābīsh of northern Kordofan; he was a magistrate and vice-president of the Kajmār branch of the Kabābīsh court.

Faḍl Allāh wad Karrīf (–1883), Mahdist amīr; he commanded a force of Fadnīya Arabs which was defeated in the Jazīra and he himself was slain by a government detachment under the *sanjaq* Muḥammad Bey Islām al-Albānī, nicknamed 'Metū Bey'.

Faḍl Allāh Muḥammad (–1934), ʿumda of the Kurtān tribe of the White Nile, a tribe which claims descent from the Jaʿlīyīn; an ancestor of his joined the Turks on their occupation of the region in 1821 and accompanied their army to al-Ubaiyaḍ.

Faḍl Allāh Bey wad Sālim (–1883), nāẓir of the Kabbābīsh Arabs and government concessionaire of transport on the road over the Bayūda between al-Dabba and Omdurman; he succeeded his father Sālim Faḍl Allāh in 1840 and ruled his tribe for forty-three years; early in his career he fought against Umm Badda abū Kindī who defeated him and raided his tribal headquarters about 1850; the Government gave him the transport concession over the Bayūda road from 1873 to 1877; in 1882–3 his refusal to join the Mahdist movement brought him into hostility with the tribes to the south who had become adherents to the cause of Muḥammad Aḥmad al-Mahdī; in a five-day battle at Jabal Umm al-Rās he was defeated and killed by the Ḥamar; he is said to have been the richest Arab chieftain in the Sudan at that time.

al-Faḍl Ḥasan (1858–1933), ʿumda of Barsī between Wad Madanī and Sennar; his father and grandfather were local notables under the Egyptian rule; he was a muqaddam in the Mahdist régime and his brother ʿAlī was an amīr under Yūnus al-Dikaim; he himself was a noted digger of wells and founder of villages; he was appointed a magistrate in 1927.

* **al-Faḍl Ḥasana** (–1945), Mahdist amīr, a Taʿā'ishī by tribe and a cousin of the amīr Aḥmad Faḍīl; his battle record came to an end with his capture at Umm Dibaikarāt in 1899; after the Anglo-Egyptian occupation he lived in retirement near Sinja; he died at Omdurman during a visit there.

Faḍl al-Marjī al-Daw (1853–1942), nāẓir of the Kawāhla of the Jazīra and president of the Kawāhla shaikhs' court in the district of Rufāʿa; he succeeded Shaikh Rahum as amīr of the Kawāhla during the Mahdist revolt and continued as head of the local administration under the Condominium régime; dismissed in 1921 for fabricating evidence in a murder case he was restored to the nāẓirship in 1927; though latterly blind and deaf he still sat at his own court and maintained control over his tribe; he died at Makka while making the pilgrimage.

Faḍl al-Mūlā Bey Muḥammad (–1890), Sudanese soldier of the Dinka tribe; he was a binbāshī in one of the black battalions in the equatorial province when Emin Pasha was governor; later promoted qā'immaqām he was in command of a force of Sudanese which separated from the main body and entered into communication with the advance agents of the Congo Free State; in a rash moment he decided to march against the Mahdists; advancing to the outskirts of Rejaf he was ambushed and killed by a Mahdist force under the amīr ʿArabī Dafaʿ Allāh.

Fafiti Yor (–1943), reth of the Shilluk tribe of the White Nile.

* **Faiyid Muḥammad** (–1885), Egyptian holy man from Qaliyūb; he came to the Sudan and set up a school in Khartoum where he was shaikh of the Aḥmadīya Islamic brotherhood; although he had a high reputation for piety he was of orthodox Sunnī views and hence opposed

to the claims of Muḥammad Aḥmad al-Mahdī; it is said that, at the sack of Khartoum, the Mahdī ordered that his life should be spared; the Dervishes, however, killed him in the general massacre and threw his body down a well over which a tomb, frequented by the pious, now stands in Gordon Avenue.

al-Falakī. *See* ISMĀ'ĪL MUṢṬAFĀ AL-FALAKĪ PASHA; MAḤMŪD AḤMAD ḤAMDĪ AL-FALAKĪ PASHA.

al-Faqīr Ismā'īl (*c.* 1850–1909), notable of the Maḥas tribe; a teacher in Dār Maḥas, he had schools in the villages of Ardwān and Tajab; in 1885, when the Mahdist army first appeared in the north, he and others were imprisoned at Dongola as hostages for the good behaviour of the people of the district whom the Mahdists ordered to dismantle the railway which the British had prolonged to 'Akāsha earlier in the year; the work done he returned to Dār Maḥas as shaikh of Ardwān and Tajab; on the establishment of the Anglo-Egyptian Government he was made 'umda of the locality.

Faraḥ Ṣāliḥ al-Ḥājj Idrīs (*c.* 1868–1946), worthy of Dār Maḥas; his father rendered useful services in hauling the ships of the Nile expedition of 1884–5 through the cataracts; appointed shaikh of Delgo, 1896, after the Mahdist defeat at Ḥafīr, he was made 'umda, 1917, and later a magistrate; his son was one of six officers of the Egyptian army who mutinied in 1924.

Faraj Allāh Pasha Rāghib (–*c.* 1893), Sudanese soldier; promoted liwā' of the Egyptian army he was one of the more senior officers under the command of al-farīq C. G. Gordon Pasha during the siege of Khartoum, 1884–5; he was placed in command of the fort at Omdurman which, after a long and gallant defence, surrendered to the Mahdists in December 1884 by permission of Gordon who was no longer able to supply it with food and ammunition; Muḥammad Aḥmad al-Mahdī, admiring his courage and skill, appointed him an amīr in which capacity he fought under the amīr Zakī Ṭamal against the Abyssinians, 1887–9; he died in Omdurman before the Anglo-Egyptian occupation.

Faraj Bey Azāzī (–1885), Sudanese soldier; entering the Egyptian army in 1849 he served as a junior officer in the Sudanese battalion in the Mexican war in 1863–7; later promoted qā'immaqām he was in command of the garrison at Kassala during the siege of the town by the Mahdists in 1884–5; the garrison finally surrendered from hunger after a prolonged resistance and he was shot in cold blood shortly after the fall of the town.

* **Faraj Pasha Muḥammad al-Zainī** (*c.* 1830–85), Sudanese soldier; he is said to have been born in Jabal Taqalī in the Nuba hills and to have been stolen from his parents by slave traders and sold in Egypt to a benevolent master who had him educated; he learnt French and Turkish and in 1852 joined the Egyptian army; he served with the Sudanese battalion in the Mexican war, 1863–7, and during the course of the campaign rose from mulāzim I to ṣāgh qōl aghāsi; after serving

at Kassala and other stations in the Sudan he retired to Egypt and lived at Ṭura; at this point information as to his movements becomes vague; it is said that the Khedive Ismā'īl suspected him of conspiracy, possibly about 1879, and had him banished to the Sudan; another story credits him with sympathy with the revolt of Aḥmad 'Urābī Pasha, 1882, when he was second in command of a Sudanese regiment and holding the rank of qā'immaqām, a rank to which he is said to have been promoted before 1881; on the creation of the new Egyptian army after the defeat of 'Urābī, he took service in it with the reduced rank of binbāshī and was for some time stationed at Muṣawwa'; on the arrival of al-farīq C. G. Gordon Pasha in Khartoum early in 1884 he was commanding the 1st Sudanese regiment in the capital, having been promoted mīrālai; as the siege of the city went on Gordon promoted him to liwā' and chief of staff and finally to farīq; he was taken prisoner by the Mahdists at the capture of Khartoum and was killed a few hours later.

Farquhar, Arthur (*c.* 1843–83), British soldier; he joined the Coldstream Guards as an ensign in 1862; in 1863 he was promoted lieutenant and in 1867 captain in the 15th Foot; he retired in 1881 with the rank of major; in 1883 he entered the Khedivial service and was appointed, with the rank of mīrālai, as chief of staff to al-farīq W. Hicks Pasha who was given command of the Egyptian army opposing the Mahdī in Kordofan; he was killed at the battle of Shaikān (Kashgil).

Fawzī Pasha. *See* IBRĀHĪM FAWZĪ PASHA.

Fechét, Eugene Oscar (1846–1925), American soldier; at the age of sixteen he enlisted in the Volunteer Light Artillery and fought in the American civil war on the Federal side before entering the United States Military Academy, 1864; he graduated in 1868 and served in the regular army in the artillery; in 1872 he joined the Egyptian general staff under General C. P. Stone Pasha and in 1873 surveyed the route from Aswān through the Nubian desert to Abū Ḥamad and Berber; finding the Khedivial service not to his liking he retired and for a short time rejoined the United States army; resigning his commission he engaged in mining and later served as United States consul at Piedras Negras, Mexico, returning to the army on the outbreak of the Spanish-American war; he retired with the rank of lieutenant-colonel in 1910 and spent his retirement at Eustis, Florida, where he died.

Felkin, Robert William (1853–1926), British doctor and traveller; born at Beeston in Nottinghamshire he was educated in medicine at the Universities of Edinburgh and Marburg, Germany; in 1878 he joined a party of missionaries of the Church Missionary Society on a journey to Uganda; arriving at Sawākin the party travelled by way of Berber and the White Nile to Uganda; in 1879 Felkin and two other members of the party returned to England via Lado, Rumbek, Daim Sulaimān, southern Dār Fūr, Kordofan, and Khartoum; he was later in correspondence with Emin Pasha when the latter was isolated by the Mahdists in Equatoria and, it was said, in 1888 endeavoured without success to induce Emin to sign a contract with the British East African Company by which the company would be granted territorial rights over Equatoria in the event of Egypt relinquishing her claims; he was the first Englishman to look upon both lakes, Albert and Victoria; in 1916 he went to live in Havelock North in New Zealand where he practised medicine until his death there; he was joint-author with C. T. Wilson of *Uganda and the Egyptian Sudan* (1882) and wrote various papers on tropical diseases.

Fergusson Bey, Vere Henry (1891–1927), British soldier; educated at Wellington College he entered the army in the ranks and in 1913 was commissioned in the Cameronians; he served in the First World War, being in 1914–16 with the West African regiment; in 1916 he was seconded to the Egyptian army and posted to the Equatorial battalion; transferring to the Sudan civil service in 1919 he was stationed at Rumbek; he was murdered by Nuong Nuer, incited by a witch-doctor named Gwek Wonding, at Lake Jur near Shambe; a biography was published by his friends in 1930.

Ferlini, Giuseppe (*c.* 1800–76), Italian doctor; born at Bologna he studied medicine at the university there and, his studies completed, left for Albania as a soldier of fortune; he later served as a doctor in the Greek insurrectionary army against the Turks; attracted to Egypt he joined the Pasha's medical service and was stationed first with the garrison at Sennar, 1830–1, then in Kordofan in 1832; in 1833 he was in Khartoum when he obtained the permission of the governor-general, ʿAlī Khūrshīd Pasha, to excavate antiquities; he appears to have been digging at Meroë through 1833 and 1834; he employed a large gang of labourers who, according to the French traveller, E. Combes, suddenly came on a massive gold statue and other highly saleable antiques; from the sale of these he drew a small fortune which enabled him to quit the Egyptian service and return to Italy; the truthfulness of his subsequent reports of his finds was questioned by I. Rosellini, the egyptologist; he severely damaged the pyramids of Meroë and could give no coherent account of what became of the treasures which he stated he found there.

Field Bey, Charles William (1828–92), colonel of the United States army; born in Woodford County, Kentucky, of an old Virginian family, he graduated from the United States Military Academy in 1849 and was posted to the cavalry; the outbreak of the American civil war in 1861 found him a captain; he joined the Confederate army and was given the rank of colonel in 1861 and brigadier-general in 1862; he was a born cavalryman and his handling of his command brought him promotion to major-general in 1864; seriously wounded in the second battle of Bull Run he surrendered at the end of the war and occupied himself in business; in 1875 he was appointed a mīrālai in the Egyptian army engineers and during the unfortunate Egyptian-Abyssinian war of 1875–6 held the post of inspector-general under Muḥammad Rātib Pasha, the commander-in-chief; he retired from the Khedivial service in 1877; in 1878 he was appointed doorkeeper of the United States

House of Representatives in the 46th Congress and from 1881 to 1885 was a government civil engineer; he had a vigorous intellect and a superb physique.

Finati, Giovanni (*c.* 1787–   ), Italian soldier of fortune; born in or near Ferrara he was intended for the Church but developed anti-clerical sentiments; in 1805–6 he was a conscript in the French army; deserting to the Turks he came to Egypt in 1809; he joined the Egyptian army and served in Arabia against the Wahhābite rebels during the war of 1811–18; in 1815 he was an instructor in the *niẓām al-jadīd*, the new regular army of the Pasha of Egypt, and narrowly escaped death in the revolt of the Albanian troops of that year; in the period 1815–20 he accompanied W. J. Bankes, the British traveller, on an expedition to Nubia which took them as far as Amka; later he worked with H. Salt and G. B. Belzoni who were excavating at Abū Simbel; other journeys included a visit to Dongola with Bankes and to Meroë with L. M. A. Linant de Bellefonds (afterwards pasha); he was in the suite of Ibrāhīm Pasha when the latter visited Sennar and Fāzūghlī in 1821–2; his subsequent career is not known; he spoke Arabic well, had become a Muslim, adopted the name al-Ḥājj Muḥammad, having visited Makka and Madīna in 1811; Bankes published his autobiography in 1830.

Firhād Bey . . . (–1842), Circassian officer in the Egyptian army during the governorship-general of Aḥmad Pasha abū Widān; he was mīrālai of the 8th regiment then garrisoning Wad Madanī; his end was mysterious; it is said on meagre authority that the governor-general, angered by his failure to pacify the Abū Rūf tribe, sought his destruction and sent poison to Saʿīd Ḥasan, accountant of the 8th regiment, who poisoned Firhād at Wad Madanī while he was drunk at a banquet; he was known as a just man.

Flaubert, Gustave (1821–80), French novelist; born and died at Rouen; with M. Du Camp he ascended the Nile by sailing boat as far as Wādī Ḥalfā in 1859; uninterested at the time in antiquities he wrote nothing which can be directly ascribed to this journey, but his subsequent work, notably his novel *Salammbô* (1862), shows evidence of Nubian inspiration.

Flower, Stanley Smyth (1871–1946), British soldier and zoologist; he joined the Artists' Rifles and was later commissioned in the Northumberland Fusiliers; after serving in India and the Straits Settlements he was appointed scientific adviser to the Government of Siam; in 1898 he became director of the zoological garden at Giza, Cairo, and later director of the zoological service of Egypt; in 1900 he accompanied an expedition led by Sir W. E. Garstin to clear the White Nile of vegetable obstructions, publishing a zoological report of the expedition; a Sudan game preservation department having been created he was honorary director, 1900–12, annually visiting the Sudan and supervising the preservation and export of game; on one of his journeys from the Sudan he brought out the surviving hounds from the Gihon hunt, celebrated by Rudyard Kipling in his *Actions and Reactions* (1909); he retired from the Egyptian service in 1924.

Floyer, Ernest Ayscoghe (1852–1903), British telegraph engineer and explorer; while serving in the Indian telegraphs he explored Baluchistan, 1876–7; he was inspector-general of Egyptian telegraphs, 1878–1903; he and his telegraph staff played an important part in maintaining communications with the Egyptian garrisons in the Sudan at the beginning of the Mahdist revolt; in 1884 he visited Dongola province with H. H. Kitchener, then in the intelligence department of the Egyptian army.

Forni, Giuseppe (–*c.* 1840), Italian chemist; born in Milan he came to Egypt and in 1818 was employed by the viceroy Muḥammad ʿAlī Pasha as manager of a nitre factory in Old Cairo; along with G. B. Belzoni he explored the ancient emerald mines in the Nubian Atbai in 1819; on the instructions of the viceroy he travelled to Sennar with the geologist G. B. Brocchi in 1825; he is said to have died in Khartoum, but the place and date of death are both uncertain; his notes of his journey to the Sudan, published in Milan in 1859, are largely cribbed from Brocchi's journal.

Fowler, Sir John, 1st Baronet (1817–98), British civil engineer; in 1871 he was appointed consulting engineer to the Egyptian Government and planned the first Sudan railway which was intended to extend from Wādī Ḥalfā to the Sixth Cataract with a branch line to Dār Fūr, but which in fact was built only as far as Sārras, thirty-three miles south of Wādī Ḥalfā, during the years 1873–6; he visited Wādī Ḥalfā in 1873 and wrote a report on the project for railways in the Sudan and for a slipway over the First Cataract at Aswān; he planned and carried through many great public works in Britain including the Metropolitan Railway in London and the Forth Bridge in Scotland.

Fox, Charles Vincent (1877–1928), British sportsman and soldier; educated at the University of Oxford he was commissioned to the Scots Guards in 1900; he served in the Egyptian army between 1908 and 1913; while stationed on the Upper Nile he practised sculling in his spare time and won the Diamond Sculls at Henley in 1910; as a political officer in the Mongalla province, 1911–13, he took part in the Beir and Anuak patrols; during the First World War he was taken prisoner and made a dramatic escape from Germany in 1917; he retired from the army in 1923; he published articles on war and sport.

Fox, William Francis (1841–1918), British engineer; a Quaker in his religious beliefs, he first worked in his father's bank, and in 1857 was articled to the engineering profession; in 1864 he founded the Atlas Engineering Company in partnership with E. Walker; in 1884 he came to Cairo on irrigation work for the Khedivial Government and his visit inspired a close interest in Sudan affairs; he visited Sawākin in connexion with a private project to build a railway to Berber, and lectured in Britain on Sudan questions, his pacific leanings urging him to endeavour to pacify that country; this was only an episode in a lifetime devoted to the cause of peace; he died in London; his biography, by J. E. G. de Montmorency, was published in Oxford in 1923.

Fraccaroli, Andrea (1854–80), Italian traveller; born in Milan of Veronese origin, the son of the sculptor Innocenzo Fraccaroli, he fought, at the age of sixteen, in the Italian legion in the Franco-German war in 1870, and in 1878 took part in the struggle of the insurgents of Herzegovina against the Austrians; in 1879 the Society for Geographical Exploration of Milan sent him to explore Dār Fūr; travelling by way of Khartoum and al-Ubaiyaḍ to al-Fāshar, he planned other journeys but was attacked by fever and returned to Khartoum where he died.

Fraser, Kenneth Grant (1877–1935), British medical missionary; he was born at Cnock Ban, Scotland, and was educated for the medical profession at Edinburgh University and the Royal Colleges; he served in the Royal Army Medical Corps throughout the First World War; in 1920 he entered the service of the Church Missionary Society and worked as a medical missionary at Yilu in the southern Sudan; he later transferred to Lui where he and his wife founded a hospital and where he died.

Fraser, Sir Thomas (1840–1922), British major-general; he joined the Royal Engineers in 1862 and was promoted brevet lieutenant-colonel in 1882; between 1882 and 1885 he was adjutant-general and quartermaster-general in the Egyptian army, and took part in the campaign of 1884–5 for the relief of Khartoum; he was promoted major-general in 1898 and in 1913 was appointed colonel-commandant of the Royal Engineers; he published *Recollections and Reflections* (1914).

Frediani, Domenico Ermenegildo (1783–1823), Italian traveller; born at Serravezza near Milan of working-class parents he entered the Neapolitan army and became a dispenser-lieutenant during the brief régime of Prince Joachim Murat; in 1817 he left for Egypt intending to collect antiquities; in Egypt he befriended G. B. Belzoni and accompanied Lord Belmore and his family on a trip to Abū Simbel and Wādī Ḥalfā in 1817; in 1820 he went with Ismā'īl Pasha's military expedition to Sennar; he was attached to Ismā'īl as a sort of tutor and, being a poet after his fashion, composed verses in the Tuscan dialect celebrating the exploits of his master; arrived at Sennar he encountered difficulties with other Europeans in the expedition, notably F. Cailliaud, who is said to have made unacknowledged borrowings from his diaries; he suffered from the delusion of grandeur, which had elements of absurdity, giving out that he was a prince; his condition developed into madness and he was taken back to Cairo where he died in hospital, a chained maniac.

Freeman, Arthur (*c.* 1854–76), British gardener, possibly the first trained gardener in the Sudan; after leaving school he entered the Royal Botanical Gardens at Kew, Surrey, in 1873; in 1875 he left England in company with L. A. Lucas who projected an exploration of Central Africa; however, in the Equatorial province Lucas's foolhardy behaviour got him into trouble with C. G. Gordon Pasha, the governor; Freeman left Lucas's service and accepted a minor appointment in the service of the Egyptian Government at Dufile where he made botanical collections which, together with those of Lucas, are preserved at Kew; falling sick, Gordon arranged to send him back to England, but he died on the journey at the Roman Catholic mission station at Berber.

Fremantle, Sir Arthur James Lyon (1835–1901), British soldier; commissioned in 1852 to the Coldstream Guards he was promoted major-general in 1882 and lieutenant-general in 1890; he commanded troops at Sawākin in the winter of 1884–5 after serving as governor of the town during the preceding summer; on the arrival of Lieutenant-General Sir G. Graham in March 1885 to command the Sawākin Field Force he was given the command of the Brigade of Guards; in 1894–7 he was governor and commander-in-chief of Malta.

French, John Denton Pinkstone, 1st Earl of Ypres (1852–1925), British soldier of Irish descent; he entered the Royal Navy in 1866 but transferred to the army and obtained a commission in the cavalry; promoted major in 1883 he served in the Nile expedition of 1884–5, fighting in various battles including Abū Ṭulaiḥ (Abu Klea); after brilliant service in the South African war he was appointed commander-in-chief of the British Expeditionary Force to France on the outbreak of the First World War; he resigned at the end of 1915 owing to criticism of his generalship and his want of tact and comprehension, and was succeeded by Sir Douglas (afterwards Earl) Haig; he had been promoted field-marshal in 1913.

* **Friend Pasha, Sir Lovick Bransby** (1856–1944), British soldier; in 1873 he joined the Royal Engineers and was promoted major in 1893; he served in the Egyptian army in the Nile campaign of 1898 and was director of works and stores to the Egyptian army in the Sudan, 1902–6, with the rank of liwā'; during the First World War he was general officer commanding in Ireland, 1914–16, and in 1916–18 was president of the claims commission for the British armies in France; he retired in 1920 with the rank of major-general.

Fū'ād I (Aḥmad Fū'ād), King of Egypt (1868–1936), born in Cairo, he was the youngest son of the Khedive Ismā'īl and the brother of Sultan Ḥusain Kāmil whom he succeeded in 1917; when the British protectorate ended he was proclaimed king in 1922; a shrewd statesman, he was a great patron of learning; under his direct initiative the Royal archives in Cairo, the source of much of the history of the Sudan in the nineteenth century, were classified and opened to students, while he liberally subsidized research in Egyptian and Sudanese studies; he was succeeded on his death by his eldest son, King Fārūq (Farouk) I.

Gaeta, Giovanni, or **Yanni** (*c.* 1770–*c.* 1798), Greek adventurer; he was one of three brothers from Zante in the Ionian islands where they worked as cannon founders; they emigrated to Egypt about 1790, were converted to Islam, and made cannons for the Mameluke rulers; Aḥmad (Giovanni) became an a<u>gh</u>ā in the army and later, about 1796, through the initiative of C. Rossetti, Austrian consul in Egypt, travelled to Dār Fūr where he took service under Sulṭān Abd al-Raḥmān Aḥmad Bukr who aspired to own artillery; Aḥmad constructed a primitive citadel at Kobbé but, accused of a desire to supplant the sultan, he was betrayed by his enemies and killed.

Gallwey, Sir Thomas Joseph (1852–1933), British military surgeon; an Irishman by origin he entered the army medical department in 1874 and was promoted surgeon-major in 1885 when he served in the Nile expedition to attempt the relief of Khartoum; in 1892 he transferred to the Egyptian army; he was appointed principal medical officer on the staff of Kitchener's armies in the Dongola and Nile campaigns, 1896–8, and was present at the battles of Ḥafīr, the Atbara, and Omdurman; after campaigning in South Africa, 1899–1901, he held important army medical administrative posts in Britain and India, retiring in 1911; he was re-employed during the First World War on home duties.

Galton, Sir Francis (1822–1911), British scientist, founder of the science of eugenics; in 1845–6 he visited Khartoum where he met the British traveller, Mansfield Parkyns; the French engineer, J. P. d'Arnaud, whom he met at Korosko, stimulated his ideas on scientific problems; he published his autobiography in 1908; a biography, by K. Pearson, appeared in 1931.

Gama, Estevam da (*fl.* 1540), Portuguese sailor, son of the more celebrated Vasco da Gama who discovered the sea route between Europe and India by the Cape of Good Hope; in 1540 he commanded a Portuguese fleet which entered Sawākin in the course of a raid on Turkish and Arab ports and shipping in the Red Sea; the Portuguese quarrelled with the shaikh of the town and sacked the place; Don Juan de Castro, a captain in the Portuguese fleet, left a description of the port and its trade.

Gand . . . (*c.* 1790–1839), French physician; he was at one time personal doctor to 'Abbās Ḥilmī Pasha, the future viceroy of Egypt, and an old friend of Aḥmad Pasha abū Widān, governor-general of the Sudan, 1838–43, with whom he campaigned against the Wahhābites in Arabia; as medical officer to the 2nd infantry regiment of the *niẓām al-jadīd* he served in the training camps of the new regular army in Egypt and afterwards accompanied the regiment to Arabia; he had fought under Ibrāhīm Pasha in the Morea, 1825–7; while stationed in Khartoum with Aḥmad Pasha abū Widān he left for Egypt only to die on the way at Abū Ḥamad whence his body was afterwards taken to France for burial; he was an unusually thin man whose long, fair moustache earned for him the nickname of 'Abū Shanab'.

Garnier, Frédéric-Benoît (1822–83), French consul; born at Andrezieux (Loire) he entered the French consular service as a dragoman; while serving as first dragoman in the consulate-general of France at Alexandria he was sent to the Sudan in 1864 to inquire into the slave trade and generally to report to the French Government on the administration of the country; he returned to Egypt in 1865; his report, though critical of the Government, is important for an understanding of economic conditions at the time; he afterwards served as a consul in several states in Asia and was consul-general at Shanghai in 1879–82 when he retired.

Garrett, Henry (–1896), correspondent of the *New York Herald* in the Dongola campaign when he died at Wādī Ḥalfā.

Garstin, Alfred Allan (1850–1937), British brigadier-general; he entered the army in 1871 and served on the staff of Lieutenant-General Sir G. Graham at Sawākin in 1885; he fought in the South African war of 1899–1902 and commanded an infantry brigade during the First World War, 1914–19.

Garstin, Sir William Edmund (1849–1925), British engineer; born in India he entered the Indian public works department in 1872; in 1892 he was appointed inspector-general of irrigation in the Egyptian Government and, shortly after, under-secretary of state in the Egyptian ministry of public works; he visited Tokar in 1892 to investigate the possibility of controlling the flood waters of the Baraka torrent; he was knighted in 1897; he projected the Aswān dam (opened 1902) and its complementary barrages; he cleared the Baḥr al-Jabal and Baḥr al-Ghazāl of vegetation obstructing navigation and the free flow of the water; it was he who first called attention to the possibility of irrigating the Jazīra, a project which he outlined in a report in 1904; the acceptance of the project by the Sudan Government led to the formation of a Sudan branch of the Egyptian irrigation department and a survey of the site; the studies which he initiated in 1905 had their result in the building of the Sennar dam and the first part of the Jazīra irrigation canal system, completed in 1925; he was adviser to the Egyptian public works department from 1905 to 1908.

Gascoigne, Sir Ernest Frederick Orby (1873–1943), British soldier; entering the Grenadier Guards in 1892 he was promoted captain in 1899 and brigadier-general in 1918; he served as a junior officer with his regiment in the Nile campaign, 1898, in the South African war, and in the First World War; he was president of the Union Jack Club in London, a famous military hostel.

Gascoigne, Frederick Richard Thomas Trench (1851–1937), British soldier; he was commissioned to the Royal Horse Guards and in 1881 toured the region of the Setīt on a hunting expedition; he fought in the Nile campaign of 1884–5 with rank of captain and later was in the South African war of 1899–1902.

Gascoigne, Sir William Julius (1844–1926), British soldier; entering the army in 1863 he served in the Egyptian war of 1882 and in the Nile campaign of 1884–5; he was promoted major-general, 1895.

Gatacre, Sir William Forbes (1843–1906), British soldier; he entered the Indian army in 1862 and after service in India and Afghanistan commanded the British division in the Nile campaign of 1897–8, taking a leading part in the battles of the Atbara and of Omdurman; in 1898 he was knighted and promoted major-general; his ill success in the South African war, 1900, caused his removal from his command; retiring from the army he was exploring the rubber forests in Abyssinia when he died of fever at Iddeni, near Gambeila; known by his troops as 'General Backacher', he was spare, middle-sized, restless, and of great strength; his wife published his biography, 1910.

Gau, François-Chrétien (1790–1853), German (naturalized French) architect; born at Cologne he studied in Paris and in 1817 went to Egypt, almost without means, pencil in hand; he travelled and made drawings in Nubia, and on his return to France published reproductions of his drawings of monuments between the First and Second Cataracts, 1823; he afterwards became a renowned architect of public buildings in France.

* **Gedge, Joseph** (–1870), British doctor, registrar at Addenbrooke's hospital, Cambridge, and demonstrator in histology in the Cambridge University Medical School; Sir Samuel Baker engaged him as medical officer to his expedition to the equatorial regions and, leaving England in 1869, he accompanied two steamers in sections which were being drawn over the Nubian desert by camel transport; he fell ill at Gondokoro and returned to Khartoum where he died.

Gentili, Andrea (–1820), Italian dispenser and physician; a native of Pergola near Ancona he spent some years in British India and at the time of his death had an English wife living at Calcutta; he accompanied the army of Ibrāhīm Pasha al-Wālī in the Arabian war, 1816–19, along with his countryman, A. Scotto, and several others who afterwards saw service in the Sudan; he lost a foot in the siege of Dar'īya and was pensioned by Ibrāhīm; tiring of inaction he followed the army of Ismā'īl Pasha to the Sudan in 1820; on the way to Sennar he died suddenly at Merowe later in the year; the British traveller, G. Waddington, recorded the suspicion of G. B. English, Ismā'īl's commander of artillery, that he was poisoned by D. Botzaris, Ismā'īl's *protomedico*, who feared him as a medical rival; Waddington wrote of him as a man of irreproachable character.

Gentz, Wilhelm (1822–90), German painter of oriental scenes; a native of Neuruppin he was a professor of the Kaiserliche Akademie of Berlin; his journey to Nubia in 1850–1 is described in his *Briefe aus Ägypten und Nubien* (Berlin, 1853).

Georges Bey. *See* DOULOGHLU, GHEORGHIOS DIMITRIOS.

Germain, Marcel (–1905), French soldier; while captain of marine artillery he was second-in-command in the mission of J. B. Marchand on the Upper White Nile, 1897–8; he was promoted commandant, 1900.

Gessi Pasha, Romolo (1831–81), Italian administrator in the Khedivial service; he was born at sea of an Italian father from Ravenna and an Armenian mother; as a young man he worked as secretary in the British Consulate in Bucharest and was later interpreter in the British army in the Crimean war, 1854–5; he fought under the command of Garibaldi in the war of 1859 against Austria; he was next employed in business at Tulcea in Rumania where he attracted the attention of Colonel C. G. Gordon who had been appointed to succeed Sir S. W. Baker as governor of the equatorial province; he accompanied Gordon to Africa, arriving at Sawākin in 1874; he circumnavigated Lake Albert in 1876 and performed valuable services as Gordon's engineer; taking umbrage at the poor recognition of his services (third-class Majīdīya decoration) he resigned and returned to Italy; with P. Matteucci he came back to the Sudan in 1877 as a private citizen on a journey of exploration to the upper reaches of the Blue Nile basin; Matteucci and he were turned back in the Banī Shanqul country by the hostility of the natives, 1878; on his return to Khartoum he re-entered the Khedivial service, Gordon having been appointed governor-general of the Sudan; made governor of the Baḥr al-Ghazāl, he fought and killed Sulaimān son of Zubair Pasha Raḥma Manṣūr in a campaign in southern Dār Fūr against rebellious slave traders; promoted pasha he was, nevertheless, discharged by Gordon's successor, Muḥammad Ra'ūf Pasha, in 1880 in circumstances amounting to disgrace; already ill from fever contracted in the Baḥr al-Ghazāl during a disastrous adventure with floating vegetation which trapped his fleet for many weeks, causing many deaths from starvation, he left Khartoum for Egypt but died at Suez; Gessi's action in killing Sulaimān and his chiefs has been the subject of controversy; Gessi himself justified the killing on the grounds of military necessity; his friend, M. Camperio, editor of *L'Esploratore* of Milan, published an account of Gessi's work (Milan, 1891); an English version (London, 1892) contains many errors of printing and translation; his standard biography, by C. Zaghi, was published in Rome, 1939; further material concerning his career in the Sudan is in the same author's *Gordon, Gessi e la riconquista del Sudan* (Firenze, 1947).

* **Geyer, Franz Xaver** (*c.* 1860–1943), Roman Catholic prelate; graduating from the University of Munich in 1880 he studied at the Verona missionary institute and was ordained priest in 1882; in 1883 he was for a short time in the Central African mission at Khartoum but left for Egypt in the general evacuation of the mission personnel on the Mahdist threat to the capital in the winter of 1883–4; he served in Egypt during the Mahdist revolt, with tours of duty to Wādī Ḥalfā and Sawākin; in 1903 in Munich he was consecrated titular bishop of Trocnade and vicar apostolic of Central Africa in succession to Bishop A. Roveggio; he filled this post from 1903 to 1921, a period which included the First World War and its difficulties for German and Austrian missionaries; he wrote *Reiseskizzen aus Ägypten und Sudan* (Stuttgart, *Ausland*, Nos. 42–9, 1884), *Durch Sand, Sumpf und Wald* (Freiburg im Breisgau, 1914), and an autobiography, *50 Jahre Auslanddeutsche Missionsarbeit* (Freiburg i. B., 1936).

al-Ghālī Tāj al-Dīn (1859–1942), notable of Dār Fūr; during the Mahdist revolt, when his brother, Bishāra Tāj al-Dīn, was head of the Habbānīya tribe, the tribe was called east to join the Mahdi's holy war; on the way thither the Habbānīya were ill treated by the Mahdi's agents, Bishāra complained, was poisoned and died; the tribe then divided, some returning to their homes, some continuing eastward with al-Ghālī; after the Mahdist defeat at Omdurman in 1898 he took refuge with a small following in the country of the Baḥr al-ʿArab, occupying himself in fishing and honey-hunting; in 1908 ʿAlī Dīnār, sultan of Dār Fūr, appointed him nāẓir of the Habbānīya; though loyal to ʿAlī Dīnār he nevertheless made his peace with the Sudan Government a few months after the fall of al-Fāshar in 1916 and remained nāẓir of his people; he was dismissed from office in 1920 and imprisoned for smuggling arms, but was reinstated in 1927 as assistant nāẓir; in 1928, on the death of Maḥmūd abū Saʿd, the holder of the post during al-Ghālī's deposition, he returned to office and was succeeded on his death by his son.

* **al-Ghazzālī Aḥmad Khawwāf** (–*c.* 1886), Mahdist amīr of the Jubārāt branch of the Taʿā'isha Baqqāra tribe; he was an early follower of Muḥammad Aḥmad al-Mahdī and was ambitious for glory; the Khalīfa ʿAbd Allāhi sent him in command of a force to subdue the Ḥumr of Kordofan who had refused to accept Mahdism; in the fighting which ensued he was killed by Manāwir Ḥabīla the Ḥumrāwī chieftain.

Gheorghiou, Michali (–1934), Greek merchant; he first came to Gedaref with the Anglo-Egyptian force commanded by C. S. B. Parsons Pasha in 1898 and was present at the battle with the Mahdists there; he settled in the town where he did much to develop trade, particularly with Abyssinia; he died in Kassala and was buried in Gedaref.

Ghulām Allāh ibn ʿĀʾid (*fl.* 1510), religious notable and genealogist who founded a seat of learning among the Shā'iqīya; among the pupils of this school, which was continued by his descendants, were ʿAbd Allāh al-ʿArakī and Yaʿqūb Muḥammad Bān Naqā, founders respectively of the ʿArakīyīn and Yaʿqūbāb families of the Jazīra; he was the author of the first part of an Arabic manuscript giving the genealogies of some of the Arab tribes of the northern Sudan; he is said to have been the first of his family to have come from Arabia to Africa; from Rikāb, one of his sons, the Rikābīya Arabs are traditionally descended; the family is said to have come originally from the Yaman where Ghulām Allāh spent his youth, and to have moved with his father over the Red Sea to the region of Dongola where he took part in the conversion of the people from Christianity to Islām; his tomb is at Old Dongola.

Gibson, Sir John Watson (1885–1947), British contractor for several large engineering works in the Sudan; he was agent for the firm of S. Pearson & Son who built the Sennar dam, completed in 1925, and was later contractor for the canalization of the Jazīra, part of which was converted into an irrigated area supplied by the dam; he was a partner in the firm of Gibson & Pauling which in 1933–4 built the Jabal Awliyā dam for the Egyptian Government; he played a leading part in the design and construction of the great floating harbours which were used during the assault by the Allied armies on the coast of Normandy in 1944; he was knighted in 1945.

Giegler (Ziegler?) Pasha . . . (–), German official in the service of the Egyptian Government; a telegraph engineer by profession, he was director of telegraphs, Khartoum, in 1875; he was promoted inspector-general of Sudan telegraphs with the title of bey in 1878, in place of Muḥammad Bey Salāma al-Bāz; Gordon Pasha, then governor-general, had a high opinion of his ability; one of his first duties, early in 1879, was to inspect the new telegraph line from Muṣawwa' to Khartoum; Gordon appointed him acting-governor-general during his absence in Dār Fūr at the end of the year, an appointment which carried with it elevation to the rank of pasha; he was in 1880 officially appointed vice-governor-general in succession to 'Uthmān Pasha Rifqī; in 1881–2 he relieved Gordon's successor, Muḥammad Ra'ūf Pasha and again acted as governor-general on Ra'ūf's recall in March 1882; the rise of Mahdism was now to try his mettle; late in 1881, while at al-Ubaiyaḍ, on the eve of the disastrous battle of Jabal Qadīr, he dispatched a force to the Nuba hills with instructions to arrest Muḥammad Aḥmad al-Mahdī; it failed; on Ra'ūf Pasha's departure from the Sudan he immediately reversed the former's passive policy towards the Mahdists and took command of the government troops campaigning in the Jazīra; in May 1882 he defeated Aḥmad Ṭaha near Abū Ḥarāz and sent his head to Khartoum; then advancing towards Sennar he inflicted several defeats upon the Mahdists; crossing the White Nile he defeated them again at al-Duwaim and captured the amīr 'Abd al-Bāsiṭ in November 1882; shortly afterwards he obtained sick leave and left the Sudan; his policy towards the Mahdist threat has been criticized for over-optimism; early in 1882 he had assured the Egyptian Government that the rebellion could be suppressed with the resources of the Sudan without the aid of reinforcements from Egypt; the government accepted his assurance and withheld reinforcements till 1883 when it was too late; he was employed in the summer of 1884 at Korosko assisting the evacuation of refugees from the Sudan; his subsequent career is not known; in appearance he was tall and had a red beard; his character was a mixture of bravery and petty-mindedness; his dislike of Italians in general, shared by Muḥammad Ra'ūf Pasha, led him into injustices towards the provincial officials R. Gessi Pasha and G. B. Messedaglia Bey who in 1880 were relieved of their posts on charges which appear to have been largely unfounded.

Giffen, John Kelly (1853–1932), American Protestant missionary; born near St. Clairesville, Ohio, he graduated from Allegheny theological seminary in 1881; he served in Egypt in 1881–99 when he came to the Sudan and worked in Khartoum except for two years (1902–3) spent at Doleib hill near the mouth of the River Sobat where he founded a mission station; he was a pioneer missionary of the United Presbyterian Church of America among the pagan Negroes of the Sudan and the first Protestant missionary to serve in the Sudan south of Khartoum after Mahdist times; he died in Khartoum; his son, M. B. Giffen, an official of the United States Government, is the author of *Fashoda: The Incident and its Diplomatic Setting* (Cambridge and Chicago, Ill., 1930).

Ginãwī Bey. *See* QINĀWĪ BEY.

Ginsberg, Albert (*fl.* 1825), Swiss mineralogist; in 1825 he travelled up the Nile valley from Egypt to Sennar and made a geological collection; he later prospected for lead and iron in the Taurus mountains, along with the Piedmontese mining engineer Boreani, during the Egyptian occupation of that region; scientific papers written by him are among the manuscripts of the British Museum in London.

Girouard, Sir Edouard Percy Cranwill (1867–1932), British soldier and engineer; born in Montreal of French-Canadian stock he first worked on the Canadian Pacific Railway and then entered the Royal Engineers, 1888; he took part in the Dongola and Nile campaigns, 1896–7, as director of railways in the Sudan, superintending the construction of the military lines which made possible Kitchener's victories; after transferring to Egypt, where he was appointed president of the state railways, he went to South Africa as director of railways during the South African war of 1899–1902; high commissioner of northern Nigeria, 1907–8, and governor and commander-in-chief of British East Africa, 1909–12, he was director-general of munitions supply, 1915–18; in this post he was chief organizer to D. Lloyd George, minister of munitions, during a critical period of the First World War; he was later managing director of the engineering firm of Armstrong Whitworth; he was knighted in 1900; although he rose in later life to positions of great responsibility, none captured the public imagination more than his leadership, while still a lieutenant, of a small band of junior officers of the Royal Engineers who, under great difficulties, laid the railways from Wādī Ḥalfā to Kerma and over the Nubian desert towards Khartoum.

Glacznik, Johann. *See* KLANCNIK, JAN.

Gladstone, William Ewart (1809–98), British Liberal statesman; he denounced Turkish cruelty to subject peoples of the Ottoman Empire and advocated the independence of the sultan's Christian provinces in the Balkans and in Asia Minor, 1875; on the defeat of the Conservative administration led by B. Disraeli, Earl of Beaconsfield, at the general election of 1880, he became prime minister for the second time, 1880–5; he supported the British military campaign against Aḥmad 'Urābī Pasha, 1882, on the grounds of freeing the Egyptian people from military tyranny; twice in 1883 he successfully countered motions of censure in the House of Commons on his Egyptian policy; he was severely criticized for his failure to take timely steps for the rescue of General Gordon and the Egyptian garrisons in the Sudan who were being menaced by the Mahdists, and for his policy of abandoning the Sudan, 1884; such was the popular feeling in Britain on these questions that his ministry, deprived of Parliamentary support, resigned in 1885, nominally on a budget debate but in fact on the question of the Sudan; he was prime minister in two subsequent administrations; as an orator and financier he was among the greatest of British statesmen; he wrote copiously on theological, philosophical, and political subjects.

Gleichen Bey, Lord Albert Edward Wilfrid (formerly Count Gleichen) (1863–1937), British major-general, son of Admiral Prince Victor of Hohenlohe-Langenburg; he joined the Grenadier Guards in 1881 and served in the Nile campaign of 1884–5 in the Guards' Camel Regiment; in 1896 he was in the Dongola campaign on special service and, transferring to the Egyptian army, in which he was promoted mīrālai, was director of intelligence and Sudan agent in Cairo, 1901–3; reverting to the British army he commanded a division in the First World War and was promoted major-general in 1919 when he retired; among his writings are *With the Camel Corps up the Nile* (1888) and *A Guardsman's Memories* (1932); he edited a collective work by various officers of the Sudan Government entitled *The Anglo-Egyptian Sudan* (1905–6).

Gobat, Samuel (1799–1879), Swiss Protestant missionary in Abyssinia, 1827–37; he afterwards became Anglican bishop in Jerusalem; born at Crémines, Switzerland, he travelled up the Nile valley in 1831 with C. Kugler to Gondar by way of Khartoum and Gallabat; war in Abyssinia combined with the death of Kugler compelled him to quit Gondar which he did via Muṣawwa'; he published an account of his journey (Paris, 1835).

Goljok Mamer (–1940), chief of the Pangom clan of the Dinka in the district of Rumbek.

Gordon Pasha, Charles George (1833–85), British soldier, major-general of the British army, farīq of the Egyptian army; born at Woolwich near London of a Scottish military family, he was commissioned to the Royal Engineers in 1852; he fought as a lieutenant in the Crimean war and earned distinction in the trenches before Sebastopol in 1855; the war over, he served on an international boundary commission in Bessarabia and Armenia, 1856–7; he was in the Chinese war of 1860 and remained after the war in the service of the Chinese Government, taking a prominent part in the suppression of the Tai-ping rebellion, 1863–4; returning to Europe he was British commissioner for the improvement of navigation on the River Danube in accordance with the terms of the Treaty of Paris, 1856; at Constantinople in 1872 he met Nubar Pasha Boghos, the Egyptian statesman, who sounded him about succeeding Sir S. W. Baker as governor of the Equatorial province; on his way from the Balkans to England he visited Egypt where the Khedive Ismā'īl Pasha appointed him governor of Equatoria at a pay of £10,000 a year of which he accepted £2,000; now a colonel he returned to Cairo early in 1874 and travelled with his staff to Equatoria by way of Sawākin and Berber, arriving at Gondokoro in April; during his two years of service on the Upper White Nile he transferred his administrative headquarters from Gondokoro to Lado, established a chain of posts along the Nile as far as Dufilé, and brought Unyoro and parts of Uganda between Lakes Albert and Ibrahim (afterwards named Kioga) within the Egyptian sphere of influence, thus furthering the work begun by Baker; he resigned in 1876 and returned once more to England, having been relieved in Equatoria by the American officer H. G. Prout Bey and succeeded by Ibrāhīm Pasha Fawzī; after making terms with the Khedive Ismā'īl he accepted appointment as governor-general of the Sudan with a mandate to suppress the slave trade and improve communications; he left Cairo in 1877 first to settle frontier disputes on the confines of Abyssinia; for this he went to Muṣawwa' by sea; at Keren he parleyed with the local chief, Wad Mikhail; from Keren he reached Khartoum via Kassala; arrived at the capital he was ceremoniously installed as governor-general on 5 May 1877; after a short stay in Khartoum he hastened to Dār Fūr where a revolt had broken out; this he suppressed and returned to Khartoum; in the winter of 1877–8 he made an unsuccessful endeavour to meet King John of Abyssinia; he set out for Abyssinia by way of Berber and Dongola intending to continue through Aswān and Berenice, thence by sea to Muṣawwa', when he was turned back by a false rumour that the Abyssinians were threatening Sennar; he therefore returned to Khartoum and from there left via Abū Ḥarāz, Gedaref, and Kassala to Keren; failing to make contact with John he then returned to Khartoum by Sawākin and Berber; at Shendi, on the way, he received a telegram from the Khedive inviting him to take part in an inquiry into the finances of Egypt which were then in a precarious state; he left Khartoum early in 1878, travelling to Cairo by Dongola and Wādī Ḥalfā; it was soon clear to the Khedive and to Gordon that he was unsuitable for this mission and Ismā'īl relieved him of the duties and permitted him to return to his post; on 30 March 1878 he left Cairo on a tour of the Egyptian possessions on the Red Sea coast which then came under the governor-generalate of the Sudan; he visited Berbera, Zaila, and Harar where he somewhat summarily dismissed Muḥammad Ra'ūf Pasha for tyranny; he had already once before dismissed Ra'ūf in 1874 from the Equatorial province; he then came back to Khartoum by Sawākin and Berber; almost immediately followed Gordon's second journey to Dār Fūr in which he organized the war against the rebel Fūrs and released slaves while R. Gessi was fighting against Sulaimān wad Zubair in the south of the province; in July 1879 he got news of Ismā'īl Pasha's deposition and himself determined to resign; leaving Khartoum on 20 July he arrived in Cairo when the new Khedive, Muḥammad Tawfīq Pasha, sent him on a mission to Abyssinia to avert an impending war; he travelled by Suez and Muṣawwa', saw King John but got no satisfaction, and returned to Cairo where the Khedive accepted his resignation, 1880; on his leaving Egypt he served in various capacities in India, China, Mauritius, and Cape Colony; in 1882 he was promoted major-general; in January 1884 the British Government dispatched him to rescue the Egyptian garrisons in the Sudan as a prelude to the abandonment of that country which by that time had been largely overrun by the forces of the Mahdists; he was again appointed governor-general of the Sudan and arrived in Cairo in

January 1884 and, hastening over the Nubian desert, reached Khartoum on 18 February; within a few weeks the city was cut off from communication with Egypt and later closely invested by the Mahdist besieging army; the wasted garrison defended the place with dogged courage until, on 26 January 1885, the Mahdists broke into Khartoum, massacred many of the inhabitants, and killed Gordon at the governor-general's palace; his unusual and unorthodox personality made a powerful impression upon his time and his actions gave rise to an enormous literature in many languages; he was capable of inspiring great devotion on the part of those who worked with him; perhaps the greatest weakness in his character was his inconsistency; his intuitive, capricious mind was ever ready to jump to conclusions, to change, to condemn, to repent; yet technically he was a good soldier and a competent, practical engineer; he was entirely selfless and without fear.

Gordon, Robert James (1786–1822), British captain of the Royal Navy and explorer; the son of an infantry captain he was born at Bawtry, Yorkshire, and entered the Royal Navy as a volunteer, 1798; he served in many parts of the world, being twice shipwrecked and once escaping from captivity as a prisoner of war in France during the Napoleonic wars; in 1807 he was commissioned as a lieutenant and in 1814 was promoted to commander; he retired from the navy with the rank of captain in 1815; in 1822 he arrived in Egypt on behalf of the African Association with the intention of ascertaining the source of the White Nile; he left Cairo in May or June 1882; F. Cailliaud met him between Aswān and Dongola; Lord Prudhoe's servant Maḥmūd accompanied him as far as Berber whence he proceeded alone; he is said to have visited the mountain regions of Kordofan, possibly the Nuba hills, though his itinerary is uncertain; falling ill of fever he managed to reach Wad Madanī where he died ten days after his arrival, and was buried, according to Prudhoe, in a spot set apart for Christians; another account ascribed his death to accidental drowning while bathing at Wad Madanī.

Gordon, W . . . Staveley (1863–1907), British officer of the Royal Engineers, nephew of Major-General C. G. Gordon Pasha; he was a captain and in charge of the Egyptian Ordnance in 1896 when the Dongola campaign began; in 1898 he superintended the assembling of the three gunboats, *Malik*, *Shaikh*, and *Sultan*, at the temporary dockyard at ʿAbidīya in preparation for the Anglo-Egyptian advance on Omdurman, at which battle he was present; he was director of stores, Cairo, 1899, and director of stores of the Egyptian army, 1901; promoted colonel, 1903, he retired, 1905.

Gorringe Bey, Sir George Frederick (1868–1945), British lieutenant-general; he received a commission in the Royal Engineers in 1888 and in 1893 was attached to the Egyptian army; he fought in the Dongola and Nile campaigns, 1896–8, and commanded a force of irregulars which defeated the Khalīfa ʿAbd Allāhi in 1899; meanwhile, he had begun on the reconstruction of Khartoum including the building of the governor-general's palace, Gordon Memorial College, and later the province offices at Wad Madanī and the governor's (now district commissioner's) office at Sinja; after serving in the South African war, in which he was aide-de-camp to Lord Kitchener, he returned to the Egyptian army and was governor of Sennar province, 1902–4; in the latter year he commanded a local military expedition to Jerok in the southern part of his province; in the First World War he commanded the 47th (London) division; he was colonel-commandant of the Royal Engineers, 1927–38.

Gorst, Sir John Eldon (1861–1911), British agent and consul-general in Egypt; a son of the politician Sir J. E. Gorst, he was born in New Zealand; his introduction to Egypt was as attaché to the British agency in 1886; he was controller of direct revenues in the Egyptian Government, 1890–2, adviser to the ministry of the interior, 1894, financial adviser, 1898–1904, and assistant under-secretary of state to the British foreign office, 1904–7, when he succeeded E. Baring, 1st Earl of Cromer, as agent and consul-general; although he was closely concerned with the financing of the reoccupation of the Sudan, his tenure of office as consul-general was too short to have permitted him much permanent influence in Sudan affairs.

* **Gostner, Josef** (1821–58), Roman Catholic missionary priest; born in Vols in the Austrian Tyrol he served as a missionary on the Upper White Nile with Bishop I. Knoblehar in 1853; on Knoblehar's death in 1858 he became vicar-general of the mission, but died in Khartoum after only three days in office; he had studied drawing when a youth and in 1854–6 superintended the construction of the mission buildings in Khartoum, traces of which still stand between the present governor's office and the Blue Nile.

Gottberg, Eduard von (*fl.* 1857), engineer; the viceroy Muḥammad Sa'īd Pasha sent him to study the cataracts of Ḥannak and Kaibār (Kajbār) with a view to improving river navigation, 1857; in his report, published 1867, he opposed any radical altering of the flow of water.

Gough, Wilfred Arbuthnot (1853–85), major in the British army; he joined the Oxfordshire Light Infantry as a sub-lieutenant in 1872 and later passed out of the staff college; in 1882 he served in the Egyptian foot police; while serving in the Nile campaign of 1884–5 he was killed in the battle of Abū Ṭulaiḥ (Abu Klea).

Graham, Sir Gerald (1831–99), British lieutenant-general; he entered the Royal Engineers in 1854 and fought in the great battles of the Crimean war, 1854–5; for outstanding bravery in the siege of Sebastopol he received the Victoria Cross; after serving in China and Canada he commanded the 2nd infantry brigade of the 1st British division in the expedition against Aḥmad 'Urābī Pasha, 1882, winning a victory at Kassassin and leading the assault on Tel el-Kebir; he was placed in command of the Sawākin Field Force which won battles at el-Teb, Hashīn, and Tamai, 1884–5; he urged without success the importance of opening the Sawākin–Berber road as a means of sending help to the beleaguered Egyptian garrisons in the Nile valley; promoted major-general in 1881 and lieutenant-general in 1884 he was colonel-commandant of the Royal Engineers, 1899; he published writings on military and other subjects; a 'life', by R. H. Vetch, was published in 1901; the promontory at Sawākin, Graham's Point, is named after him.

Granier (or **Grenier**), **Antoine** (*fl.* 1701), French priest of the Society of Jesus; with a fellow Jesuit, A. Paulet (or Paoletti), he left Egypt for Abyssinia about 1700 in search of another Jesuit priest, F. X. de Brévedent, who had gone up the Nile towards Abyssinia with C. J. Poncet in 1698 and of whom no news had been received; armed with a letter of introduction to the king of Sennar from the French consul in Egypt they duly arrived at Sennar where King Bādī III handed them over to an agent of the Abyssinian King Īyāsū (Jesus) I; the agent conducted them to the royal capital of Gondar where the king received them kindly, but the Abyssinian people being hostile to the two French priests the king hustled them back to the frontier of Sennar to save their lives; one of them died of exhaustion on the road, the other died soon after reaching Sennar.

Grant, James Augustus (1827–92), British explorer; educated at Marischal College, Aberdeen, he received a commission in the Bengal army in 1846 and fought in the Indian mutiny, 1857; in 1860 he joined J. H. Speke, also an officer of the Indian army, in a venture which had most important geographical results; the two explorers left Zanzibar in 1860 and at length arrived in the region of the south end of Lake Victoria; they then made their way northward to Uganda and Unyoro after discovering the source of the White Nile in Lake Victoria; at length, after many difficulties and hardships, they walked into Gondokoro in 1863, travelled down the Nile by steamer to Khartoum, and from Khartoum returned to England; during the journey Grant made valuable botanical and meteorological notes; he served in the intelligence department in the Anglo-Abyssinian war of 1868 when he was promoted lieutenant-colonel; his book, *A Walk across Africa* (1864) won the gold medal of the Royal Geographical Society of London.

Graves, Charles Iverson (*c.* 1837–96), American soldier in the Egyptian army; he was born in Georgia and graduated from the United States Naval Academy, 1857; in 1861 he joined the Confederate navy in the American civil war and in 1863 was appointed instructor in seamanship at the newly formed Confederate Naval Academy at Richmond, Virginia; later joining the Khedivial service he was port officer at Muṣawwa' during the Egyptian-Abyssinian war, 1875–6, and was afterwards sent on scientific duties to the Somali coast; he resigned from the Egyptian army in 1878 though (according to W. W. Loring Pasha) he was offered a high position in the Sudan; he died at Rome, Georgia.

Greaves, Sir George Richards (1831–1922), British general; receiving a commission he joined the Indian army and fought in the Indian mutiny, 1857–8; after service in several campaigns in different countries he was appointed chief of staff to Sir G. Graham in the Sawākin campaign of 1885; he was commander-in-chief, Bombay, 1890–3, retiring in 1896.

Grenfell, Francis Wallace, 1st Baron (1841–1925), British field-marshal; joining the army in 1859 he saw active service in South Africa, 1874–9; he was assistant adjutant-general to Sir G. Wolseley in the Egyptian expedition of 1882, and served in the Nile expedition of 1884–5 in command of communications with rank of brigadier-general; from 1885 to 1892 he was sirdār of the Egyptian army, succeeding Sir H. E. Wood; in 1889 he destroyed the Mahdist army of the amīr ʿAbd al-Raḥmān wad al-Najūmī at the battle of Tūshkī (Toski); during his term of duty as sirdār he reorganized the Egyptian army and consolidated the Egyptian hold on Sawākin; handing over the command of the Egyptian army to Sir H. H. Kitchener in 1892 he was governor and commander-in-chief of Malta, 1899; in 1902 he was raised to the peerage and in 1904–8 was commander-in-chief, Ireland; he was made a field-marshal in 1908.

Griffith, Francis Llewellyn (1862–1934), British Egyptologist; he was in charge of the Oxford University excavations in the northern Sudan, 1910–13; he wrote extensively on the language and inscriptions of the ancient Nubians and deciphered the Meroitic script.

Griffith Pasha, George Richard (1857–1920), British veterinary officer; he entered the army veterinary department in 1880 and served in the Egyptian war of 1882 against Aḥmad ʿUrābī Pasha and in the campaign of 1884–5 for the attempted relief of Khartoum; he served at Sawākin in 1888 and was at the recapture of Tokar in 1891; in the Dongola and Nile campaigns of 1896–8 he was principal veterinary surgeon; he was principal veterinary officer of the Egyptian army in Egypt from 1905 and in 1907 was promoted liwāʾ.

* **Grigolini, Teresina** (–1931), Italian nun of the Roman Catholic mission in the Sudan; she was stationed at the mission house in Berber in 1878, and in 1880 was posted to the mission at Dilling (Delen) of which she was appointed mother superior; in 1882 she and the other workers of the Dilling mission were captured by the Mahdists and taken first to al-Ubaiyaḍ and then to Omdurman; the Pope having released the Roman Catholic missionaries from their vows she married D. Kakorembas, a Greek subject, who was among the European captives of the Mahdists and who had been appointed amīr of the Christians; to him she bore two sons; after the end of Mahdism she continued to serve the mission in the Sudan; she died at Verona.

Grigorios abū ʾl-Faraj Bar ʿEbhrāyā (Bar Hebræus) (1226–86), Arab historian of Hebrew descent; born at Malaṭya on the Euphrates he was in later life assistant patriarch of the Jacobite Christian church; he died at Marāgha in Azarbaijan; in his *Mukhtasar taʾrīkh al-duwal* (Compendious History of the Dynasties) he maintained that, in the reign of Constantine the Great (324–37), the Christianity of the Copts had penetrated all Nubia.

Guérin, Victor (1821–91), French archaeologist of Paris; with Count de Maupas he visited Wādī Ḥalfā at the beginning of 1858 and published a description of the First and Second Cataracts in the *Bulletin of the Geographical Society of Paris,* vol. xvi, 1858.

Guthrie, Cuthbert Burrell (1883–1924), American Protestant missionary; he was born in Coin, Iowa, and graduated from Iowa State College in the agricultural department, 1908; he came to the Sudan in the same year and served all his missionary life at Doleib hill, near the mouth of the River Sobat, where he died.

Gwek Wonding (–1929), Nuer witch doctor; he incited the Nuong Nuer tribesmen to murder their district commissioner, V. H. Fergusson Bey, a Greek merchant, and sixteen Dinka carriers at Lake Jur, north of Shambé, in 1927; two patrols finally broke the resistance of the rebels, and Gwek's stronghold, the pyramid of Deng Kur, was blown up in 1928; he fled but was later killed while leading a desperate attack on government troops near the site of the pyramid.

Ḥabas͟hī otherwise **Fr. Bonaventura** (1838–), Franciscan priest; born in Khartoum of negro origin, he entered the school of the Roman Catholic mission there; later, in Cairo, he was influenced by the Franciscans and studied theology at Verona and Naples where in 1861 he made his profession; he was in Palestine, 1867–74 and was noted as a preacher in Arabic in Jerusalem, Bethlehem and al-Ramla.

Ḥabīb Allāh Muḥammad ʿAbd al-Mājid (–1929), Rubāṭābī notable; ʿumda of Kanūr near Berber and a magistrate.

Ḥabīb Bey Kaḥīl (*c.* 1873–1941), Syrian physician; a native of Beirut he was educated in the American university there and graduated in medicine; he entered the Egyptian army medical corps in 1896 and, transferring to the Sudan Government service, was quarantine officer at Sawākin and afterwards at Port Sudan, 1901–13; created a bey in 1923 he died in Beirut.

Hadji Abd-el-Hamid-Bey. *See* Du Couret, Louis-Laurent.

Hadrian, Pio Giuseppe (*c.* 1847–73), Sudanese priest of the Benedictine Order of the Roman Catholic Church; he was born somewhere on the upper reaches of the Blue Nile, possibly in Dār Berta, and at the age of four was sold into slavery; brought to Cairo he was retrieved by Roman Catholic missionaries, taken to Italy, and educated by the Benedictine monks of Subiaco; he entered the novitiate in 1861 and was ordained priest in 1872; in Italy he fell ill of consumption and was sent to the vicariate of Central Africa in an endeavour to cure him in congenial surroundings; he travelled with Bishop D. Comboni, arriving in al-Ubaiyaḍ early in 1873; he died there some weeks later.

* **Haggard Bey, Andrew Charles Parker** (1850–1923), British soldier and author; commissioned to the King's Own Borderers, 1873, he was promoted captain, 1883, when he joined the re-organized Egyptian army; he served under Lieutenant-General Sir G. Graham in transport

duties at Sawākin, 1884, and commanded the 1st battalion of the Egyptian army there, 1884–5; transferring to the Nile he commanded Egyptian troops on the southern frontier and fought at Jinnis (Giniss), 1885; on his retirement from the British army he settled in British Columbia where he died; he wrote novels, popular history, and books of sport and travel; among his writings is *Under Crescent and Star* (1895) describing his life in Egypt and the Sudan.

Haggenmacher, Gustav Adolf (1845–75), Swiss trader, afterwards official; he came to Egypt in 1865 and from 1866 to 1870 was trading in Khartoum and on the White Nile; in 1868 he married Maria Luigia, daughter of C. Contarini of Khartoum; he was then employed for three years by J. A. W. Munzinger Pasha, governor of Muṣawwaʿ and a fellow Swiss, on various missions and travels in the Sudan and in Abyssinia; he went to Europe as commissioner for Egypt at the Vienna international exhibition of 1873; returning to the Red Sea coast Munzinger appointed him in 1874 a muʿāwin or superintendent in charge of exploration, and in 1874–5 he was engaged in marking the frontier between the Sudan and Abyssinia; he met his death while accompanying Munzinger on a journey of exploration through the hostile and unknown territory of Aussa in the hinterland of the Somali coast, when he and his chief, with several of the party, were killed by Somali tribesmen. His son Adolf (*c.* 1870–1933) was an engineer on the construction of the Blue Nile bridge at Khartoum and afterwards Swiss consul in Addis Ababa.

Haig, Douglas, 1st Earl (1861–1928), British field-marshal; he joined the 7th Hussars in 1885 and later passed through the Staff College; he served in the Nile campaign as a special service officer, 1898, and fought in the battles of the Atbara and Omdurman; in the South African war of 1899–1902 he got his first experience of substantial command; he commanded the 1st British army in France in 1914–15, and from 1915 to 1919 was commander-in-chief of the British forces in France and Flanders; he was promoted to field-marshal in 1917.

al-Ḥajā Sulaimān (*c.* 1867–1923), nāẓir of the Salīm Baqqāra of the White Nile; he was appointed a magistrate in 1922.

al-Ḥajū ʿAbd al-Qādir al-Maṣiʿ (–1930), distinguished leader of the Sammānīya brotherhood; he was a member of the religious family of the Yaʿqūbāb of Sennar and a great-nephew of Shaikh al-Tūm Bān Naqā.

Haliburton (formerly **Burton**), **James** (1788–1862), British Egyptologist; he was employed on a geological survey by Muḥammad ʿAlī Pasha; he travelled to Abū Simbel, 1825, and with J. Bonomi made drawings and notes of Jabal Barkal and other sites between Semna and Meroë, 1828.

Ḥalīm Bey . . . (*fl.* 1821–5), Turkish soldier; he was second-in-command to Muḥammad Khusraw Bey Daramālī al-Daftardār in the invasion of Kordofan, 1821; on Ismāʿīl Pasha's murder at Shendi, 1822, the Daftardār left Kordofan to assume the command of the Turkish troops in the Sudan and Ḥalīm was left in command at al-Ubaiyaḍ with rank of qā'immaqām; he was succeeded in 1825 by Sulaimān Bey Kharpūtlī.

Ḥalīm, Prince. *See* MUḤAMMAD 'ABD AL-ḤALĪM PASHA, PRINCE.

Ḥamad 'Alī Ḥamad (–1946), Beja chieftain; 'umda of the Kurbāb section of the Amarar.

Ḥamad Asūsa (–*c.* 1875), Sudanese tribal leader, nāẓir of the 'Abd al-'Ālī branch of the Ḥawāzma Arabs of Kordofan; he lived near al-Birka, south-west of al-Ubaiyaḍ; he died peacefully and was succeeded by his nephew Quṭṭīya wad al-Sharīf Asūsa.

Ḥamad 'Awad al-Karīm abū Sin (–1818), Shukrī tribal leader, son of Shaikh 'Awad al-Karīm abū Sin (*fl.* 1780) and brother of Aḥmad Bey abū Sin 'Awad al-Karīm (1790–1870); he was killed in an inter-tribal fracas by Shaikh 'Alī wad Birair, causing a long blood-feud between the Shukrīya and the Baṭāḥīn; Mak Nimr of Shendi sheltered the killer.

Ḥamad Baṭrān Naṣrai (–1942), Beja notable; 'umda of the 'Āmrāb branch of the Bishārīyīn.

Ḥamad Bedein (–1932), mak of the Amira Nuba people in the eastern Nuba hills.

Ḥamad Hassai (*c.* 1790–*c.* 1850), leader of the Amarar branch of the Beja group of tribes and the great-grandfather of the present nāẓir; under him the Amarar emerged as a tribal unit with a separate identity.

Ḥamad Kirja (–1944), shartai of the Wīwī section of the Ḥamar in western Kordofan; he was a magistrate.

Ḥamad Maḥmūd (–1886), nāẓir of the Amarar tribe of the Beja peoples of the Red Sea littoral; he was killed by the Mahdist amīr 'Uthmān abū Bakr Diqna (Osman Digna), an act which sealed the hostility of the Amarar to the Mahdist cause.

Ḥamad wad al-Mak (*c.* 1772–1842), Shā'iqī chieftain and probably an officer of the irregular cavalry recruited from the Shā'iqīya tribe; the governor-general, Aḥmad Pasha abū Widān, having refused any longer to grant the Shā'iqīya relief from taxes and free fodder for their horses, caused such discontent among the tribe that Ḥamad wad al-Mak decided to emigrate with his family and retainers to Abyssinia; on the way south to the border Shaikh Aḥmad 'Awad al-Karīm abū Sin betrayed him to the government forces near Shendi and he barely escaped, leaving his wives and children behind; then, turning round and making a daring raid on the governor-general at Shendi, he turned towards Abyssinia and crossed the border; the governor-general afterwards came to terms with him and allowed him to return to his lands; however, in six months he was banished to Dongola where he died, leaving two sons and a daughter.

Ḥamad Muḥammad ʿAwad al-Karīm abū Sin (–1940), nāẓir of the Abū Sin khuṭṭ of the Shukrīya Arabs and a magistrate; he was a member of the great ruling house of the Shukrīya.

Ḥamad Bey Muḥammad Ḥamad al-Malik (1869–1934), ʿumda of Arqū and a member of the ruling house of the island; the eldest son of Muḥammad Bey Ḥamad al-Malik, he took part with his father in governing the island during the last days of Egyptian rule; the Mahdist revolt brought him ill fortune for, during the amīr Muḥammad wad Bishāra's rule in Dongola, he was taken to Omdurman on the eve of the Anglo-Egyptian occupation of Dongola in 1896 and imprisoned until his release after the battle of Omdurman in 1898; when his father retired from the duties of ʿumda in 1904 he was appointed ʿumda for the southern part of the island; he is said to have been a direct-dealing man and a great reader; the present malik, Shaikh Zubair Ḥamad al-Malik, is his son.

Ḥamad al-Naḥlān ibn Muḥammad, called **Wad al-Turābī** (1639–1704), holy man of the Bidairīya Arabs and a member of the branch of the Awlād Turābī of the Jazīra; a brother of the holy man Nanna, he became a follower of Shaikh Dafaʿ Allāh al-ʿArakī and made the pilgrimage to Makka where, according to tradition, he performed a miracle; returning to the Sudan he renounced the world and devoted himself to mysticism; he set up a *khalwa* in the village, called after him Wad al-Turābī, in the Jazīra, and here he was buried; the present guardian of his tomb is Shaikh Abū Aghā Ḥamad.

* **Ḥamad al-Nīl al-Raiyaḥ** (–1894), Sudanese religious notable of the ʿArakīyīn tribe of the Jazīra and a descendant of Shaikh Dafaʿ Allāh al-ʿArakī of Ṭaiyiba; an early adherent to the cause of Muḥammad Aḥmad al-Mahdī, he died at Omdurman and his tomb is at Abū Ḥarāz on the Blue Nile.

Ḥamad Sulaimān abū Ḥurūf (–1932), Habbānī notable, nāẓir of the Habbānīya of eastern Kordofan and a magistrate.

Ḥamdān ʿAbd al-Qādir abū Ḥusna (–1938), religious notable of the ʿArakīyīn; he died at Ḥajjāj village in the western Jazīra.

* **Ḥamdān abū ʿAnja** (*c.* 1835–88), Mahdist amīr al-umarāʾ (principal amīr), by birth a half-breed Taʿāʾishī of a freed serf community called Mandala of whom many had served under Zubair Pasha Raḥma Manṣūr on his slave-raiding expeditions and were in consequence of great military value to the Mahdī; Abū ʿAnja probably saw more fighting than any of the other great amīrs; after the fall of al-Ubaiyaḍ in 1883 he was put in command of the *jihādīya,* or regular black riflemen; he harried the doomed army of W. Hicks Pasha at the battle of Shaikān (Kashgil), 1883, and during the siege of Khartoum he captured the fort of Omdurman, 1884; after the reduction of Khartoum in 1885 he was sent to the Nuba hills to suppress opposition there; on the advance of the disaffected amīr Muḥammad Khālid Zughal through Kordofan to join the Khalīfa Sharīf who meditated a *coup d'état* against the Khalīfa ʿAbd Allāhi, Abū ʿAnja was ordered to arrest him; he pursued Khālid

as far as Bāra where the Khalīfa Sharīf and his army were surrounded and surrendered; his next command was on the Abyssinian border; with the amīr Zakī Ṭamal he invaded Abyssinia and, after beating Ras Adal in battle near Gallabat, sacked Gondar in 1887; he died, some say from poisonous medicine taken to cure indigestion, and was buried at Gallabat; others maintain that he died of cholera or typhoid fever; he was a short, dark-coloured man with a large head; of all the Mahdist amīrs he was perhaps the best fighter.

Ḥāmid Aḥmad al-Nājī (–1935), religious notable of the ʻArakīyīn and a kinsman of Aḥmad Muḥammad Ḥamad al-Nīl, ʻumda of Abū Ḥarāz; he was khalīfa of the Qādirīya brotherhood of that town, and there he died.

* **Ḥāmid ʻAlī** (–1899), Mahdist amīr, a Taʻā'ishī by tribe; a loyal follower of the Khalīfa ʻAbd Allāhi he served in several of the big battles of the day and was killed at Umm Dibaikarāt along with his leader.

Ḥāmid Khalīfa (1816–80), notable of the ʻAbābda tribe; born in Berber he became the shaikh of his branch of the tribe and was hereditary concessionnaire of the caravan route over the Nubian desert between Abū Ḥamad and Korosko to which post he was appointed in 1874 in place of his nephew, Muḥammad Ḥusain Khalīfa; several travellers, C. Chaillé-Long, F. L. James, and E. Linant de Bellefonds among them, who were his guests at various times, wrote of his hospitality and of the local authority which he possessed; he occupied a large house in Berber where he died.

Ḥāmid al-Khuwain (? *c.* 1400), traditional ancestor of the Dār Ḥāmid and of other Arab tribes of Kordofan; he is said to have been a descendant of ʻAbd Allāh al-Juḥānī and to have come to Kordofan from the north and, on the advice of Abū Zaid al-Hilālī, settled with his tribe in the Khairān in northern Kordofan (Dār Ḥāmid); other legends have it that he settled in Dār Fūr.

Ḥāmid al-Likka Muḥammad (–1929), nāẓir of the Ruwawja branch of the Ḥawāzma Arabs living round Kadugli in the northern Nuba hills.

Ḥāmid Muḥammad Jabr al-Dār (–1933), hereditary sultan of the Musabaʻāt branch of the Fūr of Dār Fūr; he was a magistrate.

Ḥāmid ʻUmrān (–1945), Beja notable; ʻumda of the Bishārīyīn who live in the valley of the Atbara.

Ḥāmid ʻUthmān Ibrāhīm (–1941), member of an old-established family which came originally from the Barbary coast; his grandfather and father had both held the post of ʻumda of Khartoum North; he was born at Ḥillat Shaikh al-Qurashī near Ḥaṣṣa Ḥaiṣa, his father being first a farmer and afterwards a merchant, and took over his father's post in 1921; in 1930 he was appointed a magistrate.

Ḥāmid Ya'qūb Ṣilaibū Tūrjuk (1876–1939), Sudanese tribal leader, shaikh of the Banī Ḥusain of Dār Fūr; he was shaikh in the reign of Sultan 'Alī Dīnār and on the Anglo-Egyptian occupation he was confirmed in the shaikhship; he did much to achieve the cohesion of the Beni Ḥusain in Dār 'Uṭāsh; he was succeeded on his death by his son Adam.

Hamilton, Sir Ian Standish Monteith Hamilton (1853–1947), British general; born at Corfu he entered the Gordon Highlanders in 1873 and in the course of much foreign service fought in the Nile campaign of 1884–5 which vainly attempted the relief of Khartoum; in the South African war of 1899–1902 he was for some time chief of staff to Kitchener and in the First World War he commanded the Allied force which landed on Gallipoli in 1915, an operation which brought him criticism; he retired in 1920; he was a ready writer on military subjects; he wrote on his Sudan days in *Listening for the Drums*, 1944.

Hamilton, James (*fl.* 1854), British traveller; in 1854, after having visited Arabia, he landed at Sawākin and thence travelled by Khōr Langeb to Kassala, Gedaref, Abū Ḥarāz, Rufā'a (where he met Aḥmad Bey 'Awad al-Karīm abū Sin), and Khartoum; he continued northward, by river to Berber and thence over the Nubian desert to Egypt; his *Sinai, the Hedjaz and Soudan* (1857) describes his journey.

* **Hamilton, William Richard** (1777–1859), British antiquarian and diplomat who travelled in Egypt in 1801–2; ascending the Nile to Aswān, south of which he met the Mameluke leader Alfī Bey, he was among the first European antiquarians to penetrate Nubia; he was afterwards under-secretary for foreign affairs and president of the Royal Geographical Society of London; he published *Aegyptian Monuments* (1809).

Ḥammād ibn 'Abd Allāh (*fl.* 1500), holy man of the Ja'līyīn Arabs and the founder of the town of al-Dāmar; the Majādhīb branch of the tribe, who form a religious confraternity at al-Dāmar, Sawākin, and elsewhere, mostly following the Shādhilīya Islamic rule, took their name from his great-grandson Ḥammād ibn Muḥammad al-Majdhūb (1693–1776); his tomb is at al-Dāmar.

Ḥammād Asūsa (–1934), nāẓir of the Baqqāra Ḥawāzma Arabs of Dār Betti in the Nuba hills; his son Muḥammad succeeded him.

Ḥammād Bey Faṭīn (–1905), nāẓir of the Daqāqīn branch of the Ḥamar Arab tribe of Kordofan at the close of the Egyptian régime; in 1883 he went over to the Mahdist cause and was appointed an amīr; in 1900, after the collapse of political Mahdism, he was reappointed nāẓir by the Anglo-Egyptian Government; on his death he was succeeded by his son 'Alī Ḥammād Faṭīn.

Ḥammād ibn Muḥammad ibn 'Alī al-Mashaikhī (1646–1730), Sudanese holy man, popularly known as Ḥammād wad umm Maryam;

he was born on Tūtī island near the site of the present Khartoum; his father was a Maḥasī and his mother a Mashaikha; his tomb is a prominent feature of Khartoum North.

Ḥammād ibn Muḥammad al-Majdhūb (1693–1776), holy man of Ja'lī descent, great-grandson of Ḥammād ibn 'Abd Allāh, founder of the town of al-Dāmar and ancestor of the Majadhīb, a religious community which has its spiritual centre at al-Dāmar and devotees in various parts of the northern Sudan; he was schooled in the practices of the Shādhilīya brotherhood in Makka and transmitted those practices to his people whose descendants mostly now follow the tenets of the Shādhilīya; his tomb is at al-Dāmar.

* **Hammām (or Ḥummām) abū Yūsuf** (*c.* 1730–*c.* 1769), notable of the Hawwāra, a Berber people who had settled in Upper Egypt and, before the end of the seventeenth century, had become arabized; the family of Hammām had by this time assumed the whole government in Upper Egypt south of Asyūṭ and the Mamelukes had been forced to cede this territory to them by treaty; Hammām also extended his authority into northern Nubia and made several visits as far south as Dār Maḥas; his rule has been variously described as just and oppressive; shortly before the accession to power of 'Alī, the enterprising bey, in Egypt, the Mamelukes attacked Hammām and killed him, though it was left to Muḥammad 'Alī's son Ibrāhīm to crush and pacify his tribe.

Hammill, Tynte Ford (*c.* 1848–94), British sailor; he entered the Royal Navy and was promoted lieutenant in 1871 and commander in 1885; in 1884 he prepared a report on the suitability of the Nile for large-scale military transport, in preparation for the advance of a British force to attempt the relief of Khartoum; he was naval transport officer at Wādī Ḥalfā during the campaign in 1885 and was later assistant director of naval intelligence at the Admiralty, London.

Ḥamūda Idrīs al-Baqqārī (–1896), Mahdist amīr; as his name indicates he came of the great cattle-owning tribe which is spread over Kordofan and Dār Fūr; he commanded a force of Mahdists at Jinnis (Giniss) in 1885 and at Tūshkī (Toski) in 1889; in 1895 he showed inactivity in his preparations to meet the Anglo-Egyptian advance and was for a time replaced by the amīr 'Uthmān Azraq; he and 'Uthmān commanded the Mahdist army in the battle of Firka (Firket) in which he was killed while charging the enemy with great courage.

Ḥamza Pasha Imām al-Khabīr (–), merchant of Dār Fūr, a brother of Muḥammad Pasha Imām al-Khabīr his ancestors were Danāqla merchants who settled in Kobbé; he and his brother were already substantial traders before the Egyptian invasion of Dār Fūr in 1874, dealing in commerce with Egypt by caravan along the Forty Days Road through the Libyan desert between Kobbé and Asyūṭ; the Egyptian occupation of Dār Fūr helped this trade and the brothers helped the Egyptians; Gordon Pasha, governor-general of the Sudan

1877–80, called him to Khartoum, got him made a bey, and thereafter enlisted his services in various posts; in 1883 he succeeded his brother as president of the court of appeal in Khartoum and was made a pasha; but the Mahdists were now threatening Khartoum and with his family he retired to Egypt where he died in poverty as a refugee in Asyūṭ.

Hankey, Algernon Alers (1863–1940), British trader of the firm of Gellatly, Hankey, Sewell & Co.; he opened agencies of the firm at Aden, Jidda, and Sawākin, with Jidda as his headquarters; he was at Sawākin in 1886; he was a son of J. A. Hankey, one of the founders of the firm, and was a member of a long line of London merchants and bankers of which a surviving member is M. P. A., 1st Baron Hankey.

Hansal, Martin Ludwig (1823–85), Austrian trader and consul; born at Gross-Thaiar in Moravia he became master at the Rennewege church school and gained a knowledge of Arabic and Ethiopian typography in the State Printing House, Vienna; coming to the Sudan in 1853 with Bishop Knoblehar's mission he was secretary to Knoblehar and teacher in the mission school at Khartoum; he later attached himself to T. von Heuglin's expedition and in 1862 was appointed Austro-Hungarian consul with orders to look after the welfare of the Catholic mission in the Sudan; he also acted for a period as consul of France and was Italian consular agent, 1876–8; a devout churchman he played the harmonium at the mission church at Khartoum on Sundays; his presence at official functions dressed in an astounding Austrian consular uniform of red coat with enormous epaulets, a long white waistcoat, and blue overalls, was an impressive sight in Khartoum; his long residence in the Sudan had led him to adopt native habits such as taking part in wedding dances; when already elderly he had the courage to marry his pupil, a half-caste Abyssinian girl of eighteen; he travelled with E. Marno in 1874–5 and wrote interesting reports of his explorations to several geographical societies of Europe; he was shut up in Khartoum during the siege and was killed by the Mahdists in the massacre which followed the taking of the city; he was a man of artistic temperament, a performer on the piano and organ, and was, as a young man, one of the founders of the Vienna Male Choir Society; on the other hand, F. L. James, who met him in Berber in 1877, called him 'a very garrulous German'; a son, Martin Albrecht Sebastien, was born in Khartoum in 1880.

Ḥārdallū. *See* MUḤAMMAD AḤMAD BEY ABŪ SIN.

Harff, Arnold, Ritter von (1471–1505), German traveller, born at Jülich near Cologne; he left Cologne in 1496 and travelled in Arabia, India, Sokotra, and Madagascar; from Cairo he ascended the valley of the Nile in an attempt to find its source; he returned to Europe in 1499 and died in Geldern: see *Die Pilgerfahrt des Ritters Arnold von Harff von Cöln durch . . . Aegypten . . . Aethiopien, Nubien* [&c.], ed. E. von Groote, Cöln, 1860, and an edition in English, *The pilgrimage of Arnold von Harff* [&c.], by M. Letts, Hakluyt Soc., 2nd series, xciv, 1947.

Harnier, Wilhelm von (1836–61), German explorer; born in Eichzell in Hesse, he arrived in Egypt in 1856 and in 1859 came to the Sudan by way of the Nubian desert, Abū Ḥamad, and Khartoum; he ascended the Blue Nile in a small boat to Roseires and afterwards returned to Egypt and Germany; after a short holiday he returned to the Sudan and with the Roman Catholic missionary, F. Morlang, explored the White Nile to a point upstream of Rejaf in 1861; he died at Holy Cross mission between Shambé and Bor as the result of an attack by a buffalo.

Harpur, Francis John (1860–1947), British Protestant medical missionary; born in Dublin where he graduated in medicine from Trinity College in 1885; for many years he was in charge of the Church Missionary Society's medical mission in Old Cairo; after visits to Arabia he worked in Sawākin in 1890 and in Omdurman, with L. H. (afterwards bishop) Gwynne, in 1899–1900; he retired in 1927 and died at Armagh, Northern Ireland.

Harrison, Sir Richard (1837–1931), British general; he entered the Royal Engineers, 1885, and in 1884 served as a colonel on the staff in the Nile campaign; he was quartermaster-general to the forces, 1897–8, and inspector-general of fortifications, 1898–1903; he published *Recollections* (1908).

Hartington, Marquess of. *See* CAVENDISH, SPENCER COMPTON, Marquess of Hartington and 8th Duke of Devonshire.

* **Hartmann, Robert** (1831–93), German naturalist of Blankenburg in the Hartz mountains; he accompanied the young Baron A. von Barnim in a journey across the Bayūda steppe from Old Dongola to Khartoum and up the Blue Nile to Fāzūghlī; his companion died at Roseires and Hartmann took the body to Europe for burial; he was later professor of anatomy at the University of Berlin; he died at Neubebelsberg; he wrote several studies on the people of the Nile valley.

Hārūn Muḥammad Tūrshain (–1899), Mahdist amīr, a Ta'ā'ishī by tribe, and a brother of the Khalīfa 'Abd Allāhi; he was killed with 'Abd Allāhi in the battle of Umm Dibaikarāt.

Ḥasab al-Nabī al-Ṭāhir (–1940), Sudanese notable, chief of the Tunjur of Dār Ḥamra in Dār Fūr; he was the first shartai from the present family and was appointed about 1885, in Mahdist times, in place of a first cousin who had died; he was in his turn succeeded by his eldest son Adam Ḥasab al-Nabī who died before the Anglo-Egyptian occupation of Dār Fūr; Adam was followed by his brother 'Abd Allāhi (died 1924) who was succeeded by 'Abd al-Raḥmān Ḥasab al-Nabī.

Ḥasab Rabbu (or **Rabbihi**) (*fl.* 1789), puppet sultan of Sennar during the final decadence of the sultanate; he ruled for a few months in 1789 in precarious authority, following Sultan Bādī V and being himself succeeded by Nawwār.

Ḥasab al-Rasūl (–1930), holy man of the family of the Awlād Muḥammad Badr of Umm Dibbān between Khartoum and Rufā'a and son of Shaikh Muḥammad Badr al-ʿUbaid; he was made khalīfa of the Jailānīya Islamic brotherhood in 1909 and in this capacity earned a wide reputation for saintliness; he conducted a large and flourishing school at Umm Dibbān and was specially interested in the treatment of the insane.

Ḥasan Pasha, Prince (1855–88), third son of the Khedive Ismāʿīl and brother of the Khedive Muḥammad Tawfīq; educated at Oxford where he received the honorary degree of D.C.L., 1872, he was for a short time a lieutenant of hussars in the German army; on his return to Egypt he joined the general staff; he served in the Egyptian-Abyssinian war in 1876 under the command of Muḥammad Rātib Pasha and was present at the battle of Gura; in October 1876 he temporarily succeeded Muḥammad Rātib Pasha as sirdār of the Egyptian army and in November was made minister of war; during the campaign of 1884–5 against the Mahdists he was appointed high commissioner for the Sudan, but his mission was rendered abortive by the evacuation of the Sudan in the spring of 1885.

Ḥasan al-ʿAbbādī (–1884), minor ʿAbbādī leader; he went over to the Mahdist cause in 1884 when Muḥammad Aḥmad al-Mahdī appointed him amīr of all Egypt; he joined the amīrs Maḥmūd Muḥammad and Aḥmad al-Hūdai in an attack on Dongola province and was killed in the battle of Kūrtī in September 1884 by a government force under Muṣṭafā Pasha Yāwar, then governor of Dongola.

Ḥasan Bey ʿAbd al-Munʿim (1834–1907), Egyptian merchant and magistrate; born at Isnā of ancient Arab stock (his family claiming descent from al-Ḥusain) he came to the Sudan in 1864 with his father who carried on trade with Egypt, the Sudan, and Abyssinia; his rising position in the Khartoum commercial community brought him to the notice of the Government by whom he was appointed a member, and later president, of the court of appeal of the Sudan, an appointment which led to the conferment on him of the title of bey; during the period of Mahdist rule he was one of the ten legal assessors appointed by the Mahdī in conformity with the precepts of Islamic law; after the establishment of the Condominium Government he was appointed a member of the board of trade; he died in Omdurman and was buried in Khartoum North.

Ḥasan ʿAlī Pasha Arnā'ūṭ (–1865), Albanian soldier in the service of Egypt; he was governor of Kordofan, 1857–9, with rank of mīrālai as his duties included the command of the regular infantry regiment based on al-Ubaiyaḍ; in 1861 he was governor of Tāka and for five weeks in 1862 again governor of Kordofan; by 1863 he had been promoted to mīrālai of the first grade and was commanding the 1st infantry regiment when he was promoted mīrlivā at 8,000 piastres a month and given command of the regular troops in the Sudan; in December 1864, on the eve of the military mutiny at Kassala, he was sent to take over command of the troops there; the revolt broke out and he was for some time besieged in the citadel which he and his loyal soldiers defended with courage and resource; he died in the town in the epidemic of fever (possibly typhus from the rotting corpses of the fallen) which followed the suppression of the mutiny.

al-Ḥasan ʿAlī Dikair (1875–1940), Shā'iqī notable of the Ḥannakāb sub-section of the Kadinkāb branch of his tribe; he was ʿumda of al-Duwaim near Merowe, a magistrate, and from 1936 president of the southern Shā'iqīya branch court.

Ḥasan Barī (–1932), Jaʿlī notable; ʿumda of al-Zaidāb.

Ḥasan al-Busrī ʿAbd Allāh al-Amīn (1865–1946), Rubāṭābī holy man whose father and grandfather were also men of religion; he was born on the island of al-Faqī al-Amīn near Jailī, between Khartoum and the Sixth Cataract.

Ḥasan Bey al-Dumyāṭī (–*c.* 1866), Egyptian engineer; he was in France learning geometry, algebra, and drawing, 1830–6, and later taught in government schools in Alexandria; in 1864 he was sent to the Sudan to make a survey for a projected railway between Sawākin and Kassala; his maps were used in a survey of Nile–Red Sea routes made by Ismāʿīl Bey Muṣṭafā al-Falakī (afterwards Pasha), 1867.

Ḥasan Hāshim (1825–79), physician; he studied in the Pharmaceutical School in Cairo and in 1847 was sent to France to continue his studies in pharmacy; later he took up medicine, specializing in obstetrics; returning to Egypt in 1862 he eventually became assistant director of the Cairo School of Medicine; on several occasions he was sent on special missions to the Sudan of which he was appointed chief medical officer in 1863.

Ḥasan ibn Ḥasūna ibn al-Ḥājj Mūsā (–1664), holy man; according to tradition his grandfather al-Ḥājj Mūsā came from Andalusia or Morocco and married a woman of the Masallamīya; he himself was born on the island of Kagoi (Kagog) between Omdurman and the Sixth Cataract and many miracles are credited to him; he made the pilgrimage to Makka and travelled for some twelve years in the Ḥijāz, Egypt, and Syria, returning at length to the Sudan where he set up at al-Dururba and Qantur al-Ḥumār in some state; he is said to have been held in honour by the Funj king, Bādī II abū Diqn wad Rubāṭ; he died from an explosion in his musket as he was attempting to shoot a crocodile; he founded the village of Wad Ḥasūna, about twenty-seven miles west of Abū Dalaiq, and is the eponymous ancestor of the Ḥasūnāb; he owned many rain reservoirs, traded, and was rich; his tomb (dangerous for liars to swear upon) is on the east bank of the Blue Nile opposite Masīd railway station.

Ḥasan Pasha Ḥilmī, called **al-Juwaisar** (–1883), mīrlivā of the Egyptian army and administrator; a soldier of Circassian origin he first came into prominence in the Sudan as a qā'immaqām during the mutiny of the 4th (Sudanese) regiment at Kassala, 1865, and as director of military works in the province of Tāka of which province he was made governor, 1866; transferred to the province of Kordofan he asked permission of Ja'far Pasha Maẓhar, then governor-general, to invade Dār Fūr, a project favoured by the viceroy Ismā'īl Pasha, but Ja'far, who preferred a less warlike policy towards the sultanate, refused, supporting his refusal by a quotation from the *Ḥadīth*; he was again governor of Kordofan on the eve of the Egyptian invasion of Dār Fūr; he took part in the invasion and was made governor of al-Fāshar, 1874; he was made general governor of Dār Fūr with rank of mīrlivā and grade of pasha, 1875; he commanded one of the two columns sent against the rebel Muḥammad Hārūn Saif al-Dīn in Jabal Sī; his contingent, heavily attacked, lost two-thirds of its strength of 1,300 men, but he retired safely with the remainder; sickness caused his transfer to Egypt, 1877, when 'Abd al-Rāziq Ḥaqqī Pasha temporarily took his place until the arrival of his short-lived successor, C. F. Rosset; he was a member of a committee formed in 1882 under the chairmanship of 'Abd al-Qādir Pasha Ḥilmī to supervise the administration of the Sudan during a critical period of the Mahdist revolt; he died a pensioner at Shubrā; he was a choleric man; the Sudanese disliked his arbitrary punishments and violent ways, but his activity while governor of Kordofan in cleaning the neglected reservoir at al-Ubaiyaḍ is still remembered.

Ḥasan Ḥilmī Bey al-Sammā' (1865–), Egyptian soldier; born in Cairo he was commissioned in 1883 and saw active service with the Nile expedition, 1884–5, having, early in 1884, left Khartoum shortly after General Gordon Pasha's arrival; in 1886 he was promoted yūzbāshī and transferred to the 13th Sudanese battalion at Wādī Ḥalfā where he assisted in frontier defence; in 1888 he joined the 10th Sudanese battalion and took part in the battles of Jummaiza (Gemmeiza), 1888, and of Argīn and Tūshkī (Toski), 1889; he was at Tokar in 1894 and took part in the Sawākin expedition of 1896 and fought at Taroi; later in the year he served in the Dongola campaign; returning to Sawākin in 1897 for a short period he was transferred to Berber to the 18th battalion with the rank of binbāshī; he took part in several minor engagements after the battle of Omdurman, 1898, and in 1901 left the Sudan for reasons of health and later served as assistant adjutant-general in Cairo with rank of mīrālai; at one time he had three brothers holding commissions in the Egyptian army.

Ḥasan Bey Ḥusnī al-Bārūdī (*c.* 1805–), soldier of the Egyptian army, a son of 'Abd Allāh Bey, one of Muḥammad 'Alī Pasha's Circassian officers; trained in the artillery he served in the Sudan and was governor of Dongola together with the northern part of the province of Berber-Ja'līyīn, 1846–51; al-Liwā' Maḥmūd Sāmī al-Bārūdī Pasha, one of the leaders of the Egyptian Nationalist movement of 1882 and a poet, was his son.

Ḥasan Pasha Ibrāhīm al-Shallālī (–1884), liwā' of the Egyptian army; during the siege of Khartoum he commanded the government troops defending the 'eastern palace' on the site of what is now

Khartoum North; during the course of a sortie commanded by Sa'īd Pasha Ḥusain al-Jimī'ābī against a Mahdist force under the Faqī Muḍāwī 'Abd al-Raḥmān, he and Sa'īd Pasha betrayed their own force to the enemy; both officers were tried by court-martial for murder and treachery and were executed.

Ḥasan Kanbal Ḥamad (*c.* 1845–1933), Bidairī notable of the Ṭaraifī clan; born at Kūrtī, the seat of the family, his father was a prominent trader in Turkish times; on his father's death in the sack of Kūrtī by a Turkish force in 1884 he became head merchant of the place; like his father hostile to Mahdism he supplied the unsuccessful Khartoum relief expedition of 1884–5 with provisions and transport; on the withdrawal of the expedition in 1885 the Mahdists occupied the district and he was afterwards beaten and imprisoned at Dongola by the amīr Yūnus al-Dikaim; eventually ransomed by his family he returned to Kūrtī where he plied what was left of his trade and (as his father before him) was prominent among the local soothsayers; in 1896, after the defeat of the Mahdists at Ḥafīr, he met H. A. Macdonald Pasha and surrendered Kūrtī to him; his trade and farms now prospered and, though too deeply committed in commerce to take a whole-time part in local government, his influence in local affairs was considerable; his brother 'Umar is the present 'umda of Kūrtī.

Ḥasan Khalīfa (fl. 1840–51), 'Abbādī notable, nephew of Baraka wad al-Ḥājj Muḥammad al-'Abbādī who was killed by government troops in 1840; fearing arrest he went to Egypt where he persuaded Muḥammad 'Alī Pasha to grant him the concessionary rights over the desert road between Korosko and Berber including the right to levy a tax of 3 rials for each camel making the journey; on his return to the Sudan he attacked and killed all the 'Āmrāb Bishārīyīn whom he found at Oneib well; the Prussian archaeologist K. R. Lepsius recorded that about 1841 some Bishārīyīn had murdered a party of Turkish soldiers and that, as protector of the road, Ḥasan Khalīfa then killed forty Bishārīyīn; 'Abd al-Laṭīf Pasha 'Abd Allāh, governor-general, obtained permission of the Egyptian Government to dismiss him and appoint his brother Ḥusain Khalīfa (afterwards Pasha) to the shaikhdom of the Desert Road, 1851.

Ḥasan Bey Khalīfa (–1900), 'Abbādī notable; he was head of the 'Abābda in the last days of Egyptian rule until Berber fell to the Mahdists in 1884; appointed an amīr by the Mahdists he then lived at Abū Ḥamad as head of those nomad 'Abābda who owed allegiance to the Mahdist cause; towards the end of the Mahdist régime the Khalīfa 'Abd Allāhi imprisoned him on suspicion of disloyalty; he died in Khartoum shortly after the Anglo-Egyptian occupation; a son, 'Abd al-Ghaffār, well known as superintendent of Sudan railways dock labourers at Port Sudan, died at Port Sudan in 1945.

Ḥasan Khalīfa (–1931), nāẓir of the Hawwāwīr, an arabicized tribe of Berber origin living in northern Kordofan; he was a magistrate and died at Abū 'Uruq.

Ḥasan Kūshī (*fl.* 1520), commander of a force of Bosnian soldiers in the army of the Ottoman sultan, Salīm I, which penetrated the northern Sudan as far as Dongola and built and garrisoned the fortresses of Aswān, Ibrīm, and Sai; on his death the force was led by Ibn Janbalān who defeated a Funj army near Ḥannak.

Ḥasan al-Maʻarak (*fl.* 1300), notable of the Rufāʻa Arabs who came up the Nile valley after the fall of the Christian kingdom of Dongola; he is said to have been of ʻIrāqī origin and to have settled with his family on the White Nile behind Kawa; from him the ʻArakīyīn are descended.

Ḥasan Makkī (–1931), notable of the Ḥasūnāb family who trace their origin to Ḥasan ibn Ḥasūna, the holy man of Andalusia (d. 1664) who married into the local Masallamīya tribe; he was ʻumda of Wad Ḥasūna village west of Abū Dilaiq in the Buṭāna; he died at Abū Dilaiq.

Ḥasan Muḥammad Khalīfa al-ʻAbbādī (1844–99), Mahdist amīr; born at Berber of the Milaikāb branch of the ʻAbābda Arabs he was the son of Ḥusain Pasha Khalīfa, last governor of the province of Berber and Dongola under the Egyptian Government; in 1894, suspecting his loyalty, the Khalīfa ʻAbd Allāhi banished him to Rejaf on a charge of having been in secret communication with his cousin, Ṣāliḥ Bey Khalīfa, the commander of irregular troops holding Murrāt wells; he returned from exile after the Anglo-Egyptian occupation but died at Omdurman a few days after his arrival from the south.

Ḥasan Muḥammad ʻUthmān (–1934), Shā'iqī notable; ʻumda of al-Zūma near Merowe, and a magistrate.

al-Ḥasan Muḥammad ʻUthmān al-Mīrghanī (–1869), son and successor of al-Saiyid Muḥammad ʻUthmān al-Mīrghanī I, founder of the Khatmīya brotherhood; born in Bāra he assumed the leadership of the brotherhood in the Sudan on his father's death in 1851; he lived mostly at Khatmīya near Kassala, where his father eventually settled, and had great influence in the eastern Sudan; his part in supporting the government during the Kassala military mutiny of 1865 after his attempts to win over the mutineers by mediation had failed probably prevented a still more serious outbreak; he died at Khatmīya; his tomb was destroyed by the Mahdists in 1885 during the assault on the garrison of Kassala but was restored after the Anglo-Egyptian Government occupied the town; at his death his son Muḥammad ʻUthmān al-Mīrghanī II, called al-Ṣughaiyar, succeeded to the leadership of the brotherhood; his daughter al-Sharīfa Nafīsa married al-Saiyid Maḥjūb al-Mīrghanī.

al-Ḥasan ibn Muḥammad al-Wazzān al-Zaiyātī (–1552), Moorish traveller from Cordoba who journeyed in North Africa and Asia Minor from 1492; falling into the hands of Venetian pirates he spent twenty years in Rome where he accepted Christianity; he later returned to Africa and died at Tunis; he wrote an account of his travels in Italian in 1526 which was printed in 1550 and was for long the chief source of information available in Europe on the interior of North Africa; there is a brief account of Nubia by him, available in English, entitled *History and Description of Africa*, edited by the Hakluyt Society, 1896.

Ḥasan Mūsā al-'Aqqād (fl. 1870–85), Egyptian merchant, a member of the trading family of 'Aqqād which played an important part in the commerce of the Sudan under the Egyptian Government; a man of some wealth he was twice banished to the Sudan; on the second occasion he had been condemned during the reign of Ismā'īl Pasha to perpetual exile at Fashoda; there is a family legend that he had incurred the Khedivial displeasure through refusal to surrender a plot of land; he was later pardoned through the influence of Aḥmad Pasha 'Urābī whom he supported during the revolt of 1882; on the failure of the revolt he was tried and banished to Muṣawwa' where later the Italians, who occupied the port in 1885, sentenced him to death, but reprieved him and allowed him to return to Egypt; his activities during the revolt of 'Urābī Pasha were obscure; at his trial evidence was brought to prove that he had accepted money from Prince Muḥammad 'Abd al-Ḥalīm, pretender to the Egyptian throne, for advancing the latter's claims, but that he pocketed the funds; the above particulars of his life have been drawn from secondary sources, some not above suspicion, and should be accepted with caution.

* **Ḥasan Pasha Rā'fat Asitānlī** (*fl.* 1843–50), mīrlivā of the Egyptian army; he was appointed governor of Dongola (with the northern part of the province of Berber) at the end of 1843 during a restaffing of the governorates of the Sudan ordered by Muḥammad 'Alī Pasha at this time; in 1844 he was temporarily transferred to the governorate of Khartoum in place of Muḥammad al-Amīn Pasha al-Arnā'ūṭ who went to Sennar; re-transferred to Dongola province he was discharged in 1846, laid off on half pay, and replaced by Ḥasan Bey Ḥusnī; in 1850 the Cairo Government was inquiring into his private financial affairs which were in confusion.

Ḥasan Rājab (–1822), tribal notable of the Hāmaj rulers of the Funj dominions and a cousin of Muḥammad wad 'Adlān, the king-maker, whom his men murdered on the eve of the arrival in Sennar of the army of Ismā'īl Pasha in 1821; Ismā'īl released him from prison and he accompanied the Egyptian expedition to Fāzūghlī, raiding the country along the River Yābūs with a force of Hāmaj cavalry early in 1822; later in the year, in the general revolt of the Sudanese following the murder of Ismā'īl at Shendi by Mak Nimr, he rose in insurrection; he and Arbāb wad Dafa' Allāh were attacked by an Egyptian force under Muḥammad Sa'īd Aghā at Abū Shōka where he was killed.

Ḥasan Riḍwān Pasha (1845–), farīq of the Egyptian army; he was born in Cairo the son of Shaikh Aḥmad Fā'id, a legal notable; in 1871 he joined the artillery school and as a junior officer fought in the Egyptian army at Tel el-Kebir, 1882, and was wounded; he entered the new Egyptian army, 1883, and was posted as officer commanding the artillery at Aswān; after serving on the staff of Lord Wolseley during the Nile campaign of 1884–5 he was promoted binbāshī and given command of the Egyptian artillery on the southern frontier; he fought in the battles of Kosha, Jinnis (Giniss), and Tūshkī (Toski); promoted qā'immaqām, 1890, he was appointed inspector-general of Egyptian artillery; mīrālai in 1895 he was governor successively of Beni Swef and of Gharbīya, having been promoted first to liwā' and later to farīq.

* **al-Ḥasan S'ad al-'Abbādī** (1844–1907), Mahdist amīr and author; a member of the 'Abābda Arab tribe he was born at Berber and educated by Shaikh Muḥammad al-Khair 'Abd Allāh Khūjalī, the future Mahdist amīr of Berber and the Ja'līyīn; on the outbreak of the Mahdist revolt he went to Kordofan to join Muḥammad Aḥmad al-Mahdī who appointed him amīr of Dār Rubāṭāb and part of the Atbai, which territory he ruled from Abū Ḥamad; during a later reorganization of the Mahdist forces the Khalīfa 'Abd Allāhi transferred him to Omdurman where he was made a religious notable; a pamphlet by him, entitled *Risālat al-'Abbādī*, was printed about 1893 on the primitive lithographic press used by the Mahdist Government at Omdurman; on the Anglo-Egyptian occupation he was appointed an Islamic judge; he died in the Ḥijāz while making the pilgrimage.

Ḥasan Ṣādiq Bey (–1885), qā'immaqām of the Egyptian army; he was governor of Sennar on the outbreak of the Mahdist revolt in the Jazīra and, with 'Abd al-Nūr Bey, the officer commanding troops, organized the defence of the town which was besieged in 1884; during the siege, owing to some disagreement among the officers, he was deposed and made a prisoner in his house while the command devolved on 'Abd al-Nūr Bey who not only successfully defended the town but attacked the Mahdists in the neighbourhood; as a result of a bold plan of action which he proposed, he was reinstated in command but was shortly afterwards killed while leading a sortie against the besieging force; though he was at one time at variance with his chief of staff the two men rivalled each other in courage, and Sennar, the last of all the Egyptian fortresses in the valley of the Sudan Nile to fall to the Mahdists, did not surrender until August 1885.

Ḥasan Bey Salāma Jarkas (*fl.* 1859–61), governor of the combined provinces of Khartoum and Sennar with authority over the muḥāfiẓate of the White Nile, 1859–61; he succeeded Arakīl Bey al-Armanī who died in Khartoum and was himself succeeded on his recall to Egypt by Muḥammad Rāsikh Bey; little is known of him beyond the comment of the Sudanese annalist that he was coarse and rough, but pious and temperate, in his ways.

Ḥasan al-Shādhilī abū'l-Ḥasan 'Alī (*c.* 1196–*c.* 1258), Islamic theologian, propagator of the tenets of the Shādhilīya brotherhood, simplicity of ritual being the keynote of his teaching; he was born probably at Ceuta and died somewhere in the Atbai while returning from a pilgrimage to Makka; the place of his burial is disputed; it was perhaps at Halus, thirty miles inland from Ḥalaib, perhaps at 'Īd al-Ḥashāb, half-way between Ḥalaib and al-Dirr.

al-Ḥasan Sulaimān (1746–*c.* 1830), last of the semi-independent rulers of Nubia, son of the kāshif Sulaimān whom he succeeded not long before W. R. Hamilton, the English traveller, arrived in Nubia in 1801; the line was descended from the Bosnian family of Kūshī or Kussa whose first representative Ḥasan was originally established by Sultan Salīm I in the sixteenth century; al-Ḥasan Sulaimān was driven out, apparently by the Mamelukes on their flight from Egypt after the massacres of 1811; with his two brothers he re-established himself at al-Dirr in 1813 whence he moved to Ishkid about 1816; he was removed finally from his post in 1818 by the Egyptian Government which was preparing the invasion of the Sudan and desired to safeguard its lines of communication.

Ḥasan al-Ṭaiyib (–1937), Shā'iqī notable, 'umda of the Ḥamdāb sub-section of the Kadinkāb Shā'iqīya in the district of Merowe.

Ḥasan Bey 'Uthmān (–1885), officer of the Egyptian army; he took part in the defence of Sennar against the Mahdists and was killed in a sortie from the town.

Ḥasanain Pasha. *See* AḤMAD MUḤAMMAD ḤASANAIN PASHA, SIR.

Hāshim Idrīs (*c.* 1873–1945), tribal leader, sultan of Dār Qimr in Dār Fūr, succeeding his father Idrīs abū Bukr in 1935; he was the thirteenth sultan of the dynasty founded by Jammār ibn Ḥasab Allāh; because of attacks by 'Alī Dīnār, sultan of Dār Fūr, he and his father were at one time forced to take refuge in Dār Zaghāwa; he was later taken prisoner by the Fūr forces and was an exile in al-Fāshar where he remained till 1913; after the defeat of 'Alī Dīnār in 1916 he submitted to the Condominium Government and Dār Qimr was incorporated in the new Anglo-Egyptian province of Dār Fūr.

Hāshim wad 'Isāwī al-Musaba'āwī (–*c.* 1812), sultan of the Musaba'āt Fūr who ruled in Kordofan and a direct descendant of Muḥammad Tumsāḥ, traditional founder of the Musaba'āwī dynasty; he warred with the local representatives of the Hāmaj overlords of Sennar, who dominated northern and central Kordofan, attacking their chief, Muḥammad abū Likailak the Hāmaj viceroy, in 1772; failing to dislodge Muḥammad abū Likailak he took advantage of the latter's death in 1776 to advance once again; now all-powerful in Kordofan he attacked the sultanate of Dār Fūr with an army of 10,000 men, chiefly Danāqla, Shā'iqīya, Kabbābīsh, and Rizaiqāt, in 1785; Dār Fūr at the time was weakened by a war with Wadā'i but, when peace was made between them, the Dār Fūr sultan Muḥammad Tīrāb successfully counter-attacked, driving Hāshim out of Dār Fūr, through Kordofan, and finally over the Nile near Omdurman; Hāshim returned to Kordofan on the heels of Muḥammad Tīrāb's retiring army and seems again to have been driven out by the forces of Dār Fūr; in 1791 he returned a second time to Kordofan where, after waging war with varying success, he was finally beaten; escaping to the north he took refuge in Jabal Jilif until driven out by the Shā'iqīya when he sought refuge with Nimr, king of the Ja'līyīn of Shendi; most of the recorded events of his life and death are uncertain and contradictory; he is said to have been implicated in a conspiracy with Nimr's brother and to have been killed by Nimr on its discovery.

* **Ḥasīb al-Ṣiddīq** (*c.* 1806–*c.* 1886), religious teacher of the family of the Majādhīb whose spiritual centre is at al-Dāmar; born at Qūz al-Funj near Berber he studied at the University of al-Azhar in Cairo, in Makka, and in Zibid in the Yaman; returning to the Sudan he was one of the teachers of Muḥammad Aḥmad al-Mahdī; he died at Qūz al-Funj.

Ḥassān Aḥmad Bey abū Sin (–1931), son of Aḥmad Bey 'Awad al-Karīm abū Sin, governor of Khartoum and Sennar (d. 1870); he was 'umda of Rufā'a where he died.

Hawker Bey, Claude Julian (1867–1936), British brigadier-general; he joined the British army in 1887 and from 1899 to 1909 was attached to the Egyptian army in which he commanded the 10th Sudanese Camel Corps with rank of mīralai; he was in 1907 appointed governor of the Red Sea province; in 1910 he joined the Turkish gendarmerie; he served in the First World War and from 1916 to 1918 was military governor of Baghdad; on the conclusion of peace he served on two European plebiscite commissions.

Hawkshaw, Sir John (1811–91), British engineer; an opponent of I. K. Brunel whose broad-gauge railways and track-laying methods he criticized; in 1863 he reported favourably on the site proposed by De Lesseps for the Suez Canal; he was requested by the Egyptian Government in 1865 to draw up a scheme to open the First Cataract to river traffic throughout the year; he sent out a party of engineers to Aswān in that year and on their investigations recommended a ship canal round the cataract, a project criticized by Sir John Fowler in 1873.

* **Hay, Robert** (1799–1863), British Egyptologist; during the years 1826–38 he was a leading member of an archaeological expedition to Egypt when he visited Sennar; his wife, a Cretan Greek whom he had bought as a slave and had educated in England, accompanied him on his travels.

Hayes-Sadler Bey, Walter (1866–1931), British soldier and administrator; commissioned to the Royal Scots Fusiliers in 1887 he was promoted captain in 1896; in 1898 he was seconded to the Egyptian army and in 1900 to the Sudan Government with the rank of binbāshī; he was governor and commandant of Fashoda, 1900, governor of Ḥalfā province, 1901–4, and director of customs, 1905–14, when he retired; he was promoted major in 1907 and mīrālai in 1912; he died at Dinard, France.

Haymes, Henry Evered (1872–1904), British military surgeon; he was commissioned to the Royal Army Medical Corps in 1899 and was promoted captain in 1902; he was seconded to the Egyptian army in 1899 and took part in the reoccupation of the Baḥr al-Ghazāl province; he died at Tonj of wounds received during an expedition in the country of the Azande.

Heath, Henry Newport Charles (1860–1915), British major-general; commissioned in 1881 he fought in the Egyptian war of 1882 and in the Nile expedition of 1884–5 in which he was present at the battle of Kirbikān, 1885; promoted captain in 1889 he later served in the South African war of 1899–1902.

Heath, John Macclesfield (1843–1911), British soldier; he joined the army in 1860 and was on the staff of al-farīq W. Hicks Pasha, but was not in the doomed army of Kordofan in 1883; he served in the Sudan in 1884 and retired in 1886 with rank of lieutenant-colonel.

* **Hedenborg, Johan** (1787–1865), Swedish physician and traveller; born in the province of Östergötland he was educated at Upsala; in 1825 he was stationed in Constantinople as medical attendant to the Swedish legation and here he began the study of natural history, antiquities, and oriental languages; he made a journey to Egypt, Syria, and Anatolia, making valuable collections, 1830–2; in 1833 he returned to Egypt and, after various travels on the Red Sea coast and in Sinai, he set out in 1834 up the Nile valley through Nubia and Dongola to Kordofan and Sennar; he and E. W. P. S. Rüppel were among the first Europeans to explore the White Nile in the region of Khartoum; his attempt to ascend the Blue Nile valley was prevented by difficulty at the mountains of the Funj near the Abyssinian frontier; worn out by hardship he returned to Egypt in 1836 bringing with him rich natural history collections which he presented to the Riksmuseum in Stockholm and ethnographical collections to the University of Upsala; he spent the greater part of his subsequent life at Rhodes in study; he died at Florence; he published an account of his travels, including his journeys in the Sudan, in Stockholm in 1843.

Hemprich, Wilhelm Friedrich (1796–1825), German naturalist; born in Glatz he joined a medical detachment in the Prussian artillery in 1814 and in 1815 saw service against Napoleon in France; discharged from the army in 1817 he resumed his medical studies which the war had interrupted; he accompanied a scientific expedition led by H. C. M. Baron von Minutoli to the northern Sudan ascending the Nile valley to Ambuqōl in 1821–3 along with C. G. Ehrenberg; he died of fever at Muṣawwaʿ during an exploration of the Red Sea coast; he collaborated with Ehrenberg in the preparation of a massive zoological survey of Nubia and Dongola (Berlin, 1828–45) in which many Sudan birds were described for the first time.

Henniker, Sir Frederick, 2nd Baronet (1793–1825), British traveller; in the winter of 1819–20 he ascended the Nile as far as Abū Simbel which he explored with all a tourist's delight; he wrote a breezy account of his journey, published in 1823, reprinted in 1824.

Henry Pasha, St. George Charles Henry (1860–1909), British major-general and liwā' of the Egyptian army; commissioned to the 8th Foot in 1880 he was seconded to the Egyptian army in 1896; he served throughout the Dongola and Nile campaigns, 1896–9, commanding the Camel Corps in the battle of Umm Dibaikarāt; after fighting in the South African war, 1900–1, he returned to the Khedivial service and in 1902–3 was governor of Kassala province; promoted liwā' in 1905, he was from 1903 to 1907 adjutant-general of the Egyptian army and officer commanding the Khartoum military district.

Henty, George Alfred (1832–1902), British journalist and novelist; after serving as a volunteer in the Crimean war, 1854–5, he adopted the career of journalist and was the correspondent of the *Standard* newspaper of London in several wars including the Abyssinian campaign of 1867–8; he published many novels including two books for young people on the Sudan: *The Dash for Khartoum: a Tale of the Nile Expedition* (1892) and *With Kitchener in the Sudan: a Story of Atbara and Omdurman* (1903), which enjoyed great juvenile popularity in their day.

Heqanekht (*fl. c.* 1250 B.C.), Egyptian viceroy of Ethiopia sometime during the reign of the XIXth Dynasty King Rameses II (1298 B.C.–1232 B.C.) who built the rock temple of Abū Simbel.

Herbert, St. Leger Algernon (1850–85), British journalist; educated at Wadham College, Oxford, of which he was a scholar, he was in the Canadian civil service, 1875–8; he was thereafter private secretary to Sir G. J. (afterwards Lord) Wolseley in Cyprus and South Africa, correspondent to *The Times* newspaper, and secretary to the Transvaal commission, 1881–2; he joined the staff of the *Morning Post* and was correspondent to this newspaper in the campaign against 'Uthmān abū Bakr Diqna (Osman Digna) on the Red Sea coast, 1884, being wounded in the battle of Tamai; while accompanying the Nile expedition as a member of the staff of Sir H. Stewart he was killed at Abū Kurū (Qubbāt) near Matamma.

Herihor (*fl.* 1090 B.C.), Egyptian high priest of Amon and viceroy of Ethiopia approximately between 1100 B.C. and 1090 B.C. under Rameses XI, XXth Dynasty king of Egypt; he himself became king about 1090 B.C. and it would appear that he assumed the office of viceroy merely as a preliminary move in the assumption of the kingship; he was the last of a line of Egyptian viceroys who ruled the northern Sudan for about 558 years.

Herodotus (*c.* 480 B.C.–*c.* 425 B.C.), Greek historian, born at Halicarnassus, a Greek colony on the coast of Asia Minor; he travelled much in the countries of the eastern Mediterranean including Egypt as far south as the First Cataract; his great work on Egypt (books 2 and 3), written about 457 B.C., contains references to Nubia and the source of the Nile.

* **Heuglin, Theodor von** (1824–76), German naturalist and Arctic explorer; born at Hirschlanden in Württemberg he was in 1852 appointed Austro-Hungarian consular agent in Khartoum; he explored the Bayūda and the region round Khartoum in 1853; with K. Reitz he went to Gedaref and on to Lake Tana in Abyssinia and to the country of Tembien which he explored; Reitz died on the way back at Dōka between Gallabat and Gedaref and Heuglin, accompanied by E. Schubert and H. Steudner, returned to Khartoum where he undertook consular duties in place of Reitz; in 1856 he was again in the Bayūda, and on the Red Sea coast in 1857; he was a member of Miss A. P. F. Tinné's expedition to the Upper White Nile in 1863 and in 1864 returned to Europe by way of Berber and Sawākin with the survivors of the expedition; he explored Spitzbergen in 1870–1; he wrote much on the geography and zoology of the Sudan.

Hewett, Sir William Nathan Wrighte (1834–88), British vice-admiral; a midshipman in 1851 he fought in the Crimean war in 1854 when he won the Victoria Cross; after service in several parts of the world he was in 1884 in command of British naval operations in the Red Sea and civil and military governor of the port of Sawākin; he assisted in the defence of the port against the Mahdist force under the amīr 'Uthmān abū Bakr Diqna (Osman Digna) in 1884 and later undertook a mission to the king of Abyssinia to arrange the evacuation of the Egyptian garrisons in the Sudan through Abyssinian territory; returning to Britain he commanded the Channel fleet, 1886–8.

Hidalgo, Stefano (1848–1918), Italian general; born at Malaga, Spain, he was commissioned to the Italian bersaglieri, 1869; while a captain serving in Eritrea he commanded a force of Eritrean troops who beat back a Mahdist attack on Agordat by a victory at Serobeti, 1892; he took part in the Italian capture of Kassala, 1894, and commanded the town, 1896; he died at Turin; he wrote *Undici mesi a Cassala* (Turin, 1910).

Hickman Bey, Thomas Edgecumbe (1859–1930), British brigadier-general; he joined the army in 1881 and was promoted major in 1896; he served in the Egyptian Camel Corps in the campaign of 1884–5 to attempt the relief of Khartoum; he was at Sawākin 1887–8 and back on the Egyptian southern frontier in 1889 in the operations against the Mahdist army led by the amīr 'Abd al-Raḥmān wad al-Najūmī; he served through the Dongola and Nile campaigns of 1896–9; he commanded the 12th Sudanese battalion in operations round Gedaref in 1898 and was present at the battles of Jadīd and Umm Dibaikarāt, 1899; promoted brigadier-general in 1902, he served in the First World War; he sat as a member of Parliament in the Unionist cause, 1910–22.

Hicks Pasha, William (1830–83), British soldier; he joined the Bombay army in 1849 and saw service in India and in the Anglo-Abyssinian war of 1867–8; having resigned from the Indian army in 1880 with rank of honorary colonel he was in 1883 appointed a farīq of the

Egyptian army and given command of a field force intended to operate against the Mahdists who had now overrun Kordofan and were threatening the Egyptian garrisons in the Nile valley; the general command of the troops in the Sudan fell to Sulaimān Pasha Niyāzī while ʿAlā al-Dīn Pasha was made governor-general for civil affairs; he arrived in the Sudan, via Sawākin and Berber, accompanied by a staff of Egyptian and European officers; on their arrival in Khartoum the intensive training of the army was begun; in April he defeated a Mahdist force at Jabalain; finding that he could not work well as chief of staff to Sulaimān Pasha Niyāzī he threatened to resign unless he were given a free hand; Sulaimān Pasha was thereupon transferred to the Red Sea littoral as governor and commander of troops there; Hicks was made commander-in-chief of the troops about to take the field; finally, in September, he was joined by ʿAlā al-Dīn Pasha and the army began its fatal march into Kordofan with al-Ubaiyaḍ as its immediate objective; demoralized and badly disciplined the army was constantly harrassed by the enemy and, suffering greatly from lack of water, was attacked and massacred by the Mahdists at Shaikān (Kashgil), near al-Rāhad; he and all his staff were killed; the cause of the tragedy has been the subject of controversy; though personally a brave man, his decision to leave the Nile valley (though desired by the Egyptian Government unacquainted with local conditions) was open to criticism on military grounds.

Higginbotham, Edwin (-1873), British civil engineer; he joined the Egyptian Government service in 1865 and in 1869 was appointed chief engineer to Sir S. W. Baker's expedition to Equatoria; he supervised the carriage of two steamers in sections over the Nubian desert via Korosko, 1869–70, and later erected the twin-screw steamer *Khedive* at Gondokoro, the first twin-screw steamer to navigate the White Nile, launched 1872; he died at Gondokoro in the following year.

Ḥijāzī ibn Maʿīn (*fl. c.* 1474), founder of the town of Arbajī in the southern Jazīra; he is said to have been a Ḥaḍarī, a term of some ambiguity which may mean simply a settler from outside the Sudan; he was possibly a slave trader from the Ḥijāz who may have made Arbajī his collecting station.

Hill Bey, Sir Henry Blyth, 6th Bart. (1867–1929), British soldier; he was seconded to the Egyptian army and fought in the Nile campaign, 1898; he was governor of Berber, 1904–6, and of the Baḥr al-Ghazāl, 1907; he was promoted mīrālai in 1905; retiring from the British army in 1908 with the rank of major he returned to active service in the First World War.

Ḥimaida Khamīs Aḥmad (-1943), nāẓir of the Missīrīya Zurruq Arabs of Kordofan since 1933; a magistrate, his seat was at Laghawa during the rains; he died in the gum forest near Abū Zabad.

Hodgson, Clement Gaukroger (1875–1944), British mechanical engineer; born in Durham he was in 1898 appointed an engineer in the railways department of the Egyptian Government and in 1899 was posted to the Sudan Military Railway; in 1906 he was promoted locomotive superintendent, a designation later changed to chief mechanical engineer; he held this post until his retirement from the Sudan civil service in 1921; he was then made consulting and inspecting mechanical engineer to the Sudan Government, and for a period was director of the State-sponsored Kassala Railway Company; he had a marked influence on Sudan railways locomotive design and maintenance for forty years.

Holled Smith, Sir Charles. *See* SMITH, SIR CHARLES HOLLED.

Holroyd, Arthur Todd (–1888), British physician and traveller; in 1836–7, following the explorations of E. W. P. S. Rüppel, he ascended the Nile to Wādī Ḥalfā and thence in December 1836 he started for Khartoum via Dongola and the Bayūda; from Khartoum he went by river to Sennar, returning to Khartoum by land through Wad Madanī and Manāqil, giving a favourable account of the productive possibilities of the Jazīra in cotton, indigo, tobacco, sugar, and grain, if irrigated by canals, thus foreshadowing the present Jazīra irrigation scheme; he then went to al-Ubaiyaḍ and thence to Khartoum; on his return to Egypt he got Sir J. Bowring to intercede with Muḥammad ʿAlī Pasha for the abolition of the practice of paying his troops in the Sudan with slaves instead of cash; he spent his later life in New South Wales, Australia; his 'Notes on a journey to Kordofan in 1836–7' appeared in the *Journal of the Royal Geographical Society* of London (1839), vol. 9.

* **Hood, Sir Horace Lambert Alexander** (1870–1916), British rear-admiral; he entered the Royal Navy in 1883 and was promoted commander in 1898; he commanded the armed river steamer *Nāẓir* in the Nile campaign, 1897–8; he was killed in the naval battle of Jutland in the First World War when his flagship, the battle cruiser *Invincible*, was blown up.

Hopkinson Pasha, Henry Charles Barwick (1867–1946), British soldier; joining the Seaforth Highlanders, 1891, he served in the 12th battalion, Egyptian infantry, and later in the camel corps, in the campaigns of 1896–8, and was wounded at Omdurman; he was director-general of the Alexandria municipality, 1917–23.

Hori I (*fl. c.* 1190 B.C.), Egyptian viceroy of Ethiopia who held office from approximately 1203 B.C. to 1180 B.C. during the reigns of Siptah, Setnekht, and Rameses III, kings of Egypt.

Hori II (*fl. c.* 1170 B.C.), Egyptian viceroy of Ethiopia; son of the viceroy Hori I he held office during the reigns of the Egyptian XXth Dynasty kings Rameses III, Rameses IV, and Rameses V, roughly between 1180 B.C. and 1160 B.C.

Hoskins, George Alexander (–1863), British archaeologist; in 1833 he travelled from Cairo by way of Aswān and Korosko over the Nubian desert to Abū Ḥamad, Berber, and the pyramids of Meroë to Shendi; here he crossed the Nile and went over the Bayūda to Jabal

Barkal, Dongola, and Wādī Ḥalfā, making archaeological drawings and notes throughout his tour; he wrote *Travels in Ethiopia* (1835).

Howard, Sir Francis (1848–1930), British major-general; born in Berlin he joined the Rifle Brigade in 1866; he commanded a battalion of the Rifle Brigade, 1894–8, when he served in the Nile campaign of 1898, fighting with his battalion at the battle of Omdurman; he commanded a brigade in the South African war and later occupied high administrative posts in England, retiring from the army in 1909; he returned to active service during the First World War as inspector of infantry; he published *Reminiscences, 1848–90* (1924).

Howard Bey, Francis James Leigh (1870–1942), British colonel; born in Delhi of a soldier father he entered the army in 1890 and from 1895 to 1905 was seconded to the Egyptian army; he fought throughout the Dongola and Nile campaigns of 1896–9 and was governor of Sawākin, 1904–5; he served in the First World War.

Howard, Hubert (1871–1898), British journalist; son of the eighth earl of Carlisle; he fought with the Cuban rebels against the Spanish and was wounded in the Matabele rebellion; he joined the Nile expedition, 1898, as a war correspondent for the *New York Herald* and (jointly with Colonel F. W. Rhodes) for *The Times* of London; after taking part in the charge of the 17th Lancers at Omdurman he was accidentally killed by a shell after the battle.

Hudson, Sir John (1833–93), British lieutenant-general; he was commissioned in 1855 and served in Persia, the Indian mutiny, Abyssinia, and Afghanistan, and in 1885–6 he commanded the Indian contingent in the Sawākin campaign; he was commander-in-chief in Bombay for a few months before his death.

Ḥūlū (*fl. c.* 1470), ancestor of the Ḥalāwīyīn Arabs, a grandson of Muḥammad Rāfaʿi, the common ancestor of all the Rufāʿa; in his time the Ḥalāwīyīn, then a wholly nomadic tribe, wandered over the south of the Jazīra.

Ḥunain Muḥammad al-Izairiq (1872–1927), religious shaikh of Sharīfī origin; he was born and died in Berber where he was the chief khalīfa of the Khatmīya brotherhood.

* **Hunt, Leigh S . . . J . . .** (1855–1933), American pioneer of irrigation, colonization, and mining projects; born at Larwill, Indiana, he began his career as a teacher in his native state and was president of the Iowa Agricultural College, 1884–6; he then bought the newspaper *Post-Intelligencer* of Seattle; in 1893 he was engaged in gold mining in northern Korea; he visited the Sudan in 1903 and became convinced of the cotton-growing possibilities of the country by the use of irrigation from the Nile; in 1904 he acquired land at al-Zaidāb in association with the Sudan Plantations Syndicate; this enterprise, derided by residents in Egypt as 'Hunt's folly', demonstrated successfully the success of growing cotton commercially in the Sudan; he was the first since Aḥmad

Mumtiz Pasha to introduce the culture of long-staple cotton to the valley of the Sudan Nile; he acquired land on the east side of Khartoum city; while in the Sudan he entertained Theodore Roosevelt, president of the United States, then on a hunting expedition; ill health compelled his retirement from the Sudan in 1910; he died at Las Vegas, Nevada.

Hunter Pasha, Sir Archibald (1856–1936), British soldier; he entered the army in 1874 and was promoted captain, 1882, colonel, 1894, and major-general, 1896; he served in the Nile campaign of 1884–5 and was wounded at the battle of Jinnis (Giniss); in 1888 he was seconded to the Khedivial army and in 1889 was present at the battle of Tūshkī (Toski); he commanded the Egyptian Frontier Field Force, 1894, to which was added the command of the Egyptian division in the Dongola campaign, 1896; in 1897 he led a flying column from Merowe through the Manāṣīr country to Abū Ḥamad, storming the village; he afterwards led his division at the battles of the Atbara and Omdurman, 1898; promoted later to full general he held high military commands in the South African war, the First World War, and in Britain; he was a member of Parliament for Lancaster, 1918–22.

Hunter Bey, William Hugh (1860–1902), British soldier; commissioned to the 72nd Foot in 1880 he transferred to the Seaforth Highlanders and was promoted major, 1899; he served in the Egyptian war of 1882 against Aḥmad 'Urābī Pasha and in the Nile campaign of 1898–9; in 1898 he was seconded to the Egyptian army and died in the Baḥr al-Ghazāl during the Anglo-Egyptian reoccupation of that area.

Ḥusain . . . (*fl.* 1800), Fulānī notable from Kano; he took part in the Fulānī holy war against Bagirmi by order of the sultan of Sokoto and being defeated fled eastward with a band of his supporters; on arriving on the banks of the Blue Nile the sultan of Sennar gave them land; his grandson was Muḥammad al-Tūm wad Shaikh Ṭalḥa.

Ḥusain Aḥmad Faraḥ (1868–1945), member of an old family, originally Rubāṭābī, long settled in the suburbs of Khartoum; he was appointed 'umda of Burrī about 1899 and held the post till his death; in 1930 he was appointed a magistrate and in 1934 vice-president of the rural district court; in later life he was described as 'a hearty old soul with a voice like a gun'.

Ḥusain al-Fīl (1861–1940), merchant, a member of the Ja'līyīn Arab tribe; he began trading in the years immediately before the outbreak of the Mahdist revolt and visited Cairo with consignments of ostrich feathers and gum arabic; during the *Mahdīya* he was appointed an amīr and was for some time the deputy of the Mahdist leader 'Uthmān wad Khālid; after the defeat of Mahdism he lived in Omdurman.

* **Ḥusain Ibrāhīm wad al-Zahra** (–1894), religious notable and poet; he was born at Wad Sha'īr near Masallamīya in the Jazīra and studied at al-Azhar University in Cairo; returning to the Sudan a man of learning he acquired great influence in the Jazīra; he duly joined

the Mahdist cause and, on the accession of the Khalīfa ʿAbd Allāhi in June 1885, he was appointed governor of Kassala when that town finally fell; he was thereafter a religious notable at Omdurman, becoming chief judge to the Khalīfa ʿAbd Allāhi in place of the judge Aḥmad wad ʿAlī in 1892, but his time was short; as a result of a disagreement with the Khalīfa over legal principles he was imprisoned till his death; he was a poet of renown.

Ḥusain Pasha Khalīfa (*c.* 1820–86), governor, and notable of the ʿAbābda Arab tribe; in 1851 he replaced his brother Ḥasan Khalīfa as government concessionaire of the caravan route over the Nubian desert from Korosko to Berber; along with his cousin Aḥmad ʿAlī he accompanied Muḥammad Saʿīd Pasha, viceroy of Egypt, on his visit to the Sudan in 1856–7, and in recognition of his services during the viceroy's tour he was granted land in the province of Idfū in Upper Egypt; from 1869 he was governor of the province of Berber and from 1871 to 1873 governor of the combined provinces of Berber and Dongola; Sir Samuel Baker praised his efficient handling of the desert transport; he was reappointed governor of Berber in 1883; in the beginning of 1884 the Mahdists began to appear in force in the region of his province and later laid siege to Berber which capitulated in June to the amīr Muḥammad al-Khair ʿAbd Allāh Khūjalī; now a prisoner of war he was summoned to appear before the Mahdī at al-Rāhad; the Mahdī received him well and appointed him amīr of the ʿAbābda tribe; he had already left Omdurman for Berber when the Mahdī died in June 1885 and the Mahdī's successor, the Khalīfa ʿAbd Allāhi, ordered him to return to Omdurman, but he escaped to Korosko; there he was tried by court-martial on a charge of responsibility for the fall of Berber but was acquitted and appointed an inspector in the Egyptian ministry of the interior; in this capacity he was placed in charge of the frontier Arabs; he died shortly afterwards in Cairo; his prominent role in the dramatic events of 1884–5 in the Sudan brought him to international attention.

Ḥusain al-Khalīfa Muḥammad Sharīf (1888–1928), pioneer Sudanese journalist, son of al-Saiyid Muḥammad Sharīf, the second khalīfa of Muḥammad Aḥmad al-Mahdī, and the Mahdī's grandson through his mother, the Sharīfa Zainab bint al-Mahdī; he was educated at Gordon Memorial College, Khartoum, from which he graduated in 1912, and was first a teacher in the Sudan Government education department; in 1917 he became editor of the Arabic weekly newspaper *al-Rāʾid al-Sudan*, a post which he held till 1919 when the journal was discontinued; he then edited the weekly *al-Ḥaḍārat al-Sūdān* owned by al-Saiyid Sir ʿAbd al-Raḥmān al-Mahdī Pasha; in 1920 this newspaper was taken over by the Sudan Government and issued twice weekly; he was its editor from 1920 till his death in Omdurman.

Ḥusain Kūmūljinalī (*fl.* 1823–4), Turkish soldier who was appointed ma'mūr of Kordofan in 1823 when Muḥammad Khusraw Daramālī, known as the Daftardār, had left Kordofan and had been formally appointed sirʿaskar of the Egyptian army in the Sudan as a result of the murder of Ismā'īl Pasha at Shendi in 1822; he was one of the Daftardār's chief officers in the expedition to Kordofan in 1821 and had taken a leading part in the battle of Bāra.

al-Ḥusain wad al-Mak al-Ḥasan (1870–1941), mak of Fāzūghlī; born at Fāzūghlī he succeeded to the makdom and in 1931 was made a magistrate and was president of the three courts of Fāzūghlī West, Tūmāt, and Berta; in 1938 he was dismissed following a conviction for having extorted a confession in a criminal case by torture; in 1939 he fled out of police supervision to Abyssinia.

Ḥusain Pasha Maẓhar (–1883), liwā' of the Egyptian army; said to have been a native of Egypt he was appointed vice-governor-general of the Sudan in July 1883 when al-farīq W. Hicks Pasha was concentrating an army on the Nile with the intention of taking the field against the Mahdī in Kordofan; he accompanied Hicks's army on its fatal march as a chief of staff; according to the diary of 'Abbās Bey Wahbī, another senior officer of the expedition, he was concerned at the confusion arising from the division of responsibility between Hicks and himself and asked that either Hicks or himself should be granted full control of the army; in a tragic letter which he wrote a few days before he was killed, and which was picked up many years later on the battlefield of Omdurman, he described in poignant terms the confusion in the Egyptian army, but magnanimously blamed nobody.

Ḥusain Bey Muḥammad Muṣṭafā (1880–1941), Sudanese officer of the Egyptian army and from 1924 of the Sudan Defence Force; he entered the Egyptian army in 1895 and fought throughout the Dongola and Nile campaigns including that against the amīr Aḥmad Faḍīl; he retired from the army in 1935.

Ḥusain Muṣṭafā Pasha (1776–1849), Ottoman commander-in-chief in the Turco-Egyptian war of 1832 and would-be ruler of the Sudan; anticipating victory the Sublime Porte nominated him wālī of Egypt, the Sudan, and Crete in place of Muḥammad 'Alī Pasha; on account of the Egyptian victory his nomination proved nominal; he died at Widdin in Serbia while muḥāfiẓ there.

Ḥusain Riḥaima (*fl.* 1810), Sudanese tribesman, a warrior hero of the Khawālda Arabs in the series of raids and counter-raids between the Khawālda and the Kawāhla on the eve of the Egyptian invasion of 1820–1.

Ḥusain Sharīf Pasha (*c.* 1859–1930), liwā' of the Egyptian army; a native of Cairo he entered the Egyptian army in 1879 as a mulāzim II; he was present at the lines of Kafr al-Dawwār and at the battle of Tel el-Kebir, in Aḥmad 'Urābī Pasha's army, 1882; he joined the cavalry in the newly created Egyptian army and fought throughout the Dongola and Nile campaigns, 1896–8, and was for a time deputy governor of Berber.

Hutton, Ronald Winder (1883–1917), British captain of the Royal Marine Artillery who was commissioned in 1901 and in 1912 seconded to the Egyptian army with rank of binbāshī; he was killed at Nitl in the Nuba hills in operations against Sultan Agabna.

Huwy (*fl.* 1350 B.C.), viceroy of Ethiopia from about 1358 B.C. to 1350 B.C. during the reign of the Egyptian XVIIIth Dynasty king Tutankhamen; he ruled the land between al-Kāb and Napata on behalf of his Egyptian sovereign.

Ibn Baṭṭūṭa. *See* ABŪ 'ABD ALLĀH MUḤAMMAD IBN BAṬṬŪṬA.

Ibn Dushain (*fl.* 1610), Sudanese judge whose just decisions earned for him the title of Qāḍi al-'Adāla; he was born at Arbajī in the Jazīra; a Shāfi'ite in doctrine he learnt law from Muḥammad ibn 'Alī ibn Qarm al-Kimānī and was later one of the four district judges appointed by Shaikh 'Ajīb the Great by order of King Dakīn wad Naiyīl (1562–77); he died at al-Dākhila where his tomb was built.

Ibn Ḥauqal (*c.* 900–*c.* 960), the popular name of Abī al-Qāsim ibn Ḥauqal, Arab geographer, the author of *al-kitāb masālik wa mamālik* which contains brief references to the Red Sea coast of the Sudan, the Beja, and Nubia; there is an English translation, *The Oriental Geography of Ebn Haukal*, by Sir W. Ouseley (1800), also a commentary in Latin, *De Ibn Haukalo Geographo*, by H. A. Hamaker (Leyden, 1822).

Ibn Jubair. *See* ABŪ'L-ḤUSAIN MUḤAMMAD IBN AḤMAD IBN JUBAIR AL-KINĀNĪ.

Ibn Khaldūn. *See* 'ABD AL-RAḤMĀN (ABŪ ZAID) . . . IBN KHALDŪN.

Ibn Mammātī. *See* AS'AD IBN AL-MUHADHDHAB IBN ABĪ AL-MILĪḤ MAMMĀTĪ.

Ibn Sa'īd. *See* ABŪ'L-ḤASAN . . . IBN SA'ĪD AL-MAGHRIBĪ.

Ibn Sulaim (or **Salīm**). *See* 'ABD ALLĀH IBN AḤMAD IBN SULAIM (or SALĪM) AL-ASWĀNĪ.

* **Ibrāhīm 'Abd al-Dāfi'** (*c.* 1800–*c.* 1882), Sudanese man of letters and poet; the Egyptian Government of the Sudan appointed him a district judge and then a muftī, posts which he held between about 1840 and 1854 until his deportation, along with others, to Egypt during the reign of Muḥammad Sa'īd Pasha (1854–63); he edited and elaborated a chronology of the rulers of the Sudan during the Funj and Egyptian periods as far as the term of office of Aḥmad Mumtāz Pasha (1871–2), a document compiled from manuscripts written by three contemporary annalists: Shaikh Aḥmad, clerk of a government warehouse, Shaikh al-Zubair wad Ḍawwa, and Shaikh al-Amīn Muḥammad al-Ḍarīr; he died in Khartoum.

Ibrāhīm 'Abd Illāh abū Sin (1880–1939), a member of the ruling house of the Shukrīya; from 1907 to 1915 he was 'umda of the Shukrīya nomads, an office which he resigned owing to illness; he was shaikh of the khuṭṭ of Rufā'a, 1926–35, and president of the local shaikhs' court.

* **Ibrāhīm wad ʿAdlān** (–1891), Mahdist official, originally a merchant of al-Ubaiyaḍ, later of Wad Madanī; on the deposition of the Khalīfa ʿAbd Allāhi's treasurer, the amīn bait al-māl, Aḥmad wad Sulaimān, in 1889, he was appointed to the post; he was a man of outstanding financial ability; he reorganized the treasury, dividing it into departments for its different functions, introducing an intelligible system of accounts and employing competent clerks and accountants with experience under the former Egyptian rule; he persuaded the Khalīfa to reopen trade with Egypt; the enormous power conferred on him by his ability and by the nature of the post itself was his undoing; he was degraded and hanged, officially for peculation and other irregularities, though some state that it was for his excessive popularity, and for his overshadowing the amīr Yaʿqūb, the Khalīfa's brother, who was jealous of his public prestige; he was succeeded as treasurer by al-Nūr Ibrāhīm al-Jaraifāwī.

Ibrāhīm Aghā, called **Abū Shanab** (–1822), Turkish soldier, commander of cavalry; he came from Egypt with reinforcements which overtook Ismāʿīl Pasha at Berber, 1821; he fell ill at Wādī Ḥalfā on the way back and died shortly after his arrival in Egypt.

Ibrāhīm Aḥmad (–1902), Maḥasī notable; he was the first ʿumda of Khartoum North under the Condominium Government; he was succeeded by his son ʿUthmān (d. 1921) who in turn was succeeded by Ḥāmid, ʿUthmān's son (d. 1941).

Ibrāhīm ʿAlī al-Amīn (–1944), shartai of the Fūr of Dār Tebella in western Dār Fūr and president of the Kergulla court.

Ibrāhīm al-Badawī (*fl.* 1821), Kahlī notable, fourth in line from the famous but little-known Shaikh al-ʿAbūdī; he was one of the Arab allies of the Hāmaj rulers of Sennar during the last days of the sultanate; rebelling against the newly established Turkish power in the Jazīra, Muḥammad Saʿīd, the Turkish dīvān efendisi on Ismāʿīl Pasha's staff, sacked the village of ʿAbūd where he lived; he became reconciled to the government, but his exactions were eventually so oppressive that he was overthrown by his own people.

Ibrāhīm Fatḥī Pasha (–1925), farīq of the Egyptian army; first appointed to the staff, he was qā'immaqām of the 7th infantry battalion from 1891 and was in command of the battalion throughout the Dongola and Nile campaigns of 1896–8 with rank of mīrālai; he was minister of national defence in 1922.

Ibrāhīm Fawzī Pasha (*c.* 1853–), liwā' of the Egyptian army; he was a cadet in the Egyptian administration of the Sudan in 1874 when he attracted the attention of Gordon Pasha, under whom he served in the Equatorial province; when Gordon returned to the Sudan in 1877 as governor-general he was promoted to qā'immaqām and saw service in the Baḥr al-Ghazāl and in Equatoria; in 1878 he was convicted of irregularities and Gordon recalled him from the post of governor of Equatoria; he was sentenced to death, but Gordon reprieved him, appointing Emin Pasha in Fawzī's stead; on Gordon's departure in 1880 he was restored to office by Gordon's successor, Muḥammad Ra'ūf Pasha; an adherent of the Egyptian nationalist cause in 1882 he was Aḥmad 'Urābī Pasha's chief of police in Cairo; G. B. Messedaglia Bey who was in Cairo immediately before the battle of Tel el-Kebir recorded the high state of public order in the city; on his return to the Sudan in 1884 with a mandate to evacuate the Egyptian garrisons in face of the Mahdist peril Gordon re-employed him, convinced that he had treated him unjustly in 1878, and Fawzī travelled to Khartoum as Gordon's personal adjutant and adviser; he commanded the Egyptian troops during the siege of Khartoum, 1884–5; on its fall his life was spared and he eked out a precarious existence at Omdurman by running a coffee house; on the Anglo-Egyptian occupation of the city in 1898 he was freed and returned to Cairo where in retirement he wrote his memoirs (Cairo, 1901).

Ibrāhīm Ḥasan wad Ḥusain (–1930), 'umda of al-Duwaim on the White Nile, by tribe a Ja'farī whose great-grandfather, Ḥasan abū 'Alī, left Egypt and settled in northern Kordofan during the rule of the Funj sultans of Sennar; his grandfather brought the tribe southward to the district of al-Duwaim; during the Mahdist régime he was a mulāzim of the Khalīfa 'Abd Allāhi and was present at the battles of Omdurman, 1898, and Umm Dibaikarāt, 1899; the Khalīfa imprisoned his father and seized his property; under the Condominium Government he became 'umda and a magistrate.

Ibrāhīm al-Kabbāshī (–1865), religious shaikh who, in spite of his name al-Kabbāshī, was in fact a Maḥasī; his tomb, together with that of his son, is at al-Qubba railway station about twenty miles north of Khartoum, and is much frequented by visiting Kabbābīsh tribesmen.

Ibrāhīm Bey al-Kabīr (–1813), Mameluke leader of one of the fugitive bands whom Muḥammad 'Alī Pasha pursued into Nubia about 1810; he died of old age at al-Urdī (Old Dongola).

Ibrāhīm Kāshif (*fl.* 1738), virtually independent ruler of Nubia from the region of Aswān to the borders of Dongola; he was the 'Baram' recorded by the Danish traveller F. L. Norden who sailed on the Nubian Nile in 1738; he was descended from Ḥasan Kūshī who with his Bosnian garrison occupied Nubia in the sixteenth century at the command of the Ottoman sultan Salīm I.

Ibrāhīm Bey Khalīl (*c.* 1844–1917), Egyptian merchant; his father came from Ibnūn al-Ḥammām near Asyūṭ and settled in Khartoum where Ibrāhīm was born; he established himself as a general merchant in the trade between Egypt and the Sudan; during Gordon Pasha's first governor-generalship (1877–80) he lent Gordon money without interest, when the treasury was exhausted, to pay discharged troops; during the siege of Khartoum, 1884–5, Gordon used to spend some of his leisure in Ibrāhīm's garden which was on the site now occupied by the zoological gardens; after the fall of Khartoum the Mahdists robbed him of his belongings and he lived quietly in Omdurman with his three sons who had been wounded in the siege of the capital; the Mahdist Government fell and, under the Condominium Government which followed, he took part in the reconstruction of Khartoum; he was a member of the board which re-allotted properties in Khartoum that had been destroyed by the Dervishes, and was later a member of the Khartoum municipal council.

Ibrāhīm al-Khalīl Aḥmad (–1898), Mahdist amīr, a brother of Maḥmūd Aḥmad, one of the principal Mahdist commanders; he raided the Tagoi region of the Nuba hills in 1892; at the battle of Omdurman in which he was killed he commanded a body of regular Mahdist infantry called, with perhaps some exaggeration, *al-jiḥādīya*, a term used in modern times by the rulers of Egypt to denote regular infantry formations.

Ibrāhīm Bey Luṭfī (–1866), soldier of the Egyptian army; he died shortly after his appointment as governor of Tāka in 1866.

Ibrāhīm Bey al-Maḥallāwī (–1885), Egyptian soldier; said to have been of pure Egyptian origin he was born at al-Maḥalla al-Kubrā and received his military education at the Cairo Military School where he was a contemporary of Muḥammad Ra'ūf (afterwards pasha); after service in the Fayyūm he was transferred to the Sudan and about 1863 appointed governor of Tāka; he was wounded in the siege of Kassala by military mutineers in 1865; after his retirement (the date of which is uncertain) he lived in Kassala and died of natural causes during the siege of the town by the Mahdists.

Ibrāhīm Maḥjūb al-Mīrghanī (–1908), member of the great religious family of the Mīrghanīya and a son of al-Saiyid Maḥjūb al-Mīrghanī (d. 1912); al-Saiyid Ibrāhīm was taken ill while passing through Wādī Ḥalfā and died there; his tomb stands in the town.

Ibrāhīm wad Maḥmūd (–1904), notorious slave dealer from Jabal Jarok on the Sudan-Abyssinian frontier near Kurmuk; he was eventually captured by a patrol of the slavery repression department of the Egyptian Government, convicted, and hanged.

Ibrāhīm Malik (–1913), Mahdist amīr; by birth a Taʿā'ishī, he fought in the great battles of the Mahdist revolt and was captured in the battle of Umm Dibaikarāt in 1899; he lived in retirement in the Taʿā'isha colony near Sinja, and there he died.

* **Ibrāhīm Bey al-Milīḥ** (*c.* 1850–1904), son of Shaikh Ismāʿīl wad al-Ḥājj Munʿim and nāẓir of the ʿAsākir branch of the Ḥamar tribe of Kordofan; on the outbreak of the Mahdist revolt in Kordofan he was made an amīr by Muḥammad Aḥmad al-Mahdī; towards the end of the Mahdist rule he fell under the displeasure of the Khalīfa ʿAbd Allāhi who threw him into prison for a time; after the Anglo-Egyptian victory at Omdurman in 1898 he took vengeance upon his oppressors and accompanied ʿAbd al-Raḥīm Bey Sālim abū Daqal who led a flying

column of anti-Mahdist tribesmen against the amīr 'Arabī Dafa' Allāh in Dār Silā.

Ibrāhīm Muḥammad 'Āmir Pasha (1882–1941), Egyptian merchant; a native of Aswān he came to the Sudan as a young employee of the firm of Georges Brahamsha and Ilyās 'Ajūrī, and in 1915 took over the Sudan interests of his employers and made a fortune; he retired to Egypt in 1932 but made frequent visits to the Sudan; he was a large subscriber to social and charitable causes and gave much to help civil aviation in Egypt; he was made a pasha of Egypt in 1938; he died in Cairo.

Ibrāhīm Bey Muḥammad Faraḥ (–1926), notable of the Ja'līyīn of Matamma, a son of al-Ḥājj Muḥammad Sulaimān Faraḥ who was nāẓir of the district of Matamma in Turkish times; he was head merchant in Dāra in Dār Fūr on the eve of the Mahdist revolt; during the Mahdist régime he was the treasurer of Matamma; the fidelity of the Ja'līyīn becoming suspect the Khalīfa 'Abd Allāhi sent the amīr Maḥmūd Aḥmad to Matamma early in 1898 to punish the inhabitants; Ibrāhīm fled in time to Dongola where he raised a force of irregulars which fought under the Anglo-Egyptian command; he visited King George V in London in 1919.

Ibrāhīm (Brāhīm) Muḥammad Ḥusain (1834–74), sultan of Dār Fūr; succeeding his father Muḥammad Ḥusain al-Mahdī in 1873 his reign was brought to an end by the invasion of Dār Fūr by Zubair Pasha Raḥma Manṣūr with his private army from the south and by the governor-general of the Sudan, Ismā'īl Pasha Aiyūb, with a regular Egyptian force from the east; at Manawāshī he was defeated and killed by Zubair; Ḥasab Allāh, his uncle, retired into the fastness of Jabal Marra to continue the struggle, but the Egyptian hold on the country soon made further resistance hopeless; Ḥasab Allāh and Sultan Ibrāhīm's brother 'Abd al-Raḥmān Shattūt submitted to the Khedivial Government and were afterwards sent to Cairo where they both died, their families being pensioned by the Government; Bōsh Muḥammad al-Faḍl and Saif al-Dīn fought on till finally in 1875 Zubair killed them both; Bōsh's son, Muḥammad Hārūn al-Rashīd, by his father's death the titular sultan, alone continued to resist.

Ibrāhīm Muḥammad Muḥammad abū Ḥijil (–1918), notable of the 'Ajībāb section of the Rubāṭāb tribe whose father was killed while serving in the Mahdist army at the battle of Tūshkī (Toski) in 1889.

Ibrāhīm Muḥammad al-Takrūrī (*c.* 1863–1943), 'umda of the north-eastern Nawāḥīya of Dār Ḥāmid in the region of Bāra in Kordofan; his great-grandfather got the nickname al-Takrūrī through his hospitality to a number of Takārīr, possibly pilgrims or refugees from the West.

Ibrāhīm Mukhaiyar (*c.* 1859–1944), Mahdist amīr of the Zaiyādīya tribe who inhabit Dār Fūr but mostly north-western Kordofan; he was wounded and taken prisoner at the battle of Umm Dibaikarāt, 1899; he died in Omdurman.

Ibrāhīm Bey Mūsā Ibrāhīm (–1931), nāẓir of the Hadendowa Beja whose tribal centre was at Mitatīb in the delta of the Gash north of Kassala; during the Mahdist régime he was an amīr under the command of ʿUthmān abū Bakr Diqna (Osman Digna); he was a son of Mūsā Ibrāhīm who with great tenacity preserved the existence of the tribe during Turkish times; he was succeeded on his death by the present nāẓir, Muḥammad Muḥammad al-Amīn Tirik; his long period of authority coincided with the spectacular development of the Gash delta as a cotton-producing area made possible by the building of a railway (completed 1924) between Haiyā Junction and Kassala; in this agricultural development the Hadendowa played a large part.

Ibrāhīm Nash'āt Bey (1853–   ), qā'immaqām of the Egyptian army; commissioned in 1875 he served with the Egyptian army in Abyssinia and was present at the battle of Gura, 1876; after fighting in the Balkans, 1876–8, he returned to Egypt and took part in the Nile campaign of 1884–5 against the Mahdists; he was a yūzbāshī in the battle of Jinnis (Giniss), 1885; transferred to the Red Sea coast he fought at Jummaiza, 1888; appointed governor of Beni Swef, 1892, he occupied several governorates in succession and in 1896 was promoted qā'immaqām.

Ibrāhīm wad Nitaifa (1852–1931), notable of the ʿArakīyīn, nāẓir of the Maʿtūq district in the western Jazīra during the last days of the Egyptian rule, a tax-collector under Mahdism and ʿumda of the ʿArakīyīn of Maʿtūq under the present government; he died at Maʿtūq.

* **Ibrāhīm al-Nūr Ibrāhīm al-Jaraifāwī** (*c.* 1854–99), Shā'iqī notable and Mahdist official, son of al-Nūr Ibrāhīm al-Jaraifāwī, who was amīn bait al-māl in Omdurman in the régime of the Khalīfa ʿAbd Allāhi; he succeeded ʿUmar Azraq as ʿāmil (popularly amīr, wālī) of the Jazīra, an administrative territory which extended from Khartoum to the Abyssinian frontier; he was later dismissed from this post and succeeded by the amīr Aḥmad al-Sunnī who held office until the fall of the Mahdist Government; he died in Omdurman and was buried in Khartoum North.

Ibrāhīm Rājī Bey (*c.* 1847–   ), mīrālai of the Egyptian army; commissioned to the horse artillery he served on the staff of the officer commanding at Alexandria; he was at Muṣawwaʿ commanding the artillery there during the Egyptian-Abyssinian war of 1875; his next service was in the Russo-Turkish war with the Egyptian contingent in 1877–8; joining the Khedivial guard in 1881 with the rank of binbāshī he served in it until the dissolution of the old Egyptian army in 1882 after Aḥmad ʿUrābī' Pasha's revolt; he continued to serve in the new army and was posted to the 7th infantry regiment with the rank of mulāzim I; he fought in the Nile campaign of 1884–5 and was present with his regiment in the battle of Jinnis (Giniss); a yūzbāshī in 1886 he was in command of the Egyptian horse artillery at Sawākin in

1887–8 and fought at Jummaiza (Gemmaiza); returning to the Nile he fought against the amīr ʿAbd al-Raḥmān wad al-Najūmī at Tūshkī (Toski) in 1889; he was afterwards inspector of warlike stores, retiring in 1902; in his later life he travelled in Europe and America.

Ibrāhīm al-Rashīd al-Diwaiḥī (–1874), religious notable, founder of the Rashīdīya Islamic brotherhood; a member of the Diwaiḥīya clan of the Shā'iqīya tribe of Dongola he became a pupil of al-Saiyid Aḥmad Idrīs and adopted the doctrines of the Aḥmadīya; his followers (called al-Rashīdīya, though not separate from the Aḥmadīya) are found chiefly in Dongola, Omdurman, Tūtī Island, and Kawa; he died at Makka; his nephew, Muḥammad Ṣāliḥ Ibrāhīm (d. 1919), succeeded him; the brotherhood has spread, among other places, to India, Syria, and Somaliland.

* **Ibrāhīm Bey Rushdī** (–1885), official in the Egyptian service; he was C. G. Gordon's secretary during the siege of Khartoum; Gordon removed him to an inferior post on a charge of stealing food belonging to the government; he was killed by the Mahdists in the capture of the city.

Ibrāhīm Bey al-Sinnārī (–1801), Mameluke of the Napoleonic period; he was undoubtedly a Sudanese from his black colour and his appearance, and he may have come from the region of Sennar as his name (no infallible guide) appears to indicate; he acted as aide-de-camp to Murād Bey in the struggle against Napoleon; after the victory of the French over the Mamelukes in the battle of the Pyramids he accompanied Murād to Upper Egypt where they resisted the southward advance of General Desaix; after the capitulation of General Menou he was murdered, along with other beys of Murād's household, on the sea-shore at Abū Qīr (Aboukir); his house at Naṣrīya in Cairo is a national monument.

Ibrāhīm Pasha al-Wālī (1789–1848), eldest son of Muḥammad ʿAlī Pasha, viceroy of Egypt; after a successful campaign against the Wahhābites in Arabia in 1816–19 his father appointed him to help his younger brother, Ismāʿīl, who had occupied Sennar early in 1821 but whom, the viceroy judged, needed the advice of a more experienced leader; he left Cairo in June 1821; while at Dongola he organized the expedition which under the command of Muḥammad Khusraw, the Bey Daftardār, conquered northern and central Kordofan; he arrived at Sennar on 22 October; here he joined Ismāʿīl in expeditions in search of slaves and gold, making a reconnaissance to the west of the Blue Nile in the region of Jabal Quraibin; taken sick of dysentery he returned to Egypt, arriving in Cairo on 6 February 1822 after a hazardous crossing of the Nubian desert; his later campaigns in the Morea and in Syria brought him to the front rank of the military commanders of the time; his contact with the Sudan was slight; there is a large literature concerning his career, mostly devoted to his later campaigns; for an account of his Sudan journey see volume 1 of G. Douin's *Histoire du Soudan égyptien* (Cairo, 1944), and volume 1 of General Weygand's *Histoire militaire de Mohammed Aly et de ses Fils* (Paris, 1936).

Idrīs Adam al-Habbānī (*c.* 1864–1927), nāẓir of the Ḥasanīya and Ḥusaināt (formerly a Mahdist amīr) who lived at al-Naʿīma near al-Qiṭaina, ruling over a widely distributed tribe.

* **Idrīs ʿAdlān Muḥammad abū'l-Kailak** (*fl.* 1826–46), Hāmaj chieftain; mak of the Funj mountains in the upper valley of the Blue Nile; he had never submitted to the Turkish Government which had been established in Sennar since 1821; about 1826 ʿAlī Khūrshid Bey, then governor of Sennar, brought about his reconciliation with the government and he was officially appointed shaikh of the Funj mountains with his seat at Gulé; his sister, Naṣra bint ʿAdlān, married Muḥammad Dafaʿ Allāh whose seat was at Ṣūraiba near Wad Madanī and who had become one of the most important shaikhs in the whole Jazīra; about 1851 ʿAbd al-Laṭīf Pasha, governor-general, dismissed Idrīs from office and put his nephew ʿAdlān in his place.

Idrīs ʿAlī Ḥalīb (1868–1936), Shā'iqī notable; he was born on Muṣāwwīʿ island near Merowe and from 1899 to 1935 (when he retired) was ʿumda of Muṣawwiʿ; he was a member of the Ṣalāḥāb section of the Kadinkāb branch of the Shā'iqīya tribe.

Idrīs Hārūn (1838–1905), Mahdist amīr; the son of a wealthy Dongolāwī merchant of Omdurman, he was related to the amīr Muḥammad ʿUthmān abū Qarja who appointed Idrīs his aide-de-camp and afterwards his second in command; he served at the siege of Khartoum, 1884–5, and with Abū Qarja against Abyssinia; he was later made controller of prisons in the Khalīfa ʿAbd Allāhi's government; present at the battle of Omdurman in 1898 he survived the defeat and fled to Kamlīn where his brother lived; there he settled and there he died.

Idrīs abū Hāshim (*c.* 1859–1935), sultan of Dār Qimr in western Dār Fūr; he was of Jaʿlī origin and was born at Qanāṭīr; he succeeded his father, Sultan Abū Bakr, in 1879; the Mahdists afterwards having overrun much of Dār Fūr, he was in 1887 summoned to al-Fāshar by the Mahdist amīr ʿUthmān Adam; he refused to obey the summons and took refuge with Sultan Yūsuf Sharīf at Abeshr, returning home after ʿUthmān Adam's death in 1889; ʿUthmān's successor, Maḥmūd Aḥmad then demanded his presence at al-Fāshar; he again refused to go and a Mahdist force sent against him was defeated by the Qimr; after this Maḥmūd came in person with a larger force; he withdrew into Dār Maṣālīṭ and thence to Abeshr, returning on Maḥmūd's departure from Dār Fūr; during the reign of Sultan ʿAlī Dīnār he had to withdraw four times to evade summonses to al-Fāshar, the capital of the Fūr sultanate; once he fled to Dār Zaghāwa, twice to the borders of Dār Qimr, and once to Abeshr where the French had now arrived and supported him with a present of 100 rifles; in the course of numerous expeditions against him ʿAlī Dīnār captured various members of his family and held them captive in al-Fāshar where some of them were found and released at the occupation of 1916; meanwhile he had moved his headquarters from Qanāṭīr to Kulbus in 1913; when the sultanate of ʿAlī Dīnār fell he gave his loyalty to the Sudan Government.

Idrīs al-Miḥaina Sulaimān (–1821), mak of the Jamū'īya tribe of the White Nile; because of his refusal to submit to the Turkish occupation, a force under Ismā'īl Pasha's dīwān efendī Muḥammad Sa'īd, aided by a friendly local chieftain Raḥama wad Rahala, advanced from Sennar to the White Nile and killed him in his house.

Idrīs wad Muḥammad al-'Arbāb, called **al-Walī** (1507–1650), holy man of great fame in the Sudan who reached the legendary age of 147 lunar years; he was known as an eminent teacher and missionary of Islam; a Maḥasī by origin he was granted land at 'Āilafūn by the kings of the Funj who held him in respect; he was the founder of the village of 'Āilafūn where he taught the doctrines of Shaikh 'Abd al-Qādir al-Jīlānī; he is said to have enjoyed the gift of prophecy and to have foretold that the sultanate of the Funj would be destroyed by internal dissension; his tomb at 'Āilafūn is a popular place of pilgrimage.

Idrīs wad Muḥammad abū'l-Kailak (–1803), Hāmaj chieftain, son of the great king-maker of the Funj sultanate; he warred against Shaikh 'Abd Allāh wad 'Ajīb of Ḥalfaiya and killed him; in the chaotic days of the decline of the sultanate he had a reputation for justice and kindness; he died in Sennar and was succeeded as vizier by his brother 'Adlān who was killed in a palace feud a few months later.

Idrīs Nāṣir (–1860), chief of the 'Abdullāb of Ḥalfaiya; he was employed by the Egyptian Government, accompanying the governor-general Aḥmad Pasha abū Widān to Tāka and other places armed with his famous sword 'Niam-Niam', a Sudanese Excalibur; there is a story that he conspired with Aḥmad Pasha to wrest the Sudan from Egypt and to hand it over to Turkey but that the premature discovery of the plot ruined all hope of its success; he died at Ḥalfaiya in the full esteem of the government and was succeeded by Shaikh Jum'a Shaikh al-Amīn.

Idrīs wad Rājab Idrīs (–1931), nāẓir of the Hāmaj of Jabal Gulé; a descendant of the viceregal line of Sennar; he was succeeded by his son, Shaikh Muḥammad Idrīs Rājab.

Idrīs ibn Sharshar ibn Ḥakīm al-Ja'lī (*fl.* 1700), malik of Arqū in the district of Dongola and founder of the line of hereditary kings of the island; a Ja'lī Arab by origin he was descended from the Hāshimāb family of al-Dāmar where he was born; he migrated to Bilād al-Duffār in Dongola and there his people multiplied, populating Arqū island.

Idrīsī. *See* Abū 'Abd Allāh Muḥammad al-Idrīsī.

Ikanj (*c.* 1860–1938), queen and rain-maker of Tirrangore (Tarengole) in the Lotuko country of Equatoria, she was married first in 1886; after a long apprenticeship in rain-making she was chosen chieftainess by her people in 1932, but though she was too old to rule actively she had great authority over the Lotuxo people in her small district, an authority which she wielded wisely.

Iles, George Ehret (1876–1933), British official; educated at Cambridge University where he studied oriental languages, he entered the Sudan political service in 1901; he was governor of the Blue Nile province, 1914–22, and of Dongola province, 1922–4, when he retired; he was one of the few British officials employed by the Sudan Government at the time who read and wrote Arabic with ease.

* **Ilyās Pasha Aḥmad Umm Birair** (–1898), wealthy merchant of Ja'lī origin who built up a substantial business in al-Ubaiyaḍ, with trade connexions in Dār Fūr and Khartoum, during the period 1865–75; his knowledge of the trade of Dār Fūr caused the governor-general Ismā'īl Pasha Aiyūb to invite him to Dār Fūr with the Egyptian army of occupation in 1875; for his services there he was appointed bey and governor of S͟hāqqa; for a short time, and in defiance of local prejudice, he was made governor of Kordofan with the civil grade of pasha; his supersession by Muḥammad Sa'īd Pasha, a Circassian, in the same year caused his intense resentment; finally, ageing and defective in sight, he went over to the cause of Muḥammad Aḥmad al-Mahdī after the capitulation of al-Ubaiyaḍ in January 1883; he is remembered for his kindness to Christian captives of the Mahdī; from the Mahdists he received no preferment and, having been suspected of treasonable relations with the Egyptian Government, he was put in prison where he died, old and blind, at the beginning of 1898; little now remains to keep his memory green in al-Ubaiyaḍ save some amusing stories of his feuds with the local Danagla.

Ilyās bey 'Īsāwī (1882–1941), Syrian official in the service of the Sudan Government; born in Jaffa of a Syrian Orthodox Christian family of Damascene origin, he was educated in the American University of Beirut whence he graduated in 1901; going to Egypt he worked for a short time on the staff of the *Egyptian Gazette* and then joined the Sudan Government finance department in Cairo in 1902; here he was on duty until 1913 when he was transferred to Khartoum as a financial inspector, retiring in 1923 with the rank of bey.

Ilyās Bey Kirīdlī (–*c.* 1862), governor of Tāka intermittently between 1845 and 1860, by origin a Cretan; he constructed much of the town of Kassala and completed the surrounding wall which had been begun during the visit of the governor-general Aḥmad Pasha Manliklī in 1844; in 1850 he ravaged the Sennaheit during a raid on the Bilen in company with the Banī 'Āmir tribesmen; after a chequered career he died at Kassala while an investigation into the disappearance of 5,000 dollars of public funds was about to be opened.

al-Imām Aḥmad Dakīn (1865–1943), member of a prominent family of the Halāwīyīn of the Jazīra; born at Takala Jubāra he was appointed 'umda of Jubāra, 1908.

* **Inger, Alexander** (–1935), Austrian soldier, afterwards said to have been a Mahdist amīr; according to the story he was the son of an Austrian officer in the Turkish service and was educated in the

Military Academy of Wiener Neustadt; wearying of garrison life in Bosnia he accepted employment in the Turkish army about 1880; he was later sent by the Ottoman Government as an intelligence officer to Egypt after the outbreak of the Mahdist revolt; here he deserted from the Turkish army and, going to the Sudan, joined the Khalīfa ʿAbd Allāhi about 1888 and became a Muslim, announcing himself as an Egyptian inspired by belief in the Mahdī, a proceeding aided by his excellent Arabic; the Khalīfa, the story goes, made him an amīr and charged him with the responsibility for the drill and equipment of his forces; he was known by the name of Sulaimān Ḥarīqa; as chief of staff to Ḥamdān abū ʿAnja and his successor Zakī Ṭamal, he took part in the Mahdist campaign against the Abyssinians, 1889; he is said to have planned and partly built the Mahdist fort of El Kakar near Khashm al-Qirba; he claimed that for three years he was governor of those parts of the Amhara province occupied by the Mahdists and that his rule came to an end only when King Menyelek (Menilik) II succeeded in uniting Abyssinia after the battle of Umm Dibaikarāt, 1899, when the last vestiges of militant Mahdism were destroyed; he then returned to Austria and bought a castle near Oradea Mare where he lived in retirement, surrounded by oriental trophies, till his death; this account of his life is drawn from an article by G. W. Bell in *Sudan Notes and Records* (Khartoum), 1937, vol. xx, and is at present unsupported by further evidence; a Karl Inger was arrested and deported from Sawākin, 1896, for attempting (on his own evidence) to reach Omdurman in order to persuade the Khalīfa to accept recognition by the Ottoman sultan as sultan of Nubia; he told the British authorities at the port that he was an ex-lieutenant of the Austrian army, born in 1868 and living at Temesvar; when arrested he wore a Dervish *jibba* and, what is interesting, called himself Sulaimān.

Inglefield, Loftus Edward Coore (1848–85), major in the British army; he joined the 32nd Foot as an ensign in 1868 and was promoted captain in 1880; he died at Wādī Ḥalfā while serving in the Nile expedition which attempted the relief of Khartoum.

Irby, Charles Leonard (1789–1845), British sailor and traveller; after serving as a youth in the Royal Navy against Napoleon he, with Captain J. Mangles, G. B. Belzoni, and others, ascended the Nile to the region of Abū Simbel in 1817–18; the account of their travels was first published in 1823; he retired from the navy with the rank of captain.

ʿĪsā, called **al-Nabī ʿĪsā** (–1888), fanatic of West African descent, possibly a Fallātī; while a Mahdist army under the amīr al-umarāʾ Ḥamdān abū ʿAnja was fighting the Abyssinians in the region of Gondar, he proclaimed himself al-nabī ʿĪsā (the prophet Jesus) and raised a revolt at Gallabat against the Mahdist rule; Abū ʿAnja defeated and killed him.

ʿĪsā ʿAbd Allāh (1855–1921), Jamarī notable, ʿumda of the Awlād abū Ḥajūl Jamrīya branch of the Jawāmaʿa of Kordofan and a much-respected man.

ʿĪsā ʿAbduh Khalīl (1860–1937), Berberine notable, born at Wādī Ḥalfā; he settled in Debeira about 1880 and later became an important contractor to the Anglo-Egyptian forces on the frontier; in 1909 he was appointed ʿumda of Debeira and afterwards became president of the Wādī Ḥalfā bench of magistrates; his son Ṣāliḥ ʿĪsā ʿAbduh is president of the Debeira village court and a prominent member of the local administration.

ʿĪsā wad Kānū (*fl.* 1660), Sudanese man of religion; a most holy man, according to the hagiographer Wad Ḍaif Allāh; he was born at Old Dongola and was by birth a Ḥaḍarī.

ʿĪsā wad al-Zain (–1947), Mahdist amīr; by origin a Taʿā'ishī, he campaigned in Dār Fūr under the command of the amīr ʿUthmān Adam and was wounded in battle outside al-Fāshar against Aḥmad abū Jummaiza who had rebelled against the Mahdists; Maḥmūd Aḥmad, having succeeded ʿUthmān Adam on the latter's death at al-Fāshar in 1889, sent him to war against the restless inhabitants of the Nuba hills; he was head amīr of Kordofan from 1893 until the eve of the battle of Omdurman in 1898 in which he fought at the head of his force of riflemen and cavalry; he came unscathed from the battles of Omdurman and Umm Dibaikarāt and spent his old age in retirement in the village of Umm Hayāya near Kosti.

Isḥāq Muḥammad Shaddād (–1938), Bidairi notable, ʿumda ʿumūm of Bāra and Dār Sahl with a long record of government service which extended from pre-Mahdist times; he died in Bāra.

Isḥāq Muḥammad Tīrāb, called **Isḥāq al-Khalīfa** (–*c.* 1785), younger brother of Muḥammad Tīrāb, sultan of Dār Fūr; on the death of the latter at Bāra his brother ʿAbd al-Raḥmān was proclaimed his successor, a step which Isḥāq did not recognize; in the course of the civil war which ensued Isḥāq was killed.

Ismāʿīl Pasha (1830–95), wālī, later khedive, of Egypt; the second son of Ibrāhīm Pasha and a grandson of Muḥammad ʿAlī Pasha, he was educated at the high school at al-Khanka in Egypt and completed his studies in Vienna and Paris; in 1863 he succeeded Muḥammad Saʿīd Pasha as wālī of Egypt; in 1865 he obtained from the Porte the cession of Sawākin and Muṣawwaʿ to Egypt and in 1867 the conferment on himself of the hereditary title of khedive; he spent the greater part of his reign in great internal reforms and external expansion; a network of railways for the Sudan was projected and many surveys made, culminating in the construction of a line from Wādī Ḥalfā southward towards Dongola, begun in 1873; Dār Fūr was conquered in 1874 and annexed to the Egyptian dominions; under his orders Sir S. W. Baker Pasha extended Egyptian territory as far as the Great Lakes, 1870–3, a work consolidated by C. G. Gordon Pasha, Baker's successor, in 1874–6; to support Gordon's activities in Equatoria he sent an expedition by sea to the Ṣomali coast with a view to opening a road from the African east coast to the Nile valley; the expedition failed owing to the hostility of Britain which supported the objections of the sultan of Zanzibar; all these schemes involved him in heavy debt which led in 1875 to the imposition of Anglo-French financial control; his dispute with the financial controllers resulted in his deposition by the Ottoman sultan in 1879 when he was succeeded by his son Muḥammad Tawfīq Pasha; he died in Constantinople; his policy and his person have given rise to an extensive literature, much of doubtful quality; while he must take the blame for landing the Egyptian Government in bankruptcy by his reckless squandering of public funds, nevertheless his attempts to benefit Egypt and the Sudan have in recent times received just recognition.

* **Ismā'īl 'Abd Allāhi al-Walī** (1793–1863), religious notable; of Dahmashī ('Abbāsī) origin he was born at al-Ubaiyaḍ and was first a pupil of al-Saiyid Ḥasan Muḥammad al-Mīrghanī, but later founded his own brotherhood, the Ismā'īlīya; a literary man and a great teacher of Islam he led a force consisting of his pupils against the people of the Nuba hills to convert them from paganism, a missionary venture celebrated by poets; he died at al-Ubaiyaḍ where his tomb, much visited, forms a prominent landmark; his son, al-Saiyid al-Makkī Ismā'īl, succeeded him in the headship of the brotherhood. He wrote about 45 books of which at least seven have been printed.

Ismā'īl 'Abd al-Nabī (–*c*. 1889), sultan of Dār Maṣālīṭ in western Dār Fūr and a member of a long line of warriors and religious teachers; on the eve of the spread of the Mahdist revolt to Dār Fūr the Egyptian Government appointed one Ḥajjām as bey of the Maṣālīṭ though Ismā'īl was popularly looked upon as the rightful ruler; taking advantage of the anarchy caused by the spread of Mahdism in the district he went to al-Ubaiyaḍ and got himself appointed amīr of the Maṣālīṭ; he was thrice attacked by Hajjām with the aid of the Fūrs but in vain; he later joined the Khalīfa 'Abd Allāhi in Omdurman, leaving his son Abū Bakr Ismā'īl to rule the amīrate; he died in Omdurman shortly afterwards.

* **Ismā'īl Pasha Aiyūb** (–1884), governor-general of the Sudan, 1873–6; he is variously said to have been a Circassian and a Kurd; rumour had it that he began his career as a musician in Muḥammad Sa'īd Pasha's band, a story possibly derived from his musical skill; the British traveller, E. A. De Cosson, wrote that he was educated at Marseilles and spoke French fluently; others have credited him with a knowledge of German; he received rapid promotion in the army and, transferred to the Sudan, was already a qā'immaqām when he was put in command of one of the columns hastening to the relief of Kassala which was besieged by Sudanese mutineers in 1865; in 1870 we find him president of the council in Khartoum and secretary to Ja'far Pasha Maẓhar, the governor-general; in this capacity he rendered useful service to Sir S. W. Baker's expedition to the Equatorial province, 1869–73; in 1872 he was in charge of a party engaged in clearing vegetable obstructions on the Upper White Nile which were hampering river communication between Baker and Khartoum; he assumed the governor-generalship in 1873 as a result of the Khedive's decision to

restore the centralized organization existing in Ja'far Pasha Maẓhar's time; the annexation of Dār Fūr had long been meditated by the Egyptian Government, and in 1874 the invasion of that sultanate by Zubair Pasha Raḥma Manṣūr with a private army forced the hand of Ismā'īl Pasha Aiyūb who quickly concentrated a regular army which, after a brief campaign, entered al-Fāshar, the capital of the Fūr sultanate, and Dār Fūr became a part of the Egyptian dominions; for his part in the war he was promoted from mīrliva' to farīq; his term of office was notable for town-planning and new public buildings in Khartoum; streets were realigned, the new palace of the governor-general was completed, and a beginning made with the reconstruction of the government offices; he was recalled to Egypt in 1876 and in the next year was succeeded by C. G. Gordon Pasha; the last eight years of his life were spent mostly in high public office; he was director of education in 1877–8 and minister of public works in 1881–2 in the ministry of Muḥammad Sharīf Pasha; he joined the cause of Aḥmad 'Urābī Pasha and was a member of the council for the defence of Cairo, but withdrew in time before the nationalist movement became involved in violence; in 1882 he was appointed to the commission which tried the leaders of the revolt; in 1883 he was minister of the interior; a man of knowledge and culture he was president of the Khedivial Geographical Society in 1883–4; in person he was tall and good-looking.

Ismā'īl ibn 'Alī abū'l-Fidā' (1273–1331), Muslim prince and historian; born at Damascus he ruled over Ḥamā in Syria; in the earlier part of his *Annals*, a valuable source for Saracen history, he makes a reference to the history of the Arabs before Islam which has some bearing upon the origin of the Arab tribes in the Sudan.

Ismā'īl al-Amīn al-Dalandūq (–1899), Mahdist amīr of the Ghudiyāt tribe who live between al-Ubaiyaḍ and the northern fringes of the Nuba hills; he fought under the command of the amīr Aḥmad Faḍil Muḥammad (who married into his family) against the Italians and afterwards against the Egyptian column under Sir C. S. B. Parsons Pasha at Gedaref and al-Dākhila in 1898; he was killed in the battle of Umm Dibaikarāt.

* **Ismā'īl al-Azharī** (1868–1947), muftī of the Sudan, 1924–32; by birth a Bidairī of the Dahmashīya branch, he was a son of Aḥmad Ismā'īl al-Azharī, the great walī who lived and taught in al-Ubaiyaḍ; himself a judge of the Islamic canon law he first served in the provinces and was later appointed an inspector of the Islamic courts, finally muftī; Ismā'īl al-Azharī the politician is his grandson and al-Saiyid Muḥammad al-Mīrghanī was his nephew.

Ismā'īl ibn Bādī IV (–*c.* 1777), puppet sultan of Sennar; he succeeded his brother Nāṣir about 1768 and earned some reputation for justice, though the real power was held by his Hāmaj vizier Muḥammad abū'l-Kailak Kamtūr; incurring the displeasure of this vizier's successor he was banished to Sawākin and was succeeded by his son, Sultan 'Adlān II.

Ismā'īl ibn al-Faqī 'Arabī (*c.* 1862–1918), Kahlī holy man; he was a noted genealogist and authority on tribal customs.

Ismā'īl wad al-Ḥājj Mun'im, called **Ismain Sakkāk** (*c.* 1795–*c.* 1850), leader of the 'Asākira section of the Ḥamar Arabs of Kordofan; he surrendered to the Egyptians who had taken al-Ubaiyaḍ in 1821 and was by them maintained as nāẓir of the 'Asākir in Kordofan, while his brother Makkī acted as head shaikh of the Ḥamar 'Asākir in Dār Fūr outside the Egyptian area of occupation; Ismā'īl lived at Firshaha and was known as a capable and just administrator; he kept the government ignorant of the true strength of his tribe (on which taxation was based) and for his refusing this information served a long term of imprisonment in al-Ubaiyaḍ; he is said to have been released owing to a threat from the Ḥamar tribe in Kordofan to withdraw into Dār Fūr; I. Pallme, the Bohemian, saw him in 1840 and called him a handsome and popular chief; the British trader John Petherick, who visited him in 1846, wrote that he had long succeeded his father to the chieftainship of the Ḥamar, that he was past his prime, and was given to drinking arrack, a habit acquired from the Turks.

* **Ismā'īl Ḥaqqī Pasha abū Jabal** (1818–82), governor-general of the Sudan; he was born in Anatolia of Kurdish ancestry; an outstanding soldier in his early days he was nicknamed 'Abū Jabal' by his men on account of some unrecorded act of bravery; in 1852 he was transferred from the governorship of the province of Qinā and Isnā to be governor-general of the Sudan in place of Rustum Pasha; his term of office was short as, owing to complaints from foreign traders in the country, he was recalled to Egypt in 1853 where he was tried for various irregularities; he stoutly defended himself against what appear to have been groundless accusations; he subsequently occupied various important posts; in the Crimean war of 1854–5 he commanded the 1st Egyptian infantry brigade before Sebastopol, and was later commander-in-chief of the Egyptian army; in 1856 he was secretary to the Royal Cabinet and in 1863 treasurer of the Royal Household, retiring in 1879; he attended a Cabinet council of which the Khedive Muḥammad Tawfīq was president, at Rās al-Ṭīn palace, Alexandria, on the eve of the bombardment of the forts by the British fleet in 1882; a son, Muḥammad Bey abū Jabal, born in 1859, was a prominent landowner and Freemason in Egypt; there is a brief life of him in Ilyās Zakhūra, *Kitāb mir'āt al-'aṣr* (Cairo, 1897), in which his name appears as Ismā'īl Ḥaqqī al-Shahīr Bābū Jabal.

* **Ismā'īl Kāmil Pasha** (1795–1822), third son of Muḥammad 'Alī Pasha, ruler of Egypt, by the daughter of the governor of Kavalla, later divorced; he was born at Kavalla, hence he appears frequently in contemporary records as *Kavālalī Ismā'īl*; in 1813 his father sent him to Constantinople to present to the sultan the keys of the city of Makka which had been liberated by Egyptian troops from the possession of the Wahhābites; in 1820 Muḥammad 'Alī entrusted him with the command of a small army being mobilized for the penetration of the Sudan; he left Cairo in July and during the summer led his force

by river through Nubia; by October the force was entering the lands
dominated by the S̲h̲ā'iqīya Arabs; these resisted the Turkish advance
in two fiercely fought battles at Kūrtī and Daija, both in November;
sending the transport laboriously by water over the Nile cataracts the
army now cut across the Bayūda to Berber which Ismā'īl entered on
8 March 1821; following the west bank of the Nile the army crossed
the river near the site of the present road bridge connecting Khartoum
and Omdurman at the end of May; finally, on 12 June, Ismā'īl entered
Sennar; here his force was beset by fever aggravated by the absence
of competent doctors; the viceroy judged it opportune to send Ibrāhīm
Pasha, his eldest son, to Sennar to help Ismā'īl with his maturer
experience; Ibrāhīm arrived at Sennar on 22 October; the two brothers
made reconnaissances for slaves and gold; leaving Sennar in December
with a force of about 1,500 men Ismā'īl visited Jabal Quraibin, Jabal
'Aqadī, and the mountains of Qaissān; meanwhile Ibrāhīm, attacked
by dysentery, returned to Cairo; he himself was exhausted by the
rigours of the climate and the intense discomfort of life deprived of all
amenities, and asked permission of his father to be relieved of his
command; after at first refusing his son's request Muḥammad 'Alī
Pasha, in October 1821, agreed to his return; Ismā'īl left Sennar with
a small suite; at Shendi he made impossible demands of the local *mak*
Nimr Muḥammad Nimr whom he treated with bad grace; Nimr concealed his anger and prepared a feast for Ismā'īl and his officers; at
a given signal fire was applied to bales of fodder which Nimr's men
had stacked round Ismā'īl's lodging; Ismā'īl and his staff were burned
to death; his remains were afterwards recovered and buried with those
of his brother Ṭūsūn in the cemetery of the Imām al-S̲h̲āfi'ī in al-Cairo.

Ismā'īl Muḥammad (–c. 1773), king of Taqalī, a member of the
royal house founded by al-Jailī abū Jarīda (*fl. c.* 1560); during his long
reign, which lasted from about 1705 to 1773, the boundaries of the
kingdom of Taqalī reached their greatest extent, attaining in the north
K̲h̲ōr abū Ḥabl and including all the country from Tukam and Turjok
in the west to Umm Ṭalḥa in the east; towards the end of his reign
Arab nomads, from whom Taqalī was to suffer much during the succeeding years, began to infiltrate into his territory; he died at a great
age and was succeeded by his son Abū Bakr who ruled till 1814.

Ismā'īl Muḥammad al-S̲h̲aik̲h̲ (–1926), Ḥamar notable, nāẓir
of the 'Asākira branch of the Ḥamar tribe of Kordofan.

Ismā'īl Muṣṭafā al-Falakī Pasha (*c.* 1830–1901), Egyptian astronomer and engineer; after schooling in Egypt he was sent by the
Egyptian Government to study physics and astronomy at the École
Polytechnique in Paris, an institution from which his brother Maḥmūd
Aḥmad Ḥamdī al-Falakī also graduated; later appointed the first
director of the new observatory built at Būlāq, he was also director
of the Cairo School of Engineering; he was in the Sudan in 1867 surveying a track for a proposed railway between Sawākin and Shendi;
he prepared a competent map of the country to accompany his report;
he was a member of many learned societies throughout the world.

Ismā'īl Rājī Bey (1862–), qā'immaqām of the Egyptian army; born in Cairo he entered the Military School in 1874 and was later commissioned to the infantry, afterwards serving on the staff; as a junior officer he was with the new Egyptian army in the Nile campaign, 1884–5; promoted yūzbāshī in 1886 he was transferred to the Sudanese field artillery and in 1887 was in command of artillery at Sawākin where he saw active service, including the battle of Jummaiza (Gemmaiza), 1888; back on the Nile in 1889 he fought in the battle of Tūshkī (Toski), 1889; in 1891 he transferred to the police and was promoted qā'immaqām in 1894; after serving as chief of police in several provinces he became a provincial governor.

* **Ismā'īl Pasha Ṣādiq** (–1876), Egyptian statesman, a native of Asyūt by a Turkish father and an Egyptian mother; as minister of finance he was held partly to blame for the financial debauchery of the government; in 1876 he was arrested by order of the Khedive Ismā'īl Pasha and taken to Dongola where he was murdered by connivance of the governor, Muḥammad Bey Almās; his grave in Dongola is known and preserved; he derived his popular name al-Mufattish (the Inspector) from the fact that he was formerly inspector-general of Egypt.

Isrā'īl Dā'ūd Binyamīn (–1915), Jewish trader; born in Baghdad he came to Egypt while a youth and there married a Jewish lady; he came to the Sudan about 1875 and set up in business as a cloth merchant; he survived the massacre of Khartoum and lived in Omdurman under the rule of the Khalīfa 'Abd Allāhi, travelling occasionally to Kordofan and Dār Fūr and becoming a Muslim; on the Anglo-Egyptian occupation he continued his business in Omdurman; visiting Dār Fūr in 1915 on the eve of the outbreak of war with the Sudan he was arrested by the agents of Sultan 'Alī Dinār and killed at al-Fāshar on suspicion of being a spy.

Istānbūlīya (popularly **Istāmbūlīya**), **Georges** (*c.* 1840–1926), Syrian Christian merchant; he was at al-Ubaiyaḍ when the Mahdists approached the town in 1882; together with most of the inhabitants he went over to the Mahdist side before the siege of the town began; during the Mahdist régime he kept a shop in Omdurman and was a clerk to the Mahdī and the Khalīfa 'Abd Allāhi; he was considerate to European captives; he survived the *Mahdīya* and died in Khartoum.

Īyāsū (Jesus) I (*c.* 1662–1706), king of Abyssinia; with his capital at Gondar he reigned from 1682 until 1706 when he was defeated in battle and killed by one of his sons; in 1692, in the course of a raid on the fringes of the kingdom of Sennar, he attacked the Shanqala on the upper reaches of the Blue Nile in the foothills of the Abyssinian mountains and the Ḍubā'īna Arabs living round the confluence of the Rivers Atbara and Setit; he is said to have been one of the few Abyssinian rulers of his age who showed any tendency towards beneficence.

Īyāsū (Jesus) II (–1755), king of Abyssinia who made a fateful intervention into the history of the Funj kingdom of Sennar; he came to the throne in 1730 and about 1738 invaded the Funj dominions;

aided by Naiyīl wad ʿAjīb, a Funj rebel, he destroyed a Funj army on the banks of the River Dinder; victory made him over-confident; lured towards Sennar by a strategem he arrived on the banks of the Blue Nile opposite the capital; here he was attacked by the Funj cavalry and badly beaten; he retreated through the valley of the Atbara to Gondar, giving out that he had won a victory over Sennar.

ʿIzz al-Dīn Aibek al-Afram (*fl.* 1276), Mameluke general; with Shams al-Dīn al-Farghānī, a brother-officer, he was sent by the sultan Baibars I to subdue the Nubians; he put the country south of Aswān to the sword while Shams al-Dīn pushed on past the Second Cataract towards Dongola; Dā'ūd, king of the Nubians, evaded capture and Shekenda, a puppet of the Mamelukes, was crowned in his stead; about 1293 he again came to Nubia, this time to set up another puppet king of Nubia, and ascended the Nile valley as far as the region of Kabūshīya.

al-Jabartī. *See* ʿABD AL-RAḤMĀN ḤASAN . . . AL-JABARTĪ.

Jabbār ʿAlī Missār (–1931), notable of the Ḥumr tribe of Kordofan; he was deputy to the nāẓir of the Ajaira division of the Ḥumr Arabs of Kordofan.

Jābir ʿAlī (–1934), tribal notable of the Ingassana negroes of the Blue Nile valley; he was a magistrate.

Jabr al-Dār Jibrīl Zarrūq (*c.* 1872–1920), nāẓir of the Aḥāmda Arabs of the White Nile valley; he succeeded the nāẓir ʿAbd al-Raḥīm Jaha who was dismissed in 1911; his father and grandfather held the nāẓirship before him.

Jabrā'īl Pasha Ḥaddād (1866–1923), Syrian administrator; born at Tripoli in the Lebanon (hence the addition of al-Ṭarābulsī to his name) he graduated from the American University, Beirut, and, coming to Egypt, joined the expedition of 1884–5 which attempted the relief of Khartoum; he was in the Egyptian ministry of the interior, 1886–1909; in the First World War which ended in 1918 by the driving of the Turks from Palestine and Syria he was made chief of the Palestine Gendarmerie under Field-Marshal Lord Allenby; he was later governor of Damascus under King Faisal's brief administration and a councillor of the king in ʿIrāq; he died at Nice; he wrote of his experiences in the Nile expedition in *Ta'rīkh al-ḥarb al-sūdānīya* (Cairo, [1888 ?]).

Jackson Bey, Ernest Somerville (1872–1943), British lieutenant-colonel, and mīrālai of the Egyptian army; he was commissioned to the Welch Regiment in 1892 and served in the Egyptian army from 1898 to 1914; he took part in the closing operations against the Khalīfa ʿAbd Allāhi in 1899 and spent most of the remainder of his service in the Sudan; after fighting in the First World War he returned to the Sudan where he farmed at Manṣūrkottī, near Dongola.

Jackson Pasha, Sir Herbert William (1861–1931), British soldier and administrator, liwā' of the Egyptian army; he joined the British army in 1881 and served in the Egyptian war of 1882 and in the Nile campaign of 1884–5; seconded to the Egyptian army in 1888 he fought in the campaigns of 1896–8 for the recovery of the Sudan; after the battle of Omdurman he commanded the Sudanese force at Fashoda in 1898 and was commandant there after Kitchener's return to Omdurman; seconded to the new Sudan Government he was governor of Berber, 1899, civil secretary and deputy governor-general, 1900–1, and thereafter governor of Dongola, 1902–22, when for a few months he was inspector-general of the Sudan, a post since abolished; he retired from the service in 1923 and farmed near Merowe; he was promoted brigadier-general in 1919 and major-general in 1922; he was knighted in 1919.

* **al-Jadail Muḥammad Jailī** (1866–1911), chief of Jabal Taroi in the eastern Nuba hills; a Muslim by religion he claimed descent from the Rubāṭāb Arabs of the Nile valley; in 1910, the year of the appearance of Halley's comet, he defied the Government; to suppress him called for the largest patrol mobilized in the Sudan since the Anglo-Egyptian occupation; escaping capture for the time he fled to Jabal Daiyar, but was finally caught and hanged.

Ja'far Bakrī al-Mīrghanī (–1944), religious notable, son of al-Saiyid Bakrī al-Mīrghanī and cousin of al-Saiyid Sir 'Alī al-Mīrghanī Pasha, present leader of the Khatmīya brotherhood; he did much to maintain the influence of the brotherhood among the Muslims of Eritrea where he spent most of his life; he died at Tessenei and was buried in Khatmīya near Kassala; al-Saiyid Bakrī Ja'far Bakrī al-Mīrghanī is his son.

Ja'far Pasha Maẓhar (–1878), mīrlivā of the Egyptian army and governor-general of the Sudan, 1866–71; of his early life little is at present recorded; he had been an officer in the Egyptian fleet, 1830–47, when he transferred to the arsenal at Būlāq as assistant director with rank of qā'immaqām; he was afterwards governor successively of a number of Egyptian provinces and in 1863 governor of the island of Thasos; already a pasha, he was in 1865 appointed vice-governor-general of the Sudan with a mission to report on the military mutiny which had broken out in Kassala and other towns in the Sudan and which was almost quelled on his arrival; he travelled to Khartoum by way of Sawākin and Kassala and made his report to Ismā'īl Pasha; on the recall of Ja'far Pasha Ṣādiq in 1866 he was appointed to the vacant post; his investiture in Khartoum took place amid solemnity, Shāhīn Pasha Kinj, then on a tour of inspection in the Sudan, attended the ceremony as the viceroy's representative; in 1867 he visited the Somali coast and recommended the Egyptian occupation of Tajūra; the mak of Jabal Taqalī made his peace with the Government; he sent samples of Sudan products, animals, and works of art to Cairo for shipment to the Paris Exhibition of 1867, the samples including the ibis bird and silver filigree work; he encouraged commerce, made useful reforms in the administration, and extended the Egyptian authority in several directions; on the appointment of Sir S. W. Baker as governor of the Equatorial province in 1869 he was helpful to Baker but warned the Khedive of the danger of employing a foreigner in this post; a man of culture he was the centre of a literary circle of Sudanese poets and men of letters in the capital; he failed, however, to carry out the Khedive's forward economic policy or to improve the finances of the Sudan Government; according to a native tradition (doubtless exaggerated) he increased the taxes six times over what they were before and collected them with brutality in order to balance his budget; as a result of his opposition to the schemes of Aḥmad Pasha Mumtāz (supported by the Khedive) to extend the cultivation of cotton, he was recalled to Egypt in 1871 leaving behind him the reputation for laborious honesty, enhanced by the rumour that he left in debt; he then held various governorships and legal appointments in Egypt and in 1876 was director of customs and president of the legislative assembly. His collected poems have not been published though his son, Muḥammad Sa'īd Bey of the appeal court, Khartoum, preserved some of them; he was probably the first governor-general of the Sudan to possess a literary knowledge of Arabic; see 'Abd al-Raḥmān Zakī, *A'lām al-jaish* (Cairo, 1947).

Ja'far Pasha Ṣādiq (*c.* 1805–), governor-general of the Sudan, 1865–6, in succession to Mīrlivā Mūsā Pasha Ḥamdī; a Circassian by birth he was promoted from the ranks in the infantry and about 1824 reached the rank of sōl qōl aghāsi; in 1829 he was a binbāshī and in 1833 a qā'immaqām in the cavalry; he probably took part in the Syrian wars against Turkey; promoted mīrlivā about 1849 he was governor of several successive provinces and in 1852 commissioner for Suez; he served in the Crimean war of 1853–5 in command of a brigade of field artillery in the Egyptian contingent assisting the Ottoman army, returning in 1855 to his commissionership at Suez; though during his stay in the Sudan there were minor administrative developments, such as the raising of Fashoda to a muḥāfiẓate, the main event was the mutiny of Sudanese troops at Kassala and elsewhere; his feeble handling of the mutiny led to his recall to Egypt and to his replacement by Ja'far Pasha Maẓhar who had been sent by the Egyptian Government to report on the outbreak; his poor health may have been another reason for his recall; he afterwards held various judicial posts and in 1879–84 was minister of justice when he retired on account of old age; Zakī Fahmī has a life of him in *Ṣafwat al-'aṣr* (Cairo, 1926).

al-Jailānī Bey al-Amīr 'Uthmān (–1883), head shaikh of the Arteiga (Beja) tribe; he succeeded his father al-Amīr 'Uthmān on the latter's death in 1863 and was himself succeeded by his own son Muḥammad, while his younger brother Maḥmūd (afterwards Bey), who had been helping him, became 'umda of Sawākin.

al-Jailī wad Adam (–1916), king of Taqalī in the Nuba hills of southern Kordofan, son of king Adam Dabbalū; he was at first the right-hand man of his brother 'Alī abū Zanait who since 1885 had been leading a desperate war of resistance to the Mahdists in the fastnesses of the eastern hills; 'Alī's cruelty at length drove Jailī to opposition and finally to revolt; in 1896 he defeated 'Alī, who fled to Jabal Daiyar in the north, and assumed the kingship; Jailī made peace with the

Khalīfa 'Abd Allāhi but, after the Anglo-Egyptian victories of 1898, refused the fugitive Khalīfa sanctuary in Taqalī territory; the Condominium Government, to which he gave grudging allegiance, confirmed him in the kingship of Taqalī; on his death he was succeeded by his son Abū Bakr who died in 1921.

al-Jailī Aḥmad al-'Abbās (–1946), son of 'Abbās wad Muḥammad Badr al-'Ubaid, the Mahdist leader; he was shaikh of the Masallamīya khuṭṭ in the district of Rufā'a and a magistrate; he died in Khartoum.

al-Jailī abū Jarīda ibn Muḥammad (*fl.* 1560), traditional founder of the present royal line of Taqalī in the Nuba hills; a son of an immigrant holy man Muḥammad al-Jailī by a daughter of a Nuba chief called Kabr-Kabr, he was a man of outstanding ability, completing the conversion of Taqalī to Islam and building a mosque the ruins of which may still be seen; he reigned from about 1560 to about 1585 and died at al-Hoi where his tomb still stands; he was succeeded by his son Sabu.

al-Jailī abū Qurun (*c.* 1600–*c.* 1665), king of Taqalī in the Nuba hills and son of King al-Jailī 'Awn Allāh; he ruled from about 1640 to about 1665; enjoying amity with the Funj kingdom of Sennar he married 'Ajaib umm Shilla, daughter of King al-Rubāṭ ibn Bādī, whose large retinue were probably the ancestors of the present Funj elements in the kingdom; later in his reign the peace was broken and Sennar made war on him when King Bādī II abū Diqn attacked Taqalī and made al-Jailī pay tribute to the Funj power; he was buried at Keraiya and was succeeded by King Muḥammad who reigned from about 1668 to about 1702.

* **Jamāl al-Dīn al-Afghānī** (1839–97), pan-Islamic agitator; born near Kabul in Afghanistan he lived in Egypt, 1871–9, and was then banished from the country; with his friend and pupil, Shaikh Muḥammad 'Abduh, he went to Paris where he published a pan-Islamic weekly newspaper in Arabic called *al-Urwa al-wuthkā* (the Indissoluble Bond) in 1884; this journal was the organ of a secret society of which the immediate aim was to end British rule in Egypt and the northern Sudan; the journal was discontinued after a few months when Jamāl al-Dīn made a brief visit to London to discuss with Lord Hartington, British secretary of state for war, and other politicians, the possibility of coming to terms with the Mahdists; it has been asserted (though the compiler has seen no supporting evidence) that the decision of the British Cabinet early in 1885 to abandon the intention of reconquering the Sudan was prompted by Jamāl al-Dīn and Muḥammad 'Abduh; after a life of politics, propaganda, and adventure Jamāl al-Dīn died in Constantinople.

James, Frank Linsley (1851–90), British explorer and hunter; with his brothers A. and W. James, together with A. Sutton, J. C. Maxwell, and a doctor, he travelled by way of the Nile valley and the Nubian desert to Berber where the party arrived in December 1877; they then ascended the Atbara river to Kassala and the country of the Setit, returning to Berber in 1878 whence they went over the Bayūda to Merowe and on through Dongola to Wādī Ḥalfā where they took ship for Egypt; at the end of 1881, accompanied by his two brothers and by G. Percy, V. Aylmer, R. B. Colvin, E. L. Phillips, and a doctor named J. Williams, he landed at Sawākin and travelled to Muṣawwaʿ via Kassala, Aicota, the country of the Basé, the Setit, and Keren, arriving at Muṣawwaʿ in April 1882; he published an account of his travels in 1883; a second edition which appeared in 1884 contains additional information.

Jameson, James Sligo (1856–88), British traveller and naturalist; after travelling in many parts of the world he served as a naturalist with H. M. Stanley's expedition to relieve Emin Pasha, 1887; on the murder of Major E. M. Barttelot he prepared to conduct the rearguard of the expedition in a search for Stanley who was believed to be in the region of the Nile valley, but died of fever at Bangala in the north-eastern part of the Congo Free State; his diary of the expedition was published in 1890.

Jāmiʿ Khair (–1929), Meidōbī notable of the Shelkota-Aurungide line; he succeeded Aḥmad Aingeru as malik of the Shelkota Meidōb after a struggle with a cousin of the male line who had set himself up as king; he himself came of the female line and, according to the Meidōb custom of matrilinear succession, was considered as the rightful heir; at this time ʿAlī ʿĪsā of the Urrtī was king of the whole district but, as ʿAlī ʿĪsā lived in al-Fāshar, he acted as ʿAlī's deputy; in 1897 the Mahdist amīr, Maḥmūd Aḥmad, having been appointed governor of Kordofan and Dār Fūr, compelled him and others to accompany him to Omdurman to assist in the resistance to the Anglo-Egyptian forces closing in on the Mahdist capital; he was present at the battle of the Atbara, 1898, in which his old leader ʿAlī ʿĪsā was killed, but did not fight at Omdurman; instead he returned to Dār Fūr with ʿAlī Dīnār who made him ruler of Jabal Meidōb; when the Sudan Government occupied Dār Fūr in 1916, Manṣūr Sulaimān was made malik of the Urrtī, and the Turrtī also became an independent district; Manṣūr was dismissed in 1923 and the Urrtī again came under Jāmiʿ Khair; unfortunately his lack of tact with his people together with the intrigues of the deposed Manṣūr led to the revolt of the Urrtī in 1928 which caused his resignation; he was succeeded by his son Muḥammad Sayaḥ.

Jawhar. *See* Abū'l-Ḥasan (Ḥusain) Jawhar ibn ʿAbd Allāh . . . al-Rūmī.

Jephson, Arthur Jermy Mounteney (1858–1908), British explorer; he accompanied H. M. Stanley through the Ituri forest to Lake Albert to the relief of Emin Pasha in 1888; he was imprisoned with Emin by Sudanese mutineers at Dufilé on the Albert Nile in August 1888; he rejoined Stanley at Kavali in February 1889 and, along with Emin, safely left Equatoria with the rest of the expedition; in 1890 he published an account of the expedition.

Jesus, king of Abyssinia. *See* Īyāsū (Jesus) I; Īyāsū (Jesus) II.

John, king of Abyssinia. *See* Yoḥannes (John) IV.

Jomard, Edmé François (1777–1862), French Egyptologist and geographer; born at Versailles he was attached to Bonaparte's expedition to Egypt, 1798–1801, and from 1828 was a member of the Institut de France; as an official of the Royal (afterwards National) Library of Paris he wrote extensively on the antiquities of the Sudan; the translation into French and the publication in 1845 of the travels of Muḥammad ibn ʿUmar al-Tūnisī to Dār Fūr owed much to his encouragement; he was for long a distinguished member of the French Academy of Inscriptions and Belles-Lettres, and was for some time director of the Egyptian educational missions in France.

Joseph . . . (*fl.* 1705), Roman Catholic missionary priest of the Franciscan order whose full name is not known; with several fellow-Franciscans he left Cairo and arrived at Sennar in 1705 in the reign of King Bādī III; a story was current at the time that he and his party poisoned the mind of the king as to the objects of a French diplomatic mission to Abyssinia headed by Le Noir du Roule to which the Franciscans were said to be opposed; whatever the truth of the story Le Noir du Roule and all but one of his suite were murdered at Sennar late in 1705 by the king's order.

Jubāra Aḥmad Jaifūn (1852–1918), nāẓir of the Shankhāb Baqqāra of the White Nile; formerly the whole tribe was under ʿAsākir abū Kalām, nāẓir of the Jimaʿa of whom the Shankhāb form part; several of his family were killed while fighting under the Khalīfa ʿAbd Allāhi at Umm Dibaikarāt, 1899; his brother ʿĪsā was ʿumda of the Shankhāb in the Kosti district.

Jubārat Allāh . . . (–1863), Sudanese soldier; he commanded the Sudanese battalion at the beginning of the Mexican campaign until his death from yellow fever at Vera Cruz when the command of the battalion devolved on the ṣāgh qōl aghāsi Muḥammad Almās.

Julianus (*fl.* 550), Alexandrine Christian priest of the Monophysite persuasion; with support from the Byzantine Empress Theodora, wife of Justinian the Great, he led a Christian mission to the Roman province of the Thebaïd about 550 and remained there for two years as bishop of Nubia; he was succeeded by Longinus.

Jumʿa wad Jadain (1856–1939), notable of the Awlād Jābir section of the Zaiyādīya tribe of Dār Fūr; during the Mahdist times he was in the cavalry of the Khalīfa ʿAbd Allāhi, and later, after the fall of the Mahdist power, he was a well-known cavalry leader under Sultan ʿAlī Dīnār in Dār Fūr; although loyal to ʿAlī Dīnār he joined the Sudan Government after the fall of al-Fāshar in 1916 and was confirmed in his position as head of the Awlād Jābir; he resigned from the shaikhship in 1932 and in 1934 was appointed one of the Zaiyādīya representatives on the Mellīt court.

Jumʻa Kyango (–1928), chief of the Golo-Buṣailī tribe of the Baḥr al-Ghazāl, and a magistrate.

Jumʻa Shaikh al-Amīn (–1882), leader of the ʻAbdullāb Arabs of Ḥalfaiya near Khartoum; succeeding Shaikh Idrīs Nāṣir he enjoyed the esteem of the Egyptian Government and was known as a serious, just man; on the outbreak of the Mahdist revolt the Government appointed him a sanjaq over a force of 400 tribesmen in the expedition commanded by ʻAlī Bey Luṭfī which attempted in vain to relieve Bāra and al-Ubaiyaḍ which were closely invested by the Mahdists; he and most of his men were killed in battle near Branku where he was buried; his successor, Shaikh Nāṣir Jumʻa, was appointed during the last days of the Egyptian Government and succeeded in weathering the Mahdist régime with full authority over the ʻAbdullāb; to him passed the hereditary sword 'Niam-Niam'; he was killed in battle against the Anglo-Egyptian forces on the Atbara in 1898.

* **Junker, Wilhelm** (1840–92), German traveller and naturalist; born in Moscow of German parents, but of Russian nationality, he studied medicine in Germany; he came to Egypt and made his way to the Sudan where he explored the lower reach of the River Sobat and the western tributaries of the Upper White Nile, 1876–8; after a period spent in Europe he returned to the Sudan and set out to explore the country of the Nile-Congo watershed, 1879; after four years spent among the Azande and Monbuttu peoples and with Emin Pasha on the Equatorial Nile, he started to return to Europe with his collections; prevented by the Mahdist revolt from returning north by the Nile valley route he made his way southward through Uganda to Zanzibar, arriving in Europe in 1887 and carrying with him Emin Pasha's journals; while his work in the field of natural history is not to be compared with that of G. A. Schweinfurth who travelled over much the same ground in the region of the Nile-Congo watershed, his writings are full of interesting information about the native people; he added much to our knowledge of the southern tributaries of the Baḥr al-Ghazāl and of the Uélé river; he discovered the River Mbomu, the important northern tributary of the Uélé.

Juraidīnī, Labīb Buṭrus (1872–1938), Lebanese scholar and journalist; he was born in Shwaifat of a Christian family and was educated at the Syrian Protestant College (afterwards known as the American University) at Beirut from which he graduated in 1891; after three years spent in teaching at the college he went to the United States and there obtained a doctorate in divinity; in 1906 he became editor of the *Sudan Times*, a newspaper published in Khartoum in Arabic and English and founded in 1903 by Khalīl Dā'ūd Thābit, afterwards editor of *al-Muqaṭṭam* of Cairo; he was in charge of the *Sudan Times* till 1925 when the Sudan Printing Press which printed this journal was taken over by McCorquodale & Co., Ltd.; he then returned to Beirut where, in straightened circumstances owing to unfortunate investments, he devoted himself to literary work.

Kabarega (–1923), *mukāma* of Bunyoro, son of Kamurasi; he began his reign on his father's death, 1869, defeating his rival brother in battle; his relations with Sir S. W. Baker Pasha who proclaimed an Egyptian protectorate over Bunyoro at Masindi, 1872, were unhappy and he compelled Baker to retire northward; he was also hostile to Baker's successor as general governor of the Egyptian Equatorial province, C. G. Gordon Pasha, whose agents he treated roughly, 1874–6; helped by Arab slave traders from the Sudan he warred successfully against Buganda; he assisted Emin Pasha when the latter was isolated by the Mahdist revolt, but attacked Emin's representative, G. Casati, 1888; hostile to the British protectorate over his country he fought against the British commissioner, Colonel Sir H. E. Colvile, who commanded a force of Sudanese troops and their Buganda allies; after eluding capture for five years he was finally taken and deposed, 1899; with Mwanga, *kabāka* of Buganda, he was banished first to British Somaliland then to the Seychelles where he embraced Christianity; released in 1923 he died at Jinja on his way home to Bunyoro; the present *mukāma* is his grandson.

Kaiku, or **Kaikun,** or **Kaikumbe** (–1881), *reth* of the Shilluk tribe living round Fashoda on the White Nile on whom the Egyptian Government had conferred the rank of bey; with a force of Shilluk tribesmen he accompanied an Egyptian army under Rāshid Bey Aymān which was attacked by the Mahdists at Jabal Qadīr in the Nuba hills and massacred; he was among the slain.

Kakwal, Anton (*fl.* 1864), Dinka youth; he was educated at the Roman Catholic mission school in Khartoum where he showed ability in languages; he later went to Europe and in 1864–5 at Brixen and Verona worked with J. C. J. Mitterrützner who was compiling a grammar of the Dinka speech published at Brixen in 1866; information about his subsequent life has not been found.

Kamāl al-Dīn Ḥusain (1875–1932), prince of the Royal House of Egypt and explorer; he travelled in the Sudan before the First World War, visiting Khartoum and the regions of the Upper White Nile; a son of Sultan Ḥusain Kamāl he declined the throne on his father's death in 1917; he was an expert on the Libyan desert in which he travelled much; in 1924–5 he set out from the oasis of Khārja and determined positions and altitudes of the principal peaks and springs of Jabal 'Uwaināt, discovered in 1923 by Aḥmad Muḥammad Ḥaṣanain Bey (afterwards pasha); he discovered and located the salt lake of Merga; in 1925–6 he explored the country between 'Uwaināt and Sarra well and determined the exact position and approximate altitude of the latter; he died at Toulouse.

Kamtūr Aḥmad (*fl.* 1750), noted shaikh of the sultanate of Sennar in the time of Sultan Bādī IV abū Shilūkh; taking advantage of the declining power of the central government he made himself the almost independent ruler of the land between Karkōj and al-Roseires in the valley of the Blue Nile; he is traditionally said to have been killed in battle with his sultan; his son Muḥammad Kamtūr was a great filibuster in the days of the Funj decay, and his descendants, known as the Kamātīr or Awlād Kamtūr, ruled the district until Turkish times, but have now almost died out.

See also MUḤAMMAD ABŪ'L-KAILAK (ABŪ LIKAILIK) KAMTŪR; MUḤAMMAD KAMTŪR.

Kamurasi (–1869), *mukāma* of Bunyoro; he ascended the throne, 1862, when he welcomed the British explorers J. H. Speke and J. A. Grant who had discovered the source of the White Nile; on his death he was succeeded by his son Kabarega who fought his way to the throne and reigned, 1869–99.

* **Kanbal,** called **al-Malik Kanbal** (–1840), Shā'iqī leader; he was in command of 1,000 Shā'iqīya irregular cavalry at Wad Madanī in 1837 when Prince von Pückler-Muskau met him and described him as black, handsome, and courteous; the tax-collecting duties of the Shā'iqīya irregulars in the Egyptian Government service made him hated among the Sudanese taxpayers; according to F. Werne he was a good soldier and generous to the poor; he was, wrote Werne, shot in the back in a brawl between the troops of Aḥmad Pasha abū Widān and some Shā'iqīya under Ḥamad wad al-Mak; Aḥmad Pasha, who greatly valued his services, had his son pensioned and educated; this son was Bashīr Bey Kanbal, an officer of the Egyptian army and later mu'āwin of the Arabs in Kordofan.

* **Kanbal Ḥamad** (–1884), Bidairi trader of the Ṭaraifī clan who was head merchant of Kūrtī, between Dongola and Merowe, and a prominent exporter of gum arabic and ostrich feathers when Kūrtī was an important trade centre containing, it is said locally, no less than seventy-five merchants engaged in the export business; he was also head of the local soothsayers; though no sympathizer with the Mahdist cause he was killed during the indiscriminate ravaging of the town by the Turks following the battle of Wad Dabash, half a mile south of the town, between Muṣṭafā Pasha Yāwar, governor of Dongola, and a Mahdist force; his son Ḥasan (d. 1933) was an influential local notable; another son, 'Umar, is 'umda of Kūrtī.

* **Kanfu Adam** (*fl.* 1840), Abyssinian governor, dajazmach of Dambeya province on the northern shores of Lake Tana; he played a leading part in raids and counter-raids against the Sudan; the Ethiopian chronicles call him good and just: 'he cut off the hands and feet of brigands and thieves, and rich and poor rejoiced'.

Kankir (–1866), *reth* of the Shilluk tribe of the White Nile; he was killed in battle with an Egyptian force under Muḥammad Bey Ḥilmī, muḥāfiẓ of the White Nile, and was succeeded by al-Ganek who assumed office in 1867.

* **Karam Allāh Muḥammad Kurkusāwī** (–1903), Mahdist amīr; a Dongolāwī by origin he was born on the island of Kurkus near Shendi; in his youth he was employed in the service of slave-raiding organiza-

tions in the Baḥr al-Ghazāl region; from here he went to al-Ubaiyaḍ in 1882–3 to join the Mahdist cause, and Muḥammad Aḥmad al-Mahdī appointed him amīr of the Baḥr al-Ghazāl province; he was put in command of a force which entered the province, occupied it, and captured the governor F. Lupton Bey and the government garrison in 1884; he was later in charge of a Mahdist force sent to suppress a rebellion of the Rizaiqāt in southern Dār Fūr; he fulfilled his mission with great slaughter; he fought in many of the Mahdist campaigns and was wounded at Firka (Firket) in 1896; in 1898, when all was lost, he took refuge with Sultan 'Alī Dīnār who later, suspecting him of intrigue, had him killed near al-Fāshar.

Kardam ibn abū'l-Dīs (*c.* 1300 ?), one of the first ancestors of the Ja'līyīn Arabs to enter the Sudan; he is traditionally said to have brought his family to Kordofan and to have settled there.

Karrār al-'Abbādī (*fl.* 1814), 'Abbādī robber, chief of the 'Ashabāb 'Abābda; he lay in the mountains of the Atbai and in 1814 plundered several caravans, mostly of Berber merchants; Muḥammad 'Alī Pasha, now in effective occupation of the Nubian Nile valley, sent several parties to catch him, but in vain.

Kāsā Tēwōdrōs (Theodore) II (1818–68), king of Abyssinia; nephew of the governor of Kwara he crushed the vice-regent, Rās 'Alī, in 1853 and, in 1855, overthrowing the ruler of Tigrai, had himself crowned as *Negus* of Abyssinia; at his coronation he swore that he would rule all the provinces that had been once a part of Abyssinia; his tyrannical rule provoked hostility and in 1861–2 the Boghos in the region of Keren threw off his yoke; in 1862 he told C. D. Cameron, British consul at Muṣawwa', that he intended to drive the Turks and Egyptians out of Matamma (Gallabat) and the Red Sea ports, and in 1864 accused Britain of helping Turkey and Egypt against him, venting his anger upon Cameron whom he imprisoned; in 1868 his stronghold, Magdala, was stormed by a British force which had landed on the Red Sea coast at Annesley Bay, and Theodore, who had long shown signs of madness, shot himself.

Kashta (*fl.* 750 B.C.), Nubian governor of Kush till about 750 B.C. and then king of Kush and Thebes which he ruled approximately 750 B.C.–740 B.C., having acquired Thebes by conquest; he was succeeded by Piankhi I and founded a line of kings of Libyan blood who ruled with varying success over Kush and Egypt for a hundred years.

Kelly Bey, Harry Holdsworth (1880–1914), British soldier and engineer; he was commissioned to the Royal Engineers in 1899 and from 1903 to 1913 was seconded to the Egyptian army during which time he was assistant director of public works in the Sudan Government with rank of qā'immaqām; he was killed in action in France at the beginning of the First World War.

Kennedy Pasha, Macdougall Ralston (1873–1924), British soldier and engineer; born at Stewarton, Scotland, he was commissioned to the Royal Engineers and from 1899 to 1909 was seconded to the

Egyptian army; in 1904, when Sawākin was being made the port for the Nile–Red Sea railway then under construction, he pointed out the superior advantages of the alternative harbour to the north which afterwards became known as Port Sudan; he was also largely responsible for the Khōr Arbaʿt water-supply line on which Port Sudan subsists; he was director of the public works department of the Sudan Government from 1906 to 1916; in 1920 he and Sir W. Willcocks were charged before the British consular court in Cairo with making a defamatory libel on Sir M. MacDonald, under-secretary of state, public works department, Egyptian Government, in which they accused the latter of falsifying figures and statistics concerning the Jazīra irrigation scheme; Kennedy was not tried but left the country; he died at Saint-Servan-sur-Mer, France.

Keppel, Sir Colin Richard (1862–1947), British admiral, son of Admiral of the Fleet the Hon. Sir H. Keppel; he entered the Royal Navy in 1875 and as a sub-lieutenant took part in the Egyptian war of 1882; he served in the naval brigade attached to the Nile expedition of 1884–5 and was for some days on board Gordon's fleet which came down to Matamma to meet the British force; promoted commander in 1895 he commanded the naval flotilla on the Sudan Nile during the Anglo-Egyptian advance against Omdurman, 1897–8; in August 1898 he had a narrow escape from drowning when his flagship, the *Ẓāfir*, suddenly sank at the entrance to the Sixth Cataract; he was promoted captain in 1899 and in 1911 he commanded the squadron which escorted King George V and Queen Mary to and from the Durbar at Delhi, a duty for which he was knighted; he was made an admiral in 1917; he was Serjeant-at-Arms in the British House of Commons, 1915–35.

Kerr, Graham Campbell (1872–1913), British official; born in Aberdeen he was educated at Durham School and Cambridge University where he was a rowing 'blue'; he entered the Sudan political service in 1901 and was governor of the Red Sea province, 1909–13 (the first civilian governor in the Anglo-Egyptian Sudan), and of Berber from 1913; he died in Edinburgh while on leave; a gateway has been built in his memory at Durham School.

Kfouri, Aziz (1874–1942), Syrian business man and farmer; born at Beirut of well-to-do Greek Orthodox parents he was educated in the French school at ʿAntūra in the Lebanon and later, while still a young man, emigrated to Egypt where he worked in commercial and agricultural enterprises; he came to the Sudan in 1899 and, making his home in Khartoum, contributed to the rebuilding of the city which had been destroyed during the Mahdist revolt; he was a pioneer of pump irrigation and ran a model farm at Khartoum North; a founder member of the Sudan chamber of commerce he was its president in 1929.

Khair Aghā . . . (*c.* 1800–   ), Sudanese officer in the Egyptian army; in 1821 or 1822 he was enrolled in the irregular formations and in 1824 or 1825 was transferred to the 9th regular infantry regiment of the niẓām al-jadīd, the new regular army created by the viceroy

Muḥammad ʿAlī Pasha; he was commissioned as a mulāzim II in 1834 or 1835; in 1848 he was transferred to the recruits' battalions for a year and on promotion to mulāzim I was posted to the 8th infantry regiment; although nothing is known of his origin or subsequent career he is noteworthy as being among the first few Sudanese to receive commissions in the Egyptian regular army in the viceroyalty of Muḥammad ʿAlī Pasha.

Khair al-Dīn Bey (*fl.* 1838), official in the service of Muḥammad ʿAlī Pasha; he served in the Egyptian navy and department of the interior and in 1838 was put in command of a mission, consisting of some naval officers and crew in three big sailing boats, charged with the discovery of the source of the White Nile; for some reason unknown the command of the mission was afterwards given to Salīm Qapūdān and he was instead made governor (altūn maʿden(i) emīni) of a colony of miners working to extract gold in the region of Fāzūghlī where he was stationed at the time of Muḥammad ʿAlī's visit in the winter of 1838–9; no mining enthusiast himself, he regarded the European prospectors as the indirect cause of his exile to those lonely parts.

Khālid Aḥmad al-ʿUmarābī (1818–1901), notable of the Jaʿlīyīn; he was born at Jabal Umm ʿAlī and was a descendant of the holy man Shaikh Ḥamad abū'l-ʿAsā, himself a near descendant of Shaikh ʿUmar wad Billāl, founder of the ʿUmarāb branch of the Jaʿlīyīn; after a youth spent in trade in Abyssinia and at Gedaref he set up in business at al-Ubaiyaḍ and prospered; his religious views caused him to transfer his allegiance from the Khatmīya to the Khalwatīya Islamic brotherhood; it is said that, so strong were his religious scruples, he avoided contact with the Turkish Government officials for fear of contracting sin; finally he handed over his business to his son Muḥammad ʿUthmān and devoted himself entirely to religion; he early made the pilgrimage; the Mahdist movement found him a ready convert and he was on intimate terms with Muḥammad Aḥmad al-Mahdī after the battle of Jabal Qadīr, 1882; when the Mahdī approached al-Ubaiyaḍ to besiege the town he appointed him amīr of the *jallāba* or Arab and Nubian townsmen who originated in the Nile valley; he took part in the main battles of the time including Shaikān (1883) and the siege of Khartoum (1884–5); after the Mahdist capture of Khartoum he settled in Omdurman where he was made custodian of enemy property and was a friendly critic of the Khalīfa ʿAbd Allāhi who respected his views; he survived the fall of the Khalīfa's régime, dying in Omdurman, his end hastened by grief at the death of Muḥammad ʿUthmān, his son.

Khālid Khusraw Pasha (*fl.* 1839–50), governor-general of the Sudan, 1845–50; he was born a free Turk in Constantinople, though he is said by some to have been of Greek origin; he joined the Egyptian army under Muḥammad ʿAlī Pasha and saw long service in the campaigns in Syria and Arabia, rising to the rank of farīq; he was governor of the Najd, 1839–40; his term of office as governor-general of the Sudan showed him as a featureless ruler, a voluminous correspondent with the government in Cairo, and a somewhat servile abettor of the viceroy's unreasoning lust for Sudan gold; as a soldier he played a better part, fighting actions against the Abyssinians in the region of Gallabat and against the Nuba; he was succeeded by ʿAbd al-Laṭīf Pasha ʿAbd Allāh.

Khālid Pasha Nadīm (–1880), liwā' of the Egyptian army; the son of ʿAbd Allāh Aghā al-ʿĀṭī he entered the army in the ranks and was soon, in 1866, given a commission as a mulāzim I; he was a binbāshī in 1874 when he began a two-years' secondment to the ministry of the interior as a secretary; in that year he came to the Sudan as president of a commission appointed to inquire into alleged malpractices of Aḥmad Mumtāz Pasha and Ḥusain Bey Khalīfa; the commission sat in Berber and Khartoum in the winter of 1874–5; he acted as deputy governor-general for Ismāʿīl Pasha Aiyūb during the latter's absence in the Dār Fūr campaign of 1875; on his return to Khartoum the governor-general complained that his deputy was unsatisfactory and he returned to Egypt by way of Dongola and Wādī Ḥalfā in 1876; he was vice-governor-general in 1877 but again returned to Egypt as the result of a disagreement with Ismāʿīl Pasha Aiyūb's successor, C. G. Gordon Pasha, who found his assistant dictatorial; he had acted for Gordon during the latter's tour of Dār Fūr; he subsequently held various provincial governorships in Egypt; he was in command of Egyptian troops in the Cretan rebellion of 1878 when he was promoted liwā' and pasha.

* **Khalīfa.** *See* ʿABD ALLĀHI MUḤAMMAD TURSHAIN KHALĪFAT AL-MAHDĪ; ʿALĪ WAD HILŪ KHALĪFAT AL-MAHDĪ; MUḤAMMAD AL-SHARĪF KHALĪFAT AL-MAHDĪ.

Khalīfa wad al-Ḥājj Muḥammad al-ʿAbbādī (1768–1828), ʿAbbādī leader; he was born at Asyūṭ and settled at Darraw; he accompanied Ismāʿīl Pasha on his journey from Aswān to Sennar at the head of an Egyptian army in 1820–1; on that occasion he had with him 700 armed ʿAbābda and 3,000 camels; for his services in the transport of army stores he was rewarded with the tax of 10 per cent. on the value of exports from the Sudan going over the Nubian desert in return for protecting the route from brigands; ʿAbbās aghā al-Bāzārlī, governor of Berber, thought that the tax was too high and attempted to persuade him to lower it; he refused; the governor, on the plea that Khalīfa had harboured a Bishārī highwayman and refused to give him up (arguing the Islamic code in the matter of sanctuary), sent to arrest him in Berber; he resisted arrest and the government troops bombarded and burnt his house in which both he and the highwayman were killed; his brother Baraka afterwards took revenge by killing the governor's brother, Sulaimān aghā.

Khalīl Aghā (*fl.* 1821), American, of unknown original name, who accompanied Ismāʿīl Pasha on the expedition to Sennar in 1820–1; G. B. English, Ismāʿīl Pasha's commander of artillery, asserted that he was probably the first individual who ever traversed the whole distance from Rosetta to Sennar by water; he was a native of New York.

Khalīl Bey al-Hindī (–1885), chief merchant of Kassala and president of the Tāka province court; he was loyal to the Egyptian cause during the military mutiny at Kassala in 1865 and died during the siege of the town by the Mahdists; his son Ḥusain Khalīl was a mu'āwin of telegraphs under Muḥammad Bey Salāma al-Bāz who was chief engineer of Sudan telegraphs on the eve of the Mahdist revolt.

Khalīl ibn al-Rūmī (*fl.* 1720), Sudanese holy man, by race a Dongolāwī Jābrī, he migrated south to Jabal Surkab near Omdurman where he lived a life devoted to religion; he later went to Dādūn where he built mosques.

Khamīs . . . (*fl.* 1748), chieftain from Dār Fūr; a skilful general he was nevertheless banished from Dār Fūr because he was said to have failed in a war against Dar Silā and Bagirmi; he fled to Sennar where Sultan Bādī IV abū Shilūkh received him kindly and took him into his service; he commanded a Funj army which, by a stratagem, won a victory near Sennar over an Abyssinian army led by King Īyāsū II about 1738; about 1747, assisted by the Hāmaj leader Muḥammad abu'l-Kailak who commanded the cavalry, he cleared the Musaba'āt overlords from Kordofan which for a time was ruled by Sennar.

* **Khashm al-Mūs Pasha.** *See* MUḤAMMAD KHASHM AL-MŪS PASHA.

al-Khātim wad Mūsā (–1914), Mahdist amīr, a Ta'ā'ishī of the Ḥāzmī branch; he assisted Muḥammad Aḥmad al-Mahdī in his assault on al-Ubaiyaḍ, 1882–3, and was later among the officers of the army of the amīr Maḥmūd Aḥmad which ravaged villages in Kordofan on its way eastward to join the Khalīfa 'Abd Allāhi's main army on the Nile in 1897; after the fall of Omdurman he commanded the Mahdist forces at al-Ubaiyaḍ; he was wounded and taken prisoner at the battle of Umm Dibaikarāt in 1899; later released, he died among his people near Nyāla in Dār Fūr.

Khātir Ḥimaidān (–1945), Mahdist amīr, by origin a Ta'ā'ishī; he commanded Mahdist troops in several of the great battles of the period and was taken prisoner by the Egyptian force at the battle of Umm Dibaikarāt, 1899; he died near Sinja.

Khidr Aghā . . . (–1823), Turco-Egyptian soldier; he was on the staff of Ibrāhīm Pasha, Muḥammad 'Alī Pasha's son, in the Sudan, 1821–2; on Ibrāhīm's return to Egypt he served under the new sir'askar, Muḥammad Bey Khusraw Daramālī, the Daftardār; he died at Berber.

al-Khidr 'Alī Kimair (–1928), commercial notable, sirr tujjār of the commercial community of Khartoum; he had been a member of the municipal council since its foundation; a Dongolāwī by birth he died in Khartoum.

Khūjalī ibn 'Abd al-Raḥmān ibn Ibrāhīm (1643–1743), a celebrated mystic, born on Tūtī island, near the site of the present Khartoum, of Maḥasī stock, he is said to have lived 101 lunar years; tradition has it that he dressed magnificently and was no respecter of persons; his tomb at Ḥalfaiya is much frequented.

Khūjalī al-Shaikh (1859–1941), Jamū'ī notable; he was born at Kararī near Omdurman in Turkish times of a wealthy commercial family and in his youth was a slave dealer serving with Zubair Bey Raḥma Manṣūr (afterwards Pasha) in Dār Fūr; he made his peace with the Anglo-Egyptian army just before the battle of Omdurman, 1898, and was shortly after made 'umda of Kararī, a post which he held till his death, which occurred in the village.

Khūrī, Yūsuf (1828–), Maronite Christian priest and traveller; born possibly in the Lebanon he was educated at the College of the Propaganda in Rome, 1842–9; leaving the college owing to sickness he went to England and taught oriental languages; among his pupils was Captain W. Peel, R.N., son of the prime minister Sir Robert Peel, with whom he made two journeys to the Sudan: the first up the Nile as far as Wādī Ḥalfā, 1850–1, the second from Korosko over the Nubian desert to Khartoum and al-Ubaiyaḍ; he wrote *Maronite Sea, Nile, the Desert and Nigritia* (1853).

Khūrshīd Pasha. *See* 'ALĪ KHŪRSHĪD PASHA.

Khushqadam al-Ẓāhirī Jaqmaq al-Rūmī (–*c.* 1488), Mameluke of supposedly Cretan origin who was bought as a child from a slave merchant called al-Aḥmadī whose name also he bore; in 1474 or 1475 he became vizier of the Sultan Qā'it, ruler of Egypt and Syria, 1468–95, and built a mosque named after him in Cairo; falling into disfavour he was banished to Sawākin where he died.

Khusraw Bey . . . (*fl.* 1854), Circassian mīrālai in the Egyptian army; having been appointed governor of Tāka in place of Ilyās Bey Kirīdlī (who was several times discharged and reappointed) he obtained European notoriety by raiding the region of Keren at the head of a large Egyptian force supported by the Beja; he pillaged Boghos and fell foul of a Roman Catholic missionary named G. Stella settled among the raided people; Stella went to Kassala to protest but, getting no satisfaction, complained to the consuls of Britain and France; the British Government intervened and Muḥammad Sa'īd Pasha withdrew Khusraw from his post and imprisoned him in Cairo; J. Hamilton, the British traveller, who passed through Kassala in 1854, stated that he was coarse in manner and appearance and no lover of Christians; the Frenchman C. Didier who was also in Kassala in 1854 felt himself ignored by the governor and vented his spleen on him.

Kinzelbach, Gottlob Theodor (1822–67), German astronomer and physicist of Stuttgart; he was a member of the expedition led by T. von Heuglin which attempted to find the lost German explorer, E. Vogel, who had disappeared in Wadā'i, 1856; he arrived in Khartoum in 1862 along with J. A. W. Munzinger; the two proceeded to al-Ubaiyaḍ but, as the sultan of Dār Fūr refused them permission to cross his territory into Wadā'i, they turned back; he was associated with the expedition of another German explorer, Baron K. K. von der Decken, who was killed by the Somali at Bardera in 1865.

* **Kirchner, Matthias** (-1912), German missionary priest of the Roman Catholic Church; a member of the Jesuit Order he came from the diocese of Bamberg in Bavaria and joined the mission in Khartoum in 1854; he went to the Upper Nile where he relieved I. Knoblehar who was in charge of the mission at Gondokoro; in 1856 he took charge of the mission school at Khartoum in place of G. Beltrame; after a short stay in Europe he returned with J. de D. Reinthaler to the Sudan in 1859 as pro-vicar apostolic of Central Africa to fill the office left vacant by the death of Knoblehar; he did not stay long; discouraged by the deaths of so many missionaries, whose places he was unable to fill, he secured permission of Propaganda to cede the vicariate to the Franciscans of Styria and in 1861 returned to Germany; he later became dean at Schesslitz and afterwards dean of Bromberg; for a time he was a deputy to the German Reichstag as a member of the Centre, 1873–6; Beltrame recorded that he was a scholar who knew Arabic and four other languages; T. von Heuglin, writing in 1863, called him the only man capable of carrying on the mission in the Sudan; when Bishop D. Comboni died in 1881 he was offered, but declined, the succession to the vicariate of Central Africa.

Kirkham . . . (-1875), Scottish adventurer; he first appeared in history as one of 'General' W. Walker's filibusters in the Nicaraguan civil war in 1855–7; he was later an instructor in Colonel C. G. Gordon's 'Ever Victorious Army' in China, 1863–4; he is next located as a sergeant in the Gordon Highlanders and later as a steward in a vessel plying in the Red Sea from which he joined the British force in the campaign of 1868 against King Theodore in Abyssinia; at the end of the war he transferred his services to Ras Kāsā, afterwards King John, as an instructor to Kāsā's riflemen; Kāsā, who was rās of Tigre, became emperor in 1871; Kirkham became a general and was entrusted with a diplomatic mission in Europe; on his return he took up farming near Asmara where he fell foul of the Egyptians who were preparing war against King John; imprisoned at Muṣawwaʻ he died there of dysentery and drink.

Kitchener, Sir Frederick Walter (1858–1912), British soldier, brother of Earl Kitchener of Khartoum; he joined the army in 1876 and was promoted lieutenant-colonel in 1896; he was director of transport in the Dongola campaign of 1896 and saw service during the Nile campaigns of 1897–9 in which latter year he commanded the Kordofan Field Force which was sent to contain the army of the K͟halīfa ʻAbd Allāhi in the region of Jadīd; he served in the South African war, 1899–1900, and in 1906 was promoted lieutenant-general; he was governor and commander-in-chief, Bermuda, 1908–9.

Kitchener, Horatio Herbert, 1st Earl Kitchener of Khartoum and of Broome (1850–1916), British soldier; born in Ireland he was commissioned to the Royal Engineers, 1870; much of his early service was spent in surveying Palestine and Cyprus for the Palestine Exploration Fund; in 1882 he entered the Egyptian army; he was in the intelligence department during the unsuccessful Nile expedition of 1884–5, in close contact with tribal affairs in the northern Sudan and on the frontier; appointed governor-general of the Red Sea Littoral in 1886, he was wounded in an action against the Mahdists at Ḥandūb near Sawākin in 1888; in that year he was made adjutant-general of the Egyptian army and held a senior command at the battle of Tū<u>sh</u>kī (Toski), 1889; his appointment as sirdār of the Egyptian army, 1892, marked the beginning of his plans for the reconquest of the Sudan; the campaign opened in 1896 with the easy reoccupation of the region of Dongola after battles at Firka (Firket) and Ḥafīr; advancing to Berber he defeated the army of the amīr Maḥmūd Aḥmad on the River Atbara in April 1898; finally, at the battle of Omdurman on 2 September 1898, he utterly defeated the main army of the <u>Kh</u>alifa ʿAbd Allāhi and broke his power; various columns under the command of his officers thereupon completed the destruction of the remaining Mahdist forces; a necessary part of his strategy was the building of military railways behind the advancing army to secure his communications and supplies; the line from Sārras to Kerma was completed in May 1897, while another line, crossing the Nubian desert from Wādī Ḥalfā, reached Abū Ḥamad in October 1897, the Atbara in June 1898, and Khartoum at the end of 1899; continuing up the White Nile with a flotilla of gunboats he arrived off Fashoda where he found a small French force which had come from the Congo basin under the command of Captain J. B. Marchand; Marchand proposed to annex the Upper Nile region to France; late in 1898 the French ultimately withdrew; his tactful handling of the Fashoda incident prevented a serious international crisis; returning to England on leave he was made a baron and received the thanks of Parliament and a Parliamentary grant; he issued an appeal to the British public for £100,000 to build and endow Gordon Memorial College, Khartoum; the sum was quickly subscribed and he became the first president of the college; the Anglo-Egyptian Agreement of January 1899 on the future status of the Sudan, signed by Lord Cromer, British agent and consul-general, and Buṭrus Pasha <u>Gh</u>ālī, Egyptian minister of foreign affairs, vested supreme military and civil powers in Kitchener as governor-general of the Sudan, but in December 1899 his appointment came to a premature end; after the British disasters in the South African war he was appointed chief-of-staff to Lord Roberts who took over the command there in December 1899; the war ended with the defeat of the Boers and the liberal Peace of Vereeniging, 1902; while on his way to his next appointment as commander-in-chief in India he visited the Sudan and officially opened Gordon Memorial College in November 1902; his work in India ended in 1909 when, after a short time as commander-in-chief in the Mediterranean, he succeeded Sir J. E. Gorst, on the latter's death, as British agent and consul-general in Egypt, a post he held, 1911–14; in 1911 he visited the Sudan, opening the Kordofan railway and attending to the affairs of the college in Khartoum; he took a big part in the decision made in 1913 to introduce a profit-sharing arrangement in the future Jazīra irrigation scheme, and himself approached the British Government to guarantee a loan to carry out the project; on the outbreak of the First World War he was at once recalled to London and made secretary of state for war; he organized a new army of over a million men, but the failure of the Dardanelles expedition, 1915, caused criticism of his methods; his difficulties were enormous and his organizing ability contributed to the eventual victory of the Allies; he was drowned at sea while going on a mission to Russia; there is an extensive literature about his campaigns in the Sudan; his official biography, by Sir G. C. A. Arthur, appeared in 1920.

* **Klancnik, Jan** (*fl.* 1853–70), Slovene trader from the Austrian province of Carniola; he came to the Sudan as a lay brother attached to the Roman Catholic mission in 1853; he was a cooper by trade but had also worked as a carpenter, weaver, charcoal burner, and lime burner; by 1862 he had left the mission and had gone into trade on the Upper Nile, exploring the outer fringes of the Azande country; G. Lejean, G. Schweinfurth, and other travellers in the area mention his activities; Schweinfurth asserted that he engaged in the slave trade.

Klein, Franz (–1885), Hungarian Jewish tailor; he came to Khartoum and in 1868 married Melania, daughter of the Venetian trader C. Contarini, and was converted to the Roman Catholic faith; he was for many years the official tailor to successive governors-general and a popular figure among the foreign community in the city; he was killed in the massacre of Khartoum in the presence of his wife and children.

Klootz, Gustav (–1886), German ex-soldier, said to have been a non-commissioned officer in the Prussian Uhlans; he came to the Sudan as the orderly of Count G. B. von Seckendorff, one of the officers in the army of W. Hicks Pasha, in 1883; he deserted from the Egyptian army to the Mahdists on the eve of the battle of Shaikān and was given the name of Muṣṭafā; deserting later from Omdurman he begged his way to Gallabat where he died on his way to Abyssinia.

Knight, Edward Frederick (1852–1925), British journalist; educated at Oxford University he was called to the English Bar in 1879; he was correspondent to *The Times* newspaper in many wars, including the Dongola and Nile campaigns, 1896–8; among many books on his experiences he wrote *Letters from the Sudan* (1897).

* **Knoblehar (Knoblecher), Ignaz** (1819–58), pro-vicar apostolic of the Roman Catholic mission to Central Africa; a Slovene, born at Skocijan (St. Kanzian or St. Cantian) near Trieste his name was originally Knoblehar though he used the germanized form, Knoblecher; he studied at Rudolfswerth and Laibach and at the College of Propaganda in Rome; entering the Jesuit Order he sought a missionary career and was priested in 1845; when Pope Gregory XVI instituted the vicariate apostolic of Central Africa in 1846, Knoblecher left for the Sudan with the first missionaries having at their head M. Ryllo, the first pro-vicar apostolic; the party arrived in Khartoum, 1848; on the death of Ryllo a few months after his arrival, Knoblecher succeeded him; in Khartoum

the missionaries founded a school for young negroes bought in the slave market; in the same year he went up the White Nile on a mission which failed owing to obstruction from traders who opposed it; he nevertheless reached Mount Rejaf; in 1850 he returned to Europe where he founded a society to assist the mission, the Marienverein zur Beförderung der Katholischen Mission in Central Afrika, and collected helpers and funds; he returned to the Sudan in 1852, arriving in Khartoum with an iron barque, *Stella Matutina*, bought in Egypt and brought up-river; again, this time with A. Vinco, he ascended the White Nile and founded a mission at Gondokoro in 1852 and another in 1854 at a point between Shambé and Bor which he named Heiligencreuz (Holy Cross), the site of which is still called Kanīsa (Arabic for a Christian church); both mission stations were afterwards abandoned; while on the Upper Nile he explored the country up to Mount Logwek; in 1856 he sent eight negro youths to Europe for theological training; he left the Sudan on another visit to Europe in 1857 and died shortly after at Naples; he was succeeded as pro-vicar by M. Kirchner; a man of learning and an expert linguist, he assisted J. C. J. Mitterrützner in the latter's studies in the Bari language; his life was written by Mitterrützner entitled *Dr. Ignaz Knoblecher* (Brixen, 1869); for an account of his travels see *Jahresbericht des Marienvereines* (Vienna, 1852–7).

Kœnig Bey, Mathieu-Auguste (1802–65), French orientalist; born in Paris he early applied himself to the study of oriental languages and came to Egypt, 1820, later travelling to Sennar under the auspices of the Royal Geographical Society of Paris and settling ultimately in Egypt where he was successively a teacher of French at the Egyptian Staff College, tutor to the children of the viceroy Muḥammad ʿAlī Pasha, and latterly private secretary to Muḥammad Saʿīd Pasha, his former pupil, 1854–63; he translated many works of physical and military science from French into Arabic; he died in Alexandria.

Koettlitz, Reginald (1861–1916), British physician and explorer; registered in 1884 he was a surgeon aboard S.S. *Discovery* and was medical officer to the Jackson-Harmsworth expedition to Franz-Josef Land; he and Lord Lovat accompanied a scientific expedition led by H. Weld Blundell from Addis Ababa over the Abyssinian highlands to the valley of the Blue Nile, Omdurman, and Egypt, 1898–9; he wrote an account of the journey in the *Scottish Geographical Magazine*, vol. 16, 1900; he contributed notes on geology and anthropology to Weld Blundell's account in the *Geographical Journal*, vol. 15, 1900; he spent his later years in South Africa where he died.

Kokorembas, Dimitri (1847–1915), Greek trader who was in business in the Sudan at the outbreak of the Mahdist revolt; finding himself a captive at Omdurman he renounced his religion, took the Islamic name ʿAbd Allāh, and was appointed amīr of the Christians in the town; while thus employed he married Teresina Grigolini, an Italian nun who as a captive had been dispensed from her religious vows; by her he had two sons, Giuseppe and Giorgio, who became Italian citizens;

after the fall of Mahdism he stayed on in the Sudan, dying at Omdurman where the former amīr was buried with Christian rites in the Coptic Orthodox cemetery.

Kotschy, Theodor von (1813–66), Austrian botanist; born at Ustron in Austrian Silesia, he first intended to become a pastor in the Evangelical Church but later preferred a scientific career, having shown an early bent for botany; he accompanied an expedition led by J. von Russegger to Asia Minor and Africa in 1835 as botanist and zoologist; Muḥammad ʿAlī Pasha, viceroy of Egypt, employed the expedition to examine the mineral resources of his dominions; the party left Cairo late in 1836 and travelled over the Nubian desert to Khartoum; Kotschy made journeys to al-Ubaiyaḍ and the northern Nuba hills, to the White Nile near Khartoum, and to the region of the River Tūmāt and the Banī Shanqul, 1837–8, making botanical collections; he returned with the party to Cairo whence all but he left for Europe; leaving Cairo for a second journey to the Sudan he again visited Kordofan, 1839–40; after occupying for many years a minor post in an Austrian museum his talents were at last recognized and he was appointed to a well-paid scientific post in Vienna where he died.

* **Kovalevsky, Egor Petrovitch** (1811–1968), Russian colonel, geologist, and traveller; born in the district of Kharkov he became a mining engineer and made extensive journeys in Siberia and the Balkans; charged by Muḥammad ʿAlī Pasha to prospect for gold and to introduce modern mining methods, he ascended the Nile valley in 1847 and in the winter of 1847–8 explored the gold-bearing region of Dār Berta on the borders of Abyssinia; there he established a sand-washing plant, but his mission failed; he afterwards undertook various diplomatic missions for the Russian Government in Asia; he died at St. Petersburg; his account of his journey to the Sudan was published in Russian (St. Petersburg, 1849) with a French version entitled *Voyage dans l'intérieur de l'Afrique.*

Krapf, Johann Ludwig (1810–81), German Protestant missionary; returning from a second journey in Abyssinia he entered the Sudan at Gallabat, 1855, and thence travelled by way of Sennar to Egypt; C. Cuny met him with the Coptic patriarch of Abyssinia at Dongola, 1858; see his *Travels* (1860).

Kretschmer, Robert (1818–72), German painter of animals; he came from Burghof in Schweidnitz and worked in Leipzig; he visited the eastern Sudan with Ernest, Duke of Saxe-Coburg-Gotha, in 1862 and wrote an account of the journey (Leipzig, 1864).

Krockow von Wickerode, Carl, Count (–), German traveller; he came to the eastern Sudan in 1864 on a hunting expedition and travelled by Sawākin to Kassala, Algeden, the Setit, Gedaref, and Gallabat, returning via Kassala to Sawākin; he wrote *Reisen und Jagden in nord-ost Afrika, 1864–1865* (Berlin, 1867).

Krump, Theodor (*fl.* 1700–2), German Roman Catholic priest of the Franciscan Order; originating from Bavaria he came to Cairo and with a party of several other missionary priests set out for Abyssinia; travelling by way of Isnā, Selīma Oasis, Mushū, and Dongola they arrived at Sennar in 1701; he returned with some of the party by the same route in 1702, others of the party, including the Jesuit A. Grenier and A. Paulet (or Paoletti), continued the journey into Abyssinia; his account of the journey, published in Augsburg in 1710, contains an important description of Sennar and the Funj dominions.

Kuchūk 'Alī (–1869), Turkish adventurer, commonly known as Kuchūk 'Alī Aghā from the fact that he had probably been a soldier; he was for several years engaged in trade on the Upper White Nile and in the Baḥr al-Ghazāl where he had a station near the site of the present village of Wau; this and other properties he sold to the government; he was later appointed a sanjaq in command of 400 local irregular troops in a force led by al-Ḥājj Muḥammad al-Hilālī who had been given the mission of occupying the district along the Baḥr al-'Arab on the southern borders of Dār Fūr; he quarrelled with al-Hilālī and died on the road, perhaps of a natural death, though Zubair Pasha Raḥma Manṣūr, who himself served in the Baḥr al-Ghazāl in his youth, asserted that he was poisoned.

Kwal Arob (–1945), chief of the Ngork Dinka of south-west Kordofan; he died at Abyei on the Baḥr al-'Arab.

Kwanieret Awur Akoldit (–1934), Shilluk notable, a descendant of Reth; he was chief of Nun near Kodok, the former Fashoda.

Kyriakos (*fl.* 722), king of the Nubians; in 722 he marched northward into Egypt with a large army to avenge the insult which the Arabs under 'Amr ibn al-'Āṣī had inflicted on the Nubian Christians in the century before by sacking Old Dongola and forcing the inhabitants to pay tribute; at the urgent request of the Coptic Patriarch (whom the Arabs tactfully released from prison in Egypt) he withdrew his army to Nubia.

Labakh. *See* FAḌL ALLĀH, called LABAKH.

Lafargue, Ferdinand (*c.* 1800–71), French veterinary officer and trader; a native of Bordeaux he studied veterinary science at the school at Alfort, then emigrating to Egypt he was employed as a veterinary officer at Zagazig; he gave up this post and came to the Sudan to trade in 1834, remaining in the country till his death; he lived chiefly at Berber which he preferred to Khartoum, of whose European residents he had a poor opinion on account of their endless petitions and protests to various European consuls; during his long commercial career in the Sudan he built up a profitable business, trading in gum arabic and ivory; he had travelled on the White Nile with F. Werne, J. P. d'Arnaud, and G. Thibaut in 1840–1 and had a trading station at Gondokoro which he visited annually; he accompanied Bishop I. Knoblehar on a voyage up the White Nile in 1848, passing the rapids near Rejaf which had baffled Salīm Qapūdān; he was commercial agent for Prince Muḥammad ʿAbd al-Ḥalīm, uncle of the Khedive Ismāʿīl; he had an Abyssinian wife and kept a spacious house at Berber visited by many travellers; he died at Berber.

La Kéthulle de Ryhove, Charles de (1865–1903), Belgian official and explorer; as the first Belgian resident to the Sultan Rāfaʿi at Bomu he conducted, with Commandant T. Nilis, a reconnaissance to the confines of the Baḥr al-Ghazāl in 1894, making a treaty with Sultan Ḥāmid wad Mūsā of the Faroghé tribe and founding a post of the Congo Free State (afterwards abandoned) on the River Adda, a tributary of the Baḥr al-ʿArab; he died at Bockryck in Belgium.

* **Lambert Bey, Charles** (1804–64), French engineer; born at Valenciennes he was educated in mining engineering at the École Polytechnique of Paris; imbued with the doctrines of the Saint-Simonians he left for Egypt with other members of that group in 1833 and engaged in constructional work at the Delta Barrage; in 1838–9 he accompanied Muḥammad ʿAlī Pasha to the Sudan where the viceroy entrusted him and another French engineer named Lefèvre with prospection for gold and the establishment of mines in the district of Fāzūghlī in the Blue Nile valley in collaboration with the Italian mineralogist, Boreani; the viceroy also instructed him to examine the possibility of building a railway to connect the iron deposits of Kordofan with the Nile; he was later director of the school of engineering at Būlāq.

Lamson, Robert Schuyler (–1876), American soldier in the Khedivial service; he was on the staff of Muḥammad Rātib Pasha, commander of the Egyptian army which was defeated by the Abyssinians at Gura in March 1876; shortly afterwards, holding the rank of binbāshī, he was sent on a mission to Dār Fūr where he died of fever near al-Fāshar.

Landeghem, André (1876–1943), Belgian captain in the service of the Congo Free State; in February 1903, with a small detachment of Congolese troops, he arrived at Tambūra; this force formed part of a 'scientific' mission under Commandant C. Lemaire; he attained Daim Zubair intending to visit Ḥufrat al-Naḥās, but difficulties with the Sudan Government prevented this and he returned to the Congo; Lemaire with the remainder of his mission arrived at Mvolo and shortly after retired south when the post was occupied by Sudan Government troops.

Landor, Arthur Henry Savage (1865–1924), British explorer, grandson of W. S. Landor the poet and prose writer; born in Florence he travelled in many parts of the world; in 1906 he entered the Sudan on foot from western Abyssinia and walked from Gambeila to Tawfīqīya; continuing by ship to Mushraʿ al-Raq he walked by way of Wau to Zemio and eventually completed the crossing of Africa; see his autobiography, *Everywhere* (1924).

Lanzon, Amabile (*fl.* 1862–8), Maltese trader, nephew of A. Debono; J. Petherick, British vice-consul in Khartoum, had him arrested and sent to Cairo on a charge of dealing in slaves, 1862; his friends raised counter-charges against Petherick and he was acquitted for lack of reliable evidence against him; the proceedings so weakened the prestige of the British vice-consulate in Khartoum that the British Government suppressed it; he died about 1868 on the Upper White Nile and his corpse was buried in Khartoum where he was survived by a young wife, Sophie, a daughter of the French trader G. Thibaut.

Largeau, Victor Emmanuel Étienne (1866–1916), French brigadier-general; while a captain he served in the Congo-Nile expedition, led by J. B. Marchand, which ended in the Fashoda Incident, 1898; he took a leading part in the campaign against Dār Maṣālīṭ after the massacre of a French column commanded by Captain Fiegenschuh and the death of Colonel Moll; he fought in the First World War and died of wounds received in the fighting round Verdun.

Laṭīf Efendi. *See* DEBONO, ANDREA.

* **Lefèvre . . .** (–1839), French mining engineer, one of the party of the philosophical sect of Saint-Simonians who came to Egypt to work for Muḥammad ʿAlī Pasha; he accompanied another French engineer, C. Lambert, in the suite of Muḥammad ʿAlī during the viceroy's visit to the Sudan in 1838–9; he probably prospected for silver at Jabal Moya and had no more luck in his prospections for gold in the mountains of Fāzūghlī where he died a few months later.

Legnani, Calisto (*fl.* 1878–87), Italian trader and consular agent; he was born at Menaggio near Como and emigrated to Egypt; he was Italian consular agent in Khartoum during the last years of the Egyptian régime; the Italian explorer P. Matteucci met him in Khartoum in 1878 and he was still carrying out his consular duties there in 1881; having left the Sudan on the outbreak of the Mahdist revolt he returned later to Sawākin where in 1887 he was consular agent; he was afterwards Italian consul at Trieste.

Lehoux, Pierre-François (1803–92), French painter, he accompanied the archaeological expedition of J. F. Champollion to Abū Simbel and Wādī Ḥalfā in the winter of 1828–9.

Lejean, Guillaume (1828–71), French traveller; a Breton from Plouégat-Guérand in Finisterre where he was born and where he died, he first entered local government and was secretary to the council of the prefecture of Morlaix; he collaborated with A. de Lamartine on the journal *Pays* in the revolutionary year 1848, but decided to devote his energy to travel; he made his first visit to the Sudan, 1860, when he landed at Sawākin and went by Kassala to Khartoum; in company with the Italian naturalist, O. Antinori, he toured Kordofan and ascended the estuary of the Baḥr al-Ghazāl, then went up the White Nile to Gondokoro where fever overtook him, 1861; after a visit to France he went to Abyssinia where in 1863 he was held a prisoner by the Emperor Theodore; in 1864 he was appointed consul of France at Muṣawwaʿ and landed at Sawākin charged by Napoleon III with a mission of exploration and observation; from Sawākin he travelled to Kassala, making careful notes, and from Kassala went on by Keren to Muṣawwaʿ; he afterwards travelled in India, Mesopotamia, and the Balkans; his writings on the geography of the Sudan are numerous.

Lemaire, Charles (1863–1926), Belgian soldier, born at Cuesmes; he was in charge of a scientific expedition, perhaps not without political implications, to the country of the Azande in 1902–4; he occupied Mvolo between Rumbek and Amādi, but shortly afterwards retired when the post was occupied by troops of the Sudan Government; he died at Etterbeek in Belgium.

Lemay, Gaston (1843–1911), French vice-consul in Khartoum, 1882, and temporarily at Sawākin, 1883–4, under the agent and consul of France in Egypt; he was promoted to consul-general, 1907, and retired, 1911 when he died.

Le Noir du Roule, Janus (–1705), French diplomat; formerly vice-consul of France in Tripoli on the Barbary coast, he was vice-consul in Cairo when Louis XIV charged him with the mission of entering into diplomatic relations with the emperor of Ethiopia; before starting from Cairo he ran foul of the Jesuit missionaries who hindered the enterprise; finally he set out in 1704 with a party which included A. Lippi, L. Macé, Bayard, and two French servants; travelling with a caravan bound for Ethiopia the mission left Asyūṭ and journeyed by way of the Khārja and Salīma oases, regaining the Nile at Mushū; at Dongola they received a letter from Bādī III, king of the Funj, permitting the passage of the mission through his kingdom; they arrived at Sennar in May 1705; here Le Noir du Roule and all his French attendants with him were murdered at the instigation of King Bādī, a crime which has been attributed to the influence of Latin Missionaries; on the news of the murder reaching Paris the French Government ordered all Nubians to be dismissed from the French service.

Lenormant, Charles (1802–59), French archaeologist; a nephew of Mme Récamier and originally an inspector of fine arts in France, he accompanied the archaeological expedition of J. F. Champollion to Abū Simbel and Wādī Ḥalfā in 1828–9; he was later a member of the Institut de France and editor of *Le Correspondant*.

Leo Africanus. *See* AL-ḤASAN IBN MUḤAMMAD AL-WAZZĀN AL-ZAIYĀTĪ.

Leontides, Nikólaos (–1885), Hellenic consul in Khartoum, originally from Leros in the Dodecanese islands; he was killed in the massacre at Khartoum; General C. G. Gordon, who likened him to the classical Leonidas, commended him to the king of the Hellenes as one 'who has behaved worthy of his ancestor of Thermopylae'.

Lepsius, Karl Richard (1810–84), German Egyptologist; son of the archaeologist K. P. Lepsius he came from Naumberg; after a promising scientific career he was placed at the head of a Prussian archaeological expedition to the Sudan and neighbouring countries, 1842–5; the expedition visited Nubia and Sennar, 1843–4, travelling from Egypt to Wādī Ḥalfā in 1843 then, returning to Korosko, crossed the Nubian desert to Berber and Khartoum which it reached in February 1844; Lepsius with H. Abeken continued to Sennar; on the homeward journey the party went by Meroë and, crossing the desert to Jabal Barkal, visited Dongola and Wādī Ḥalfā where they arrived in July 1844; a massive record of the monuments found by the expedition was published in Berlin, 1849–59; an English translation of his letters describing the journey appeared in 1853; his interest in the Nubian language is shown in his *Nubische Grammatik* (Berlin, 1880).

Le Saint, Joseph-François-Marie (1833–68), French explorer; he was born at Landivisiau in the department of Finisterre; in 1853 he joined the French army as a volunteer and served in the infantry, rising to sergeant-major, 1857; wounded at the battle of Solferino in 1859, he received his commission on the field; he was discharged in 1864 and turned to geographical exploration; although the journeys of J. H. Speke and J. A. Grant had revealed the main configuration of the Nile watershed, the region between the Upper White Nile and the west coast of Africa was still largely unexplored; Le Saint proposed to explore this region and, with the support of the Geographical Society of Paris, arrived in Egypt late in 1867; travelling to Khartoum he made for the upper reaches of the White Nile but died of fever at the Poncet brothers' trading post at Abū Kūka between Shambé and Bor in January 1868.

Leslie, Armand (1845–83), British doctor; born in Ireland he was medical officer to the Poti and Tiflis Railway Company in the Caucasus, 1868–72; in 1876–7 he was in Serbia working for the British National Society for Aid to the Sick and Wounded in War, and in the Russo-Turkish war of 1877–8 he became principal medical officer of the Society attending to the Turkish wounded; he was sent to Egypt in 1883 to help in an outbreak of cholera; on the formation of an army under General V. Baker Pasha to take the field against the Mahdists on the Red Sea coast he was appointed chief of the medical department and was killed in the first battle of el-Teb.

Lesseps, Ferdinand-Marie de, Viscount (1805–94), French diplomat and founder of the Suez Canal; born at Versailles, a cousin of the Empress Eugénie, he was occupying a diplomatic post in Egypt when he visited the Sudan in 1856–7 with the Viceroy Muḥammad Saʿīd Pasha; from Khartoum he visited Jabal Awliā and the ruins of Soba, describing his journey in *Souvenirs de Quarante Ans* (Paris, 1887) of which an English translation appeared in the same year.

Lesseps, Théodore-Antoine-Lopez de la Sainte Trinité (1802–74), French diplomat, brother of F. M., Viscount de Lesseps; he joined the diplomatic corps and in 1822 left France with his father who had been appointed consul-general of France in Syria; shortly afterwards he undertook a mission in Egypt for his father; with A., Baron d'Uxküll, P.,

Count de Medem, he ascended the Nile to Wādī Ḥalfā and travelled overland as far as Semna in 1822–3; in 1860 he retired from the diplomatic corps and was made a senator.

Letorzec, Pierre Constant (*fl.* 1820–4), French traveller; after service in various French ships he was a midshipman of the first class in 1819 when he signed a contract with his fellow townsman, F. Cailliaud of Nantes, to accompany the latter on his journey to Sennar; he was with Cailliaud throughout the journey, 1820–3, when he ascertained the geographical positions of the more important places on the route; on his return with his companion to France he obtained in 1824 a captain's ticket in the French merchant navy.

Lewin Bey, Henry Frederick Elliott (1872–1946), British soldier; he received a commission in the Royal Artillery, 1894, and in 1901–11 served in the Egyptian army; he was assistant military secretary to Sir F. R. Wingate Pasha, governor-general of the Sudan and sirdār of the Egyptian army, 1907–8, and from 1909 was military secretary with rank of qā'immaqām; he served in the First World War and retired from the British army in 1929 with the rank of colonel and honorary brigadier-general; he married in 1913 a daughter of Field-Marshal Earl Roberts, V.C., now Countess Roberts, and had one son (in the Irish Guards) killed in 1940 in the Second World War.

Lewis Bey, David Francis (1855–1927), British colonel and mīrālai of the Egyptian army; born at Buttington near Welshpool he joined the army in 1875 and from 1886 to 1900 was seconded to the Egyptian army; he fought throughout the Dongola and Nile campaigns, 1896–9; in the Dongola campaign he commanded the 1st Egyptian brigade and in the campaigns of 1897–8 he led the 3rd Egyptian brigade; after the Mahdist defeat at Omdurman, 1898, he was put in command of a force, supported by the gunboat *Malik* and the steamer *Dal*, which destroyed an army under the amīr Aḥmad Faḍīl at Dākhila south of Roseires; he commanded an infantry brigade at the battle of Umm Dibaikarāt in 1899 in which the Khalīfa 'Abd Allāhi was killed and the remnants of his army scattered and taken prisoner; from 1898 to 1900 he was governor of Sennar; he retired from the British and Egyptian armies in 1900; in 1907 and 1909 he was correspondent for *The Times* in Morocco; in 1914, on the outbreak of the First World War, he returned to the colours and raised the 16th battalion of the Royal Warwickshire Regiment; he spent his later years in local government.

L'Hôte, Nestor (1804–42), French archaeological draughtsman; born at Cologne he entered the French customs service and afterwards became an Egyptologist; he accompanied the archaeological expedition led by J. F. Champollion to Abū Simbel and Wādī Ḥalfā in 1828–9 as a draughtsman.

Linant de Bellefonds Pasha, Louis-Maurice-Adolphe (1800–83), French engineer and explorer; a Breton from Lorient, the son of a naval lieutenant, he came to Egypt as a draughtsman with the French archaeological mission of the Comte de Forbin, 1818; he later entered the service of Muḥammad ʿAlī Pasha who charged him with various engineering and exploring duties; he followed in the wake of the Egyptian army to Sennar, 1821–2; difficulties in the Pasha's service caused him to resign when he returned to the Sudan under the auspices of the British African Association, ascending the White Nile to al-Ais (Kawa), about 150 miles south of Khartoum, then the northernmost limit of the Shilluk people, in 1827; in 1831–2, having returned to the service of the viceroy, he made two explorations of the Atbai in an unsuccessful search for gold; in the course of these explorations he examined and mapped the country between Wādī al-ʿAllaqī and Shendi; he now entered upon a long and useful career as a public servant of Egypt, becoming a bey in 1847, minister of public works in 1869, and a pasha in 1873; he initiated many irrigation projects and was one of the pioneers of the Suez Canal; he married an Abyssinian lady; two sons, Auguste-Édouard and Ernest, both served under C. G. Gordon Pasha in Equatoria; Auguste died of fever at Gondokoro in 1874; Ernest, who gallantly left a promising position in Egypt to replace his dead brother, was killed in a fight with the Bari.

Lindsay, Alexander William Crawford, 25th Earl of Crawford and 8th Earl of Balcarres (1812–80), British antiquarian and historian; he travelled in Nubia as far south as the Second Cataract in 1836–7, a journey which he described in *Letters on Egypt* (1838).

Liotard, Victor Théophile (1858–1916), French colonial administrator; after serving as a naval dispenser he joined the colonial service, 1887; in 1891 S. de Brazza, governor of the French Congo, appointed him head of a mission to establish French sovereignty over the Ubanghi-Shari region and neighbouring unoccupied territories; his mission encountered the opposition of the Belgian and Anglo-Egyptian authorities; nevertheless he occupied the country north of the Uélé and in 1896 crossed the Nile–Congo watershed and established French posts at Tambura and Daim Zubair, an operation which facilitated the passage of the Marchand expedition to Fashoda, 1897–8; as the first governor of the Haut-Oubanghi territory from 1894 he was the ultimate chief of Marchand's expedition and the agent whereby this territory came into French possession; after a colonial career of great usefulness to France he retired, 1910.

Lippi, Agostino (1678–1705), Zantiote physician; he was attached as physician and naturalist to the diplomatic mission of Le Noir du Roule which Louis XIV sent from Egypt to the emperor of Abyssinia; he was murdered with others of the mission at Sennar by order of the Funj king Bādī III.

Litchfield, George (1854–1945), British Protestant missionary; he was ordained in 1878 and in the same year joined R. W. Felkin and other missionaries on a journey to Uganda by way of the Nile valley; the party landed at Sawākin and travelled through Berber, Khartoum, and Equatoria, reaching Uganda in February 1879; after service in India and South Africa he became a parish priest in England.

Lithgow, Stewart Aaron (1833–99), British surgeon major-general; commissioned as an assistant surgeon to the army medical staff in 1855 he served in the Indian mutiny, 1857–9, and in 1884 was promoted deputy surgeon-general; he was deputy surgeon-general in the Nile campaign, 1884–5, and was principal medical officer to the Sudan Frontier Force, 1885–6; in 1891 he was promoted surgeon major-general.

Lloyd Bey, Hesperus David Watkiss (1872–1915), major in the British army and qā'immaqām in the Egyptian army; he was commissioned to the Cameronians (Scottish Rifles) in 1893 and was promoted captain in 1899; from 1898 to 1908 he was seconded to the Egyptian army and in 1901 entered the Sudan Government service; he was appointed governor of Kordofan, 1908; he was killed in the battle of Neuve Chapelle in France during the First World War.

Lockett, Samuel Henry (1837–91), American soldier; born in Virginia he entered the United States Military Academy and graduated in 1859; in the civil war of 1861–5 he served on the Confederate side and achieved the rank of colonel of engineers; at the end of the war he taught mathematics and engineering latterly at the State University of Louisiana; joining the Egyptian army in 1875 he was sent to Muṣawwaʿ to make a topographical survey of the country inland of that town in preparation for an Egyptian offensive against Abyssinia; his work was interrupted by his appointment as an engineer staff officer to the army which Muḥammad Rātib Pasha led to its doom at Gura in 1875; in 1877 he directed the preparation of the great map of Africa by officers of the Egyptian general staff; this map embodied the results of the latest explorations and surveys in the Sudan; he returned to the United States in 1878 and was later employed at the University of Tennessee, in the construction of the pedestal of the Statue of Liberty in New York harbour and in engineering work in South America; he died at Bogotá, Colombia.

Logan Pasha, Maxwell Hannay (1873–1947), British soldier; he received a commission in the West Yorkshire Regiment in 1894 and was promoted captain in 1901; between 1909 and 1919 he was seconded to the Egyptian army in which he rose to the rank of liwā'; he took part in operations against the Beir and Anuak, 1912, and in the Nyima hills, 1917; he was appointed chief staff officer and adjutant-general of the Egyptian army in Khartoum, 1917–19; he retired from the British army in 1923 when he was commanding the regimental depot at York.

Logwit lo Ladu, Franz (1848–66), Bari youth, born at Gondokoro; he was among the first of the Bari people to become Christian; in 1853–60 he attended the Roman Catholic mission school at Gondokoro and later went to Holy Cross station (now called Kanīsa and, like Gondokoro mission, later abandoned); in 1863 he was living at Brixen in the Tyrol where he helped Canon J. C. J. Mitterrützner in the preparation of the latter's grammar of the Bari language (Brixen, 1867); he himself wrote an elementary German-Bari dictionary and corrected other works on the Bari language by Mitterrützner and F. Morlang; he died at Brixen.

Loiso, Nikolaus Loiso (–1913), Greek contractor and landowner; born at Limassol, Cyprus, he came as a young man to Egypt where he built up a business, acting as a contractor to the Anglo-Egyptian army during the Dongola and Nile campaigns, 1896–8; Kitchener's opinion of his worth was expressed in the gift of a jewelled signet pin; soon after the reoccupation of Omdurman he set up in business there with branch houses in Wādī Ḥalfā, Aswān, and Lower Egypt, in partnership with his four brothers, Petros, Mikhailis, Konstantinos, and Aristides, the last of whom fought in the Greek army in the Balkan war, 1912; he was at one time president of the Hellenic community in the Sudan, but later moved his business activities to Egypt where he died.

Lomoro Xujang (1853–1912), chief of the Lotuxo of Tirrangore in Equatoria; he was the son of Xujang (or Amoyya, the 'Moy' of Sir S. W. Baker) who was chief of Tirrangore after the religious kingdom of Lotuxo had split into two parts; he entered the warrior class about 1873 and so great was his personal prestige that he was appointed by his people to succeed Chief Lajaru on the latter's death in 1892; by occasional fighting, but chiefly by bluff, he extended his authority over most of the true Lotuxo and over neighbouring tribes; his astute mind prompted him to co-operate with the Uganda Government which in 1898 sent Colonel (afterwards Major-General Sir) J. R. L. Macdonald on a patrol to the Lotuxo country and later established a post at Ikoto; his dictatorship led to opposition from his own people; he was killed by a spear-thrust and his kingdom was divided.

Longfield Bey, William Elrington (1874–1942), mīrālai of the Egyptian army and lieutenant-colonel of the British army; commissioned to the Royal Engineers he was transferred to the Egyptian army and in 1901 retransferred to the Sudan Government with rank of binbāshī; he was promoted qā'immaqām, 1905, and mīrālai, 1914; in 1906 he was appointed deputy director of the Sudan Government Railways, his designation being changed to deputy general manager, 1908; he was engaged on railway survey and construction, notably of the Atbara–Red Sea line, 1904–5; in the First World War he was for a time Chief Royal Engineer at Alexandria; he retired in 1922.

Longinus (*c.* 540–*c.* 600), Christian priest of the Monophysite Church of Egypt; he succeeded Julianus as bishop of Nubia; he baptized the king of the Alodæ, *c.* 580.

Lorenzato, George (Ghiorghios Lorenzatos) (1872–1945), Greek merchant; born on the island of Cephalonia he came to the Sudan, 1896, where he worked with A. H. Capato at Sawākin until 1901; he then started trading in partnership with his brother, A. Lorenzato, first at Sawākin, then at Port Sudan; he was president of the Hellenic national committee at Port Sudan from its foundation.

Loring Pasha, William Wing (1818–86), American soldier; born at Wilmington, North Carolina, of an old Massachusetts family, he fought as a volunteer against the Red Indians in Florida; educated for the Bar he nevertheless preferred soldiering, fought in the American-Mexican war of 1847, and in 1848 was made a lieutenant-colonel of the regular army; in the American civil war of 1861–5 he served on the Confederate side and rose to be major-general; the war over he entered the banking business, but in 1869 joined the Khedivial service and was appointed inspector-general of the Egyptian army with rank of liwā'; in 1875 he was in command of Egyptian coast defences; he was appointed second in command and chief of staff to Muḥammad Rātib Pasha in the disastrous campaign of 1876 against the Abyssinians; in his book, *A Confederate Soldier in Egypt* (New York, 1884), he attributed the Egyptian defeat to disorganization of the staff; promoted farīq he left the Egyptian service in 1879 and retired to the United States; he died in New York.

Losi, Giovanni (1834–82), Italian missionary priest; born at Caselle Landi near Lodi he came to Khartoum, 1873, and in 1874 went to al-Ubaiyaḍ where he was Superior of the newly founded mission till 1878 and again in 1881–2; between 1878 and 1881 he was at another mission established at Dilling in the Nuba hills; he opposed Bishop D. Comboni in matters of missionary policy and after Comboni's death was for a short time acting head of the Central African missions; he died of scurvy during the siege of al-Ubaiyaḍ by the Mahdists; he was an accomplished craftsman and church decorator.

Lovat, Simon Joseph Fraser, 14th Baron. *See* Kœttlitz, Reginald.

Lowe, David (1849–81), British physician; born at Skene in Aberdeenshire he graduated in medicine and practised in Scotland; he left for Cairo in 1872 as assistant to a Dr. Grant established there in private practice; he later joined the Egyptian Government service and was employed on various missions in the Sudan including a tour to get information on the slave traffic and a turn of duty on Egyptian cruisers in the Red Sea engaged in hunting slave traders; he accompanied McKillop Pasha's fleet to the Somali coast and was later appointed assistant judge in the slave court at Muṣawwaʿ; in 1875 he joined the Soudan railway at Wādī Ḥalfā as medical officer and went with a party of surveyors to find a trace for a railway from al-Dabba to al-Fāsh̲ar, 1875–6; Ismāʿīl Pasha Aiyūb, then governor-general of the Sudan, next appointed him chief medical officer of the Sudan, 1876; there he worked on under C. G. Gordon Pasha, who changed his designation to inspector-general of hospitals, till 1880 when he became medical inspector to the sanitary board at Alexandria.

Lowry-Corry (Somerset), 2nd Earl of Belmore (1774–1841), British peer; in 1816–17, with an aristocratic party, he ascended the Nile to Wādī Ḥalfā and Abū Ṣīr in the course of a grand tour of Egypt; the magnificence of his equipage drew jealous comment from less favoured Europeans.

Lucas, Louis Arthur (1851–76), British traveller; in 1875 he set out to explore the Congo basin, travelling by way of Khartoum and Equatoria; in 1876 he accompanied C. G. Gordon Pasha, then governor of Equatoria, from Duffile on an exploration to Unyoro; his arrogance towards the natives roused the hostility of Gordon; ill health finally caused him to abandon his onward journey and he returned to Khartoum; while on his way back to England he died on shipboard between Sawākin and Suez and was buried at Jidda.

Lugard, Frederick Dealtry, 1st Baron Lugard of Abinger (1858–1945), British administrator; he joined the army and fought as a junior officer in the Afghan war, 1879–80; his connexion with the Sudan was a modest one, for in the Sawākin campaign of 1885 he was second in command to J. Willcocks, afterwards General Sir J. Willcocks, who was in charge of the mule corps in the Indian contingent under Lieutenant-General Sir G. Graham; he was afterwards famous as an administrator in Uganda and pre-eminently in Nigeria where he evolved the principles of indirect rule described in his book, *The Dual Mandate in British Tropical Africa* (1922).

Lumbroso, Giacomo (–1885), Italian postal official of Jewish extraction; originating from Leghorn he came to the Sudan in 1861 as a cashier of the Sudan Bank; on the liquidation of the bank in 1873 C. Addà, whom the Egyptian Government charged with the extension of postal facilities to the Sudan, gave him a postal appointment in Khartoum; he was promoted postal inspector of the Sudan by L. Santoni, then director of posts in Upper Egypt and Nubia, in 1878; he was killed by the Mahdists in the sack of Khartoum, or perhaps committed suicide during the massacre.

Lupton, Frank Miller (1854–88), British administrator in the Egyptian Government service; born at Ilford, Essex, he entered the merchant service, 1878; while at Sawākin, 1879, he accompanied a caravan and rode to Berber and Khartoum where he joined the staff of C. G. Gordon Pasha, governor-general of the Sudan, who appointed him first as officer in charge of government steamers on the Nile then deputy to Emin Bey, general governor of the Equatorial province, 1880; shortly afterwards Muḥammad Ra'ūf Pasha, Gordon's successor, appointed him governor of the Baḥr al-Ghazāl in succession to R. Gessi Pasha; first going to Khartoum for instructions he took up his quarters at Daim Sulaimān (wad Zubair) with Saʻtī Efendi, an Egyptian officer, as his assistant; from 1882 he resisted the Mahdists and their Dinka allies who were encroaching upon the Baḥr al-Ghazāl from the north; Saʻtī soon left him for Khartoum which he afterwards deserted for the Mahdi's camp; the Mahdists finally closed in under the amīr Karam Allāh Muḥammad Kurkusāwī who captured him and had him led captive to Omdurman where he lingered in great misery and died in delirium; he had two daughters by his wife Zainūba, an Abyssinian, formerly a slave of F. Rosset Pasha; his widow later married Ḥasan Zakī, a medical officer of the Egyptian army.

Lyall, Charles Elliott (1877–1942), British official; born in Simla he was educated at Oxford University and appointed to the Sudan political service, 1901; he was made governor of the Red Sea province, 1914, of Ḥalfā province, 1914–17, and of Kassala province, 1917–21; finally he was civil secretary, 1921–6, when he retired; he died at Burnham, Buckinghamshire.

Lynes, Hubert (1874–1942), British rear-admiral and naturalist; he entered the Royal Navy, 1887, and rendered distinguished service in the First World War, retiring 1922; he travelled in the Sudan, 1913–14 and 1920–2, making zoological collections; his *Birds of Northern and Central Dar Fur* appeared in *Ibis*, 1924–5.

* **Lyons, Sir Henry** (1864–1944), British archaeologist and soldier; commissioned to the Royal Engineers, 1884, he was in 1890 posted to Cairo where he made a study of archaeological method; he was later attached to the Egyptian army when he saw service on the Sudan frontier, an opportunity which gave him time for archaeological field-work; he cleared and surveyed several temples of the twelfth and eighteenth dynasties at Buhen near Wādī Ḥalfā and recovered important inscriptions; at Wādī Ḥalfā he rebuilt the Nile gauge; in 1895–6 he cleared and surveyed the buildings on the island of Philæ, later to be submerged under the Aswān reservoir; he led the geological and cadastral survey of Egypt, 1897–1909; he retired from Egypt in 1909 and entered upon another period of distinguished public service; his principles of preserving antiquities are embodied in his *Archaeological Survey of Nubia* (1907, &c.).

Lyttleton, Sir Neville Gerald (1845–1931), British general; he entered the Rifle Brigade, 1865, and in the Nile campaign of 1897–8 commanded the 2nd British brigade; he commanded a division in the South African war and was in 1904–8 chief of the general staff and first military member of the army council.

Macauley, Sir George Bohun (1869–1940), British railwayman; he entered the Royal Engineers, 1889, and in 1896 was transferred to the Egyptian army; in 1897 he became assistant director and chief engineer of the Sudan Military Railway (from 1902 Sudan Government Railways) and general manager, 1897–1906; during his term of office as general manager the Red Sea line was built and railway headquarters and workshops established at Atbara; he was general manager of the Egyptian State Railways, 1907–19; during the First World War he built military railways in Sinai and Palestine and was promoted brigadier-general; he was adviser to the Egyptian ministry of communications, 1919–22, when he retired.

Macdonald Pasha, Sir Hector Archibald (1853–1903), British soldier; he joined the army as a private in 1870 and in 1880 was promoted second lieutenant for gallantry in the field; a veteran of the Nile campaign of 1884–5, he served many years in the Egyptian army and fought at Sawākin, 1888, Tūs͟hkī (Toski), 1889, and Tokar, 1891; he commanded the 2nd Egyptian brigade in the Dongola campaign of

1896 and the 1st Egyptian brigade in the Nile campaigns of 1897–8; his handling of his command in the battle of Omdurman was masterly; after a short period in India he saw service in the South African war, 1900–2; he was promoted major-general in 1900; as a result of an opprobrious accusation preying on his mind he shot himself in Paris.

Macdonald, Sir James Ronald Leslie (1862–1927), British major-general; commissioned to the Royal Engineers in 1882 he surveyed the route for the Kenya and Uganda railway and in 1893 was made commissioner for the Uganda Protectorate; having assisted in quelling a mutiny of Sudanese troops in Uganda in 1897 he led a small column from Mount Elgon northward to the Lotuxo (Latuka) country which he reached in the autumn of 1898; here he met with a friendly reception from the Lotuxo chief, Lomoro Xujang; after serving in various parts of Asia he was general officer commanding in Mauritius, 1909–12.

Macé, Louis (*c.* 1680–1705), French linguist, said to have been a good horseman and courageous; employed as secretary to the diplomatic mission of J. Le Noir du Roule sent by the French monarch Louis XIV to the court of the king of Abyssinia, he was murdered with other members of the mission at Sennar.

Macfarlane, Donald Alexander (1880–1944), British merchant; in 1896 he entered the Glasgow office of the trading firm of Gellatly, Hankey, Sewell & Co. (changed in that year to Gellatly, Hankey & Co.) and in 1917 came to the Sudan, having been shipwrecked on the way by a torpedo from a German submarine; first employed in the firm's office at Port Sudan he was appointed managing director of the firm in the Sudan in 1925; in 1933 he was transferred to the London office; in 1934 he became a managing director there, and in 1938 a director; he retired from the business in 1942.

Macgregor, Robert Menzies (1882–1946), British engineer; after spending his early life as an irrigation engineer in India, his services were lent to the Sudan Government in 1923; in 1925 he was appointed British delegate on the Nile commission, and in 1926 irrigation adviser to the Sudan Government; he visited Addis Ababa in 1929 to negotiate with the emperor of Abyssinia a proposal by the Egyptian Government to build a dam over the Blue Nile at Lake Tana.

Machell, Percy Wilfrid (1862–1916), British soldier; he joined the army in 1882 and was promoted captain in 1888; after serving in the Nile campaign of 1884–5 he was transferred to the Egyptian army in 1886; a force under his command captured Khōr Mūsā in 1888, and he fought at Tūshkī (Toski), 1889, and at Tokar, 1891; he commanded the 12th Sudanese battalion, 1891–5; promoted major in the British army in 1893 he retired from it in 1896; his later service in the Egyptian army was spent in administrative posts; he was an alderman on the London County Council, 1912–13.

Maciek (Joseph) Deng Col (–1945), an influential chief of the Bor Gok Dinka on the Upper White Nile, and a magistrate; he was buried near Bor.

MacIver, David Randall (1873–1945), British archaeologist and anthropologist; in 1900–6 he was a research student at Oxford University and in 1907–10 director of the Eckley B. Coxe Junior archaeological expedition of the University of Philadelphia to Egypt and the northern Sudan; he spent his later years in archaeological research in Italy; among his writings are *Karanog* (Oxford, 1910) and *Buhen* (Oxford, 1911).

McKerrell Bey, Augustus de Ségur (1863–1916), British soldier; he received a commission in the army in 1884 and in 1893–1903 served in the Egyptian army; he was at Sawākin, 1884–5, in the fighting on the frontier in 1886, and in the Dongola and Nile campaigns of 1896–9; he was governor of Dongola, 1900–1, and of Berber, 1902–3; later a brigadier-commandant, he was killed in the First World War.

McKey Bey, Charles K . . . (1869–1941), British soldier and official; he joined the British army in the ranks and was later, when a sergeant, seconded to the Egyptian army; for gallantry in the field during the Dongola campaign of 1896 he was promoted second lieutenant of the Middlesex Regiment; he served in the ensuing Nile campaigns of 1897–8; in 1902 he was appointed to the Sudan customs service and from 1914 to 1919 was director of customs.

McKillop Pasha, Henry Frederick (*c.* 1825–79), British sailor in the Khedivial service; he entered the Royal Navy, 1841, and served in the Crimean war, taking part in the capture of Kertch and Yenikale, 1855, for which he was promoted commander; promoted captain, 1862, he later retired and joined the service of the Khedive Ismāʿīl in whose Government he held the posts of port captain of Alexandria and comptroller-general of Egyptian ports and lights; in the war against Abyssinia, 1875–6, he commanded an Egyptian naval squadron in the Red Sea; in September 1875, under orders of the Khedive, his squadron arrived off the mouth of the River Juba on the Somali coast and Egyptian troops were landed at Kismayu; when the British Government protested on behalf of the sultan of Zanzibar, Ismāʿīl Pasha, who claimed the Somali coast as far as the Juba mouth, explained that the expedition had been sent to open communications with the Equatorial province (whose governor, C. G. Gordon Pasha, had advised communicating with the coast); in the face of British objections, however, Ismāʿīl Pasha gave in and McKillop's expedition was recalled; he was afterwards promoted to the rank of *farīq al-baḥr* and was appointed a member of the Egyptian council of state; promoted a retired rear-admiral in the Royal Navy, 1878, he died in Cairo in the following year.

McNeill, Sir John Carstairs (1831–1904), British major-general; he joined the Bengal native infantry in 1850 and served during the Indian mutiny, 1857; in the Maori war in New Zealand he was awarded the Victoria Cross; after service in Canada and West Africa he commanded a brigade in the Sawākin campaign of 1885 and was criticized for lack of caution in the battle of Tofrik; he retired in 1890.

McNeill, Tennent (1887–1921), British inspector, Sudan political service, from 1912; in 1917 he was transferred to Dār Fūr where at Nyāla he was killed during an insurrection by a fanatical faqī named ʿAbd Allāh al-Sihainī.

Madanī Aḥmad al-Ḥasan (1860–1938), Jaʿlī tribal worthy; he was ʿumda of Umm Shōka and shaikh of khaṭṭ; a large landowner, he resigned his public offices in 1937 when his khuṭṭ was incorporated in the qism of the Funj.

Madanī ibn ʿUmar ibn Sarḥān, called **al-Ḥājar** (*fl.* 1650), Moslem holy man, a nephew of the noted religious leader, Shaikh Ṣughaiyarūn; the certitude of his teaching obtained for him the title of al-Ḥājar (The Rock); he was buried at al-Qūz where his tomb was known as Qubbat al-Ḥājar.

Madanī al-ʿUrḍī (1860–1940), tribal notable of the Shanābla Arabs of the Jazīra; born at Nidyāna he was appointed shaikh of the second khuṭṭ of Ḥaṣṣa Ḥaiṣa district in 1911 and a senior notable in 1929; he was president of the Shanābla court at Masallamīya; a wealthy cultivator and merchant, he suffered heavily from the Mahdists in his early manhood.

* **Madībbū Bey ʿAlī** (–1886), chief of the Rizaiqāt tribe of southern Dār Fūr; in 1878–9 he helped R. Gessi Pasha, governor of the Baḥr al-Ghazāl, in the latter's struggle against Sulaimān, son of Zubair Pasha, who was in revolt against the Egyptian Government; on the outbreak of the Mahdist revolt he left his country and visited Muḥammad Aḥmad al-Mahdī at Jabal Qadīr, 1882, and returned to Dār Fūr a convinced believer in the Mahdī; he harassed the government troops under R. C. von Slatin Bey at Shaqqa and in 1883 killed Aḥmad Bey Dafaʿ Allāh and Muḥammad Yāsīn who had been captured by the Mahdists at al-Ubaiyaḍ and sent to him for execution; later, however, he opposed the Mahdist amīr Karam Allāh Muḥammad Kurkusāwī who had been ordered by the Khalīfa ʿAbd Allāhi to occupy Shaqqa where Madībbū ruled; Karam Allāh picked a quarrel with him and sent him to al-Ubaiyaḍ where he was killed by order of the amīr Ḥamdān abū ʿAnja; he was succeeded by his son Mūsā Madībbū.

See also MŪSĀ MADĪBBŪ.

Madigan, Cecil Thomas (1890–1947), Australian explorer; after serving in Sir Douglas Mawson's Antarctic expedition of 1911–14, followed by service in the First World War as an engineer, he returned to Oxford University as a Rhodes Scholar; in 1920–1 he was a member of the staff of the geological survey of the Sudan, making various reconnaissances in connexion with water supply and assisting the commission which studied the hydrography of Lake Tana; he left the Sudan in 1921 to take up a geological post in the University of Adelaide, a post which he held till his death; his widest-known work was his systematic exploration of the desert centre of Australia.

Mahdī. *See* MUḤAMMAD AḤMAD AL-MAHDĪ.

Mahdī Ḥasab Allāh (–1944), chief of the cattle-owning tribe, the Mahrīya, living between Kuttum and Jabal Marra in western Dār Fūr.

Maḥjūb ʿAbd al-Raḥmān Zaiyād (1872–1939), Shā'iqī notable from the Shā'iqīya tribesmen settled in the district of Shendi; during the Mahdist revolt his father served the Khalīfa ʿAbd Allāhi; he himself was appointed shaikh of the Rubāṭāb tribesmen in the district in 1899 and ʿumda in 1905; in 1920 he fell from a camel and broke his neck, but recovered after a year; he played an important part in the construction of the irrigated basin at al-Basābīr, 1932–3; he retired from public life in 1938 in favour of his brother al-Tūm.

Maḥjūb al-Buṣailī (*fl.* 1860–70), Upper Egyptian trader, said to have been a member of the well-known Aswānlī family of the Buṣailīya; he traded on the White Nile and Baḥr al-Ghazāl, and several European travellers have left impressions of him; Miss A. P. F. Tinné and her party made a long stay at his stations in the Baḥr al-Ghazāl in 1863.

Maḥjūb al-Mīrghanī (*c.* 1825–1912), religious leader, second son of al-Saiyid Muḥammad Sir al-Khātim al-Mīrghanī and grandson of al-Saiyid Muḥammad ʿUthmān I, founder of the Mīrghanīya (Khatmīya) brotherhood in the Sudan; he married Nafīsa, daughter of al-Saiyid al-Ḥasan al-Mīrghanī; he died at Khartoum North where his tomb stands.

Maḥjūb al-Saiyid Ismāʿīl al-Walī (–1929), religious dignitary; a son of the celebrated saint Ismāʿīl ʿAbd Allāhi al-Walī, he was the head of his father's brotherhood in al-Ubaiyaḍ.

Maḥmūd ʿAbd Allāh al-Maḥallāwī (*fl.* 1859–92), Egyptian slave trader and afterwards anti-slavery inspector; by birth a Jaʿfarī from the governorate of Isnā in Upper Egypt he was brought up in Khartoum by his father, a merchant engaged in trade between Egypt and the Sudan; he was in Kassala in 1859 when he was conscripted into the army; to avoid military service he escaped to the camp of ʿUmāra wad Nimr, the Jaʿlī desperado living on the Abyssinian border, and accompanied ʿUmāra on some of his raids; in 1863 he profited from the amnesty accorded to the Nimrāb, through the influence of friends in Cairo, and went to Egypt; he later returned to the Sudan where he engaged in slave-raiding in the Nuba hills; the governor of Fashoda made him chief of the elephant and ostrich hunters in the governorate; then, after a period in trade in Gedaref, he joined his brother Muḥammad Bey ʿAbd Allāh al-Maḥallāwī in Dār Fūr in 1877; here he was appointed a muʿāwin of the sub-governorate of Shaqqa and was later made an anti-slavery inspector by R. Gessi Pasha, a post which he held till 1884 when he was captured along with F. Lupton Bey in the Baḥr al-Ghazāl in 1884; making his way to the eastern Sudan he escaped from the Mahdist lines to Sawākin about 1892 and returned to Egypt where he lived in retirement.

Maḥmūd ʿAbd al-Karīm abū Saʿd (1858–1927), notable of the Riyāfa section of the Habbānīya tribe, he was born at Kalaka in southern Dār Fūr; his brother Shimais was nāẓir of the Habbānīya under the Egyptian Government; during the Mahdist revolt, when the amīr ʿUthmān Adam came to Dār Fūr, he was one of his tribe to answer the call to go east and join the Holy War; afterwards made an amīr he commanded a body of his own tribesmen at the battle of Omdurman, 1898, whence he fled with the Khalīfa ʿAbd Allāhi to Shurqaila in Kordofan; seeing the hopelessness of the Khalīfa's cause he and a number of his fellow tribesmen gave themselves up to the Anglo-Egyptian forces; he lived in Omdurman until 1920 when the governor of Dār Fūr invited him to return to Dār Fūr and replace the nāẓir al-Ghālī Tāj al-Dīn who had been imprisoned for malpractices; there he served his people well and in 1923 was made a magistrate; he died at Buram.

Maḥmūd ʿAbd al-Saiyid (–1920), faqī of the Jimaʿa of eastern Kordofan; he lived all his life in Dār al-Jimaʿa round Jadīd; he possessed a fine manuscript copy of the Qur'ān.

Maḥmūd abū Adam ʿAlī Rikat (–1944), notable of the Beja and ʿumda of the Sindereit clan of the Amarar; he died at Musmār.

* **Maḥmūd wad Aḥmad** (*c.* 1865–1906), Mahdist amīr, a nephew of the Khalīfa ʿAbd Allāhi; he was born at Kalaka in south-western Dār Fūr and in 1891 was appointed amīr of Kordofan and Dār Fūr in place of ʿUthmān Adam who had died in 1889 after the Mahdist invasion of Dār Maṣālīṭ; in 1892 he sternly repressed a revolt against him at al-Nahūd; later transferred by his uncle to guard the northern approaches of the Sudan against a threatened advance by the Anglo-Egyptian forces, he was largely responsible for the massacre of the Jaʿlīyīn townsmen of al-Matamma in 1898; brave but stupid, and lacking experience in warfare against a disciplined enemy, he was utterly defeated in the battle of the Atbara by an Anglo-Egyptian army led by the sirdār, al-farīq H. H. Kitchener Pasha; taken prisoner after the battle he died in captivity at Rosetta.

Maḥmūd wad Aḥmad al-ʿArakī (*fl.* 1510), an early ancestor of the ʿArakīyīn Arabs; disgusted with the prevailing lawlessness and paganism obtaining at the time of the conquest of the Jazīra by the Funj he went to Egypt where he studied the Mālikite code of Islamic law and on his return to the Sudan set up a school or 'castle' on the White Nile, hence his nickname al-Rajul al-Quṣaiyar (the Man of the Castle); he is said to have had seventeen schools between al-Ais (Kawa) and Tūtī Island and to have concentrated on the proper enforcement of the divorce laws.

* **Maḥmūd Aḥmad Ḥamdī al-Falakī Pasha** (1815–85), Egyptian astronomer; educated with his brother, Ismāʿīl Muṣṭafā al-Falakī (afterwards Pasha), at the École Polytechnique, Paris, he occupied an honoured place in the scientific life of Egypt; in 1860, at the request of the scientists of France, he came to Dongola to observe an eclipse of the sun and was the first to fix the latitude of Old Dongola; he was minister of public works in Aḥmad ʿUrābī Pasha's ministry, 1882, and was head of the Egyptian schools administration, 1884–5.

Maḥmūd Bey Aḥmadānī (–1883), Egyptian official; formerly governor of Khartoum, he was killed at the battle of Shaikān (Kashgil) while accompanying the army of W. Hicks Pasha as a civilian.

Maḥmūd al-'Ajamī Ḥamza (–1919), notable of the Raḥmāb branch of the Mīrafāb tribe of the Berber district, son of al-'Ajamī Ḥamza, nāẓir al-qism of Berber and shaikh of Rās al-Wādī in Turkish times; he was appointed ḥākim al-khuṭṭ of Rās al-Wādī, an area which extended along the east bank of the Nile from Berber to the mouth of the Atbara river; when the great shaikh, Muḥammad al-Khair 'Abd Allāh Khūjalī of Berber went over to the Mahdists in 1883, he joined him; he later fought in many of the battles of 1884–5 including Abū Ṭulaiḥ (Abu Klea) and was appointed an assistant to the amīr Zakī Ṭamal, Mahdist governor of Berber; falling out with the Khalīfa 'Abd Allāhi he and his brothers were imprisoned in Omdurman and were at length freed by the Anglo-Egyptian army in 1898; appointed 'umda of his native district he remained in office till his death.

Maḥmūd 'Alī Bey (–1889), shaikh of the Faḍlāb branch of the Amarar Beja tribe inhabiting the Red Sea hills; on the eve of the outbreak of the Mahdist revolt on the coast he was engaged in inter-tribal war with the Ḥamdāb branch of the Hadendowa tribe, probably over the control of the local section of the Sawākin–Berber road, a source of revenue to a camel-owning tribe; the Egyptian garrison at Sinkat intervened on the side of the Ḥamdāb; about 1883 he was granted the title of bey by the Egyptian Government and waged war against the Mahdist forces under the command of 'Uthmān abū Bakr Diqna (Osman Digna); he fought alongside the Anglo-Egyptian column in the battle of Tamai in 1884; two of his sons went over to the Mahdists in 1888 when the tribes friendly to the government were growing restless as he was regarded by the tribal leaders as an upstart.

Maḥmūd 'Alī al-Dādinjāwī (*c.* 1866–1922), notable of Dār Fūr; his father, 'Alī Bey al-Dādinjāwī, had been tutor to Ibrāhīm Muḥammad Ḥusain, afterwards sultan of Dār Fūr (1873–4), and superintendent of the market at al-Fāshar; on the collapse of the Mahdist movement Maḥmūd threw in his lot with 'Alī Dīnār who had made himself sultan; he was one of the most notable figures in Dār Fūr during the greater part of 'Alī Dīnār's reign; in 1902 'Alī Dīnār sent him to attack Sanīn Ḥusain of Kabkabīya, but he was quickly and heavily defeated; again in 1907 he was sent in joint command with Adam Rijāl with a large force against Sanīn and this time was victorious; he fought against the Maṣālīṭ, the Rizaiqāt, and the French; ranking as a malik and holding the courtesy title of *abo*, he was much respected for his honesty and bluntness; in the Anglo-Egyptian campaign of 1916 against 'Alī Dīnār he remained faithful to the sultan until the latter's flight from al-Fāshar when he accepted the new order and faithfully served it till his death.

Maḥmūd Bey al-Amīr 'Uthmān (1855–1937), head shaikh of the Arteiga tribe of the Beja group and a magistrate; he first helped his elder brother al-Jailānī, who had succeeded to the shaikhship in 1863, and on Jailānī's death in 1883 became ʿumda of Sawākin; he did not join the Mahdist movement but actively assisted the Anglo-Egyptian authorities at Sawākin; in 1895 he was created bey; he was largely responsible for the peaceful state of Port Sudan during the political disturbances of 1924.

Maḥmūd Ḥusnī Pasha (*c.* 1852–), liwā' of the Egyptian army; brought up in Cairo where he received his military education at the school of engineering and the cavalry school, he was commissioned mulāzim II, 1874; after some years as an instructor at the military school he served in the Nile campaign of 1884–5 and then in various staff posts; in the Dongola and Nile campaigns he fought in the battles of Firka (Firket) and Ḥafīr, 1896, Atbara and Omdurman, 1898, and Umm Dibaikarāt, 1899; now a qā'immaqām he was posted in 1900 to Omdurman where he served until his retirement with rank of mīrālai; in 1905 he was promoted liwā' on becoming amīr al-ḥājj for that year.

* **Maḥmūd wad Khalīl wad ʿAbd al-Wāḥid** (–1885), Mahdist amīr, an uncle of Muḥammad Aḥmad al-Mahdī; he commanded the Mahdist forces holding al-Ubaiyaḍ after its fall while the main Mahdist army encamped at al-Rāhad, 1883; in 1885 he visited Omdurman when he heard of a mutiny which had broken out among the black troops in al-Ubaiyaḍ; quickly returning to Kordofan he pursued the mutineers to Jabals Ghulfān and Nyima and, while endeavouring to storm Ghulfān, was killed.

Maḥmūd Muḥammad (–1884), Mahdist amīr; in 1884 Muḥammad Aḥmad al-Mahdī sent him with reinforcements from al-Ubaiyaḍ to join the amīr Aḥmad al-Hūdai who had been badly mauled by Muṣṭafā Pasha Yāwar, governor of Dongola, at al-Dabba and al-Hatānī in July; he was ordered also to assume the amīrship of Dongola; instead he was killed at Korti in September by a government force led by Muṣṭafā Pasha Yāwar; in the same battle fell the amīr Aḥmad al-Hūdai.

Maḥmūd Musa ʿAbd al-Raḥmān (–1931), shaikh al-mashāyikh of the residential suburbs of Khartoum and a magistrate; he was a Jaʿfarī of Egyptian origin.

Maḥmūd Ṣabrī Pasha (1852–), liwā' of the Egyptian army; born at Alexandria he was commissioned to the engineers, 1871, and was in the survey parties of R. E. Colston Bey and H. G. Prout Bey in Kordofan and Dār Fūr, 1874–6; his own work on these surveys included a map with Arabic indications entitled *Carte du nord de Dar-For;* while an engineer on the Soudan railway C. G. Gordon Pasha had him promoted qā'immaqām, 1879; he was inspector-general of gendarmerie during Aḥmad ʿUrābī Pasha's revolt, 1882 and, when governor of Manūfīya, was made a pasha, 1894.

Maḥmūd wad Sharaf al-Dīn Ḥamad (–1935), Beja chieftain; ʿumda of the Bishārīyīn of the Atbara valley; he died at Baʿaluk north-west of Qūz Rājab.

Maḥmūd Ṭāhir Pasha (*fl.* 1874–83), Egyptian soldier; he was

governor of Kordofan from about 1874 to 1878 when the Khedivial
Government removed him from office on a charge of dishonesty; in the
Superior Order approving his discharge he is described as 'ex-prisoner
in Sennar'; he was afterwards reinstated and was sub-prefect of police
in Cairo when in October 1883 he was appointed, with rank of liwā',
to command Egyptian troops in the eastern Sudan; arriving at Sawākin
he attempted the relief of Tokar which was besieged by a Mahdist
force under 'U<u>th</u>mān abū Bakr Diqna (Osman Digna); landing his force
at Trinkitat he advanced towards Tokar, but his troops were utterly
defeated by the Mahdists at el-Teb on 4 November 1883; among the
slain were Commander L. N. Moncrieff, British consul at Sawākin;
Maḥmūd Pasha escaped to his ships and was afterwards convicted of
negligence by a court martial.

Mahon Pasha, Sir Bryan Thomas (1862–1930), British soldier,
commissioned in the 8th Hussars, 1883, he was seconded to the Egyptian
army in 1893 and served in the Dongola and Nile campaigns, 1896–9;
in 1900 he left the Sudan for the South African war where he ably
commanded a column which relieved Mafeking; returning to the Sudan
he was governor of Kordofan, 1901–4; after service in India he fought
in the First World War as a divisional general on Gallipoli (1915),
Macedonia (1915–16), and was commander-in-chief, Ireland (1916–18),
rising to full general; he was knighted in 1922.

Maḥū Bey Urfalī (–1828), Turkish cavalry officer and governor;
by origin a Kurd (his name Maḥū is a Kurdish familiar variant of
Muḥammad), he distinguished himself as a cavalry officer in the army
of Ibrāhīm Pasha in the Arabian war of 1818–19 and was transferred
to the Sudan late in 1821 as governor of the regions of Berber, Shendi,
and the Rubāṭāb in place of Aḥmad A<u>gh</u>ā; he arrived early in 1822
and at once began making arrangements for the transit of slaves by
water through his province which lay between the slave-raiding areas
to the south and the military camps of Upper Egypt where the slaves
were destined as recruits for the viceroy's new regular army; he twice
attacked the Jamīlāb tribesmen on the west bank of the Nile and
executed some of their <u>sh</u>ai<u>kh</u>s; he was himself attacked by the Ja'līyīn
under Mak Nimr before the latter fled to the River Setit; having
stamped out the last Sudanese resistance in his province he was suddenly called to Khartoum by the death of the mīrālai 'U<u>th</u>mān Bey
Jarkas, governor of the province of Sennar, in March 1825; he took
over the governorate of Sennar, leaving al-Ḥājj Amīn A<u>gh</u>ā in charge
of Berber; during his short period as acting governor he showed
courtesy and moderation in his dealings with the people who had been
alienated by the brutality of 'U<u>th</u>mān Bey and his troops; he raided
the region of Gedaref for corn and did much to resettle the peasants
on their land in the Jazīra whence they had fled from fear of the Turks
and their grinding taxation; he was relieved early in 1826 by 'Alī
<u>Kh</u>ūr<u>sh</u>īd A<u>gh</u>ā (afterwards Pasha) who had been appointed governor,
and was recalled to Egypt where the viceroy had need of his experience;
his memory is kept alive in the Sudan by a great tree which used to
stand near the site of the present dockyard of the Egyptian irrigation

service on the White Nile near Khartoum under which the Bey is credited by local tradition with holding merry picnics, and by wells which he dug north-east of Berber; his connexion with the establishment of long-staple cotton in Egypt is now said to be mythical.

* **Maillet, Benoît de** (1756–38), French diplomat and traveller; he was born at St. Mihiel and died at Marseilles; he was consul-general of France in Egypt from 1692 and was intimately concerned with the land trade routes to Sennar, Dār Fūr, and Abyssinia; the missions of C. J. Poncet and J. Le Noir du Roule, both of which traversed the Sudan, occurred during his consulship.

Maiwurno. *See* Muḥammad Bello Maiwurno.

Majak Akot (–1936), chief of the Gonijor section of the Malwal Dinka tribe of Equatoria.

Makīn wad al-Nūr (–1889), Mahdist amīr; by origin an ʿArakī he was a brother of the amīr ʿAbd Allāh wad al-Nūr; he fought under the command of ʿAbd al-Raḥmān wad al-Najūmī on the southern border of Egypt, 1887–9, and in 1889 was engaged with the amīr ʿAlī wad Saʿd in bringing up reinforcements from Dongola for Wad al-Najūmī's intended invasion of Egypt; he died of wounds received at the battle of Tūshkī (Toski) and was buried in the hills above the temple of Abū Simbel.

* **al-Makkī Ismāʿīl al-Walī** (–1906), religious notable, son of al-Saiyid Ismāʿīl ʿAbd Allāhi al-Walī, founder of the Ismāʿīlīya religious brotherhood; to al-Makkī fell the leadership of the brotherhood when Muḥammad Aḥmad al-Mahdī secured his loyal support at the outbreak of the Mahdist revolt; he marched with the Mahdī from Kordofan to the siege of Khartoum in 1884; he was greatly trusted by the Khalīfa ʿAbd Allāhi.

Makkī Munʿim abū'l-Milīḥ (–1870), nāẓir of the Ḥamar Arabs on the borders of Kordofan and Dār Fūr; he was a son of al-Ḥājj Munʿim, nāẓir of all the Ḥamar; he held office from 1850 till his death, waging perpetual inter-tribal warfare with the neighbouring people including the Kabābīsh whose shaikh, Faḍl Allāh wad Sālim, he defeated about 1850; he was as good an administrator as he was a successful warrior; he found his tribe divided and united it sufficiently to withstand the shock which the next twenty years were to give to its unity; he extended the Ḥamar tribal boundaries and made Umm Shanqa his seat; he had thousands of tebeldi trees hollowed for conversion into water reservoirs and exploited the gum arabic resources of his country, and, in consolidating the Ḥamar people, he held the balance nicely between Turk and Fūr; his son al-Milīḥ succeeded him.

Malcolm Pasha, George John (*c.* 1824–84), British sailor; he entered the Royal Navy, 1842, and served in the Baltic naval operations in the Crimean war, 1855; promoted captain, 1866, he retired, 1873, and entered the Ottoman service with the grade of pasha and the high-sounding designation of director-general of the abolition of the slave trade and judge of the slave courts, 1878; as head of the Egyptian anti-slave trade police in the Red Sea he applied himself with zeal to the suppression of the trade, arresting the relatives of Abū Bakr Pasha, governor of Zaila; C. G. Gordon Pasha, then governor-general of the Sudan, was opposed to his appointment, objected to his arrests which Gordon considered over-zealous and administratively injudicious, and resented the fact that the costs of Malcolm's police was a charge against the dwindling revenue of the Sudan Government; Gordon released the relations of Abū Bakr, whereupon Malcolm resigned and Gordon assumed responsibility for the suppression of the slave trade both in the Red Sea and in the Sudan; he was promoted rear-admiral, 1882.

al-Malik ʿAwad Allāh. *See* ʿAWAD ALLĀH, called AL-MALIK ʿAWAD ALLĀH.

al-Malik Kanbal. *See* KANBAL, called AL-MALIK KANBAL.

al-Malik ʿUthmān (–1931), Maḥasī notable; ʿumda of al-Madik (East) in Dār Maḥas.

Malik Yāsīn (*c.* 1850–1940), ʿumda of the Masaʿdāb section of the Jimaʿa Baqqāra of the White Nile, a magistrate and member of the Baqqāra court; he belonged to the old ruling family of the Masaʿdāb.

Malte-Brun, Victor-Adolphe (1816–89), French geographer; he wrote much on the quest for the source of the White Nile.

Malzac, Alphonse de (–1860), French hunter and trader; he asserted that he had been secretary to the Comte de Rayneval, ambassador of France at Rome; the Vicomte F. M. de Lesseps, who met him in Khartoum in the winter of 1856–7, merely recorded that he had abandoned diplomacy for elephant-hunting; J. Petherick stated that he was formerly attaché to the French embassy at Athens and that he knew much about the fauna of the White Nile; he was an associate of Petherick with whom he occupied hunting stations jointly; in his ivory (and, it is said, slave-raiding) expeditions he explored the country west of the White Nile and founded Rumbek in 1857–9; for some time his base of operations was Shambé; according to C. Piaggia, who came across him in the region of Rumbek, he gave slaves to his retainers in place of wages; T. von Heuglin wrote of him as a scoundrel and added that, when he (von Heuglin) was Austrian consul in Khartoum, he deprived de Malzac of the rights of Austrian protection but that he crawled back into favour with von Heuglin's successor, J. Natterer; he died in Khartoum after a long illness, fortified by the Sacraments of the Latin Church; he left a widow and one daughter, Ginevra Ottilia, born out of wedlock in 1856 and christened in Khartoum 1860; on his death his trading stations passed to F. Binder; a paper by him on the flow of the White Nile and its tributaries was published in the *Bulletin of the Geographical Society of Paris*, June 1862.

Manāwir Ḥabīla (–*c.* 1887), Ḥumrāwī chieftain of the Kāmilī branch; a prominent tribal figure in Dār Ḥumr in western Kordofan during the latter days of the Egyptian rule, he refused to join the Mahdist movement and killed al-Ghazzālī Aḥmad Khawwāf whom the Khalīfa ʿAbd Allāhi sent to subdue the Ḥumr about 1886; he was later killed by the Mahdist amīr Bishārī Muḥammad Raida at Hegeiwa near Muglad.

Mangin, Charles-Marie-Emanuel (1866–1925), French general; born at Sarrebourg he entered the French army in 1885 and served in the colonial forces until 1914; he was under Captain J. B. Marchand in the French mission of 1896–8 to the Upper Nile; while Marchand was at Fashoda (now Kodok) he explored the country to the east of the White Nile, entering the region of the Beni Shanqul and thence making his way southward to Gore in the western Abyssinian highlands; in the First World War he commanded a division and finally the 10th army group in France.

Mangles, James. *See* IRBY, CHARLES LEONARD.

Manṣūr ibn al-Saiyid Aḥmad Zabad al-Baḥr, called **al-Hardān** (*fl.* 1300), traditional ancestor of the Kināna Arabs, said to have descended from Ḥamza, youngest son of the Prophet's grandfather, ʿAbd al-Muṭṭalib; as a result of a family quarrel he is said to have left Makka with his younger brother ʿAbd Allāhi for Egypt and from there to have passed up the Nile valley to the Sudan, marrying into the Maḥass tribe of Nubians and becoming the ancestor of most of the Kināna.

Manṣūr Sulaimān (1864–1940), malik of Dār Urrtī on the desert fringes of northern Dār Fūr; in 1914 he fled from Dār Fūr to Kordofan fearing for his life as the Kufra caravan had called at ʿAin Saraif, made exhorbitant demands, and had complained to the sultan of Dār Fūr when he had failed to supply them with all they asked; on the occupation of Dār Fūr by the Anglo-Egyptian forces in 1916 he returned along with the new administration and was re-elected malik of Dār Urrtī independent of Jamiʿ Khair, malik of Mīdōb; in 1923 he was dismissed for inefficiency and for refusing to arrest two kidnappers; he was banished to Mellīt and Dār Urrtī was placed under Jamiʿ Khair; in 1926, however, Manṣūr Sulaimān returned to Jabal Mīdōb and began to plot to regain his position, thereby causing unrest among the Urrtī which came to a head in 1928, after which he was elected dimlig of the Teukeddi and Usuti sections of the Urrtī under Jamiʿ Khair; after 1933 old age and ill health caused him to lose much of his zeal for politics.

Maqbūl Muḥammad al-Zain (*c.* 1852–1918), ʿumda of the Ḥasanīya living in the neighbourhood of Kawa on the White Nile; he grew wealthy with increasing age.

al-Maqrīzī. *See* TAQĪ AL-DĪN AḤMAD IBN ʿALĪ . . . AL-MAQRĪZĪ.

Marchand, Jean-Baptiste (1863–1934), French soldier and explorer; born at Thoissey, Aisne, he entered the French army in 1883 and in 1888 began a series of African explorations which lasted till 1899; as captain in command of a small expedition charged by the French Government with the exploration of the Upper Nile then under the control of the Mahdists, he arrived at Loango in 1896 and ascended the Congo and Oubangui rivers; at the head waters of the M'Bomu the expedition dismantled a small steamer, the *Faidherbe*, which they carried in sections over the Nile–Congo watershed and assembled and launched on the River Sué, within the borders of the Sudan, 1897; the party, composed of a handful of French officers and sergeants and a detachment of Senegalese troops, then descended the Sué and Jur rivers to the Baḥr al-Ghazāl, establishing depots at Fort Hossinger (Tambura), Fort Gouly (on the Sué), and Fort Desaix (Wau); on 10 July 1898 the expedition arrived at Fashoda (the present Kodok) where they hoisted the French flag and defeated a Mahdist force which had come up the White Nile in steamers; hearing that a party of Europeans had established themselves at Fashoda, Kitchener, who had recently won the battle of Omdurman, set out with a flotilla of gunboats for the south; arrived at Fashoda he asked Marchand to withdraw, but Marchand refused and remained at Fashoda for six weeks until ordered by the French Government to withdraw after a settlement with the British Government; the Fashoda Incident, as it was called, almost led to war between the two nations; leaving Fashoda Marchand with the main body of his party travelled up the Sobat, Pibor, and Baro rivers to the limit of navigation where the *Faidherbe* was sunk near Gambeila; the remainder of the expedition travelled to Europe by way of the Nile; the main body finally crossed Abyssinia and arrived at Jibūtī in 1899; during the First World War Marchand was a brigadier-general and in 1917 was promoted divisional general; he led his command with distinction in some of the bitterest fighting in France; the Fashoda Incident gave rise to an enormous literature, mostly French, of no enduring merit, save some excellent accounts of the expedition by some of its members.

Marcian (Flavius Marcianus) (391–457), emperor of the Eastern Roman Empire who reigned from 450 till his death; the Thebaid was so often raided by the Nubians that he was forced to make an unfavourable peace with them in 451.

al-Marḍī abū Rūf. *See* YŪSUF AL-MARḌĪ ABŪ RŪF.

Mari Bey, also called **Békir Aghā, Békir Bey** (*c.* 1790–*c.* 1860), French soldier in the Egyptian army; a Corsican by origin (he was born at Fiumorbo) and an adventurer by choice, he served in the army of Napoleon, according to himself as a colonel, according to others as a drummer, hence his nickname 'Le Colonel Tapin'; General Weygand in his *Histoire Militaire de Mohammed Aly et de ses Fils* (1936) describes him as having been an infantry captain in the Grande Armée; he was at all events an old companion in arms of O. J. A. Sève (Sulaimān Pasha al-Faransāwī) by whose influence he was appointed an instructor in the new regular army, the *niẓām al-jadīd* of the Viceroy Muḥammad 'Alī; he fought under Ibrāhīm Pasha in Arabia and in the Morean campaign of 1825–7; in 1834 he was on the staff of Aḥmad Pasha abū Widān in Arabia, becoming a commandant in ʿAsīr and governor of Jidda; he was afterwards prefect of police in Cairo with rank of qā'immaqām and bey; about 1853, in the reign of ʿAbbās I, he fell into disgrace and was banished for a time to Khartoum where the French traveller C. Didier met him in 1854; his wife's tomb is by the side of that of Aḥmad Pasha abū Widān in ʿAbbās Street; he was a yellow-faced, comical little man of bilious temperament.

Marinelli, Vincenzo (1820–92), Italian painter; born at San Martino d'Agri, Lucania, he studied first letters and mathematics and then painting at Rome; travelling abroad he worked for King Otto I in Greece and for Muḥammad Saʿīd Pasha in Egypt; he accompanied the viceroy to the Sudan in the winter of 1856–7; he settled in Naples where he taught in the Institute of Fine Arts and where he died; his visit to the Sudan inspired several of his paintings of oriental scenes.

* **Mark** (*c.* A.D. 1–*c.* A.D. 70), Christian evangelist, one of the twelve disciples of Jesus Christ and the traditionally accepted author of the Second Gospel; he was possibly in Egypt between A.D. 50 and A.D. 60; he was the traditional missionary of Egypt and Nubia and the founder of the church of Alexandria, hence many churches in those countries have been dedicated to him, both in early Christian and in modern times.

Marling, Sir Percival Scrope (1861–1936), British colonel; he joined the army in 1880 and was with the mounted infantry in the Sawākin campaign of 1884, fighting in several engagements with the Mahdists including the second battle of el-Teb, Tamai, and Tamanib, in the last of which his gallantry won him the Victoria Cross; he served in the Nile campaign of 1884–5 and was present at the battle of Abū Ṭulaiḥ (Abu Klea); promoted captain in 1886 he saw further service in the South African war and First World war; retiring from the army he was high sheriff of the city of Gloucester, 1923; he wrote *Rifleman and Hussar* (1931).

Marno Bey, Ernst (1844–83), Austrian explorer and administrator; he was born and bred in Vienna and, after travelling in Abyssinia, came to Khartoum in 1867; in 1870 he attempted without success to ascend the Blue Nile valley to the country of the Galla and succeeded only in reaching Fadāsī; he explored the Baḥr al-Zarāf in 1872 on his way to join Sir S. W. Baker at Gondokoro; after a period in Europe he returned to the Sudan in 1874 and, while with C. G. Gordon Pasha at Lado, explored the region between the Nile and the Yei, and accompanied C. Chaillé-Long on an exploration of the country of the Makraka Niam-Niam (Azande) on the Nile–Congo watershed in 1875; after exploring in Kordofan in 1875–6 he entered the service of the Egyptian Government and was in 1878 appointed governor of Gallabat; he held this post for a few months only, for in 1879–80 he was employed with a fleet of steamers clearing vegetable obstructions from the Baḥr al-Jabal; promoted bey, he was made governor of Fāzūghlī in 1881; he died in Khartoum; a son, Jakob Ernst, by his Abyssinian wife Catherine Zainab, was baptized at the Roman Catholic mission, Khartoum, in

1881; he contributed many papers to Austrian and German journals, mostly on his explorations and on natural history; he also published two larger works: *Reisen im Gebiete des Blauen und Weissen Nil . . . 1869 bis 1873* (Vienna, 1874), and *Reise in der Aegyptischen Aequatorial-Provinz und in Kordofan . . . 1874–1876* (Vienna, 1879).

Martyr, Cyril Godfrey (1860–1936), British lieutenant-colonel; he entered the army in 1880 and served in the Nile campaign of 1884–5 and fought at Abū Ṭulaiḥ (Abu Klea); transferring to the Egyptian army he was present at the battles of Jummaiza, Tūshkī (Toski), and at the reoccupation of Tokar; he served in the Dongola campaign of 1896 as assistant adjutant-general; reverting to the British army he went to Uganda where in the latter half of 1898 he helped to quell a mutiny of Sudanese troops; he then led a small column down the Albert Nile, reaching Rejaf in November, and, assisted by Congo Free State troops, pushed on to Bor whence the Mahdist garrison retired north-westward; prevented by serious *sudd* blocks in the river from attempting to join the Anglo-Egyptian forces in the north, he retired to Bedden near Rejaf and established posts at Fort Berkeley, Afuddo, and Wadelai; he served in the South African and First World wars.

al-Mās (or **Almās) Bey Muḥammad** (*fl.* 1873–9), Circassian soldier in the Egyptian army; he was transferred from the governorate of Kordofan to that of Dongola in 1873; it is said that he was a party to the murder of Ismā'īl Pasha Ṣādiq, the Egyptian minister of finance, whom the Khedive Ismā'īl banished to Dongola in 1876; F. L. James, the British traveller who met him in Dongola in 1878, wrote of him as an old Turk who, in spite of his long service in the Sudan, spoke Arabic with difficulty; he was appointed governor of Sennar in 1879.

al-Mās (or **Almās) Bey Mursī** (1859–1941), Sudanese soldier; born among the Dinka of the Baḥr al-Ghazāl he received no schooling until he was enrolled in the army in 1873; he fought in most of the battles of the Mahdist period including Jummaiza, 1886, Tūshkī (Toski), 1889, the reoccupation of Tokar, 1891, and in all the important battles of the Dongola, Nile, and Kordofan campaigns of 1896–9; after the reoccupation he saw service in the Niam-Niam, Nyima, and south Kordofan patrols; promoted qā'immaqām in 1911 he retired from the army in 1915 after no less than forty-three years with the colours.

Masi, Lorenzo (*fl.* 1821–2), Italian engineer; a native of Leghorn, he came to Egypt and entered the service of Muḥammad 'Alī Pasha, founding a school of surveying at Būlāq about 1820 which G. B. Brocchi visited in 1822 and praised; he followed the military expedition of Ismā'īl Pasha to the Sudan and with G. Segato mapped the country east of the Rivers Nile and Atbara, 1821–2; he was later employed as a surveyor on the Maḥmūdīya canal and designed the fresh-water canal at Suez; he collaborated with Segato in the publication of *Saggi pittorici . . . nel Egitto* (Firenze, 1827).

* **Mason Bey, Alexander McComb** (–1897), American sailor in

the Khedivial service; he was a graduate of Annapolis Naval College and was later a naval officer in the Confederate fleet in the American civil war of 1861–5; he entered the service of the Egyptian Government in 1870 and was first employed as an officer in the Khedivial steamer service plying between Alexandria and Constantinople; he was afterwards appointed to the Egyptian General Staff with rank of qā'immaqām and in this capacity worked with E. S. Purdy, a fellow American, on surveys in 1874; he followed H. G. Prout as acting governor of the Equatorial province, 1876–7; during this period he made scientific reconnaissances of the White Nile between Dufile and Lake Albert, a reach of the river traversed, but not surveyed, by W. H. Chippendall and C. M. Watson in 1874–5; he also, in 1877, made a thorough reconnaissance of Lake Albert itself which R. Gessi had circumnavigated, but not surveyed, in 1876; he discovered the Semliki river; in 1878 he resigned from the army and was given a post in the survey department of the Egyptian Government when he came to the Sudan and surveyed the country between Wādī Ḥalfā and Berber of which he compiled a map; early in 1878 he visited Berber and Muṣawwaʿ to discuss the slave trade with the governors there on his appointment as chief of the anti-slave trade organization on the Red Sea coast; he was in the Fayyūm during the revolt of Aḥmad ʿUrābī Pasha, 1882; in 1883 he sat on a commission, of which ʿUmar Luṭfī Pasha was chairman, to consider the future of the Soudan railway; he was appointed governor of Muṣawwaʿ in 1884 and accompanied Vice-Admiral Sir W. N. W. Hewett to Abyssinia as the Egyptian Government representative; he retired in 1885 and died in Washington, D.C.

Massaia, Lorenzo Guglielmo (1809–89), cardinal of the Roman Catholic Church; he entered the Capuchin (Franciscan) Order in 1825; in 1846 he was appointed first Vicar Apostolic for the Galla in Abyssinia; after having been expelled from Abyssinia he visited Europe and returned to his mission among the Galla; leaving Cairo in 1851 he travelled through the Sudan by way of Korosko, Berber, and Khartoum where he was well received by the governor-general ʿAbd al-Laṭīf Pasha ʿAbd Allāh; while in Khartoum he obtained an unfavourable impression of the conduct of the Roman Catholic mission there; leaving Khartoum late in 1851 he attempted in vain to penetrate Abyssinia by way of the Blue Nile and was forced to proceed by Gallabat and Gondar; in his *In Abissinia e fra i Galla* (Florence, 1895) he gives an interesting account of the neighbourhood of Roseires; after many years working among the Galla he was made a cardinal in 1884; he died in Naples.

Massari, Alfonso Maria (1854–92), Italian naval officer; while a lieutenant he accompanied the explorer P. Matteucci on a journey across Africa from Khartoum to the west coast, 1880–1; he was afterwards employed in the Congo Free State.

al-Masʿūdī. *See* ABŪ'L-ḤASAN ʿALĪ AL-MASʿŪDĪ.

* **Mather, Sir William** (1838–1920), British cotton-spinner and

benefactor; he was chairman of the firm of Mather & Platt, Ltd., of Manchester, a trustee of Gordon Memorial College, Khartoum, and several times a member of Parliament in the Liberal interest; in 1902 he presented to Gordon Memorial College the plant and tools for equipping a complete mechanical workshop for industrial training.

Mathias Pasha, Hugh Brodrick (1863–1912), British doctor; entering the Royal Army Medical Corps, 1886, he served in the Egyptian army and took part in the Nile campaign of 1898; after an absence at the South African war, 1899–1902, he returned to the Egyptian army and was appointed principal medical officer, Sudan medical department, and promoted liwā', 1909; he had retired from the British army with rank of lieutenant-colonel in 1906, in which year the title of the post was changed to director-general, Sudan medical department; he died in Khartoum.

Matteucci, Pellegrino (1850–81), Italian explorer and doctor; he was born at Ravenna and pursued his medical studies at the University of Bologna; with R. Gessi (afterwards governor of the Baḥr al-Ghazāl and Pasha) he entered the Sudan in 1877 in an attempt to explore western Abyssinia; travelling up the valley of the Blue Nile to the country of the Beni Shanqul the two explorers were compelled by the hostility of the tribes and by lack of means to abandon the project and return to Khartoum; after travels in Abyssinia he returned to the Sudan with a young naval officer, A. M. Massari, in 1880 in an attempt to cross Africa from east to west; Matteucci and Massari, financially aided by Prince Giovanni Borghese and with scientific instruments provided by the Egyptian Government, left Khartoum in April 1880, and after fourteen months, following the route through Kordofan, Dār Fūr, and Wadā'i to Kano, they descended the Niger to the west coast; Matteucci died of fever in London on his way back to Italy; see *I Viaggi di Pellegrino Matteucci in Africa* (Turin, 1932).

Matthews Pasha, Godfrey Estcourt (1866–1917), British soldier; entering the Royal Marines, 1884, he was promoted captain, 1894; in 1896 he was seconded to the Egyptian army and served in the Nile campaigns of 1897–8; in 1900 he was assistant civil secretary, Sudan Government, and in 1901 was appointed commandant of an expedition to remove vegetable obstructions impeding navigation on the Upper White Nile; he was administrator of Fashoda, 1902–3, and governor of the Upper Nile province, with his capital at Tawfīqīya and afterwards at Fashoda (renamed Kodok), from 1904 to 1910; he had been promoted mīrālai, 1903, and liwā', 1909; after a few months reversion to the British army he returned to the Egyptian army as commandant of the military district of Khartoum, finally rejoining the British army, 1913; promoted colonel and then brigadier-general during the First World War he died of wounds received at the battle of Arras.

Maud, William Percy (–1903), British journalist and artist; he was correspondent of the *Graphic* illustrated journal in the Nile campaigns, 1897–8.

Maude, Sir Frederick Stanley (1864–1917), British soldier; born at Gibraltar the son of General Sir F. Maude, V.C., he joined the army in 1884 and served in the Khartoum relief expedition of 1885; after service in the South African war he served in staff appointments in Canada and Britain; in the First World War he was a divisional commander on Gallipoli and finally a commander of the army of Mesopotamia which drove the Turks from Kut al-Amara and entered Baghdad, 1917; he died in Baghdad, supposedly of cholera.

Mayya (–1897), Lotuxo chieftain; on the splitting of the Lotuxo religious kingdom during the first half of the nineteenth century he became chief of one part and Xujang became chief of the other; he was murdered in Ilyeu.

Maxwell Pasha, Sir John Grenfell (1859–1929), British general; he entered the army in 1879 and fought as a junior officer at Tel el-Kebir, 1882, and in the Nile campaign of 1884–5; he transferred to the Egyptian army, 1886, and served three years on the southern border of Egypt; he commanded the 3rd Egyptian brigade in the Dongola campaign, 1896, and the 2nd Egyptian brigade in the Nile campaign, 1897–8; he was the first governor of Khartoum under the new Condominium administration, 1898–9; he was knighted in 1900; after service in South Africa he commanded British troops in Egypt, 1908–12, and again 1914–16; he concluded his military career in high appointments in Ireland and England, being promoted full general, 1919; he died in Cape Town.

* **Maxwell, Sir William** (–1928), British journalist; he was war correspondent of the *Standard* newspaper of London in the Nile campaign of 1898 and in other parts of the world; he later served on other newspapers and was a director of public companies; he wrote several books on his travels.

Mboro Bekobo (–1943), chief of the Ndogo tribe of the Baḥr al-G͟hazāl; a magistrate and president of the Wau area group court and of the Buṣailīya panel court.

Medem, Piotr (Pierre) de, Count (*fl.* 1838), consul-general of Russia in Egypt; he was travelling in Nubia in 1838 on the tracks of the viceroy Muḥammad ʿAlī who was visiting the Sudan; in his dispatches to Nesselrode, his Foreign Minister, he drew a sombre picture of the misery of the Egyptian serfs under Muḥammad ʿAlī.

Melly, André (1802–51), Liverpool merchant of Swiss origin; in 1850–1 he visited the Sudan with his wife, two sons, and a daughter, travelling by way of Wādī Ḥalfā, Dongola, and the Bayūda, finally reaching Khartoum; he died during the return from Khartoum to Egypt and was buried near Abū Dīs, forty miles south of Abū Ḥamad, where his grave may still be seen near the railway; his *Khartoum and the Blue and White Niles* was published in 1851; see his *Lettres d'Égypte et de la Nubie* (1852), edited by his son.

Menyelek (Menilik) II (–1913), king of Shoa and afterwards (1889–1913) king of all Abyssinia; after having defeated several Italian columns in a series of battles culminating with that of Adowa in 1896, he took advantage of the strained relations between Britain and France to urge territorial claims in the region of the Upper White Nile; early in 1898 a force sent by him occupied the region of Lake Rudolf; his general, a Russian named Boulatowich, claimed to have extended Menyelek's dominion as far south as latitude 3° north; another Abyssinian general, Rās Tasama, led a small force with the French expedition of the Marquis de Bonchamps and planted the Abyssinian flag at the confluence of the Sobat and the White Nile also in 1898; Tasama failed, however, to join forces with the French expedition of Captain J. B. Marchand then on its way from the Congo valley to Fashoda; Menyelek, seeing the Anglo-Egyptian power firmly established in the valley of the Upper Nile, did not press his claims and in 1902 signed the Anglo-Italian-Abyssinian treaty which delimited the frontiers of the Sudan.

Merymes (*fl.* 1380 B.C.), Egyptian viceroy of the northern Sudan between about 1412 B.C. and 1370 B.C. during the reigns of the Egyptian kings Thothmes IV and Amenophis III of the XVIIIth Dynasty.

Messedaglia Bey, Giacomo Bartolomeo (1846–93), Italian soldier and administrator; born in Venice (his father was an officer in the army of Garibaldi) he enlisted as a volunteer in the Piedmontese army in 1859 and was promoted sergeant, 1865; he fought in the war of 1866 against Austria and was present at the battle of Versa; discharged from the army as medically unfit in 1869, he worked for some time in Asia Minor as an engineer and archaeological excavator; he went to Egypt in 1876 and was employed by the Egyptian general staff; in 1878 he was posted to the Sudan and appointed by C. G. Gordon Pasha, then governor-general of the Sudan, as governor of Dāra in Dār Fūr, a province conquered by the Egyptian Government in 1874; after fighting against the rebel leader, Muḥammad Hārūn al-Rashīd, he was appointed general governor of Dār Fūr with rank of mīrālai, 1879; in 1880 he was discharged and called to Cairo to answer charges of irregularity, his place being taken by R. C. von Slatin Bey; after a trial he was honourably acquitted; he accompanied Lieutenant-Colonel J. D. H. Stewart on a tour of inspection to the Sudan in 1882; the two officers travelled to Khartoum and returned to Egypt by Kassala and Muṣawwaʿ early in 1883; he assisted Stewart in the compilation of the latter's report on the Sudan; he was chief of the intelligence branch of General V. Baker Pasha's ill-fated army on the Red Sea coast and was wounded in the battle of Ander Teb (el-Teb), 1884; he was next transferred to the Egyptian army intelligence service at Korosko and Wādī Ḥalfā during the Nile campaign of 1884–5; retiring from the Egyptian army in 1887 he returned to Upper Egypt as war correspondent of the newspaper *La Riforma* of Rome; in 1891 he retired to Pisa and there died; his maps of Dār Fūr and other parts of the Khedivial possessions were serious contributions to geography; his biography, with those of other Italians in Khedivial employ in the

Sudan, was published by his nephew L. G. Messedaglia as *Uomini d'Africa* (Bologna, 1935).

Messuwy (*fl.* 1210 B.C.), Egyptian viceroy of the northern Sudan who held office roughly between 1225 B.C. and 1209 B.C. under the Egyptian kings Menephthah, Amenmeses, and Sethos II of the XIXth Dynasty whose capital was Thebes.

Metaxas, Nikolaus (1879–1946), Greek business man; he was born in Egypt of a family which came from Cephalonia; he first went to the Congo in 1907, in the days of the Free State, and built up business interests in the Kilo-Moto district; he later formed the firm of Metaxas & Macris and in 1924 the Société du Haut-Uélé et du Nil of which he was managing director; this concern was engaged in general trade and motor transport operation between the Sudan and the Belgian Congo; he was president of the Hellenic community in Khartoum, 1934–7; in 1946 with his brother he established the banking business of N. Metaxas & Co., Ltd., Khartoum.

* **Miani, Giovanni** (1810–72), Italian explorer; born at Rovigo of humble parents he went to Venice to learn wood-carving and while there studied music and wrote an opera, *Un Torneo a Tolemaide*, played in Pavia, 1843; he took part in the defence of the Roman Republic, 1848, and in 1849 emigrated as an exile to Egypt; with help from the Egyptian Government he explored the country of the Bari on the Upper White Nile as far south as the Aswa river in quest of the reputed lake (afterwards known as Lake Albert), 1859–60; he then returned to Europe where he engaged in controversy over the recent discovery of the source of the White Nile by J. H. Speke and J. A. Grant; he returned to Egypt as curator of a zoological museum founded by the Khedive Ismā'īl, 1870; intent on exploring the unknown country west of the Upper Nile valley, he left Khartoum in 1871 for Shambé whence he travelled to the region of the Uélé, but died on the journey at Nangazizi near the present site of Niangara in the Belgian Congo; he was the first to explore the basin of the Uélé river as far south as the Bomokandi river.

Midwinter Pasha, Sir Edward Colpoys (1872–1947), British railwayman; he entered the Royal Engineers in 1892 and in 1897 arrived in the Sudan on transfer to the Egyptian army; here he joined a band of junior engineer officers under Lieutenant E. P. C. Girouard, the youthful director of Kitchener's military railways; he worked at the railhead of the line being built across the Nubian desert from Wādī Ḥalfā to Abū Ḥamad and the Atbara on the heels of the advancing Anglo-Egyptian army, 1897–8; he was present at the battle of Omdurman in 1898; in 1906 he succeeded C. B. Macauley as director of the Sudan Government Railway, the designation of his post being changed in 1908 to that of general manager; he was so employed until 1925 when he was succeeded by A. C. Parker; a member of the governor-general's council, 1913–25, he had great influence on transport policy in the Sudan; from 1925 to 1932 he was controller of the Sudan Government office in London; promoted captain in 1903 he retired from the British army in 1907; he was a liwā' of the Egyptian army; he devoted the years of his retirement to religious and social work.

Mihaira bint ʿAbūd (*fl.* 1820), daughter of Wad ʿAbūd, shaikh of the Suwārāb branch of the Shā'iqīya Arabs; at the battle of Kūrtī in 1820 between the Shā'iqīya and the invading Turks under Ismāʿīl Pasha Kāmil, she was seated on a camel at the rallying point for the Shā'iqīya army; on the defeat of the Shā'iqīya she escaped from the battlefield surrounded by their cavalry; the Suwārāb, together with the Ḥannakāb Shā'iqīya under malik Subair, shortly afterwards made peace with the Turks, while the ʿAdlānāb under malik Shaʿūs gave in later at Shendi.

Mīkhā'īl Luṭf Allāh al-Shāmī (–*c.* 1880), Syrian Christian trader on the White Nile where he seems to have had big business interests; he was under Austrian consular protection but is said to have traded under the British flag, perhaps from about 1863; he died a bachelor in the Sudan; Ḥabīb Pasha Luṭf Allāh was his brother.

Milḥam Bey Shakūr (1850–1911), Syrian official; of a Lebanese Protestant family he was educated in the National College, Beirut, and came to Egypt in 1881 in connexion with Miss Whateley's Anglican mission schools; he later entered the Egyptian civil service and was posted to the war office, rising ultimately to the post of Arabic secretary to the sirdār; he served in the intelligence department in the Nile campaign, 1884–5, and was present at the battles of Jinnis (Giniss), 1885, and Tūshkī (Toski), 1889; he was Arabic secretary in the Eastern Sudan Field Force and accompanied the troops at the battles of Jummaiza, 1888, and Tokar, 1891; he was assistant director of military intelligence in the campaigns for the recovery of the Sudan, 1896–8.

Mills, Wilfred L . . . (–1946), British missionary of the Baptist Church; born in England he began missionary work in the southern Sudan, 1913, founding a mission station at Melut where he worked till 1920; he then married and opened another station at Heiban in the Nuba hills, he and his wife building houses and a school with their own hands; he later founded a third station at Abri among the Koalib Nuba people; from 1930 till his retirement in 1945 he was field superintendent of the Sudan United Mission in the Nuba hills; he and his wife translated much of the New Testament into the Koalib Nuba language; he died in Auckland, New Zealand.

Mīrghanī. *See* AḤMAD ʿUTHMĀN AL-MĪRGHANĪ; BAKRĪ AL-MĪRGHANĪ; AL-ḤASAN MUḤAMMAD ʿUTHMĀN AL-MĪRGHANĪ; IBRĀHĪM MAḤJŪB AL-MĪRGHANĪ; JAʿFAR BAKRĪ AL-MĪRGHANĪ; MAḤJŪB AL-MĪRGHANĪ; MĪRGHANĪ MUḤAMMAD SUWĀR AL-DHAHAB; MUḤAMMAD SIRR AL-KHĀTIM AL-MĪRGHANĪ; MUḤAMMAD ʿUTHMĀN AL-MĪRGHANĪ I; MUḤAMMAD ʿUTHMĀN AL-MĪRGHANĪ II; ʿUTHMĀN TĀJ AL-SIRR AL-MĪRGHANĪ.

Mīrghanī Muḥammad Suwār al-Dhahab (*c.* 1860–1920), Mahdist amīr; born in New Dongola of the famous religious family bearing his name, and son of Ṣāliḥ Suwār al-Dhahab, a holy man of al-Ubaiyaḍ, he joined the Mahdist cause and was present at the battle of Firka (Firket), 1896; he died in New Dongola.

Mitchell, Lebbens H . . . (1834–), American mining engineer in the Egyptian service; from Boston, Mass., he joined the Federal army at the outbreak of the American civil war and was employed as a topographical engineer; he resigned his commission in 1864; joining the Egyptian general staff in a scientific capacity he made a geological survey of the country between the Nile and the Red Sea, 1874; in 1877 he arrived at Muṣawwaʿ to conduct a geological and mineralogical survey of the country between that port and the Abyssinian highlands; while so engaged he and his party were captured by Abyssinian raiders and taken to King John in the interior; after great suffering and the loss of all his effects he was released and regained Muṣawwaʿ, while his Egyptian staff were kept for some time longer in captivity by the Abyssinians.

Mitford, Bertram Reveley (1863–1936), British major-general; commissioned to the Buffs (East Kent Regiment) in 1882 he joined the Egyptian army in 1886 and took part in the patrolling and fighting on the southern border of Egypt, 1886–91, and afterwards served in the Dongola and Nile campaigns, 1897–8, and in the Kordofan Field Force, 1899; he served in the South African war, 1899–1902, and commanded a division in France during the First World War.

* **Mitterrützner, Johann Chrysostomus Josef** (1818–), Austrian theologian and orientalist; born at Tils near Brixen in the Tyrol he entered the Augustinian Order in 1843, and in Rome in 1856 came under the influence of I. Knoblehar, vicar apostolic of Central Africa; in 1856 he visited the Sudan where he journeyed to the Roman Catholic missions on the Upper White Nile and studied languages; on his return to Europe he compiled grammars of the Bari and Dinka languages with the help of the Bari youth, Francesco Logwit lo Ladu and the missionary F. Morlang; he wrote *Die Dinka-Sprache* (Brixen, 1866), *Die Sprache der Bari* (Brixen, 1867), and a life of A. Haller, a missionary who died in Khartoum (Innsbruck, 1855).

Moir Bey, James Philip (1872–1934), British engineer officer and postal official; he entered the Royal Engineers in 1892 and served in the Nile campaign, 1898; after service in the South African war and in southern Nigeria he was appointed director of posts and telegraphs in the Sudan Government in 1912, a post he held until 1922; he retired from the army in 1929 with the rank of colonel after spending the years 1925–9 as chief engineer of air defence formations in the territorial army in England; he was a mīrālai of the Egyptian army.

Moldiang Logunu, also called **Alessandro Molodian** (*c.* 1911–45), Bari notable, chief of Belinian and Illibari and since 1935 a magistrate; educated at the Roman Catholic school at Rejaf he was a Christian and was known as a progressive chief.

Moncrieff, Lynedoch Needham (*c.* 1848–83), British sailor; he entered the Royal Navy in 1863 and after serving for some years afloat fought in the Zulu war in South Africa, 1879–80; after acting as British consul at Jidda, he was appointed consul at Sawākin, 1882; he was killed in battle near Tokar when accompanying an Egyptian force under Maḥmūd Ṭāhir Pasha which was destroyed by the Mahdists.

Montuori, Luigi (1798–1857), founder of the Roman Catholic church in Khartoum; he was born at Avellino near Naples and entered the Vincentian Order; in 1839 he left Italy for Abyssinia, entering the country by way of Assab; after vicissitudes in the Abyssinian highlands, he was expelled by the Coptic bishop, Abūna Salāma, and took refuge in Gondar where he met B. van Cuelebroeck, Belgian consul-general in Egypt, who was travelling in Abyssinia at the time; the two left Gondar at the beginning of 1842 and, travelling by Qalʿa al-Naḥl, arrived at Abū Ḥarāz whence they completed the journey to Khartoum by river, entering the capital in May 1842; helped by Van Cuelebroeck's good offices with the governor-general, Aḥmad Pasha abū Widān, he set up a church and school and obtained a piece of land on the south side of the town as a Christian cemetery; according to G. Lejean his mission was opposed by some of the European residents of Khartoum; he left Khartoum in September 1844 for Abyssinia, leaving another priest, G. Serrao, who had joined him shortly before, to continue his work; Serrao himself abandoned the mission in 1845 and returned to Europe shortly after; Montuori died in Naples.

Morant Bey, Hubert Horatio Shirley (1870–1946), British soldier; he received a commission in the Durham Light Infantry, 1889, and during 1898–1908 served in the Egyptian army, including the Nile campaign of 1898, and later a period as governor, Ḥalfā province; he was promoted captain in 1899; he retired from the Egyptian army with the rank of qā'immaqām; he fought in the First World War and himself raised and commanded the 10th battalion of the Durham Light Infantry; he commanded a territorial brigade in France, 1918, and was promoted brigadier-general; he retired in 1927.

Morès, Antoine-Amedée-Vincent-Manca de Vallombrosa de, Marquis (1858–96), French sympathizer with the Mahdist cause; he was born in Paris of an ancient family established in Sardinia in the fourteenth century; after a short time in the French army he farmed in the United States of America from 1883 and then went to Tonkin where he attempted, without success, to build a railway to Yunnan to counteract British influence from Burma; returning to France he threw himself into the political movement of General Boulanger; his violence and anti-semitism cost him several duels; in 1893 he carried out a propaganda campaign in French North Africa and in March 1898 arrived at Tunis intent on joining the Mahdists in the Sudan; avoiding the French frontier posts, which had been ordered to stop him, he set out southwards with a small following of guides and servants; after undergoing much fatigue he was attacked by the Tawāriq for loot not far from al-Awtīya, and killed.

Morice Bey, James (–1884), British official in the Khedivial service; he was inspector-general of the Egyptian coastguard service when in 1883 he volunteered for service in V. Baker Pasha's military expedition to the Red Sea coast; appointed paymaster-general to the force, he was killed in the disastrous battle of el-Teb; he was a brother of Sir George Morice Pasha, controller-general of Egyptian lighthouses.

Morpurgo, Isachetto (*c.* 1820–*c.* 1890), Austrian Jewish merchant of a family domiciled in Alexandria where he himself was born; his business interests brought him to the Sudan where we find him with the British traveller, M. Parkyns, on the way from al-Ubaiyaḍ to Cairo, 1848; during the revolt of Aḥmad ʿUrābī Pasha in 1882 he and his brothers fled from Alexandria and took refuge with their cousin E. (Baron) Morpurgo, the industrialist of Trieste; Isachetto set up in business in Milan where he died; his son became Italian minister of posts.

Morris, John Ignatius (1842–1902), British major-general; entering the Royal Marines in 1859, he was deputy assistant adjutant-general in the Sawākin Field Force, 1884–5; he was later Admiralty recruiting officer and deputy adjutant-general, Royal Marines.

Mosconas, Dimitrios (1837–95), Greek trader and student of Egyptology; he was born on the island of Leros in the Dodecanese and was a self-taught, self-made man; he for some time explored in the Equatorial province where he met Emin Pasha, the governor; in 1880 he was trading at Sawākin; in 1882 he was engaged in sinking wells between Kassala and Gedaref but found little water; he served under General V. Baker Pasha in the Red Sea campaign of 1883–4, and in 1884–5 was present in the Nile campaign as a dragoman on the staff of General Lord Wolseley; an intelligent and cultured man, he devoted himself to the study of Ancient Egyptian hieroglyphics, history, and scarabs on which he wrote several books and pamphlets, and exhibited models of mummies of the Pharaohs at the Chicago World Fair, 1892; he died in Alexandria; a son, Lieutenant G. Mosconas, was killed while serving under Baker at the battle of el-Teb, 1884.

* **Mosgan, Bartholomäus** (1823–58), Roman Catholic missionary priest from the diocese of Laibach (Liubliana) then in Austria; he came to the Sudan with I. Knoblehar, the first vicar-apostolic of Central Africa, in 1851 and was among the first members of the mission on the Upper White Nile; he was at Gondokoro in 1853, and in 1854, with Knoblehar's encouragement, he founded the mission station of Holy Cross (called also Heiligencreuz, Santa Croce) situated between Shambé and Bor; as the superior of this mission he was host to the Italian explorer C. Piaggia; born at Kappel in Carinthia, he died at Holy Cross; his mission station was abandoned in 1859; the site is still locally called Kanīsa (church).

Mourikis, Konstantinos (1867–1939), Greek trader; born in the Morea, he came to the Sudan with his brother Christos about 1899 and founded a shop and ferry on the White Nile near Qūz abū Jumʿa; the settlement which grew up round his shop developed into the modern town to which the local people gave the name of Kosti after the abbreviated version of his Christian name; he died in Athens; another brother, Nikolaus, also a pioneer in the development of the White Nile trade, died in Khartoum in 1947.

Mubārak ʿAbd Allāh Mubārak (–1943), ʿumda of the Rashaida in the Kassala province and a magistrate; he died at Atbara.

* **Muḍawī ʿAbd al-Raḥmān** (–1899), Islamic judge and Mahdist amīr; by birth a Maḥasī, a son of Shaikh ʿAbd al-Qādir Muḥammad ʿAbd al-Raḥmān, he was educated at al-Azhar University, Cairo, and became a follower of Shaikh Idrīs Muḥammad al-Arbāb of al-ʿĀilafūn; caught up in the general enthusiasm for the cause of Muḥammad Aḥmad al-Mahdī, he assisted the amīrs ʿAbbās and Ṭāhir, sons of Muḥammad Badr al-ʿUbaid, in the siege of Khartoum, 1884–5; fearing the Khalīfa ʿAbd Allāhi he fled to Abyssinia in 1887, then, after making the pilgrimage, he returned to al-Azhar; after the Anglo-Egyptian occupation of the Sudan he was appointed Islamic judge at Dongola; he died at Khartoum and was buried at al-ʿĀilafūn where his tomb stands; he was familiarly called al-faqī Muḍawī.

Muḍawī ibn Barakāt ibn Ḥammād ibn al-Shaikh Idrīs (–1684), holy man; he is said to have introduced the Muslim religion into al-ʿĀilafūn and neighbouring villages on the Blue Nile between Khartoum and Kamlīn.

al-Muḍawī Muḥammad al-Miṣrī (–*c.* 1684), holy man of Shendi; among other works he wrote four commentaries on al-Sanūsī's *Umm al-barāhīn.*

Muḍawī Qāsim Allāh (–1938), Masallamī notable; ʿumda of the Masallamīya of the Jāzīra.

Muddaththir Ibrāhīm al-Ḥajjāz (1855–1937), religious notable; a Jaʿlī by origin, he went to the Ḥijāz as a boy and returned to the Sudan during the Mahdist revolt; he served first Muḥammad Aḥmad al-Mahdī, and later the Khalīfa ʿAbd Allāhi, as a clerk and was the keeper of the latter's privy seal; during the First World War he played a part in the rising of the Sharīf Ḥusain of Makka against the Turkish rule in 1916; he made the pilgrimage many times and in 1926 sat on the Islamic council; he was a poet of some fame; he died at Berber.

Muḥammad Bey ʿAbd Allāh ʿAdlān (1881–1945), qā'immaqām of the Sudan Defence Force; educated at the military school, Cairo, he was commissioned to the Egyptian army and as a junior officer saw service in 1899 in the last operations against the Khalīfa ʿAbd Allāhi; he served in many of the minor wars and patrols of the early years of the Condominium Government including those of the Niam-Niam, 1905; Jabal Nyima, 1908; and the Nuer, 1917 and 1920; promoted qā'immaqām in 1930, he retired in 1931; he died in Cairo.

Muḥammad Bey ʿAbd Allāh al-Maḥallāwī (–1885), Egyptian merchant originally from Isnā; a brother of Maḥmūd ʿAbd Allāh al-

Maḥallāwī; he was sirr tujjār and president of the town council of Shaqqa in Dār Fūr; after the closing of the governorate of Shaqqa he moved to Khartoum where, during Gordon Pasha's second governorship-general in 1884, he was appointed officer of a volunteer detachment to aid in the defence of the city; he was killed by the Mahdists when the city fell.

Muḥammad ʿAbd Allāh Yaʿqūb (*c.* 1864–1936), Maḥasī notable; his father ʿAbd Allāh Yaʿqūb was (jointly with Zubair Dīyāb al-Malik) deputy of the Maḥas at the court of the Khalīfa ʿAbd Allāhi and died in 1903; Muḥammad was ʿumda of Jeddī when blindness latterly overtook him.

Muḥammad ʿAbd al-Ḥalīm Pasha, Prince (1831–94), younger brother of Muḥammad Saʿīd Pasha, viceroy of Egypt; educated at the high school at al-Khānka, he was in Paris completing his studies in 1844–8; he held various posts under Muḥammad Saʿīd Pasha including those of minister of war and governor-general of the Sudan; he was sent on a tour of inspection to the Sudan in 1856 accompanied by E. Rossi, his personal physician; during his brief tour he visited Nubia and Kordofan and spent two weeks on the White Nile; appointed governor-general, he held effective office for about three weeks only, when an outbreak of cholera led to his return to Egypt; during his term of office he amalgamated the provinces of Berber and Dongola and changed the borders of Kordofan uniting it with several outlying territories; on his departure from Khartoum he left ʿAlī Pasha Jarkas as his deputy; he was a man of energy and was the first to send a steamer over the Nile cataracts from Egypt as far as Khartoum whence it was used in trading voyages to Fāzūghlī and to points on the White Nile; he was a pioneer in the attempt (ultimately unsuccessful) to develop commerce with the natives of the White Nile and for this purpose employed a French agent, F. Lafargue; he later became involved with Ismāʿīl Pasha over the succession to the throne of Egypt and retired to Constantinople where he died.

Muḥammad ʿAbd al-Karīm (–1891), Mahdist amīr; an uncle of Muḥammad Aḥmad al-Mahdī he, together with another of the Mahdī's uncles, ʿAbd al-Qādir wad Satī, and the amīrs Aḥmad Sulaimān and Saʿīd Muḥammad Faraḥ, were banished by the Khalīfa ʿAbd Allāhi to Fashōda for championing the cause of the Mahdī's family against the dictatorship of the Khalīfa; arrived at Fashōda they were all killed.

Muḥammad ʿAbd al-Mājid (–1929), religious shaikh known for his piety; by origin a Jaʿlī of the ʿUmarāb branch, he was a member of the board of ʿulamāʾ of Omdurman.

* **Muḥammad ʿAbd al-Mutʿāl Aḥmad al-Idrīsī** (–1936), Arab leader; born in ʿAsīr in Arabia of Dongolāwī and Yamanī blood on his mother's side, he was a grandson of Shaikh Aḥmad ibn al-Idrīs who lived at Makka at the end of the eighteenth century and who had among his pupils al-Saiyid Muḥammad ʿUthmān al-Mīrghanī I, founder of the Khatmīya brotherhood in the Sudan, and the original Sanūsī;

he studied at al-Azhar University, Cairo, and then lived for a period in Dongola and afterwards in the Western Desert with the Sanūsīya, returning in 1903 to 'Asīr; in 1910 he rebelled, without success, against the Turkish Government; he entered the First World War in 1916 as leader of the tribesmen of 'Asīr under the amīr Ḥusain of Makka; he died, as did his father al-Saiyid 'Abd al-Mut'āl Aḥmad al-Idrīsi, at Dongola.

Muḥammad 'Abd al-Raḥīm abū Daqal (–1932), nāẓir of the Gharaisīya branch of the Ḥamar Arabs of western Kordofan; son and successor to 'Abd al-Raḥīm Bey abū Daqal.

Muḥammad 'Abd al-Raḥmān (1791–1866), holy man and tribal notable of the Maḥas of al-'Ailafūn on the Blue Nile; a follower of the cult of Shaikh Idrīs Muḥammad al-Arbāb (1607–50); his son 'Abd al-Qādir Muḥammad became a prominent figure in local government on the Blue Nile during the Egyptian rule.

Muḥammad ibn 'Abd al-Ṣādiq ibn Māshir al-Rikābī, also called **al-Hamīm** (*fl.* 1580), religious man, a contemporary of the great Shaikh Idrīs wad Muḥammad al-Arbāb and a disciple of Shaikh Muḥammad Tāj al-Dīn al-Bahārī; he seems to have spent his active life in the Jazīra and was buried at Jabal Mandara, about half-way between Kamlīn and the Atbara river, where his tomb stands.

* **Muḥammad 'Abduh** (*c.* 1849–1905), Egyptian reformer of remote Turkish origin; a pupil, and afterwards a colleague, of Jamāl al-Dīn al-Afghānī, he was implicated in the revolt of Aḥmad 'Urābī Pasha and exiled from Egypt, 1882; he went to Paris and there in 1884 joined with Jamāl al-Dīn al-Afghānī in publishing *al-'urwah al-wuthqah* (the Indissoluble Bond), the organ of a pan-Islamic society whose immediate object was the removal of the British from Egypt and the northern Sudan; returning to Egypt, he was later appointed muftī and a member of the legislative council; he was a reformer of the Islamic University of al-Azhar and a revivalist of Arabic literature; he visited the Sudan in the winter of 1904–5; his influence on theological and political reform made him one of the outstanding figures of modern Egypt; there are numerous lives of him; C. C. Adams's *Islām and the Modern World* (1933) is the best account in English of his doctrines.

* **Muḥammad Bey 'Abūd** (–1935), a native of Sawākin, he was mu'āwin 'Arab of the Red Sea hills and a magistrate; he died at Shendi whither he had gone for treatment of an illness; his son Ibrāhīm is an officer in the Sudan Defence Force.

* **Muḥammad Adam Sa'dūn** (–1886), notable of the 'Abd al-Raḥmānāb branch of the Amarar tribe of the Beja people dwelling in the Red Sea hills; he and his branch of the tribe were the first of the Amarar to declare themselves adherents to the Mahdist cause; he was killed in an inter-tribal fight with the Hadendowa in khōr Arba't.

Muḥammad wad 'Adlān (–1821), vizier and king-maker of the Funj kingdom during its last days; a member of the Hāmaj ruling class, he was a grandson of the great Muḥammad abū'l-Kailak and came to power in 1808; he dominated the titular King Bādī VI ibn Ṭabl, who had been deposed then reinstated shortly before the arrival of the invading Turkish army under Ismā'īl Kāmil Pasha at Sennar in 1821; he had weakened his position by maintaining a feud with his cousin Ḥasan wad Rājab whose supporters murdered him on the eve of the Turks' approach to the capital.

Muḥammad wad 'Adlān (–1904), religious fanatic; calling himself al-nabī 'Īsā (The Prophet Jesus), he stirred up trouble at Sinja in 1904 and murdered a police officer; he was killed in action against government police.

Muḥammad Aḥmad Pasha (*fl.* 1820–1), Turkish officer in the army of Muḥammad 'Alī Pasha; he served as a binbāshī in the expedition of Ismā'īl Pasha to Sennar, 1820–1, commanding a force of 400 Turkish musketeers in battles against the Shā'iqīya at the end of 1820; he took part in the Turkish assault on Jabal Kilgū near Fāzūghlī in December 1821 when he was made kāshif of Ḥālfaiya; in 1822 he was transferred to Damascus of which city he was appointed pasha.

* **Muḥammad Bey Aḥmad** (1845–1931), Sudanese soldier; born at Sawākin, he was of Turkish origin on his father's side; a self-educated youth, he joined the army in the ranks and soon won promotion; the outbreak of the Mahdist revolt was his opportunity; he fought in the battles of el-Teb (Anderteib) and Tamai (1884), Hashin and Tofrik (1885), Ḥandub and Jummaiza (1888), and Tokar (1891), when he was promoted qā'immaqām and later commandant of police at Sawākin; on the formation of the Red Sea province after the Anglo-Egyptian occupation of the Sudan, he became commandant of the province police; in 1900 he assisted F. Burges Pasha in the capture of the Mahdist amīr 'Uthmān abū Bakr Diqna (Osman Digna) who for two years had skilfully avoided arrest; in 1911 he accompanied the governor-general, Sir F. R. Wingate Pasha, to the Somali coast; he retired from the active list in 1913 with the rank of mīrālai; during the First World War he was in the Yaman with C. J. Hawker Bey arranging the exchange of prisoners of war; he was one of the finest Sudanese officers of modern times.

Muḥammad Aḥmad al-'Aqqād (–1870), Egyptian trader of a family settled in Aswān; he was engaged in trade on the White Nile and was said to be under the personal patronage of the Khedive Ismā'īl; he did big business under the trading name of Agad [*sic*] & Co. of Khartoum, of which firm he was head and his brother Mūsā Bey al-'Aqqād a partner; in 1865 the firm acquired the business of A. Debono, the Maltese trader; on his death the management of the firm went to his son-in-law Muḥammad abū Su'ūd Bey al-'Aqqād.

Muḥammad Aḥmad Badawī (–1941), Ja'lī notable; shaikh of al-Zaidāb (South).

Muḥammad Aḥmad Bakhīt (–1929), 'umda of the Jubārāb section of the Ja'līyīn near Berber; he died at Jubārāb village.

Muḥammad Aḥmad Faraḥ (–1934), Ja'lī notable; 'umda of Matamma near Shendi.

Muḥammad Aḥmad Nubāwī (*c.* 1867–1925), nāẓir of the Banī Jarrār tribe of the White Nile; the family got the name Nubāwī from the fact that his grandfather was born in the Nuba hills; his tenure of office was unhappy; he was dismissed in 1904 when he lived at Bāra and was succeeded by his brother Ḥāmid (d. 1915); reappointed nāẓir in 1917, he was again, and finally, dismissed in 1919 when the office lapsed and the tribe was decentralized under its various 'umdas.

* **Muḥammad Aḥmad ibn al-Saiyid 'Abd Allāh, al-Mahdī** (1848–85), Sudanese religious leader and founder of the Mahdist movement in the Sudan; he was born at Ḍarār, among the islands of Arqū in the district of Dongola; his father, a local boat-builder, claimed descent from the family of the Prophet; after leaving a Qur'ānic school at Omdurman he went to Abā island on the White Nile where his father was then buiildng boats; here as a young man he began a career of study and meditation; he early attached himself to the religious brotherhood of the Ismā'īlīya and became a pupil of S͟haik͟h Muḥammad S͟harīf Nūr al-Dā'im; as one of the *as͟hrāf* by descent he started with a hereditary reputation which was enhanced by his piety and asceticism; disagreeing with his teacher and reproving him for worldliness he left Abā with a few disciples and lived near by; in 1875 he transferred his religious allegiance to S͟haik͟h al-Quras͟hī wad al-Zain of the Sammānīya brotherhood; about 1880 he toured Kordofan and found the state of the country irreconcilable with his religious beliefs which were now progressing towards the stage of political intervention; the nomadic tribes outside the direct influence of the Egyptian government were ravaged by internal warfare and the whole country was exasperated by the mal-administration of the government whose rule was more venal and incompetent than deliberately oppressive; the clumsy attempts of the government to suppress the slave trade had provoked resentment in a country whose economy was based on slavery; the turbulent population of the Central Sudan was ripe for the secular adventure of a concerted revolt which it had been denied since the foundation of foreign government sixty years before; he represented the only apparent hope of Sudanese unity and freedom; in May 1881 he announced his divine mission and summoned the people to fight the infidel Turks as a first step towards the introduction of a purified society based on Islamic precepts; his teaching combined elements found in the Wahhābite and Sanūsī movements, including the return to primitive Islam, opposition to innovations and foreign influences, prohibition of pilgrimages to tombs, of the veneration of saints, and of music and tobacco; the strong element of mysticism in his teaching appealed to a people traditionally receptive to Ṣūfism; after successfully resisting several feeble attempts of the government to arrest him he retired with his followers to the Nuba hills and in 1882 massacred a force of 7,000 troops under Rās͟hid Bey Aymān at Jabal Qadīr; in 1881, after the example of the Prophet, he chose four caliphs: 'Abd Allāhi

Muḥammad Tūrshain to represent Abū Bakr; ʿAlī al-Hilū to represent ʿUmar; Muḥammad Sharīf, his son-in-law, to represent ʿAlī; while the fourth Caliphate was offered to Muḥammad al-Mahdī, head of the Sanūsīya brotherhood of Jaghbūb in Libya, who declined the nomination; his former teacher, Muḥammad Sharīf Nūr al-Dā'im, and the orthodox brotherhood of the Mīrghanīya excommunicated him, but it was soon clear that he was supported by a Sudan-wide revolt; the rebellion of Aḥmad ʿUrābī Pasha which convulsed Egypt in 1882 hindered the government from taking vigorous action against him; after destroying a second government force, led by Yūsuf Pasha Ḥasan al-Shallālī, in the Nuba hills, he unsuccessfully attacked al-Duwaim on the White Nile; he then marched on al-Ubaiyaḍ, the capital of Kordofan, defended by an Egyptian garrison under Muḥammad Saʿīd Pasha, and personally conducted the siege of the town which, along with Bāra, fell in January 1883; the government, now thoroughly alarmed, began to put Khartoum in a state of defence and sent an army under al-farīq W. Hicks Pasha to recapture Kordofan; Hicks and his army were destroyed at Shaikān (Kashgil), in October 1883; by the spring of 1884 the Mahdists had overrun the Baḥr and Ghazāl province and, though government troops won temporary successes in small actions in the Jazīra, only the bigger garrison towns, Khartoum, Sennar, and Kassala, held out against the rebels; in the eastern Sudan the Mahdists won a series of victories including the crushing defeat of an Egyptian army commanded by V. Baker Pasha at el-Teb in February 1884; the Mahdist horde now assembled before Khartoum where the Mahdī arrived from Kordofan in October; after a gallant resistance, inspired by al-farīq C. G. Gordon Pasha who had been sent by the government to attempt the withdrawal of the beleaguered garrisons, Khartoum fell and Gordon was killed on 26 January 1885; a small British column advancing over the Bayūda to the help of the garrison arrived too late and, after some hard fighting at Abū Ṭulaiḥ (Abu Klea) and Matamma, retreated to Dongola; the Mahdī's dominions now reached from Dār Maḥas to the Upper White Nile and from Dār Fūr to the Red Sea coast; Sennar and Kassala still held out, but these last government strongholds fell during the year and the effective control of the Anglo-Egyptian power was confined to Wādī Ḥalfā and Sawākin; the Mahdī did not long survive these sweeping triumphs; he had taken up his residence in Omdurman where he died on 22 June 1885, and his temporal powers were assumed by the Khalīfa ʿAbd Allāhi who converted the Mahdī's religious state into a military dictatorship; the Mahdī's followers have organized themselves into an influential brotherhood under the present leadership of his son, al-Saiyid Sir ʿAbd al-Raḥmān al-Mahdī Pasha.

* **Muḥammad Aḥmad Bey abū Sin,** called **Ḥārdallū** (1830–1917), Shukrī poet and tribal chieftain; born at Rufāʿa the son of Aḥmad Bey ʿAwad al-Karīm abū Sin, governor of Khartoum and the Jazīra, he lived the nomad life of his tribe, settling at Raira in the Buṭāna in 1850 when he began to compose romantic poetry dedicated to ladies in general and in particular to al-Ḥamdīya bint abī Khanaijir; the Egyptian Government appointed him shaikh al-mashāyikh of the region

west of the River Atbara adjoining the nāẓirate of his brother, S̲h̲aik̲h̲ 'Alī Aḥmad abū Sin, who was succeeded by their elder brother, S̲h̲aik̲h̲ 'Awaḍ al-Karīm Aḥmad abū Sin, afterwards Gordon's pasha; on the outbreak of the Mahdist revolt he joined the Mahdī's cause and was for some time stationed round Tokar where he composed nostalgic verse expressing his longing for his Buṭāna home and family; after the Anglo-Egyptian occupation he returned to his beloved Raira where he ruled till his death; he was a tall, spare man with a slight beard; his poems have achieved a wide celebrity in the Sudan.

Muḥammad Aḥmad abū Sin (-1932), S̲h̲ukrī notable of the branch of the ruling house of Abū Sin settled in the region of Gedaref of which he was 'umda and a magistrate.

Muḥammad 'Alī Pasha (1769–1849), pasha of Egypt; he was born at Kavalla in the Turkish province of Drama in Macedonia of Rumelian Turkish (not Albanian) stock originating from Anatolia; he came to Egypt in 1801 as a binbās̲h̲ī in command of a Macedonian detachment of the Ottoman army to make war against the French invaders under Napoleon Bonaparte; by his astuteness and his sword he became master of Cairo and then of Egypt during the anarchy which followed the withdrawal of the French; in 1805 the Sublime Porte recognized him as governor of Egypt, later made hereditary in his family; in 1819 he actively prepared an expedition to occupy the Sudan where he hoped to find precious metals, specially gold, and slaves with whom to form his new regular army; in 1820 an army led by his son Ismā'īl Kāmil Pasha advanced up the Nile valley and at the end of the year beat the S̲h̲ā'iqīya in two pitched battles; continuing its march to the confluence of the Blue and White Niles the army crossed to the Jazīra of Sennar; the decadent Funj kingdom fell without resistance and Ismā'īl entered the capital, Sennar, in 1821; in the same year another Turkish force, under the command of Muḥammad K̲h̲usraw, the Bey Daftardār, crossed the Bayūda steppe from al-Dabba and, after destroying a force led by Musallim, the Fūr governor of Kordofan, at Bāra, occupied al-Ubaiyaḍ; it was not until the winter of 1838–9 that Muḥammad 'Alī visited the Sudan; leaving Cairo in October 1838 with a numerous suite including several Europeans, he travelled by way of Dongola and the Bayūda to Khartoum where he solemnly proclaimed the abolition of the slave trade; he then ascended the Blue Nile to Fāzūg̲h̲lī near which he founded what was intended to be the city of Muḥammadapolis; gold was the main object of his journey and he intensified the search then being made to find gold in the mountains nearby; disappointed in the results of the prospections, but not yet disillusioned as to the prospect of its ultimate discovery, he returned to Egypt through Berber and over the Nubian desert in the spring of 1839; he actively supervised the administration of the Sudan under its successive commanders and governors-general; it was on the Sudanese slaves that he counted to replenish his armies which fought in Greece, Arabia, and Syria; he initiated in the Sudan a vast experiment in economic exploitation, introducing new crops such as indigo, creating a boat-building industry, and organizing the export trade of the country by means of a closed state monopoly; the scarcity of capable assistants and the crushing weight of taxation, however, did much to ruin the success of his schemes in the Sudan; by 1848 he was suffering from senile decay and was succeeded by his son Ibrāhīm Pasha; he died in 1849.

Muḥammad ʿAlī al-Ḥadd (–1934), Shukrī notable and magistrate; he was ʿumda of Fau which lies between Gedaref and the Blue Nile; he died at Gedaref.

Muḥammad ʿAlī Pasha Ḥusain (–1884), Egyptian soldier of Kanzī origin; born at Manjara village at the Mughran adjoining Khartoum, he served as a junior officer in the Sudanese battalion under Marshal Bazaine in Mexico, 1863–7; on the outbreak of the Mahdist rebellion he had risen to field rank and during the defence of Khartoum in 1884 was mīrālai in command of the 1st Sudanese infantry regiment which occupied the entrenchments guarding the eastern approaches to the capital; one of Gordon Pasha's most trusted and capable officers, he was promoted liwāʾ and put in command of a force which was sent up the Blue Nile in steamers to attack the Mahdists under the amīr al-Ṭāhir wad Muḥammad Badr al-ʿUbaid concentrated at Umm Dibban; the force landed near al-ʿĀilafūn and in the darkness was ambushed and cut to pieces; Muḥammad ʿAlī was among the killed.

Muḥammad ʿAlī al-Ikhaidir (–1938); ʿumda of the Majānīn Arabs living in the neighbourhood of Bāra.

Muḥammad ʿAlī Karam Allāh (*c.* 1870–1947), Sudanese notable; of Maḥasī origin, he came of a family of public men, his father and grandfather having both held the post of nāẓir of the *qism* (sub-district) of Khartoum under the former Egyptian Government; he himself while a youth was one of the bodyguard of the Khalīfa ʿAbd Allāhi at Omdurman; on the Anglo-Egyptian occupation of the Sudan, he was appointed ʿumda of Khartoum, 1899; he was dismissed in 1912 after conviction for assault; in 1924, amid popular acclamation, he was reinstated in his office which he held till his death which occurred in Khartoum.

Muḥammad ʿAlī al-Naʿīm (–1930), ʿumda of Abū Tija in the Funj area of the Blue Nile valley; he was a member of the ʿAqalīyīn branch of the Rufāʿa Arab tribe.

Muḥammad ibn ʿAlī ibn Qarm al-Kīmānī (*fl. c.* 1550), holy man who came to the Sudan in the early days of the Funj rule and taught in turn at Arbajī, Sennar, and Berber where he died; he was widely known as a teacher of theology and Islamic law; Wad Ḍaif Allāh the hagiographer writes of him as one of God's own miracles; he was also known as al-Miṣrī al-Shāfiʿī.

Muḥammad ʿAlī Ṭaha Duwaiw (–1931), notable of the Jazīra; ʿumda of Amārāt Duwaiw and a magistrate; by tribe a Jaʿlī, he died at Amāra Ṭāha near Ḥaṣṣa Ḥaiṣa.

* **Muḥammad Bey Almās** (*c*. 1815–   ), Sudanese soldier whose name is also (wrongly) spelt al-Māẓ; he entered the Egyptian army in the ranks in 1834 and rose to commissioned rank; he commanded the Sudanese battalion in Mexico after the death of Binbāshī Jubārat Allāh in 1863; for his services in the campaign the Archduke Maximilian of Habsburg awarded him the Mexican Imperial decoration of Our Lady of Guadeloupe, while at a review held in Paris in 1867 on the return of the battalion to Europe Napoleon III, emperor of the French, awarded him the cross of Officer of the Legion of Honour; promoted mīrālai after his return to Egypt, he was posted to the Sudan in 1869 to command the 2nd Sudanese infantry regiment.

Muḥammad al-Amīn (–1903), fanatical faqī originating from Bornu; in 1903 he proclaimed himself to be the Expected One and in the Jimaʿa district of eastern Kordofan rose in revolt; he was captured by mīrālai (afterwards General Sir) B. T. Mahon Bey, governor of Kordofan, and hanged at al-Ubaiyaḍ.

Muḥammad al-Amīn ʿAbd al-Ḥalīm (*c*. 1865–1946), Mahdist amīr; a Jaʿlī by tribe, he was born at Abū Jimrī near Sennar; joining the Mahdist movement, he fought under the amīr ʿUthmān Azraq in the north and was present in the Mahdists' raids on Jammai (Gemai, Gammai) and Murrāt wells, 1893; in the latter action he was wounded; he was again wounded in the battle of Firka (Firket), 1896; his tale of battles ended with the Atbara and Omdurman, 1898; he died in Omdurman; small in stature, he was known for his wisdom and gentleness.

Muḥammad al-Amīn wad ʿAjīb, called **Wad Mismār** (–1790), viceroy of the kings of Sennar over the ʿAbdullāb Arabs of Qarrī; in 1784, allied with the Shukrīya, he sacked the town of Arbajī founded in 1474; he continued the customary feud between the viceroys of Qarrī and Sennar and was killed by the partisans of ʿAbd Allāh wad ʿAjīb of Ḥālfaiya.

Muḥammad al-Amīn Pasha al-Arnā'ūṭ (*fl.* 1843–6), Albanian soldier in the service of Muḥammad ʿAlī Pasha wālī of Egypt; he was on the staff of Aḥmad Pasha abū Widān, governor-general of the Sudan, with rank of mīrālai; it was said that in 1843 he betrayed Aḥmad Pasha to Muḥammad ʿAlī after the former had entered into treasonable correspondence with ʿAbd al-Majīd, the Ottoman sultan, with the object of detaching the Sudan from Muḥammad ʿAlī's dominion and bringing it under the direct rule of the sultan; at the end of 1843 he was promoted to mīrlivā, made a pasha, and appointed governor of Khartoum together with Shendi, Matamma, and the southern half of the former province of Berber and the Jaʿlīyīn; in 1844 he was transferred to the province of Sennar whose capital was then Wad Madanī; the Prussian archaeologist, K. R. Lepsius, recorded that he was inactive during the Sudanese military mutiny at Wad Madanī in that year, one Rustum Efendi taking the initiative against the mutineers; in 1846 the minister of war, Cairo, was pressing him for a debt of 52,658 piastres and 10 paras which he was alleged to owe to the government.

Muḥammad al-Amīn Baʿshūm (–1935), Jaʿlī notable; ʿumda of Kabūshīya.

* **Muḥammad al-Amīn al-Ḍarīr** (*c.* 1877–1933), religious notable; born on Tūtī island, the son of al-Amīn Muḥammad al-Ḍarīr, shaikh al-Islām during the concluding years of the Egyptian rule, he was a member of the board of ʿulamāʾ of Omdurman and a teacher at the Maʿhad al-ʿIlmī institute in that town from about 1901; he built the mosque known after his father's name in 1916; it was rebuilt in red brick in 1947.

Muḥammad al-Amīn al-Jaʿlī (–1945), religious teacher of the Jaʿlīyīn; he was the leader of the Qādirīya brotherhood in Berber where he died.

Muḥammad abū ʿĀqla ʿAbd Allāh (*fl.* 1882), nāẓir of the ʿArakīyīn of Wad Madanī and neighbourhood; he was an important shaikh having two shaikhs of qism under his authority; in 1882, while the government was disputing with the Mahdists the control of the Jazīra, he received an order from the governor-general ʿAbd al-Qādir Ḥilmī Pasha to arrest Zubair wad ʿAbd al-Qādir, nāẓir ʿumūm of all the Jazīra; on Zubair's execution by drowning in the Blue Nile it is asserted by one of his descendants that the government appointed him to Zubair's post, an office which he cannot have held long since the Mahdists overran the Jazīra in 1884.

Muḥammad wad Arbāb (–1887), Mahdist amīr, a Takrūnī negro of Gallabat on the Sudan-Abyssinian frontier; he was killed in local war against the neighbouring Abyssinian chief.

Muḥammad al-Arbāb wad Dafaʿ Allāh Aḥmad (–1854), only surviving son of the Arbāb Dafaʿ Allāh Aḥmad Ḥasan, the turbulent Hāmaj filibuster of the last days of the sultanate of Sennar; he submitted to the Egyptian Government and was allowed to own property round Ṣūraiba near Wad Madanī; he married Naṣra bint ʿAdlān, daughter of ʿAdlān Muḥammad abū'l-Kailak; by 1840 he was probably the most important man between Khartoum and Sennar and in 1845 was chosen, with Shaikh ʿAbd al-Qādir wad al-Zain, nāẓir ʿumūm of the Sudan, to visit the viceroy Muḥammad ʿAlī in Egypt; on his death he was succeeded by his son ʿAdlān Muḥammad Dafaʿ Allāh (d. 1879).

Muḥammad al-Asyūṭī (*fl.* 1821), Islamic judge from Upper Egypt who accompanied the expedition of Ismāʿīl Pasha to Sennar, 1820–1; he was one of a party of learned and religious men sent by Muḥammad ʿAlī to assist the pacification of the Sudan by persuasion.

Muḥammad ʿAwad al-Karīm abū Sin (*fl.* 1821), tribal leader of the Shukrīya, a son of ʿAwad al-Karīm (*fl.* 1780) whose shaikhship he inherited; although recognized by the tribe as their shaikh, he refused to have any dealings with the Turks who occupied the Blue Nile valley in 1821 but retired to the remote regions of the Atbara, leaving his brother Aḥmad ʿAwad al-Karīm (later bey) to represent the tribe in the Turkish local administration.

Muḥammad Bābikr (–1942), ʿumda of the third khuṭṭ of the Shukrīya whose seat was at Abū Shām, north-east of Rufāʿa.

* **Muḥammad al-Badawī** (–1911), religious notable; of Dongolāwī (ʿAbbāsid) origin he was born at al-Ubaiyaḍ and educated at al-Azhar University, Cairo; after spending a few years as a teacher of religion at al-Fāshar and Umm Shanqa in Dār Fūr, he joined the Mahdist movement at al-Ubaiyaḍ; under the Mahdist régime he became an Islamic judge at Berber where he earned a reputation for his just judgements; he fell out, however, with the Mahdist governor of the place, whereupon the Khalīfa ʿAbd Allāhi summoned him to his side in Omdurman where he lived during the rest of the Khalīfa's rule; on the Anglo-Egyptian occupation he was appointed president of the board of religious notables; his tomb is in the Mūrada district of Omdurman.

* **Muḥammad Badr al-ʿUbaid** (*c.* 1810–84), religious leader, a member of the Ibrāhīmāb branch of the Masallamīya Arabs of Umm Dibbān on the Blue Nile; he was received into the Jailanīya brotherhood and he met the religious leader al-Saiyid Muḥammad ʿUthmān al-Mīrghanī at Makka while on the pilgrimage, about 1840; he founded a settlement at Umm Dibbān in 1847 and built a mosque there in 1857; here he achieved a great reputation as a teacher; he died while on his way to meet Muḥammad Aḥmad al-Mahdī in Omdurman; his sons ʿAbbās and al-Ṭāhir were devoted adherents to the Mahdist cause, the latter gaining a victory over Muḥammad ʿAlī Pasha Ḥusain, one of Gordon's best officers, between al-ʿĀilafūn and Umm Dibbān in 1884.

Muḥammad Bayūmī (*c.* 1801–*c.* 1852), Egyptian schoolmaster; born at Dashūr in the province of Giza, he became a master in the School of Engineering at Būlāq; in 1826 he went to France and stayed there nine years learning engineering and mathematics; having got his diploma he returned to Egypt and was again a master at the School of Engineering then under C. Lambert Bey; he afterwards transferred to the directorate of education where he worked with Rifāʿa Bey Rāfiʿ al-Ṭahṭāwī, the great translator, in writing and translating school textbooks; dismissed from his post along with Rifāʿa Bey in the reactionary régime of the viceroy ʿAbbās I in 1850, the two were banished to Khartoum with other suspected persons under the pretext that they were to found a school there; he died in Khartoum.

* **Muḥammad Bello Mai Wurno** (*c.* 1876–1944), Hausa chieftain; he was the son of Attahira, sultan of Sokoto, who claimed to be a descendant of ʿUthmān Dan Fodio, the great Fulānī sultan who was reigning at the time of the British occupation in 1903; in company with Mai Aḥmad, amīr of Meisau, he set out eastward in flight from British interference and in response to apocalyptic beliefs regarding the advent of a new mahdī and the prophecy that the Fulānī people would thenceforward dwell near Makka; with a considerable following the two chieftains journeyed through Wadāʾi into the Sudan where Mai Aḥmad became head of the Fallāta settlement south of Sinja in the Blue Nile valley; Mai Wurno arrived on the Nile about 1906 when

Shaikh Muḥammad al-Tūm, son of Shaikh Ṭalḥa, a noted pioneer from West Africa, welcomed him and invited him to establish the village which is called after his name; the villagers refer to him as their sultan.

Muḥammad wad Bilail (–1939), notable of Port Sudan, a magistrate.

Muḥammad wad Billāl (–1885), Mahdist amīr, by birth a Dongolāwī he joined the Mahdist cause and fought against the British column at the battle of Abū Ṭulaiḥ (Abu Klea) in which he was killed.

Muḥammad wad Bushāra (*c.* 1861–98), Mahdist amīr; a Taʿā'ishī by birth he was the son of the holy man the amīr Bushāra ʿAlī and a near relative of the Khalīfa ʿAbd Allāhi; he was born in the village of Barkas near Dāra in Dār Fūr and as a young man went with his father to join the Mahdī after the fall of al-Ubaiyaḍ, 1883; he fought in the great battles of the early *Mahdīya* including Shaikān (Kashgil), 1883, and the assault on Khartoum, 1885; he was second in command to the amīr ʿUthmān Adam in the campaign against Yūsuf Ibrāhīm, the rebel sultan of Dār Fūr, 1888; his youth prevented his succeeding ʿUthmān Adam on the latter's death in 1889 and, being unable to work harmoniously with the amīr Maḥmūd Aḥmad, ʿUthmān Adam's successor, the Khalīfa ʿAbd Allāhi appointed him second in command to the amīr Yaʿqūb Muḥammad Turshain in Omdurman; he was later made governor of Dongola in succession to the amīr Yūnis wad al-Dikaim and held that post until the fall of Dongola to the Anglo-Egyptian forces, 1896, when he was wounded in the battle of Ḥafīr; retreating to Matamma, where he reorganized his shattered army, he was later killed in the battle of Omdurman.

Muḥammad ibn Dafaʿ Allāh ibn Muqbal al-ʿArakī, called also **Abū Idrīs** (*fl.* 1560), Sudanese religious teacher; the hagiographer Wad Ḍaif Allāh wrote that he was a shaikh al-Islām and very famous; he was buried at Abū Ḥarāẓ on the Blue Nile; it was in his time that Shaikh Muḥammad Tāj al-Dīn al-Bahārī came to the Sudan, it was said from Baghdad; his brother ʿAbd Allāh ibn Dafaʿ Allāh al-ʿArakī was also a holy man of note.

Muḥammad Dālī or **Dalīl Baḥr** (*fl.* 1450), Tunjur-Fūr sultan of Dār Fūr; he was the traditional ancestor of the two leading family groups, the Musabaʿāt and the Kunjāra, who successively controlled Kordofan.

Muḥammad al-Ḍarīr ibn Idrīs ibn Dūlīb, called also **Dūlīb Nesi** (*fl. c.* 1500), Sudanese mystic; he was apparently a Dongolāwī, the word *nesi* meaning son's son in the Dongolāwī dialect of the Nubian language; he was a man of energy and asceticism, holding retreats on Jabal Bursī on the borders of Dār Shā'iqīya; he was buried at al-Dabba.

Muḥammad al-Ḍaw (–1919), Khāldī tribesman; in his younger days he was an officer in the Mahdist army; he was murdered in the course of a private quarrel; his son ʿUmar (d. 1945) was shaikh of the Khawālda khuṭṭ in the southern Jazīra.

Muḥammad Dawra (–1732), sultan of Dār Fūr; in 1722 he succeeded his father, Aḥmad Bakr Mūsā, and reigned till his death when he was followed by his son, 'Umar Layla (Lele).

Muḥammad Dīyāb Raḥma (*fl.* 1821), malik of the Bidairāb branch of the Rubāṭāb at the time of the invasion of the Sudan by the army of Ismā'īl Pasha, 1820–1; he lived on Muqrāt island near Abū Ḥamad and, according to G. B. English, the American commander of Ismā'īl's artillery, had a wide reputation for his courage, morals, and generosity.

Muḥammad Dīn (–1841), chief of the Hadendowa Beja at the time of the Egyptian occupation of the delta of the Gash; many stories are told of his long resistance to the conquerors and to their influence, how he refused to speak Arabic, how he destroyed a force under 'Alī Khūrshīd Pasha in 1831–2; finally in 1840 Aḥmad Pasha Abū Widān, 'Alī Khūrshīd's successor to the governorship-general, invaded Tāka and after fighting the Hadendowa arrested him and his nephew Mūsā by a stratagem and sent them with other Hadendowa notables in chains to Khartoum where he died in captivity of small-pox.

Muḥammad wad Dūlīb, called **The Younger** (*fl.* 1730), Sudanese genealogist and part-author of a manuscript compilation on the history of the Arab tribes of the Sudan of which he wrote the last part; the other contributors were Ghulām Allāh and Muḥammad wad Dūlīb the Elder; he was buried at Khūrsī in Kordofan; the Duwālīb family of Kordofan take their name from him.

Muḥammad Fāḍil Pasha (1871–1941), liwā' of the Egyptian army and military engineer; born in Cairo, he was educated at al-Azhar University and at the School of Languages, entering the military school in 1889; he was commissioned mulāzim II in 1891; he served throughout the Dongola and Nile campaigns of 1896–8 in the Egyptian engineers and fought in the battles of Firka (Firket), Ḥafīr, the Atbara, and Omdurman; for many years he commanded the Egyptian engineer battalion operating the railways in the Sudan; promoted liwā' in 1923, he retired in 1924; in 1925 he defended those cadets of the Khartoum military school who were on trial before a court-martial for mutiny; he was a man of many interests, a poet of some competence, and the author of a book on palmistry.

Muḥammad al-Faḍl 'Abd al-Raḥmān (–1839), sultan of Dār Fūr, grandfather of 'Alī Dīnār (*c.* 1865–1916); he was raised to power in 1802 as a minor with a guardian; in his early years he defeated Adam, sultan of Wadā'i, and harried the Rizaiqāt; in 1821 his overlordship of Kordofan came to an end when a Turkish army under Muḥammad Khusraw the Bey Daftardār defeated the Fūr army at Bāra and killed his deputy, the Maqdūm Musallam; shortly afterwards he received a letter from Muḥammad 'Alī Pasha calling on him to capitulate; his defiant reply is said to have dissuaded the Pasha from attempting to invade Dār Fūr; he was buried in the ancestral cemetery of the Fūr kings on Jabal Marra and was succeeded by his son, Muḥammad Ḥusain al-Mahdī.

Muḥammad Faḍl Allāh (–1938), Mahdist amīr of the Taʿā'isha Baqqāra tribe; taken prisoner in the battle of Abū Ḥamad in 1897, he lived to a good old age and died in Omdurman.

Muḥammad wad al-Haila (*c.* 1867–1939), Ḥasanī notable of Turʿa al-Khaḍra; he took an insignificant part in the Mahdist revolt as a muqaddam and, on the setting up of the present government, he was made ʿumda of the Ḥasanīya round Turʿa al-Khaḍra and of the Shanabla in the locality; in 1913 the Nuba Jaʿlīyīn of al-Turʿa were added to his administration.

Muḥammad al-Ḥājj Aḥmad (–1937), Maḥasī notable; he was shaikh of the village of Burrī al-Maḥas (adjoining Khartoum) where he died.

Muḥammad ibn al-Ḥājj Ḥabīb al-Rikābī (*fl.* 1650), mystic who lived on al-Qashābī island near Dongola; he was one of the most venerated saints of the Rikābīya and a traditional descendant of Shaikh Ghulām Allāh ibn ʿĀid.

Muḥammad ibn Ḥamad ibn Idrīs al-Faḍlī, called **Bān al-Nuqā (Bān Naqā)** (*fl.* 1550), founder of the religious family of the Yaʿqūbāb who have two branches, one near Sennar, the other near Shendi; he was generally believed to have been of the Razqīya Arabs by tribe, but, though his exact origin is obscure, his mother was said to be Sudanese; he enjoyed great prestige in the Funj sultanate of Sennar and was in favour at the court of Sultan Naiyīl; he died and was buried at al-Waʿar near Sennar.

Muḥammad Bey Ḥamad al-Malik (1845–1908), son of al-Malik Ḥamad of the ruling house of Arqū; the Turks appointed him kāshif of Arqū sometime between 1871 and 1873 during the governorship of Ḥusain Pasha Khalīfa; on the Mahdist occupation of the district he remained and, such was his authority among his people, was regarded by the Mahdists as an amīr; only on one occasion did the Khalīfa ʿAbd Allāhi suspect his loyalty; he was summoned to Omdurman, and was cleared of suspicion; on the Anglo-Egyptian occupation of 1896, he was appointed ʿumda of Arqū.

Muḥammad Ḥāmid Shikkū (–1941), ʿumda of the Dirās section of the Missīrīya Arabs of Kordofan.

Muḥammad Hārūn al-Rashīd Saif al-Dīn (–1880), rebel sultan of Dār Fūr; he was a son of Bōsh ibn Muḥammad al-Faḍl and belonged to the royal line; he succeeded to the leadership of the resistance movement on the death of his father in battle in 1875 and continued the struggle against the Egyptian occupying forces; in 1877 he headed an open revolt and after several successes invested Dāra, al-Fāshar, Kabkabīya, and Qūlqūl; he was, however, defeated by an Egyptian army under ʿAbd al-Rāziq Pasha Ḥaqqī at Burush between Umm Shanqa and al-Fāshar; al-Fāshar was thus relieved and Hārūn fled to Jabal

Marra where R. C. von Slatin Bey, then governor of Dāra, defeated him; he recovered from his defeat and again raised an army but was finally defeated and killed in an ambush near Kabkabīya by a government force under al-Nūr Bey Muḥammad ʿAnqara, governor of Qūlqūl; on his death his cousin ʿAbd Allāhi Dūd Banja was regarded by his people as the legitimate sultan of the Fūr.

Muḥammad Pasha Ḥasan (–1885), Egyptian merchant and government official; he was born at Idfū in Upper Egypt and came to the Sudan when young; here he built up a considerable business, rising to be chief merchant in Khartoum about 1883; on his arrival in Khartoum in February 1884 Gordon Pasha conferred on him the rank of pasha and appointed him financial secretary, a post which he held throughout the siege; he was killed by the Mahdists during the sack of the city.

Muḥammad Ḥasan Minyāwī (–1946), Egyptian merchant who during the first years of the present government was one of the most important merchants in Khartoum; his mother, Zainūba al-Minyāwīya, was a remarkable woman; she took a leading part in the family business at the latter end of the Egyptian rule and in 1884, while shut up in the capital during the siege by the Mahdists, gave much help to C. G. Gordon Pasha, supplying him with her large stocks of corn; it is even said that Gordon in gratitude created her a bey; she survived the Mahdist régime and maintained her own pavilion at the annual *mūlid al-nabī* celebrations in Khartoum during the early years of the Condominium Government.

Muḥammad abū Ḥijil (*c.* 1827–87), Rubāṭābī notable, son of the malik Abū Ḥijil whom Ismāʿīl Pasha, son of Muḥammad ʿAlī Pasha, made chief of all the Rubāṭāb tribe; about 1871 Ḥusain Bey K͟halīfa, then governor of the united provinces of Berber and Dongola, appointed him muʿāwin al-idāra of Dongola to act in place of ʿUt͟hmān Bey who had been discharged for irregularities; he is said to have been a successful ruler; in 1876, acting on instructions from the governor, Almās Bey Muḥammad, he is said to have been responsible for the strangling of Ismāʿīl Pasha Ṣādiq, the Egyptian minister of finance, whom the Khedive had banished to Dongola; he later joined the Mahdist cause; two of his sons died before him: Mūsā, who was killed fighting on the Mahdist side in the battle of Kirbikān, 1885, and Muḥammad, killed in battle at Tūs͟hkī (Toski) while fighting under the banner of the amīr al-umarāʾ ʿAbd al-Raḥmān wad al-Najūmī, 1889; a third son, ʿUmar, was killed in the defence of Abū Ḥamad against an Egyptian force commanded by A. Hunter Pasha, 1897.

Muḥammad al-Hilālī (–1872), freebooter and faqī; originating from Lake Fitri in Bagirmi, he remained in the Sudan on his way back from the pilgrimage; he had been to Egypt where it is said that he had told the Khedive Ismāʿīl that he had conquered parts of Dār Fūr and wished to take possession of the copper mines of Ḥufrat al-Naḥās;

the Sudan Government provided him with a small force with which he occupied points in the Baḥr al-Ghazāl in collaboration with the Turkish ex-trader (now temporary official) Kuchūk ʿAlī; he quarrelled with Kuchūk ʿAlī who mysteriously died; his overbearing conduct towards the traders in the Baḥr al-Ghazāl in the name of the government angered Zubair Raḥma Manṣūr, the future pasha, who attacked and defeated him; he was shortly after killed by Zubair's henchman Rabīḥ Faḍl Allāh.

Muḥammad Bey Ḥusain Khalīfa (1837–77), ʿAbbādī notable, eldest son of Ḥusain Pasha Khalīfa, governor of Berber and Dongola, 1869–73; his father's dismissal from his governorship in 1873 had repercussions on his son who until that year had been government transport concessionaire over the Nubian desert; the Khedive Ismāʿīl declared him incapable of holding the concession which was then given to his uncle, Ḥāmid Khalīfa; before his dismissal he had been assisting in a survey for a railway between Berenice and Berber; he was born at Abū Ḥamad and died at Dirāw.

Muḥammad Ḥusain al-Mahdī (–1873), sultan of Dār Fūr, a son of Sultan Muḥammad al-Faḍl ʿAbd al-Raḥmān and the first sultan of the Fūr to use firearms, introducing military instructors from Tunis; he was possibly responsible for the death of the French doctor, C. Cuny, who set out from Egypt in 1858 to explore Dār Fūr; he made the usual war against the Rizaiqāt in the south of his territories; he sent an army under the shartai ʿAbd Allāh and the vizier Khalīl against a party of Egyptian Arabs who had raided northern Dār Fūr, and captured their leader, ʿUmar al-Miṣrī, whom the sultan mercifully sent back to Egypt, an act which so impressed Muḥammad Saʿīd Pasha that he sent the sultan presents; he reigned from 1839 till his death when he was succeeded by his son Ibrāhīm Muḥammad Ḥusain; he was said to have been a literate and pious man.

Muḥammad Ḥusain Rās al-Tūr (–1945), ʿumda of Qimr in south-western Dār Fūr and a magistrate; he died at Nyāla.

Muḥammad Ibrāhīm Arbāb (1860–1937), Bidairī notable; from 1908 he was shaikh of Affāt near al-Dabba.

Muḥammad Imām wad Ḥabūba (–1896), chieftain of the Ḥalāwīyīn of the Jazīra; the Egyptian Government appointed him nāẓir of the southern district of the Khartoum province about 1870; he was afterwards removed from his post as a result of a petition against him from some villages alleging oppression, and the government thereupon made his half-brother Abū Sin shaikh al-qism, and Karam Allāh, the Jaʿlī, nāẓir of the whole district south of Khartoum; he was reinstated in 1877 and died peacefully in his village; a forceful character, he stimulated tribal consciousness among his people and many tales are told of his bravery and his litigation with the neighbouring Ḍubāsīyīn.

Muḥammad Pasha Imām al-Khabīr (–1883), merchant of Dār Fūr; he came of original Dongolāwī stock long settled at Kobbé, at the southern end of the Darb al-Arbaʿīn caravan route between Asyūṭ and northern Dār Fūr, and here the family had built an extensive export and import business; he and his brother Ḥamza Imām al-Khabīr (since Pasha) had welcomed the Egyptian conquest of Dār Fūr, 1874–5, and he was shortly after appointed president of the council at al-Fāshar; about 1877 Gordon Pasha, then governor-general of the Sudan, called him to Khartoum to fill the post of president of the court of appeal; about 1879 Gordon appointed him governor of western Dār Fūr, though he was afterwards temporarily dismissed for malpractices; the outbreak of the Mahdist revolt saw him back in Khartoum where in 1882 he commanded a body of reinforcements which the Government was sending to Bāra and al-Ubaiyaḍ; on their arrival they found Bāra already besieged by the Mahdists and, on the investment of al-Ubaiyaḍ, they deserted from the doomed town and joined the enemy; he survived the siege and died a natural death in the Mahdī's camp shortly after.

Muḥammad ibn ʿĪsā ibn Ṣāliḥ al-Bidairī, called **Sūwār al-Dhahab** (*fl.* 1504), religious leader of the Dahmashīya section of the Bidairīya Arabs; the original home of his ancestors was Makka, his grandfather having come from the Holy City to teach the Qur'ān; the young Muḥammad travelled to Andalusia and thence made his way by the North African coast to Egypt, settling for some time at Aswān where his descendants still survive; his missionary zeal brought him finally to Dongola where the historian al-Talmisānī al-Maghribī met him about 1504; here he preached the tenets of the Qādirīya brotherhood and his followers greatly multiplied in this former Christian region; pupils came to him from places as far distant as Tlemcen; at Old Dongola he converted a former Christian church into a mosque still used by his descendants; his pupils included ʿAbd al-Raḥmān wad abū Malāḥ, the father of Shaikh Khūjalī, the saint of Ḥalfaiya.

Muḥammad Iṣāgha (–1941), shaikh of Tūmāt in the ʿumudīya of Abū Naʿama in the Funj district of the Blue Nile; by tribe he was of the Banī Ḥasan branch of the Rufāʿa al-Hūī.

Muḥammad Bey Islām al-Albānī (–1885), Albanian soldier in the Egyptian army, nicknamed 'Metu Bey'; while a sanjaq in command of a force of Turkish cavalry in the Jazīra, he defeated and killed the Mahdist amīr Faḍl Allāh wad Karrīf, 1883; he was killed in the Mahdist assault on Khartoum.

Muḥammad al-Jaʿlī (*fl. c.* 1530), traditional ancestor of the kings of Taqalī in the Nuba hills; little is known of him save that he was a poor man of great piety and that he came to Taqalī from the Nile valley; so impressed were the Nuba by his peaceful ways and holiness that they received him among them and accepted Islām; his son Abū Jarīda, whose mother was the daughter of the chief Kabr-Kabr, succeeded him in the chieftainship and, to indicate his foreign blood, was named al-Jailī.

Muḥammad Bey Jumʿa (1888–1940), qā'immaqām of the Sudan Defence Force; born in Dongola of Fūr descent, he entered the Egyptian army from which he was later transferred to the Sudan Government service as a sub-ma'mūr, in which capacity he served in the province of Sennar; in 1918 he was promoted yūzbāshī, in 1923 ma'mūr; in 1937, two years before his retirement, he reached the rank of qā'im-maqām; he died in Cairo.

Muḥammad Junqul Baḥr (*fl. c.* 1650), sultan of the Musabaʿāt, a branch of the Fūr who ruled in Kordofan; in the reign of the Fūr sultan, Mūsā Sulaimān (1637–82), he laid claim to the throne of Dār Fūr, but without success; Sultan Hāshim wad ʿĪsawī al-Musabaʿāwī (d. *c.* 1812) was his grandson.

Muḥammad al-Kāhil (*fl. c.* 1000), traditional ancestor of the Kawāhla Arabs; he is said to have been the first Arab to enter the Sudan—an ambitious claim—having been driven out of Arabia by the Banī ʿAbbās; he is credited with having defeated the *Anaj* or original inhabitants near Qarrī and made the people of the surrounding country effectively Muslim; he is also said to have lived for ninety years and to have been buried with his son ʿAbd Allāhi at Jabal Jilif in the Bayūda.

Muḥammad abū'l-Kailak (abū Likailik) Kamtūr (*c.* 1710–76), king-maker and general of the Funj sultanate of Sennar; although of Hāmaj descent he was probably partly Arab, possibly Jamūʿī; he was largely responsible for the victory of the Funj army over the Abyssinians, 1744; with Khamīs, a disaffected Fūr commander banished from Dār Fūr, he led a Funj army into Kordofan and, after severe fighting against the Musabaʿāt, the Fūr overlords, conquered the region about 1744; here he maintained himself as mek of Kordofan for thirty years at the cost of hard fighting; his preoccupations in Kordofan did not prevent him from heading a revolt against King Bādī IV abū Shilūkh of Sennar, his own sovereign, and deposing him in 1761; from henceforward the sultans of Sennar were but puppets in the hands of the powerful Hāmaj viziers; his numerous descendants wasted the sultanate with civil war which lasted until the Egyptian occupation of 1821.

Muḥammad Kamtūr (–1820), one of the leading Hāmaj notables of Sennar in the last days of the Funj kingdom; he was engaged in continual civil war and intrigue until he was killed by a rival, Muḥammad wad ʿAdlān, a son of Muḥammad abū'l-Kailak.

* **Muḥammad al-Khair ʿAbd Allāh Khūjalī** (–1888), Mahdist amīr and religious teacher; a Jaʿlī of Berber, he was at first known as Muḥammad al-Dakkair; Muḥammad Aḥmad al-Mahdī sat at his feet for several years before continuing his studies under the celebrated shaikh, Muḥammad Sharīf Nūr al-Dā'im, leader of the Sammānīya brotherhood; on the outbreak of the Mahdist revolt his former pupil appointed him amīr of Berber and of the Jaʿlīyīn; in 1884 he laid siege to Berber whose garrison, under the governor, Ḥusain Pasha Khalīfa, surrendered after a half-hearted defence; in 1885 he moved up from

Berber on the heels of the retreating British force which had attempted in vain to relieve Khartoum, and held temporary command in Dongola; he was amīr of Berber and of the Ja'līyīn until his death when the amīr 'Uthmān wad al-Dikaim, brother of the more famous Yūnus, replaced him.

Muḥammad Khair al-Arqāwī, called **al-Khairī** (–1862), Dongolāwī trader and freebooter; born on Arqū island, he was trading in dates at Kaka on the White Nile when his store was looted by Shilluk tribesmen; finding no redress from the government, he collected a private army of about 500 men, mostly Danāqla, and waged war on the Shilluk, selling captives in the market at Khartoum and buying arms with the proceeds; finally Fashoda, then the Shilluk centre, gave in to him and, once master of the Shilluk, he offered to pay the government a yearly toll of cattle in return for the official recognition of his overlordship; his continued ravaging of the Shilluk caused the latter to appeal to Khartoum for protection by virtue of the former annual tribute which they paid to the government; the government sent a force under Yūsuf Ḥasan al-Shallālī (afterwards Pasha) to aid the Shilluk; on its approach Muḥammad Khair fled to Fungor, the daughter of whose chief he had married, and sought the help of his allies, the Baqqāra Arabs, in the neighbourhood; the circumstances of his death are not clear; according to one account he was treacherously killed by his wife's father, according to another source Yūsuf al-Shallālī, being unable to follow him into Kordofan, asked Wad Taimā to capture him; this Wad Taimā did and sent his head to Khartoum; Idrīs, Muḥammad Khair's deputy, tried to hold the dead man's followers together but failed, and the force dissolved into small parties which continued slave-raiding in the Baḥr al-Ghazāl.

Muḥammad Khālid al-Mak Nimr (–1938), Ja'lī notable of the old ruling house of the Nimrāb and a direct descendant of 'Abd al-Salām, fourth kinglet of Shendi; he was a magistrate and a member of the Shendi court.

* **Muḥammad Bey Khālid Zughal** (–1903), Mahdist amīr al-umarā', a cousin of Muḥammad Aḥmad al-Mahdī; he began life as a humble merchant and was afterwards a government official in Dār Fūr after the Egyptian occupation; in 1879 he was governor of Shaqqa and assisted in the suppression of the revolt of Sulaimān wad Zubair; in 1882 he was acting governor of Dāra and a bey; when Muḥammad Aḥmad al-Mahdī had captured al-Ubaiyaḍ and the Egyptian garrisons in Dār Fūr were isolated from all help from the Nile valley, R. C. von Slatin Bey, governor of Dār Fūr, sent him to interview the Mahdī at al-Ubaiyaḍ; he arranged the surrender of Von Slatin and the transfer of Dār Fūr to the Mahdist cause; the Mahdī then appointed him governor in Von Slatin's stead; after the Mahdī's death his relations with the Khalīfa 'Abd Allāhi were unhappy; he was banished to Rejaf for alleged complicity in the attempted rebellion of the Khalīfa Muḥammad al-Sharīf, 1889; with the amīr Muḥammad 'Uthmān abū Qarja he was released by the Belgians on their occupation of the town, 1897;

he made his way to Dār Fūr where he excited the suspicion of Sultan ʿAlī Dīnār who had him killed; he was a big, stout man, wealthy before the *Mahdīya*, and no fanatic.

* **Muḥammad Khashm al-Mūs Pasha** (*c*. 1850–*c*. 1912), Sudanese soldier; a Shā'iqī by tribe, he was a son of Shaikh Muḥammad Sibair and was born near Kūrtī; when a youth he enrolled in the Shā'iqī cavalry which then formed part of the Egyptian irregular forces in the Sudan; he was later promoted sanjaq and served in garrison duties; C. G. Gordon Pasha liked him and appointed him in command of troops at the frontier station of Fadāsī; during the siege of Khartoum, 1884, he commanded a flotilla of Gordon's steamers which steamed down to Matamma to meet the British column which was attempting the relief of the city; he himself went inland and met the relieving force at Jakdūl wells; two of his sons were killed by the Mahdists in the sack of Khartoum, 1885; the city having fallen, he retreated with the British army to Dongola; he was then stationed at Wādī Ḥalfā on military duty; already a bey, the Khedive Muḥammad Tawfīq promoted him pasha in 1885; he spent his retirement at Maʿad al-Khabīr in Egypt where he built a mosque and where he died.

Muḥammad Khūjalī al-Hitaik (–1885), Maḥasī notable, the last qāḍī of Khartoum under the Egyptian rule; he was killed by the Mahdists in the massacre of Khartoum.

Muḥammad Khusraw Pasha (*c*. 1757–1855), Turkish wālī of Egypt, 1801–3, and afterwards grand vizier of the Ottoman Empire; while in Egypt he formed a regiment of Sudanese and clothed them in uniforms similar to those of the French army.

* **Muḥammad Bey Khusraw al-Daramalī, al-Daftardār** (–1833), Rumelian Turkish soldier and official in the service of Muḥammad ʿAlī Pasha; though apparently originating from Drama in Macedonia, he appears to have been bred in Constantinople as he was frequently called 'Asitānalī' (Arab. al-Istānbūlī); the title Daftardār signifies that he served Muḥammad ʿAlī as intendant of finance and held the lands register, the key to land taxation, an office to which he had been appointed by the Ottoman sultan; he had married Nāzlī Ḥānim, a daughter of Muḥammad ʿAlī, and enjoyed the full confidence of the Pasha; while governor of the Saʿīd (Upper Egypt) he was given command of an Egyptian army destined for the conquest of Kordofan which was then under the sway of the kings of Dār Fūr; leaving the Nile at al-Dabba in August 1821 his force marched across the Bayūda through Abū Ḥarāza to Bāra near which he routed an army led by the maqdūm Musallam, the Fūr governor of Kordofan, who was killed in the battle; he then occupied al-Ubaiyaḍ unopposed; gazetted governor of Kordofan directly responsible to Muḥammad ʿAlī, he laid the foundations of a military administration and raided the Nuba hills for slaves; on the assassination of Ismāʿīl Pasha, Muḥammad ʿAlī's son, by Nimr king of Shendi late in 1822 he was ordered, as senior Turkish commander in the Sudan, to avenge Ismāʿīl's death and to quell a threatened

Sudanese rising in the Nile valley; leaving al-Ubaiyaḍ early in 1823, he made for the Nile and burnt Matamma, Shendi, Kabūshīya, and al-Dāmar, massacring the inhabitants; with the help of Maḥū Bey Urfalī, governor of Berber and of the Ja'līyīn, he defeated Nimr at Nasūb in the Buṭāna, causing the latter to flee to the Abyssinian frontier; having given the Ja'līyīn up to slaughter, he hacked his way, killing and burning as he went, to Sennar, where he arrived in June 1823; having cowed the inhabitants of the Nile valley, he led a raid over the Atbara, fought the Hadendowa, systematically devastated the Gash delta, and placed garrisons at important points between Tāka and Sennar; the Bishārīyīn and Shukrīya alone continued to resist; on the arrival in Khartoum in September 1824 of his successor, 'Uthmān Bey Jarkas al-Birinjī, mīrālai of the 1st regular infantry regiment, he handed over the command of the Turkish troops in the Sudan and, with a portion of them, left for Cairo; arrived in Egypt, he resumed his office of governor of the Sa'īd and was, from 1825, minister of war; from time to time Muḥammad 'Alī sought his advice in council on Sudan affairs; an educated man, handsome and courtly, he made a route map of the Egyptian-occupied parts of the Sudan; A. Cadeau, a French military instructor who served in al-Ubaiyaḍ in 1824–8, in the course of an odious comparison with his successor in Kordofan, recorded his organizing ability and care for his troops; many stories (perhaps exaggerated with the passage of time) are told in the Sudan of his cruelty; he died at Jazīra Muḥammad near Cairo.

Muḥammad Kurra [not **Qurra'a**] (–1804), Fūr statesman; nothing is known of his origin other than that Muḥammad ibn 'Umar al-Tūnisī denied that he was a slave; he was the devoted servant of Sultan Muḥammad al-Faḍl, for whom he was first regent, after the death of al-Faḍl's father, Sultan 'Abd al-Raḥmān Aḥmad Bukr, in 1799, and then vizier; he warred against Hāshim wad 'Īsāwī al-Musaba'āwī, finally driving him from Kordofan and restoring that province to direct Fūr rule; he was killed in a fight with his enemies who had intrigued against him at court and who had gained the sultan's ungrateful approval of their action; his name Kurra is derived from the Fūr word meaning 'long', an allusion to his height.

Muḥammad Madanī Dushain (*fl.* 1680), grandson of the Shāfi'ite holy man Dushain wad Ḥamad called al-Qāḍī al-'Adāla, the Just Judge; himself a mystic, he is regarded as the founder of the family group of the Madanīyīn who gave their name to the town of Wad Madanī which grew up round his tomb; he first settled at Abū Ḥarāza where he was befriended by the 'Arakīyīn and later transferred with his disciples to the site of Wad Madanī; his descendants have been prominent as religious teachers.

Muḥammad al-Māḍī abū'l-'Azā'im (1870–1936), Egyptian religious leader and founder of the 'Azmīya brotherhood; born at Dusūq, he went thence to Maṭarīya in al-Mīnyā province, now the seat of the brotherhood; he entered the Egyptian education department, 1893, and served, among other places, at Sawākin; he was transferred to the Sudan

Government education department, 1902, and taught at Wādī Ḥalfā, Omdurman, and, from 1905 to 1915, at Gordon Memorial College, Khartoum, when he founded a mission at Burrī on the outskirts of the capital; he left the Sudan, 1915, on account of his political views, and lived at al-Minyā; he had a popular reputation in Egypt for holiness and had his own *mūlid* in Cairo; originally a Shādhilī he strove for religious simplicity and was hostile to the hereditary religious shaikhs and to superstition; attributed to him are two books: one on the first principles of following the Prophet, the other on the ʿAzmīya brotherhood and heavenly inspiration; his followers call themselves the ʿAwāzma.

Muḥammad abū Madyan (*c.* 1803–*c.* 1847), claimant to the throne of Dār Fūr; he claimed to be a son of Sultan ʿAbd al-Raḥmān Aḥmad Bukr and a brother of Sultan Muḥammad Faḍl; ill treated by his reigning brother and disappointed that his claim to the throne was unrecognized, he was in Cairo in 1820 on the eve of the Egyptian invasion of the Sudan probably soliciting the help of Muḥammad ʿAlī Pasha to gain his throne with Egyptian armed assistance; Muḥammad ʿAlī, however, temporarily abandoned his intention of occupying Dār Fūr and Muḥammad abū Madyan returned thither where he made his peace with Sultan Muḥammad Faḍl; nevertheless the sultan treated him with suspicion and confined him to his home near al-Fāshar whence in 1833, after narrow escapes from pursuing Fūr horsemen, he and his younger brother arrived at al-Ubaiyaḍ where they were honourably received by the governor; Muḥammad ʿAlī met him when the former visited the Sudan in 1838–9 and afterwards invited him to Egypt; in 1843 the viceroy, now free of his military preoccupations in Syria, returned to his original project of invading Dār Fūr which an Ottoman firman of 1841 had included within his dominions; an expedition was fitted out in Cairo and Muḥammad abū Madyan left for the Sudan, but the death of the governor-general, Aḥmad Pasha abū Widān, in 1843 put an end to the operation and the luckless claimant returned to Egypt where he died.

Muḥammad Māhir Pasha (1854–1909), Egyptian soldier and geographer; educated in the school of engineering and in the military school, Cairo, he was commissioned in 1874 and employed by the geographical section of the general staff then under the command of al-farīq C. P. Stone Pasha; soon after the Egyptian conquest of Dar Fūr he accompanied al-mīrālai R. E. Colston Bey on a survey of Kordofan; the party left Cairo in December 1874 and, travelling by the Nile valley route to al-Dabba, struck inland to al-Ubaiyaḍ where Colston, injured in an accident, gave over the command to H. G. Prout Bey who led the party into Dār Fūr, 1875; in 1876 most of the party returned to Cairo, but Muḥammad Māhir stayed in the Sudan as governor of the district of Bor and Latuka in the Equatorial province, 1876–8; the revolt of Aḥmad ʿUrābī Pasha broke out while he was employed in the geological survey section of the general staff, 1878–82, and he enrolled in the reconstituted Egyptian army; having formed a Sudanese regiment, he saw service in the campaign of 1884–5 against the Mahdists on the Red Sea coast, taking part in the battle of Tamai and being promoted binbas̲h̲ī for valour on the field; in 1885 he was appointed assistant governor of Sawākin; promotion was now rapid; he was qā'immaqām, 1886, mīrālai, 1888, and liwā', 1892; he was sub-governor of the southern frontier of Egypt, 1889–92, and was in 1893 appointed under-secretary of state for war and marine; his retirement from office is said to have been a consequence of an incident at Wādī Ḥalfā wherein the Khedive 'Abbās Ḥilmī Pasha criticized the efficiency of the British troops there; he was governor of Cairo from 1894 till his death; his sons Aḥmad Māhir Pasha and 'Alī Māhir Pasha were afterwards well-known statesmen; his cartographical work in the Sudan was an important contribution to the geographical knowledge of the country; he assisted in the construction of the great map of Africa prepared by the Egyptian general staff in 1877.

Muḥammad Maḥmūd 'Alī (1898–1944), notable of the Dadinja Fūr; he was made s̲h̲artai of Qūz Baina in Dār Fūr, 1933, and president of al-Fās̲h̲ar court, 1935; he died while on pilgrimage to the holy places of Arabia.

Muḥammad al-Majd̲h̲ūb, called **al-Kabīr** (*fl.* 1720), religious notable of the Majād̲h̲īb branch of the Ja'līyīn; he introduced into the Sudan the principles of the S̲h̲ād̲h̲ilīya brotherhood; his son, Ḥamad al-Majd̲h̲ūb, is said to have been the founder of the town of al-Dāmar; his grandson, Muḥammad al-Majd̲h̲ūb al-Ṣug̲h̲aiyar, continued the family influence over the religious life of al-Dāmar where they formed a theocracy.

Muḥammad al-Majd̲h̲ūb, called **al-Ṣug̲h̲aiyar** (1796–1833), grandson of Muḥammad al-Majd̲h̲ūb who founded the S̲h̲ād̲h̲ilīya religious brotherhood in the Sudan; he was born at Matamma near Shendi and, arrived at manhood, took his place as leader of the brotherhood in the Sudan; in the town of al-Dāmar he dominated a community devoted to the teaching and practice of the Order; in 1823, during the Turkish reprisals for the murder of Ismā'īl Pasha by Nimr, king of Shendi, the mosque of the brotherhood was burnt and he was forced to flee to Sawākin and thence to Makka where he studied for nine years; on his return to the Sudan he taught at Sawākin, spreading his influence among the Beja; among his disciples on the Red Sea coast were S̲h̲aik̲h̲ Yāsīn of Sawākin and S̲h̲aik̲h̲ 'Alī Diqna, uncle of 'Ut̲h̲mān abū Bakr Diqna (Osman Digna), the Mahdist amīr; returning to al-Dāmar about 1832, he died there shortly afterwards.

* **Muḥammad Ma'nī Bey** (–c. 1881), Syrian civil official; he came to the Sudan about 1852 and is said to have been vice-governor of Khartoum under Aḥmad Bey 'Awaḍ al-Karīm abū Sin, 1860–70; when in 1872 the district of Fāzūg̲h̲lī was detached from the province of Sennar and placed under its own mudīrīya, he was appointed its first governor; at the time of his appointment the governor-general, Ismā'īl Pasha Aiyūb, reported that he had been at one time cotton inspector at Khartoum and had a wide knowledge of the Sudan; from Fāzūg̲h̲lī he went on to be governor of Khartoum from which post he was removed for negligence in 1878 and replaced by Aḥmad Bey abū Zaid;

his next appointment was to the governorship of Berber where in 1879 he entertained the Russian explorer W. Junker; according to an informant he was murdered with several others at Berber by an unknown assailant; his two sons, Ḥasan and Ḥusain, are said by the same informant to have been killed in the siege of Khartoum.

Muḥammad Mihrī (–1925?), Turkish translator and official; of Kurdish origin, he belonged to a tribe located in the region of Sulaimānīya; he began his career as a teacher of Turkish and Persian to the children of Prince Muṣṭafā Fāḍil, son of Ibrāhīm Pasha al-Wālī, viceroy of Egypt; he then served as a translator in the Sublime Porte, and later as town governor of Khūī on the Persian frontier; after a further period of service as a translator to the Porte, he retired to Egypt where he died; in 1912–13 he accompanied Prince Yūsuf Kamāl on a visit to the Sudan and wrote an account of his journey in Turkish entitled *Sūdān seyāḥatnāmesi* (A Journey to the Sudan), translated into Arabic as *Riḥla Miṣr wa'l-Sūdān* (Cairo, 1914), and also into Persian.

Muḥammad Muḥammad (–1943), ʿumda of the Sinkātkināb clan of the Banī ʿĀmir tribe; he died at Kassala.

Muḥammad Muḥammad Masʿūd ʿAbd al-Raḥmān (–1878), holy man, founder of the Raḥmānīya, a branch of the Darqawīya religious brotherhood; he built a zāwiya (place of prayer) at Makka, 1857, and afterwards preached through the country from Sawākin to Muṣawwaʿ where his khalīfa, Aḥmad al-Hajūnī al-Ghafrūnī, broke away and founded an offshoot, the Ghafrūnīya.

Muḥammad Mukhtār Pasha (1835–97), Egyptian soldier; born at Būlāq and educated in France and Egypt, he graduated from the Egyptian Military School and was attached to the general staff; on his way to duty in Harar in 1875 he surveyed a road between Sawākin and Sinkāt assisted by his fellow officer ʿAbd Allāh Fawzī and the civilian ʿAbd al-Ḥalīm Ḥilmī; in 1880, having been appointed chief of staff to the Egyptian army in the Sudan, he surveyed a road from Abū Ḥarāza to Gedaref and Kassala and proposed a line of wells along the Gedaref–Kassala portion; Muḥammad Ra'ūf Pasha, then governor-general, approved the project and employed D. Mosconas in 1882 to dig the wells, a venture not attended by success; the dissolution of the general staff following the revolt of Aḥmad ʿUrābī Pasha in 1882 left him temporarily without official employment, a period which he filled by writing and lecturing; in 1883 he was governor of Muṣawwaʿ in place of Khūrshīd Bey Pertew and was then director of the Sudan bureau in Cairo, an agency for transacting all work concerning the Sudan during the Mahdist revolt; after a short time as assistant-adjutant-general of the Arabic section of the Egyptian war office, he was promoted liwā' in 1886; he was finally appointed to the controllership of the Khedivial household and there he served his Khedive until his death; he wrote several papers on geographical subjects and contributed to the making of the map of Africa prepared by officers of the general staff in 1877.

Muḥammad al-Mukhtār 'Abd al-Raḥmān al-Shanqīṭī (–1882), holy man, trader and traveller, known as Wad al-'Āliya; born at Tashīt, Algeria, he introduced the tenets of the Tījānīya brotherhood into the Sudan whence West African holy men, such as the Hausa Saiyid 'Umar Janbū, spread the brotherhood in Kordofan and Dār Fūr; he is said to have been employed by the sultan of Dār Fūr as his agent in Cairo and to have acted as emissary between the sultan and the Ottoman Government (the agent of the sultan of Dār Fūr at the time appears in the Egyptian State papers as Muḥammad Shanqīṭī al-Sinighālī who, on his return from Egypt to al-Fāshar in 1858, carried presents from Muḥammad Sa'īd Pasha to the sultan); he was popularly credited with having admitted the viceroy Sa'īd Pasha to membership of the Tījānīya brotherhood; he travelled widely, living at one period at Sawākin, going thence to Berber with Zain al-'Ābidīn al-Maghribī; on the latter's death he settled among the Ja'līyīn near Qūz where he died; his writings include a *dīwān*, *Mūlid insān al-kāmil* (both printed), and *Kitāb al-wāridāt* in manuscript.

Muḥammad Bey Murābiṭ (*fl.* 1836–9), mīrālai of the regular infantry regiment which he was sent from Egypt to form from Sudan negroes in 1836 for service in Arabia and which was given the number 25th; in 1837 he was transferred to the 1st regiment which had been in the Sudan since 1824, and was at the same time appointed governor of Kordofan in succession to Yūsuf Bey; he was relieved of his post in 1839 and all his staff officers together with nine other officers and Coptic clerks were brought to trial for maladministration.

Muḥammad Bey Mūsā Ibrāhīm (–1933), nāẓir of the Hadendowa; he had been already in effective leadership of the tribe for several years before the death of his father Mūsā Ibrāhīm in 1884 at an advanced age; he fell out with the Mahdist amīr 'Uthmān abū Bakr Diqna (Osman Digna) by whom he was imprisoned only to be forcibly rescued by the Hadendowa; he fled to Eritrea where in 1892 an Italian court-martial sentenced him to five years imprisonment for intriguing with his old enemy, Osman Digna; he afterwards returned to the Sudan and was reinstated in the leadership of the tribe by the Anglo-Egyptian Government towards the end of the Mahdist rebellion, but was dismissed and exiled to Muḥammad Qūl shortly after the reconquest for being implicated in highway robbery; he died an old man in the delta of the Gash where he had gone to spend his old age; after a short interval, he was succeeded by Ibrāhīm Bey Mūsā, another son of the nāẓir Mūsā Ibrāhīm.

Muḥammad Muṣṭafā al-Marāghī (1881–1945), grand qāḍī of the Sudan, 1908–19, a graduate, and afterwards rector, of al-Azhar University, Cairo; he was a follower of Shaikh Muḥammad 'Abduh, and supported the law of 1936 which modernized much of the teaching at al-Azhar; in 1925 he was injured by sulphuric acid maliciously thrown at him.

* **Muḥammad Nādī Pasha** (1836–), liwā' of the Egyptian army; he was a mu'āwin in the Sudan Government when in 1867 he was

promoted qā'immaqām; in 1869 he undertook a hazardous mission to Dār Fūr ostensibly diplomatic but in reality to prepare a military report on routes and water-supplies for a future invading army; on his return he was appointed deputy governor of Khartoum; he fought in the Egyptian-Abyssinian war, 1876, and was promoted liwā'; he was a successful general governor of Harar and its dependencies, 1880–2.

Muḥammad ibn Naṣr al-Tarjamī al-Ja'lī, called **Abū Sinaina** (*fl.* 1670), Sudanese holy man; born at al-Buwaiḍ, he settled at Arbajī where he taught and where he was buried.

Muḥammad Nu'mān al-Jārim (1882–1943), grand qāḍī of the Sudan, 1932–40; a native of Rosetta, he was educated in Islamic law in Cairo and was appointed to the Sudan in 1912; he served as a provincial judge in the Islamic courts until 1916 when he returned temporarily to Egypt to fill a similar appointment at Ṭanṭā; returning to the Sudan in 1932 on his appointment as grand qāḍī, he retired from active legal duties in 1943 very shortly before his death at Ṭanṭā; he was a student of history and an authority on the teaching of Arabic in the Sudan.

* **Muḥammad al-Nūr wad Ḍaif Allāh** (–1809), historian; of the Faḍlīyīn branch of the Ja'līyīn Arab tribe, he lived at Ḥalfaiyat al-Mulūk; he was the author of an important work called *al-Ṭabaqāt wad Ḍaif Allāh* which he wrote about 1805 in robust, colloquial Sudan Arabic; the work consisted of a collection of biographies of Muslim saints in the Sudan; two editions, by Ibrāhīm Ṣādiq and Sulaimān Dā'ūd Mandīl, were published in Cairo, 1930; Sir H. A. MacMichael has a partial translation into English, with introduction and notes, in his *History of the Arabs in the Sudan* (1922); translated extracts by S. Hillelson will be found in *Sudan Notes and Records*, vols. vi and vii 1923–4.

Muḥammad Nūr al-Dīn (*fl. c.* 1830), official and landowner; originally a Coptic Christian, he came to the Sudan as secretary or accountant to 'Alī Khūrshīd Pasha, governor-general, and is said to have been converted to Islam by a holy man of Abū 'Ushar in the Jazīra; after retiring from the government service he acquired land in the Blue Nile valley, founded the villages of Kamlīn and Imāra wad Rāwa, and at Kamlīn owned an indigo factory.

Muḥammad Nūr Muḥammad (1855–1943), a Maḥasī worthy who claimed descent from the Naṣrāb; he was 'umda of Sonkī in Dār Sukkōt and was prominent as a cattle contractor to the government during the Nile campaigns of 1896–7; in 1913 he became blind and his son Muḥammad Muḥammad Nūr became 'umda.

Muḥammad Nuṣḥī Pasha (*c.* 1838–1903), liwā' of the Egyptian army; a Turk by birth, he was educated in Egypt and was then sent to Berlin to learn military science; on his return he was commissioned in 1860; he served in the Egyptian contingent attached to the Ottoman army in the Russo-Turkish war of 1877–8; promoted binbāshī, 1877, and qā'immaqām, 1883, he served in the Sudan from 1880, when he was on garrison duty in Khartoum till 1883, having during this time been promoted mīrālai; in 1884 he was shut up in Khartoum with C. G. Gordon Pasha, commanding the 1st battalion of the 5th infantry regiment; towards the end of the siege Gordon put him in command of a flotilla of government steamers which steamed down to Matamma and met the British column which had crossed the Bayūda in the vain hope of relieving the capital; he thereupon, with the rest of the ships' company, retreated to Dongola with the British army; promoted liwā', he retired from the army, 1885; he was president of a commission which sat in Egypt in 1887 to investigate the circumstances of the fall of Khartoum; he was later appointed amīr of the Egyptian annual caravan to Makka.

Muḥammad Qirdī (–1934), Fallātī notable; shaikh of the Fallāta at Sawākin where he died.

Muḥammad Ramlī Surūr (–1930), Abdullābī notable; 'umda of Wad Ramlī between Khartoum and the Sixth Cataract, and a magistrate; he died at Khartoum North.

* **Muḥammad Rāsikh Bey** (*c.* 1834–83), soldier and administrator; he was born at Ḥillat Yūnus near Berber; his father was a member of the Khūfāb family who inhabited the village; his real name was Muḥammad al-Ṭāhir; while a youth he went to Cairo to join his brother who was at al-Azhar University; in Cairo he attracted the attention of Prince Ḥaidar Pasha by whose help he received a primary education; the Egyptian Government then sent him first to Constantinople and then to Berlin to undergo a military education; he returned to Constantinople where he married a Turkish lady and picked up the name Rāsikh which he used henceforth; from there he went back to Egypt; his subsequent career was spent entirely in the Sudan; he was governor of Khartoum and Sennar, 1861–3, when Mūsā Pasha Ḥamdī, who had been made governor-general, requested his removal in favour of Aḥmad Bey 'Awad al-Karīm abū Sin; he seems to have been governor of Muṣawwa', 1868–71, deputy general manager of the Soudan railway, 1877, governor of Sennar, 1878–81, and governor of Sawākin, 1881–2; he is said to have died in Khartoum in the next year and to have been buried in the cemetery now in 'Abbās avenue; both the dates and appointments of his career are subjects of discrepancy.

Muḥammad Rātib Pasha (–1920), field-marshal of the Ottoman Empire and sirdār of the Egyptian army; a Circassian by origin, he received his military education in Cairo and afterwards in France; he was employed in Constantinople until about 1863 when he returned to Egypt; in 1864 he was promoted liwā' and in 1867 was appointed sirdār; the disaster to the Egyptian army which invaded Abyssinia in 1875 under the command of S. A. Arendrup Bey caused the Khedive Ismā'īl to dispatch a larger army under Muḥammad Rātib Pasha later in the year; this army, based as was Arendrup's on Muṣawwa', advanced into the highlands of the Hamasien where at Gura it was heavily defeated in March 1876; his American staff accused him of lack of co-operation and caprice, while he blamed the defeat on the Americans; the broken force retreated to Muṣawwaʿ; he continued to hold the sirdārship (with an intermission of one month late in 1876 when Prince Ḥasan superseded him) until 1879 when he was raised to field-marshal; he was minister of war and marine in Nubar Pasha's ministry in 1888.

Muḥammad Ra'ūf Pasha (*c.* 1832–88), liwā' of the Egyptian army and governor-general of the Sudan; he served in the equatorial province under Sir S. W. Baker Pasha and was commandant of the garrison of Gondokoro; he also saw service in Unyoro and Uganda; Baker had a poor opinion of his efficiency, but C. Chaillé-Long Bey wrote well of his administration at Gondokoro; he acted as governor of the Equatorial province between Baker's departure and Gordon's arrival, 1873–4, and was governor of Harar, 1875–8; in 1880 he succeeded Gordon as governor-general of the Sudan; a few months later, possibly persuaded by his deputy, Giegler Pasha, a bitter disliker of Italians, he removed R. Gessi Pasha, governor of the Baḥr al-Ghazāl, and G. B. Messedaglia Bey, governor of Dār Fūr, on charges of corruption, charges of which both were subsequently acquitted; in 1881 Muḥammad Aḥmad al-Mahdī proclaimed his mission and the government sought to arrest him at Abā island on the White Nile; he sent two ill-assorted missions to this end; the first was turned away, the second, using armed force, was massacred by the Mahdī's supporters at Abā; his failure to stem the rising tide of Mahdism caused his recall and replacement by ʿAbd al-Qādir Pasha Ḥilmī in 1882; while in office he built a mosque called after his name in Khartoum and evoked admiring envy by his skill at baccarat; he was one of a commission appointed for the trial of Aḥmad ʿUrābī Pasha and his fellow nationalists, 1882; he died at Mīnyā; he was said to be a Berberine on his father's side, and his mother (of whom he ever spoke with affection) was Abyssinian; he was a swarthy, handsome man.

Muḥammad Ṣādiq Yaḥya Pasha (–1944), Egyptian soldier; he served with Lord Kitchener in the cavalry during the Dongola and Nile campaigns, 1896–8; during the First World War he was for three years liaison officer to the governor of the Red Sea province and was decorated by the British Crown for his services during the operations in the Ḥijāz in 1916–17.

Muḥammad abū Ṣafīya. *See* ʿAbd al-Ṣamad abū Ṣafīya.

Muḥammad Saʿīd Pasha (1822–63), wālī of Egypt, 1854–63; a son of Muḥammad ʿAlī Pasha, he was educated by French tutors and came early under European cultural influences; on his accession to power he prohibited the importation of slaves into Egypt; he gave concessions for the construction of the Suez Canal, to the Eastern Telegraph Company, and to the Bank of Egypt, all three concessions having importance for the Sudan; he was prodigal of money and began the reckless floating of loans which his successor, Ismāʿīl Pasha, continued on a disastrous scale; the financing of the still-born expedition of Count

P.-H.-S. d'Escayrac de Lauture in 1856 to discover the source of the Nile alone cost him £500,000; he visited the Sudan in the winter of 1856–7 by way of Korosko and the Nubian desert; on his arrival in Khartoum he first contemplated the abandonment of the Sudan but later changed his mind and issued various edicts reorganizing the political framework of the government; he abolished the governorate-general and made each province mutually independent and directly responsible to the government in Egypt; he abolished the slave trade, standardized taxation, and appointed advisory councils to assess and collect taxes; he ordered the acceleration of communications with Egypt by the creation of a postal service and planned a railway from Wādī Ḥalfā to Khartoum; apart from the abolition of the governorate-general these measures were not carried out; he returned to Egypt over the Bayūda; in spite of his feckless nature he seems to have had a genuine affection for the black Sudanese troops whom he employed in his bodyguard.

Muḥammad Sa'īd Pasha Wahbī (–1883), liwā' of the Egyptian army; he is said to have been of Circassian origin; in 1872–3 he was a binbāshī in the eastern Sudan; in 1873–4 he served his first term as governor of Kordofan when the Khedive commended him for his work in passing troops and stores through his province for the conquest of Dār Fūr; in 1879 he was temporarily governor of Tāka when in the same year, on the recommendation of C. G. Gordon Pasha, then governor-general of the Sudan, he was promoted liwā'; in 1879 he was again appointed governor of Kordofan; in 1882 the forces of Muḥammad Aḥmad al-Mahdī were concentrating in the Nuba hills; he led a reconnaissance of government troops from al-Ubaiyaḍ which returned without having closed with the enemy; the Mahdist horde now came out of the hills and besieged al-Ubaiyaḍ where he commanded the garrison; after a stout defence and with the garrison reduced by hunger the town surrendered; he was taken prisoner with several other senior officers, and, suspected of treachery by the Mahdists, he was taken to 'Allūba and there killed.

Muḥammad ibn al-Saiyid 'Abd Allāh (–1883), Mahdist amīr, brother of Muḥammad Aḥmad al-Mahdī; he fought at the side of his more distinguished brother from the beginning of the latter's ministry and was present at the small battle with Egyptian troops at Abā island in 1881 and at Jabal Qadīr in 1882; he led the Mahdist army in the siege of al-Ubaiyaḍ and was killed in the assault on the town.

Muḥammad al-Saiyid al-Barbarī (–1946), merchant of Egyptian origin; he arrived in Sawākin from Suez in 1903 and was employed as a rivetter on the construction of the Red Sea railway; thereafter he engaged in trade, buying property in the new town of Port Sudan and progressively expanding his business interests; in the First World War the Sudan Government charged him with the supply of grain to the Ḥijāz; in his prime a magistrate, he was a connoisseur of pearls and precious stones and a liberal benefactor, building at his own expense the minaret of the Port Sudan town mosque.

Muḥammad Bey Salāma al-Bāz (*fl.* 1840–85), telegraph engineer; he was educated in the School of Engineering, Cairo, and then sent to England, 1847–55, to study mechanics; on his return he entered the telegraphic service of the Egyptian State Railways and from 1874 to 1878 was chief engineer of the telegraph between Aswān and Wādī Ḥalfā; in 1875–6, in consequence of the Khedive's complaints of interruptions on the Sudan telegraphs, he made an inspection of the Sudan lines; he was then transferred and replaced by E. A. Floyer, the future inspector-general of Egyptian telegraphs; of nationalist leanings, he was head of the Egyptian posts and telegraphs during the rising of Aḥmad ʿUrābī Pasha, 1882, and on this account suffered temporary dismissal; he was director of Sudan telegraphs in 1884–5; he was known as an efficient engineer and a fluent speaker of English.

Muḥammad Bey Salīm (1848–94), physician; he studied medicine in Munich, 1862–9; he later served as a medical officer with the Sudan garrisons and held various subsequent appointments in Egypt including a senior medical post in the Suez Canal administration.

Muḥammad Sālim (–1930), Kabbā<u>sh</u>ī chieftain; <u>sh</u>ai<u>kh</u> of the Dār Ḥāmid section of the Kabbābī<u>sh</u> tribe living in the district of Dongola.

Muḥammad Sanbū (–1919), West African fanatic; in December 1918 he persuaded some tribesmen of the Hadendowa Beja to attack Kassala; in the course of the attack some unresisting Egyptian troops were murdered; a force of the Eastern Arab Corps pursued and killed him.

Muḥammad al-Sanūsī (–1910), sultan of Dār Kūtī, having been installed by Rabīḥ Zubair before the latter moved his headquarters from Dār Fertīt to Bornu in 1890, hoping by this to keep open his communications with the Baḥr al-<u>Gh</u>azāl; Muḥammad got arms from the Crampel mission, massacred in 1891, then made an alliance with the French; on Rabīḥ's death in 1900 many of Rabīḥ's veterans transferred their allegiance to him until he had a standing army of 4,000 with which he raided for slaves and devastated the surrounding country; in December 1910, feeling French pressure, he prepared to seek a new capital in the mountains of Jallāb when he was shot in a small affray with a French detachment under Captain Modat.

Muḥammad ibn Sarḥān al-ʿŪdī, called **al-Ṣu<u>gh</u>aiyarūn** (*fl.* 1614), religious teacher, born on Tarnag island in the <u>Sh</u>ā'iqīya country, he professed ṣūfism and followed the teaching of <u>Sh</u>ai<u>kh</u> Idrīs ibn al-Arbāb; he is said to have performed miracles; at the invitation of Bādī abū Rubāṭ, master of the household to Sultan ʿAdlān I wad Aya of Sennar, he went south to al-Fijaija where the sultan gave him lands; here he built a mosque where he taught many pupils including some future famous men; he was buried at al-Qūz al-Mutraq, opposite the plain of Umm Wizīn; he was one of the great Islamic saints of the Sudan.

Muḥammad Bey <u>Sh</u>afīq al-Ḥaḍarī (1866–1940), Egyptian soldier; born at Maṣṭūr in Egypt, his father was chief engineer of the province of Manūfīya; he entered the army in 1884 and in the same year saw service at Sawākin in the Mahdist war; he was on the line of communications during the Nile campaign of 1884–5 and was present at the battle of Jinnis (Giniss), 1885; promoted binbās̲h̲ī, he served throughout the Dongola and Nile campaigns, 1896–9, and in the Nyima patrol, 1908; retiring with rank of qā'immaqām in 1918, he lived in Khartoum North where he died.

Muḥammad al-S̲h̲aikh (–1874), notable of the Ḥamar tribe of Kordofan; he was for long a leader of irregular Arab formations in the Egyptian service; he took part in the opening of the campaign for the invasion of Dār Fūr but died a few days after the Egyptian forces had begun the advance towards al-Fās̲h̲ar.

Muḥammad S̲h̲arīf Pasha (1823–87), statesman and soldier; born in Cairo of Circassian parentage, he was educated at al-K̲h̲ānka and afterwards pursued military studies in France; he married a daughter of Colonel Sève, the famous Sulaimān Pasha al-Faransāwī; a liwā' of the Egyptian army, he held many high civil appointments; under Ismāʻīl Pasha he was minister of foreign affairs; in September 1881 a military mutiny called for a new ministry; he became prime minister but resigned in February 1882; on the collapse of the ʻUrābī revolt he again headed a ministry in September 1882 and adopted a militant policy against Muḥammad Aḥmad al-Mahdī which culminated in the crushing defeats of Generals W. Hicks and V. Baker, 1883–4; in January 1884, believing that it was still possible to defeat the Mahdī, he and his ministry resigned rather than sign the Khedivial decrees for the evacuation and abandonment of the Sudan which had been drafted under pressure from the British Government; he died at Gratz and was buried in Alexandria.

❋ **Muḥammad al-S̲h̲arīf, K̲h̲alīfat al-Mahdī** (–1899), son-in-law of Muḥammad Aḥmad al-Mahdī who in 1881, at the outset of his mission, appointed him to represent ʻAlī ibn abī Ṭālib, the Fourth Caliph of orthodox Islam; he was at this time entering early manhood; he is said to have killed W. Hicks Pasha, commander of the Egyptian army at the battle of S̲h̲aikān (Kas̲h̲gil), 1883; he fought under a red flag during the siege of Khartoum, 1884–5; during the rule of the K̲h̲alīfa ʻAbd Allāhi he was kept in the background and never allowed much authority, though in 1889 he attempted without success to oppose the military dictatorship into which ʻAbd Allāhi had converted the Mahdī's religious state; in November 1898 he surrendered to the Anglo-Egyptian Government and with the Mahdī's sons, al-Bus̲h̲rā and al-Fāḍil, settled at S̲h̲ukkāba in the Jazīra; on the grounds that he was collecting a force, chiefly of Kināna, to rejoin the K̲h̲alīfa ʻAbd Allāhi then in Kordofan, the three were arrested at S̲h̲akkāba; while under arrest an attempt was made to rescue them; incriminating evidence having been produced, they were tried by court-martial and shot.

Muḥammad al-S̲h̲arīf Muḥammad Faqīr (1869–1947), Maḥasī notable who claimed ancient Arab descent; a refugee during the

Mahdist rule, he returned to his native district after the battle of Firka (Firket), 1896, and was appointed ʿumda of Koyeka in the qism of Sukkōt; his father (d. 1918) was ʿumda before him.

Muḥammad al-Sharīf Nūr al-Dā'im (–1908), religious notable; a descendant of Shaikh Aḥmad al-Ṭaiyib wad al-Bashīr who introduced the Sammānīya brotherhood into the Sudan, he taught in a village near Abā island on the White Nile where he expounded the Sammānīya way of life; Muḥammad Aḥmad al-Mahdī was at one time his pupil and was received into the Sammānīya brotherhood but afterwards transferred his allegiance to Shaikh al-Qurashī wad al-Zain who lived near Masallamīya; on the outbreak of the Mahdist revolt he supported the government, and General Gordon conferred on him the grade of pasha; he was taken prisoner by the Mahdists in the capture of Khartoum in 1885 but was honourably treated by the Mahdī whose service he now joined; after the Anglo-Egyptian occupation of Omdurman in 1898 he continued to live at the village of Shaikh al-Ṭaiyib near by till his death.

Muḥammad Sirr al-Khātim ʿAbbās (–1933), grandson of the renowned religious teacher Shaikh Muḥammad Badr al-ʿUbaid of Umm Dibbān; in 1920 he was appointed shaikh of the Masallamīya khuṭṭ and was a magistrate; he died at Umm Dibbān, the family seat.

Muḥammad Sirr al-Khātim al-Mīrghanī (–1917), eldest son of al-Saiyid Muḥammad ʿUthmān al-Mīrghanī I; on his father's death he carried on the latter's religious work in the Sudan and afterwards in Egypt where he died; late in 1883 he returned from Egypt to Sawākin to attempt to win over the revolting Beja tribes of the Red Sea hinterland to the cause of peace, but his efforts were unavailing; he was succeeded on his death by his son, al-Saiyid Muḥammad abū Bakr.

Muḥammad Bey Sulaimān (*c.* 1822–82), Sudanese officer in the Egyptian army which he joined, probably in the ranks, in 1846; he served as a sergeant-major and afterwards as a mulāzim and yūzbāshī in the Sudanese battalion in Mexico, 1863–6; promoted binbāshī on his return to Egypt, he was later promoted qā'immaqām and in 1877 commanded a regiment in Dār Fūr where he was officer commanding the town of Dāra; in 1879 he commanded the Egyptian troops at Qūlqūl and was killed in Dār Fūr at the beginning of the Mahdist revolt; he is said to have been a cultivated man of high character.

Muḥammad abū Suʿūd Bey al-ʿAqqād (–1881), Egyptian trader and official, born near Cairo of the noted trading family of al-ʿAqqād; he was at school with Muḥammad Ra'ūf, the future governor-general of the Sudan, and came to Khartoum when a young man to join the trading firm of al-ʿAqqād & Company of which his father-in-law, Muḥammad Aḥmad al-ʿAqqād, was head; on Muḥammad's death in 1870 Abū Suʿūd took his place in this concern which occupied a number of trading stations, leased from the government, in the Equatorial province; having a stake in the slave traffic, he opposed the mission of Sir S. W. Baker Pasha whom the Khedive Ismāʿīl had appointed in 1869 to the governorship of the Equatorial province with a mandate to destroy the slave trade; Baker found himself continually in conflict with Abū Suʿūd's agents until in 1873 he advised the government to arrest him and try him on a charge of slave trading; incriminating documents were sent by Baker to Cairo; Abū Suʿūd complained of Baker's high-handed action in ruining his business, and the prosecution was dropped; Baker's successor, Colonel (afterwards Major-General) C. G. Gordon Pasha, appreciating Abū Suʿūd's great local influence, appointed him lieutenant-governor of Gondokoro in 1874, but later in the year found him engaged in private trade and discharged him; he was appointed director of accounts in the central treasury in Khartoum in 1878; Muḥammad Ra'ūf Pasha, then governor-general, sent him on an errand to Abā island on the White Nile to attempt to persuade Muḥammad Aḥmad, who had not long before proclaimed his divine mission, to desist; the errand failed; he was then sent back to Abā with a force to arrest the Mahdī; the force was set upon by the Mahdī's followers and Abū Suʿūd barely escaped with his life to Khartoum where he found himself exposed to the anger of the relatives of the fallen soldiers; he died shortly after in circumstances which suggest poisoning.

Muḥammad al-Ṭāhir al-Majdhūb (1863–1930), Mahdist amīr; born at Sawākin the son of Shaikh al-Ṭāhir al-Ṭaiyib Qamar al-Dīn al-Majdhūb, he joined the Mahdist movement with his father and was for long the adviser of ʿUthmān abū Bakr Diqna (Osman Digna), commander of the Mahdist forces in the eastern Sudan, as well as qāḍī and muftī at ʿUthmān's headquarters; he was present at the battle of Omdurman when he surrendered to the victors; his later life was spent at Ḥamar Adaleib on the Atbara river where he was known for his learning and piety.

Muḥammad al-Ṭaiyib al-Baṣīr (–1908), Mahdist amīr and man of religion; he was a member of the Ḥalāwīyīn tribe of the Jazīra where he first met Muḥammad Aḥmad al-Mahdī; the Mahdī married his daughter and he became the Mahdī's chief agent in the Jazīra; he unsuccessfully attacked the Shā'iqī leader, Ṣāliḥ al-Mak, at Fadāsī in 1883, but made him prisoner at Masallamīya in 1884; after winning subsequent victories in the Jazīra he with his Ḥalāwīyīn tribesmen went north to the siege of Khartoum, 1884–5; after the fall of the city he served on the Abyssinian border and later in the northern Sudan under the amīr al-umarā' ʿAbd al-Raḥmān wad al-Najūmī from 1887; in 1898 he was in the region of Gedaref when he joined forces with the amīr Aḥmad Faḍīl; with Ahmad he retreated to the west after the defeat at al-Dākhila near Roseires and was captured by the Anglo-Egyptian forces near Renk; he died among his own people in the Jazīra.

Muḥammad Tāj al-Dīn al-Baghdādī, called **al-Bahārī** (*c.* 1520–*c.* 1600), holy man; he is said to have been born in Baghdad, to have made the pilgrimage to the Holy Places, and thence to have come to the Sudan about 1555, living at Wad al-Shaʿīr in the Jazīra where he married and lived for seven years; he was reputed to have travelled to Jabal Taqalī in the Nuba hills; he introduced to the Sudan the ṣūfist tenets of the Qādirīya brotherhood and was one of the great Islamic saints of the Sudan.

Muḥammad Tāj al-Dīn Ismā'īl (–1910), sultan of Dār Maṣālīṭ in western Dār Fūr, 1905–10, and uncle of Abū Bakr Ismā'īl al-Maṣālāṭī, his predecessor, who was defeated and captured by the forces of 'Alī Dīnār, sultan of Dār Fūr, 1905; he successfully raised a revolt against the Fūr; although 'Alī Dīnār had his captive, Abbukr Ismā'īl, killed, nevertheless the former proposed peace, and in 1907 peace was made; but now a more powerful opponent appeared; a French column under Captain Fiegenschuh entered Dār Maṣālīṭ but was destroyed by the inhabitants, 1909; an avenging French force under Colonel Moll was attacked and Moll killed, but the remainder of the beaten French column recovered, counter-attacked, and heavily defeated the Maṣālīṭ, killing Muḥammad Tāj al-Dīn; he was succeeded by Muḥammad Baḥr al-Dīn Abū Bakr, the eldest surviving son of Abū Bakr Ismā'īl.

Muḥammad Ṭalḥa (–1933), shaikh 'amm of the Baṭāḥīn of Abū Dilaiq in the Buṭāna between the Nile and Atbara rivers; he was succeeded on his death by his son Ṣiddīq (b. 1898).

Muḥammad Tawfīq Bey (–1884), qā'immaqām of the Egyptian army; although known as 'al-Miṣrī' (the Egyptian) he is said to have been of Cretan origin, though H. C. Jackson in his *Osman Digna* (1926) called him a Cretan Jew; educated in the French School in Cairo, he joined the army and was eventually promoted to qā'immaqām; his appointment as governor of Sawākin in February 1883 proved his worth; placed in command of a force opposing the Mahdist amīr 'Uthmān abū Bakr Diqna (Osman Digna) in the Red Sea hills, he defeated the Mahdists at Erkowit but was later shut up in Sinkāt; after a long siege, during which his small garrison was reduced to starvation, he and his troops tried to cut their way out of the town but were surrounded and killed after a desperate resistance; he was a cultured man and a good sportsman with the rifle.

Muḥammad Tawfīq Pasha, Khedive of Egypt (1852–92), son of Ismā'īl Pasha whom he succeeded on the latter's deposition in 1879; his reign was marked by foreign control of the country, the consequent rebellion headed by Aḥmad 'Urābī Pasha, 1882, and the evacuation and temporary abandonment of the Sudan, 1884–96; he relied largely on the advice of Sir E. Baring (afterwards Lord Cromer), British agent and consul-general in Egypt; in 1891 he inspected the Egyptian forces at Wādī Ḥalfā; he was succeeded on his death by 'Abbās Ḥilmī Pasha.

Muḥammad Tīrāb Aḥmad Bukr (–1785), sultan of Dār Fūr after his brother Abū'l-Qāsim Aḥmad Bukr; Browne, the English traveller, wrote that he earned the name 'Tīrāb' from his habit of rolling in the dust while a child; the son of Sultan Aḥmad Bukr Mūsā, he conquered the grandee Hāshim wad 'Īsawī al-Musaba'āwī in

Kordofan and drove him to the valley of the Nile; returning homeward, he died at Bāra after reigning for thirty years, 1752–85, in barbaric splendour; he is said to have devoted ten years of his reign to religion and study; on his death civil war broke out between rival claimants to the throne, but eventually his brother ʿAbd al-Raḥmān Aḥmad Bukr succeeded him.

Muḥammad al-Tūm Faḍl Allāh Sālim (*c.* 1868–1938), elder brother of Sir ʿAlī al-Tūm and the latter's right-hand man and envoy for many years; a jovial and warm-hearted man, he was affected by paralysis in old age.

Muḥammad Tūm Zubair (–1944), secular leader of the branch of the religious family of the Yaʿqūbāb who live near Sennar, a family founded by Muḥammad ibn Ḥamad, called Bān al-Nuqā (*fl.* 1550); he died at Sabīl village.

Muḥammad Tūtū (–1946), mak of the Moro hills and head of the southern Nuba administration.

Muḥammad ʿUmar al-Bannā (–1919), poet and man of letters; a Jaʿlī by origin, he was born at Rufāʿa where he studied religion, having as his teachers S̲h̲aik̲h̲s Ḥusain wad al-Zahra and Yūsuf wad Naʿma; he then completed his education at al-Azhar University, Cairo; one of the earliest followers of Muḥammad Aḥmad al-Mahdī, he was called to an official position at Omdurman where he became court poet to the K̲h̲alīfa ʿAbd Allāhi; after the Anglo-Egyptian occupation of 1898 he was appointed an Islamic judge and was afterwards an inspector of Islamic law courts; he died at Omdurman; he enjoyed a wide reputation in the Sudan for his verses and his literary virtuosity; a son, S̲h̲aik̲h̲ ʿAbd Allāh, was a lecturer in Arabic literature in Gordon Memorial College, Khartoum.

* **Muḥammad ibn ʿUmar ibn Sulaimān al-Tūnisī** (1789–1857), traveller to Dār Fūr and Wadāʾi; a member of a learned Tunisian family, his grandfather, Sulaimān (d. 1797), settled in Sennar where he married and had a son, Aḥmad Zarrūq; another son, ʿUmar, Muḥammad's father, studied at al-Azhar University, Cairo, and visited his father in Sennar and his relatives in Tunis where Muḥammad was born; ʿUmar settled in Sennar and afterwards in Dār Fūr where Muḥammad joined him in 1803; here Muḥammad was welcomed by the vizier, Muḥammad Kurra, and stayed for eight years; he then moved to Wadāʾi where he enjoyed the patronage of Sultan Ṣābūn; finally he left via Murzuk and Tripoli for Tunis where he arrived in 1813; after a short period he went on to Cairo; he served under Ibrāhīm Pasha as a regimental imām in the war in the Morea; in 1832 he was appointed to the staff of the School of Medicine at Abū Zaʿbal where he met Dr. A. Perron, the translator of the two books he wrote on his travels: that on Dār Fūr, entitled *Tas̲h̲ḥīd̲h̲ al-ad̲h̲hān bi sīrat bilād al-ʿArab wa'l-Sūdān*, was published by Perron in Paris in 1850, while a French translation by Perron had been published there in 1845 and an abridgement, by B. St. John, in London in 1854; the Arabic original of his

journey to Wadā'i (containing many references to Dār Fūr) has been lost; there is a translation by Perron (Paris, 1850); al-Tūnisī gave the world the first detailed description of Dār Fūr; his work is reliable but unmethodical.

Muḥammad 'Uthmān (–1934), nāẓir of the Missirīya Arabs of Dār Fūr; a magistrate.

Muḥammad 'Uthmān 'Abd al-Raḥmān al-Nūr (–1944), notable of the Inqarrīyāb in the neighbourhood of Berber and a relation by marriage of al-Saiyid Sir 'Alī al-Mīrghanī Pasha, present head of the Khatmīya brotherhood; he was 'umda of Artūlī where he died.

Muḥammad 'Uthmān Diglel (–1931), deputy nāẓir of the Banī 'Āmir round Tokar; he died at 'Aqīq.

* **Muḥammad 'Uthmān al-Ḥājj Khālid** (–1899), Mahdist amīr; born at Jabal Umm 'Alī of the 'Umarāb branch of the Ja'līyīn Arabs, the son of the pious Khālid Aḥmad al-'Umarābī, he was a young merchant when the Mahdist revolt broke out; the Khalīfa 'Abd Allāhi recognized his political talent and sent him as an envoy to the court of King Menyelik II of Abyssinia to negotiate a frontier settlement; the king gave him an Abyssinian lady for his wife; never a keen Mahdist, he threw in his lot with the advancing Anglo-Egyptian army in 1898 and later accompanied Kitchener to Fashoda; he died shortly after his return; his father, disconsolate at his son's death, survived him barely two years.

Muḥammad 'Uthmān Idrīs (–1929), shaikh of Tangasi between Dongola and Merowe; a Shā'iqī.

Muḥammad 'Uthmān al-Mīrghanī I, known as **al-Khātim** (1792–1853), one of the greatest religious leaders of the Sudan; founder of the Khatmīya Islamic brotherhood and the first member of his family to settle in the Sudan; born at al-Ṭā'if, he was educated at Makka and came to the Sudan from Egypt in 1817; at Bāra he lived for some time, married, and, among other children, begat al-Saiyid al-Ḥasan Muḥammad 'Uthmān al-Mīrghanī, his successor; he finally settled at Khatmīya, a village which he founded near Kassala in 1840 when the Turks set up an administration in the region; he also travelled to Muṣawwa'; he is said to have lent his great influence towards the pacification of the Sudan after the Turkish invasion of 1820–1; he returned to the Ḥijāz via Sawākin and Jidda and died in Makka; upon his death his eldest son, al-Saiyid Muḥammad Sirr al-Khātim, who carried on his father's work, went to Egypt and died there in 1917 when he was succeeded by al-Saiyid Muḥammad abū Bakr.

* **Muḥammad 'Uthmān al-Mīrghanī II,** called **al-Ṣughaiyar** (1819–86), head of the Islamic brotherhood of the Khatmīya; a son of al-Saiyid al-Ḥasan Muḥammad 'Uthmān al-Mīrghanī and a grandson of al-Saiyid Muḥammad 'Uthmān al-Mīrghanī I, founder of the brotherhood, he was called al-Ṣughaiyar to distinguish him from his grand-

father; he was a man of ability, active in forwarding the cause of the brotherhood, and much sought after as a mediator in disputes, a traditional role of the Mīrghanī family; in 1869 he succeeded his father as head of the brotherhood; during the opening phase of the Mahdist revolt, he strove hard in the cause of peace; he remained at Khatmīya until after the fall of Khartoum in January 1885, and his presence undoubtedly prolonged the resistance of the government garrison in Kassala; a friend of Gordon Pasha, he forwarded the pasha's letters to Egypt and left his own wife and daughter at Shendi to maintain his influence for peace in the Nile valley; the two ladies showed great courage and independence under the Mahdist rule; his exertions finally told on his health and he left Kassala a sick man convinced, as an orthodox Sunnī Muslim, that reconciliation with the Mahdist movement was not possible; for some time he was too ill to leave Sawākin, but finally arrived in Egypt where he had an audience with the Khedive Muḥammad Tawfīq Pasha; he died shortly after in Cairo; his two sons, al-Saiyid Aḥmad and al-Saiyid 'Alī, successively followed him in the leadership of the brotherhood.

Muḥammad 'Uthmān abū Qarja (–1916), Mahdist amīr, a Dongolāwī originally from al-Qiṭaina; he was a pilot of a river boat belonging to Ḥamad al-'Aqqād of the trading house of 'Aqqād & Co.; another source represents him as being a typical freebooter of the time, serving in the slave-raiding organization of Idrīs Abtar and at one time under Zubair Raḥma Manṣūr; he was one of the first adherents to the Mahdist cause and was a valuable leader in the Mahdī's battles in the Nuba hills, 1881–2; he played a leading part in the destruction of W. Hicks Pasha's army at Shaikān (Kashgil), 1883, in the fighting on the Blue Nile, 1883–4, and in the siege of Khartoum, 1884–5; appointed an amīr al-umarā' and supreme ruler of the Jazīra, he was now at the height of his power; he next saw active service with the amīr 'Uthmān abū Bakr Diqna (Osman Digna) before Sawākin; having quarrelled with 'Uthmān Diqna he now quarrelled with Aḥmad wad Hilū whom he replaced as leader of the Mahdist forces covering Kassala against the Italians; he was later recalled to Omdurman; implicated in the Khalīfa Muḥammad Sharīf's abortive revolt, he was banished to Rejaf where he remained a prisoner until his release by the Belgians on their occupation of the place, 1897; on the break-up of the Khalīfa's empire he made his way to Dār Fūr with the amīr Muḥammad Bey Khālid Zughal; here he lived at al-Fāshar whence he later returned to his home at Umm Ghanim on the White Nile where he became 'umda of the local Danāqla under the Anglo-Egyptian Government; illness prompted him to move to Omdurman where he died.

Muḥammad Yāsīn Muḥammad (–1883), shaikh al-mashāyikh of the Egyptian province of Kordofan, the last to hold that post; he was a member of an important Dūlābī family and came from Khūrsī; his father, Muḥammad Dūlīb, had held the post before him for many years; Mūsā Ḥamdī Pasha (governor-general of the Sudan, 1862–5) reorganized the local administration, the post of shaikh al-mashāyikh was suppressed, the duties distributed among four nuẓār, and Muḥammad Yāsīn was appointed a muʿāwin at the provincial headquarters at al-Ubaiyaḍ; here he was captured in the assault on the town by the Mahdists in 1883, deported to Shaqqa in Dār Fūr, and there killed on his arrival by Madibbū Bey ʿAlī, chief of the Rizaiqāt.

Muḥammad Yūsuf. *See* Cuzzi, Giuseppe.

Muḥammad Zain Ḥasan (*c.* 1873–1903), Mahdist amīr; born in Dār Taʿā'isha, he came to Omdurman as a boy and was made an assistant to the amīr ʿUthmān abū Bakr Diqna (Osman Digna) whom he accompanied to Gallabat and Sawākin where he saw much fighting; later, while still a youth, he was made an amīr and sent with a force of regular Mahdist infantry (jihādīya) and irregular Arab cavalry to Abū Ḥamad where in 1897 he put up a spirited defence against an Egyptian infantry brigade supported by artillery under the command of A. Hunter Pasha which had advanced along the Nile from Merowe; he was, however, quickly overcome, reinforcements from Berber having failed to arrive in time; he himself was taken prisoner and was a captive at Rosetta whence he was released in 1901; he died in Omdurman.

Muḥammad Zuhrī Pasha (1855–1915), farīq of the Egyptian army; born in Cairo, he attended the Paris exhibition of 1867; commissioned mulāzim II, he was posted to the general staff and served in the Egyptian contingent assisting the Ottoman army against the Russians, 1877–8; he entered the re-created Egyptian army in 1882 with the rank of ṣāgh qōl aghāsi and in 1885 served in the Nile campaign; in 1887 he was given the command of the 6th infantry battalion serving against the Mahdists on the southern frontier; promoted liwā', he was assistant adjutant-general in the Dongola and Nile campaigns of 1896–8.

Muḥyī al-Dīn al-Amīn (–1947), religious notable of the Khūjalāb, and descendant and khalīfa of Shaikh Khūjalī ibn ʿAbd al-Raḥmān ibn Ibrāhīm (d. 1743); his family was by origin of the Maḥas of Tūtī island off Khartoum; he died at Khartoum North.

Mukhtār ʿAwad Ḥāmid (*c.* 1846–1936), Jābrī notable; born at Zawrāt village near Dongola, his father was nāẓir of the government warehouse at Dongola during the Egyptian régime; sent to Egypt for his education, his father died, and he was sent back to the Sudan where C. G. Gordon Pasha employed him as a muʿāwin at the palace in Khartoum; the Mahdists took him prisoner and he was for some time under surveillance at Omdurman; released from custody, he returned to Dongola where about 1896 he entered the Egyptian intelligence service under F. R. Wingate Pasha who about 1900 sent him to Dār Fūr to carry a letter to Sultan ʿAlī Dīnār; about 1907 he was appointed ma'mūr ʿarab at Dongola and was later given the rank of ṣāgh; he retired in 1921 and died at Dongola.

Mukhtār Badrī Sharīf (*c.* 1877–1941), Maḥasī notable; born at Ṣuwārda, his father (d. 1896) was amīr of Dār Sukkōt during the *Mahdīya*; after the Anglo-Egyptian occupation of the region in 1896

Mukhtār became ʿumda of Ṣuwārda and later president of the majlis court.

Mukhtār ibn Muḥammad Jawdat Allāh (*fl.* 1670), holy man, born at al-Zalaṭa in northern Kordofan; he was killed by Junqul, sultan of the Musabaʿāt overlords from Dār Fūr, and his death was by some considered a martyrdom which led to divine repercussion on Junqul and his descendants.

Mukhtār Muḥammad Maḥmūd (–1947), physician; born in Kassala, he was educated at Gordon Memorial College and the Kitchener School of Medicine in Khartoum, graduating in medicine in 1929; he joined the Sudan medical service, being one of the first practitioners to graduate in the Sudan; a medical officer, then senior medical officer, he was appointed medical inspector in 1946; he took a serious but unostentatious part in public life; a great gardener, he won the Banksian horticultural medal in Khartoum in 1947; he died at Merowe.

Müller, Johann Wilhelm von, Baron (1824–60), Austrian consul-general in Central Africa; in 1847 he arrived in Egypt with A. E. Brehm, the German zoologist, as his secretary and companion; together they ascended the Nile valley to Dongola and Merowe and thence over the Bayūda to Matamma and Khartoum; from here they reached al-Ubaiyaḍ in May 1848, visiting Jabal Taqalī; they returned from Khartoum to Cairo in two boats provided by Khālid Khusraw Pasha, the governor-general; while on his way southward through Nubia he continued the surveys of A. von Prokesch-Osten as far as Dongola.

Mumtāz Pasha. *See* AḤMAD MUMTĀZ PASHA.

Munʿim wad Sālim al-Ṭaraishī (–*c.* 1830), tribal worthy of the ʿAsākira branch of the Ḥamar Arabs of Kordofan, founder of the greatness of the Ḥamar tribe; popularly known as al-Ḥājj Munʿim, for he made repeated pilgrimages to Makka, he was a born administrator; when the forces of Dār Fūr took al-Ubaiyaḍ in 1796 he accompanied them; he warred against the Zaiyādīya from Umm Badr and expelled them; he survived the occupation of the plains of Kordofan by the Turks in 1821 and by them was maintained as nāẓir of the ʿAsākira; on his death he was succeeded by his son Ismāʿīl wad al-Ḥājj Munʿim.

Munro, Patrick (1883–1942), British official of the Sudan political service which he joined in 1907; he was governor of Dār Fūr, 1923–4, and of Khartoum, 1925–9, when he retired; in 1931 he entered the British Parliament as member for Llandaff and Barry, South Wales, in the Conservative interest, and was a Junior Lord of the Treasury from 1937 till his death.

* **Munzinger Pasha, Johann Albert Werner** (1832–75), Swiss administrator and explorer; born at Olten in the canton of Soleure, he was the son of a deputy to the cantonal diet who later became president of the Swiss Confederation; he was educated at Berne, Munich, and Paris and finally in Cairo where he went to study Arabic; here he

joined a French trading concern which enabled him to visit Kordofan, Boghos, and the ports of the Red Sea; in 1861–2 he collaborated in T. von Heuglin's expedition in search of the lost German explorer, E. Vogel, who had disappeared in Wadā'i in 1856; leaving the expedition in northern Abyssinia, he explored the head waters of the Gash and Atbara, completing his tour in Khartoum, then regaining the expedition, he succeeded von Heuglin as its leader and made an unsuccessful attempt to enter Dār Fūr; in 1864 he was appointed French consul at Muṣawwaʿ in succession to G. Lejean, a post he held till 1870; French interests at this time being closely linked with the Roman Catholic missions in the interior, he went frequently to Keren to which place he became romantically attached, marrying a wife from the Boghos people and assuming Turkish dress and habits; after a short visit to Europe he returned to Muṣawwaʿ in 1865 as acting British consul (in addition to his French consulship) after Consul C. D. Cameron had been imprisoned by King Theodore of Abyssinia; he was later political assistant to Colonel Merryweather who made the preliminary survey for the British military expedition to Magdala, 1867; an unsuccessful attempt on his life was made in 1869; for some reason, perhaps because he was disappointed at the slowness of his advancement in the French service or because of a Germanic dislike of France at the opening of the Franco-German war, he left the French service and, after consulting Aḥmad Mumtāz Pasha, then governor of the eastern Sudan, entered the Khedivial service with grade of bey and in 1871 was appointed governor of Muṣawwaʿ; he at once began an aggressive policy towards Abyssinia; in 1873 all Egyptian territory from the Somali coast to the River Setit was combined in one province under his command and Sawākin was included within his boundary; as governor of the newly constituted province he was active in promoting telegraphs and railway surveys; the Khedive Ismāʿīl Pasha corresponded frequently with him and on occasion reproved him for wasting time on particular aspects of administration which the Khedive did not consider important; on the eve of the Egyptian-Abyssinian war he, his wife and child, his assistant G. A. Haggenmacher, and others, were killed by Somali tribesmen while leading an expedition through Aussa to join Menelik, governor of Shoa, against King John; he wrote *Ostafrikanische Studien* (Schaffhausen, 1864) and contributed various papers to geographical journals.

Muqbal al-ʿArakī (*fl.* 1540), wandering Sharīfī holy man from the Ḥaḍramawt who settled among a colony of ʿArakīyīn Arabs at Bīr Sirrār near Bāra; he married an ʿArakīya girl and by process of juxtaposition became the ancestor from whom not only the ʿArakīyīn but all the Rufāʿa Arabs now claim Sharīfī descent.

Murie, James (1832–1925), British naturalist and physician; born in Glasgow, he was pathologist to the Glasgow Royal Infirmary; a lively interest in zoology led to his joining J. Petherick, then British consul in Khartoum, as naturalist and medical officer in Petherick's journey to the Upper White Nile to meet the northward-bound explorers J. H.

Speke and J. A. Grant, 1861–3; he was present at Gondokoro when the two explorers arrived from Uganda, having discovered the source of the White Nile in Lake Victoria; he devoted the rest of his long life to medical practice and zoology on which latter he published many papers, mostly in the *Proceedings of the Zoological Society*, London; he died at Rochford, Essex.

Mūsā ʿAbd Allāh (*c.* 1870–1939), ʿumda of the Kawāhla in the valley of the White Nile; a brother of ʿAbd Allāh Jād Allāh, formerly nāẓir of all the Kawāhla, he came from Omdurman when young, was made ʿumda in 1922, and lived at Shiqaiq, near al-Duwaim.

Mūsā ʿAbd al-Rasūl (–1929), Fūr chieftain; shartai and magistrate of Jabal Sī, west of al-Fāshar in Dār Fūr; he died at Geldak village.

Mūsā Adam (–1896), Beja notable, shaikh of the Shīʿayāb; he was killed in battle by the Mahdists near Obo in the Red Sea hills when part of his tribe joined the Mahdist cause, though the remainder, including his own family, adhered to the government.

Mūsā Aḥmad Rijba al-Asʿad (–1931), ʿumda of the Ghulāmāb section of the Ḥasanīya Arab tribe of the White Nile, and a magistrate; he died at al-Qiṭaina.

Mūsā Bey al-ʿAqqād (–1867), Egyptian trader originally from Aswān; he was a brother of Muḥammad Aḥmad al-ʿAqqād with whom he was trading in partnership under the name of Agad [*sic*] & Co. of Khartoum, a firm which had important interests on the White Nile during the last twenty years before the Mahdist revolt.

* **Mūsā Pasha Ḥamdī** (*c.* 1810–65), governor-general of the Sudan, 1862–5, and mīrlivā of the Egyptian army; by origin a Circassian, he entered the Egyptian army and made his name in various campaigns in Syria and the Sudan; he appears to have been a junior officer in the fighting round Gallabat against the Abyssinians in 1837–8, and in 1844 was 1st adjutant to Aḥmad Pasha Manliklī (Mānliklī) in the war against the Beja in which he shared his leader's reputation for cruelty; sometime before 1851 he was governor of Kordofan when he led an expedition against Mek Nāṣir ibn Abbukr of Jabal Taqalī in the Nuba hills; in 1851 he was appointed deputy governor-general when he seems to have led a raid on the Ḥalanqa and the Shukrīya of the Buṭāna; he had returned to Egypt and was governor of Girga when in 1856–7 he accompanied Muḥammad Saʿīd Pasha, wālī of Egypt, to the Sudan; in 1862 he took office as governor-general following a reversal of Muḥammad Saʿīd's policy of provincial decentralization and the return to a more centralized administration involving the re-establishment of the governorate-general which had been abolished in 1857; shortly before his assumption of office he secured the removal of the governor of the combined province of Khartoum and Sennar, Muḥammad Rāsikh Bey, and the cutting up of this area into two separate provinces; one of his first acts as governor-general was to clear the Abyssinian border of the

incessant raids made into Sudan territory; he led a reconnaissance in force during the winter of 1862–3 to Dunkur while Egyptian detachments raided Wahni and the mountains of Wolkait, burning Mai Qubba on the Setit, the headquarters of the refugee Ja'līyīn under the son of Mak Nimr; in his internal policy he was less successful and his method of collecting taxes was resented by the people; he died of small-pox in Khartoum; his domed tomb is the westernmost of the two big tombs standing in 'Abbās avenue; his character has been the subject of dispute; T. von Heuglin called him energetic, experienced, and well disposed towards Europeans; his successor, Ja'far Pasha Ṣādiq, wrote that he was a drunkard and corrupt, J. Petherick, that he was a cruel monster, while, according to G. Lejean, he was the hangman of the Baqqāra and the chief slaver of the Sudan; all are agreed that he was a forceful character; he was a man of substance, owning lands in the Fayyūm; he is said to have been the first to introduce a carriage to Khartoum in which he rode preceded by runners in the manner of the pashas of Egypt; he was one of the few governors-general of the Sudan to attain the grade of Rumeli beylerbeyisi in the pashalik; Khōr Abū Nikhṣira or Nukhṣur is said to have got its name from the nickname given him by the Sudanese in reference to his big nose.

Mūsā Ḥāmid (–1932), shaikh of the Khasa clan of the Banī 'Āmir tribe on the borderlands between the Sudan and Eritrea.

Mūsā wad Ḥilū (–1885), Mahdist amīr, a member of the Daghaim Baqqāra Arabs of the White Nile; brother of the Khalīfa 'Alī wad Ḥilū, he came of a family of religious ascetics; he was serving in the Mahdist army before Khartoum, 1884, when he was given command of an army sent to oppose the advance of the British column coming over the Bayūda from Dongola; the two forces met at Abū Ṭulaiḥ (Abu Klea) where he was killed.

Mūsā Ḥinaitir (–1934), 'umda of the Ma'ālīya Arabs of Kordofan and a magistrate.

Mūsā Ibrāhīm (–1884), nāẓir of the Hadendowa who occupy the country between Sawākin and Kassala, nephew of Nāẓir Muḥammad Dīn who resisted the occupation of the delta of the Gash by the Turks; Aḥmad Pasha abū Widān in a raid on Tāka in 1840 captured young Mūsā and his uncle and sent them in chains to Khartoum; released about 1841 he took over the control of the tribe from his father and ruled for over forty years, consolidating the supremacy of the Hadendowa among the neighbouring tribes; the massacre of Beja chiefs by another governor-general, Aḥmad Pasha Manliklī, in 1844 ended open Hadendowa resistance to the government but did not weaken Mūsā's authority; he visited the Ḥijāz and Khartoum and went several times to Egypt; his relations with the government were on the whole correct, though he was occasionally imprisoned or flogged by the governors of Tāka; latterly he and his tribe became openly disaffected and became strong adherents to the Mahdist cause; but old age now overtook him and the practical leadership of the tribe passed to his son, Muḥammad Bey Mūsā Ibrāhīm.

* **Mūsā Madibbū** (–1920), head shaikh of the Rizaiqāt tribe of southern Dār Fūr; he succeeded his father Madibbū Bey 'Alī who was killed by the amīr al-Nūr Bey Muḥammad 'Anqara during the Mahdist rule; he was summoned to Omdurman by the Khalīfa 'Abd Allāhi who, when R. C. von Slatin Bey escaped to Egypt in 1895, imprisoned him as an old friend of Slatin's and a suspected accessory to his escape; he was not present at the battle of Omdurman in 1898, having fled that day with his family; while they were returning to their lands they were caught by the Missīrīya but were released after about a year; on his return to Dār Rizaiqāt late in 1899 'Alī Dīnār, sultan of Dār Fūr, did not immediately demand tribute but in 1900 ordered the Rizaiqāt to produce ivory; as this was not forthcoming he went to 'Alī Dīnār to explain the reason; 'Alī Dīnār, though his old companion of Mahdist times, threw him into prison and released him in 1901 only after he had handed over his slaves, arms, and most of his horses; he henceforward ignored the demands of the sultan who sent his general, Tīrāb Sulaimān, with an army against the Rizaiqāt who fled to the Baḥr al-'Arab and Dār Ḥumr; he and his people returned at the end of 1901; from now on his relations with the sultan were hostile and intermittent war continued till the fall of 'Alī Dīnār; on several occasions the Sudan Government tried without success to arrange a settlement between the disputants; he was a passive ally of the Sudan Government during the campaign of 1916; he was succeeded on his death by his son Ibrāhīm Mūsā Madibbū, the present nāẓir.

Mūsā Sulaimān (–1682), sultan of Dār Fūr; successor of Sultan Solon (or Solong), founder of the dynasty; he ascended the throne in 1637 and ruled till his death when he was succeeded by his youngest son, Aḥmad Bukr (or Bukkur) Mūsā.

* **Musā'd Jaidūn** (*c.* 1861–1934), tribal notable of the Riyāfa section of the Ḥabbānīya Arabs of Dār Fūr; born at Kalaka, he was educated in the khalwa of the Faqī Muḥammad 'Alī, father of the Khalīfa 'Abd Allāhi, at Minalkhairāt in Dār Rizaiqāt; he afterwards accompanied his teacher to Dār al-Jima'a west of al-Duwaim on the White Nile and later joined Muḥammad Aḥmad al-Mahdī at Jabal Taqalī in the Nuba hills, 1882; he followed the Mahdī to al-Ubaiyaḍ where he was present at the fall of the town, 1883; the Khalīfa 'Abd Allāhi made him a mulāzim; from Omdurman he went north where he served under the amīr 'Abd al-Raḥmān wad al-Najūmī; military duty then took him to fight the Italians in Eritrea; he was present at the battle of Ḥafīr, 1896; at the battle of Omdurman, 1898, he fought under the amīr 'Abd al-Bāqī 'Abd al-Wakīl, but afterwards, with Mahmūd 'Abd al-Karīm abū Sa'd and other Ḥabbānīya, he deserted the Khalīfa's cause at Umm Ruwāba; from 1899 until 1920 he remained a political prisoner in Omdurman and then returned to Kalaka with Maḥmūd 'Abd al-Karīm abū Sa'd when the latter was made nāẓir of the Ḥabbānīya; he himself was made 'umda of the Riyāfa section; he resigned in 1932.

Musā'd Muḥammad (1862–1936), notable of the Shanābla of the Jazīra, shaikh of the 1st khuṭṭ which includes Naiyīl, Amāra Ja'līyīn, and Fadāsī; he was a tax collector for the Mahdists; on the Anglo-Egyptian occupation he was made shaikh of the Shanābla khuṭṭ about 1901 and rendered valuable help to the government during the rising of ʿAbd al-Qādir Muḥammad Imām wad Ḥabūba in 1908; he was president of the local court from 1908 and a senior notable from 1929.

Musallam . . . (–1821), maqdūm (governor) of Kordofan on behalf of the sultan of Dār Fūr; he was of aristocratic Fūr birth and was reputedly good-looking; according to the manuscript of an unidentified, probably French, traveller to al-Ubaiyaḍ in 1825, he was caught in adultery with one of the sultan's wives and escaped castration only by blaming the woman who was thereupon blinded; the sultan ʿAbd al-Raḥmān Aḥmad Bukr sent him with an army to drive out the Musabaʿāt under Hāshim wad ʿĪsawī; this he accomplished about 1799 after great difficulty, compelling Hāshim to flee the country; he ruled Kordofan, justly according to some, with the help of his Kunjāra (Fūr) regular troops; he was defeated and killed by a Turkish army under Muḥammad Khusraw Daramalī, the daftardār of the Pasha of Egypt, at Bāra; his wife survived him, living quietly in al-Ubaiyaḍ.

Muṣṭafā Bey . . . (–1841), mīrlivā of the Egyptian army with grade of bey, and from about 1837 governor of Khartoum; in 1837–8 he led a slave-raiding expedition in the Nuba hills when he subdued the negroes of Jabal Shaibūn whose villages he burnt; he gave Prince H. L. H. von Pückler-Muskau, who met him in Khartoum, an account of Jabal Taqalī, its people, and institutions; he died of fever in Khartoum after returning from another tour in Kordofan and was succeeded by Mūsā Bey Ḥamdī, afterwards Pasha and governor-general of the Sudan.

Muṣṭafā Aḥmad al-Salāwī (–1885), judge, son of Aḥmad al-Salāwī, an Egyptian; his father came to the Sudan with the army of Ismāʿīl Pasha in 1821 as a muftī; on his death his son succeeded him in the judiciary; he became corrupt, changing the judges in the Sudan who failed to bribe him; aggrieved litigants complained to the viceroy, Muḥammad Saʿīd Pasha, during the latter's visit to Khartoum in 1856–7; he was imprisoned and deported to Egypt, but in 1862 was pensioned and allowed to return to Khartoum; in 1865 he was appointed qāḍī of Khartoum; he died, or was killed, in the siege of Khartoum by the Mahdists.

Muṣṭafā Ḥasan (*c.* 1852–1924), Jaʿfarī notable, ʿumda of the khuṭṭ of Shawwāl on the White Nile; he was employed for many years as firewood collector for the Sudan Government.

Muṣṭafā Pasha Kirīdlī (*fl.* 1840–50), Turkish governor of Cretan origin; he was raised to the pashalik in 1843 and from then till 1848 was governor of Kordofan with rank of mīrlivā; it is believed (but the evidence is uncertain) that he had already been governor of Kordofan from about 1833 to 1837 and mīrālai commanding the 1st infantry regiment, and that he had been governor of Sennar, 1837–40; accompanied by 400 bāshī-būzuq, 1,000 Ḥamar horse, and some Ḥawāzma

Arabs, he raided the Nuba hills in 1847; he resided for some time in Bāra, leaving his qā'immaqām at al-Ubaiyaḍ to transact the routine duties of government; J. Petherick draws a pleasant picture of him, then a little past the prime of life, as an old friend; according to Petherick, who probably got the story from him, he was kidnapped while a youth and sold into slavery in Egypt; he entered the army and won promotion in the Syrian war.

Muṣṭafā Muḥammad al-Maghribī (1842–1922), Tunisian merchant and camel contractor; born in Tunis, he owned a caravan of 100 camels which annually made the desert journey from Tunis to Dār Fūr and back, bringing silks and fezzes and taking in exchange ostrich feathers, ivory, and honey; unpopular with the French, who proclaimed a protectorate over Tunis in 1881, he settled in al-Fāshar, making several journeys to his former home; at the beginning of the Mahdist revolt he found himself shut up in al-Ubaiyaḍ and, on its fall early in 1883, became a follower of Muḥammad Aḥmad al-Mahdī and was later appointed chief clerk of the northern amīrate under the amīr Yūnus al-Dikaim; his opposition to what he considered the inordinate demands of the amīr 'Abd al-Raḥmān wad al-Najūmī, who was preparing his ill-fated expedition to Egypt, resulted in his imprisonment in Omdurman for three years; after the Anglo-Egyptian occupation he became a government contractor and was the first to introduce a steam-driven corn mill into the Sudan; he died at Omdurman.

Muṣṭafā Qalgham (*c.* 1856–1931), emissary and notable of Dār Fūr; a Takrūrī by origin, he was an officer in Sultan 'Alī Dīnār's forces and the husband of the sultan's sister, Mairam Tāja; before 1913 he was in command of the post of Jabal Ḥilla on the eastern border of the sultanate; holding no permanent command and having no great influence or power, he was sent on an embassy to Dār Sūla in 1915 to arrange a marriage between Ḥamza, one of the sultan's sons, and the daughter of Bakhīt Rīsha; absent at the time of the Anglo-Egyptian occupation, he joined 'Alī Dīnār after the fall of al-Fāshar, 1916; 'Alī Dīnār sent him as an envoy to mīrālai H. J. Huddleston Bey; he did not return and made his peace with the new government; in 1917 he became a government assessor and rendered valuable services in the early days of the Dār Fūr administration; a member of the al-Fāshar native court, he was highly esteemed by the people.

Muṣṭafā al-Subkī (–1860), physician; his origin is uncertain, but he was probably an Egyptian; he was sent from Egypt to study medicine in France, 1832–8; he specialized in ophthalmology and, on his return to Egypt, taught this subject in the School of Medicine, Cairo, until 1849 when he was transferred to Khartoum where Rifā'a Bey Rāfi' al-Ṭahṭāwī had been made headmaster of a new school; on the closure of this school in 1854 he returned with his chief to Cairo and in 1856 resumed his former duties at the School of Medicine.

Muṣṭafā Yāwar Pasha, Sir (–1914), liwā' of the Egyptian army; of Circassian origin, after receiving a good education he entered the army and, on the new viceroy, Ismā'īl Pasha, attempting to lessen the influence of the Mameluke class in Egypt, he was sent to the Sudan in 1864; on his arrival in Khartoum he was promoted yūzbāshī; from Khartoum he was posted to Kordofan where he was stationed for some years as a civil official; he is also said to have served in Sennar and Dār Fūr; in 1877 he was appointed governor of Khartoum and was later transferred to the combined governorate of Berber and Dongola; in December 1883, shortly before the arrival of Gordon Pasha in the Sudan, he was removed in favour of Ḥusain Pasha Khalīfa who had already been governor in 1871–3; Ḥusain Pasha, however, capitulated to the Mahdists at Berber in May 1884 and he was reinstated; the rising tide of Mahdism having overflowed into his province, he fought several battles against the Mahdist forces in which the amīrs Aḥmad al-Hūdai and Maḥmūd Muḥammad were killed at Kūrtī in September 1884; on the arrival soon after of the British column on its way to attempt the relief of Khartoum, he rendered valuable services on the line of communications for which he was knighted by Queen Victoria; when the Dongola province was in process of being evacuated by the retreating British column he returned to Egypt, his place being taken by his deputy, Jawdat Efendi (later Bey); his departure was hastened by the opinion of the British commander-in-chief, Lord Wolseley, that he was obstructive; Wolseley also wrote of him as energetic, pious, and incorruptible; he died in retirement in Egypt.

Mutesa I (*c.* 1839–84), kabāka of Buganda; he came to the throne in 1857 while a youth and proved a capable ruler, maintaining his state intact at a time when the first Europeans were coming among his people; in 1861 he invited the British explorers J. H. Speke and J. A. Grant, who had discovered the source of the White Nile, to visit Buganda where they arrived in 1862; he at first welcomed Sir S. W. Baker Pasha when the latter sought to establish an Egyptian protectorate over Buganda in 1872, but fighting soon broke out between the soldiers of both sides and Baker withdrew to Foweira; when C. G. Gordon Pasha, Baker's successor as general governor of the Egyptian Equatorial province, arrived in Gondokoro to take up his duties in 1874 he found a messenger from Mutesa with letters; Gordon sent his officer, C. Chaillé-Long Bey, with a friendly message to Mutesa whom Chaillé-Long got to sign an undertaking accepting Egyptian protection; in 1875 Mutesa entertained H. M. Stanley who was on a journey across Africa from east to west; he obstructed Gordon's attempts to extend the Egyptian sway over his lands; he was at first favourable to the establishment of Christian missions possibly as a counter-balance to Egyptian political influence, but his enthusiasm later cooled; on his death he was succeeded by his son Mwanga (*c.* 1866–1903); the present kabāka, Mutesa II, is his great-grandson.

Muzzi Bey, Giacomo (1822–   ), Italian postal official in the Khedivial service; he came from Bologna to Egypt in 1846 and was associated with T. Chini in a private postal company in Egypt, the Posta Europea, which had a monopoly guaranteed by the State; in 1864 he proposed to Ismā'īl Pasha the introduction of postage stamps, the first issue of which appeared in 1866; in 1865 the Egyptian Government took over the Posta Europea and he was appointed director-general of the Egyptian Postal Service, a post which he held till 1876 when he was succeeded by A. Caillard Pasha (1876–9), who was himself succeeded by W. F. Halton Pasha (1879–87); Muzzi's colleagues, L. Santoni, C. Addà, J. Lumbroso, S. Mei, and Giegler (afterwards Pasha), played an important part in the development of postal and telegraphic services in the Sudan.

Mwanga (*c.* 1866–1903), *kabāka* of Buganda; a son of Mutesa I, he reigned intermittently, 1884–97, when he was finally deposed; in 1885 he invited Roman Catholic missionaries from the south to settle in his Buganda but afterwards turned against all foreigners, killing Bishop J. Hannington and many of his own people who were Christian converts; in 1888 he determined to destroy all Christians and Muslims but failed; deprived of the support of his people, he fled to join some Arab traders to the south of Lake Victoria; returning to make a bid to regain his throne, he was unsuccessful and took refuge in German East Africa but escaped thence and joined Kabarega, the *mukāma* of Bunyoro; he was captured by the British in 1899 and deported along with Kabarega to the Seychelles where he died; his remains were buried in Buganda in 1910; he was succeeded by Sir Daudi Chwa II who reigned 1897–1939.

Myers, Arthur Bowen Richards (1838–1921), British surgeon; born at Tenby, he joined the Army Medical Corps and in 1883 was assistant surgeon in the Coldstream Guards; he accompanied a big-game hunting trip by some officers of the Guards to the country of the River Setit and the Ḥamrān, 1874–5; he wrote *Life with the Hamran Arabs . . . a Sporting Tour* [*&c.*] (1876).

Nachtigal, Gustav (1834–85), German explorer; in 1869 he was sent on a mission to the sultan of Bornu; thence he travelled through Wadā'i, Dār Fūr, and Kordofan, arriving in Khartoum, 1874; he later took part in explorations in Togoland and the Cameroons on behalf of the German Government; he died at Cape Palmas; his *Sahara und Sudan* (Berlin and Leipzig, 1889) contains an account of Dār Fūr on the eve of its occupation by Egypt.

Na'īm . . . (–1812), Rubāṭābī robber of Mughrāt near the present village of Abū Ḥamad; he attained great riches by robbing caravans crossing the Nubian desert; he thus drew upon himself the anger of the 'Abābda, the traditional lords of the Nubian desert road, who killed him in his lair; it is said that his head was carried to Egypt and his ears sent to the viceroy Muḥammad 'Alī Pasha who was then in the Ḥijāz.

Na'īm 'Abd Allāh al-Kirail (1884–1940), 'umda of the Muḥammadīya branch of the Kawāhla Arabs of the White Nile; born at Wad Kirail in the neighbourhood of al-Duwaim of a well-known family, he helped the government in quelling the rising of 'Abd al-Qādir Muḥammad Imām wad Ḥabūba in the Jazīra in 1908.

Na'īm Surkattī (1870–1940), notable of the Rikābīya section of the Duwālīb tribe of Kordofan and nāẓir of the northern hills; he took only a small part in the Mahdist revolt; the Khalīfa 'Abd Allāhi fined and imprisoned him for suspected sympathy with the pro-government Kabābīsh; taken prisoner to Omdurman, he was eventually released; after the fall of the Khalīfa's régime in 1898 he collected the scattered Nuba people of the region; when al-Ubaiyaḍ was reoccupied he was employed by the new government to settle disputes between the Koja Nuba and afterwards naturally assumed the leadership; on the opening of the court of the northern hills in 1936 he was made its president; he died at al-Sōdarī.

al-Naiyīl (–1554), sultan of the Funj, son of 'Umāra Dūnqas who founded the dynasty; he reigned from 1543 till 1554, succeeding his brother, Sultan 'Abd al-Qādir, and being himself succeeded by Sultan 'Umāra abū Sakaikīn; his reign is said to have been peaceful.

al-Naiyīl Zain al-'Ābidīn (–1935), 'umda of Ṣarrāf between Gedaref and Gallabat; by race he was a Mīmāwī (the Mīma are possibly a combination of Tawāriq and Dār Fūr negro elements) and he ruled a community of western Sudanese; he died at Ṣarrāf.

Nanna wad 'Abd al-Raḥmān Ḥamad (*fl.* 1650), Bidairī holy man of the Awlād Turābī, brother of the better-known Ḥamad al-Naḥlān ibn Muḥammad, known as Wad al-Turābī; he was a follower of Shaikh Idrīs Muḥammad Arbāb; said to have lived 150 lunar years, he has a prominent tomb at Hilālīya on the Blue Nile.

Nāṣir ibn Abbukr (*c.* 1801–*c.* 1865), mak of Taqalī in the Nuba hills who reigned 1844–59; the eldest surviving son of Abū Bakr ibn Ismā'īl (1773–1814), he tried to wrest the throne from his uncle, al-Mariut ibn Ismā'īl, but was unsuccessful and fled to Khartoum where he convinced the government that he was the rightful king; according to another account he was captured in the Nuba hills in a raid by Muṣṭafā Pasha al-Kirīdlī, governor of Kordofan, 1843–8, and promised Muṣṭafā that, if he were released and troops placed at his disposal, he would take Taqalī and pay tribute to the government; he returned to Taqalī and killed Mariut, but, instead of acting on his word, settled the black troops of his Egyptian allies in the enjoyment of lands and wives at Taqalī and killed their officers; he paid no tribute and successive governors of Kordofan tried in vain to dislodge him; in 1858, for example, he ambushed and massacred a punitive expedition commanded by 'Uthmān Bey al-Sinnārī; the government thereafter left Taqalī alone; Nāṣir, virtually independent, grew in power and several of the surrounding Arab tribes paid tribute to him; power made him a tyrant and his people became hostile to him; about 1864 his nephew, Adam Daballū, seized the throne and he fled to Khartoum where he had no difficulty in making his peace with the government, offering a gold chain as an act of surrender; possibly over-estimating his political value, Shāhīn Pasha Kinj, then on a tour of inspection to the Sudan, led him in triumph to Egypt in July 1864 and Ismā'īl Pasha gave him a sword and robe; Count R. du Bisson, in a somewhat spiteful reference, suggested that his surrender and the consequent fuss were fabricated by Mūsā Pasha Ḥamdī, then governor-general, for his own greater glory; Nāṣir returned to the Sudan at the end of the year and was given land at Ma'tūq in the western Jazīra where he shortly afterwards died; a man of great physical strength, many stories are told of his cruelty.

Nāṣir ibn Bādī IV (–1768), sultan of Sennar, brother of Ismā'īl who succeeded him; he himself succeeded his father, Bādī IV abū Shilūkh, who had been deposed by the Hāmaj vizier, Muḥammad abū'l-Kailak Kamtūr; he ruled from 1761 till 1768 when the vizier deposed and exiled him; he attempted to revolt, failed, and was killed; he was said to have been a learned man.

Nāṣir Ibrāhīm al-Mak (1856–*c.* 1910), Jamū'ī notable; born near Jabal Ḥinaik, the tribal seat, he took over the rule of the tribe from his brother, the nāẓir Sulaimān Ibrāhīm, during C. G. Gordon Pasha's first governor-generalship (1877–80); during the Mahdist régime he was made amīr of his tribe in 1884 and later served with his men under Ḥamdān abū 'Anja in the Abyssinian wars; at Omdurman in 1898 he fought under the green banner; the new government confirmed him in his post of 'umda of the Jamū'īya about 1899.

Nāṣir al-Makkī (–1933), Shā'iqī notable, 'umda of the rural areas of Shendi; 'Uthmān Nāṣir, shaikh of Muwais, is his son.

Nāṣir Muḥammad al-Amīn (*fl.* 1790–1821), manjil or viceroy of Ḥalfaiyat al-Mulūk, ruling under the nominal authority of the puppet sultan of Sennar but actually under the Hāmaj vizier Idrīs wad Muḥammad abū'l-Kailak who, after killing Shaikh 'Abd Allāh wad 'Ajīb al-Fīl in 1799, placed him in power; his father had been killed by the partisans of Shaikh 'Abd Allāh in 1790; he surrendered to Ismā'īl Pasha on the latter's arrival at Ḥalfaiya in May 1821.

Nāṣir wad Muḥammad abū'l-Kailak (–1798), son of the great Muḥammad abū'l-Kailak, vizier of the Funj sultans of Sennar; like his father, he was a king-maker; he occupied Sennar in 1788 and was killed in a faction-fight at Abū Ḥarāz where he was buried; the chronicler recorded that he was generous but unjust and latterly grew luxury-loving.

Nāṣir wad Nimr Bishāra (–*c.* 1897), nāẓir of the Ḥasanīya and Ḥusaināt of the White Nile and a member of the ruling house of the Ḥasanīya; his father, who was nāẓir in Turkish times, was imprisoned and his office was thereupon sold to the highest bidder; he succeeded to the headship of the tribe after a relative, 'Alī Miraimī, had been dismissed by the Khalīfa 'Abd Allāhi; about 1889 he accompanied the Mahdist army fighting round Gallabat while Idrīs al-Ḥabbānī remained at home as his deputy; he and 'Alī Miraimī were killed in a fight with Hawāwīr raiders.

Naṣr al-Dīn Baḥr (–1938), Fūr notable of the Kunjāra branch, and a member of the celebrated house of Baḥr; he was nāẓir of the central khuṭṭ of the district of Gedaref where he died.

Naṣr al-Dīn abū'l-Kailak (1761–c. 1837), mak of Berber; by tribe a Mīrafābī, about 1814 he went to Arabia to take a consignment of horses to the army of Muḥammad 'Alī Pasha then fighting the Wahhābites; the hereditary mak was 'Alī wad Timsāḥ, his nephew from whom he had usurped the power; during his absence in Arabia the forces of Shendi seized Berber and placed 'Alī wad Timsāḥ in authority as mak; he had no option but to remain with Muḥammad 'Alī Pasha with whom he went to Egypt where he stayed until the invasion of the Sudan by Ismā'īl Pasha in 1820–1; he accompanied the invading army and Ismā'īl Pasha installed him as kāshif of Berber while the deposed 'Alī wad Timsāḥ was executed at Sennar in 1822 for conspiracy; G. B. English, Ismā'īl's commander of artillery, described him as a very tall, big man; his son, 'Abd al-Mājid Naṣr al-Dīn, was a Mahdist amīr; there is a portrait in G. A. Hoskins, *Travels in Ethiopia* (1835).

Nāṣra 'Adlān (*c.* 1810–*c.* 1852), daughter of 'Adlān Muḥammad abū'l-Kailak, the Hāmaj chieftain, and brother of Idrīs wad 'Adlān, shaikh of the Funj mountains; she married Muḥammad Dafa' Allāh Aḥmad of Ṣūraiba who became an important shaikh in the Jazīra; on account of her royal descent she retained the title of sultana; she was said to have been dignified and regal in manner and to have had considerable local authority; the women of her household provoked the censure of some visitors and satisfied the desires of others.

Nastasen (*fl. c.* 315 B.C.), king of Kush, crowned at Napata (Jabal Barkal) but ruling from Meroë; he was the last of the line of Napatan kings founded by Alara and Kashta, and the last king to be buried at Nūrī; the story of his coronation, journey northwards and skirmishes with local tribes, shows that the effective northern boundary of his kingdom was at the Third Cataract; this is the last known, long historical account of a Sudanese king written in Egyptian hieroglyphic; it was written on a stela originally set up at Jabal Barkal but found in 1853 by W. von Schlieffen at New Dongola; this king was formerly dated some 200 years earlier owing to the supposed identity of a name in his inscription with that of the Persian king Cambyses II.

Nathan, Sir Matthew (1862–1939), British soldier and colonial governor; he entered the Royal Engineers in 1880 and served in the Nile campaign of 1884–5, drawing up a careful report on the Soudan railway which ran from Wādī Ḥalfā southward to Sārras; he afterwards held various governorships in British possessions abroad.

Natterer, Josef (*c.* 1820–62), Austro-Hungarian vice-consul at Khartoum, 1860, and a strong opponent of the slave trade; born in Vienna, the nephew of the naturalist Johann Natterer, he inherited the family love of science; in 1848 his energy prevented the wrecking of the Vienna natural history museum by the revolutionary mob; in 1855 he started on his travels to Nubia and the Sudan, returning in 1858 with a collection of animals and birds for the Schönbrunn menagerie; after a short while he returned to the Sudan, having been appointed vice-consul at Khartoum in place of T. von Heuglin; he wrote to his relatives that he had made a fortune by speculation and intended to return to Europe to devote himself entirely to science, but he died of fever in Khartoum; in 1867 his brother Johann, a pioneer of daguerrotype, caused to be erected in the cemetery of the Roman Catholic mission at Khartoum a memorial plaque surmounted by the figure of an angel which evoked superstitious awe from the heathen; he was succeeded in the vice-consulate by M. L. Hansal.

Naubonnet, Émilienne (1819–77), French religious sister of the Roman Catholic Church; a native of Pau, she joined the Order of St. Joseph of the Apparition and after long experience in Cyprus and Syria came to the Sudan in 1875 as provincial mother superior; she was stationed at the new mission house at Dilling in the Nuba hills and afterwards died in Khartoum.

* **Na'ūm Bey Shuqair** (1863–1922), Syrian official in the service of the Egyptian and Sudan Governments; born at Shwaifat in the Lebanon of a Syrian Orthodox Christian family having among its members Sir Sa'īd Pasha Shuqair, he graduated from the Syrian Protestant College (afterwards the American University), Beirut, in 1883; emigrating to Egypt, he joined the Nile expedition in 1884 and was in the service of the army on the frontier of the Sudan until 1887; he was in the intelligence department of the Egyptian army, 1890–1900, when, on the transfer of the department to the Sudan Government, he was appointed director of the historical section, an office which he held till his death; he accompanied the sirdār, H. H. Kitchener Pasha, on inspections of the frontier in 1890 and 1893 and to Sawākin in 1891 and 1892; he was present at the battle of Tokar, 1891; he assisted in the escape of R. C. von Slatin Bey from Omdurman and was himself created a bey; as a member of the intelligence department, he was at the battles of Firka and Ḥafīr (1896) and Omdurman (1898); in 1905 he was sent on a mission to Sinai in connexion with a frontier dispute with Turkey and was a member of the Sinai boundary commission; he was again in the Sudan in 1906 for the opening of the Red Sea railway and in 1909 for the opening of Port Sudan harbour; he rendered valuable services to the Allies in the First World War; he wrote a history of the Sudan in Arabic entitled *Tārīkh al-Sūdān* (Cairo, 1903), an indispensable work based on native authorities and his own vast experience of the recent history of the country; he also wrote a history of Sinai (1916) and several smaller works including a collection of Arabic proverbs.

Nawwār (–1790), puppet sultan of Sennar; he reigned for a short period in 1790, succeeding another puppet named Ḥasab Rabbu, or Rabbihi; his death in Sennar was attributed to the powerful Hāmaj vizier Nāṣir wad Muḥammad abū'l-Kailak who feared his ability; he was followed by Bādī VI wad Tabl II, the last of the sultans of Sennar.

Nehi (*fl.* 1460 B.C.), Egyptian viceroy of Ethiopia during the reigns of Hatshepsut and Thothmes III of the XVIIIth Dynasty; he held office about 1500–1435 B.C.

* **Neufeld, Karl** (1856–   ), German merchant, born at Fordon near Bromberg; he came to Egypt in commerce and in 1887 accompanied a convoy of arms from Egypt for the Kabbābīsh with the intention of making easy money by buying gum arabic; leaving Wādī Ḥalfā for the south, he was captured in the Wādī al-Qa'ab west of Dongola by the Mahdists and sent to Omdurman where he was held a captive, often in chains, until his release by the Anglo-Egyptian army after the battle of Omdurman in 1898; while a prisoner he married an Abyssinian lady called Umm Shūl; he returned to the Sudan after the occupation and later set up as a tourist agent in Aswān; in 1914 he returned to Germany on the outbreak of the First World War; he married an Englishwoman, the daughter of a Norwich tailor, in 1880; his subsequent fate is unknown; his book, *A Prisoner of the Khaleefa* (1899), describes his experiences in the Mahdist grip.

Newbold, Sir Douglas (1894–1945), civil secretary, Sudan Government; educated at Oxford University, he entered the Sudan political service in 1920 after four years' active service in the First World War, of which he spent three years in the Near East; in 1923 he carried out his first desert exploration, from northern Kordofan to Bīr Naṭrūn; in 1927, with W. B. K. Shaw, he continued the exploration from Bīr Naṭrūn northward to the oases of Nukhaila and Salīma, in a vain search for the fabled oasis of Zarzūra, reaching the Nile at Wādī Ḥalfā; his third journey was undertaken as a member of an expedition led by Major (afterwards Brigadier) R. A. Bagnold in 1929–30 from Baḥrīya oasis to Jabal 'Uwaināt and on to Wādī Ḥalfā; appointed governor of Kordofan in 1933 and civil secretary in 1939, he died in Khartoum; his contributions to the geography of the Libyan desert were published in *Sudan Notes and Records* (Khartoum), vii, 1924; xi, 1928 (jointly with W. B. K. Shaw), and in *The Geographical Journal*, lxxviii, 1931.

Newbolt, Sir Henry John (1862–1938), British barrister, author, and poet; of his poems two have the Sudan as their theme: 'Vitaï Lampada' and 'The Nile'.

Newcombe Bey, Edward Osborn Armstrong (1874–1941), British major of the Royal Engineers and railwayman; commissioned in 1893, he served in the Egyptian army in the Dongola and Nile campaigns, 1896–9, and in the South African war, 1899–1902; he held the post of traffic manager, Sudan Railways, 1906–26, broken by service in the First World War, 1914–17; he retired from the British army, 1912, and from the Sudan civil service, 1926; he was one of a small body of Royal Engineers who played a great part in the development of railways in the Sudan.

Nhial Acuol (–1935), head chief of the Luac Dinka in the swamp region of the Upper White Nile; he was a magistrate.

Nickerson Bey, George Snyder (1873–1911), British captain in the Royal Army Medical Corps; commissioned in 1898, he joined the Egyptian army and served in the campaign against the Khalīfa 'Abd Allāhi in Kordofan, 1899; promoted captain in the British army, 1901, he entered the Sudan Government service, 1905, and from 1909 till his death was governor of Sennar; he was killed by a fall from his horse at Sinja.

Nikolaos (*c.* 1874–1939), Greek Orthodox bishop of Nubia; born at Yanina in the Epiros, he was bishop of Nubia, 1919–26, when he transferred to the bishopric of Hermopolis (Ṭanṭā); he afterwards became Patriarch of Alexandria.

Nilis, Théodore (1851–1905), soldier and explorer in the service of the Congo Free State; born at Brilow, Westphalia, he joined the Congo service and in 1893 commanded an expedition which travelled north along the Nile–Congo divide towards Ḥufrat al-Naḥās; a flood in the River Adda, a western tributary of the Baḥr al-ʿArab, and a threatened Mahdist attack from the north, prevented him from reaching his goal; he died at Ixelles, Belgium.

Nimr ʿAlī Julla (–1924), nāẓir of the Ajaira branch of the Ḥumr tribe of Kordofan who dwell in the region of Mujlad; he and his father ʿAlī, later nāẓir ʿumūm of the Ḥumr, were both mulāzimīn to the Khalīfa ʿAbd Allāhi; his son Bābū (ʿUthmān) ʿAlī Julla rules the combined Missīrīya and Ḥumr under the name of the nāẓirate of the Missīrīya.

Nimr Muḥammad Nimr (*c.* 1785–*c.* 1846), last of the Jaʿlī kings of Shendi; he had a stormy youth among the chaos which accompanied the bloody Hāmaj domination over the decaying sultanate of Sennar; he spent part of his boyhood as an exile among the Baṭāḥīn, returned to Shendi, and won his way to power when he was made mak about 1802, having been recognized as heir since about 1795; he submitted with a bad grace to Ismāʿīl Pasha when the Turkish army reached Shendi in 1821 on its way to Sennar; in 1822 he assassinated Ismāʿīl and his staff at Shendi and fled to the Buṭāna; Muḥammad Khusraw Daramalī the Daftardār, hastening from Kordofan with a punitive force, ravaged the country of the Jaʿlīyīn and routed him and his allies in battle at Naṣūb near Abū Dilaiq; he fled with his followers to the Setit where they formed a buffer state in relation with the king of Tigrai and with Sōfī as their centre; he was excluded from the general amnesty of ʿAlī Khūrshīd Bey in 1829; as his power declined he moved farther into the mountains, to Mai Qubba on the Baḥr al-Salām, and collected a band of desperadoes who impartially attacked Turks and Abyssinians and interrupted the Gondar–Sennar trade route; in 1832 the Turks occupied Gallabat and curbed his raiding range; in 1834 his followers, aided by Abyssinians, attempted in vain to raid Sennar; he paid a secret visit to Shendi about 1840 hoping to find buried family treasure, but without success; by 1844 he was decrepit and blind, and his son ʿUmāra wad Nimr carried on the struggle against the Turks; the bedraggled remainder of the Nimrāb were finally amnestied by Ismāʿīl Pasha and returned to Shendi about 1865.

Norden, Friderik Ludvig (1708–42), Danish sailor and traveller; born at Glückstadt, he graduated as a naval lieutenant at Copenhagen,

1732; afterwards promoted captain, he served in the British navy as a volunteer and was elected a member of the Society of Arts, London; after several years of touring in Europe he left for Egypt in 1737 with an order from the Danish Government to draw monuments; he ascended the Nile as far as al-Dirr in Nubia, being hindered from going farther by the hostility of the inhabitants; he returned to Cairo in 1738; his *Voyage d'Égypte et de Nubie* (Copenhagen, 1752–5) has been translated into English and German.

Northcote Bey, Cecil Stephen (1878–1945), British major; he was seconded from the Egyptian army to the Sudan Government service in 1912, he was governor of Mongalla province, 1918, and of the Nuba mountains province, 1919–27, with the rank of mīrālai; he retired from the Sudan, 1928.

Northumberland, Duke of. *See* PERCY, SIR ALGERNON, 4th Duke of Northumberland.

Nubar Pasha Boghos (1825–99), Armenian Christian statesman in the Egyptian service; born in Smyrna and educated in Europe, he was a nephew of Boghos Bey Yusufian who was Muḥammad 'Alī Pasha's foreign secretary; he himself was minister for foreign affairs, 1867 and 1875–6, and was prime minister, 1878–9 and 1884–8; his policy towards the Sudan was dictated by opportunism; he died in Paris; his character has been maligned by those jealous of his ability; he was, however, debarred by his Franco-Levantine upbringing and outlook from being in full sympathy with contemporary Egyptian nationalist feeling; two of his near relatives were prominent in the Sudan: Arakīl Bey al-Armanī, governor of Khartoum and Sennar, 1857–9, and Arakīl Bey Nubar, governor of Muṣawwa', 1874–5.

Nūl (–1723), sultan of Sennar; he was the first sultan not of the royal line founded by Sultan 'Umāra Dūnqas; he succeeded Ūnsā III wad Bādī III in 1718 and was himself succeeded on his death by his son, Bādī IV abū Shilūkh; he is recorded as a just and peaceful ruler.

al-Nūr al-Birair (1872–1923), religious notable of the Ja'līyīn who lived at Shabasha, and a son of the great Shaikh al-Birair wad al-Ḥasīn whose tomb stands in the village; a member of the Sammānīya religious brotherhood, he was a man of learning and influence.

al-Nūr al-Dīn Pasha (*fl.* 1854), Turkish governor of Sawākin, then subject to the governor of Jidda, 1854; J. Hamilton, who passed through Sawākin in 1854, wrote of him as energetic yet popular; trained in a government department at Istānbūl, he had established a town council at Sawākin in accordance with the new (tanẓīmāt) organic law, and regularly consulted it.

al-Nūr Ḥanwa (–1931), nāẓir of the Ḥalafa branch of that portion of the Ḥawāzma tribe which lives in the eastern Nuba hills; he died at Umm Burembeika.

* **al-Nūr al-Jaraifāwī.** *See* IBRĀHĪM AL-NŪR IBRĀHĪM AL-JARAIFĀWĪ.

al-Nūr Bey Muḥammad (–1905), Sudanese soldier of the Egyptian army; born and educated at Sennar, he entered the army and was at length commissioned as mulāzim II; after service with Sir S. W. Baker in Equatoria and Uganda, 1869–73, he commanded a battalion of Mugharba (men from the western Sudan and from the Barbary Coast) in the province of Tāka; promoted mīrālai, he commanded the troops in the Equatorial province when he was in 1882 posted to the north; he fought the Mahdists in the Sennar campaign of 1884 when Gordon Pasha appointed him governor of Sennar; he defended his province with determination but lost both legs in battle and was captured by the Mahdists and taken to Omdurman, 1885; the Khedive 'Abbās II, on his visit to the Sudan, 1901–2, decorated him and awarded him a pension.

* **al-Nūr Bey Muḥammad 'Anqara** (1836–1920 ?), Mahdist amīr; by origin a Dongolāwī, he was brought up in the house of the malik Ṭanbal Muḥammad Idrīs of Arqū and, curiously enough, claimed descent from the Shā'iqī kings; he enlisted as a private in the cavalry and served under Mūsā Pasha Ḥamdī in the latter's reconnaissance on the Abyssinian border, 1862; he was afterwards discharged from the army and entered the service of Zubair Raḥma Manṣūr, the Ja'lī freebooter, in the Baḥr al-Ghazāl; Zubair recognized his fighting qualities and made him his chief of staff in the Dār Fūr campaign of 1874–5; he afterwards served Zubair's son Sulaimān in slave-raiding expeditions; deserting to the government with 2,000 men, Gordon Pasha promoted him qā'immaqām with grade of bey and made him first governor of Lado, 1877, and then governor of Qūlqūl and Kabkabīya in western Dār Fūr, 1878; the citadel which he built at Kabkabīya stands to-day; promoted mīrālai, he defeated and killed the Fūr pretender, Sultan Hārūn, 1880, cutting off Hārūn's head with his own hands; in 1882 he was in command of the government forces besieged in Bāra by the Mahdists to whom he surrendered the town in January 1883; appointed an amīr by the Mahdī, he was one of the leaders of the Mahdist army in the battle of Abū Ṭulaiḥ (Abu Klea), 1885; he later fought under the amīr al-umarā' Ḥamdān abū 'Anja; he surrendered with his black riflemen to a force under C. S. B. Parsons Pasha at Gedaref, 1898; he spent his old age at Omdurman.

al-Nuwairī Aḥmad (–1943), notable of the Shanābla Arabs, 'umda of Naiyīl near al-Ḥaṣṣa Ḥaiṣa; his son Aḥmad succeeded him on his death.

* **Nyigilö** (–*c.* 1860), chief of the Bari round Gondokoro, a son of Chief Moldiang; he was helpful to the French trader A. Brun-Rollet in 1844; he visited Khartoum in 1845; in 1854 he was present at the killing of the Savoyard trader A. Vaudey by the Bari at Gondokoro; he himself was killed by the people of Illibari for his failure to produce rain.

Obeid. *See* 'UBAID.

O'Connell Bey, James Ross (1863–1925), British soldier; he entered the army in 1884 and was promoted captain in 1892; having been seconded to the Egyptian army, he took part in the Dongola and Nile campaigns, 1896–9, and fought at Firka (Firket), Ḥafīr, Omdurman, and Umm Dibaikarāt; he was governor of Kordofan, 1903–7, with rank of mīrālai; he retired from the British army with rank of major.

O'Donovan, Edmund (1844–83), British journalist, son of J. O'Donovan, the Irish scholar; his calling as a newspaper correspondent took him to Merv in central Asia, and in Constantinople he was arrested on a charge of having insulted the sultan; he came to the Sudan, clothed in Turkish costume, as war correspondent of the *Daily News* of London and joined the army of W. Hicks Pasha; he was killed in the battle of Shaikān (Kashgil).

* **Ohrwalder, Josef** (–1912), Austrian priest of the Roman Catholic mission to Central Africa; born at Lana in the Tyrol, he came to Cairo in 1880 and with Bishop D. Comboni and two other missionaries entered the Sudan by way of Sawākin and Berber; he was stationed at the mission house at Dilling in the Nuba hills where, with other members of the mission, he was captured by the Mahdists and brought to al-Ubaiyaḍ, 1882; at Omdurman, where he was finally held captive, he made a precarious living by weaving; with two nuns, Sisters E. Venturini and C. Chincharini, he escaped to Egypt, 1892; after his escape he visited Vienna and met the family of R. C. von Slatin Bey who was still a prisoner at Omdurman; he returned to Omdurman after the Anglo-Egyptian occupation in 1898 and died there; his account of his adventures, translated and edited by F. R. Wingate, appeared as *Ten Years' Captivity in the Mahdi's Camp, 1882–92* (1892); a version in German was published at Innsbruck (1892).

Okeir 'Īsā Mūsā (–1946), notable of the Amarar Beja of the Red Sea hinterland; he was 'umda of the Muḥjan section living west of Port Sudan.

Okud Mūsā (–1919), Banī 'Āmir worthy, 'umda of the Ad Hasri clan, the only clan of the Banī 'Āmir in the Sudan to contain members of the tribal ruling caste; he was a leader of exceptional character and during both the Mahdist times and the present government wielded greater power than the nāẓir himself.

Oliphant, Sir Laurence James (1846–1914), British general; commissioned 1866, he served in the Nile campaign, 1885; he was general officer commanding Northern Command, England, 1907–11.

Omar. *See* 'UMAR.

O'Nial, John (1827–1919), military surgeon; born at Killaloe, Ireland, he joined the medical staff of the British army as assistant surgeon, 1852; promoted deputy surgeon-general, 1880, he served in the Sudan campaigns of 1884–6; in 1885 he was made surgeon-general, retiring in 1887.

Onslow, George Thorp (1859–1921), British major-general; he entered the Royal Marines, 1876, and was promoted captain, 1884; he served in the Sawākin campaign of 1884–5 and fought at Ḥashīn, Tofrek, and Tamai; he served also in the South African war of 1899–1902 and in 1906 was made colonel-commandant.

Ori, Leopoldo (1830–69), Italian physician; born at Cascina in Tuscany, he studied medicine at Florence where he graduated in 1854; he came to Egypt in 1856, entered the government medical service, and was appointed medical officer of health, Khartoum, 1858; in 1861, on the death of A. Peney, he became chief medical officer to the troops in the Sudan; encouraged by the progressive-minded governor of Khartoum and Sennar, Arakīl Bey al-Armanī, he drew up plans for improving the sanitary condition of Khartoum which included the building of a wall along the river bank and the construction of drains; he organized an effective vaccination service and improved the military hospital at Khartoum; his reforming zeal provoked the hostility of the new governor-general, Mūsā Pasha Ḥamdī, who availed himself of a recent decree of the viceroy, transferring to him the control of the medical service of the Sudan, to replace Ori by a more amenable medical officer, said to have been a Syrian Christian of low financial morals, presumably before the appointment of G. D. Douloghlu to the post; deprived of his living, he took to exploration and big-game hunting and in 1864 was collecting live specimens for the Turin Zoological garden and exploring the fauna of the Blue Nile and Atbara basins as far as the Abyssinian plateau; he went to Egypt in that year with a collection of wild animals for King Victor Emanuel II of Italy; he assisted in preparing Sudanese exhibits for the Paris exhibition of 1867; reinstated in that year as chief medical officer in the Sudan, he was assembling a collection for Ismāʿīl Pasha when he died of phthisis at Abū Ḥarāz on the Blue Nile; he left a collection of manuscripts most of which were destroyed in Cairo by ignorant hands.

Orler, Rodolfo (1892–1946), Italian bishop of the Roman Catholic Church; he was born at Vulcan, Michigan, of parents who came to the United States of America from the valley of Primiero near Trent in northern Italy; educated at Brescia and Verona, he was ordained priest in 1916; in 1920 he joined the mission in the Baḥr al-Ghazāl; later, while recuperating in Italy, he was for some time in charge of the training school for lay brothers at Thiene near Vicenza; in 1931, after a few months at Port Sudan, he was appointed assistant-general of the society and superior of the mother house of the African missions in Verona; he was made a bishop on his appointment as vicar apostolic of the Baḥr al-Ghazāl in 1933, a charge which he held till his death at Wau.

Orlowsky, Jan (1835–75), Polish engineer; he was posted as chief engineer of the Sudan about 1874 but died shortly after of fever at Khartoum; he was succeeded by A. Chélu, afterwards Pasha.

Osman. *See* ʿUTHMĀN.

Oswald, J . . . S . . . (–1893), British merchant; he was working in the Jidda office of the firm of Wylde, Beyts & Co. about 1884 when that firm was absorbed by Gellatly, Hankey, Sewell & Co., and he joined the service of the latter firm; he appears to have been at Sawākin till 1888; F. Power, correspondent of *The Times* newspaper, who met him at Jidda in 1883, wrote that he was 'a wonderfully nice fellow'; he died of cholera at Jidda during the epidemic of 1893.

Ounsa. *See* Ūnsā.

Owen, Edward Roderick (1856–96), popularly known as 'Roddy' Owen; a major in the British army and an explorer, he won the Grand National Race in 1892 as a gentleman rider; in 1893 he went to Uganda where he was sent with Captain R. Portal to bring to Uganda a force of 600 mutinous Sudanese, the remainder of Emin Pasha's army which H. M. Stanley had left at Toro; he was for some time besieged by the Sudanese who terrorized the country-side, but in the end they followed him to Uganda in 1894 when he hoisted the British flag at Wadelai; he served in the Dongola campaign, dying of cholera at Ambuqōl wells.

Owen Pasha, Roger Carmichael Robert (1866–1941), British soldier and administrator; born at Writtle, Essex, he entered the army in 1888; in 1902 he was seconded to the Egyptian army and in 1903 transferred to the Sudan Government; he was director of the intelligence department of the Egyptian War Office and Sudan agent in Cairo, 1905–8; in 1906 he served on the Sinai boundary commission; he was governor of Mongalla, 1908–18, when he saw active service as a political officer in several minor military operations such as the Beir patrol (1912) and in the Lafite and Lokoia mountains; he retired from the service of the Sudan Government with the Egyptian rank of liwā' and the British rank of lieutenant-colonel in 1918 when he was appointed governor of the Egyptian desert and oases; he died in Cairo; he published an English translation of J. C. Mitterrützner's *Die Sprache der Bari* in 1908.

Oyler, David Smith (1881–1934), American missionary of the United Presbyterian Church; born in Nortonville, Kansas, he graduated from Xenia Theological Seminary, 1909, when he came to the Sudan; he served at Doleib hill on the River Sobat, 1909–27, when he returned to the United States and for the rest of his life was a pastor at Cutler, Illinois, where he died; he published several studies of the customs of the Shilluk people among whom he lived.

Paez, Pedro (1564–1622), Spanish priest of the Jesuit Order and missionary to Abyssinia; Volume III of his *Historia Æthiopiae* (edited by C. Beccari in *Rerum Æthiopicarum*, xvi-xix, 1905) contains interesting references to the Funj sultanate of Sennar and its relations with Abyssinia.

Page, Charles Herbert (1866–1938), British marine engineer; appointed to the Egyptian coastguard service, 1894, he transferred to the Egyptian War Office, 1895, and served in the dockyard at Shallāl where the Nile flotilla which played so important a part in the campaigns of 1896–8 was based; in 1901 he was transferred to the Sudan

Government as assistant director of the newly constituted steamers and boats department; he assisted in experiments, which, however, proved unsuccessful, to open the rivers Atbara, Rāhad, and Dinder to seasonal steam navigation; he retired in 1918 and died at Kempsey, Worcestershire.

Pain, Olivier (1843–84), French journalist; born at Troyes, he worked on the staff of the Socialist newspapers *Mot d'Ordre* and *L'Affranchi* of Paris; for participating in the defence of the Paris Commune he was deported to New Caledonia whence he escaped to Europe, installing himself at Geneva where he wrote for left-wing newspapers; he then went as a newspaper correspondent to the Russo-Turkish war of 1877–8; he returned to France under the amnesty of 1879 and joined the staff of *L'Intransigeant*; in this capacity he went to Egypt, attracted by the news-value of the Mahdist revolt; evading the frontier authorities, he travelled to Dongola and over the Bayūda to al-Ubaiyaḍ in August 1884 with the intention of obtaining an exclusive interview with the Mahdī for *L'Intransigeant*; the Mahdī, failing to comprehend his mission, kept him captive; he died while accompanying the Mahdist army marching from al-Ubaiyaḍ to the siege of Khartoum; his death provoked a violent anti-British outcry in France where the gutter press attributed his death to British intrigue; only the good sense of the British and French Governments averted a political crisis.

Pallme, Ignaz (1810–41 ?), Austrian trader; born at Rumburg, Bohemia, he went to Egypt as a merchant; in 1837 he started on a journey to the Sudan and went via Dongola to al-Ubaiyaḍ; after travelling in Kordofan and in 1839 accompanying a military expedition sent by the Turkish governor of the province to the Nuba hills to capture slaves for the army, he returned by way of Berber and the Nubian desert in Cairo in 1841; he died shortly afterwards in Cairo; his *Beschreibung von Kordofan* (Stuttgart and Tübingen, 1843) appeared in an English translation as *Travels in Kordofan* (1844).

Palmer, Sir Arthur Power (1840–1904), British general; he entered the Indian army in 1857 and served in many campaigns on the frontier and in the Anglo-Abyssinian war in 1868; in 1885 he was with the Indian contingent in the Sawākin campaign; promoted full general in 1899, he was commander-in-chief in India, 1900–2.

Palmer Pasha, Henry Douglas (1867–1946), British soldier; while a captain in the Royal Marines, he was seconded to the Egyptian army, 1900; he served in the Sudan and was later assistant adjutant-general, and ultimately financial secretary, on the headquarters staff of the Egyptian army; he retired from the British army, 1910, and in 1914 was promoted liwā'; rejoining the Royal Marines in the First World War, he was badly wounded at Gallipoli, 1915; he finally retired from the British army with rank of lieutenant-colonel, 1919.

Panehsi (*fl.* *c.* 1134 B.C.), Egyptian viceroy of Ethiopia during the reigns of Rameses X and Rameses XI, XXth Dynasty kings of Egypt; he was in office roughly 1120–1100 B.C.

Parke, Thomas Heazle (1857–93), British physician; born at Drumsna, Eire, he graduated in medicine and joined the Army Medical Department in 1881; in 1882 he was serving in Egypt and in 1884–5 was medical officer to the naval brigade in the British column which attempted without success to relieve Khartoum then besieged by the Mahdists; his garrison duties in Egypt were interrupted by his joining the expedition of H. M. Stanley to rescue Emin Pasha on the Albert Nile; in 1890 he attended Emin and, after fulfilment of the mission, returned to duty in Egypt; he died at Alt-na-Craig, Scotland, soon after his retirement from the Royal Army Medical Corps; his professional writings include contributions on hygiene and pathology; he also published accounts of his experiences in Africa.

✱ **Parkyns, Mansfield Harry Isham** (1823–94), British country gentleman and traveller; born at Ruddington, Nottinghamshire, he arrived in Abyssinia in 1843 and thence, late in 1845, made his way to the Sudan, passing down the valley of the Setit where he met Nimr Muḥammad Nimr, formerly mak of Shendi, and then crossed the Atbara to Gedaref; from here he went by Abū Ḥarāz to Khartoum; here the details of his stay in the Sudan become vague, for he left no precise record; he relates that, being temporarily short of money and liking the life, he spent several months as a down-and-out in the market; in Khartoum he met Sir F. Galton, the British anthropologist, in the winter of 1835–6 and with him made a short voyage on the White Nile; he afterwards travelled to Kordofan; in company with an Austrian Jewish merchant named I. Morpurgo he left al-Ubaiyaḍ in January 1848 and crossed the Bayūda to Dongola whence he made for Cairo, returning to England in 1849; he collected manuscripts and birds and made useful notes of the Sudan tribes and their customs; the part of his travels which concerns the Sudan is briefly described in his *Life in Abyssinia* (1853).

Parr Pasha, Sir Henry Hallam (1847–1914), British major-general and liwā' of the Egyptian army; he was commissioned to the 13th Light Infantry, 1865, and after service in South Africa fought in the Egyptian war, 1882; joining the Egyptian army, 1883, he was given command of the newly raised 9th Sudanese battalion; in 1884 he was commandant of Sawākin and was present at the battle of Tamai; he was serving on the line of communication of the Nile expedition in 1885, mostly as commandant, Shallāl; in 1885–8 he was adjutant-general and second in command of the Egyptian army, a post which he left owing to bad health and in which he was succeeded by H. H. Kitchener Pasha (afterwards sirdār); continuing sickness caused his retirement in 1902; his autobiography, edited by Sir C. Fortescue-Brickdale, appeared in 1917.

Parsons Pasha, Sir Charles (1855–1923), British major-general; he joined the army and served in South Africa, 1877–9, and again in the first Boer war, 1881; he next fought in the Egyptian war, 1882; in the Dongola campaign of 1896 he commanded the Egyptian artillery; in 1897 he was governor and officer commanding troops at Sawākin, while in 1898–9 his command was extended to Kassala and the Red Sea littoral; he was in command of a small force of the Egyptian army which was sent to Muṣawwaʿ by sea and thence marched to Kassala to take over the defence of the town from the Italians, 1897; early in 1898 he patrolled as far as the Atbara river and later in the year, after a difficult crossing of the Atbara, he defeated the Mahdists at Gedaref and received the surrender of the commander, al-Nūr Bey Muḥammad ʿAnqara; he then entrenched himself in Gedaref and beat off an attack by the amīr Aḥmad Faḍīl; leaving the Egyptian army, he fought in the South African war, 1900–1; he commanded the regular forces in Canada, 1902–6.

Paser I (*fl. c.* 1320 B.C.), Egyptian viceroy of Ethiopia during the reigns of kings Ay and Haremheb of the XVIIIth Dynasty; he served approximately 1350–1320 B.C.

Paser II (*fl. c.* 1250 B.C.), Egyptian viceroy of Ethiopia during the reign of the XIXth Dynasty king Rameses II, the builder of the rock temple of Abū Simbel, who reigned about 1298–1232 B.C.

Paulet (or **Paoletti**), **A . . . .** *See* GRANIER, ANTOINE.

Paulis, Albert (1875–1933), Belgian soldier in the service of the Congo Free State; in 1904 he took over from C. Lemaire the command of the Free State politico-scientific mission in the Yei basin.

* **Pearse, Henry Hiram S . . .** (–1905), British journalist; he was war correspondent of the *Daily News* in the Nile campaign, 1884–5, and war artist and correspondent to the *Graphic* in the Dongola campaign, 1896; he wrote much on hounds and hunting.

Pearson, Charles William (1847–1917), British missionary of the Church of England; born at Whitehaven, he entered the merchant navy and was later chief officer on an Indian mail steamer; called to the religious life, he entered the Church Missionary College, Islington, 1876; in 1878, along with R. W. Felkin and G. Litchfield, he travelled to Uganda by way of Sawākin, Berber, and Khartoum; he returned to Europe by the overland route from the Great Lakes to Zanzibar, 1879; at the time of his death he was vicar of Walton, Buckinghamshire.

Pearson Pasha, Hugh Drummond (1873–1922), British soldier and surveyor, a liwā' of the Egyptian army, and a lieutenant-colonel of the British army; born in London, he was commissioned to the Royal Engineers, 1892; in 1904 he was seconded to the Egyptian army and joined the Sudan Government survey department with the rank of qā'immaqām; in 1905 he was appointed director of surveys, a post which he held till his death; in 1917–19 he served in the Palestine campaign in the First World War; while serving as British commissioner on the Anglo-French commission which was demarcating the frontier between Dār Fūr and Wadā'i, he fell ill and died at Umm Dafog.

Pearson, Weetman Dickinson, 1st Viscount Cowdray (1856–1927), British contractor; as head of the firm of S. Pearson & Son he was responsible for the construction of many great engineering works in various parts of the world, including the Sennar dam, completed 1925; from 1895 to 1910 he was a member of the British Parliament; he was made a baron, 1910, and in 1917 a viscount; his biography, by J. H. Spender, appeared in 1930.

* **Pedemonte, Emanuele** (1802?–67), Roman Catholic priest of the Jesuit Order; born at Genoa, he entered the Society of Jesus, 1818, and came to the Sudan with Bishop I. Knoblehar with whom he worked in Khartoum and on the Upper White Nile from 1848 till 1852 when he was recalled to Europe; he died at Naples; he was a handsome man with an enormous beard reaching to his waist; the date of his birth is doubtfully given as 1792 by one source which credits him with having been a soldier in Napoleon's army.

Peel, Sir William (1824–58), British sailor, son of Sir R. Peel, prime minister; he entered the Royal Navy, 1838, and was promoted captain, 1849; he commanded the Naval Brigade at the siege of Sebastopol, 1855, and received the first Victoria Cross awarded; he died in the Indian mutiny; in 1851, being on half-pay, he set out with J. Churi (i.e. Yūsuf Khūrī), a Syrian Maronite educated in Rome, on a visit to the Sudan in order to explore the interior of Africa; the travellers reached Khartoum by way of the Nubian desert route and thence visited al-Ubaiyaḍ where both caught fever; they returned to Egypt at great speed in the winter of 1851–2, travelling by the same route as that by which they had come; he published *A Ride through the Nubian Desert* (1852).

* **Peney, Alfred** (–1861), French physician and explorer; born at Saint-Genix-sur-Guiers in Savoy and educated at Montpellier and Paris, he became secretary to A. B. Clot Bey, chief of the Egyptian public health council; in 1850 he was appointed chief medical officer to the Egyptian troops in the Sudan; in Khartoum he married a Galla lady in 1855 and by her had several children, all christened at the Roman Catholic mission there; he was to have been medical officer in the abortive expedition of P.-H.-S. d'Escayrac de Lauture to discover the source of the Nile, 1856; fired to explore the upper reaches of the White Nile on his own account, he left Khartoum with the Maltese trader A. Debono to examine the country between Gondokoro and the Albert Nile; his failure to return caused anxiety and search parties were sent out; A. Antognoli found him dying near the site of Fort Berkeley; Peney's contribution to extending the world's knowledge of Central Africa was valuable; he explored the valley of the Yei to the west and entered the Lotuko country to the east, making a careful and relatively accurate map.

* **Pennazzi, Luigi, Count** (1838–95), Italian traveller; born in Havana, Cuba, he made a journey with Lieutenant G. Besone from Muṣawwaʿ through Kassala to Khartoum in 1880, returning to the coast by Kassala and Sawākin; he died in Madrid.

Penton Pasha, Richard Hugh (1863–1934), British military surgeon; he was seconded from the Royal Army Medical Corps to the Egyptian army, 1892, and served in the Dongola and Nile campaigns, 1896–8; he was principal medical officer of the Egyptian army, 1899–1905, with rank of liwā'; in the First World War he held senior administrative posts in France, 1915–19; he retired from the British army with the rank of colonel.

Percy, Sir Algernon, 4th Duke of Northumberland and 1st Baron Prudhoe (1792–1865), British sailor and antiquary; he entered the Royal Navy in 1805 and in 1862 was promoted admiral; in 1829 he travelled from Cairo to Sennar and wrote an informative account of his journey in the *Journal of the Royal Geographical Society* of London, vol. v, 1835.

Perrotta, Carmelo (1875–1942), Italian engineering contractor; born at Caltagirone in Sicily of a family of Milanese origin, he entered the Italian army engineers and served in the Italo-Abyssinian war, 1896; on his return he stayed in Egypt and worked on the construction of the Aswān dam; soon after the Anglo-Egyptian occupation of the Sudan he came to Khartoum as an engineering contractor and engaged in various constructions including Gordon Memorial College and the river embankment; he was president of the Italian community in Khartoum for several years till 1920 when he left for Egypt where he died.

Petherick, John (1813–82), Welsh mining engineer, trader, and explorer; he came from Glamorgan and, going to Egypt, entered the service of Muḥammad 'Alī Pasha in 1845 and was employed until 1848 in a fruitless search for coal deposits in Upper Egypt, the Red Sea hills, and Kordofan; quitting government service, he lived at al-Ubaiyaḍ and traded in gum arabic from Kordofan, 1848–53; when the gum trade began to suffer from over-supply aggravated by the development of gum exports from the west coast, he transferred his activities to the White Nile and to the ivory trade; while engaged in this trade he explored the rivers Jur and Yalo and arrived at the borders of the country of the Azande, 1853–8; in 1858 he was appointed British vice-consul in Khartoum; taking his first leave to Britain in 1859, he married the lady who was to accompany him on many travels and in the same year was invited by the Royal Geographical Society of London to take charge of an expedition to succour J. H. Speke and J. A. Grant, the explorers, who were shortly expected to enter the Sudan from the south; accompanied by his wife, the doctors C. M. Brownell and J. Murie, and a youth named Foxcroft, he ascended the White Nile in 1862 but, misjudging the probable time of arrival of Speke and Grant at Gondokoro, went on a trading expedition to the west, returning to Gondokoro in 1863 only to find that the explorers had already arrived and had no need of his services; his failure to meet them did his reputation harm; having shown perhaps excessive zeal in reporting suspected cases of slave trading to the British consul-general in Egypt, he was accused by A. Lanzon, A. Debono's nephew, of having himself engaged in this trade; the British Government, in doubt as to the truth of these allegations and counter-allegations, suppressed the vice-consulate in Khartoum, 1864; he left the Sudan in 1865; F. T. Buckland, in a premature obituary occasioned by rumours of his death, called him 'a kind-hearted, plucky, powerfully built specimen of true John Bull' (*The Field*, No. 527, 1863); he wrote *Egypt, the Soudan and Central Africa* (1861) and (jointly with his wife) *Travels in Central Africa* (1869).

Petronius (*fl.* 24 B.C.), Roman prefect of Syene, the modern Aswān; the Ethiopians having raided Syene, Petronius led his legion south and retaliated by destroying Napata.

Peyton, Sir William Eliot (1866–1931), British general; he joined the army in the ranks of the 7th Dragoon Guards and received a commission in 1887; seconded to the Egyptian army, he fought in the Egyptian cavalry in the Dongola and Nile campaigns, 1896–8; he was later an army corps commander in France in the First World War, retiring in 1930.

Pfund, Johann Gabriel (1813–76), German botanist, a native of Hamburg; he accompanied the survey missions of R. E. Colston Bey and H. G. Prout Bey to Kordofan and Dār Fūr, 1875–6; he died at al-Fā<u>sh</u>ar.

Phipps Pasha, Pownoll Ramsay (1864–1932), British soldier and administrator; born in Brighton, he entered the British army from which he was seconded in 1899 to the Egyptian army; he joined the Sudan Government in 1903 and was private secretary to Sir F. R. Wingate, the governor-general, 1903–4; he was civil secretary, Sudan Government, 1905–14, when he retired; he was promoted mīrālai, 1907, and liwā', 1909.

Piaggia, Carlo (1827–82), Italian trader, mechanic, and explorer; he was born at La Badia di Cantignano near Lucca and came to the Sudan in 1856 as caravan leader to some traders in the Baḥr al-<u>Gh</u>azāl; in 1863–5 he explored the country of the Azande and in 1876 travelled in the region of Lake Kioga and the Victoria Nile; he died at Karkōj on the Blue Nile while on a journey of exploration to the River Sobat; although a man of little book learning he was a careful explorer; G. A. Schweinfurth, who himself explored the Nile–Congo watershed, paid him the tribute of having lifted the veil of fantastic mystery which had hitherto enveloped the Azande.

Piankhi (*fl.* 730 B.C.), Nubian king, born at Napata; he succeeded Kashta, conqueror of Thebes, about 751 B.C.; he overcame Meroë and installed a branch of his family on the throne there; he invaded Lower Egypt and imposed a tribute on it, overawing the Nile valley from Meroë to the approaches to the delta, 731–708 B.C.; he rebuilt the temple of Amon-Ra originally built in the New Kingdom at Jabal Barkal; he was succeeded by King Shabaka.

Playfair Bey, Norman Ernest (1867–1914), British soldier; an officer of the King's Own Scottish Borderers, he was commissioned, 1888, and promoted captain, 1899, when he retired from the British army; he had already served in India when he was seconded to the Egyptian army, 1891–6, and, after campaigning against Kabarega in the Uganda Protectorate, 1898–1900, he returned to the Egyptian army and was governor of Sawākin, 1903.

Pliny (Gaius Plinius Secundus) (*c.* 23–79), Roman writer; born at Como in north Italy, he was employed in various military and administrative posts in the Roman Empire; he was killed by an eruption of Mt. Vesuvius which he had gone on shore to examine; famous among his works is a voluminous encyclopaedia and gazetteer entitled *Natural History*, of which book 5, chapter x, contains references to Nubia.

Poncet, Ambroise (1835–68), Savoyard trader, brother of J. Poncet and nephew of A. Vaudey; born at Saint-Jean-de-Maurienne, he and his brother came to the Sudan in 1851 and worked with their uncle; they nearly lost their lives when Vaudey was killed in a fight with the Bari at Gondokoro in 1854; they now took over Vaudey's business and traded as A. & J. Poncet Frères of Khartoum, carrying on commerce, chiefly in ivory, in the region west of the Upper White Nile where they had stations in the Dinka-Nuer country; Ambroise died in Alexandria and the firm was dissolved in 1872; the Poncet brothers undertook explorations of importance; they were the first Europeans from the Upper White Nile to reach the tributaries of the Congo, and they were among the few foreigners in the Sudan at the time who were not suspected of participation in the slave trade.

Poncet, Charles-Jacques (–1706), French surgeon who established himself in Cairo about 1687; little is known of his early life except that he was born in the Franche-Comté; invited by the emperor of Abyssinia to treat him for a skin disease, he left Cairo in 1698 in company with Father C. F. X. de Brévedent and travelled by way of the Western Oases touching the Nile at Mus͟hū near Arqū; from Dongola they crossed the Bayūda to Khartoum and Sennar, reaching Gondar in 1699; here de Brévedent died; having treated the emperor, he returned to Egypt via Axum and Muṣawwaʿ; he died in Iṣfahān.

Poncet, Joseph (1804–59), French trader; born at La Thuile in the Savoy, he was the father of Ambroise and Jules Poncet; on the death of their uncle, A. Vaudey, he came to the Sudan to help his sons to reorganize the estate; after two years of work and travel he died in Khartoum.

Poncet, Jules (1838–73), brother of Ambroise Poncet; on the dissolution of the firm of A. & J. Poncet Frères of Khartoum in 1872, he returned to Europe but died in Paris a few months later.

Poore, Sir Richard (1858–1930), British admiral; he served as a junior officer in the naval brigade in the Nile campaign of 1884–5 and was responsible for warping the steamer *Naṣīf al-K͟hair* through the Second Cataract; a lieutenant, 1885, he was rear admiral, 1903, and admiral, 1911; he was commander-in-chief at the Nore, 1911–15, retiring from the Royal Navy, 1917.

Potagos, Panayotis (1838–1903), Greek traveller; a physician by profession, he was born at Vytina in Greece and graduated in medicine at Athens; beginning his travels in 1867, he visited Mesopotamia, Persia, Afghanistan, and the Gobi desert, journeying thence through Siberia to Russia, Egypt, Arabia, and India; from India he returned to Egypt, ascended the Nile valley, and visited southern Dār Fūr in the course of a journey from al-Ubaiyaḍ towards the region of the Uélé basin which he explored in 1876–7, penetrating to a point farther south than G. Schweinfurth did; he returned northward by way of Shambé where he joined the Nile; he published an account of his travels entitled *Περίληψις Περιηγήσεων* (Athens, 1883), translated into French as *Dix Années de voyage dans l'Asie Centrale et l'Afrique Équatoriale, 1867–77* (Paris, 1885); he left unpublished manuscripts.

Potter, Maurice (1865–98), Swiss painter; born at Geneva and trained at Geneva and Paris, he developed a felicity in portraying Arab and oriental subjects, exhibiting his pictures mostly in Paris; in 1897 he joined the politico-scientific French mission which, first under Bonvalet, then under Bonchamps, travelled through Abyssinia to Gambeila in an attempt to make contact with the mission of J. B. Marchand which was on its way from the Congo basin to Fashoda; Potter, with the Russian Colonel Artamanoff and Dejazmatch Tasama in command of a small column of Abyssinian troops, leaving the main party at Gore, set out for the Nile; reaching the mouth of the Sobat they planted the Abyssinian and French flags, missed Marchand, and, their supplies exhausted, returned towards the Abyssinian highlands; on the way back he was killed by a spear thrown by some Anuak hidden in the long grass; throughout this trying journey he made an entomological collection and sketches outstanding for their ethnographic faithfulness.

* **Pourpe, Marc** (–1914), French airman; he piloted the first aircraft to enter the Sudan, arriving at Khartoum near the site of the present aerodrome east of the city on 12 January 1914; he had flown direct from Abū Ḥamad, no small feat in those days; a large and uncontrollable crowd welcomed him on a piece of desert which had been cleared for him; he was followed by Lieutenant-Colonels Sir F. McLean and A. Ogilvie in a float seaplane; they had left Alexandria on 3 January and, after thirteen engine failures, arrived in Khartoum on 13 March; Pourpe, flying a Morane-Parasol aircraft, was shot down behind the French lines in the Somme area by German aeroplanes in the First World War.

Power, Frank le Poer (–1884), British journalist; he accompanied a fellow journalist, E. O'Donovan, to the Sudan via Sawākin in 1883 as war artist for the *Pictorial World* and correspondent for *The Times*; intending to go to Kordofan with Hicks Pasha's army, he left the expedition at al-Duwaim owing to dysentery and returned to Khartoum; here he was appointed British consul in December 1883; deciding to remain in Khartoum, he and Herbin of *Le Bosphore Égyptien* of Alexandria were shut up in the beleaguered town; the two journalists finally left with Lieutenant-Colonel J. D. H. Stewart in the steamer

ʻ*Abbās*, but all three were killed by Manāṣīr tribesmen between Abū Ḥamad and Merowe; his letters to *The Times*, written before and during the siege, were published by his brother in 1885.

Prideaux, William Francis (1840–1914), British colonel of the Bombay Staff Corps; he was a member of the mission headed by H. Rassam which endeavoured to treat with King Theodore of Abyssinia for the release of European prisoners held by him; he left Muṣawwaʻ with the mission in 1865 and travelled to Abyssinia via Keren, Kassala, and Gallabat; arrived at Theodore's headquarters the mission was itself held captive, 1866–8; he later served in the foreign department of the Government of India and was a competent bibliographer, archaeologist, and numismatist.

Primrose, Everard Henry (1848–85), British soldier, younger brother of A. P., 5th Earl of Rosebery, prime minister of Great Britain, 1894–5; joining the Grenadier Guards, 1868, he was promoted lieutenant-colonel, 1878; in 1879 he was military attaché at Vienna; a colonel in 1882, he took part in the Nile expedition, 1884–5, and died at Abū Fāṭima during the latter part of the campaign.

Prior, Melton (1845–1910), British war artist and correspondent; from 1868 he was on the staff of the *Illustrated London News* and from 1873 was correspondent for that journal; after following the Ashanti war, 1873, and the Russo-Turkish war, 1878, he was in the campaigns round Sawākin, 1884; illness kept him aboard ship at Trinkitat and prevented his presence at the disastrous defeat of the Egyptian army at the first battle of el-Teb; he was, however, at the second battle there and later at Tamai; he accompanied the Nile expedition of 1884–5 and was with the Desert Column in the battles of Abū Ṭulaiḥ (Abu Klea) and Matamma, 1885; S. L. Bensusan edited his autobiographical *Campaigns of a War Correspondent* (1912).

Procopius (*c.* 499–565), Byzantine historian; in his *History of the Wars* he described the Blemmyes and Nobates on the southern frontier of Byzantine Egypt.

Prokesch-Osten (the Elder), Anton von, Count (1795–1876), Austrian traveller and diplomat; born at Gratz he entered the army and fought in the wars against Napoleon, 1814–15; between 1827 and 1830 he made a careful survey of the Nile valley between Aswān and Wādī Ḥalfā continued by Baron J. W. von Müller; he later held high diplomatic posts in the Austro-Hungarian service, including ambassadorships at Berlin and Constantinople, and died at Vienna; his son Anton wrote of his father's work (Leipzig, 1874).

Prout Bey, Henry Gosslee (1845–1927), American soldier on the Egyptian general staff; he was born in Fairfax County, Virginia; in 1863, at the age of eighteen, he enlisted in the Federal army during the American civil war and served with the army of the Potomac till the end of the war; he then graduated in civil engineering from the University of Michigan, 1871; while still at college he led an expedition in south-western Colorado which brought him to the attention of General W. T. Sherman, head of the United States army, who recommended him to the Khedive; he joined the Khedivial service in 1872 as a binbāshī of engineers; he was second in command to R. E. Colston Bey on a reconnaissance of Kordofan, 1875, and took over command after Colston was invalided at al-Ubaiyaḍ; he then led the expedition into Dār Fūr; he made valuable reports on Kordofan and Dār Fūr including the results of topographical surveys and astronomical calculations; promoted qā'immaqām and transferred to Equatoria, he was governor of that province in 1876 in succession to C. G. Gordon Pasha who was appointed governor-general of the Sudan; while holding this post he supervised the transport of the component parts of the steamer *Khedive* on the backs of negro porters from the neighbourhood of Rejaf to a point upstream of the Fola rapids where she was assembled and launched on the Albert Nile; he then resigned his commission in the Egyptian army and returned to the United States where he was editor of *The Railroad Gazette*, 1887–1903, and later president of the Hall Switch and Signal Company of Garwood, New Jersey; he retired from business in 1915 when he devoted his time to writing a biography of George Westinghouse, published in 1922.

Prudhoe, 1st Baron. *See* PERCY, SIR ALGERNON, 4th Duke of Northumberland and 1st Baron Prudhoe.

* **Pruyssenaere de la Wostyne, Eugène de** (1826–64), Belgian traveller; born at Ypres of a noble Flemish family, he came to Egypt, 1856, and in 1857 ascended the Nile valley, visiting Berber and Khartoum, returning to Cairo early in 1858; in the same year he returned to the Sudan, leaving again for Egypt in October 1860; his third journey began in 1861; arrived in Khartoum, he joined a hunting expedition in the south; in February 1862 he was in Sennar when he became enamoured of an Abyssinian girl whom he married at the Roman Catholic mission at Khartoum in 1864; he made a voyage on the Upper White Nile with J. Petherick, returning to Khartoum; in 1863–4 he explored the Blue Nile basin; falling ill, he started out for Khartoum but died on the way at Ḥarb al-Dunyā near Karkōj and was buried on the island in front of the village; his wife, who married again, died in 1867.

Psammetichus I (Psammētik), Egyptian king of the XXVIth Dynasty, contemporary with the first four successors of Taharqa in Ethiopia; Meroë then replaced Napata as the Nubian capital though Napata remained the religious capital until its destruction by the Roman prefect Gaius Petronius, 23 B.C.

Ptolemy (Claudius Ptolemaeus) (*fl.* 139–61), Graeco-Egyptian astronomer and geographer, a native of Egypt and a resident of Alexandria; among his writings of interest to the Sudan is his *Geographia*, of which book 4 contains a description of the Nile as far south as the site of the present Berber; to him is commonly attributed the first clearly expressed suggestion as to the origin of the White Nile in the twin lakes (Victoria and Albert) by the Mountains of the Moon

(Ruwenzori), although each of these localities had been separately suggested by prior geographers; the maps attributed to him have had a great influence over geographical speculation.

Pückler-Muskau, Herman Ludwig Hendrik, Prince von (1785–1871), German traveller, artist, and horticulturalist; born at Muskau in Lusatia, he travelled to Egypt, bought an Abyssinian girl named Maḥbūba in the slave market of Cairo, and with her toured Upper Egypt where the viceroy Muḥammad ʿAlī Pasha received him at Asyūṭ; he then visited the Sudan, arriving at Khartoum in 1837 and ascending the Blue Nile to Wad Madanī; returning to Europe, he brought Maḥbūba with him to Vienna; the prince was a romantic character and a handsome man; vol. iii of his *Aus Mehemed Ali's Reich* (Stuttgart, 1844) contains an account of Nubia and the Sudan.

* **Purdy Bey, Erastus Sparrow** (1838–81), American soldier in the Khedivial service; born in the State of New York, he spent his early life in California; he fought on the Federal side in the American civil war, 1861–5, and in 1870 joined the Egyptian general staff with rank of qā'immaqām; later in the same year he led a scientific expedition which surveyed Upper Egypt between the Nile and the Red Sea; in 1873 he reconnoitred the country between Berenice and Berber; in 1874–6 he was in command of a survey party which travelled from Dongola south-westward to al-Fās͟har and on to Ḥufrat al-Naḥās in a general reconnaissance of the newly acquired Egyptian province of Dār Fūr; he was promoted mīrālai for his services in these missions; he was sued for debt in Cairo in 1874; discharged from the army during retrenchment in 1878, he was re-employed in a civilian post as a cadastral inspector, 1879–81, when he was finally discharged, ill, and still in debt; he died in Cairo; parts of his reports are printed in the publications of the Egyptian general staff and in the bulletins of the Khedivial Geographical Society of Cairo.

Qādīm Jirū (–1937), paramount chief of the Kuwālīb eastern Jabals district of the Nuba hills of Kordofan; he was a magistrate.

Qalā'ūn, al-Malik al-Manṣūr Saif al-Dīn . . . al-Alfī (*c.* 1220–90), Baḥrī mameluke ruler of Egypt and Syria; he invaded Nubia and in two battles beat the native king Shamamum but was able to maintain his authority there only so long as his armies remained; though he gained no permanent success in Nubia, he forced the king to resume payment of the ancient tribute.

Qarīb Allāh Ṣāliḥ al-Ṭaiyib (1871–1936), religious leader; by tribe a Jamūʿī, he was *k͟halīfa* of the Sammānīya religious brotherhood whose branch of the order was called by his followers the Qarībīya; a grandson of Aḥmad al-Ṭaiyib wad al-Bas͟hīr, who introduced the order into the Sudan, he succeeded his cousin ʿAbd al-Maḥmūd Muḥammad al-S͟harīf Nūr al-Dā'im, 1915; he made the pilgrimage many times and in 1931 built his own mosque in Omdurman where he died; a tomb has been built over his grave.

al-Qidail (–1911), mak of Tagoi in the eastern Nuba hills; in 1910 he defied the Sudan Government, fled to Jabal Daiyar, was caught, and hanged.

Qināwī Bey . . . (–1883), Egyptian trader; he had worked with R. Gessi Pasha in the Baḥr al-Ghazāl and was one of a number of merchants suspected of having been engaged in the slave trade; it is said that 'Alā' al-Dīn Pasha Ṣiddīq intended to appoint him governor of the Baḥr al-Ghazāl had al-Ubaiyaḍ been captured from the Mahdists; he accompanied the army commanded by W. Hicks Pasha into Kordofan and was killed at the massacre of Shaikān (Kashgil).

* **al-Qurashī wad al-Zain** (–1878), shaikh of the religious brotherhood of the Sammānīya; by birth a Bazai, he was related on his mother's side to the Ḥalāwiyīn among whom he lived near al-Ḥaṣṣa Ḥaiṣa; to his *khalwa* came Muḥammad Aḥmad, the future Mahdī, as a pupil after the latter's breach with Shaikh Muḥammad al-Sharīf Nūr al-Dā'im; Muḥammad Aḥmad stayed till 1878 and married his daughter, the future mother of al-Sharīf 'Alī al-Mahdī; he did not long survive the departure of his pupil and on his death Muḥammad Aḥmad, as an act of piety, helped to build his tomb.

* **Rabīḥ Aghā** (*fl.* 1821–49), Sudanese soldier of unknown origin who received a commission in the niẓām al-jadīd, the new regular army which Muḥammad 'Alī Pasha created from Egyptian serfs and Sudanese slaves; enrolled in the 7th infantry regiment in 1821 or 1822, he was commissioned in 1840 as mulāzim II in the 2nd infantry regiment and in 1849 was promoted mulāzim I; of his subsequent career nothing is known.

* **Rabīḥ Faḍl Allāh,** also called **Rabīḥ Zubair** (1845–1900), slave trader and freebooter; he was probably of Hāmaj origin and was born in an undesirable quarter of Khartoum named Salāmat al-Bāshā on the south-east side of the town; here he received the elements of a Qur'ānic education and went to the Baḥr al-Ghazāl, while a young man, as assistant head of a slave-trading concern; when the government took over his firm he worked for Zubair Raḥma Manṣūr, greatest of all the freebooters in the Baḥr al-Ghazāl, and was in service with Zubair's son Sulaimān when the latter was defeated by R. Gessi Pasha in 1879; taking with him some of Sulaimān's men, he fled to the country of the Azande where he founded a sultanate, 1880–4; in 1885, dressed in the patched clothes of the Mahdist warrior, he invaded Dār Banda and lived on the country; in 1891 he massacred the French mission of P. Crampel then, marching northward into Wadā'i, he was beaten in battle by the sultan; moving to the west, he set himself up over the pagan people of the Chad; appearing in Bornu in 1894, he was joined by Ḥaiyātu, ruler of Adamawa, who married his daughter but who was killed by Rabīḥ's son Faḍl Allāh in a quarrel, 1899; in this year he destroyed another French mission, that of the naval lieutenant Bretonnet, at Togbao; the French now took effective steps to overcome him

and he was killed by a force under E. Gentil, governor of the S͟hārī, near Lake Chad; see Dujarric, G., *La vie du Sultan Rabah* (Paris, 1902).

Raddi, Giuseppe (1770–1829), Italian naturalist, a physician by profession; he accompanied J. F. Champollion on an archaeological mission to Abū Simbel and Wādī Ḥalfā in the winter of 1828–9 as a member of the Italian expedition under I. Rosellini which joined forces with that of Champollion; an eccentric with an unkempt beard, he was the butt of the jokes of the party; he fell ill and died at Rhodes on his way back to Italy; he made collections of plants and fossils for Italian museums.

* **Rāfaʿi** (*c.* 1850–*c.* 1910), Azande chief; he was the son of Chief Kasanga; he himself was chief of the Bandia, a large Sudanic and Bantu tribe which, although keeping its own chiefs of the Baza clan, adopted the Zande language and customs; with the help of Zabiri (Jabir), the great Bandia chief to whom he was the lieutenant, he strengthened his position among the Anzakara, Azande, and other tribes on the River Shinko, a tributary of the Mbomu; he later won the support of the filibuster Faḍl Allāh Rabīḥ during the latter's brief sultanate, 1880–4; he had died before 1912 when the expedition of the Duke of Mecklenburg found his son ʿItmān (ʿUt͟hmān) ruling in his place; a village on the River Shinko bears his name.

Rāg͟hib Bey Ṣādiq (–1883), Egyptian soldier; he was a binbās͟hī on the staff of Muḥammad Rātib Pasha in the Egyptian-Abyssinian war of 1875–6; his diary of the campaign which ended in the defeat at Gura is in the Royal archives in the Abdin Palace, Cairo; promoted mīrālai, he commanded the 4th infantry regiment in W. Hicks Pasha's army of Kordofan, 1883; early on the march from the White Nile he seized the wells of S͟haṭṭ; he was killed with almost all his regiment in the battle of S͟haikān (Kashgil).

Raḥal Ardu (–1917), mak of Jabal Kadūglī in the Nuba hills; he was succeeded on his death by his son Muḥammad.

Raḥma, called **al-Arbāb** (*fl.* 1784–1821), powerful s͟haikh of the Maḥas of ʿĀilafūn on the Blue Nile; he was ruler of the Jazīra under the Funj sovereignty and was a hard disciplinarian, exacting death as a penalty for disobedience in carrying out his orders; he joined in the Hāmaj rising which superseded the Funj kings, and helped to defeat al-Amīn Musmār at Hilālīya, 1784; about 1804 he fought against Muḥammad Kamtūr, and on the coming of the Turks in 1821 was one of the few local leaders who remained loyal to the puppet ex-sultan Bādī VI.

Raḥma Muḥammad Manūfal (1850–1909), Mahdist amīr, a tribal notable of the Awlād Raḥma branch of the Jawāmaʿa Arabs of Kordofan; he took a leading part in the siege of Bāra, 1882; with his tribesmen he fell upon a government force commanded by ʿAlī Bey Luṭfī at Kāwa on the White Nile as it was marching to the relief of the Egyptian garrisons of al-Ubaiyaḍ and Bāra; after severely defeating this force he returned to his tribal lands; on the Anglo-Egyptian occupation of Kordofan he resumed cultivation and the collection of gum arabic; his son ʿAbd al-Qādir wad Raḥma inherited his father's shaikhdom.

al-Raiyaḥ ʿAlī Nafiʿ (1892–1940), ʿumda of Wad al-Murād; an ʿArakī by tribe, he was born at Wad al-Mansī.

Rajab Idrīs ʿAdlān (– *c.* 1881), shaikh of Jabal Funj; appointed 1857, he was jealous of his hereditary rights and in 1861 complained to the viceroy Muḥammad Saʿīd Pasha of the arbitrary manner in which taxes were being collected from his people; Idrīs Rajab Idrīs, nāẓir of Jabal Gule (d. 1931), was his son.

Rājab Muḥammad wad ʿAdlān (–1821), notable of the last days of the Funj sultanate of Sennar; a son of Muḥammad wad ʿAdlān killed by Ḥasan wad Rājab, a rival noble, in 1821, he was one of the delegates of Sultan Bādī VI who surrendered to the Turks on their approach to Sennar later in the year; Ismāʿīl Pasha, the Turkish commander, accorded him pardon and put him in charge of troops sent to arrest Ḥasan wad Rājab; in spite of Ismāʿīl's clemency, he was suspected of intrigue against the Turks who killed him in his bed at Sennar.

Ramaḍān ʿAlī (–1916), one of the military commanders of ʿAlī Dīnār, sultan of Dār Fūr; he commanded a rubaʿ of the sultan's army; in 1911 he succeeded Adam Rijāl as commander-in-chief but never attained the power or prestige of his predecessor; in 1913 he led a Fūr army against the ever-rebellious Rizaiqāt; at first successful, his army was defeated and scattered at the battle of Kanfūsa; in 1916 he and his brother Sulaimān commanded the sultan's troops opposing the Anglo-Egyptian army at the battle of Birinjīya; after the battle his banner and robe were found beside his dead horse, and it was later learned that he had died of wounds in the action.

Rameses II (1298 B.C.–1232 B.C.), Egyptian king of the XIXth Dynasty who waged successful war against the Nubians whom he subjugated, and who built the rock temple of Abū Simbel; his identification with the pharaoh of the Hebrew Bible is a subject of controversy.

Ramessenakht (*fl.* 1150 B.C.), Egyptian viceroy of Ethiopia during the reign of the XXth Dynasty king Rameses VI.

Rānfī . . . (–1803), puppet sultan of Sennar who was placed or the throne on the temporary deposition of Sultan Bādī VI wad Ṭabl II in 1803; it appears (though accounts differ) that he ruled for a few weeks only and was then killed in Sennar by a hostile faction led by Muḥammad wad Nāṣir, called Abū Rīsh.

Rāshid Bey Aymān (–1881), Egyptian soldier, governor of Fashoda on the White Nile; he left the White Nile with a force which included Shilluk tribesmen under the Reth Kaiku and C. Berghof, inspector for the suppression of slavery; his object was the destruction of the Mahdist power in the Nuba hills; his force was destroyed and himself killed at the battle of Jabal Qadīr.

Rāshid Pasha Rājab (–1876), Egyptian soldier; while governor of the eastern Sudan, 1875, he established a military post at Jīra on the River Setit near the Abyssinian border as one of a chain of forts between Keren and Gallabat to protect the Sudan from Abyssinian incursions; promoted liwā', he commanded the 2nd infantry brigade under Muḥammad Rātib Pasha in the Egyptian-Abyssinian war of 1875–6 and died of wounds received in the battle of Gura; al-liwā' W. W. Loring Pasha, his American companion-in-arms, praised him.

Rassam, Hormuzd (1826–1910), Assyriologist and British agent; he was born at Mosul the son of Chaldaean Christian parents; he held various political appointments at Aden and Muscat and took part in excavations of ancient Assyrian remains; he headed a mission which was sent to Abyssinia to endeavour to secure the release of prisoners held captive by King Theodore; the mission landed at Muṣawwaʿ in 1865 and travelled to Abyssinia via Keren, Kassala, and Gallabat; on arriving at the court of Theodore, he and his companions were themselves made captive and were released only on the arrival of a British military expedition; he wrote *A Narrative of the British mission to Theodore . . . with notices of the countries traversed* (1869).

Ra'ūf Pasha. *See* MUḤAMMAD RA'ŪF PASHA.

Rawlinson, Sir Henry Seymour, 1st Baron Rawlinson of Trent (1864–1925), British soldier; commissioned to the King's Royal Rifle Corps, 1884, he was promoted captain, 1891, and major, 1899; he served in the Nile campaign of 1897–8 and was present at the actions on the Atbara and at Omdurman, 1898, as deputy assistant adjutant-general; in the South African war, 1899–1902, he was chiefly engaged in staff duties; in the First World War he rose quickly to senior commands; he was a divisional commander in France in 1914, and in 1915–18 commanded an army group; a member of the war council, he was British military representative on the supreme war council at Versailles, 1918–19; from 1920 to 1925 he was commander-in-chief in India; promoted major-general in 1909, he was made full general in 1917 and created a baron.

Ready, Sir Felix Fordati (1872–1940), British general; he received a commission in the Royal Berkshire Regiment, 1891, and was promoted captain, 1902; seconded to the Egyptian army, 1898–1900, he fought in the battles of the Atbara and Omdurman, 1898; after service in the South African war, 1899–1902, and in France in the First World War, he was appointed director of personal services at the War Office, London, 1921; promoted general in 1934, he was quartermaster-general to the forces, 1931–5, when he retired.

Reed Bey, Horatio B . . . (1836–1888), American officer on the Egyptian general staff; born in New York he received a commission in the 5th United States Artillery, 1861, and in the civil war he fought on the Federal side rising to the colonelcy of a New York cavalry regiment, 1864; he retired from the United States army, 1870, and entered the Khedivial service; appointed second in command to R. E. Colston Bey who was charged with a survey mission in Kordofan, 1874, he was invalided before the mission reached Dongola and was replaced by H. G. Prout Bey.

* **Reinisch, Leo** (1832–1919), Austrian philologist; born at Osterwitz in Styria, he was private secretary to the Emperor Maximilian of Mexico, 1866–7, and thereafter devoted his life to learning; he was much interested in the Hamitic languages and their various affinities in the Sudan; his works include studies of the Beja and Nuba languages; he died at Lankowitz in his native province.

* **Reinthaler, Johann de Ducla** (–1862), Austrian priest of the Franciscan Order of the Roman Catholic Church; he joined the mission to Central Africa, 1859, and was for a short time stationed at Shallāl with the Jesuit, M. Kirchner, then pro-vicar apostolic, and then returned to Europe; in 1861 the pro-vicariate apostolic was transferred from the Jesuits to the Franciscans and in the same year he was appointed to the office; he returned to Africa and, after a visit to the mission stations on the Upper White Nile, fell ill and died at Berber.

Reisner, George Andrew (1867–1942), American Egyptologist; among many distinguished posts he held was the professorship of Egyptology in the University of Harvard; born at Indianopolis, Indiana, he was educated at Harvard and after prolonged archaeological work in Egypt was appointed director of the Harvard-Boston archaeological expedition to the northern Sudan, 1905; he was archaeological director of the archaeological survey of Nubia undertaken by the Egyptian Government, 1907–9, and later made important discoveries in the course of excavations at Kerma, Jabal Barkal, Nūrī, Qurrū, Semna, and Bajrawīya, leading to a great increase in our knowledge of ancient Egyptian and Meroïtic times; he died in his camp at the Pyramids of al-Jīza, Cairo; his wife, M. B. Reisner, herself an accomplished archaeologist, assisted him in much of his field-work and publication.

* **Reitz, Konstantin** (1819–53), Austrian consul at Khartoum, 1851–3; an influential and slightly eccentric figure in the capital, he was a great hunter and horseman and was noted for his furious energy; in 1851 he accompanied Mūsā Ḥamdī Pasha on a military expedition against the Ḥalanqa and Shukrīya tribes between Kassala and the valley of the Atbara; he was agent for a company formed to introduce small steamers for commercial purposes on the White Nile; he died of fever in Khartoum on his return from a journey to Abyssinia with T. von Heuglin, who succeeded him as consul; nothing is known of his origin; Yūsuf Khūrī, the Maronite companion of Sir W. Peel, who came across him in Khartoum in the winter of 1851–2, wrote that he had a Polish heart and a Jewish head, a pleasantry aimed at his morals but which suggests that he may have come from the Polish province of Galicia.

Renaud de Châtillon (1148–87), French crusader; born at Châtillon-sur-Indre, he went with the army of Louis le Jeune on the First Crusade; captured by the Saracens in 1160 while still a boy, he was held captive for sixteen years when he learnt Arabic; after having secured his freedom by ransom, he renewed the fight against the Muslims; in 1182 he conceived a daring raid on the Red Sea into the heart of Islam at Mekka and Madīna and had a fleet of galleys carried in sections overland by friendly Arabs to the gulf of ʿAqaba where they were assembled and launched; the Frankish fleet then set out and passing down the coast raided ʿĀīdhāb (Old Sawākin), 1182; the Franks destroyed a Muslim pilgrim fleet in the harbour, then, riding inland towards the north, captured a rich caravan on its way to Quṣair; during the period 1182–3 the Franks were masters of the Red Sea; Islam was now roused to the menace in its midst; in Egypt the Saracens prepared a fleet which sailed out and destroyed the Frankish ships, 1183; Renaud was defeated near Madīna but escaped to his fief, for he was lord of al-Karak (Crac, Kerak), Montréal, and Transjordan; captured later by Sultan Ṣalāḥ al-Dīn Yūsuf ibn Aiyūb I (Saladin) at the battle of the Horns of Ḥaṭṭīn, he was executed; his name is perpetuated in the Palestinian village of al-Rayna.

Rendel, George Wightwick (1833–1902). *See* ARMSTRONG, SIR WILLIAM GEORGE, Baron Armstrong of Cragside.

ha-Reubeni, David (*c.* 1490–*c.* 1540), Jewish adventurer; born possibly in Khaibar in Central Asia, possibly in Europe, he told the Pope and others that he had been sent by his brother, whom he claimed to be the king of a mythical Hebrew tribe, to obtain Palestine from the Muslims; he wrote memoirs, whose authenticity has been questioned, in which he stated that he visited the Sudan in 1530, travelling from the Red Sea coast to Sennar and thence to Dongola and Egypt; he was a swarthy dwarf who dressed in oriental clothes; of Reubeni there is an extensive literature in many languages; for a critical examination of his claim to have travelled in the Sudan see A. Z. Eshkoli, *The Memoirs of David ha-Reubeni* (Jerusalem, 1940, in Hebrew), and S. Hillelson in *Sudan Notes and Records* (Khartoum), xvi, 1933.

Rhodes, Francis William (1851–1905), British soldier and journalist, brother of Cecil Rhodes; he joined the army in 1873 and served in the Nile campaign of 1884–5; he was promoted colonel in 1889; he was correspondent of *The Times*, jointly with H. Howard, in the Nile campaign of 1898 and was wounded at the battle of Omdurman; prominent in the South African war, he died at Capetown.

* **Ricci, Alessandro** (–1832), Italian doctor, draughtsman, and traveller; born at Sienna, he accompanied the archaeological expeditions of W. J. Bankes (1815) and Baron H. C. M. von Minutoli (1818–21) to Upper Egypt and Nubia as a draughtsman; he travelled to Sennar with Ismāʿīl Pasha's army, 1820–1; leaving his fellow traveller, L. M. A. Linant de Bellefonds, at al-Dāmar, he hurried back to Sennar to replace A. Scotto, who had died there, as medical attendant to Ibrāhīm Pasha, 1821; his timely ministrations probably saved Ibrāhīm's life; an Italian

member of Ismā'īl's suite went mad shortly after and Ricci accompanied him to Egypt; he left a valuable manuscript account of his journey to Sennar published by A. Sammarco as *Alessandro Ricci e il suo giornale di viaggio* (Cairo, 1930); in 1828–9 he took part in the Tuscan archaeological expedition to Nubia led by I. Rosellini and died at Luxor from a scorpion bite.

Richardson, John Soame (1834–1895), British major-general; commissioned in 1854 in the 12th Foot, he served in the Crimean war, 1854–5, and in the Maori war in New Zealand, 1860–1 and 1863–4; in 1865 he retired from the British army and in 1876 was appointed to command the forces in New South Wales; on the intervention of Britain in the Mahdist revolt in 1884 the Government of New South Wales sent a force to assist the Home troops campaigning on the Red Sea coast and he was given command of it; the New South Wales contingent landed at Sawākin early in 1885 and joined Lieutenant-General Sir G. Graham's field force; owing, however, to the decision of the British Government to discontinue active operations against the Mahdists, it had little fighting and was soon withdrawn with the rest of Graham's field force; the contingent was dressed in khaki uniform, then a novelty, as Richardson considered the official red to be an unserviceable colour.

Richardson, Robert (1779–1847), British physician and traveller; he accompanied the Earl of Belmore in a journey to Nubia, 1816–17, visiting Wādī Ḥalfā and Abū Ṣīr rock; he wrote *Travels* (1822).

Richardson, William Stewart (*c.* 1832–1901), British major-general; he entered the army, 1852, and served in the Indian mutiny, 1857–9, the Egyptian war, 1882, and the Nile campaign, 1884–5.

* **Rifā'a Bey Rāf'i al-Ṭahṭāwī** (1801–73), Egyptian translator; born at Ṭahṭa in Upper Egypt, he was educated at al-Azhar University, Cairo, and at Paris; after ten years studying in France, he was appointed director of the office of translation, founded in 1842 on the initiative of Muḥammad 'Alī Pasha at Cairo, and later became principal of the school of foreign languages there; he translated many foreign learned works into Arabic; the accession of 'Abbās Pasha Ḥilmī in 1849 resulted in a reactionary régime; he and several of his colleagues were dismissed from their posts in 1849 and in 1850 banished to Khartoum ostensibly to found a school there but in reality to remove a body of men suspected of modernism; he and those of his colleagues who survived returned to Egypt in 1854 on the accession of the liberal Muḥammad Sa'īd Pasha who recalled them; his Sudan experiences are recorded in his book *Manāhij al-albāb al-miṣrīya*. After his return from Khartoum, he became editor of *Rawḍat al-madāris*, a government educational journal.

Rigolet, Charles (*c.* 1853–   ), French soldier, sub-lieutenant of the French army on the unattached list; he entered the Khedivial service and was employed in 1878–9 as governor of Dāra and then of Shaqqa in Dār Fūr; ill from dysentery he resigned, and Gordon Pasha, then governor-general of the Sudan, who considered him to be unsuited for the hard life of a provincial administrator, accepted his resignation; his manuscript notes and diary are in the archives of the Geographical Society of Paris.

Rivelet, Geneviève (–1875), French religious sister, mother superior of the Roman Catholic Mission in Khartoum where she died.

Rokeby, Langham (*c.* 1838–73), British officer of the Royal Marines; lieutenant, 1859, and 2nd captain, 1867, he retired from the army, 1870; entering the Egyptian telegraphic service, he arrived at Sawākin in October 1870 with A. M. Rolfe, a telegraph engineer, to restore and complete the telegraph line between Sawākin and Kassala; they repaired the line as far as Kassala where Rokeby arrived in May 1871, Rolfe having died in Kassala a fortnight before; Rokeby began clearing the ground for laying the line to Berber and by August had finished 100 miles of the work when failing health caused his resignation; he reached Cairo where he died in February 1873; see *Narrative of an expedition from Suakin to the Soudan; compiled from the journal of the late Captain Langham Rokeby by Francis Parry* in the *Journal of the Royal Geographical Society*, xliv, 1874.

Rolfe, Ernest Neville (1847–1909), British admiral; a sub-lieutenant, 1867, and lieutenant, 1871, he saw service in the Ashanti war, 1873–4, and on the Congo and Niger, 1874–6; in 1884, while a commander in the Royal Navy, he led the naval brigade under Lieutenant-General Sir G. Graham in the second battle of el-Teb (Andateib) where a British force gained a victory over the Mahdists; for his services in this campaign he was promoted captain; he accompanied Vice-Admiral Sir W. N. W. Hewett on a mission to King John IV of Abyssinia in connexion with the withdrawal of Egyptian garrisons from the Sudan through his territory; raised to flag rank in 1899, he was promoted admiral in 1907 when he retired.

* **Rosellini, Ippolito** (1800–43), Italian egyptologist; born in Pisa, at whose university he was a professor, he was head of an archaeological expedition sent by the Government of the Grand Duchy of Tuscany to Egypt and Nubia; in 1828–9 the mission joined forces with that of J. F. Champollion, visiting Wādī Ḥalfā and describing the rock temple of Abū Simbel.

Rosset Pasha, Charles-Frédéric (–1879), trader, afterwards government official; nothing has been found concerning his origin; he seems to have lived in the Sudan since about 1860; he was the agent in Khartoum for C. G. Gordon Pasha when the latter was governor of Equatoria, 1874–6, and was at various times acting vice-consul for both Britain and Germany in Khartoum; when Gordon became governor-general in 1877 he combined his consular duties with those of Gordon's private secretary; it is said that he led the party at the governor-general's office which was opposed to 'Uthmān Pasha Rifqī, vice-governor-general, 1878, whom Gordon suspected of irregularities; in 1879 he was appointed governor of Dār Fūr where he went at once to join R. Gessi Pasha who at the time was engaged in suppressing the revolt of Sulaimān wad Zubair, but died three days after his arrival at al-Fāshar, by poison it was alleged by some unsupported contemporary opinion; P. Matteucci wrote that he had an elegant house in Khartoum and that his wife Maria, a daughter of Mussu, a Maltese resident in Khartoum, was pretty and *simpatica*, possessing an English education and an Italian gracefulness.

Rossi Bey, Elia (1816–92), Italian physician; born at Ferrara, where he studied medicine, he came to Egypt in 1838, entered the government medical service, and was posted to the army; in 1856 he accompanied Prince Muḥammad ʿAbd al-Ḥalīm to the Sudan on the latter's appointment as governor-general, and served in the Sudan until about 1865; he wrote a number of medical papers; his experiences in the Sudan are embodied in his *La Nubia ed il Sudan* (Constantinople, 1858).

Rossignoli, Paolo (1852–1919), Italian missionary priest of the Roman Catholic Church; he was born at Frascati and studied in Rome; he came to the Sudan, 1880, and was sent to the mission station of Delen (Dilling), 1881, and later to al-Ubaiyaḍ where he was captured by the Mahdists on the fall of the town, 1883; after eleven years in captivity, in which he kept a cook-shop in Omdurman, he escaped to Aswān, 1894; promoted canon he died in Rome; he wrote *I miei dodici anni di prigionia in mezzo ai Dervisci del Sudan* (Mondovi, 1898).

Rott, Gottfried (–1883), Swiss schoolmaster at Asyūṭ; W. E. Gladstone, British prime minister, and the Anti-Slavery Society, complimented him for having discovered a number of slaves being smuggled over the Darb al-Arbaʿīn road from Dār Fūr for sale in Egypt; the Egyptian Government afterwards appointed him an inspector for the suppression of slavery and sent him to Dār Fūr where R. C. von Slatin Bey, governor, 1881–3, employed him in intelligence duties; he sickened soon after at Dāra and died at al-Fāshar; he was a competent Arabic scholar.

Roulet, Édouard (*c.* 1868–1928), French soldier; while serving as a captain of marine infantry, he was given command of the rear-guard of the Marchand expedition and the task of reinforcing the French occupation of the Upper White Nile and Baḥr al-Ghazāl; he arrived at Tambura, 1898, and founded a military post at M'bia; he occupied Mushraʿ al-Raq and, in spite of Dinka hostility, installed his troops at Ayak on the Rohl and at Shambé on the Nile; as a result of the Anglo-French agreement, 1899, he received orders from his government to evacuate the Baḥr al-Ghazāl, and left Tambura for the Congo, 1900, while one of his officers, Lieutenant A. de Q. de Tonquedec, returned to France by Shambé and the Nile; he was afterwards promoted colonel.

* **Roveggio, Antonio Maria** (1858–1902), prelate of the Roman Catholic Church, titular bishop of Amastri, and vicar apostolic of Central Africa; he was born at Colonia Veneta near Verona and was ordained priest at Vicenza, 1884, being one of the first ten who professed in the newly formed Society of the Sons of the Sacred Heart of Jesus (F.S.C.J.), popularly known as the Verona Fathers; he was elected vicar apostolic of Central Africa, and consecrated bishop, 1895; the Mahdist rule and

the war of reoccupation prevented his entering Khartoum before January 1900; he endeavoured to obtain for the mission the old site between the present governor's office and the Blue Nile whereon were the ruins of the church and school buildings which had been occupied by the mission from 1848 to the end of 1883, but in this was unsuccessful; he died at Berber on a train while on his way to Cairo; he was buried first at Berber and afterwards, in 1904, re-interred in the Roman Catholic church at Aswān.

Roversi, Alfonso (–1882), Italian inspector for the suppression of slavery; he came from Bologna and was a Protestant by religion; appointed inspector in the Nuba hills in 1881, he accompanied Bishop D. Comboni on a journey between the Nuba hills and the Baḥr al-Ghazāl, and assisted in the compilation of Comboni's map of Jabal Nuba published by the Italian Geographical Society (Rome, 1882); on the coming of Muḥammad Aḥmad al-Mahdī to the Nuba hills, he led a successful raid upon slaves allied with the Mahdī but, when the Mahdists captured the Roman Catholic mission at Dilling, 1882, he sought safety with the rebels and (according to L. Bonomi) became a Muslim and took the name of Manṣūr; he fell sick of dysentery and died in November 1882.

al-Rubāṭ I wad Bādī I (–1642), sultan of Sennar, of the royal line founded by 'Umāra Dūnqas; he ascended the throne in 1614, having succeeded his father Bādī I Sīd al-Qūm; during his reign the Abyssinians made several raids into Sennar territory; he was followed on his death by his son, Bādī II abū Diqn.

al-Rubāṭ II wad 'Adlān (–1789), puppet sultan of Sennar; he reigned for only a few weeks between the equally powerless puppets Bādī V and Ḥasab Rabbu, or Rabihi; he was killed in the endless civil war of the time, the plaything of powerful Hāmaj nobles who disputed the control of what was left of the sultanate.

Rugman, Sir Francis Dudley (1894–1946), British official; after serving as a soldier throughout the First World War, 1914–19, he qualified as a chartered accountant, 1920, and in the same year entered the Sudan civil service as an inspector in the finance department; he was financial secretary and a member of the governor-general's council, 1934–44, when he retired; at the time of his death he was serving with the Allied forces in Germany.

Rundle Pasha, Sir Henry MacLeod Leslie (1856–1934), British general; commissioned in the Royal Artillery, 1876, he fought in the Egyptian war, 1882, and transferred to the Egyptian army; in 1883–4, with Major (afterwards Field-Marshal Lord) Kitchener, he made various reconnaissances in Dongola province and in the Nubian desert to mobilize the nomad tribes against the rising Mahdist power; he served in the Nile campaign of 1884–5 and again in the Frontier Force, 1885–7; he fought at Tūshkī (Toski), 1889, under the sirdār Sir F. W. (afterwards Lord) Grenfell Pasha, and in the Dongola and Nile campaigns, 1896–8, as chief of staff and adjutant-general to Kitchener who succeeded Grenfell; he led a force from Omdurman to relieve an Egyptian force under C. S. B. Parsons Pasha besieged in Gedaref by the Mahdist amīr Aḥmad Faḍīl Muḥammad, 1898; he left the Egyptian army at the end of the Mahdist war and fought in the South African war, 1900–2; after filling high military administrative posts in Britain, he was governor and commander-in-chief, Malta, 1905–15; his slow-but-sure methods earned him the nickname 'Sir Leisurely Trundle'.

Rüppel, Eduard Wilhelm Peter Simon (1794–1884), German naturalist; born at Frankfurt-am-Main, he received a scientific education and travelled much in Europe; he left Cairo in October 1822 and travelled via Dongola and the Bayūda to the northern approaches to Kordofan; he visited Jabal Barkal and Napata then returned to Cairo; in the autumn of 1823 he set out through Dongola to Shendi and Sennar, returning to Dongola early in 1824 via Shendi and the ruins of Meroë; after spending the summer in the region of Dongola and Dār Sukkōt, he spent the winter of 1824–5 in a journey over the Bayūda to Kordofan, returning thence to Dongola and Egypt when, after travels to various points on the Red Sea coast, he arrived in Europe in 1827; he thereafter devoted himself to an academical career in Germany; he died at Frankfurt-am-Main; his *Reisen in Nubien, Kordofan und dem petraischen Arabien* (Frankfurt-am-Main, 1829) records his journeys in the Sudan.

Russegger, Josef von, Ritter (1802–63), Austrian geologist and traveller; born at Salsburg, he became director of coal mines in Hungary and a leading authority on mining geology; in 1838 he was commissioned by Muḥammad 'Alī Pasha to explore the mineral resources of the Sudan and visited Jabal Taqalī in the Nuba hills and the mountains of Fāzūghlī in the Blue Nile valley in a prospection for gold; his over-optimistic reports on the prospects of finding gold were countered by the distinctly pessimistic reports of the Italian Boreani whom the viceroy had also sent to the Sudan to search for precious metals; accepting Russegger's opinion the viceroy thereupon spent much energy and money in a fruitless quest for Sudan gold; besides several papers on the geology of the Sudan he wrote *Reisen in . . . Afrika* (Stuttgart, 1841–9).

Rustum Bey . . . (–1833), Turkish governor of Kordofan and mīrālai commanding the 1st regular infantry regiment whose headquarters were at al-Ubaiyaḍ; he was inspecting the troops in the province of Sennar and visiting 'Alī Khūrshīd Bey (later Pasha), governor of Sennar, when he died in Khartoum.

Rustum Pasha Jarkas (–1852), governor-general of the Sudan from January to May 1852 in succession to 'Abd al-Laṭīf Pasha 'Abd Allāh; he instituted a council (majlis al-aḥkām) with powers of appeal and other functions similar to those established in Egypt; he barely had time to inspect his territory, beyond visiting Wad Madanī, whence he returned, a sick man, to die in Khartoum; his grave is in the cemetery in ʿAbbās avenue, immediately to the west of the tomb of Aḥmad Pasha abū Widān; he was succeeded by Ismāʿīl Pasha Ḥaqqī abū Jabal.

Rustum Nājī Bey (–1875), qā'immaqām of the Egyptian army; he was second in command to mīrālai S. A. Arendrup Bey in the Egyptian-Abyssinian war of 1875–6; Arendrup's force left Muṣawwaʿ in the autumn of 1875 for the highlands of Hamasien and was destroyed by an Abyssinian army at Gundet; Rustum was killed with his chief; several times wounded, he fell after making a gallant attempt to rally his men.

* **Ryllo, Maximilien** (–1848), Polish priest of the Jesuit Order in the Roman Catholic Church; he was born in the Russian province of Lithuania and received his theological education in Rome where he was in 1845 appointed rector of the Collegio Urbano; in the same year the Board for the Propagation of the Faith created the vicariate of Central Africa, confirmed by Pope Gregory XVI in 1846; the Austrian Imperial family led the contribution of funds, the mission was placed under the protection of an Austrian consulate at Khartoum, and Ryllo was made the first pro-vicar of the mission; with a party of other missionaries he left Cairo in 1847, travelling by Dongola and over the Bayūda; he died in Khartoum four months after his arrival in the town; his grave in the old mission garden was destroyed during the Mahdist régime.

Saba, Constantin (1875–1923), Syrian merchant of a Greek Orthodox family of Aleppo where he was born; coming to Khartoum in 1902, he set up in business in Omdurman where he imported gold and silver bullion and exported ivory and ostrich feathers to the United Kingdom; he settled in Egypt in 1917 and died in Cairo.

Sabatier, Louis (*fl.* 1840–1), French explorer; little is known of him other than from the journals of J. P. d'Arnaud and F. Werne whom he accompanied on the second voyage, led by Salīm Qapūdān in 1840–1, to attempt the discovery of the source of the White Nile; he is said to have been an engineer by profession; he lived formerly in Texas and was able to pass as an American or Frenchman.

Ṣābūn Keppi (–1932), mak of the Atoro hills in the eastern group of the Nuba hills of Kordofan.

Ṣābūn Muḥammad (–1944), notable of the Rizaiqāt tribe of the Baqqāra Arabs, a cousin of Shaikh ʿUqail al-Dinkāwī, nāẓir of the Rizaiqāt in Mahdist times; he was ʿumda of Dobo, near al-Fāshar in Dār Fūr, where he died.

Sacconi, Pietro (1840–83), Italian merchant; born at Borgonovo near Piacenza, he pursued commerce round the world; between 1870 and 1880 he was in business in the Sudan; he later established a commercial house in Harar and, while exploring the Ogaden, was killed by Somali tribesmen.

Saʿd Allāh Saʿdān (–1898), Mahdist amīr, by tribe a Taʿāʾishī, though his mother was a negress from Dār Fertyt; while fighting under the command of the amīr Aḥmad Faḍīl Muḥammad outside Gedaref against a government force led by C. S. B. Parsons Pasha, he was defeated, 1898; he retreated with Aḥmad Faḍīl to the Blue Nile where he was killed by a shell from an Egyptian gunboat at the battle of Dākhila near Roseires later in the year.

Saʿd al-Nūr. *See* AḤMAD SHAṬṬA.

Ṣafīya bint al-Mak Ṣubair (*fl.* 1820), daughter of Mak Ṣubair, leader of the Ḥannakāb clan of the Shāʾiqīya tribe; he commanded the Shāʾiqī army in the battle of Jabal Daija (Dager) against the Turks under Ismāʿīl Pasha, 1820; on the defeat of the Shāʾiqīya Ṣafīya, who was present at the battle, was captured by the Turks; Ismāʿīl, impressed by her bravery, treated her with respect and sent her back to her father under a truce, dressed in rich Turkish clothes; she persuaded her father to make an armistice with the Turks resulting in the Ḥannakāb Shāʾiqīya entering the Turkish service as irregular cavalry.

Ṣaga Krestos (Zaga Christ) (1610–38), Abyssinian prince, son of Yaʿkob Malak Sagad (Jacob) II who was killed in 1607; his mother, fearing for her son's life, sent him to Sennar where he was well received by the sultan al-Rubāṭ (reigned 1614–42); his story was that the sultan turned against him for his refusal to marry his daughter and he fled to an unidentified neighbouring ruler named Sālim or Salīm who gave him asylum; Susenyos (Socinius), a hostile king of Abyssinia, sent a force to capture him, but it failed to do so; finally he escaped to Cairo where the pasha treated him well; after living in Jerusalem where he embraced the Latin Catholic faith, Pope Urban VIII invited him to Rome whither he went in 1632; he died at Reuil near Paris of pleurisy and (it is said) of debauchery as a guest of Cardinal de Richelieu; it is possible that he was an impostor and that the above account of his origin is a fabrication.

Sagar, John Warburton (1878–1941), British official; educated at the University of Cambridge, he served for a year as an assistant master at Loretto school and in 1903 entered the Sudan political service; he was governor of Kordofan, 1917–21, and of Ḥalfā province, 1922–4, when he retired.

Saʿīd Pasha. *See* MUḤAMMAD SAʿĪD PASHA

Saʿīd Bey ʿAbd Allāh (1864–1935), mīrālai of the Egyptian army; by birth a Taqalāwī from the Nuba hills, his family was settled in Khartoum after Mūsā Pasha Ḥamdī's raid on Jabal Taqalī, 1863–4, and in Khartoum he was born; he joined the regular army in the ranks and was stationed at Amideb on the eastern frontier, 1880–5, when with the survivors of the Egyptian garrisons he was withdrawn to Egypt as sergeant-major of reserve police; commissioned in 1888, he fought at Jummaiza (Gemaiza) and Tūshkī (Toski), 1889, Tokar, 1891, and in the battles of the Dongola and Nile campaigns, 1896–8, promoted yūzbāshī, 1894, binbāshī, 1906, and qāʾimmaqām, 1912, he retired on promotion to mīrālai, 1918; for some years he commanded the reservists' cantonment at Kassala; his last years were spent at al-Buwaida near Qal'a al-Naḥl where he was a magistrate; he died at al-Buwaida.

Sa'īd Bey 'Abd al-Qādir (–1883), mīrālai of the Egyptian army; he commanded the 2nd regular infantry regiment in the army of Kordofan under W. Hicks Pasha and was killed in the battle of Shaikān (Kashgil).

Sa'īd 'Abd al-Raḥmān Jamāl al-Dīn (–1924), Ja'lī notable; he was a magistrate and 'umda of Shendi where he died.

Sa'īd 'Awad al-Jidd (–1931), religious notable of the Khawālda; a follower of the tenets of the Sammānīya brotherhood as was his father who was known for his great spiritual powers; he died at al-'Ifaina.

Sa'īd Pasha Huṣain al-Jimī'ābī (–1884), liwā' of the Egyptian army, a member of the Jimī'āb section of the Ja'līyīn; he was officer commanding Egyptian troops at al-Dūwaim in 1883 during the operations against the Mahdists on the White Nile; in 1884, during the earlier part of the siege of Khartoum, C. G. Gordon Pasha appointed him in command of the bāshī-būzuq troops defending the city; while leading a force to attack Ḥalfaiya, the present Khartoum North, he with Ḥasan Pasha Ibrāhīm al-Shallālī attempted to betray their force into the hands of the Mahdists but failed in their object; arrested by their own troops, they were tried by court-martial for murder and treachery and were executed.

* **Sa'īd Bey Juma'** (–1912 ?), soldier of the Egyptian army; he was born and died in the Fayyūm; he was governor of al-Fāshar in Dār Fūr, 1879–84; R. C. von Slatin Bey, who had been appointed governor-general of Dār Fūr in 1881, found that he had been dismissed from the governorship in 1880 and, as he had to carry on the administration, reinstated him; Slatin wrote of him as an intriguer and unpopular with the officers but a brave man, greatly attached to Dār Fūr, and famed for his rich vocabulary of bad language; he defended al-Fāshar with gallantry when the town was besieged by the Mahdists, surrendering with the garrison when defence was no longer possible; Muḥammad Aḥmad al-Mahdī appointed him commander of the Mahdist artillery and, with Yūsuf Manṣūr, formerly a mulāzim of the Egyptian army, as his second in command, he was responsible for the bombardment of Khartoum, 1884; he survived the régime of the Khalīfa 'Abd Allāhi and retired to spend his old age in the Fayyūm; he was a very tall man.

Sa'īd Muḥammad Faraḥ (–1891), Mahdist amīr; of Funj origin, he was born at Tangasi in the neighbourhood of al-Dabba and became nāẓir of the Funj colony in those parts under the Egyptian Government; on the rise of the Mahdist movement he changed sides and became amīr of the local Funj; he saw active service against the Anglo-Egyptian forces on the northern frontier, but was not in the Mahdist army which invaded Nubia and met its end at Tūshkī (Toski); a member of the party which resented the dictatorship of the Khalīfa 'Abd

Allāhi and his exclusion of the Mahdī's family from all authority, he was banished to Fashoda where he and other Mahdist notables were killed; his son, Shaikh Aḥmad Sa'īd Muḥammad, is president of the Funj court of al-Dabba.

Sa'īd Naṣr Pasha (1839–1905), soldier of the Egyptian army who spent the greater part of his working life in civil posts; educated in France, including a period at the military academy of Saint-Cyr and in the French army, he returned to Egypt in 1861; among the various administrative posts he held was that of French secretary to the governor of the Red Sea littoral, 1880–1; he was later honorary president of the Mixed Courts in Egypt and a pasha.

Sa'īd Pasha Shuqair, Sir (1868–1938), Syrian official in the service of the Egyptian and Sudan Governments; born at Shwaifat in the Lebanon of a distinguished Protestant family, he was educated at the Syrian Protestant College, afterwards known as the American University, in Beirut and after graduating taught Arabic there, 1886–9, and was the joint author of an Arabic grammar; in 1889 he emigrated to Egypt and was for a short time a journalist on the staff of the Cairo newspapers *al-Muqaṭṭam* and *al-Muqtaṭaf*, but before the year was out he entered the Egyptian Government service; he was employed in the ministry of finance under A. (afterwards Viscount) Milner, then in Sawākin under Sir H. H. (afterwards Earl) Kitchener, who had him transferred to the intelligence department in Cairo; in 1900 he was put in charge of the accounts of the newly formed Sudan Government and from 1907 to 1921 was director-general of accounts; from 1921 till his death he was financial adviser to the Sudan Government; he played an unobtrusive but decisive part in the organization of the Sudan finances; in 1919 the amīr Faisal invited him to reorganize the Syrian financial service; he afterwards went to England to advise the British Government on financial questions concerned with Syria and its share of the Ottoman debt; he was promoted bey, 1907, pasha, 1909, and was knighted by King George V, 1924.

al-Saiyid Aḥmad al-Saiyid Timsāḥ al-Kadarū (*c.* 1863–1926), 'umda of al-Kadarū eight miles north of Khartoum; by tribe a Dūlābī, his father worked for Zubair Bey Raḥma Manṣūr (afterwards pasha) in the Baḥr al-Ghazāl and Dār Fūr and earned his nickname Timsaḥ (crocodile) from his great height and strength; he served in the Mahdist régime as leader of the local Dūwālīb and was for five years in Equatoria under the amīr 'Arabī Dafa' Allāh, returning to Omdurman about 1891; he led his men at the battle of Omdurman, 1898; a short time afterwards the new government appointed him 'umda of Kadaru where he served till his death.

Saiyid al-'Awad Nabrī (1858–1922), Dūlābī notable, 'umda of Omdurman; he was succeeded first by his son 'Abd al-Raḥmān and then by another son, Maqbūl, the present 'umda.

Ṣalāḥ al-Dīn Yūsuf ibn Aiyūb (Saladin) (1138–93), Kurdish ruler of Egypt and Syria, leader of the Muslim resistance to the Frankish

Crusades; he sent two expeditions against Northern Nubia; in the second of them an army commanded by his elder brother, Aiyūb al-Malik al-Mu'aẓẓam Shams al-Dawla Turānshāh, setting out from the Yaman, invaded Nubia in 1173 and sacked Qaṣr Ibrīm (Primis).

Ṣāliḥ 'Alī al-Dadinjāwī (1875–1939), notable of Dār Fūr; born in al-Fāshar, his paternal ancestors included mulūk and warriors of renown; his great-great-grandfather Malik Mūsā was killed in warfare with the sultanate of Wadā'i, his great-grandfather Malik Ḥamad Wir was killed at Umm Dam fighting against the Funj, and his grandfather Malik Ibrāhīm was killed at the battle of Bāra, 1821, fighting the Turks; on his mother's side his great-grandmother was a daughter of the Fūr sultan 'Abd al-Raḥmān Aḥmad Bukr who reigned 1785–99; as a young man he was taken to Omdurman by the Ta'ā'isha and in 1899 he returned to Dār Fūr with Sultan 'Alī Dīnār by whom he was held in high favour; in 1907 he went to Makka with the sultan's first caravan; while passing through Khartoum he saw General Sir F. R. Wingate, governor-general of the Sudan, and apparently gave him some sort of guarantee for the sultan's behaviour which later got Ṣāliḥ into trouble; when he returned to al-Fāshar in 1908 he found that Tīrāb Sulaimān, 'Alī Dīnār's military commander, had been put to death, his own brother Malik Maḥmūd was in disgrace, and he himself had been deprived of most of the lands which the sultan had given him as a mark of favour; he remained at Qūz Baina until the dethronement of 'Alī Dīnār in 1916 and, it is said, declined several offers by the sultan to reinstate him at al-Fāshar; after the occupation of the capital by government troops, he helped to obtain the surrender of his brother Maḥmūd and then went back to retirement at Qūz Baina emerging into the limelight in 1926 when he was chosen 'umda of al-Fāshar; in 1928 he was made president of al-Fāshar court; he continued to administer his charge with wisdom and ability until within a short time of his death.

Ṣāliḥ ibn Bān al-Nuqā (Bān Naqā) (1681–1753), religious teacher of the family of the Ya'qūbāb descended from Muḥammad ibn Ḥamad Bān al-Nuqā (*fl.* 1550); he was one of the founders of that branch of the family which lives near Shendi; the hagiographer Muḥammad al-Nūr wad Ḍaif Allāh in the *Ṭabaqāt wad Ḍaif Allāh* describes his great religious influence in the northern part of the Funj sultanate.

Ṣāliḥ Bey Faḍl Allāh al-Kabbāshī (–1887), shaikh of the Kabbābīsh Arabs of northern Kordofan; when the bulk of his tribesmen had joined the Mahdist cause he, with a handful of loyal Kabbābīsh, resisted, cutting off small parties of Mahdists during the Nile campaign of 1884–5; his headquarters in 1885 were at Jabal al-'Ain; in 1887 he inflicted a reverse upon the amīr 'Abd al-Raḥmān wad al-Najūmī and the Egyptian Government sent him arms few of which ever reached him; in May 1887 'Uthmān Adam, the Mahdist governor of Kordofan, sent a force against him commanded by Faḍl 'Adlān; a battle took place at Umm Badr where after an initial victory he was beaten; he fled towards Jabal al-'Ain but was overtaken and killed.

Ṣāliḥ Ḥammād (–1939), Mahdist amīr, a prominent leader from the Ta'ā'isha tribe; he was for a time the Mahdist governor of the Jazīra with his seat at al-Kamlīn; his character provoked the popular saying *Ṣāliḥ 'adal, al-jidād qadal*; he had a reputation for being just.

Ṣāliḥ Bey Hijāzī (–1897 ?), qā'immaqām of the Egyptian army; in 1855 the viceroy Muḥammad Sa'īd Pasha, with a view to the suppression of the slave trade, ordered the establishment of a muḥāfiẓate on the White Nile; Ṣāliḥ Hijāzī, then a yūzbāshī, was appointed the first muḥāfiẓ with headquarters at Fashoda and a post at the mouth of the River Sobat; appointed in December 1855, he was dismissed for negligence in connexion with a revolt of the Dinka, but was reinstated in February 1863 on the request of Mūsā Pasha Ḥamdī, the new governor-general; about 1876 he was ma'mūr of Dāra in Kordofan; his subsequent career is ill recorded; in 1884 Gordon Pasha asked the Council of Ministers for the third grade to be conferred on him, and in 1891 he was a pensioner with rank of qā'immaqām.

Ṣāliḥ Bey Ḥusain Khalīfa (–1893), 'Abbādī notable, shaikh of the 'Abābda of Korosko and first cousin of Ḥusain Pasha Khalīfa, governor of Berber and Dongola under the Egyptian administration; during the Mahdist revolt he raised a force of irregulars for the Egyptian army, but his efforts were hindered by a feud between his men and those under a fellow 'Abbādī, Bashīr Bey Jubrān; he raided in wide sweeps south of the Egyptian border outposts and in 1891 captured an outpost of Abū Ḥamad and killed Sulaimān Nu'mān wad Qamar, the Manṣūrī chieftain who killed Lieutenant-Colonel J. D. H. Stewart in 1884; while patrolling the desert road between Abū Ḥamad and Korosko he was attacked by the Mahdist amīr 'Uthmān Azraq who killed him at Murrāt wells; his younger brother 'Abd al-'Aẓīm (afterwards Bey) succeeded him in command.

Ṣāliḥ Idrīs (–1914), nāẓir of the Banī 'Āmir tribe who graze on the Eritrean border of the Sudan.

* **Ṣāliḥ Pasha al-Mak** (*c.* 1828–90), liwā' of the Egyptian army; a Shā'iqī, born at Merowe, he joined the Shā'iqīya irregular cavalry and served the Egyptian Government in the Jazīra and elsewhere, leading various tax-collecting patrols; promotion came rapidly and he soon became sanjaq; on the outbreak of the Mahdist revolt he had orders to join the army of Yūsuf Pasha Ḥasan al-Shallālī which was afterwards destroyed by the Mahdists at Jabal Qadīr, 1882, but his orders were cancelled and he was sent to join in the defence of the Jazīra; here he fought many actions, raising the siege of Sennar, 1882, and defeating and killing the amīr Aḥmad al-Makāshfī at Jabal Saqadī, 1883; promoted sirsūwārī, he remained in the Jazīra, attacking and being attacked, until finally in February 1884 he was besieged in Masallamīya by the amīr Muḥammad al-Ṭaiyib wad al-Baṣīr; after a stout defence he surrendered with much stores and the steamer *Muḥammad 'Alī*; Gordon Pasha, himself shut up in Khartoum, was unable to do more than express his confidence in him by promoting him liwā' and recommending his elevation to the grade of pasha; two of his sons,

al-Binbāshī Muḥammad Ṣāliḥ and Ḥāmid Ṣāliḥ, were killed in the defence of Khartoum; he was imprisoned until Khartoum fell when the Mahdī released him; he was later allowed to tour the country collecting the dispersed Shā'iqīya tribesmen; while on one of these tours he died near al-Qiṭaina; Ḥamad Bey Ṣāliḥ al-Mak, ex-officer of the Egyptian army and Sudan Defence Force, and politician, is his son.

Ṣāliḥ Muḥammad al-Ghubshāwī (–1939), shaikh and magistrate in the neighbourhood of Rashād in the Nuba hills.

Ṣāliḥ Qawālalī (*fl.* 1854), Egyptian soldier of Macedonian origin; he was qā'immaqām of the 3rd regiment of the line in the Sudan in 1854 when his efficiency, and ability to read and write both Arabic and Turkish, secured his nomination as governor, Sennar, by a committee of senior officers sitting in Khartoum.

Ṣāliḥ Suwār al-Dhahab (–*c.* 1875), religious notable of Ja'lī ('Abbāsī) stock; he was born at Dongola of the celebrated religious family bearing his name; about 1817 he accompanied al-Saiyid Muḥammad 'Uthmān al-Mīrghanī I from Dongola to Bāra and thence to al-Ubaiyaḍ where he died before the outbreak of the Mahdist revolt; his tomb at al-Ubaiyaḍ contains also the remains of al-Saiyid Ibrāhīm, son of al-Saiyid Muḥammad 'Uthmān al-Mīrghanī I; of his own two sons Muḥammad died at al-Ubaiyaḍ during the Mahdist occupation and Ibrāhīm, who became a Mahdist amīr, was killed at Matamma in the massacre of the Ja'līyīn by the amīr al-umarā' Maḥmūd Aḥmad in 1898.

* **Salīm I** (1467–1520), Ottoman sultan, known as Yāvūz (the inexorable, inflexible) Sultan Salīm; in 1517 he conquered Egypt from the Burjī Mamelukes and within a few months sent Turkish troops to garrison Sawākin and Muṣawwa'; in 1520 a force of Bosnian troops penetrated to Dongola and the region as far as Jabal Barkal; this force defeated a Funj army near al-Khandaq; the Turks occupying Sawākin were the forebears of many present-day inhabitants of the town, while Bosnian and Magyar detachments left their traces in the region of Wādī Ḥalfā.

Salīm Pasha Arnā'ūṭ (*c.* 1808–*c.* 1862), Albanian officer in the Egyptian army; his military career of thirty-five years was spent mostly with the Egyptian forces in Syria and in the Sudan; he was probably the Salīm Bey who served in the Crimean war before Sebastopol as mīrālai in command of the 19th infantry regiment; after his return to Egypt he was appointed commandant of the Sa'īdīya fortress built by the Viceroy Muḥammad Sa'īd Pasha near the Delta Barrage; he retired in 1861 and died in the Islamic year 1278.

Sālim Faḍl Allāh (–1840), shaikh of the Kabbābīsh Arabs of northern Kordofan; in the winter of 1838–9 Muḥammad 'Alī, Pasha of Egypt, then on a tour to the Sudan, summoned him to Khartoum and gave him and his tribe several concessions as to freight charges over the Bayūda of which the Kabbābīsh were the principal camel convoyers; he was succeeded by his son Faḍl Allāh wad Sālim Bey.

Sālim Naiyīl abū Daqal. *See* ʿAbd al-Raḥmān Bey Sālim abū Daqal.

* **Salīm Qapūdān** (*fl.* 1839–42), Turkish sailor; while a frigate captain with rank of binbāshī he was appointed by Muḥammad ʿAlī Pasha to command three expeditions to explore the White Nile; the first voyage was undertaken in 1839–40 with Salīm in command of the party, Sulaimān Kāshif, a Circassian officer, in command of the troops, and Faiẓ Allāh Qapūdān, second in command to Salīm; with them were the frigate captain Baumgarten, a Swiss, and G. Thibaut, a Frenchman, as engineer; the expedition reached a point on the White Nile 7° south latitude; the second expedition which was undertaken in 1840–1 ascended the Sobat 100 miles upstream of the mouth of that river, and then proceeding up the White Nile reached Gondokoro; on this expedition Salīm had with him the French engineer, J. P. d'Arnaud, the French-American L. Sabatier, and the German F. Werne; a third expedition, again accompanied by d'Arnaud, was made in 1842 when after reaching 4·42° of latitude the party returned after much privation; the rapids near Rejaf proved an insuperable barrier to the second and last voyages; Salīm is said to have been a short, thick-set man; though a good practical navigator his reports are not informative on the scientific side.

Salīm Pasha Ṣā'ib al-Jazā'irlī (*fl.* 1843–54), liwā' of the Egyptian army and governor-general of the Sudan; of his origin little is known other than that he served in the Sudan as ma'mūr of Fāzūghlī on the Blue Nile for a period from 1843 and later, in 1853–4, was employed as a ma'mūr ashghāl (probably administrative engineer on construction) on the railway then being built by Robert Stephenson from Alexandria to Cairo and Suez; he succeeded Ismāʿīl Ḥaqqī Pasha abū Jabal as governor-general of the Sudan in 1853; during most of his term of office he was confined to Khartoum by sickness which compelled his replacement in 1854 by al-Liwā' ʿAlī Pasha Sirrī al-Arnā'ūṭ.

Salīm Bey Shumaiyīl (1874–1933), Syrian official; born in Liverpool and educated at the Jesuit College and French School of Law, Beirut, he joined the Egyptian civil service and was in the ministry of war, 1894–8; in 1898–1910 he was in the finance department of the Sudan Government, and from 1910 until his death in Cairo he was secretary to the Koubbeh Gardens Company.

Salīm Bey ʿŪnī (–1883), Egyptian soldier; he commanded the 1st regular infantry regiment with rank of mīrālai in W. Hicks Pasha's army of Kordofan and was killed at the battle of Shaikān (Kashgil).

Salīm Bey Yūsuf ʿAṭīya (1878–1925), Syrian physician; born in Bainū, Akkār, in the Lebanon of a Protestant family, he was educated at the American University, Beirut, and afterwards studied medicine in the College of Physicians and Surgeons, Baltimore, United States; from 1898 to 1904 he served in the medical corps of the Egyptian army, then, transferring to the Sudan Government service, was medical officer in charge of the hospitals at Wādī Ḥalfā and Omdurman, 1905–20, when he retired; he died at Sūq al-Gharb in the Lebanon.

Salisbury, 3rd Marquess of. *See* CECIL, ROBERT ARTHUR TALBOT GASCOYNE, 3rd Marquess of Salisbury.

Salmān al-Ṭawwālī, called **al-Zaghrāt** (*fl.* 1520), holy man, by tribe a Ja'lī; 'Alī, called Abū Dilaiq, was among his pupils; he died, wrote Wad Ḍaif Allāh the hagiographer, at the age of 120 and was buried at Wad Saq Urta near Rufā'a; a number of his descendants live on the Blue Nile between Rufā'a and al-Kamlīn.

Salt, Henry (1780–1827), British traveller and collector of antiquities; in 1809–11 he was on a mission in Abyssinia on behalf of the British Government and was British consul-general in Egypt in 1815–27; a vigorous, restless man, he was an ardent student of antiquities; he had already toured with Lord Valentia as the latter's secretary and draughtsman and had visited Sawākin in 1806; he discovered the inscriptions at Abū Simbel in 1817; his passion for the collection of antiquities brought him into competition with B. Drovetti, the consul-general of France, and there were moments when British and French foreign policy in Egypt was diverted to serve the archaeological purposes of the two great collectors.

al-Samarqandī . . . (*fl.* 1550), genealogist; though his genealogies are much quoted in the Sudan, nothing is known either of his origin or his authenticity save by conjecture; he was possibly an itinerant religious man attracted by the newly established sultanate of Sennar; of his original work no trace seems to exist to-day, though there are many copies which purport to be genuine.

al-Sammānī al-Bashar (*c.* 1885–1946), Fallātī notable of southern Dār Fūr; he was born at Jiddād of the Ikka section of the Fallāta and during the Mahdist times was taken to Dār Bergo (now in French territory); he was shaikh of the Osmāna section of the tribe in 1916 when the Sudan Government occupied Dār Fūr, and in 1920 was made 'umda of the Juba section under the nāẓir Abū Ḥamaira; in 1931 he was appointed nāẓir of the Fallāta and in 1935 was made a magistrate; in 1937 he was appointed president of the Kalaka and Fallāta courts and vice-president of the Baqqāra confederate court; he died at Nyāla.

al-Sammānī Birair (*c.* 1851–1946), religious notable of the Ja'lī tribe and one of the principal shaikhs of the Sammānīya brotherhood in the Sudan; the son of Shaikh al-Birair wad al-Ḥasīn he was one of four brothers eminent in religion and he himself was the father of twenty-three sons and twenty daughters; on his death his religious mantle fell on his son Muḥammad al-Sammānī Birair; he died at the foot of Jabal Arashkūl north-west of al-Dūwaim.

Sanīn Ḥusain (*c.* 1847–1909), holy man and Mahdist; tracing his descent from the old Arab tribe of the Khazraj, his grandfather came to Dār Tāma on the western side of the present Wadā'i–Dār Fūr frontier as a stranger sharīfī; hearing of the reputation of Muḥammad Aḥmad al-Mahdī he and his followers went to Omdurman in 1885 to swear allegiance to him; he joined the army of the amīr Ḥamdān abū 'Anja, then waging war in the Nuba hills, and was fighting there,

1885–7; he next fought under Ḥamdan abū ʿAnja against the Abyssinians, 1887–9; when the amīr ʿAbd al-Qādir Dalīl went to western Dār Fūr he accompanied him and in 1891 was left in charge of Kabkabīya district; he was still there on the collapse of the Mahdist régime in the Nile valley; faithful to the Mahdist cause he gathered round him a strong fighting force; ʿAlī Dīnār, now sultan of Dār Fūr, sent several armies against him but all were defeated until in 1909 he was besieged in Kabkabīya and killed.

Sanjar Bey Urfalī (–1874), Turco-Egyptian soldier; he was governor of the eastern Sudan and Red Sea littoral during the brief period from October 1873 until his death.

* **Santoni, Licurgo Alois** (*fl.* 1865–98), Italian postal official; he joined the Egyptian postal service, 1865, and was director of posts in Upper Egypt and Nubia, *c.* 1878–98; he accompanied C. G. Gordon Pasha to the Sudan, 1878, and organized the postal service on the line of communication of the military expedition of 1884–5 which attempted the relief of Khartoum; he retired, 1898; for some years he was secretary-general of the Khedivial Geographical Society; his autobiographical *Alto Egitto e Nubia* (Rome, 1905) contains interesting chapters on the Gordon period.

al-Sanūsī Aḥmad Muḥammad (–1899), Mahdist amīr of the Taʿāʾis͟ha branch of the Baqqāra and half-brother of the K͟halīfa ʿAbd Allāhi; he was killed at the battle of Umm Dibaikarāt.

Ṣāqib . . . (*fl.* 1562), holy man traditionally said to have come from Makka; he was the ancestor of the As͟hrāf of Rufāʿa district on the east bank of the Blue Nile; there is a story that he was brought to the sultanate of Sennar by the deposed Sultan Dakīn wad Naiyīl, who reigned 1562–77, in order to intercede for him with the people, and that S͟haik͟h ʿAjīb wad ʿAbd Allāh al-Manjilak gave him land at Umm Aqārib, now called al-S͟harāfa.

Sartorius Pasha, George (1840–1912), British soldier in the British, Indian, and Egyptian armies; commissioned a lieutenant in the Royal Artillery, 1857, he was promoted captain, 1869; transferring to the Bombay Staff Corps, 1868, he was released for service with the Ottoman army where he fought through most of the Russo-Turkish war of 1876–8 and was made a pasha; having been a fellow officer of V. Baker Pasha in Turkey, he served under Baker in the Sudan; seconded to the Egyptian army, he was chief of staff and second in command to Baker in the campaign of 1883–4 on the Red Sea coast against the Mahdists under the amīr ʿUt͟hmān abū Bakr Diqna (Osman Digna); arriving at Sawākin with his chief and staff late in 1883, he was present at the disastrous defeat of el-Teb; his wife, Ernestine Sartorius, who was at Sawākin with her husband, wrote a lively account of life there entitled *Three months in the Soudan* (1885).

Sāʿtī Bey abū'l-Qāsim (–1884), qāʾimmaqām of the Egyptian army; he served in the Baḥr al-G͟hazāl in 1878 and in 1878–9 was with R. Gessi Pasha in the various campaigns in southern Dār Fūr; he took part in the defence of Khartoum against the Mahdists, 1884; in patrols south of Khartoum he burnt Kalakla, made a daring attack on a Mahdist force at Maḥū Bey's (now Gordon's) Tree, and attacked al-Qiṭaina where he was killed along with three of his officers; his death was a serious loss to Gordon Pasha.

Savage-Landor, Arthur Henry. *See* LANDOR, ARTHUR HENRY SAVAGE.

Sayce, Archibald Henry (1845–1933), British archaeologist; he was professor of Assyriology in the University of Oxford, 1891–1919; he visited the Sudan in 1908–9 and helped the Condominium Government to formulate its policy on the excavation and preservation of antiquities.

Saxe-Coburg-Gotha, Duke of. *See* ERNST, DUKE OF SAXE-COBURG-GOTHA.

Schnitzer, Eduard Carl Oscar Theodor, known as **Emin Pasha** (1840–92), physician and official; a German Jew of Protestant Christian parents, he was born at Oppeln in Silesia; after studying medicine in Germany he practised his profession in Albania and Anatolia as a medical officer in the Ottoman service, adopting Turkish dress, customs, and the name Mehemet Emin (Arabic Muḥammad al-Amīn); crossing to Egypt he travelled over the Nubian desert by way of Korosko and Berber, arriving penniless in Khartoum in 1875; the members of the European community assisted him to set up in private practice in the capital in 1876 when Colonel C. G. Gordon invited him to the Equatorial province as a medical officer; Gordon liked him and appointed him chief medical officer of the province, but from the first employed him in other administrative work including a mission to Uganda and Unyoro; in 1878 he was appointed governor of Equatoria, a post which he held till 1889; even before the rise of the Mahdist movement he was cut off from the world save for occasional visits to Khartoum; he explored the Lotuka and Unyoro country and made valuable contributions to the natural history of the region; when Khartoum fell in January 1885 and the Egyptian army withdrew to the north his isolation was complete; he found himself hemmed in on his northern border by a Mahdist force under the amīr ʿArabī Dafaʿ Allāh; to crown his troubles a mutiny broke out among his own troops; with great fortitude he maintained a semblance of administration until 1888–9 when, apparently against his will, he was rescued by the explorer H. M. Stanley with whom he and a remnant of his troops and civilian staff retired to Zanzibar; in 1887 he had been promoted liwā' and pasha; he later joined the German service in East Africa and was murdered by Arab slave traders near the Stanley Falls in what is now the Belgian Congo while on a journey of exploration; he was a clever administrator in unusually difficult circumstances; besides being a competent scientist he was an accomplished musician; punctilious and careful in dress, he was short-sighted and wore a beard; during his service in the Sudan he observed the practice of Islam; his career inspired an extensive literature printed mostly in English and German.

Schuver, Jan Maria (1852–83), Dutch explorer; born at Amsterdam, he was a man of substance and an untiring champion of the Sudanese slaves; after being correspondent of the *Standard* newspaper of London in the Russo-Turkish war of 1876–8 he wandered for a year in Armenia and Kurdistan then, after a stay in England, came to the Sudan, 1881; travelling by way of Berber and Khartoum he explored the Blue Nile basin including the country of the Berta as far as Fadāsī and mapped the sources of the Rivers Yābūs, Tūmāt, and Yāl; in 1883 he explored and mapped the desert country immediately north-west of Omdurman; going south he next explored the country of the Dinka of the Baḥr al-Ghazāl where he was murdered; his writings consist of papers, chiefly on his explorations, to various learned journals of Europe.

Schweinfurth, Georg August (1836–1925), German naturalist and explorer; born in Riga, he was educated at German universities, specializing in botany; in 1864 he came to Egypt whence he travelled along the Red Sea coast from Quṣair through Sawākin to Muṣawwaʿ and thence by Kassala, Gallabat, and Abū Ḥarāz to Khartoum, collecting botanical specimens; in 1868 he again came to the Sudan; landing at Sawākin, he journeyed through Berber to Khartoum where he was assisted by Jaʿfar Pasha Maẓhar, then governor-general; he then ascended the White Nile and Baḥr al-Ghazāl, reaching the Azande region and penetrating the hitherto unexplored country to the south, discovering the Uélé river, 1870–1; he then returned north by way of the Rohl river and Dār Fertīt to Berber and Sawākin; in 1874–83 he explored various districts of Egypt and Arabia, chiefly in relation to botany; he was the first president of the Khedivial Geographical Society of Egypt, founded by Ismāʿīl Pasha in 1875, and director of the Cairo museum, 1880–9; he afterwards settled in Berlin devoting the rest of his long life to the study of African subjects; during 1891–4 he made botanical expeditions in Eritrea; he published a large body of writings covering almost the whole range of natural history; his best-known book is *Im Herzen von Africa* (Leipzig, 1873), translated into many languages.

Scott, Douglas Alexander (1848–1924), British major-general; commissioned to the Royal Engineers, he served in the Egyptian war, 1882; he was managing director of the Soudan Railway during the Nile campaign, 1884, when the line was extended from Sarras to ʿAkāsha; promoted colonel, 1889, he held various technical appointments in Britain and in 1921 was made colonel-commandant, Royal Engineers.

Scott-Moncrieff, Colin Campbell (1883–1908), British official; he entered the Sudan political service in 1906 and, while serving in the Blue Nile province as a sub-inspector, was killed at Tujr near al-Ḥaṣṣa Ḥaiṣa by the followers of ʿAbd al-Qādir Muḥammad Imām wad Ḥabūba, a former Mahdist, who had revolted against the government.

Scotto, Antonio [Agostino ?] (–1821), Italian physician; Genoese by origin he came to Egypt and was, with his compatriot, A. Gentili, a member of the medical service in Ibrāhīm Pasha's army in the Arabian war in 1816–18 as Ibrāhīm's personal doctor; he served

Ibrāhīm in the same capacity during the latter's journey to Sennar, 1821; at Sennar, while his master was prostrate from dysentery, he himself died, possibly from blackwater fever assisted by *delirium tremens*.

Scudamore, Francis (1859–1939), British journalist; as correspondent of *The Times* newspaper of London with the army of V. Baker Pasha on the Red Sea coast he narrowly escaped death in the first battle of el-Teb, 1884; he was correspondent of the *Daily News* in the Dongola and Nile campaigns, 1896–8, and was present at the battle of the Atbara, 1898; Sir A. Conan Doyle described him as small, Celtic, mercurial, full of wit and go; he wrote *A Sheaf of Memories* (1925).

Seckendorff, Götz Burkhard von, Baron (–1883), major in the German army and a member of an old German family; he was attached to the British expedition against King Theodore in Abyssinia in 1867–8 on which he wrote his experiences (Potsdam and Leipzig, 1869); he was a volunteer on the staff of W. Hicks Pasha in the fatal advance of the Egyptian army into Kordofan and was killed at the battle of Shaikān (Kashgil); his German servant G. Klootz deserted to the Mahdists and died in 1886 while attempting to escape to Abyssinia.

Segato, Girolamo (1792–1836), Italian explorer and chemist; born at Vadana in the Bellunese, he arrived in Egypt to occupy a commercial post, 1818; turning explorer, he and L. Masi, an engineer, travelled to Sennar on the heels of the army of Ismā'īl Pasha in 1821–2 and mapped the country bounded by the rivers Atbara, Baraka, and Blue Nile; the map was afterwards lost; he and Masi are said to have also explored the region between Wādī Ḥalfā and the confluence of the Blue and White Niles but to have been refused permission to join Ismā'īl Pasha at Sennar; the diary of his Sudan journey was destroyed by fire in Cairo, while the remainder of his papers disappeared during the Austro-German occupation of northern Italy, 1917–18; after 1823 he devoted his energies in Florence to African cartography and to experiments in the petrification of corpses; he died in Florence.

Seligman, Charles Gabriel (1873–1940), British anthropologist; of Jewish origin he began his career as a physician; he made anthropological expeditions to various parts of the world; in 1909–10, 1911–12, and 1921–2 he was in the Sudan assisting to fill the almost complete blank in African anthropology; he held distinguished academical posts including the professorship of ethnology in the University of London; his *Pagan Tribes of the Southern Sudan* (1932) was the result of an invitation by the Sudan Government to make an ethnographic survey of the region; his wife, Brenda Z. Seligman, herself an authority on the linguistics of the Nuba hills, accompanied him on his tours in the Sudan.

Selous, Frederick Courtenay (1851–1917), British hunter; born in London, he went in 1871 to South Africa where for nearly twenty years he hunted big game; he hunted in the Baḥr al-Ghazāl in 1911; he was killed while fighting in the British army in the east African campaign of 1917.

Seneca (Lucius Annæus Seneca) (*c.* 4 B.C.–A.D. 65), Roman moral philosopher and politician; he was born at Cordoba in Spain, the son of Annæus Seneca the rhetorician; after many years of devotion to letters he entered Roman public life, but being unfortunate in his choice of party he was condemned to death by the Emperor Nero; among his writings is a work, *Quæstiones Naturales*, in which there is a description of the *sudd* region of the White Nile and a possible reference to Lake No, information which he may have derived from the legionaries whom Nero sent to discover the source of the Nile.

Seni (*fl.* 1520 B.C.), viceroy in Ethiopia of the Egyptian kings Thothmes I and Thothmes II of the XVIIIth Dynasty; he served 1537 B.C.–1500 B.C.

Senkovsky, Osip Ivanovitch (1800–59), Polish orientalist and traveller; born at Vilna, he studied oriental languages and was attached as a dragoman to the Russian Embassy at Constantinople in 1821 when, under the auspices of the Imperial Academy of St. Petersburg, he came to Egypt; he ascended the Nile to the Second Cataract, possibly in search of news of Ismā'īl Pasha's military expedition to Sennar, but was not allowed to go farther south; on his return to Russia in 1822 he was made professor of oriental languages in the University of St. Petersburg, where he died; his complete works were published in Russian (1858), but an extract in French from the notes of his journey to Nubia appeared in *Nouvelles Annales de Voyages* (Paris, 1822), xvi.

Sethauw (*fl.* 1250 B.C.), Egyptian viceroy of Ethiopia during the reign of the XIXth Dynasty king Rameses II; he is known to have been in office from before 1261 B.C. till after 1233 B.C.

Sety (*fl. c.* 1205), another of the Egyptian viceroys of Ethiopia; he served King Rameses Siptah, holding office approximately 1209 B.C.–1203 B.C.

Sève Pasha, Octave-Joseph-Anthelme, otherwise **Sulaimān Pasha al-Faransāwī** (1788–1860), French soldier, reorganizer of the Egyptian army; a lieutenant in the army of Napoleon, he was discharged after Waterloo and came to Egypt in 1816; the viceroy Muḥammad 'Alī Pasha charged him with the creation of a regular army on Western models; the *niẓām al-jadīd*, as his new force was called, gave a good account of itself in the wars in Greece and Syria; several of the infantry regiments in this new force were composed of Sudanese slaves captured in raids, such as the 1st regiment which, after training in Egypt, came to the Sudan in 1824; he later became farīq and pasha.

Shā'a al-Dīn wad al-Tuwaim (*fl. c.* 1550), traditional founder of the house of Abū Sin, an eminent family of the Shukrīya Arabs who live between the Blue Nile and the Atbara; tradition has it that he was carried off by the Funj to Sennar and grew up under the protection of the Funj sultans, marrying the sultan's daughter Bayākī by whom he had a son called Naiyil; he afterwards settled, so the story runs, at Jabal al-Jailī where his children, each the founder of a separate family of the Shukrīya, were born; his grave is pointed out at Jabal al-Jailī.

Shabaka (*fl. c.* 708 B.C.), Nubian king of Ethiopia and Egypt; he succeeded Piankhi whose conquests in Egypt he extended to the Mediterranean, transferring his capital from Napata to Thebes; he apparently went to help the Hebrew king Hezekiah against the Assyrian hordes of Sennacherib and was succeeded by his nephew Shabataka.

Shabataka (*fl.* 700 B.C.), Nubian king of Ethiopia (Kush) and Egypt approximately 699 B.C.–684 B.C. following King Shabaka; he was in his turn succeeded by Taharqa (Tirhaqa).

* **Sh̲āhīn Pasha Kinj** (–*c.* 1879), soldier and statesman; born of Turkish blood, he joined the Egyptian army and was promoted qā'immaqām during the reign of ʿAbbās I; he served in the Crimean war of 1853–5 as second-in-command of the 18th infantry regiment in the Egyptian contingent; in 1855 he was promoted mīrālai of the 2nd infantry regiment in place of ʿUt̲h̲mān Bey on the ground that the latter was a bad organizer; he was governor of Cairo in 1866; he was a member of a military mission sent to France in 1866–7 by Ismāʿīl Pasha in connexion with the modernization of the Egyptian army and, by now a farīq, was present at a review held in Paris by Napoleon III in 1867 to welcome the Sudanese battalion on its way back to Egypt from the Mexican war; in the same year he visited the Sudan to inquire into the circumstances of the mutiny of Sudanese troops which had broken out at Kassala and Sawākin in 1865; minister of war in 1869, he again visited the Sudan in 1871 to inspect the eastern Sudan then governed by Aḥmad Mumtāz Pasha; in 1875 he was appointed first director of the Soudan railway which was being built from Wādī Ḥalfā towards Dongola; his functions were administrative, not technical; encountering many difficulties, notably in the supply of labour, he asked to be relieved of his post only seven months after his appointment, and was succeeded by Muṣṭafā Fahmī Pasha; he followed the khedive Ismāʿīl Pasha into exile in 1879 as a member of his suite and shortly afterwards died in Rome.

Shakespear Bey, Arthur Bucknall (1850–98), British soldier; commissioned to the Royal Marine Artillery, he transferred to the Egyptian army in 1883 and served in the Nile campaign of 1884–5, being present in the battles of Kirbikān, 1885, Jummaiza (Gemaiza), 1888, and Tūs̲h̲kī (Toski), 1889; promoted major in 1888, he returned in 1891 to the Royal Marine Artillery of which he became paymaster in 1897.

Sh̲ākir (*fl.* 1300 ?), ancestor, possibly legendary, of the S̲h̲ukrīya Arabs; according to tradition he and his people migrated westward to Morocco and afterwards returned to the east and founded a home round Jabal Barkal, near the present Merowe, whence the tribe ultimately moved up the Nile to the country where it now dwells.

Sh̲alai Kh̲ūjalī Kaiwat, called **Abū Afīya** (–*c.* 1835), chief of the Awlād Kāhil (the united Arab tribes of the Kawāhla, Ḥasanīya, and Ḥusaināt); though nominally subject to the sultans of Sennar and occasionally paying tribute, he was an absolute ruler within his own jurisdiction; he had his own qāḍī and clerk; he survived the coming of the Turks in 1821, but the new government seems to have been intent on limiting his power since it stationed its own qāḍīs at certain villages in his nāẓirate; on his death he was succeeded by his son Bis͟hāra wad S͟halai.

S͟hammār ibn Muḥammad ibn ʿAdlān al-S͟hā'iqī (*fl.* 1730), holy man; he was born and he died at Arbajī; the hagiographer Wad Ḍaif Allāh calls him a learned jurisconsult in both the S͟hāfiʿīte and Mālikite codes.

* **S͟haʿūs . . .** (*c.* 1780–), malik of the ʿAdlānāb branch of the S͟hā'iqīya Arab tribe; he was a commander in the S͟hā'iqī army which was defeated by the Turks under Ismāʿīl Pasha near Kūrtī in 1820; a few days later he led the S͟hā'iqīya in a second battle with the Turks which took place at Jabal Daija (Dager), at which his daughter Ṣafīya was captured; unlike his fellow chiefs he did not immediately surrender but retired to Shendi where he later made his peace with the conqueror; a shrewd care for the future of his people, combined with a respect for Turkish fire-power, induced him to submit; Ismāʿīl, admiring his soldierly qualities, enlisted him in the Turkish army and made him a bulūk-bās͟hī over the 140 ʿAdlānāb who had surrendered with him; his energy in putting down the rebellion of the ʿAbdullāb of Ḥalfaiya while Ismāʿīl was engaged in Sennar in 1821 was rewarded by the grant of ʿAbdullāb lands which he and his men held on a military tenure; G. B. English, the American chief of Ismāʿīl's artillery, described him as a large, stout man with a pleasing face and the reputation of being the greatest warrior of the neighbourhood.

Shute, Sir Cameron Deane (1866–1936), British general; he received a commission in the Welch Regiment, 1885, and was promoted captain in the Rifle Brigade, 1895; he served in the 2nd battalion of the Rifle Brigade in the Nile campaign of 1898 and fought at Omdurman; he commanded the 5th corps of the 3rd army in France, 1918–19; in 1931 he was promoted to full general when he retired.

Ṣiddīq ʿĪsā Saʿd (–1935), merchant of Omdurman where he lived and died; a Kanzī by origin, he was a member of the municipal council and a magistrate.

al-Ṣiddīq al-Mahdī (–1899), fourth son of Muḥammad Aḥmad al-Mahdī; he was killed in the battle of Umm Dibaikarāt.

al-Ṣiddīq Sulaimān Bushāra Mas͟haik͟ha (1878–1933), s͟haik͟h of the Zanārk͟ha branch of the Bakrīya tribe; born in Khartoum, where his father was a farmer and trader, he was a tax-collector in Mahdist times; in 1907 he was chosen by his people to be their s͟haik͟h.

* **Sienkiewics, Henryk** (1846–1916), Polish novelist, better known as the author of *Quo Vadis?*; his writings include *W Pustyni i w Puszcze* (Warsaw, 1912), translated into English as *In Desert and Wilderness*

(London, 1912); this children's story about a Polish boy and an English girl in the Mahdist revolt is the only known Polish contribution to the romantic literature of the Sudan.

Silko (*fl. c.* 550), Ethiopian ruler of the Nobades; he is said to have founded the town of Old Dongola and to have adopted Monophysite Christianity.

Simāwī wad Timsāḥ umm Badda, called also **Jarijīr** (–1891), head shaikh of all Dār Ḥāmid at the close of the Egyptian rule; on the outbreak of the Mahdist revolt he joined the rebel cause and took part in the defeat and killing of the Kabbābīsh leader, Ṣāliḥ Bey Faḍl Allāh al-Kabbāshī, 1887; he later served under the amīr al-umarā' 'Uthmān Adam in Dār Fūr where he died.

Skirmunt, Stanislaus (1857–1921), Polish agriculturist; born at Kolodne near Pinsk, he entered the agriculture department of the Sudan Government in 1904 as deputy inspector for the rubber plantations then being developed (though without success at the time) in the Baḥr al-Ghazāl region; he established a government experimental farm at Wau (Fort Desaix); appointed a deputy assistant director in the woods and forests department, 1905, he was in 1910 promoted deputy assistant director of woods and forests; in 1915 he was transferred to the game preservation department as acting superintendent and from 1920 was superintendent; he died at Merowe.

* **Slatin Pasha, Sir Rudolf Karl von, Baron** (1857–1932), Austrian officer in the service of the Egyptian and Sudan Governments; born near Vienna of a minor aristocratic family believed to have been originally Jewish, he visited the Sudan as a youth in 1874–6 when he worked for a time for C. F. Rosset, German vice-consul, in his business in Khartoum, and travelled to Kordofan, returning to Austria in 1876 to continue his military career; he served as a lieutenant in the Bosnian campaign of 1878 when he was invited by C. G. Gordon Pasha, who was now governor-general of the Sudan, to join his staff; he resigned from the Austrian army and came to Khartoum where he was appointed a finance inspector later in the same year; in 1879 he was made governor of Dāra in southern Dār Fūr in place of C. Rigolet who had been invalided from the service; in 1881, on the recommendation of Muḥammad Ra'ūf Pasha, Gordon's successor to the governorship-general, he was appointed governor of Dār Fūr on the transfer of 'Alī Bey Sharīf and promoted qā'immaqām and bey; while at Dāra he had helped R. Gessi Pasha against the rebel Sulaimān wad Zubair and had taken a part in the defeat of the pretender sultan Muḥammad Hārūn al-Rashīd; the rise of Mahdism, and finally the destruction of the Egyptian army of W. Hicks Pasha at Shaikān (Kashgil) in November 1883, isolated his province from all outside help; after fighting a series of actions against the Mahdists, who were now overrunning Dār Fūr, he surrendered at Dāra in March 1884; for eleven years he remained in captivity at Omdurman, a period during which he gained a profound knowledge of Mahdism and of the tribes of the Sudan; he escaped in 1895, fleeing by camel northward over the Nubian desert to safety;

rejoining the Egyptian army he served under Kitchener Pasha in the Dongola and Nile campaigns as assistant director of military intelligence; in 1898 he was knighted by Queen Victoria and promoted liwā' of the Egyptian army with elevation to the grade of pasha; from 1900 to 1914 he was inspector-general of the Sudan; he was created a baron of the Austrian Empire in 1906 and in 1907 was promoted farīq of the Egyptian army; the outbreak in 1914 of the First World War rendered his position as an Austrian subject in the Sudan Government anomalous and he resigned; during the war he was president of the Austrian Red Cross organization and in 1919 was a member of the Austrian delegation to the peace conference; he revisited the Sudan in 1931 and met many of his old friends and former enemies; *Fire and Sword*, the story of his adventures, has been translated into many languages.

Slessor, Herbert (1863–1946), British lieutenant-colonel; while a captain in the Royal Marine Artillery, he transferred to the Egyptian army, 1896, and served in the Nile campaigns of 1897–8, being for a time commandant of railhead at Kerma; he returned to the British army, 1898, and retired, 1909; he was superintendent of the Royal Naval School of Music, 1914–18, and recruiting staff officer, Southampton, 1919–21.

Sloggett, Sir Arthur Thomas (1857–1929), British lieutenant-general; commissioned to the Royal Army Medical Corps, 1881, he was lieutenant-colonel, 1896, when he was appointed senior medical officer to the British troops in the Dongola campaign, 1896, and to the 1st brigade, British division, in the Nile campaign, 1898; he was dangerously wounded at the battle of Omdurman; promoted lieutenant-general, 1914, he was director-general of the Army Medical Service throughout the First World War and colonel-commandant, Royal Army Medical Corps, 1921–8; he retired in 1928 and went into business.

Smith Pasha, Sir Charles Holled (1846–1925), British major-general; he entered the army in 1865 and as a captain fought in the Egyptian war of 1882; in 1883 he transferred to the Egyptian army and served in the Nile campaign of 1884–5; he was a brigade commander under Major-General Sir F. W. Grenfell at the battle of Jummaiza (Gemaiza) in 1888; from 1888 to 1892 he was governor of the Red Sea littoral in succession to H. H. Kitchener Pasha who had been incapacitated by a wound received in action with the Mahdists at Ḥandūb; in 1891 he recaptured Tokar and Afafit; leaving the Egyptian army he was commandant of the forces in Victoria, Australia, 1894.

Smith, Sir Grafton Elliot (1871–1937), British anatomist and anthropologist; born at Grafton, New South Wales, he was educated at the Universities of Sydney and Cambridge; he was professor of anatomy at the University of Manchester, vice-president of the Royal Society, and a member of many learned societies; he wrote much on archaeological anatomy including contributions on the anthropological side of Nubian archaeology; he took part in the archaeological survey of Nubia begun by the Egyptian Government in 1908.

Smith Bey, Guy de Herriez (1869–1904), British soldier; commissioned in the East Yorkshire Regiment, 1888, he transferred to the Indian army, 1892, and fought in Waziristan, 1894–5; after further active service in Uganda, 1895, he was seconded to the Egyptian army, 1896, and fought in the Dongola and Nile campaigns, 1896–9, as an officer in the 11th Sudanese battalion; he was governor of Sennar, 1901.

Smith, William Dunlop (1865–1940), British veterinary officer; he received a commission in the Army Veterinary Service in 1892 and served throughout the Dongola and Nile campaigns as a veterinary lieutenant; after further service in the South African and First World Wars he was appointed director-general of the Army Veterinary Service in 1921; he retired in 1925.

Smith-Dorrien, Sir Horace Lockwood (1858–1930), British general; entering the army in 1877, he fought in the Zulu war, 1879, and the Egyptian war, 1882; in the Nile campaign of 1884–5, he was present at the battle of Jinnis (Giniss), 1885; joining the Egyptian army, he was second-in-command of the 13th (Sudanese) battalion of the Egyptian army at the battle of Omdurman, 1898, and was present at Fas͟hōda later in the year when the sirdār, Sir H. H. Kitchener Pasha, accompanied by an Egyptian army detachment, confronted a small French force under Captain G. B. Marchand; he was made governor of Omdurman province, 1898, and was designated by Kitchener to succeed him, but he preferred to seek service elsewhere; he held high command in the South African war, 1899–1901, in India, 1901–7, and in England, 1907–14; in the First World War he commanded the 2nd corps at Mons, 1914, and in 1915 was given command of the 2nd army; knighted, 1907, he was governor of Gibraltar, 1918–23.

Snow, Sir Thomas D'Oyly (1858–1940), British lieutenant-general; he entered the army, 1879, and was in the British column which in 1884–5 attempted without success to relieve Khartoum; he was present in the battle of Abū Ṭulaiḥ (Abu Klea) and severely wounded at al-Qubbat; he served as a staff officer in the British army in the Nile campaign of 1898 with rank of major; after service in the First World War he was promoted lieutenant-general, 1918.

Sogaro, Francesco (1839–1912), prelate of the Roman Catholic Church; born at Lonigo near Vicenza, he entered the religious life at the age of eighteen; in 1882 he succeeded D. Comboni (d. 1881) as vicar apostolic of the missions to Central Africa and visited Khartoum, returning to Cairo in June; on the approach of the Mahdist armies to Khartoum and the capture of the missions at Dilling and al-Ubaiyaḍ, he returned to Khartoum in the autumn of 1883 to supervise the evacuation of the mission from the capital; this completed, he left in December for Cairo which became the seat of the vicariate apostolic till the end of the Mahdist rule; he took a leading part in the establishment in 1885 of the Congregation of the Sacred Heart of Verona in support of the African missions; he later held important posts in Rome including that of president of the Academy of Nobles of the Church; he died in Rome.

Sonnini de Manoncour, Charles-Nicolas-Sigisbert (1751–1812), French naturalist and traveller, son of a Roman father; he travelled in Egypt, 1777–80, and wrote of Nubia in his book of travels, (Paris, 1799), which has been translated into English, German, and Russian.

Soule, Cora Blanche (1875–1945), American missionary; born in New Bloomfield, Pennsylvania, she trained as a nurse and came to the Sudan in 1921; she spent all her missionary life under the United Presbyterian Board at Nāṣir on the River Sobat where she did a notable work for orphan girls; she died in Malakal.

Soulié . . ., legendary, but non-existent, Frenchman whom the Parisian press (see *Le Temps* of 23 November 1883) credited with having served in the French army; according to the story he came to Egypt, left after the bombardment of Alexandria, 1882, for the Sudan where he joined the Mahdist cause, and was appointed commander of the Mahdī's forces; similar romantic legends rose concerning General Gordon and Uthmān abū Bakr Diqna (Osman Digna).

Sowerby Bey, Maurice Eden (1874–1920), British lieutenant-colonel and mīrālai of the Egyptian army; gazetted to the Royal Engineers in 1894, he was transferred to the Egyptian army in 1898; in 1901 he was made traffic manager of the Sudan Military Railway (title changed to Sudan Government Railways, 1902) and chief engineer, 1906; he held this post till 1915 when he assisted in the building of military railways in Palestine under Sir C. B. Macauley; he was afterwards under-secretary to the ministry of communications of the Egyptian Government.

Spada, Lorenzo (*fl.* 1878), Italian artisan; said to have been originally a watchmaker from Pinerolo near Turin he became superintendent of the government arsenal at Khartoum where several visitors saw him in 1877–8; he assembled and repaired steamers and did all manner of engineering work; he was a successful trainer of native artisans, mostly negroes educated in the Roman Catholic mission school and speaking a little Italian; in his spare time he taught engineering in the mission school; his pupils afterwards assisted in the defence of Khartoum and were later artisans in the Mahdist fleet; information about his private life is altogether lacking; an only daughter died, apparently in Khartoum, about June 1878.

Sparkes Pasha, William Spottiswode (1862–1906), British colonel; he entered the army in 1881 and was promoted captain in 1888; in 1894 he was seconded to the Egyptian army and fought in the Dongola and Nile campaigns, commanding the fourth battalion; in 1899 he was governor of Fashōda; in 1900 he was promoted colonel in the British army to which he reverted in 1904; he was in command of a detachment of the Egyptian army which between 1901 and 1903 occupied the Baḥr al-Ghazāl province; arriving at Mushraʿ al-Raq in December 1900, he raised the British and Egyptian flags at Wau early in 1902 and established posts at Wau, Tonj, Rumbek, and Shambé.

Speke, John Hanning (1827–64), British explorer; formerly an officer in the Bengal army; he accompanied Sir F. R. Burton on an exploration in 1856–8 which resulted in the discovery of Lakes Tanganyika and Victoria; on a second expedition, undertaken with J. A. Grant, he set out from Zanzibar for the interior and in 1862 found, as he suspected, that the White Nile issued from Lake Victoria; this settled a geographical dispute of many centuries; the two explorers, continuing northward through Uganda, reached Gondokoro in 1863; here they met Sir S. W. and Lady Baker and with them descended the Nile to Khartoum; he accidentally shot himself; his *Journal of the Discovery of the Source of the Nile* (1863) contains references to the Sudan part of their journey.

Stack, Sir Lee Oliver Fitzmaurice (1868–1924), British soldier and administrator; educated at Clifton and Sandhurst, he joined the British army in 1888 and retired from it in 1910 with rank of major-general; in 1899 he was transferred to the Egyptian army and in 1902 commanded the Shambé Field Force, a punitive expedition on the Upper White Nile; he was re-transferred to the Sudan Government in 1904 and was Sudan agent and director of military intelligence, Cairo, 1908–14; in 1914–17 he was civil secretary to the Sudan Government, and in 1917 he succeeded Sir F. R. Wingate as sirdār of the Egyptian army and governor-general of the Sudan; he was assassinated in Cairo.

Stamboulieh, George. *See* ISTĀNBŪLĪYA, GEORGES.

Stanley, Sir Henry Morton (1841–1904), explorer and journalist whose name at birth was John Rowlands; British by birth, he became an American, but reverted later to British citizenship; after several years of notable exploration in Central Africa he took command of an expedition to the Egyptian Equatorial province where the governor Emin Pasha (E. C. O. T. Schnitzer) and his staff had been cut off from the outer world by the Mahdist revolt in the Sudan; starting from the mouth of the River Congo in 1887, he ascended that river to the point now called the Stanley Falls and thence marched through the dense tropical forest to Lake Albert; in April 1888 he and Emin met; finally, in April 1889, after much delay and argument, he left Wadelai with Emin, G. Casati the Italian explorer, Vita Ḥasan, an Egyptian Government doctor, and those of the garrison and their families who wished to leave; the party followed the route leading round the western shore of Lake Victoria and in December reached Bagamoyo on the east coast where they were succoured by the German authorities; the literature about Stanley and the Emin expedition (chiefly in English and German) is large, and in part controversial.

* **Stanton Bey, Edward Alexander** (1867–1947), British soldier, colonel in the British army, and mīrālai of the Egyptian army; he joined the Oxfordshire Light Infantry, 1887, and after secondment to the Egyptian army served in the Dongola and Nile campaigns, 1896–9; he was governor of Khartoum, 1900–8, when he retired from the Egyptian army; he afterwards held high official positions in Canada and in Britain; he served in the First World War and was military

governor of the Phoenician district of Palestine, 1918–20; though no philatelic expert, he designed in 1897, on the instructions of the sirdār, the first 'camel' postage stamps of the Sudan, issued in 1898.

Stanway, Christopher William (1879–1945), British official; he entered the British civil service in 1900 and in 1905 was posted to the newly formed army accounts department; he was assistant financial adviser, British army of the Rhine, 1919–20, with rank of major and was on the staff of the financial adviser, Egyptian Expeditionary Force, 1920–1; in 1921 he joined the Sudan civil service as an audit inspector and from 1928 until his retirement in 1933 was auditor-general; he died by misadventure at Deepway, Devon.

Steer, George (1909–44), British journalist; he arrived in Khartoum in July 1940 with rank of captain and was employed in propaganda designed to rouse the Abyssinians against the Italian rule; he introduced a news sheet printed in Khartoum called *Bandarachin* (Our Flag) which was distributed behind the Italian lines; he also directed pamphlets in Italian against the defenders of Keren, 1941; he accompanied the Emperor Haile Selassie from Khartoum to Addis Ababa to start a news service in the Abyssinian capital; later promoted lieutenant-colonel, he was killed in a motor accident during the war against the Japanese in Burma; his *Sealed and Delivered* (1942) describes his experiences in the Sudan.

Steevens, George Warrington (1869–1900), British journalist; he joined the staff of the *Daily Mail*, visited India whence he wrote the brilliant essays *In India*, and as a war correspondent followed the advance of the Anglo-Egyptian forces from Wādī Ḥalfā to Omdurman, 1897–8; he died in the siege of Ladysmith in the South African war; his *With Kitchener to Khartoum* (1898) is an amusing account of the Nile campaign.

* **Stella, Giovanni** (1800–1869), Italian priest of the Lazarist Order of the Roman Catholic Church; a Piedmontese by origin, he went by way of the Nile valley and Kassala to open a mission among the people of Boghos in 1851 and lived at Keren; his wisdom endeared him to the people who were suffering from raids by both the Egyptians and the Abyssinians; after a raid on the Bilen people by an Egyptian force he protested to Khusraw Bey, governor of Tāka, but finding this of no avail carried his protest to the viceroy, Muḥammad Saʿīd Pasha; his prestige among the people grew until he became their adviser, almost their ruler; in 1864 he met Count R. du Bisson but did not share the enthusiasm of his superior, Monsignor Biancheri, vicar-apostolic of Abyssinia, for the French adventurer; in 1864 he again went to Kassala in a vain attempt to secure redress from the governor, Ibrāhīm Bey al-Maḥallāwī, for the ill treatment of his people; similar ill success met a protest to the acting-consul of France at Muṣawwaʿ; he is said to have been expelled from Keren by J. A. W. Munzinger in 1869, but the fact and the date are both suspect; whatever the truth, his death was hastened by grief.

Stephenson, Sir Frederick Charles Arthur (1821–1911), British general; he served in the Crimean war of 1853–5 and in 1883 commanded the army of occupation in Egypt; in 1884 he organized Sir G. Graham's expedition for the relief of Tokar and the defence of Sawākin; his recommendation that the Sawākin–Berber route be taken by the force intended to relieve Khartoum was rejected by the British Cabinet and the Nile route, favoured by Lord Wolseley the commander-in-chief, was adopted; he commanded the frontier field force, 1885–7, and defeated the Mahdists under the amīr ʿAbd al-Raḥmān wad al-Najūmī at Jinnis (Giniss), 1885; he was promoted colonel of the Coldstream Guards, 1892, and from 1898 till his death was constable of the Tower of London.

Stern, Henry Aaron (1820–85), Jewish missionary; born in Hesse-Cassel, Germany, he entered the Hebrew College of the London Jews' Society, 1842; after missionary work among the Jews and Muslims in Asia Minor and Persia, he was ordained a priest of the Church of England; in the course of several missionary journeys he went to Abyssinia, travelling by way of the Nile, 1859; he was held captive by King Theodore, 1863, and freed, 1868.

* **Steudner, Herrmann** (1832–63), German naturalist from Greiffenberg in Silesia; in 1862 he travelled with T. von Heuglin and E. Schubert from Gondar via Gallabat to Khartoum; he accompanied the expedition of Miss A. P. F. Tinné to the Baḥr al-Ghazāl and died at Wau.

Stevani, Francesco (1840–1917), Italian general; born at Nibbiano near Piacenza he joined the army and fought in the Italian wars of independence against Austria, 1859, 1866; while colonel of bersaglieri he was in command of a column which defeated a Mahdist force at Tukruf and occupied Kassala, 1895; he died at Sassari.

Stevenson, Alexander Gavin (1871–1939), British major-general; he entered the Royal Engineers in 1891 and was promoted captain in 1901; he served in the Dongola and Nile campaigns, 1896–8, and (except for a short period in 1898 when he commanded the gunboat *Metemma*) he was locomotive superintendent, Sudan Military Railway; after serving in the South African war, 1900–1, and in the First World War, he was engineer-in-chief at Army Headquarters in India, 1928–32, when he retired.

Stewart, Sir Herbert (1843-85), British major-general; as assistant adjutant-general of the British cavalry in the Egyptian war of 1882, he secured Cairo after the battle of Tel el-Kebir; he commanded the cavalry brigade at the second battle of el-Teb under Lieutenant-General Sir G. Graham in 1884; in the Khartoum relief expedition of 1884–5 he was given command of the desert column which crossed the Bayūda from Kūrtī to Matamma and gave battle to a Mahdist army at Abū Ṭulaiḥ (Abu Klea) on 17 January 1885; two days later, in action at al-Qubbat, he was mortally wounded.

Stewart, John Donald Hamill (1845–84), British lieutenant-colonel; he was appointed a cornet in the 11th Hussars, 1865; in 1882, while serving in Egypt, he was instructed to prepare a report on the Sudan where Muḥammad Aḥmad al-Mahdī was defying the Egyptian Government with success; with G. B. Messedaglia Bey, formerly governor of Dār Fūr, he reached Khartoum in December 1882 when the fall of Bāra and al-Ubaiyaḍ was imminent; the two officers left Khartoum in March 1883 by way of Sennar, Kassala, and Muṣawwaʿ; his *Report on the Soudan* (1883) was the result; he returned to the Sudan with C. G. Gordon Pasha, arriving in Khartoum in February 1884; here he assisted Gordon and was wounded during the siege; in September he left the doomed city in the steamer *ʿAbbās* with F. Power of *The Times* and Herbin of *Le Bosphore Égyptien* and a party of Khartoum residents in an attempt to run the blockade and reach Egypt; the steamer ran (or was run) aground between Abū Ḥamad and Merowe and he, with Herbin, Power, and others, was killed by the Manāṣīr tribesmen.

Stigand Bey, Chauncey Hugh (1877–1919), British soldier and administrator; born at Boulogne-sur-Mer, where his father was British consul, he joined the army and saw service in Burma, British Somaliland, and British East Africa; in 1910 he entered the Egyptian army and was posted to the Upper White Nile where he took over the Lado enclave from the Belgians as the result of an international agreement; he was later in charge of the Kajo Kaji district; promoted major in 1915, he served in the Dār Fūr campaign of 1916 against ʿAlī Dīnār; he was governor of the Upper Nile province, 1917–18, and in 1919 was appointed governor of Mongalla province; he was murdered with Binbāshī R. F. White and Sergeant Macalister shortly after by tribesmen of the Aliyāb section of the Dinka Negroes at Pap between the River Lau and the White Nile; he was buried at Tombé; a ready writer, he published *Administration in Tropical Africa* (1914), *Equatoria: the Lado Enclave* (1923), and was a frequent contributor to *Sudan Notes and Records* and other journals on geography and natural history.

Stone, Charles Pomeroy (1824–87), American soldier; born at Greenfield, Massachussetts, he entered West Point Military Academy, 1841, and was gazetted lieutenant, 1845; he fought in the American-Mexican war of 1846–7 and on the Federal side in the American civil war in which he was engaged 1861–4, rising to brigadier-general; his war career was marred by unfounded charges of military incompetence; mustered out of the army, ill and exhausted, 1864, he was employed as a mining engineer, 1865–9; the most important work of his life was now to begin; between 1870 and 1883 he served in the Egyptian army with rank of farīq as chief of the general staff; in this capacity he organized and collated many surveys of the Sudan including those of R. E. Colston, A. McC. Mason, Muḥammad Māhir, Muḥammad Mukhtār, H. G. Prout, and E. S. Purdy; he superintended the preparation of the great map of Africa published by the Egyptian general staff in 1877 and embodying the latest explorations by the Khedivial and other geographers; he was at the side of the Khedive Muḥammad Tawfīq Pasha throughout the revolt of ʿAḥmad ʿUrābī Pasha, 1882, and has been criticized for failure to foresee the gravity of the situation which the revolt caused; on his return to the United States he again became a managing engineer and, among other duties, was construction engineer for the laying of the foundations of the Statue of Liberty in New York harbour; he died in New York City.

Stopford, Sir Frederick William (1854–1929), British general; he was gazetted to the Grenadier Guards, 1871, and served in the Egyptian war, 1882, and in Lieutenant-General Sir G. Graham's Sawākin Field Force, 1885; after serving in the South African war, 1899–1902, he was appointed director of military training at the War Office, London, 1904; in the First World War he was a corps commander at the Suvla Bay landing at the Dardanelles, 1915.

Strabo (*c.* 64 B.C.–*c.* 21 B.C.), geographer and historian; born in Pontus on the southern shore of the Black Sea, of Greek descent on his mother's side, he seems to have spent his life in travel and study; in 24 B.C., in company with Ælius Gallus, Roman governor of Egypt, he ascended the Nile; his *Geographia* in seventeen books has survived almost complete; it contains references to Nubia and the valley of the middle Nile.

Stuart-Wortley, Edward James Montagu (1857–1934), British soldier; after serving in the Anglo-Afghan war of 1879–80, he fought as a lieutenant at Tel el-Kebir and in the Nile campaign of 1884–5 he was aboard one of Gordon's steamers which arrived off Khartoum too late to be of help; in 1898 he commanded a force of irregular Sudanese troops which advanced up the east bank of the Nile and took part in the skirmishing which preceded the battle of Omdurman; he served in the South African war and the First World War, retiring a major-general, 1919.

Subair . . . (*fl.* 1821), Sh̲ā'iqī notable, leader of the Ḥannakāb branch of the Sh̲ā'iqīya Arabs; in the years of anarchy which followed the incursion of the refugee Mamelukes into the Sudan in 1812, he fought against Malik Ṭanbal Muḥammad Idrīs of Arqū and, together with the other Sh̲ā'iqī chiefs, resisted the Turks under Ismā'īl Pasha at the battles of Kūrtī and Jabal Daija (Dager) at the end of 1820; his territory reached from Ḥannak to Merowe; making his peace with the Turks, he and his men joined the Turkish service as bās̲h̲ī-būzuq and accompanied Ismā'īl in his raid on the negroes of the Upper Blue Nile in 1821.

al-Ṣug̲h̲aiyarūn. *See* MUḤAMMAD IBN SARḤĀN AL-'ŪDĪ, called AL-ṢUG̲H̲AIYARŪN.

Sulaimān . . . (*fl.* 1795), semi-independent kās̲h̲if of Nubia, vaguely tributary to the wālī of Egypt; the title of kās̲h̲if was hereditary and dated possibly from the original Ḥasan Kūs̲h̲ī (*fl.* 1520); he was succeeded by his son Ḥasan Sulaimān.

Sulaimān ibn 'Abd al-Malik ibn Marwān (*fl.* 750 ?), traditional Arab ancestor of the Funj; he is said to have entered Abyssinia as a fugitive from the Caliph Abū'l-'Abbās al-Saffāḥ and thence to have reached the Sudan where he married the daughter of a local king.

Sulaimān Aḥmad abū-Karūq (1881–1942), ʿumda of Kūrtī, a magistrate since 1932 and president of the Kūrtī branch court since 1936; a member of the Suwārāb branch of the Shāʾiqīya tribe, he was born and died at Kūrtī.

Sulaimān wad Aḥmad al-Maʿqūr (*fl. c.* 1550 ?), legendary figure of Dār Fūr, son of Aḥmad, the eponymous ancestor of the Tunjūr tribe who is traditionally claimed to have been sultan when Islam began to be introduced into the country; by some the family is held to be of Tuwāriq, by others of Daju, even ʿAbbāsid, origin, but the history of the Tunjūr and Daju royal houses is confused and uncertain.

* **Sulaimān Bey Amīn abū ʿIzz al-Dīn** (1872–1933), Syrian official in the civil services of the Egyptian and Sudan Governments; born at al-ʿAbbādīya, Mount Lebanon, of a Druse family, he was educated at the Friends' High School at Brummāna and at the Syrian Protestant College (afterwards the American University) at Beirut whence he graduated in 1895; he joined the Egyptian civil service, transferring later to that of the Sudan where he served as an inspector in the finance department; while in Khartoum he founded, and was the president of, the Druse Educational Society, a body devoted to assisting the education of Druse youths; retiring in 1921, he died in Beirut as the result of a motor accident; he published *Ibrāhīm Bāshā fīʾl-Sūriyā* (Beirut, 1925) and left a history in manuscript of the leading Druse families.

Sulaimān al-Bāzārlī, called **Sulaimān al-Jundī** (–1839), Kurdish officer in the service of Muḥammad ʿAlī Pasha and brother of ʿAbbās Aghā, governor of Berber and the Jaʿlīyīn; he was on his way from Egypt to the Sudan when he was killed at a spot afterwards called Talʿat al-Jundī in the ʿAtbāī by an ʿAbbādī chief called Baraka wad al-Ḥājj Muḥammad in revenge for the killing of Baraka's brother Khalīfa by ʿAbbās Aghā; Baraka was later caught and killed by a government patrol.

Sulaimān Pasha al-Faransāwī. *See* SÈVE, OCTAVE-JOSEPH-ANTHELME.

Sulaimān Ḥarīqa. *See* INGER, ALEXANDER.

Sulaimān Bey ʿĪsā (1893–1944), qāʾimmaqām of the Sudan Defence Force; born at Sawākin during the Mahdist revolt, of a Nuba father and a Shāʾiqīya mother, he was educated at Gordon Memorial College and the Khartoum Military School; commissioned in 1913, he was a yūzbāshī in 1917 and a ṣāgh in 1930; he was at one time on the staff of the Military School and served much in Dār Fūr; he died while serving with his unit in Libya during the Second World War.

Sulaimān Ishaiqir (1857–1922), shaikh of the Sharak section of the Jimaʿa of the White Nile; he acted as guide to the force which destroyed the Mahdist army at Umm Dibaikarāt, 1899; he was principal adviser to Shaikh Aḥmad al-Badawī ʿAsākir abū Kalām, nāẓir of the Jimaʿa, until the latter's death in 1917.

Sulaimān Bey Kharpūtlī (*fl.* 1825–43), Turkish soldier; he was appointed governor of Kordofan and officer commanding the troops there in place of Ḥalīm Bey; his slave raids into the Nuba hills cost him heavy losses among his men; in 1827 he was relieved by Salīm Bey and succeeded by Rustum Bey in 1828; in 1843 a Sulaimān Bey (believed to be the officer noticed here) was made governor of Sennar, promoted mīrlivā, and elevated to the grade of pasha.

Sulaimān Muḥammad al-Ḥājj al-Zubair (1895–1943), shaikh of the northern khuṭṭ of Khartoum province, a great-grandson of Zubair Pasha Raḥma Manṣūr and grandson of Sulaimān Bey wad Zubair; born in Jailī of Jimīʿābī stock, he became ʿumda of the place; in 1930 he was made president of the Jailī court and in 1938 shaikh of khuṭṭ; he was chiefly concerned with the administrations of Zubair Pasha's estates.

Sulaimān abū Nimr (*c.* 1841), ʿAbbādī tribesman, of a family in feud with the house of Khalīfa whom the Turkish governor of Berber had killed in 1828: Khalīfa's brother, Baraka wad al-Ḥājj Muḥammad, killed Sulaimān, the governor's brother, in revenge; Baraka then fled with his men to the remoteness of the ʿAtbāī, east of the Berber-Korosko road; ambitious for fame Sulaimān abū Nimr proposed to the governor-general, Aḥmad Pasha abū Widān, to punish Baraka; Aḥmad Pasha lent him a force of Mugharba irregulars and, led by guides from the ʿĀmrāb Bishārīyīn (on whom Ḥasan Khalīfa, Baraka's nephew, later took bloody reprisal), Sulaimān tracked Baraka to Ḥajar al-Zarqā and there cut off his head; the grateful governor-general arbitrarily appointed Sulaimān concessionaire of the Desert Road, though the viceroy, Muḥammad ʿAlī Pasha, had already given the concession to Ḥasan Khalīfa; over-confidence was Sulaimān's undoing; he now prepared to ravage the Ariyāb Bishārīyīn who had been Baraka's allies and who had married one of their girls to him; issuing from Berber with his ʿAbābda levies he attacked the Ariyāb at their wells, killed many and scattered the rest; the ʿAbābda, heavy with loot, regained the Nile valley before the Ariyāb could recover, but from here onwards the Ariyāb shadowed the raiders, and three days south of Abū Ḥamad they ambushed the ʿAbābda and killed Sulaimān; thus was Baraka's death avenged.

Sulaimān Pasha Niyāzī (*c.* 1822–), farīq of the Egyptian army; of Circassian origin, he began his military career as a young soldier in the army of Muḥammad ʿAlī Pasha and later, as a junior officer, saw service in the Egyptian contingent in the Crimean war of 1853–5; promoted mīrlivā he served as chief financial officer at Muṣawwaʿ during the Egyptian-Abyssinian war of 1875–6; on the recall of the governor-general ʿAbd al-Qādir Pasha Ḥilmī to Egypt early in 1883 he replaced him in his military functions, the civil government being allotted to ʿAlā al-Dīn Pasha; he commanded an Egyptian army assembled on the White Nile for the purpose of resisting the forward movement of the

Mahdist forces from Kordofan and with 5,600 men won a battle at al-Marābiʿ near Abā island in April 1883; in July he was removed from his command on representations from Farīq W. Hicks Pasha who had been put in command of a field force intended for the recapture of al-Ubaiyaḍ and Bāra; Hicks had threatened to resign unless he was given sole command of troops in the Sudan Nile valley; he was appointed governor of the Red Sea littoral, which post he held till his supercession by mīrlivā Ḥusain Wāṣif Pasha early in 1884; his governorship was unfortunate; he intervened disastrously in the military affairs of the Red Sea region, attempting to buy off the Mahdist leader, the amīr ʿUthmān abū Bakr Diqna (Osman Digna), with favours, and achieving nothing but added hostility to the Egyptian Government; his measures to relieve the gallant Muḥammad Tawfīq Bey, besieged with a small garrison in Sinkāt, were ineffectual.

Sulaimān Nuʿmān wad Qamar (*c.* 1865–91), Manṣūrī chieftain whose village lies on the bank of the Nile near the present railway station of al-Kāb between Abū Ḥamad and Karīma; siding with the Mahdists, he and others killed a party of Europeans escaping from Khartoum in the steamer *ʿAbbās*, including Lieutenant-Colonel J. D. H. Stewart, F. Power, and Herbin, in 1884; he eluded a British river column under General Sir H. Brackenbury which burnt his village in 1885, but was killed by a force of ʿAbābda irregulars under the command of Ṣāliḥ Bey Ḥusain Khalīfa during a raid on the district.

Sulaimān abū Rūf (*fl.* 1841), shaikh of the Rufāʿa Arabs of the ʿAṭīsh, a country lying between the Blue Nile and the Dinder rivers; for some offence the Turkish Government imprisoned him in Khartoum where he died; the Rufāʿa Arabs, convinced that he had been poisoned, rose in rebellion led by his sons; Aḥmad Pasha abū Widān sent Firhād Bey, mīrālai of the 8th regiment stationed at Wad Madanī, to investigate the cause of the revolt and try to pacify the tribesmen; mistaking Aḥmad Pasha's orders, he captured and put Sulaimān's sons in chains; his brother escaped and went to Khartoum where he complained to the governor-general.

Sulaimān Solong or **Solon** (*c.* 1550–*c.* 1637), sultan of Dār Fūr, the first of a line of rulers which ended with sultan ʿAlī Dīnār in 1916; one tradition makes him a descendant of Muḥammad Dālī (*fl. c.* 1450); he ruled Dār Fūr from 1596 to 1637, conquering Kordofan and for a time extending his dominions over Sennar; he was succeeded on his death by his son Mūsā Sulaimān and was buried on Jabal Marra in what was to become the ancestral cemetery of the Fūr sultans.

Sulaimān Bey wad Zubair (–1879), son of Zubair Pasha Raḥma Manṣūr; during his father's forced absence in Egypt after 1875 he looked after his business affairs in southern Dār Fūr and the neighbouring regions, for Zubair Pasha had considerable commercial interests over a wide area; the anti-slavery measures taken by the government upset the local economy which was based on the institution of slavery, alienated the traders (many of whom were engaged in the slave trade), and added to the indignation excusable in a son whose father was virtually banished from the Sudan; to endeavour to make him see reason C. G. Gordon Pasha, then governor-general, met him, appointed him vice-governor of Shaqqa and afterwards of the Baḥr al-Ghazāl, and gave his chief assistants minor government posts; he appeared reconciled to the government, but in a short while began to resist government measures; declared a rebel, he was pursued by R. Gessi Pasha and, after several pitched battles, captured; on the ground that he was attempting to escape Gessi had him shot, an action which has been criticized as unjust.

al-Sunnī Faḍl Allāh Muḥammad (*fl.* 1821), shaikh of the Kabbābīsh Arabs of northern Kordofan; he submitted, along with Ismā'īl wad al-Ḥājj Mun'im of the 'Asākira Ḥamar tribe, to the Turkish conquerors of Kordofan in 1821.

* **Surūr, Daniele Deng** (–1899), the first member of the Dinka tribe to be ordained priest of the Roman Catholic Church; originating from the region of the Baḥr al-'Arab, he was while a boy caught by slave traders and with his mother taken to al-Ubaiyaḍ; there he was rescued by Bishop D. Comboni who had him educated in Khartoum and Beirut; in 1885 he went to Cairo where he was ordained priest; he worked at the Roman Catholic School at Sawākin, 1888–91, and in 1891 toured Europe collecting money for the Central African missions; at Cracow, for instance, he preached in French to a large congregation in the cathedral; he died in Cairo; he was a competent linguist, had a fair mastery of classical Arabic, and was familiar with several European languages as well as his native Dinka.

Sutherland Bey, Alic (1863–1947), British soldier; he was commissioned in 1885 in the 91st regiment (Argyll and Sutherland Highlanders) and in 1896 was promoted captain; after fighting on the north-west frontier of India, 1897–8, he served in the Egyptian army, 1900–7; he was governor of the Baḥr al-Ghazāl, 1905–6, when he took part in the Niam-Niam patrol of 1905; in 1907 he was governor of the Berber province with headquarters at al-Dāmar; he left the Egyptian army with rank of mīrālai and in 1912 retired from the British army as a major; rejoining the colours on the outbreak of the First World War, he was on the staff of the British army in France, 1914, and lieutenant-colonel of the 12th service battalion of his old Highland regiment.

Suwār al-Dhahab. *See* Mīrghanī Muḥammad Suwār al-Dhahab; Muḥammad wad 'Īsā Suwār al-Dhahab; Ṣāliḥ Suwār al-Dhahab.

Ṭabl I (–1589), sultan of Sennar, a descendant of the royal line established by 'Umāra Dūnqas; he succeeded Sultan Dakīn wad Naiyīl and was himself succeeded by Sultan Ūnsā I; he reigned in peace from 1577 till his death.

Ṭabl II (–1788), puppet sultan of Sennar; he owed his precarious throne to the Hāmaj king-maker Shaikh Nāṣir wad Muḥammad abū'l-

Kailak who made him nominal sultan in place of another transitory puppet named Awkal; he was killed in battle near Shendi while fighting against the rebel chieftains Muḥammad al-Amīn wad al-ʿAjīb and Abū Riḍā, and was succeeded by his son Bādī V.

Tabran, Giuseppina (1841–74), Roman Catholic religious sister; of Syrian Christian extraction (she came of a Greek Catholic home in Tiberias) she was educated in Jerusalem, joined the Order of the Sisters of the Apparition, and taught in Palestinian schools; she came to the Sudan with Bishop D. Comboni in 1871 and was the first mother superior of the mission to Central Africa; she died in Khartoum.

Tādrus Bey Nākhla Jirjis (1852–85), Coptic Egyptian merchant and official; he was born in Wad Madanī, his father having been forced by the Egyptian Government to emigrate to the Sudan in view of the reluctance of Egyptian officials at the time to serve there; while his father became chief clerk to the garrison at Wad Madanī, young Tādrus also joined the government service and ultimately became a senior financial official; he was in Khartoum when C. G. Gordon Pasha arrived in February 1884 to assume his second governorship-general of the country, and Gordon made him superintendent of finance during the siege of the city; he was killed with Gordon and many others in the sack of Khartoum in January 1885; his son, ʿAbd al-Masīḥ Tādrus (d. 1933), was president of the Coptic community in Omdurman.

Ṭaha ʿAlī Surij (–1930), Shā'iqī notable; he was ʿumda of al-ʿArak in the neighbourhood of Kūrtī and a magistrate; he was succeeded on his death by his son Muḥammad Ṭaha ʿAlī.

Taharqa (*fl. c.* 670 B.C.), Nubian king, the Tirhakah of the Hebrew Bible; he succeeded his brother Shabataka and continued the war against the Assyrian invaders of Egypt; he was later himself defeated by Esarhaddon and Asshurbanipal, the son and grandson of Sennacherib, and was driven back to Upper Egypt and thence to Napata; he built temples at Jabal Barkal and Semna; he reigned from approximately 689 B.C. to 663 B.C. and was buried at Nūrī where his pyramid may be seen; Tanutamon, last of the Nubian kings of both Kush and Egypt, followed him on the throne.

Ṭāhir Adam Dabbalū (–1925), son of Adam Dabbalū, king of Taqalī in the Nuba hills; he with the rest of his family were prisoners of the Mahdists after his father had fallen into their power; he escaped from custody towards the end of the Mahdist régime and lived a quiet life making the pilgrimage several times; he was famous locally as an ʿālim and as the greatest authority of his time on the history of Taqalī.

al-Ṭāhir Muḥammad Badr al-ʿUbaid (1854–1907), Mahdist amīr and judge, a Masallamī by origin, one of the sons of the great religious shaikh, Muḥammad Badr of Umm Dibbān, a man deeply attached to the Jailānīya brotherhood; he and his brother ʿAbbās took a prominent part in the fighting in the northern Jazīra against the government in 1884 when they heavily defeated Muḥammad 'Alī Ḥusain, Gordon's 'fighting pasha', in a battle between al-'Āilafūn and Umm Dibbān, he then moved up to the siege of Khartoum and thence went to serve in the Mahdist army of the north, escaping the defeat of Tūshkī (Toski), 1889, by timely flight; he was captured by the Anglo-Egyptian army at the battle of Firka (Firket), 1896, and changed sides, accompanying the sirdār's army as commander of the Masallamīya irregular troops; he died at Umm Dibbān.

Ṭāhir Nūrain (1871–1937), shartai of Dār Suwainī and Artag westward of al-Fāshar in Dār Fūr; during the Mahdist period he joined the army of the amīr Maḥmūd Aḥmad on its march from Dār Fūr to Omdurman in 1897, but he never reached the capital; returning to Dār Fūr, he was at length appointed shartai by Sultan 'Alī Dīnār who had seized power in 1899, but was shortly afterwards deposed in favour of his son; 'Alī Dīnār reinstated him and he remained shartai till 1936 when, afflicted by gout, he retired; he is said to have spent a year at the bottom of a well in Sultan 'Alī Dīnār's time for having shown cowardice in face of some enemy.

* **al-Ṭāhir al-Ṭaiyib Qamar al-Dīn al-Majdhūb** (*c.* 1822–89), member of the religious family of the Majādhīb; born at Matamma and educated in religion at al-Dāmar, the ancestral home of the Majādhīb, he went to Sawākin about 1854 and there set up as the local khalīfa of the family cult, founding a small mosque and collecting followers; he went over to the Mahdist cause about 1882 when 'Uthmān abū Bakr Diqna (Osman Digna), his fellow townsman, brought him a letter from Muḥammad Aḥmad al-Mahdī; except for a visit to the Khalīfa 'Abd Allāhi in Omdurman in 1885, shortly after the death of the Mahdī, he was at 'Uthmān's side throughout the series of battles waged by the Mahdists against the Egyptian and British armies in the Red Sea littoral, 1884–5; he was later appointed an 'āmil; one of his sons was killed by the Amarar tribesmen at Tamai; he himself died at Tokar.

* **al-Tai Sa'īd** (–1932), shaikh of khuṭṭ of Rufā'a and himself a Rufā'ī; during the Mahdist régime he was a friend of R. K. von Slatin Bey whom he helped to escape in 1895.

al-Ṭaiyib Aḥmad al-Bannānī (*c.* 1832–1902), trader of Moroccan origin on his father's side; his father, who came from Fez, entered the Sudan as an aghā in the force of Mugharba irregulars which formed part of the invading army of Ismā'īl Pasha in 1820–1; settling at Berber, he took a wife of the Ja'līyīn and entered into commerce, chiefly in the supply of slaves to Egypt; al-Ṭaiyib was born in Berber and carried on his father's business to which he added a native soap manufactory; he was on friendly terms with Muḥammad Aḥmad al-Mahdī, and there is a family tradition that the Mahdī intended to send him with a caravan to assume the amīrship of Morocco but that the Mahdī's temporal successor, the Khalīfa 'Abd Allāhi, cancelled the plan.

* **al-Ṭaiyib Aḥmad Hāshim** (*c*. 1857–1924), muftī of the Sudan; born at Berber of the Jawdalāb branch of the Jaʿlīyīn Arabs, he studied in the khalwa of Shaikh Muḥammad al-Khair Khūjalī and became a clerk in the Islamic court of his native town at the end of the Egyptian régime; on the establishment of Mahdist rule he became secretary to the amīr ʿUthmān Muḥammad Shaikh al-Dīn, brother of the Khalīfa ʿAbd Allāhi, and tutor to al-Saiyid Muḥammad ʿAbd Allāhi, the Khalīfa's son; on the Anglo-Egyptian occupation he was first Islamic judge at Khartoum and from 1900 till his death muftī of the Sudan.

al-Ṭaiyib wad Ḥamdūn (–1883), Mahdist amīr, popularly known as al-Shaikh al-Ṭaiyib, and by tribe a Jaʿlī; he was killed near Wad Madanī in battle with a government force under Ṣāliḥ Bey al-Mak (afterwards Pasha).

al-Ṭaiyib Muḥammad Badr (–1929), one of the younger sons of Shaikh Muḥammad Badr al-ʿUbaid of Umm Dibbān, not to be confused with an elder son of the same name who died in 1878; he was a magistrate and president of the Kamlīn bench; he ruled the east bank of the Blue Nile opposite Kamlīn until his death at Umm Dibbān.

al-Ṭaiyib Muḥammad Badr al-ʿUbaid (–1878), holy man, son of the great religious teacher Shaikh Muḥammad Badr al-ʿUbaid, founder of the village of Umm Dibbān on the Blue Nile near Khartoum; a man of great piety, he died before his father; his tomb is near Umm Dibbān.

al-Ṭaiyib Muḥammad al-Ṭaiyib Aḥmad al-Baṣīr (–1945), notable of a distinguished religious family of the Ḥalāwīyīn tribe in the neighbourhood of al-Ḥaṣṣa Ḥaiṣa where he died; like his forebears he was a leader of the Sammānīya brotherhood.

al-Ṭaiyib Nimr (–1935), Ḍubānī notable; he was ʿumda of Sōfī Bashīr, in the former eastern khuṭṭ of the district of Gedaref, peopled largely by the Ḍubānīya; he died at Gedaref.

al-Ṭaiyib al-Qurashī (1864–1942), religious notable of the Sammānīya brotherhood, son of Shaikh al-Qurashī wad al-Zain, one of the teachers of Muḥammad Aḥmad al-Mahdī, and grandson of a Bazai from West Africa; his elder brother, ʿAbd al-Raḥmān (who joined the Mahdī early), died in 1890 when he was succeeded by his son al-Zain who died in 1898; after which al-Ṭaiyib succeeded as khalīfa; he lived at Ḥillat al-Shaikh al-Qurashī whose tomb the Mahdī helped to build.

al-Ṭaiyib Ṣāliḥ (*c*. 1883–1934), notable of Dār Fūr; he was born at ʿUbaid in Dār Galla, the son of Ṣāliḥ Donkusa, who was shartai of Dār Galla before him; he took part in several wars during ʿAlī Dīnār's reign and served under various of the sultan's commanders; he fought in the campaign against Abū Bakr Ismāʿīl, sultan of Dār Maṣālīṭ, and marched with Adam Rijāl against the Kenīn and the Badaiyāt; he took part also in the expedition against Sultan Nūrain of the Zaghāwa Kabga; he was appointed shartai about 1914 on the deposition of his brother Ḥasan by Sultan ʿAlī Dīnār, and on the conquest of Dār Fūr did not come in to make his peace with the new government till September 1916; he visited Khartoum in 1922.

Tāj al-Dīn Ismā'īl (-1910), sultan of Dār Maṣālīṭ in western Dār Fūr; he succeeded his brother Abū Bakr Ismā'īl who was killed by Sultan 'Alī Dīnār in 1907; he warred against the French and in 1910 killed Colonel Moll at Darūtī, but was himself killed by Moll's column which successfully counter-attacked; he was succeeded by his nephew Muḥammad Baḥr al-Dīn, the present sultan.

Takping Malwal (-1943), chief of the Cic Adar branch of the Dinka in the neighbourhood of Yirrol; he was a magistrate.

Talbot Pasha, Milo George (1854–1931), British soldier; he joined the Royal Engineers, 1873, and was attached to the Egyptian army during the Nile campaign, 1897–9; he was director of surveys, Sudan Government, 1900–5, with rank of liwā' when he retired; during the First World War he was again attached to the Egyptian army, 1916, and was employed by the Sudan Government.

Tamar Aghā . . . (*c.* 1820–1911), he is said to have been the son of a Turkish official, who visited Katūl in northern Kordofan, by a local lady of the jabal; his uncle al-Ḍaw was formerly 'umda of Katūl; he himself was appointed 'umda in 1841 and for seventy years retained his office; during the Mahdist revolt he remained at Katūl till 1885 then spent some years in Dār Fūr in Mahdist employ; he was wounded in the battle of the Atbara while fighting under the amīr Maḥmūd Aḥmad in 1898; on the Anglo-Egyptian occupation he was reinstated at Katūl; his kinsman Tamar Aghā Dōka, later 'umda of Katūl, died in 1931.

Tambura, son of Riwa (-1913), chief of the Anungo group of the Azande; on the death of his father at the hands of his own nephew Sanango in inter-tribal fighting, he was taken to Daim Zubair by an Arab chief called Rawātī who had been the ally of his father's murderer; Rawātī cared for the young prisoner and made him his drummer, hence the possible derivation of his name from tanbūr, a lute, drum; freed with his brother Gedi on the occupation of Daim Zubair by government troops about 1878, the Egyptian Government acknowledged his title to the chieftainship, and with Gedi's help he made war against 'Īsā, successor of Sanango, and recovered all his father's former territory; he was deposed by the Condominium Government in 1911 when he was succeeded by his son Renzi.

Ṭanbal Ḥamad Ṭanbal (1840–1922), malik of the ruling house of Arqū, eldest son of al-Malik Ḥamad, grandson of Ṭanbal who was malik at the time of the Turkish occupation, and brother of Muḥammad Bey Ḥamad al-Malik; in 1885 he was appointed ruler of Arqū by the Egyptian Government at the time of the retreat of the British army from Dongola as the result of its failure to relieve Khartoum; his efforts to organize a native administration came to nothing as the Mahdists began to overrun the old Dongola province; he fled with his family to

Egypt and settled at Shallāl where he remained till 1896, when Dongola was cleared of the Mahdists and he returned home; he lived at Arqū till his death.

Ṭanbal Muḥammad Idrīs (1780–1843), malik of Arqū island near New Dongola Town and last of the virtually independent mulūk of the ruling house; he was crowned in 1810 at Arqū and ruled all the land between Ḥannak and Khandaq; he fought the Maḥas and the Shā'iqīya in a series of confused encounters and with difficulty avoided the ravages of the fugitive Mamelukes who, fleeing from Upper Egypt, were battening on the people of the region; the coming of the Turks in 1820 put an end to his independence and he became thereafter kāshif of Arqū under the Turkish governors of Dongola.

Tannyon, Louis de (*fl.* 1860–7), French hunter; he was employed by Prince Muḥammad 'Abd al-Ḥalīm as his huntsman-in-chief; in 1860 the prince had a small steamer of 30 horse-power put on the White Nile with de Tannyon as her captain; this was probably the first steamer to navigate that river; J. F. M. Le Saint the French explorer, who was on his fatal journey to the Upper White Nile, met him with A. Castelbolognesi in Cairo in 1867.

Tanutamon (–*c.* 653 B.C.), Nubian king of Kush and Egypt about 663 B.C.–653 B.C. in succession to Taharqa; he reoccupied Memphis, compromised with the vassals of Assyria in the Nile delta, and temporarily expelled the great Assyrian ruler Asshurbanipal; after their victory the Nubians clung for a while to Egypt, but about 654 B.C. Tanutamon lost Thebes and retired south to the cataracts where he reigned over Kush till the following year; thus was brought to an end in Egypt the line of kings of possibly Libyan descent who had dominated it for a century; he was buried at Kurru.

Taqī al-Dīn ibn 'Alī . . . al-Maqrīzī (1364–1442), Arab historian; an official of the Government of Cairo, he wrote works on Egyptian history and other subjects; we owe to him the preservation of the account of Christian Nubia by Ibn Sulaim or Ibn Salīm; his work, *al Khiṭāṭ*, contains an account of Nubia and the country to the south.

al-Ṭaraifī Aḥmad al-Raiyaḥ (–1857), 'Arakī notable; his father, Shaikh Aḥmad al-Raiyaḥ, brought the fugitive 'Arakīyīn back to their homeland in the Blue Nile valley in 1830 after their reconciliation with the Egyptian Government; they had fled in the early days of the occupation to the southern Buṭāna to escape the exactions of the new rulers.

Tasama (*fl.* 1898), Abyssinian general, nephew of the Emperor Menyelek (Menelik) II; the collapse of the Government of the Khalīfa 'Abd Allāhi saw both France and Abyssinia ready with territorial claims on the Sudan; while Captain J. B. Marchand was leading a French expedition from the Congo basin to Fashoda, Menyelek proposed to annex the land east of the White Nile as far as Khartoum, a claim previously maintained by the Emperor Theodore II; in 1898 Tasama with a column of Abyssinian troops, accompanied by several Frenchmen from the mission of the Marquis de Bonchamps and a Russian colonel named Artamanoff, marched from the Abyssinian highlands along the Baro and Sobat rivers to the confluence of the White Nile and Sobat and here planted the French and Abyssinian flags; failing to join the Marchand expedition from the Baḥr al-G͟hazāl, and anxious for his men who were being decimated by the unaccustomed climate, he retreated into Abyssinia.

Tawfīq Pasha. *See* MUḤAMMAD TAWFĪQ PASHA.

Taylor Bey, Adrian Aubrey Charles (1876–1915), British soldier; commissioned to the Royal Dublin Fusiliers in 1897, he was promoted captain in 1902; he joined the Egyptian army in 1903 and was appointed inspector in the Baḥr al-G͟hazāl province with rank of binbās͟hī; promoted qā'immaqām in 1908, he was acting governor of Sennar in 1911–13 when he reverted to the British army; at the time of his death he was attached to the Egyptian police.

Taylor, James Bayard (1825–78), American diplomat, traveller, and translator of *Faust*; he was born at Kennett Square, Pennsylvania, and died in Berlin; he visited the Sudan in 1851–2, travelling southward from Korosko over the Nubian desert to Berber and Khartoum, whence he sailed up the White Nile to Kawa; on his return journey he crossed the Bayūda to Dongola; he later became United States ambassador in Berlin; he published *Life and Landscapes from Egypt to the Negro Kingdoms of the White Nile* (1854); his wife wrote his *Life and Letters* (1884).

Teleki von Szék, Sámuel, Count (1845–1916), Hungarian explorer, born in Transylvania; with the Austrian naval officer L. von Höhnel (afterwards admiral) he discovered Lake Rudolf in 1886–8; in later life he took a prominent part in public affairs and geographical studies in Hungary.

* **Terranova, Filippo** (*c.* 1820–67), Italian physician; a native of Somacatino, Caltanisetta, Sicily, he was the son of a doctor who left Sicily as a political exile after the suppression of the revolution of 1820 and came to Egypt and settled in Cairo; Filippo followed his father to Egypt in 1838 when he seems to have joined the government medical service; in 1852 or 1853 he came to Khartoum with A. Vaudey and L. Cremona; for the next two years he traded in the Dinka and Nuer country and in 1854 established a trading station ten days upstream of the mouth of the Sobat; with A. Debono he ascended the Sobat in 1855 and reached the old Bonjiac post near the present Akobo post, the farthest point then reached by European explorers; he died in Cairo leaving a family since domiciled in Egypt.

Theodore, King of Abyssinia. *See* KĀSĀ TĒWŌDRŌS (THEODORE) II.

Thibaut, G[eorges ?] (1795–1869), French trader; born in Paris, F. Werne's statement that he was a Parisian street urchin was said by G. Lejean, who met him at Sawākin in after years, to be untrue;

he was more probably an officer or non-commissioned officer in the French army; after having served two years with the Greek insurgents in their war of independence, 1822–3, he changed sides and joined the staff of Sulaimān Pasha al-Faransāwī (O. J. A. Sève) at Aswān as an instructor in the *niẓām al-jadīd*, the new Egyptian regular army trained on European lines; later leaving this employment he entered the service of the trader, J. M. F. Vaissière, and with him came to the Sudan in 1826; eventually setting up as a trader on his own account he collected big game which he took to the zoological gardens of London and Paris; he was known in England as the first to import live giraffes which he deposited in the zoological garden in Regent's Park; in London he met Sara, a slave girl from Kordofan, whom he married and brought back with him to the Sudan; under the name of Shawqī Ibrāhīm he ascended the White Nile as an engineer in two voyages of discovery led by Salīm Qapūdān, 1839–41; the Swiss Baumgarten, who served as a captain on the first of these expeditions, took him on the recommendation of the governor-general, Aḥmad Pasha abū Widān; Thibaut has been accused of stealing Baumgarten's notes and publishing them in his own name after the latter's death; he was for forty years French consular agent in Khartoum where he was a notable figure in the European community; he wore Turkish dress and was at home in the Arabic language and local customs; he and all his family died within a week from the plague.

Thomson Bey, Douglas Stokes Brownlie (1879–1939), British official; born in Dublin, he was commissioned as a lieutenant in the Royal Army Medical Corps, 1904, and was promoted captain, 1907; in 1905 he joined the Egyptian army and was later appointed medical officer on a commission investigating the kala-azar disease in the Sudan; in 1910 he left the Sudan medical department and became a junior inspector in the political service; he was commissioner, Port Sudan, 1928–32, when he retired with the ranks of mīrālai and major.

Thothmes I (*fl.* 1525 B.C.), Egyptian king of the XVIIIth Dynasty who led an army into the northern Sudan and subdued the rebellious Nubians.

Thothmes (*fl.* 1360 B.C.), Egyptian viceroy of Ethiopia from about 1370 B.C. to 1352 B.C. under the Egyptian king Akhenaten of the XVIIIth Dynasty.

Thruston, Arthur Blyford (1865–97), British soldier; gazetted to the Oxfordshire Light Infantry, 1884, he served for a short period in India and Egypt; in 1890–1, while seconded to the Egyptian army, he fought on the Red Sea coast against the Mahdists; he served in the Uganda protectorate, 1893–5, and in the Dongola campaign, 1896, on special attachment to the Egyptian Camel Corps; returning to Uganda in 1897 as commandant of the Uganda Rifles, he was killed by Sudanese mutineers, the remains of Emin Pasha's army; his account of his campaigns was published after his death as *African Incidents* (1900).

Thury (*fl. c.* 1540 B.C.), Egyptian commandant of Buhen near the site of the present Wādī Ḥalfā, and viceroy of Ethiopia in the time of the kings of the XVIIIth Dynasty; he held office roughly from 1551 B.C. to 1528 B.C. during the reigns of kings Amenophis I and Thothmes I.

Thwaites, Guy (1877–1917), British major in the Army Service Corps who was seconded to the Egyptian army in 1914; he was drowned off Renk when the steamer *Amāra* turned turtle and sank.

Tibn Sa'd al-Nūr (*c.* 1870–1932), Fūr worthy of the Kunyanga branch; born at Birinjil, his father held the family title and was vizier to sultans Ḥusain and Ibrāhīm and was killed in the fighting against the invading forces of Zubair Bey Raḥma Manṣūr in 1874; his elder brother then succeeded to the title and went with his followers to join the Khalīfa 'Abd Allāhi at Omdurman; he was afterwards killed at Gedaref; Tibn accompanied him as far as al-Ubaiyaḍ and after three years returned to Dār Fūr where about 1888 he was appointed shaikh of Birinjil; on the assumption of the throne by Sultan 'Alī Dīnār in 1899, he succeeded to the family title and occasionally acted as deputy for the sultan when the latter was absent from his capital; on the Anglo-Egyptian occupation of Dār Fūr in 1916 he fled with 'Alī Dīnār but soon came into al-Fāshar to make his peace with the new government; he then retired to Birinjil as a private citizen under Shartai Adam Taw; in 1929 he was appointed 'umda of Nyāla; in his hereditary capacity of malik al-naḥās or somindogola he was warden of the sultan's war drums and held wide lands by reason of his office.

Tidrick, Ralph (1875–1914), American Protestant missionary; born in Bedford, Iowa, he graduated from Tarkio College, 1906, and after a year studying agriculture in Iowa State College he came to the Sudan; here he worked on the Sobat river under the United Presbyterian Board; he died through a mauling received from a lion.

al-Tījānī Yūsuf Bashīr (1912–37), poet and journalist; he was born at al-Maknīya near Jabal Umm 'Alī of the Jawdalāb branch of the Ja'līyīn Arab tribe and was educated at the Ma'had al-'Ilmī school at Omdurman; he afterwards became editor of the journal *Mir'āt al-Sūdān*, and published poems in this and other journals; he died at Omdurman; his collected poems were published by 'Alī al-Birair and others as *Ishrāq al-naẓm al-Tījānī Yūsuf Bashīr* (Cairo, 1942).

Timsāḥ Simāwī Jarajīr (–1932), nāẓir of Dār Ḥāmid and a member of the ruling house of the dār and a magistrate; his son Muḥammad Timsāḥ is the present nāẓir.

* **Tinné, Alexandrina Petronella Francina** (1839–69), Dutch explorer; she was the daughter of P. F. Tinné, formerly a diplomat and colonial official in the Dutch service and later a trader in Liverpool and a naturalized British subject; she was born at The Hague, the richest heiress in Holland, and spent much of her short life in travel; accompanied by her mother, the Baroness H.-M.-L. van S. Capellen, and her aunt, Miss A. van S. Capellen, two Dutch women servants, Baron d'Ablaing, T. von Heuglin, and H. Steudner, she left Cairo in

January 1862 by the overland route to the Sudan; the party left Khartoum in a fleet of steamers and boats early in 1863 to explore the Upper White Nile; reaching Gondokoro they returned to Khartoum where her aunt was left behind mortally ill; the party then returned southward and travelled on the lower reach of the Sobat and the Baḥr al-Ghazāl; striking inland they journeyed via Wau to the borders of the Azande country; her mother and Steudner, together with the two Dutch servants, died of fever; the survivors left the Sudan by way of Berber and Sawākin in March 1864; she was murdered by the Tuwāriq in the Fazzān while on an expedition to the interior of the Sahara; about the only profitable outcome of her tragic journey in the Sudan was the botanical collection from the Baḥr al-Ghazāl described by T. von Kotschy and J. Peyritsch (Vienna, 1867).

Tippetts, Sydney Atterbury (1878–1946), British official; educated at the University of Oxford; he joined the Sudan political service, 1902; he was governor of Wādī Ḥalfā, 1917–22, and of the Red Sea province, 1922–7, when he retired; a suburb of Wādī Ḥalfā town is named after him al-Daim Tippetts; he was later bursar of Bradfield College, Berkshire.

Tīrāb (or **Tairāb**) **Sulaimān** (–1908 ?), one of the chief military commanders of Sultan ʿAlī Dīnār of Dār Fūr; he normally commanded a rubaʿ, a complete tactical unit including a varying number of riflemen, mounted men, and spear men; his own rubaʿ consisted of 800 riflemen and 200 horsemen; he also commanded ʿAlī Dīnār's bodyguard; the Fūr expedition against the Rizaiqāt of southern Dār Fūr was under his command; after defeating them and killing Ṣūbāshī ʿUqail, one of their leaders, and sending his head to al-Fāshar, he would have attacked the Ḥumr and Ḥamar tribes of Kordofan had not Liwā' (afterwards General Sir) B. T. Mahon Pasha, governor of Kordofan, mobilized a small force of the Camel Corps with Maxim guns and gone at once to the frontier where the presence of this detachment checked Tīrāb's aggressive plans; on his return to al-Fāshar he found himself in disgrace for having killed Ṣūbāshī ʿUqail without orders; he was removed from command of the sultan's bodyguard and thrown into prison; his fate is uncertain, but later, in 1908, a military intelligence report mentions a Tairāb who was governor of Kalaka in that year, though there is nothing to show whether he was the Tīrāb recorded here.

Tirhaqa, Tirhakah. *See* TAHARQA.

Tonquedec, Aymard de Quengo de (1867–1943), French officer of Marine Infantry, born at Glénac, Morbihan; while serving with a Senegalese regiment he was in the rearguard of the Marchand expedition to the Upper Nile; he left Fort Desaix (Wau) in March 1899 and marched and fought his way to Shambé where he maintained himself until November 1899 when he received orders from his government to withdraw; he and his detachment then descended the Baḥr al-Jabal in canoes and, after an arduous passage through a series of reed barriers, met an Egyptian flotilla and continued by steamer to Khartoum where he arrived in February 1900; he retired in 1917 with the rank of lieutenant-colonel and died at Susa, Tunis.

Tossitza, Mikhail (1787–1856), consul-general of Greece in Egypt, 1833–54; born at Metsovo in the Epirus, his family moved to Kavalla; here he became a friend of Muḥammad ʿAlī, the future viceroy of Egypt; on the creation of the Hellenic state he was appointed its first diplomatic representative in Egypt; in 1838–9 he accompanied Muḥammad ʿAlī to Khartoum and Fāzūghlī; he carried on a big trading business centred in Alexandria and died in Athens.

Trampas, Panayotis (–1919), Greek trader, captive at Omdurman during the Mahdist rule; he was decorated by the Emperor Franz Josef of Austria for protecting Christian nuns.

Trevisan, Paolo (*fl.* 1480), Venetian diplomat; he travelled to Abyssinia about 1480, possibly by way of Nubia and the Sudan; on his return he wrote *De Nili origine* (1483), a work since lost.

Trotti, Bentivoglio Lodovico, Marquess (1830–1915), Italian nobleman and revolutionary; a patrician of Milan, he fought on the popular side in the 'Five Days' of 1849 and was exiled; in 1851 he accompanied Count E. Dandolo to the Sudan, visiting Nubia and Khartoum; he served in the Sardinian army in the war of 1859 against the Austrians and from 1891 was a senator.

Tuḥāmī Jalāl al-Dīn Bey (*c.* 1835–), official; born at Umm Bakal near Kūrtī of Ḥalanqa origin, he was educated in the Roman Catholic mission school at Khartoum, learning English and French; he was later appointed a clerk at the British consulate, Khartoum, and about 1873 joined the clerical staff of Ismāʿīl Pasha Aiyūb, the governor-general; while in Cairo, whither he had been sent on duty, he was attached to the staff of C. G. Gordon Pasha whom he accompanied to the Sudan in 1874; he became private secretary to Gordon with grade of bey; while in Dār Fūr he led a punitive force against the maqdūm Saʿd Argūn whom he defeated at Haiyaih wells north of al-Fā<u>sh</u>ar; Ḥasan Ḥilmī Pasha al-Juwaisar, then governor of Dār Fūr, accused him of taking bribes; he was sentenced and exiled to Lado; becoming blind he was ultimately released and retired to Cairo where the Khedive granted him a pension; in 1884 Gordon met him in Cairo and invited him to return with him to Khartoum, but he remained in Egypt where he was of use to Gordon; he died in Beirut after making the pilgrimage to Makka.

al-Tūm ʿAlī al-Tūm Faḍl Allāh (1897–1945), nāẓir ʿumūm of the Kabbābī<u>sh</u> Arabs of northern Kordofan; he was the son of Sir ʿAlī al-Tūm Faḍl Allāh Sālim whom he succeeded on his father's death in 1938; he deputized for his father when the latter went to England in 1919, and in 1934, on the creation of the Kabbābī<u>sh</u> native administration, he was appointed its wakīl; with him the headship of the tribe had been vested in his family for ten generations; he died at Ḥamrat al-<u>Sh</u>ai<u>kh</u> and was succeeded by his son ʿAlī.

al-Tūm Faḍl Allāh Sālim (–1883), paramount shaikh of the Kabbābīsh Arabs; about 1879, with permission of C. G. Gordon Pasha, then governor-general, Ilyās Pasha wad umm Birair, governor of Kordofan, deposed him and appointed his brother Ṣāliḥ Faḍl Allāh Sālim (later Bey) in his place; shortly afterwards Gordon cancelled this arrangement and reappointed al-Tūm, who was nāẓir at the outbreak of the Mahdist revolt; hostile to the Mahdist régime he was killed by the Mahdists at al-Ubaiyaḍ a short time after the fall of the town.

al-Tūnisī. *See* MUḤAMMAD IBN ʿUMAR IBN SULAIMĀN AL-TŪNISĪ.

Tūrī Yaʿqūb (–1924), ʿumda of the Salamāt branch of the Missīrīya (Ḥumr-Falaita) tribe of Kordofan; the tribe pastured round Mujlad and Kailak where he died.

Ṭūsūn ʿAlī Pasha Yeghen (1793–1826), Turkish commander; born at Kavalla in Macedonia, he was first cousin of Muḥammad ʿAlī Pasha; he was one of Ismāʿīl Pasha's senior officers in the march to Sennar, 1820–1; when Ibrāhīm Pasha returned to Egypt, 1821, he appointed him as his personal deputy in the Sudan under Ismāʿīl Pasha; he was also officer commanding the Turkish troops at Sennar; in 1822 he led a force from Jabal Quraibin via Jabals Ghūl and Darwī to the White Nile in the Dinka country, a march of fourteen days; after a week's rest the force returned by Jabals Tābī and Quraibin to Sennar; he proved a popular commander; he was recalled soon after to Egypt, but not before he had led a punitive expedition against the Shukrīya for non-payment of tribute; he was promoted pasha in 1824.

ʿUbaid al-Ḥājj al-Amīn ʿAbd al-Qādir (1904–32), born in Omdurman of Maḥasī origin he was educated at Gordon Memorial College, Khartoum, and entered the Sudan railways; in 1923 he left the railway service and became a clerk in the prisons department; in 1924 he joined the White Flag league, an organization of Sudanese in favour of political independence; the movement having been declared illegal he was arrested; while in prison in Khartoum he took part in a mutiny; after serving his sentence he was banished to Wau; released in 1931 he was engaged as a clerk in the district office at Wau where he shortly afterwards died.

Ueberbacher, Anton (1827–58), Austrian priest of the Roman Catholic Church; born at Natz near Brixen he came to the Sudan in 1854; in 1855 he was superior of the mission station of St. Mary at Gondokoro; on his death there from fever he was succeeded by F. Morlang; he was a student of the Bari language and helped J. C. J. Mitterrützner in the compilation of the latter's Bari grammar.

* **Ulivi, Nicola** (*c.* 1792–1852), Italian collector of natural history specimens and (according to contemporary rumour) a slave trader; he was by origin a Tuscan; G. Melly inspected his collections in Khartoum in 1850; he died in Khartoum; by his wife Maḥbūba, an Abyssinian, he had several children including Ginevra who married L. Cremona, Maria

Anna Adriana, baptized at the Khartoum Roman Catholic mission, 1843, and two other children: a boy, Francesco, and a baby girl, who both died within a month of their father's burial.

Ullmann, Josef (1829–57), Austrian merchant from Steinschoenau in Bohemia; he died in Khartoum.

'Umar Aḥmad umm Fārūq (*c*. 1874–1929), Missīrī notable; 'umda of the Awlād abū Nu'mān branch of the Missīrīya Arabs of Kordofan.

'Umar Aḥmad Makkī (–1947), imām of the principal mosque at Omdurman; he was a Ja'lī by birth.

'Umar abū 'Alī (–1938), Beja worthy; 'umda of the Shebodināb section of the Hadendowa tribe who live between the Red Sea hills and the Nile; he died at Musmār.

'Umar 'Aṭīya (1881–1942), Egyptian religious shaikh; he entered the service of the Sudan legal department in 1907 when he was appointed an assistant qāḍī; qāḍī in 1908 and province qāḍī in 1923, he was made inspector of Islamic courts in 1934; he retired in 1937.

'Umar Azraq (–1946), Mahdist amīr, no relation of 'Uthmān Azraq; he was born at Maknīya near Maḥmīya of the 'Umarāb branch of the Ja'liyīn Arabs and as a young man joined the Mahdist movement at its beginning; he succeeded Muḥammad 'Uthmān abū Qarja as amīr of the Jazīra; after the fall of the Mahdist Government he lived on at Omdurman where he was among the last surviving chiefs of Khalīfa 'Abd Allāhi's régime.

'Umar al-Bashīr Baṭrān (1877–1942), tribal chieftain of the Bidairāb section of the Rubāṭāb, a son of Shaikh al-Bashīr Baṭrān who was head man and judge of Abū Ḥamad district in Turkish times; he was 'umda of Muqrāt near Abū Ḥamad from 1917 and president of the Rubāṭāb shaikhs' court from 1934.

'Umar Bey Fakhrī (–1866), soldier of the Egyptian army; he was deputy governor-general under Mūsā Ḥamdī Pasha and in 1865 was acting governor-general between the death of Mūsā Ḥamdī and the arrival in Khartoum of Ja'far Pasha Ṣādiq; as a result of his lack of energy in quelling the military mutiny which broke out in Kassala and Sawākin in 1865 he was degraded to the rank of deputy governor of a province; he shortly afterwards died.

'Umar al-Faqīr al-Nimr (–1929), notable of the Nimrāb section of the Mīrafāb tribe; he was 'umda of Sallam north of Berber.

'Umar Jamīl (*c*. 1866–1943), cavalry leader under 'Alī Dīnār, sultan of Dār Fūr, by tribe a Ḥalbāwī; his military career was damaged by having his right leg broken in war with the Kenīn, and when he tried to take the field against the Rizaiqāt in 1913 he had to retire; while the Anglo-Egyptian army was entering al-Fāshar in 1916 he was in the south engaged in leading raiding parties against the Fūr and Birgid and met the new government only just before 'Alī Dīnār's death; he was imprisoned until he gave up the loot which he had taken in his raids; having helped in the recovery of cattle during a patrol to the Beni Ḥalba which he accompanied, he was released and returned home; in 1928 he was appointed assistant nāẓir of the Beni Ḥalba and vice-president of the Beni Ḥalba court, but was dismissed for misdemeanour in 1930; between 1937 and 1941 he was exiled to al-Fāshar for intriguing against his nāẓir.

'Umar Janbū (–1918), holy man of Hausa descent; a prominent member of the Tījānīya brotherhood in Dār Fūr and Kordofan, he was a disciple of Muḥammad al-Ṣaghīr ibn al-Saiyid 'Alī of Tlemcen; he was living at al-Fāshar under the protection of the sultan 'Alī Dīnār when he came under suspicion of using witchcraft to cause the sultan's death and had to flee in 1908 to al-Ubaiyaḍ; here and at Omdurman he spent the rest of his life with occasional pilgrimages to Makka where he died.

'Umar Layla (Lele) Muḥammad Dawra (–1739), sultan of Dār Fūr in succession to his father Muḥammad Dawra; he ruled from 1732 until his death in battle against Ṣābūn, sultan of Wadā'i, when his uncle Abū'l-Qāsim Aḥmad Bukr (or Bukkur) reigned in his stead.

'Umar wad al-Mak Nāṣir (*c.* 1835–1928), notable of the ancient dynasty of the Funj; born at Sennar he lived most of his life at al-Jailī in the district of Sennar; when the Mahdists besieged Sennar in 1884–5 he took part in the defence of the town as second-in-command to his brother Tāj al-Dīn.

* **'Umar al-Makāshfī** (–1883), Kahlī notable, brother of Aḥmad al-Makāshfī who was killed fighting against government troops under Ṣāliḥ Bey al-Mak at Jabal Saqadī; he was one of the Mahdist commanders at the battle of al-Marābi' near Abā island on the White Nile and was killed in the battle.

'Umar Muḥammad 'Abbās (–1945), Maḥasī notable and magistrate; he lived and died at Burrī, a suburb of Khartoum.

'Umar Muḥammad al-Daw (–1945), Khāldī chieftain; shaikh of the Khawālda khuṭṭ in the southern Jazīra; his father Muḥammad (d. 1919) was a Mahdist amīr; he died at al-Nuwila.

'Umar Muḥammad Ḥijāzī (*c.* 1821–1915), Egyptian artisan, popularly known as 'Umar al-Muhandiz (the engineer); he was born at Ṭahṭa of a Sudanese mother; his father emigrated to the Sudan where he cultivated at Manjala near Khartoum, dying about 1879; young 'Umar learnt brick-making and helped build the mosque erected in the city during the governor-generalship of Ismā'īl Pasha Aiyūb (1873–6); he was afterwards made chief foreman of government buildings, a post which involved travelling widely in the country; he was caught in the siege of al-Ubaiyaḍ by the Mahdists, 1882–3, but was soon employed by the Mahdī and by the Khalīfa 'Abd Allāhi for whom he built the bait al-māl, the Khalīfa's mosque, and helped in the building of the Mahdī's tomb and of fortifications at Gallabat; after the Anglo-Egyptian occupation he was employed by the military works department as foreman of brick kilns at Jaraif and worked on the construction of Gordon Memorial College and other public buildings.

'Umar Muḥammad abū Ḥijil (–1897), Mahdist amīr of the Rubāṭāb tribe and a member of a leading Rubāṭābī family; his father, Muḥammad abū Ḥijil, had been vice-governor of Dongola under the Egyptian Government; joining the Mahdist cause he was killed in the defence of Abū Ḥamad against an assaulting force under A. Hunter Pasha which had come by forced marches from Merowe to seize this strategic point.

'Umar ibn Nāṣir ibn Bādī (1836–1929), notable of the Funj, grandson of Bādī VI wad Ṭabl II, last sultan of Sennar; he lost no less than eight sons in the defence of Sennar against the Mahdists, 1884–5; a surviving son was Nāṣir wad al-Mak 'Umar al-Funjī.

'Umar Rushdī Pasha (–1898), by origin a Turk he joined the Egyptian army and served with the survey missions of R. E. Colston Bey and H. G. Prout Bey in Kordofan and Dār Fūr, 1874–5, and contributed to the cartographical work of the general staff; as a binbāshī in S. A. Arendrup Bey's ill-starred force in Abyssinia, 1875, he refused to surrender and led his men safely back to Muṣawwa'; after holding high judicial posts he died in Cairo.

'Umar Ṣāliḥ (–1897), Mahdist amīr, of Ta'ā'isha Baqqāra origin; he disembarked at Lado from three steamers and nine barges in 1888 with the intention of destroying the forces of Emin Pasha, Egyptian governor of Equatoria; he sent an ultimatum to Emin which was intercepted by Egyptian mutineers who decided to fight; he then seized Rejaf and killed Ḥamad Aghā, the mutineers' governor, after his men had run away; he attacked Dufile and held it for a brief period, but was driven out by mutineers under Salīm Bey; he was killed in battle against the Belgians at Rejaf.

'Umar al-Sanūsī 'Alī, called **Wad Baqādī** (–1857), holy man of the Kawāhla of the Jazīra, grandson of the faqī 'Alī al-Ḥamūda (d. 1803); his son, Aḥmad wad 'Umar wad Baqādī, was a friend of Muḥammad Aḥmad al-Mahdī.

'Umar Ṭūsūn, Prince (1872–1944), Egyptian landowner and historian; a grandson of Muḥammad 'Alī Pasha, he was born at Alexandria; educated in the Khedivial palace and afterwards in Switzerland, France, and England, he spoke and wrote English, French, and Turkish fluently; he was much interested in the Sudan and advocated its retrocession to Egypt; among his many publications dealing with the Sudan are *Buṭūlat al-urṭat al-sūdānīya fī ḥarb al-Maksīk* (Alexandria, 1933), an account of the Sudanese battalion under Marshal Bazaine in Mexico, and *Tārīkh mudīrīyat khaṭṭ al-istiwā' al-miṣrīya* (Alexandria, 1937), dealing with the history of Egyptian Equatoria.

'Umāra Dūnqas (Dūnqus) (–1553), founder of the Funj sultanate of Sennar; he created the town of Sennar and made it his capital; in alliance with the local Arab tribes he defeated and slew the Nubian Christian kings of Soba and al-Qarrī; his sultanate finally extended from Dongola to the mountains of Fāzūghlī and from the Abyssinian border to the Nuba hills; he ascended the throne about 1504 and reigned till his death when he was succeeded by his son 'Abd al-Qādir; there is much uncertainty about the origin of the Funj and the events leading up to his accession to power.

'Umāra wad Nimr Muḥammad (–1863), Ja'lī refugee chieftain; he was the son of Nimr Muḥammad Nimr, last king of Shendi who died in exile at Mai Qūbba on the Baḥr al-Salām in 1846; on the death of his father he became the leader of the outlawed band of Ja'līyīn desperadoes and continued the struggle against the Turks with whom he fought many battles; with a force of Abyssinians he raided Tāka and attacked the Hadendowa, 1850; he laid claim to Sūq abū Sin (Gedaref) as part of the kingdom of Tigre to which he was allied; he bartered women for arms with Ilyās Bey, governor of Tāka; in 1857 Muḥammad Sa'īd Pasha granted an amnesty to the Nimrāb exiles, but before he received the news he had seized the Egyptian customs post at Dōka and had been declared an outlaw; the Egyptians burnt his village, Mai Qūbba, in 1863 in the course of a reconnaissance of the Abyssinian border commanded by Mūsā Ḥamdī Pasha; he escaped only to be mortally wounded in another fight with an Egyptian patrol in the same year.

'Umāra abū Sakaikīn (–1562), sultan of the Funj dominion of Sennar; he succeeded King Naiyīl in 1554 and was himself succeeded on his death by Dakīn wad Naiyīl; it was in his reign that the powerful manjil or viceroy of al-Qarrī, Shaikh 'Ajīb wad 'Abd Allāh al-Kāfūta, was appointed.

Umm Badda Simāwī (*c.* 1870–1944), 'umda of the Ḥabābīn tribe of the Dār Ḥāmid tribal group of Kordofan, a member of a family which had ruled in Dār Ḥāmid for four generations; he was a magistrate.

* **Umm Maryam.** *See* 'Abd al-Qādir wad Umm Maryam; Ḥammād ibn Muḥammad ibn 'Alī al-Mashaikhī.

Ūnsā I (–1598), sultan of the Funj of Sennar; of the royal line of 'Umāra Dūnqas, he succeeded Sultan Ṭabl I on the latter's death in 1589 and ruled till his own death when Sultan 'Abd al-Qādir II succeeded him.

* **Unsā II wad Nāṣir** (–1688), nephew of Sultan Bādī II abū Diqn whom he succeeded to the Funj sultanship of Sennar in 1677; a great famine ravaged the land during his reign; his son Bādī III al-Aḥmar succeeded him.

Ūnsā III wad Bādī III (–1718), last sultan of Sennar of the royal line founded by 'Umāra Dunqas about 1504; he ascended the throne in 1715; frivolous and immoral, he was deposed by the southern Funj and possibly died of small-pox in Sennar.

Urben, Percy Walter (1885–1943), British postal official; he entered the British Post Office as a learner in 1900 and during the First World War served in the Royal Navy, rising from ordinary seaman to lieutenant-commander; he returned to the Post Office after the war and in 1922–6, and again in 1928–31, was seconded to the posts and telegraphs service of the Sudan, first as head of the traffic department, later, in 1931, as director; after three months in office he returned to the British postal service from which he resigned in 1942; during the Second World War he was a colonel of the Home Guard.

'Uthmān Adam, called also **'Uthmān Jānū** (*c.* 1866–89), Mahdist leader; a Ta'ā'ishī by tribe, he was a relative of the Khalīfa 'Abd Allāhi; he showed unusual military talent at an early age and about 1886 was an amīr and governor of Kordofan where he gained a reputation for chivalry; he mobilized the Mahdist force which fought the Kabbābīsh and which killed their leader Ṣāliḥ Bey Faḍl Allāh at Jabal al-'Ain in 1887; later in the same year he joined the amīr Karam Allāh Muḥammad Kurkusāwī in Dār Fūr, defeating the adherents of Sultan Yūsuf Ibrāhīm, killing Yūsuf in battle in Jabal Marra, capturing Shaqqa, and defeating another rebel force near Dāra; he was next appointed ruler of Dār Fūr and Kordofan with the elevated rank of amīr al-umarā'; he ruled with a rod of iron; after a bitter struggle with the fanatic Aḥmad abū Jummaiza of the Maṣālīṭ tribe he destroyed his following near al-Fāshar in 1889; he died shortly afterwards and was succeeded by the amīr Maḥmud Aḥmad.

* **'Uthmān Azraq** (–1898), Mahdist amīr; of Dongolāwī stock (he was no relation of the amīr 'Umar Azraq) he served in the northern theatre of war during the Mahdist régime under the amīr 'Abd al-Mājid Naṣr al-Dīn and was wounded at the battle of Jinnis (Giniss) in Dār Sukkōt in 1885; in 1887 he ambushed the German trader K. Neufeld in Wādī al-Qa'ab west of Dongola; escaping by flight from the disaster of Tūshkī (Toski), in 1889, when his commander 'Abd al-Raḥmān wad al-Najūmī was defeated by a government force under the sirdār F. W. Grenfell Pasha, he led a daring raid on Murrāt wells and killed Ṣāliḥ Bey Ḥusain Khalīfa, the 'Abbādī shaikh who commanded the post there, in 1893; he commanded the Mahdist army at Firka (Firket), 1896, and was wounded at Ḥafīr later in the year; recalled to defend the approaches to the Sixth Cataract (which the Khalīfa 'Abd Allāhi later decided not to defend) he led a force of regular Mahdist troops in the battle of Omdurman in which he was killed.

* **'Uthmān abū Bakr Diqna** (*c.* 1840–1926), Mahdist amīr al-umarā'; though he claimed 'Abbāsī descent, his ancestors on his father's side were said to have been Kurds from Diyārbakr who were soldiers in the army which the Ottoman sultan Salīm I sent to occupy Sawākin about 1518 and who inter-married with the local Beja population; his mother was of the Bishārīyāb branch of the Hadendowa Beja tribe; a mistaken rumour was current during his lifetime that he was of French origin born at Rouen; having embarked in the family business of sea trading with the Arabian coast, he was caught about 1877 by a British ship-of-

war in the act of carrying slaves from the Sudan; he was handed over to the Egyptian authorities by whom he was imprisoned; financially ruined by the incident, he developed a life-long hatred of Turks and British; a sympathizer with the aims of Aḥmad 'Urābī Pasha, he attempted without success to create a disturbance at Sawākin but was forced by the leading merchants to leave, so went to Berber where he set up as a broker; he joined the cause of Muḥammad Aḥmad al-Mahdī and was in al-Ubaiyaḍ early in 1883; appointed an amīr, he returned to the Red Sea hills and gathered the Beja tribesmen to the Mahdī's now victorious cause; he besieged and destroyed the small garrison of Sinkāt commanded by Qā'immaqām Tawfīq Bey al-Miṣrī, 1884; various forces of Beja whom he organized, but did not usually lead, fought a series of battles with the Egyptian and British troops on the coast; at el-Teb (Andatteib), between Tokar and the harbour of Trinkitat, they annihilated an Egyptian force under the incompetent Maḥmūd Ṭāhir Pasha in 1883 and Tokar was besieged and taken; early in 1884 another Egyptian force under V. Baker Pasha ran away and was butchered at el-Teb; a third battle was fought there within a few days when for once the Mahdist tribesmen were defeated by a British column under Sir G. Graham; at Tamai Graham won another victory, but at some cost, in March 1884; in 1885 battles were fought between the British and Mahdists at Hashīn and Tofrik; after these heroic encounters the fighting on the Red Sea coast degenerated into occasional skirmishes and small actions, and 'Uthmān Diqna was recalled in 1886 to Omdurman; the fighting fervour of the tribesmen was now spent by continual war and in 1891 Colonel Sir C. Holled Smith recaptured Tokar; 'Uthmān Diqna retired to Adarama on the Atbara, returning to make an ineffectual raid on Tokar district in 1895; although present at the battles of the Atbara and Omdurman, 1898, he took no active part, and after the Mahdist defeat at Omdurman fled to the Red Sea hills where he was finally captured in 1900; he was imprisoned, first at Rosetta, then at Ṭura, finally, on account of his health, at Wādī Ḥalfā, 1908, where he devoted himself to religious contemplation; in 1924, now an old man, he made the pilgrimage to Makka, returning to die at Wādī Ḥalfā; his exploits attracted much attention in the European press; a biography by H. C. Jackson appeared in 1926.

'Uthmān wad al-Dikaim (–1898), Mahdist amīr; of Ta'ā'ishī blood, he was a brother of Yūnus al-Dikaim and a cousin of the Khalīfa 'Abd Allāhi; he was appointed amīr of Berber in place of Muḥammad al-Khair 'Abd Allāh Khūjalī who died in 1888 and was killed at the battle of Omdurman.

'Uthmān Ghālib Pasha (–1893), liwā' of the Egyptian army; while a mīrālai he commanded the 1st infantry regiment of the 1st brigade in Muḥammad Rātib Pasha's campaign in Abyssinia, 1876.

'Uthmān wad Ḥamad (*fl. c.* 1670), Shā'iqī patriot; he freed the Shā'iqīya Arabs from the domination of the Funj, defeating the Funj viceroy of al-Qarrī and his army of 'Abdullāb.

'U<u>th</u>mān Bey Ḥasan (-1816), Mameluke leader, commander of one of the fugitive bands of Mamelukes pursued into Nubia by Muḥammad 'Alī Pasha in 1812; he died in Dongola.

'U<u>th</u>mān Ḥasan 'Abd Allāh (1876-1937), chief merchant of Karīma; born at Dongola he claimed <u>Sh</u>arīfī descent from a great-grandfather who emigrated from Makka; during the Mahdist rule he traded between Omdurman and Dongola and later between Omdurman and Sawākin; in 1919 he made Karīma the centre of his business.

* 'U<u>th</u>mān Ḥi<u>sh</u>mat (-1885), qā'immaqām of the Egyptian army; during the siege of Khartoum he commanded the 1st battalion of the 5th infantry regiment whose mīrālai was Ḥasan Bey Bahnassāwī; while defending his section of the defences he was killed in the Mahdist assault of the city.

'U<u>th</u>mān Bey 'Iffat (1854-1940), Egyptian soldier; he was commissioned originally in the engineer corps and then served as a staff officer in the Cairo military district; promoted binbā<u>sh</u>ī in the 9th Sudanese infantry battalion at Wādī Ḥalfā, 1895, he served in the Dongola campaign, 1896; on the capture of Dongola he remained to command the Egyptian troops there, having been promoted qā'immaqām; in 1900 he was given command of the 6th infantry battalion at Khartoum till he retired in 1902.

'U<u>th</u>mān Bey Jarkas (-1825), sir'askar of Sennar, his name is also recorded as 'U<u>th</u>mān Bey al-Birinjī; formerly a Mameluke a<u>gh</u>ā in the service of Muḥammad 'Alī Pasha, he held the post of <u>ch</u>amā<u>sh</u>īrjī (literally washerman) on his personal staff; on the formation of the niẓām al-jadīd, the new regular army, in 1821 he was chosen, though entering middle age, for training to be an officer of this force; after finishing his training in European military drill, he was made binbā<u>sh</u>ī of the 20th battalion and in 1823 promoted mīrālai of the 1st infantry regiment; in 1824 he was appointed commander-in-chief of Sennar on the departure of Muḥammad Bey <u>Kh</u>usraw the Daftardār; he set out for the Sudan with his regiment and on the way suppressed a rebellion of peasants in Upper Egypt; marching via Dongola and the Bayūda he entered the village of Omdurman in September with the first regular troops ever seen there; camping on the site of the present city of Khartoum, where he made a military post, he went on to Wad Madanī, then the capital of Sennar province, or rather military district; returning to Khartoum he died there of consumption in March 1825 and was succeeded by Maḥū Bey, governor of Berber; the testimony of the Sudanese chronicler makes him a monster of violence and injustice.

'U<u>th</u>mān Pasha Jarkas (-1860), Circassian soldier in the service of Egypt; in 1857, with rank of mīrlivā, he was appointed to command the troops in the Sudan; after his death the command of the Sudan garrisons was distributed among the provincial governors as part of the policy of decentralization announced by the viceroy Muḥammad Sa'īd Pasha in Khartoum in 1857.

Uthmān Manṣūr (–1941), Kanzī notable, shaikh of the third qism of Khartoum province.

'Uthmān Muḥammad al-Khair (–1944), Islamic judge who lived and served latterly in Berber where he was a native; by tribe a Bidairī from al-Ghubush, Berber, he was a relative of Shaikh Aḥmad al-Ja'lī al-Ḥājj Ḥamad and son of Muḥammad al-Khair 'Abd Allāh Khūjalī, Mahdist amīr and governor of Berber.

'Uthmān Rifqī Pasha (1839–86), deputy governor-general of the Sudan and farīq of the Egyptian army; he was a Circassian volunteer born in the Caucasus; after a military education in Egypt, he was commissioned as mulāzim II in 1857; his promotion was unusually rapid, for he was promoted qā'immaqām in 1861 at the age of twenty-two; he was for a short time on administrative duty on the Red Sea coast before he took part in the suppression of the Greek rebels in the Cretan insurrection of 1866–7; then followed regimental duty in Egypt, including command of the 11th infantry regiment; he was offered the post vacated by Muḥammad Ra'ūf Bey (afterwards pasha) in Equatoria in 1873 but declined it; he was promoted liwā' in 1875 when he was given the command of the 1st brigade under the sirdār, Muḥammad Rātib Pasha in the unfortunate war against Abyssinia in 1875–6; he was commissioner for Muṣawwa' and Sawākin and officer commanding troops in the eastern Sudan in 1877, when he was transferred to Khartoum as deputy governor-general and commander-in-chief of troops in the Sudan, duties which he took over in 1878; his relations with the Governor-General C. G. Gordon Pasha were unhappy and he was soon recalled to Egypt suffering from bad health and was succeeded by Giegler Pasha; from 1879 to 1881 he was minister of war when he was opposed by the partisans of Aḥmad 'Urābī Pasha who wished to have an Egyptian appointed in his place; he was superseded early in 1882 by 'Urābī Pasha on the formation of a new Cabinet led by Maḥmūd Sāmī Pasha al-Bārūdī and banished to Constantinople; while in exile he is said to have refused an offer by the sultan 'Abd al-Ḥamīd of the command of a Turkish division to take the field against the Egyptian nationalists; on the defeat of 'Urābī Pasha's army later in 1882, he returned to Egypt and in 1883 was a member of a government commission on railways in the Sudan; he spent his remaining years in retirement; active and a born horseman, his last months were clouded by a painful illness which he bore with courage.

* **'Uthmān Shaikh al-Dīn 'Abd Allāhi al-Ta'ā'ishī** (*c.* 1880–1900), Mahdist amīr, son of the Khalīfa 'Abd Allāhi; in spite of his youth he was one of the principal Mahdist leaders at the battle of Omdurman where with the amīr 'Uthmān Azraq he commanded the regular troops; he was wounded, and his father was killed, at the battle of Umm Dibaikarāt in 1899; taken prisoner, he died in captivity at Rosetta.

'Uthmān Bey al-Sinnārī (–1858), mīrālai of the Egyptian army; he was in command of the 2nd infantry regiment when he was appointed deputy governor-general in February 1855; in March 1855 Muḥammad

Sa'īd Pasha, the viceroy, wrote to the minister of war informing him that he had written to the governor-general to discharge 'Uthmān Bey from the command of his regiment on the ground that he was a bad disciplinarian; in a later letter the viceroy ordered his replacement by Shāhīn Bey Kinj; in February 1856 he was appointed governor of Kordofan and ordered to march against the mak of Jabal Taqalī, Nāṣir ibn al-Mak Abbukr; in the course of the expedition he was killed, his army destroyed, and only 200 survivors reached al-Ubaiyaḍ; his name, al-Sinnārī, has given rise to the supposition that he was of Sudanese origin, though his name does not appear among the available lists of early Sudanese officers, and it is known that more than one Turkish officer was nicknamed after the territory where he had served; he was also called 'Uthmān al-Izairiq.

'Uthmān Sulaimān Qamar (–1934), Manṣūrī notable; 'umda of the Manāṣīr and a magistrate.

'Uthmān Tāj al-Sirr al-Mīrghanī (–1903), religious notable, third son of al-Saiyid Muḥammad Sirr al-Khātim al-Mīrghanī and grandson of Muḥammad 'Uthmān who founded the Mīrghanīya brotherhood in the Sudan; he married al-Sharīfa Maryam al-Mīrghanīya, granddaughter of the founder; he died at Sawākin where a tomb perpetuates his memory.

* **Vaissière, Joseph-Marie-François** (1786–*c.* 1845 ?), French soldier and trader; born at Castres, he served as an officer in the army of Napoleon; he was made a chevalier of the Legion of Honour, 10 April 1815, and he probably fought during the campaign of the Hundred Days; on the dissolution of the Imperial army he went to Egypt where he was engaged as an army instructor, 1816; he accompanied Ibrāhīm Pasha as aide-de-camp in the Arabian war of 1816–18, and as an expert in siege artillery took a leading part in the reduction of Dar'īya, 1818, on whose capture he was promoted qā'immaqām; Ibrāhīm Pasha sent him to carry the news of the victory to his father who rewarded him with a gratuity of 50,000 dollars; he was not, however, retained in the Egyptian army but embarked upon a commercial career; between 1823 and 1828 he made frequent journeys between Egypt and Kordofan whence he exported gum arabic, ostrich feathers, and (according to some) slaves; A. Cadeau, instructor to the 1st infantry regiment at al-Ubaiyaḍ, wrote to the French consul-general in Egypt that his conduct failed to maintain the good name of France; he made two journeys between Egypt and Abyssinia through the Sudan with camel convoys carrying coffee and trade goods; he was one of the first European merchants to penetrate Abyssinia by way of the Nile valley and is said to have made a fortune in commerce; in 1832 he was staying in Abyssinia living the life of a prosperous trader; he probably visited France in 1834, but was back in Egypt in 1839; the date and place of his death are uncertain; the registers of the Roman Catholic mission in Khartoum record that Joseph Vissier [*sic*] had a daughter, Judith Rose, born 1837 and christened 1842; another entry records Yacob Vessier (Gallus) [*sic*] as having a son, Alexandre, born 1844.

Valentia, Viscount. *See* ANNESLEY.

Vallom . . . (–1896), British engineer; he was chief superintendent of engines and workshops at Wādī Ḥalfā, 1886–96, when he died in the cholera epidemic which raged there in the latter year; he was responsible for the maintenance of rolling stock of the Sudan railway during the interval between the two wars, and on the opening of the Dongola campaign in 1896 was superintendent of railway construction; though a small man of no fame or influence, his careful husbanding of the material under his charge made possible the early start in the construction of Kitchener's military railways towards Kerma and Khartoum.

Vandeleur, Cecil Foster Seymour (1869–1901), British soldier and explorer; gazetted to the Scots Guards in 1889, he served in Uganda and in the expedition to Dufile in 1895–6; in 1897 he was a member of the Niger–Sudan expedition; he was in the Egyptian army in the Nile campaign, 1898, and fought in the battles of the Atbara and Omdurman where he was wounded while serving in the 9th Sudanese battalion; he wrote *Campaigning on the Upper Nile and Niger* (1898); a biography, by Sir F. I. Maxse, appeared in 1905.

Vandeleur, John Ormsby (1832–1908), British major-general; he entered the army in 1851 and served in the Egyptian war of 1882 and in the Nile campaign of 1884–5 which attempted without success to relieve Khartoum; he was promoted major-general in 1887.

Vanian, Soukias (1840-1915), Armenian merchant; born at Egin in the vilāyet of Kharpūṭ in Anatolia, he went to Egypt in 1862, setting up in business with his uncle in Cairo; shortly after the entry of the Anglo-Egyptian forces into Omdurman in 1898, he opened a shop there which he transferred in 1899 to Khartoum, founding the firm afterwards known as S. & S. Vanian, Ltd.; he was in business in Khartoum until 1915 when, suffering from ill health, he went to Cyprus to attempt a cure; he died at Nicosia.

* **Vaudey, Alexandre** (1814–54), Savoyard trader, uncle of A. and J. Poncet, the explorers and traders on the Upper White Nile; he was secretary to A. B. Clot Bey 1837–49 and, sharing his employer's fall, turned to trading in the Sudan; with J. Petherick he was engaged in the gum arabic trade in Kordofan in 1850 and later traded independently, importing trade rifles and ironmongery and exporting ivory; he was appointed pro-consul (i.e. vice-consul) of Sardinia in Khartoum and was the first to hold this office which he occupied till his death; in 1851 he visited his native land and brought back with him his two nephews, A. and J. Poncet, to the Sudan; he was on a trading expedition to Gondokoro with them when he was killed in an incident with the Bari people, his nephews barely escaping with their lives; such was the trust placed in him by the inhabitants of St. Jean-de-Maurienne, his native village, that he formed from their number a commercial company for hunting elephants on the White Nile.

Vayssière, Jean-Alexandre (1817–61), French soldier and trader; he was born at Espalion and joined the French army in which he served as a lieutenant of light cavalry, partly on active service in Algeria; he abandoned his military career to seek adventure in Egypt where through the patronage of A. B. Clot Bey he was appointed a ṣāgh qōl aghāsi at the ministry of war about 1845; he resigned from this post in 1847, and after an archaeological tour to Arabia with T. J. Arnaud he turned to big game hunting on the Upper White Nile where he was traced about 1850 when he established a trading station slightly downstream of Gondokoro; he was again there in 1857 when, after a visit to Espalion in 1856, he closed his station and transferred his activities to the Baḥr al-Ghazāl where he founded another station and where he died on his return to Lake No after accompanying O. Antinori and C. Piaggia on an exploration to the country of the Jur; the identity of Vayssière has been confused with that of J. M. F. Vaissière.

* **Venturini, Elisabetta** (–1937), nun of the Roman Catholic mission to Central Africa; she came to the Sudan in 1881 and was one of the sisters who nursed R. Gessi Pasha during his illness in Khartoum; transferred later in 1881 to the mission at Dilling in the Nuba hills, she was with the rest of the mission staff taken prisoner by the Mahdists and conveyed first to al-Ubaiyaḍ then to Khartoum whence she escaped with Fr. J. Ohrwalder and Sister C. Chincharini to Egypt in 1892; after the pacification of the Sudan she returned to her former work and served in the missions at Khartoum, Omdurman, and Atbara; she died in ripe old age in Khartoum.

Vigoureux . . . (*fl.* 1823–39), French soldier and trader; he was said by the malicious, if amusing, F. Werne to have been a corporal in the Napoleonic army; he distinguished himself in Arabia in 1824 where he was serving with the 2nd infantry regiment of the *niẓām al-jadīd*; he afterwards resigned, or was discharged, from his post as army instructor with the regiment in Kordofan about 1840 when he traded in gold and (wrote Werne) in slaves.

Villiers, Frederic (1852–1927), British war artist; born in London and educated in France, he was war artist for the *Graphic* illustrated journal in several wars, including the Sawākin campaign, 1884, and the Nile campaign, 1884–5, when he was present at the battles of Abū Ṭulaiḥ (Abu Klea) and Qubbat; he was the operator of the first cinematograph camera used in the history of warfare when he accompanied the Turko-Greek war of 1897; he returned to the Sudan in 1898, as war artist for the *Globe*, to follow the campaign which ended in the battle of Omdurman; after further campaigning and sketching in the Boer and Balkan wars he followed his calling in the First World War; among his books are *Pictures of many Wars* (1902) and *Villiers: his Five Decades of Adventure* (1921).

* **Vinco, Angelo** (1819–53), Italian priest of the Roman Catholic Church; born at Cerro near Verona and trained in the Istituto Mazza at Verona, he came to the Sudan in 1848 with I. Knoblehar, apostolic vicar, and

the Genoese Jesuit E. Pedemonte; in 1849 he went back to Europe and in 1851, having returned to the Sudan, with Knoblehar founded a mission station at Gondokoro in 1852; from here he made several local explorations of the Bari country, reaching the River Koss eastward of Torit; he died at Libo while preparing an exploration to the south; G. (afterwards Cardinal) Massaia, who met him in Khartoum, wrote that he was a great man though not by his temperament suited to the work. G. Lejean called him 'the perfect type of Christian missionary in the Sudan'.

Vita Ḥasan (1858–93), Jewish pharmaceutical dispenser; born in Tunis, the son of a dragoman at the Sardinian consulate there, he began his education in Alexandria; poverty compelled him to leave school at the age of fifteen when he entered the pharmaceutical business, becoming at the age of nineteen manager of a dispensary in Cairo belonging to the physician of the widow of the viceroy ʿAbbās Pasha; helped by this connexion he entered the government medical service and in 1880 was transferred from al-ʿArīsh to the Sudan as a dispenser; he arrived at Lado in January 1881 on attachment to the staff of Emin Pasha, governor of Equatoria; he served under Emin for ten years and with him marched out to safety at Bagamoyo in 1889; he died of an illness caused by his privations on the long journey from Equatoria; Emin called him 'good as gold, but flightly, hot-headed and a babbler'; he wrote an account of his adventures with Emin entitled *Die Wahrheit über Emin Pascha* (Berlin, 1893) and assisted G. Casati in the compilation of a comparative table of southern Sudan languages printed in volume 1 of Casati's *Dieci anni in Equatoria* (Milan, 1891).

Vizetelly, Frank (1830–83), British war correspondent, editor, and artist; he was editor of the Parisian journal *Le Monde Illustré*, 1857–9; he was present as a war correspondent at the battle of Solferino, 1859, and with Garibaldi's expedition of 1860 against the Kingdom of Naples; in 1859 he began a long connexion with the *Illustrated London News* which he represented in the Sudan in 1883 when he performed the unusual feat of walking the whole distance from Sawākin to Khartoum where he joined the doomed army of W. Hicks Pasha which was on the point of setting out for Kordofan; he was killed in the massacre which was called the battle of Shaikān (Kashgil); had all gone well he intended to continue walking south through Africa sketching for the *Illustrated London News*; he was described as of portly but soldier-like presence; a biography by his relation, H. Vizetelly, was published in 1893.

Vossion, Louis (1847–1906), French consular official; in 1877, through the influence of a former fellow student of the Military School at Saint-Cyr who later commanded the cavalry of the last king of Burma, he entered the Burmese service; leaving Burma the French Government sent him on a mission to the Sudan where he visited Kordofan and Dār Fūr in 1880–2, during which period he was French vice-consul in Khartoum in 1881; he died at Cape Town while serving there as French consul-general.

Wad al-Baṣīr. *See* MUḤAMMAD AL-ṬAIYIB AL-BAṢĪR; AL-ṬAIYIB MUḤAMMAD AL-ṬAIYIB AḤMAD AL-BAṢĪR.

Wad Bishāra. *See* MUḤAMMAD WAD BISHĀRA.

Wad Ḍaif Allāh. *See* MUḤAMMAD AL-NŪR WAD ḌAIF ALLĀH.

Wad Ḥabūba. *See* 'ABD AL-QĀDIR MUḤAMMAD IMĀM WAD ḤABŪBA; MUḤAMMAD IMĀM WAD ḤABŪBA.

Wad Ḥasūna. *See* ḤASAN IBN ḤASŪNA IBN AL-ḤĀJJ MŪSĀ.

Wad Ḥilū. *See* AḤMAD WAD ḤILŪ; 'ALĪ WAD ḤILŪ KHALĪFAT AL-MAHDĪ; MŪSĀ WAD ḤILŪ.

* **Wad al-Baṣīr.** *See* MUḤAMMAD AL ṬAIYID AL BAṢĪR.

Wad al-Malik 'Awad Allāh (–1895), Mahdist amīr of the Rubāṭāb tribe from 1886 when he succeeded al-Ḥājj Aḥmad of whom the tribesmen complained to the Khalīfa 'Abd Allāhi; in 1889 he came over to the Egyptian Government and asked for pardon; his son Rājab, a mulāzim in the bodyguard of the Khalīfa, was killed the battle of Omdurman, 1898.

Wad umm Maryam. *See* 'ABD AL-QĀDIR WAD UMM MARYAM; ḤAMMĀD IBN MUḤAMMAD IBN 'ALĪ AL-MASHAIKHĪ.

Wad al-Najūmī. *See* 'ABD AL-RAḤMĀN WAD AL-NAJŪMĪ.

Wad al-Nūr. *See* 'ABD ALLĀHI WAD AL-NŪR; MAKĪN WAD AL-NŪR.

Wad al-Turābī. *See* ḤAMAD AL-NAḤLĀN IBN MUḤAMMAD, called WAD AL-TURĀBĪ.

Wad al-Zahra. *See* ḤUSAIN IBRĀHĪM WAD AL-ZAHRA.

Waddington, George (1793–1869), British traveller and church historian; in 1821 he travelled from Wādī Ḥalfā to Merowe and back in company with the Reverend B. Hanbury and with him published an account of their journey called *Journal of a Visit to some Parts of Ethiopia* (1822); he later became dean of Durham and warden of Durham University.

Walhousen, François (1865–98), Belgian captain commandant in the service of the Congo Free State; he was in command of a small column which occupied various posts on the retreat of the Mahdists from the region of Lado and the Nile–Congo watershed; he was drowned in the Nile between Lado and Rejaf.

Walker, Craven Howell (1878–1939), British consul; born at Wellington, Surrey, and educated at the University of Oxford; after schoolmastering in England and Cairo, he joined the Sudan civil service as a commercial inspector, 1905; he was appointed British consul for Western Abyssinia, 1911, and lived at Dunkur and Gambeila; he served in the Dār Fūr campaign, 1916, retiring in 1928 from the consular service; he died suddenly while travelling by train in England.

Walker, Sir Harold Bridgwood (1862–1934), British lieutenant-general; in 1884 he received a commission in the Duke of Cornwall's Light Infantry, of which he was later colonel, and saw service in the river column of the Nile expedition of 1884–5; in 1885–6 he was with the frontier force and was present at the battle of Jinnis (Giniss), 1885; after serving in the First World War he was promoted lieutenant-general in 1923 and held a senior command in India in 1924–8, when he retired.

Watson, Allan (1887–1920), British captain of the Royal Medical Corps; commissioned in 1914 and promoted captain in 1915, he was seconded to the Egyptian army with the rank of binbāshī and served on the Sudan sleeping-sickness commission from 1919; he died at Tambura.

Watson Pasha, Sir Charles Moore (1844–1916), British soldier; he entered the Royal Engineers, 1866, and in 1874–5 was employed with Lieutenant W. H. Chippendall in mapping the White Nile from Gondokoro to within a short distance of Lake Albert on instructions from C. G. Gordon Pasha, then governor of Equatoria; he served in Egypt and the Sudan, 1882–6, when he was appointed governor of the Red Sea littoral with headquarters at Sawākin; he was knighted, 1905, and promoted colonel, 1906, and was afterwards deputy inspector of fortifications, and a major-general; S. Lane-Poole wrote his biography (1919).

Wauchope, Andrew Gilbert (1846–99), British major-general; he entered the Royal Navy and was a midshipman in 1860; he later obtained his discharge and in 1865 received a commission in the Black Watch; after service in Cyprus, 1878–80, and in the Egyptian war of 1882, he fought as a captain in the Nile expedition of 1884–5 and commanded the 1st British brigade in the campaign of 1897–8 for the recovery of the Sudan; he was killed in the battle of Magersfontein during the South African war; General Sir A. G. Wauchope, high commissioner for Palestine and Transjordania, 1931–8, was his nephew.

Weld Blundell. *See* KOETTLITZ, REGINALD.

Wellby, Montagu Sinclair (1866–1900), British soldier and explorer; he was commissioned to the cavalry in 1886 and in 1894 and 1895 undertook two journeys to the interior of Somaliland; in 1896 he made the hazardous journey from Kashmir through Mongolia to Peking; in 1898, starting from Addis Ababa, he went south along the chain of Abyssinian lakes until he arrived at the north end of Lake Rudolf which had been first reached by the Hungarian explorer Count Teleki von Szék in 1887; from here he walked round the eastern side and southern end of the lake and made for the rivers Akobo and Sobat; his explorations added much to the then existing knowledge of the little-known south-eastern Sudan; he was killed in the South African war.

* **Wellcome, Sir Henry Soloman** (1853–1936), British chemical manufacturer and benefactor; by birth an American citizen, he became a

British subject in 1910; born in a log cabin about 125 miles from Milwaukee, the son of an itinerant missionary, he spent his boyhood among the Dakota Indians; he was educated at frontier schools and developed an interest in pharmacy; he settled in England in 1880 and there he built up with his partner the important firm of Burroughs & Wellcome, manufacturing chemists; he was the donor of the Wellcome Tropical Research Laboratories, Gordon Memorial College, Khartoum, 1900, and a steamer, the *Lady Baker*, fitted as a floating laboratory for use on the Upper Nile, 1906; he began in 1901 to conduct archaeological and ethnological explorations in the Sudan and from 1910 to 1914 discovered a number of ancient Ethiopian sites at four of which he excavated; his interest in the site at Jabal Moya near Sennar continued till his death; he was a member of the governing board of Gordon Memorial College.

Wentawuat (*fl. c.* 1150 B.C.), Egyptian viceroy of Ethiopia, perhaps during the reigns of the XXth Dynasty kings Rameses VI, Rameses VII, and Rameses VIII; if so he held office roughly from 1157 B.C. to 1142 B.C.

Werne, Ferdinand (*fl.* 1840), German serving in the Sudan Government; he came from Embscherbruch in Westphalia and was a brother of J. Werne of the Egyptian medical service who died in Khartoum; he may have been a lawyer by calling, though from his own account he was a ship's captain and an engineer; after some time in Greece, possibly engaged in the fighting during the insurrection, he came to the Sudan in 1839; he took part in the military expedition of Aḥmad Pasha abū Widān to Tāka in 1840 and described how he superintended the building of a dam across the Gash at Kassala to bring the Hadendowa to submission by diverting the water down the Atbara, and how the Hadendowa (it was more probably the flood) breached the dam; in 1840–1 he took part with other Europeans in the second voyage of discovery to the Upper White Nile commanded by Salīm Qapūdān which attained the region of Gondokoro; though his books reveal a bitter, malevolent, and vain personality, they are useful authorities for the period; his *Feldzug von Sennar nach Tāka* (Stuttgart, 1851), describing the Tāka campaign and the then little-known country in the line of march, was translated into English as *African Wanderings* (1852); *Reise durch Sennar, nach Mandera, Nasūb, Gheli* (Berlin, 1852) contains a description of the Buṭāna; his voyage to discover the source of the White Nile is covered in his *Expedition zur Entdeckung der Quellen des Weissen Nils* (Berlin, 1848), of which there is an English translation, *Expedition to discover the sources of the White Nile* (1849).

Wesersatet (*fl.* 1430 B.C.), Egyptian viceroy of Ethiopia under the XVIIIth Dynasty kings Amenophis II and afterwards Thothmes IV; each of these viceroys took the title of 'King's son of Kush, governor of the Southern Lands'.

White, Sir George Stuart (1835–1912), British soldier; he saw his first campaigning in the Indian mutiny, 1857, and later won the Victoria Cross in the second Afghan war, 1878–80; he served in the

Nile expedition, 1884–5, and in the South African war became famous for his defence of Ladysmith, 1899–1900; in 1903 he was made a field-marshal.

White, Richard Finch (1880–1919), British soldier; gazetted to the Essex Regiment, 1900, he transferred to the Egyptian army, 1913, and was promoted major, 1915; while serving as a binbāshī in Equatoria he was killed by the Aliyāb Dinka at Pap with C. H. Stigand Bey.

* **Whitehead, George O . . .** (1894–1941), British schoolmaster who lived for some time at Loka in Equatoria and made a study of the Bari people; he published a collection of Bari fables (1932) and wrote on the Bari and other topics in *Sudan Notes and Records*.

Wild, James William (1814–92), British archaeologist who was attached to the Prussian expedition led by K. R. Lepsius which visited Nubia and Sennar, 1843–4; he was later decorative architect to the Great Exhibition of 1851 in London and curator of the Soane Museum.

Wilkinson Pasha, Ernest Berdoe (1864–1946), British soldier and administrator; born in Dublin, he joined the British army; transferring later to the Egyptian army, he saw service with the Kassala irregular Arab troops in the eastern Sudan, 1898; he commanded the Camel Corps, 1899–1903, with rank of mīrālai; seconded to the Sudan Government, he was governor of the Jazīra, 1903–4; of Kassala, 1904–7; and of Berber, 1908–10; he was director of agriculture, 1910–14 when he retired with the British rank of lieutenant-colonel and the Egyptian rank of liwā'; he died at Bramley near Guildford, Surrey.

Wilkinson, Sir John Gardner (1797–1875), British explorer and archaeologist; arriving in Alexandria from England in 1821, he spent altogether twelve years in Egypt and Nubia, twice ascending the Nile to the Second Cataract, and visiting Abū Ṣīr rock in 1822; in 1848–9 he returned to Nubia and travelled between Wādī Ḥalfā and Jabal Barkal.

Willcocks, Sir James (1857–1926), British general; born and commissioned in India, he joined the Army Transport Department there in 1884 and served in the Indian contingent in the Sawākin campaign of 1885 in command of the Mule Corps; he was knighted in 1900; he commanded the Indian army corps in France in the First World War but resigned in 1915 owing to differences with Field-Marshal Sir D. (afterwards Earl) Haig; he died in India; his autobiography appeared in 1925.

Willcocks, Sir William (1852–1945), British engineer; after serving in the Indian public works he transferred to the employ of the Egyptian Government public works department in which he worked from 1883 to 1897; he designed the Aswān dam (completed 1902) and irrigation works in 'Irāq; his great interest in the development of irrigation in the Nile valley and his opposition to official views led him into ill advised controversy with fellow engineers; with Colonel R. Kennedy, formerly director of works, Sudan Government, he was in 1920 sentenced by a British consular court, Cairo, for a defamatory libel on Sir M. MacDonald, then under-secretary of state in the Egyptian public works department, in which he had accused the latter of falsifying figures and statistics concerning the Jazīra irrigation scheme; he spent his latter years in Cairo; a sound engineer, his strong individualism makes his many reports on Nile irrigation projects of engineering and historical value.

Williams, Charles (1838–1904), British journalist; he was the first editor of the *Evening Standard* and of the *Evening News* of London, 1881–4; he then spent several years as a correspondent of the *Standard* in several parts of the world including the Nile campaign, 1884; the Nile campaign of 1898 brought him back to the Sudan, this time as a correspondent of the *Daily Chronicle*, and he was wounded in the battle of Omdurman; he was founder and president (1896–7) of the Press Club in London; in 1892 he published a life of Sir H. E. Wood, sirdār of the Egyptian army.

* **Wilson, Sir Charles** (1836–1905), British soldier and cartographer; he received a commission in the Royal Engineers in 1855; he had already distinguished himself as a military and archaeological cartographer and was a Fellow of the Royal Society before his appointment as military attaché to the British agency in Egypt in 1882; he was chief of the intelligence department in the Nile campaign of 1884–5 which attempted in vain to relieve Khartoum; he was later director-general of the ordnance survey of the United Kingdom; his books include *From Korti to Khartoum* (1885), the story of the Desert Column.

Wilson, Charles Thomas (1852–1917), British Protestant missionary; born in Adelaide, Australia, he was educated at Oxford and was ordained deacon in 1875; in 1876, as a member of the Church Missionary Society, he travelled from Zanzibar to Uganda which he reached in 1877; here he was joined by R. W. Felkin who had come via Sawākin, Khartoum, and the Nile valley with a small party of fellow missionaries of the Church Missionary Society; with Felkin he returned to England by Equatoria, southern Dār Fūr, Kordofan, and Sawākin in 1879; he died at Clifton; he wrote, jointly with Felkin, *Uganda and the Egyptian Soudan* (1882).

Wilson Pasha, Cyril Edward (1873–1938), British soldier, son of Major-General Sir C. W. Wilson; joining the army in 1893, he was seconded to the Egyptian army in 1898–1900 and in 1902; he fought in the Nile campaign, 1898; in 1902 he transferred to the Sudan Government with rank of mīrālai and was governor of Sennar (with headquarters at Wad Madanī), 1904–8; in 1907 he moved his headquarters to the newly formed provincial capital of Sinja, since reduced to a district station; he was governor of Khartoum, 1908–13, and of the Red Sea province, 1913–22, when he retired with ranks of liwā' and colonel; during the First World War Sir R. F. Wingate, in command of allied operations in the Ḥijāz, appointed him his representative at Jidda where he rendered useful service as British agent, 1916–19.

Wilson Pasha, Reginald Sutcliffe (1873–1932), British soldier; born in Liverpool, he received a commission in the Lancashire Fusiliers, 1897, and fought in the Nile campaign, 1898; after service in the South African war, 1899–1900, he was seconded to the Egyptian army, 1903, and transferred to the Sudan Government, 1905; promoted qā'immaqām and mīrālai, he was governor of the Nuba mountains province, 1914–18, when he was promoted liwā'; he died at Willaston, Cheshire.

Wilson, William J . . . (*c.* 1835–), American military doctor; in 1865 he joined the Ohio 13th cavalry towards the end of the American civil war; he remained in the army after peace had been restored and in 1874 was serving as post surgeon at Fort Bayard, New Mexico; in 1875–7 he was on leave of absence to serve in the Egyptian army and was wounded at the battle of Gura in the Egyptian-Abyssinian war, 1876; he rejoined the United States army and was last traced as post surgeon at the Plattsburg Barracks, New York, with rank of captain.

* **Wingate, Orde Charles** (1903–44), British soldier, cousin of General Sir R. F. Wingate, governor-general of the Sudan, 1899–1916; commissioned to the Royal Engineers, 1923, he was promoted captain, 1936; from 1928 to 1933 he served in the Sudan Defence Force as a binbāshī; in 1938 he was serving in Palestine against Arab guerillists; it was in the Second World War that he won world-wide fame as a guerilla leader; in 1940–1 he was a member of Brigadier D. Sandford's military mission operating against the Italians in the heart of Ethiopia, an operation which was organized in the Sudan; transferred to the Burma front, his rise was spectacular, being promoted from major to brigadier in 1942 and shortly after to major-general when he trained and led into battle a force which successfully fought the Japanese in small composite units, each tactically self-sufficing and independent of any line of communications; he was killed in an air accident during the fighting.

Wodehouse Pasha, Josceline Heneage (1852–1930), British general; he was commissioned to the Royal Artillery, 1872, and saw service in Zululand and Afghanistan; in 1883 he joined the Egyptian army when he served on the Sudan frontier and on the Red Sea coast where he commanded a battery of guns in the second battle of el-Teb (Andeteib), 1884; in the Nile campaign of 1884–5 he was employed on the line of communication and later was stationed at railhead, 'Akāsha, as commandant; he fought and won the action at Arqīn near Wādī Ḥalfā, 1889, and at Tūshkī (Toski), shortly after, he commanded the infantry division under the sirdār, Sir F. W. (afterwards Baron) Grenfell Pasha; from 1888 to 1894 he was governor of the Egyptian frontier province, a temporary military government with its headquarters at Aswān, and in 1899 he was promoted liwā'; leaving the Egyptian army he served on the north-west frontier of India; he was appointed governor and commander-in-chief, Bermuda, 1907, and was later in command of the northern army, India.

Wolseley, Garnet Joseph, 1st Viscount Wolseley (1833–1913), British field-marshal; he joined the army in 1852 and served in many wars and countries; he was in the Crimean war, 1854–6, the Indian mutiny, 1857–9, and with rising seniority he was given command of an expedition which he skilfully conducted against King Koffee of Ashanti, West Africa, 1873–4; he next went to South Africa and there retrieved the dangerous situation brought about by a series of Zulu victories over the British forces; his chief title to fame was as a re-organizer of the British army; while quartermaster-general at the War Office, London, he carried through reforms in the face of strong opposition from the Duke of Cambridge, the commander-in-chief; he was next placed in command of an expeditionary force against Aḥmad ʿUrābī Pasha who had seized power in Egypt; landing at Ismāʿīlīya in the Suez Canal he won the battles of Kassassin (Qaṣṣāṣīn) and Tel el-Kebir, 1882, occupying Cairo; for his part in the war he was promoted general and created a baron; in 1884 he led the Nile expedition, an operation which attempted, too late, to save Khartoum which was besieged by the Mahdists; choosing the Nile route in opposition to that from Sawākin to Berber, advocated by some, he organized a force which ascended the Nile to Dongola; from al-Dabba a column of picked troops under Major-General Sir H. Stewart cut across the Bayūda and regained the Nile slightly downstream of Matamma; a fiercely contested battle was fought at Abū Ṭulaiḥ (Abu Klea) and a less important action at Qubbat in January 1885; the fall of Khartoum on 26 January 1885 made any further advance useless, and the column, led by Sir R. H. Buller (in place of Stewart, killed at Abū Ṭulaiḥ), retreated to al-Dabba; another force made a reconnaissance up the Nile towards Abū Ḥamad and fought the battle of Kirbikān in which Major-General W. Earle, the commander, was killed; finally, during the first half of 1885, the whole force retired northward, fighting and winning a rear-guard action at Jinnis (Giniss) in Dār Sukkōt on the way, but abandoning the whole of the Sudan except Wādī Ḥalfā, Sawākin, and a part of Equatoria to the Mahdists; at Sawākin a field force of British, Indian, and Australian troops assembled early in 1885 to reinforce the garrison; this force, led by Lieutenant-General Sir G. Graham, fought several pitched battles against the Mahdists (chiefly Beja tribesmen) under the amīr ʿUtẖmān abū Bakr Diqna (Osman Digna); Graham's army, like that on the Nile, was withdrawn as a result of the policy of the British Government to abandon active military operations in the Sudan; Wolseley, now a viscount, was for five years (1890–5) commander-in-chief, Ireland, when he was appointed commander-in-chief of the British army, a post which he held, 1895–9, when he effected nothing short of a revolution in British military organization; he died at Mentone, France; his most widely known works are *The Soldier's Pocket Book* (1869) and his autobiography, *The Story of a Soldier's Life* (1903); his official biography was published in 1924.

Wood, Sir Henry Evelyn (1838–1919), British field-marshal and sirdār of the Egyptian army; he entered the Royal Navy, 1854, and fought as a midshipman in the Crimean war in the naval brigade under

Sir W. Peel, the traveller to Kordofan; in 1855 he transferred to the army and in 1858 won the Victoria Cross in the Indian mutiny; a major-general, 1882, he served under Lord Wolseley in the Egyptian war, and on the abolition of the old Egyptian army by Khedivial decree he became sirdār of the new army; he commanded the line of communications in the Nile campaign of 1884–5, having been succeeded as sirdār by Sir F. W. Grenfell; on his return to Britain he held various high military administrative appointments; he was made a field-marshal, 1903; he wrote several books on military subjects and two books of reminiscences: *From Midshipman to Field-Marshall* (1906) and *Winnowed Memories* (1917); C. Williams published a biography (1892).

Woodward Bey, Francis Willoughby (1872–1926), British soldier; born in Bombay, he entered the army in 1893 and served in the South African war, 1899–1902; from 1906 to 1916 he was seconded to the Egyptian army, a period spent almost entirely in the Sudan political service to which he was attached in 1907 as a junior inspector; promoted mīrālai, he was governor of the Upper Nile, 1911–16, when he went to serve in the First World War; he was promoted colonel, 1924.

* **Wright, Henry Charles Seppings** (–1937), British artist and war correspondent; he was present in many wars in many parts of the world; he was war artist for the *Illustrated London News* in the Dongola campaign, 1896; among his books is *Soudan, '96* (1897).

Wright, Henry Thomas Richard Somerset (1884–1916), British soldier; commissioned to the Manchester Regiment, 1903, and promoted captain, 1914, he was seconded to the Egyptian army; while serving as a binbāshī he was killed at Dabbis in the Dār Fūr campaign.

Württemberg, Friedrich Paul Wilhelm von, Prince (1797–1860), German traveller from Karlsruhe; having served in the Prussian army and visited America, he travelled in the Sudan, 1839–41; he ascended the Nile valley in 1839–40 with a suite of huntsmen and at Khartoum stayed with the governor-general, Aḥmad Pasha abū Widān; he then journeyed in Dār Berta and the country south of Fāzūghlī, shooting and making botanical collections; F. Werne described him as a fat, jovial man with a raucous, military voice; he died at Mergentheim in Württemberg.

Wylde, Augustus Blandy (*fl.* 1878–90), British trader; he was for many years working on the Red Sea coast; the British missionary R. W. Felkin, who met him in the desert between Sawākin and Berber in 1878, stated that he was bringing a consignment of wild animals from Khartoum to the coast and refers to him as formerly British consul [*sic*] at Jidda; he was at Sawākin in 1884 possibly in connexion with the provisioning of the troops there; in the same year he was attached to Vice-Admiral Sir W. N. W. Hewett's mission to Abyssinia which endeavoured to secure the evacuation of the beleaguered Egyptian garrisons from the eastern Sudan through Abyssinian territory; in 1888 he and W. F. Fox, the Quaker engineer, wrote to the Marquess of Salisbury advocating the lifting of restrictions on trade with the interior of the Sudan then in Mahdist hands; the local military command, however, forbade the two men to land at Sawākin as their project was contrary to British military policy; a cotton plantation which he had founded on the coast north of the town was destroyed by Mahdist raiders; in 1890 he was British vice-consul at Sawākin; his writings include *'83 to '87 in the Soudan* (1888); his brother Jack was associated with him at Sawākin where he was in charge of the affairs of the firm of Wylde, Beyts & Company which had establishments also at Suez and Jidda.

Wyllie, Alexander (1884–1917), British captain in the Royal Scots Fusiliers; commissioned in 1905, he was seconded to the Egyptian army in 1913 and died at Dilling in the Nuba hills while serving as a binbāshī.

Yambio (–1905), sultan of the Azande; about 1860 he, with his father Bazimbe and a large Azande following then living west of the River Yubo, migrated east to the present Yambio area, subduing *en route* the then occupying tribe; in 1881 he totally defeated a mixed force of government troops and tribesmen, but was captured in 1882 by Rifā'ī Aghā, an officer of F. Lupton Bey, governor of the Baḥr al-Ghazāl; though neutral during the Mahdist revolt he was hostile to the Anglo-Egyptian Government which followed the end of Mahdism; he was wounded in an endeavour to escape from a patrol which arrived at his village in February 1905 and died in hospital three days later; on his death the sultanate was divided among his descendants.

Ya'qūb Muḥammad Bān Naqā (Bān al-Nuqā) (*fl.* 1570), religious teacher, founder of the Sennar branch of the Ya'qūbāb religious family; he was a khalīfa of the holy man Muḥammad Tāj al-Dīn al-Baghdādī called al-Bahārī and was a missionary of al-Bahārī's ṣūfist teaching in the Jazīra; his tomb is at al-Ḥumr near Sennar.

Ya'qūb Muḥammad Tūrshain (1855–98), Mahdist amīr, half-brother of the Khalīfa 'Abd Allāhī and a member of the Jubārāt branch of the Ta'ā'isha Baqqāra tribe; he joined Muḥammad Aḥmad al-Mahdī during the latter's march from the White Nile to the Nuba hills in 1881 and took an active part in the siege of al-Ubaiyaḍ and the defeat of the army of W. Hicks Pasha at Shaikān (Kashgil) in 1883; he held an important command in the besieging forces before Khartoum, 1884–5; on the death of the Mahdī he became chief of staff of the Mahdist armies, an appointment which made him virtually second in power to his brother 'Abd Allāhi; latterly, however, his position was weakened by his nephew, 'Uthmān Shaikh al-Dīn, 'Abd Allāhi's eldest son, who was given command over the jiḥādīya or regular troops and most of the firearms; he was killed in battle at Omdurman, 1898; he was a fine figure of a man, thick-set and light in colour, and intellectually alert.

Ya'qūb ibn Mujallī al-Mashaikhī (*fl. c.* 1592), holy man; born in Upper Egypt, he is said to have entered the Jazīra in the early days of the Funj sultanate of Sennar; the sultan gave him his daughter in marriage, and land near Ḥalfaiya where his tomb was built.

Yaʿqūb abū Zainab (–1940), Mahdist amīr; a Taʿāʾi<u>sh</u>ī by tribe, he fought in most of the big battles of the *Mahdīya* and was wounded at the battle of Umm Dibaikarāt, 1899; he died in Omdurman.

Yāqūt ibn ʿAbd Allāh al-Ḥamāwī (1179–1229), greatest among the ʿAbbāsid geographers, he lived about the same time as Abū Ṣāliḥ the Armenian; in his geographical dictionary *Muʿjam al-buldān* he supplemented Abū Ṣāliḥ's account of Nubia and the Beja.

Yarrow, Sir Alfred Fernandez (1842–1932), British engineer, founder of the firm of Yarrow & Co., Ltd., shipbuilders; he constructed shallow-draught stern-wheel river steamers for the Nile campaign of 1884–5; the design of these steamers has greatly influenced Nile shipbuilding practice.

Yāsīn Muḥammad Dūlīb (–1857), notable of the Dūwālīb family which had its centre at Bāra in Kordofan; he was <u>sh</u>aikh al-ma<u>sh</u>āyi<u>kh</u> of Kordofan during the governorship-general of <u>Kh</u>ālid Pasha <u>Kh</u>usraw (and possibly earlier) until his death in the cholera epidemic of 1857.

Yāsīn Yūsuf (–1916), nāẓir ʿumūm of eastern Kordofan; he was succeeded by Aḥmad ʿUmar Ḥawwār al-<u>Sh</u>aikh.

Yohannes (John) IV (1839–89), emperor of Abyssinia; as Rās Kāsā (called also Abba Bazbaz) he first came into prominence as ruler of Tigre; during the advance of the British column through Abyssinia to attack Theodore, 1868, he helped the British with supplies; in 1872, having made himself master of Abyssinia, he was crowned King of Kings at Axum; in 1875, war having broken out with Egypt, he lured two Egyptian armies, based on Muṣawwaʿ, into the highlands of Hamasien and there destroyed them at Gundet (1875) and Gura (1876); peace was concluded after much delay in 1879 with C. G. Gordon Pasha as Egyptian emissary; the rise of the Mahdist movement in the Sudan now drew him to the side of Egypt and as a result of a mission led by Vice-Admiral Sir W. N. W. Hewett in 1884 he agreed to assist the retirement of the Egyptian garrisons lying along the Sudan frontier through Abyssinian territory, an operation carried out with partial success, 1884–5; early in 1887 an Abyssinian army under Rās Alūla advanced towards Muṣawwaʿ which the Italians had occupied since 1885 and annihilated an Italian force at Dogali on the coastal belt; meanwhile war with the Mahdist power broke out in full fury; in 1885 a brigand from the Sudan sacked an Abyssinian church, a gesture to which Rās Adal, governor of Amhara, replied by cutting up a small Mahdist force under the amīr Wad Arbāb at Gallabat; a powerful force under the command of the amīr Ḥamdān abū ʿAnja next invaded the Abyssinian mountains and, after defeating Rās Adal, sacked Gondar, 1887; smarting under this setback Yohannes counter-attacked; early in 1889 he reached Gallabat on the frontier at the head of an army estimated to have consisted of 20,000 horse and 130,000 foot and at once attacked the Mahdist army of about 85,000 men under the amīr Zakī Ṭamal; he was killed by a chance shot during the battle when the Mahdists were on the point of being defeated; his own army, discouraged by the death of their emperor, left the field and the fight was turned into a Mahdist victory; Zakī did not pursue the retreating Abyssinians and the war relapsed into frontier skirmishing whence it had begun; he was succeeded by Menyelek (Menilik) II.

Yol Kur (–1942), ʿumda of the Bawom Dinka of Renk, a magistrate and president of the Bawom Dinka court.

Younghusband, Sir George John (1859–1944), British major-general, brother of Sir F. Younghusband, the traveller in Turkestan and the Pamirs; he entered the army, 1878, and served as a lieutenant in the Sawākin campaign, 1885; he then served in India, in the South African war, 1899–1902, in which he was severely wounded, and in the First World War; he was appointed keeper of the Jewel House, Tower of London, 1917; his Sudan experiences are recorded in his *Forty Years a Soldier* (1923); he was a prolific writer.

Ypres, 1st Earl of. *See* FRENCH, JOHN DENTON PINKSTONE, 1st Earl of Ypres.

Yuni (*fl.* 1280 B.C.), Egyptian viceroy of Ethiopia on behalf of the kings of Egypt; he held office approximately 1300 B.C.–1280 B.C. during the reigns of the XIXth Dynasty kings Sethos I and Rameses II; he is the Regent Ani in G. M. Ebers' novel of Ancient Egypt *Uarda* (Leipzig, 1867).

Yūnus al-Dikaim (1816 ?–1936), Mahdist amīr al-umarā', cousin of the Khalīfa ʿAbd Allāhi; he joined Muḥammad Aḥmad al-Mahdī at Jabal Qadīr at the end of 1881 and occupied small posts in the siege of al-Ubaiyaḍ, 1882–3, and before Khartoum, 1884–5; among his earlier campaigns was his mission to obtain the adherence of the Rizaiqāt in southern Dār Fūr; here he captured Shaikh ʿUqail al-Jangāwī and brought him a prisoner to al-Ubaiyaḍ where he was executed; after the death of the Mahdī in 1885 he crushed the dissident Jimaʿa in Kordofan and the Arabs of Dār Muḥārib on the White Nile; he was later recalled to Omdurman in disgrace for his failure to suppress a rising at Gallabat; after a period in Omdurman he was appointed governor of Dongola in 1889; his exactions distressed the people; he held high command in the Mahdist armies at the battle of Omdurman, 1898, and at Umm Dibaikarāt (where he was wounded), 1899; he spent his old age at Omdurman where he died at the reputed age of 120; a typical Baqqārī, spare and handsome in his youth when he was a great elephant hunter, and in his prime a competent commander of the Khalīfa's horsemen.

Yūsuf ʿAbd Allāh abū Sin (–1937), Shukrī notable of the paramount family which has taken a leading part in local administration in the country between the Blue Nile and the Atbara during the last century; he was ʿumda of Shimāliyāb near Gedaref; he died at Wad Madanī.

Yūsuf ʿAnqara (–1896), Mahdist amīr, by tribe a member of the Taʿā'isha Baqqāra and a near relative of the Khalīfa ʿAbd Allāhi; he was killed at the battle of Firka (Firket) while leading the jihādīya or regular Mahdist riflemen.

Yūsuf Pasha Ḥasan al-Shallālī (–1882), liwā' of the Egyptian army; of Kanzī (Nubian) extraction, he was born at Manjara near al-Muqran, Khartoum; sub-governor of Rohl district in Equatoria about 1876–8, he first came to notice as a result of his efficient handling of troops in R. Gessi Pasha's operations against Sulaimān wad Zubair in southern Dār Fūr in 1878–9 for which he was promoted liwā', 1879; the Government having learnt of the defeat and death of Rāshid Bey Aymān at the hands of the Mahdists at Jabal Qadīr in the Nuba hills in December 1881, fitted out an expedition of 4,000 men of which he was given the command; most of this force went by river to Fashoda and thence marched inland; arrived near the scene of the first disaster the force was set upon by the Baqqāra and utterly destroyed; he was among the dead.

Yūsuf Ibrāhīm Muḥammad (–1888), puppet sultan of Dār Fūr, son of Sultan Ibrāhīm Muḥammad Ḥusain who was killed in the battle of Manawāshī by Zubair Bey in 1874; joining the Mahdist cause, the amīr Muḥammad Khālid Zughal left him as amīr al-umarā' of Dār Fūr when he was still a young man, but he worked for Fūr independence and rose in rebellion against the Mahdist rule; he was defeated in battle by the amīr al-umarā' 'Uthmān Adam in 1887 and again in 1888 when, after an engagement near al-Fāshar, his army was broken and he fled towards the Marra mountains; he was later killed near Kabkabīya by 'Uthmān Adam's uncle, Aḥmad al-Khitaim; his brother Abū Khairāt then declared himself the Fūr sultan and joined the revolt of the fanatic Aḥmad abū Jummaiza, but his own followers rebelled against him and killed him in 1889.

Yūsuf Jubāra al-Imām (–1935), Rufā'ī notable, shaikh of Abū 'Ushar khuṭṭ in the northern Jazīra; he died at Ḥaṣṣa Ḥaiṣa.

Yūsuf al-Marḍī, called **Yūsuf abū Rūf** (*c.* 1870–1942), nāẓir of the Abū Rūf who live southward of Sennar; when the remnant of the Abū Rūf were taken captive to Omdurman during the Mahdist régime, he was made a mulāzim in the Khalīfa 'Abd Allāhi's army and was later present at the battle of Omdurman, 1898; the Condominium Government appointed him nāẓir of the Rufā'a al-Hūī; in 1904 he was deposed and imprisoned on a charge of helping to screen a murderer; after various changes of fortune he was made 'umda of Sairū, 1919.

* **Yūsuf Muḥammad al-Amīn al-Hindī** (*c.* 1865–1942), religious leader; his great-grandfather came from the Ḥijāz, the family claiming descent from the Prophet through his daughter Fāṭima, the wife of the Caliph 'Alī; his father, al-Sharīf Muḥammad al-Amīn, travelled to the Ḥijāz and Egypt seeking religious instruction; he returned to the Sudan about 1840 and taught at Thamanīyāt near al-Jailī; Yūsuf, as a young Mahdist officer, took part in several battles in the eastern Sudan and after the Anglo-Egyptian occupation powerfully assisted the new régime in the restoration of the country; he married a daughter of Zubair Pasha

Raḥma Manṣūr; his numerous followers, the Hindīya, are an offshoot of the Sammānīya brotherhood; age and infirmity latterly compelled his withdrawal from public life when he devoted himself to religion and scholarship, collecting material (still unpublished) for a great history of the Arab tribes in the Sudan; he was buried at Burrī on the east side of Khartoum under a conspicuous dome.

Yūsuf Muḥammad al-Malik (1881–1944), notable of Ja'lī descent; from 1927 he was 'umda of Badin near Arqū in Dongola district, a magistrate and, since 1935, president of the Arqū court.

Yūsuf Muḥammad Zaid Tar Juk (*c.* 1876–1946), notable of Dār Fūr; he was born near Umm Shanqa of the Kuwādik sub-section of the Shafālīq branch of the Banī 'Umrān Arabs and traced his descent six generations back from 'Abd al-Raḥmān Kaduk who brought his people to Dār Fūr and thence to Shaflūq and was thus the ancestor of the Shafālīq; he was a village shaikh in 1914 when Sultan 'Alī Dīnār promoted him to be shartai of Umm Shanqa in succession to his cousin Yūsuf 'Abd al-Rāziq; he made his peace with the Sudan Government during the campaign of 1916 against 'Alī Dīnār; he was appointed a magistrate in 1923 and in 1930 was made vice-president of the Umm Kidāda native court.

Yūsuf Sālim (–*c.* 1894), Mahdist amīr; a member of the Falaita branch of the Ḥumr of Kordofan, he served under the amīr al-umarā' Maḥmūd Aḥmad in Dār Fūr and died a natural death in al-Ubaiyaḍ.

* **Yūsuf abū Shara** (–*c.* 1802), shaikh of the 'Arakīyīn of the Jazīra; from him most of the present leading men of the tribe are descended.

Yūsuf Shuhdī Pasha (–1899), liwā' of the Egyptian army; of Circassian origin, he was educated in Cairo and at the age of fourteen was sent to Berlin to study medicine, but changed to military science; returning to Egypt, he was promoted yūzbāshī in 1863 and mīrālai in 1875; he was aide-de-camp to Prince Ḥasan in the Egyptian-Abyssinian war of 1875–6; he fought in Serbia against the nationalists in 1876 and held senior command in the Egyptian contingent in the Russo-Turkish war of 1877–8 when he was promoted liwā' on the field; in 1882, after the collapse of the Egyptian nationalist movement, he was a member of the court which tried Aḥmad 'Urābī Pasha; on the formation of the new Egyptian army he was given command of the 2nd brigade; he was at Wādī Ḥalfā in 1886 as head of an Egyptian Government commission to examine the possibilities of reopening trade and communication with the Sudan, a commission in which he was also the representative of the Turkish high commissioner in Egypt, al-Ghāzī Mukhtār Pasha; he was minister of war and marine, 1893–4, when he retired.

Yūsuf Surūr Pasha (1819–1902), liwā' of the Egyptian army; born at Kafr al-Maiyāsra near Fāraskūr, he was commissioned to the regular army in 1843 and promoted binbāshī in 1857; he then served as a professor of the Turkish language, geography, and engineering at the military school; after experience in provincial administration in Egypt he came to the Sudan on military inspection duties in 1871 with rank of mīrālai; in 1873 he inspected garrisons in the eastern Sudan and established a military post with a battery of artillery at Senheit, the modern Keren; he was director of stores and twice governor of Giza; as Khedive's commissioner charged with surveillance of the Sudan frontier, he delivered his last report in 1887 when he retired; he died at his birthplace.

Yūsuf ʿUthmān (–1946), ʿumda of the Laḥāwīyīn nomad Arabs who now pasture along the valley of the River Atbara near al-Fāshar.

Zaga Christ. *See* Ṣaga Krestos.

Zaidan, Jurjī (1861–1914), Syrian scholar and journalist; born at Beirut of a poor Christian family, he was largely self-taught but spent some time at the Syrian Protestant College where he received the diploma in pharmacy; he went shortly after to Egypt where he first worked on the staff of the newspaper *al-Zaman* and then served as a dragoman in the Nile expedition of 1884–5 for the relief of Khartoum; he settled in Cairo where he taught and was attached to the *Maqtaṭaf*; he wrote many books, mostly on Arab literature and history, besides twenty-two historical novels of which two concern the Sudan: *Asīr al-Mutamahdī* (Cairo, 1892) and *al-Mamlūk al-Shard* (Cairo, [ ]); he died in Cairo.

* **Zain al-ʿĀbidīn** (*fl.* 1818–28), Tunisian traveller; in 1818 or 1819, having finished his studies at al-Azhar University, Cairo, he set out for the Sudan where he (like Muḥammad ibn ʿUmar ibn Sulaimān al-Tūnisī) spent about ten years as a professional religious teacher; he first went to Sennar and Kordofan and thence to Dār Fūr and Wadā'i; finally, about 1828, after three years in Wadā'i, he returned to Tunis via Fazzān; the manuscript in which he wrote his experiences is believed to be lost; a Turkish translation was published in Istānbūl in 1846, and this was translated into German by G. Rosen, entitled *Das Buch des Sudan* (&c.) (Leipzig, 1847); his book is a valuable supplement to that of al-Tūnisī.

al-Zain ibn Bān al-Nuqā (1705–75), religious teacher, son of Ṣāliḥ ibn Bān al-Nuqā of whom the hagiographer Muḥammad al-Nūr wad Ḍaif Allah writes with reverence; he was known for his diligent reading of the Qur'ān by night and day.

al-Zain ibn Ṣughaiyarūn (–1675), holy man; born in the country of the Shā'ikīya he followed the teaching of his more famous father, Muḥammad ibn Sarḥān al-ʿŪdī, called Ṣughaiyarūn.

Zainab bint al-Mahdī (–1947), distinguished lady, daughter of Muḥammad Aḥmad al-Mahdī and wife of Muḥammad al-Sharīf Khalīfat al-Mahdī, the Mahdī's son-in-law and second caliph; a son, Ḥusain al-Khalīfa Muḥammad Sharīf (d. 1928), was editor successively of the newspapers *al-Rā'id al-Sūdān* and *Ḥaḍārat al-Sūdān*.

Zainūba al-Minyāwīya. *See* MUḤAMMAD ḤASAN MINYĀWĪ.

Zakarīyā (*fl.* 833), king of the Nubians; in 833 he decided to cease paying tribute to the Muslims which his predecessor Kānūn had promised to pay by treaty with the Arab general 'Abd Allāh ibn Jahān in 831, and prepared to fight the caliph Mu'taṣim over the question; he sent his son Feraki to discuss the dispute with the caliph who ordered the tribute to be lightened, and war was averted for a time.

Zakarīyā Bey . . . (–1877), qā'immaqām of the Egyptian army, of Circassian origin; he commanded one of two columns sent by C. G. Gordon Pasha, governor-general of the Sudan, to Jabal Sī to attempt to quell the rebellion of Muḥammad Hārūn al-Rashīd who had assumed the title of sultan of Dār Fūr; attacked by the Fūr rebels his entire force of 800 men and two cannon was lost and himself killed.

* **Zakī Ṭamal** (–1892), Mahdist amīr al-umarā'; he was a member of the Mandala half-Ta'ā'isha serf community to which also belonged the amīr Ḥamdān abū 'Anja; he saw much active service in command of Mahdist armies in Dār Fūr; with Ḥamdān abū 'Anja, whom he served and afterwards succeeded, he invaded Abyssinia and won a victory near Gondar, 1887; he reached the height of his fame in 1889 when an army under his command won a decisive victory over a huge Abyssinian host at Gallabat after King John, the enemy leader, had been killed; he was later accused by the amīr Aḥmad wad 'Alī Aḥmad of conspiring to hand over Kassala to the Italians; summoned to Omdurman for investigation of the charge he was stoned to death.

* **Zakī 'Uthmān** (–1898), Mahdist amīr; a Ta'ā'ishī of the Jubārāt branch which produced many leading warriors of the Mahdist régime; he was amīr of Berber where he earned the nickname of Abū Farrār (Father of Quicksilver); he was killed at the battle of Omdurman.

Zemio (Zemoi Ikpiro) (*c.* 1842–1917), Azande chief, son of Chief Tikima; he began his rule about 1885 and, by a series of victories over the Bandia and other chiefs of the Azande, made himself the most powerful chief of the Anunga group situated in the Mbomu valley in what is now the Ubangui-Chari district of French Equatorial Africa; a town on the Mbomu river is named after him.

Zenkowski, Joseph. *See* SENKOVSKY, OSIP IVANOVITCH.

Zichy, Wilhelm, Count (–1875), officer of the Austrian cavalry, of Hungarian origin; after having fought in the wars of 1859 and 1866 in northern Italy he left the army seized with a desire for big-game hunting and perhaps pressed by creditors at home; he went to Muṣawwa' in 1875 and with Arakīl Bey Nūbār, governor of the town, toured unknown Dankalia; returning to Muṣawwa' he joined the Egyptian force under S. A. Arendrup Bey and died of wounds received in the battle of Gundet in which Arendrup and Arakīl were killed.

Zīyāda ibn al-Nūr ibn al-Shaikh Muḥammad walad 'Īsā (*fl.* 1660), religious man who taught during the reign of Sultan Bādī II abū Diqn walad Rubāṭ with whom he stood in high favour; he died at Old Dongola.

al-Zubair ʿAbd al-Qādir wad al-Zain (1826–82), notable of the Yaʿqūbāb religious family of Sennar and shaikh al-mashāyikh under the Egyptian rule, 1857–63, in succession to his father, Shaikh ʿAbd al-Qādir wad al-Zain, who had held the post from 1826; during the governorship of Arakīl Bey al-Armanī (1855–8) he fell foul of the government and fled to Cairo where he was for some time a muʿāwin in the department of the interior; returning to the Sudan Mūsā Ḥamdī Pasha, the governor-general at the time, reorganized the local administration and in 1863 appointed him nāẓir over all the district nāẓirs (nuẓār aqsām) of the Jazīra; Jaʿfar Pasha Mazhar, governor-general 1866–71, made him president of the court of appeal in Khartoum; he served in various other capacities, but after the outbreak of the Mahdist revolt in 1881 his unpopularity became a source of embarrassment to the government; suspected of intriguing with the Mahdī he was arrested at Ṭalḥa in the Jazīra by order of the then governor-general, ʿAbd al-Qādir Pasha Ḥilmī, and (it is alleged by some) was shortly after drowned by some sailors in the Blue Nile near Sennar or, according to others, he was recalled to Khartoum and there murdered in prison.

* **Zubair Dīyāb al-Malik** (*c.* 1850–1910 ?), hereditary malik of the Maḥas, son of the malik Dīyāb who exercized authority in the reign of ʿAbbās Pasha; a ma'mūr under Muṣṭafā Pasha Yāwar, governor of Dongola during the Nile campaign, 1884–5, he fled to Egypt from the Mahdists who destroyed his property; in 1894 he submitted to the government of the Khalīfa ʿAbd Allāhi who appointed him amīn bait al-māl of Dār Maḥas; along with ʿAbd Allāh Yaʿqūb he was for some time deputy of the Maḥas at the court of the Khalīfa; he again fell under the disfavour of the Mahdists who arrested him for treason, but he escaped in 1896 and joined the Egyptian gunboats which were ascending the Nile in pursuit of the Mahdist forces; the new government appointed him shaikh of Koka.

al-Zubair wad Musāʿd (–1937), notable of the Jaʿlīyīn; he was ʿumda of ʿAliyāb and president of the shaikhs' court at al-Dāmar; after 1918 poor health compelled him to leave the detailed work of his ʿumudīya to his son Muḥammad Sharīf al-Zubair.

al-Zubair Pasha Raḥma Manṣūr (1830–1913), farīq of the Egyptian army, trader and administrator; born near al-Jailī of the Naʿamāb section of the Jimīʿāb branch of the Jaʿlīyīn Arabs he was educated in Khartoum and in 1856 set out for the southern Sudan to trade; for several years he traded and raided for slaves in the country of the Baḥr al-Ghazāl and in the lands of the Azande in the interior; he rationalized the trade in slaves and placed it on a proper commercial footing; by 1865 he was virtually master of the Baḥr al-Ghazāl, ruling over a large territory with his seat at Bayyu, now called Daim Zubair; checked by government interference from unrestricted trading intercourse along the White Nile, he sought other avenues for the export of merchandise and slaves and in 1866 made a treaty with the Rizaiqāt Baqqāra to open up a trade route through southern Dār Fūr to Kordofan; in 1869–72 he fought and beat Muḥammad al-Hilālī, a government-sponsored filibuster in the Baḥr al-Ghazāl, and in 1872 killed Sultan Tikma and conquered his country; quarrelling with the Rizaiqāt he prepared in 1873 for a more ambitious project, the conquest of Dār Fūr, ostensibly on behalf of the Khedivial Government which conferred on him the governorship of the Baḥr al-Ghazāl with grade of bey; setting out with his well-equipped private army he invaded southern Dār Fūr and in 1874 defeated and killed the Fūr sultan Ibrāhīm Muḥammad al-Ḥusain at the battle of Manawāshī and occupied Dār Maṣālīṭ, Tāma, Qimr, and Sūla, even penetrating Wadā'i; the brilliance of his leadership eclipsed the modest exploits of the regular Egyptian army with which he was co-operating, and he fell out with Ismā'īl Pasha al-Aiyūb, the governor-general and commander-in-chief of the expedition; suspecting Ismā'īl of attempting to rob him of the fruits of his victories he went to Cairo in 1875 to present his complaint, but once there the Khedive Ismā'īl forbade him to return; he was, however, created a pasha; in 1877 he served with the Egyptian contingent in Rumelia in the Russo-Turkish war; the death of his son Sulaimān at the hands of R. Gessi Pasha in 1879 further alienated him from the Egyptian Government; nevertheless in 1883 he raised a force of black troops in Egypt for dispatch to the Sudan to assist in the war against Muḥammad Aḥmad al-Mahdī but disagreed with the terms of service and did not take command but stayed in Egypt; suspected (most probably without foundation) of having relations with the Mahdī, the British occupying power in Egypt had him sent to Gibraltar out of harm's way, 1885–7; in 1899, at the request of the governor-general, Sir R. F. Wingate Pasha, he returned to the Sudan and for the rest of his life was a valuable counsellor of the new government and a progressive farmer of his large estate at al-Jailī.

* **Zucchinetti, Paolo Virginio** (*fl.* 1876–80), Italian adventurer; of unknown origin he is said to have been a retired officer of the Italian army and to have afterwards been employed by the Egyptian Government as a veterinary inspector when he published a report entitled *Epizotia equina* (Alexandria, 1876); he came to the Sudan, possibly attached to the Roman Catholic mission, in 1877, and afterwards travelled with Bishop D. Comboni in Kordofan; leaving the mission he set out with the intention of walking to the Cape of Good Hope but got no farther than Equatoria, where he got into trouble with Emin Bey, and forthwith returned northward via the Baḥr al-Ghazāl; here he joined R. Gessi Pasha's expedition against Sulaimān wad Zubair as a doctor but soon quarrelled with Gessi and continued to Kordofan; C. G. Gordon Pasha, who met him at al-Ubaiyaḍ, thought poorly of him; P. Prada called him a know-all and doubt-all; Giegler Pasha had him expelled from the Sudan in 1880 for plotting against the state, an impressive charge; he is said to have returned to his former calling of veterinary inspector in Egypt and to have later set up as a printer in Cairo; he died at sea while returning to Italy.

*** Zughal.** *See* MUḤAMMAD BEY KHĀLID ZUGHAL.

Zuhrab Pasha, Sir Edward Henry (1850–1909), farīq of the Egyptian army; born at Brusa in Anatolia and educated in Constantinople, he was an aide-de-camp to Prince Ḥasan in the Egyptian–Abyssinian war, 1875–6, and to Lord Wolseley in the Nile campaign, 1884–5; promoted farīq, 1905, he was under-secretary of state for war, 1893–1905 when ill health compelled his retirement.

*** Zurbuchen, J . . .** (–1881), Swiss physician; he was stationed at Wādī Ḥalfā as a medical inspector in the Egyptian Government medical service when C. G. Gordon Pasha, who met him at al-Ubaiyaḍ in 1879, appointed him principal medical officer in Dār Fūr; R. C. von Slatin Pasha, who travelled with him from al-Ubaiyaḍ to Dāra, described him as having a long, black beard and spectacles; he died suddenly on his return to Khartoum.

NOTES AND CORRECTIONS

Figures preceding notes indicate the pages referred to.

NOTES AND CORRECTIONS

ix. 'Āmil. l.2, *add* The Mahdi introduced the term in place of Amīr in 1883

ix. Bāshī. l.5, *read* Maghāriba

x. Bey. l.9, *add* The title became extinct in Egypt after 1952, though it is still, like Pasha, used informally by servants as a term of respect

x. Efendī. l.4, *for* now *read* subsequently; l.9, *add* since about 1945 the term has been replaced by Saiyid, q.v.

xii. Mu'allim. l.3, *add* the term is used informally of a senior artisan instructor-foreman

xii. *Add* **Mubāshir** (Arab). Chief accountant, invariably a non-Muslim, in the Egyptian government of the Sudan, 1820–1885

xiii. Mudīr. l.6, *add* During the military regime, 1958–64, the office of provincial governor was divided between a military area commandant (*mumath thil al-ḥukūma*, literally government representtive) and a civil chairman of the provincial executive council (*ra'īs al-majlis al-tanfīdhī li'l-mudīrīya*). The succeeding parliamentary regime reunited the office by abolishing the military area commandant and altering the designation from *mudīr* to *muḥāfiẓ*

xiii. Mufattish. l.2, *add* The general-purposes district commissioner disappeared with the promulgation of the Provincial Administration law (*Qānūn idārat al-mudīriyāt*), 1960, and his duties were distributed among a variety of local government officers, including the town clerk (*ḍābiṭ majlis al-baladī*) in the larger towns and the local government inspector (*mufattish ḥukūmat al-maḥallīya*) in rural areas. The latter continues to hold all the powers formerly exercised by the district commissioner but by delegation from the various central government ministries and organs

xiii. Muqaddam. ll.1–3, *delete* Used of . . . Fur sultans; *add* Used of a subordinate officer of the Mahdist army until 1883 when the Mahdi changed the designation to Naqīb. Maqdūm, a variant of Muqaddam, was used of a vizier or senior political representative of the sultans of Darfur.

xiii. *Add* **Nā'ib** (Arab). In its legal acceptation a magistrate, judge-substitute. The term came to be used of all the judges during the Mahdist regime except of the chief judge, the Qāḍī al-Islām

xiv. Qāḍī. l.2, *add* Qāḍī al-Islām, head of the judiciary during the Mahdist period

xv. Saiyid. l.1, *add* From about 1945 universally used as the residuary equivalent of Mister, replacing Efendī

xvi. *Add* **Ustādh.** Residuary honorific for all teachers (cf. French *professeur*) and members of the professions. In formal university parlance its use is restricted to academically accredited professors, though the growing informal use of Brufisīr may herald the devaluation of Ustādh in this sense. A teacher who is academically a doctor is addressed as Duktūr. The current Egyptian practice of using Ustādh semi-jocularly in addressing, e.g., taxi drivers and bosom companions, as roughly synonymous with 'Old Boy', has not yet penetrated the Sudan

2. *Add*: **'Abbās Bey** [?Hilmi] (–1883), Egyptian official of the rank of qā'im maqām; he was a customs officer at Sawākin in 1882 when he was appointed mu'āwin to the governor general, 'Alā al-Dīn Pasha Ṣiddīq whom he accompanied on the disastrous campaign of W. Hicks Pasha against the Mahdist forces in Kordofan; he was killed with his chief on the battlefield of Shaikān (Kashgil); his diary, now in Windsor Castle library, describing the march through Kordofan, was published as 'Yawmiyāt 'Abbās Bey' (ed. 'Abd al-Raḥmān Zakī) in *Majallat al-jam'īyat al-miṣrīya li'l-darāsāt al-ta'rīkhīya*, Cairo, iii, pt. 2, 1950, pp. 71–156; there is a MS. English translation in the Sudan Archive, School of Oriental Studies, Durham.

2. 'Abbās Bey Wahbī. ll.5–7, *delete* his diary . . . Omdurman

4. 'Abd Allāh al-Dūma. l.1 *and passim for* al Fāshar *read* al-Fāshir

5. 'Abd Allāh Jād Allāh. l.1, *for* –1929) *read* –1961); l.4, *add* he died at Omdurman

5. 'Abd Allāhi Muḥammad Tūrshain, Khalīfat al-Mahdī. l.1, *name to read* 'Abd Allāhi Muḥammad Khalīfat al-Ṣiddīq; l.40, *delete* on, *add* at Abu Rukba near

7. 'Abd Allāh ibn Sa'd ibn abū Sarḥ. l.1, *for* abū *read* abī

10. 'Abd al-Ḥalīm Musā'd wad al-Hāshimī. l.5, *here and passim for* Najūmī *read* Nujūmī

14. 'Abd al-Qādir wad umm Maryam. l.1, *read* Maryūm

14. 'Abd al-Qādir Muḥammad 'Abd al-Raḥmān. l.13, *for* Muḍāwī *read* Muḍawwī

17. 'Abd al-Raḥmān wad al-Najūmi. ll.1,14, *read* Nujūmī

23. Abū Qarja. *Insert cross reference*: Abū Qarja. *See* Muḥammad 'Uthmān abū Qarja

23. Abū'l Qāsim Aḥmad Hāshim. l.11, *add* his writings include a diwan, *Rawḍ al-ṣafā' fī madḥ al-Muṣṭafā* ( ); *see* al-Muddath thir abū' l-Qāsim Hāshim, *Fatḥ dhi'l'marāhim fī ta'rīkh . . . Abū' l-Qāsim Aḥmad Hāshim* (Cairo 1946)

24. Abū Sin. ll.1–9 *and passim for* Sin *read* Sinn; *for* 'Awad *read* 'Awaḍ

25. Adam Dabbalū. l.1, *read* Adam umm Dabbalū

27. Adham Pasha al-'Arifī. l.1, *name to read* Adam Pasha al-'Arīfī; l.19, *add* he is said to have come from the 'Arīfīya branch of the Dār Ḥāmid tribe of Central Kordofan in spite of his nickname al-Taqalāwī, from Taqalī, a Nuba kingdom

27. 'Adlān. l.1, *insert* Nāṣra 'Adlān

28. Agati, Pietro. l.12, *for* 'Pietrino' *read* 'Pierino'

29. Aḥmad wad 'Alī wad Aḥmad. l.2, *after* was *add* a brother of Ḥāmid wad 'Alī wad Aḥmad and; l.7, *delete words* he . . . stead, *add* Aḥmad was appointed governor of al-Qaḍārif

30. Aḥmad al-'Awwām. l.5, *delete and add* siege he wrote a sympathetic treatise on the authenticity of the claims of Muḥammad Aḥmad al-Mahdī entitled *al-Risālat al-musammāh bi nasīḥat al-'Awwām*; l.8, *for* history *read* work

31. Aḥmad Bey Dafa'Allāh. l.1, *add after name* al-'Awaḍī

33. Aḥmad al-Hūdai. l.1, *read* Hudai; l.2, *read* Yāwar

34. Aḥmad Ismā'īl al-Azharī. l.3, *after* al-Ubaiyaḍ *add* second son of Ismā 'īl 'Abd Allāhi al-Walī; l.6, *read* Mālikite

35. Aḥmad al-Makāshfī. l.1, *read* Aḥmad al-Mikāshfī

35. Aḥmad Pasha Manliklī. l.5, *read* Kavālalî

39. Aḥmad Sulaimān. l.1, *date to read* –1891)

39. Aḥmad al-Sunnī. l.10, *add* his son Ibrāhīm al-Sunnī was also 'umda of Wad Madanī retiring in 1936

40. Aḥmad al-Ṭaiyib wad al-Bashīr. l.1, *add date of birth* (*c.* 1742; l.12, *add* entitled *al-Ku'ūs al-mutra'a fī manāqib al-sādat al-arba'a* (Cairo, 1959), and a biography, *Azāhir al-riyāḍ fī manāqib al-'ārif bi' llāh al-Shaikh Aḥmad al-Ṭaiyib* (Khartoum, 1954)

40. Aḥmad 'Urābī Pasha. l.1, *after* Pasha *add* al-Ḥusainī, called al-Miṣrī

41. Aḥmad 'Uthmān al-Mīrghanī. l.1, *for* –1926) *read* –1928); l.3, *for* al-Ḥasan 'Uthmān *read* 'Uthmān al-Ḥasan, called al-Aqrab

41. Aḥmad Pasha abū Widān. l.1, *for* Widān *read* Adhān

45. 'Alī 'Awaḍ al-Karīm abū Sin. l.2, *for* brother *read* son

45–46. 'Alī Dīnār Zakariyā Muḥammad al-Faḍl. l.29, *add* in his letters preserved in the Public Record Office, Khartoum, he followed a simplified form of Ottoman usage; he styled himself *ḥaḍarat jallālat*

amīr al-mu'minīn fī Dār Fūr al-Sūdān and cited his royal genealogy; he published a *diwān al-madīḥ fī-madḥ al-nabī al-milīḥ* (Khartoum, 1331/1913); see A. B. Theobald, *Ali Dinar, last Sultan of Darfur* (1965)

47. **'Alī wad Ḥilū K̲h̲alīfat al-Mahdī.** l.1, *name to read* 'Alī ibn Muḥammad Ḥilū K̲h̲alīfat al-Fārūq, called 'Alī wad Ḥilū

47. **'Alī Jaifūn.** l.1, *for* Jaifūn *read* Jifūn; *dates to read* (1812–98); l.15, *delete* sāg̲h̲ qōl ag̲h̲āsi, *add* binbāshī; *see* 'Umar Ṭūsūn, *Buṭūlat al-urtat al-sūdānīya al-miṣrīya fī ḥarb al-Maksīk* (Alexandria, 1933)

48. **'Alī Julla.** 1,16, *add* he died at Mujlad

51. **'Alī al-Rūbī Pasha.** l.12, *add* he died at Sawākin where his tomb stands

54. **Amery Bey, Harold François Saphir.** l.6, *after* published *add English-Arabic vocabulary for the use of officials* (Cairo, 1905), and

55. **al-Amīn Muḥammad al-Ḍarīr.** l.1, *name to read* Muḥammad al-Amīn al-Ḍarīr; l.6, *read mumayyiz*; l.10, *name to read* al-Amīn Muḥammad al-Ḍarīr

58-59. **Arakil Bey Nubar.** l.1, *name and dates to read* Arakil Bey Abro (1832–75)

60. **Arendrup, Søren Adolph.** l.1, *dates to read* (1834–75)

62. **'Asākir wad abū Kalam.** l.1, *for* abū *read* abī

63. **Aumont, Louis-Marie-Joseph.** l.2, *date of death to read* –81)

68-69. **Baker Pasha, Sir Samuel White.** l.8, *for* Ninian *read* Finian

70. **Bak̲h̲īt Bey Batrākī.** l.13, *add see* 'Umar Ṭūsūn, *Buṭūlat al-urtat al-sūdānīya al-miṣrīya fī ḥarb al-Maksīk* (Alexandria, 1933)

72. **Bankes, William John.** l.3, *for* Sennar *read* Dār al-Sukkōt

75. **Bas̲h̲īr Bey Kanbal.** l.1 *and passim read* Kanbāl

76. **Baumgarten.** l.1, *name to read* Baumgärtner

77. **Beltrame, Giovanni.** ll.8–9, *delete* came back … died, *add* was appointed superior of the Mazza institutions, 1900, and died at Verona

80. **Binder, Franz.** l.1, *dates to read* (1824–75); ll.4–5, *delete* he was acting … 1859; l.9, *add* he died at Borberek near Hermannstadt (Sibiu) now in Rumania; see K. Binder, *Reisen und Erlebnisse eines Siebenburger Sachsen* (Hermannstadt, 1930)

83. **Bonomi, Luigi.** ll.7–9, *delete* who … Dongola, *add* who led Bonomi and his fellow-missionaries into captivity; in June 1885 he escaped from al-Ubaiyaḍ to Dongola

84. **Botta, Paul-Émile.** l.7, *for* Anchères *read* Achères

88-89. Brugsch Bey, Heinrich Karl. l.1, *for* Bey *read* Pasha

89. Brun-Rollet, Antoine. ll.19–20, *delete* in 1856–7 . . . died, *add* he died in Khartoum

95-96. Capellen, Henriette Marie Louise van Steengracht. l.1, *add date of birth* (1796–

96. Casanova, Lorenzo. l.1, *after* hunter *add* employed before 1869 as a keeper at the zoological gardens in the Prater, Vienna

97. Casolani, Annetto. l.1, *dates to read* (1817–66); ll.6–8 *delete* he disagreed . . . volunteering, *add* on being urged by the College of the Propaganda to hasten his departure, not having his plans ready to start from Tripoli through the Saharan oases, he resigned in favour of M. Ryllo who had chosen the Nile route, and volunteered

99-100. Chermside Bey, Sir Herbert Charles. l.1, *for* Bey *read* Pasha

100. Chippendall, William Henry. l.1, *read* Chippindall

100-01. Clayton Pasha, Sir Gilbert Falkingham. l.11, *add* his papers are preserved in the Sudan Archive, School of Oriental Studies, University of Durham

101. Clot, Bey, Antoine-Barthélemi. l.7, *for* was discharged *read* resigned in disgust

102-03. Combes, Edmond. l.1, *name and dates to read* Combes, Jean Alexandre [Edmond] (1812–48); l.6, *for Jaune read Joanne*; l.12, *add* he died in Damascus

107. Cuzzi, Giuseppe. l.19, *after* Italy *add* his memoirs, edited by H. Resener, appeared as *Funfzen Jahre Gefangener des falschen Propheten* (Leipzig, 1900); ll.21–22 *delete* Zaghi . . . him, *add* see C. Zaghi, 'Gordon e il dramma di Khartum', *Riv.Stor.Ital.*, fasc. 3–4 (Rome, 1951)

110-11. Debono, Andrea. l.1, *dates to read* (1821–71); l.20, *add* see S. B. Galea, *Andrea de Bono* (Valletta, 1933)

113. Didier, Charles. l.9, *delete* died, *add* committed suicide

117. Du Couret, Louis-Laurent. l.15, *add* See R. L. Hill, 'Louis du Couret', *French Studies*, Oxford, ix, 1955, pp. 143–53

119. Ehrenberg, Christian Gottfried. l.1, *after* naturalist *add* born in Delitzsch near Leipzig

119. Elliott Smith, Sir Grafton. *Read* (*twice*) Elliot

119. Emiliani dei Danziger Bey, Francesco. l.1, *after* Francesco *add* Germanico Pietro; l.3, *after* Udine *add* in 1866, while serving in the Austrian marine artillery, he was suspected of being an Italian nationalist, arrested and sent to Dalmatia until peace was made; he went to Egypt where he worked at the Suez canal and in Cairo where in 1875;

l.12, *add* L. Messedaglia, 'Francesco Emiliani', *Ce Fastu, riv. soc. filol. friuliana*, Udine, xxvi, 1950, pp. 89–100

120-21. Escayrac de Lauture, Pierre-Henri-Stanislas d', Count. l.13, *add* See P. Durand-Lapie, *Le Comte d'Escayrac de Lauture . . . sa vie et ses oevres* (Paris, 1899)

121. Evliyā Çelebi (Evliyā Muḥammad Dervīsh). l.4, *after* 1938 *add* in modern Turkish by an editor ignorant of Sudanese topography

122. Fabricius (Favrkios) Pasha, Dimitrios. l.1, *read* Favrikios

123. al-Faḍl Ḥasana. l.1, *read* Faḍl al-Ḥasana

123-24. Faiyid Muḥammad. l.9, *to read* stands in Shāri' al-Jāma' a (formerly Shāri' Ghūrdūn); on his tomb, however, his name is recorded as Muḥammad Faiyid

124-25. Faraj Pasha Muḥammad al-Zainī. l.23, *add* see 'Umar Ṭūsūn, *Buṭūlat al-urta al-sūdānīya al-miṣrīya fī ḥarb al-Maksīk* (Alexandria, 1933)

130. Friend Pasha, Sir Lovick Bransby. ll.4–5, *delete* in the . . . 1902–6 *and add* 1900–04, and of Egyptian public works, 1905

133. Gedge, Joseph. ll.6–7, *for* Gondokoro *read* Tawfīqīya

134. Geyer, Franz Xaver. l.9, *read* Trocmade

135. al-Ghazzālī Aḥmad Khawwāf. l.1, *delete* Khawwāf, *add* Khawf

141. Gostner, Josef. ll.3–5, *delete and add* White Nile with I. Knoblehar, 1853; on Knoblehar's death, 1858, he was appointed pro-vicar apostolic; he died in Khartoum after only three days in office and was succeeded by M. Kirchner; he had studied drawing when a youth; l.8, *add* J. C. Mitterrützner wrote a short life in *Ein Blatt der Erinnerung an die Missionäre aus* Tirol, 1853–1882 (Brixen, 1890)

143. Grigolini, Teresina. l.1, *add date of birth* (1853–; ll.7–8, *read* Kokorembas

144-45. Haggard Bey, Andrew Charles Parker. l.11, *add* he was a brother of Sir Henry Rider Haggard the novelist; a third brother, Edward Arthur (1860–1925) also a novelist, served at Sawākin in the British army, 1885–6

147. Ḥamad al-Nīl al-Raiyaḥ. ll.4–5, *delete* and his . . . Nile, *add* where his tomb stands prominently in the cemetery named after him

147-48. Ḥamdān abū 'Anja. l.1, *date of death to read* –89)

148. Ḥāmid 'Alī. *Delete* ll. 1–4, *add* Ḥāmid wad 'Alī wad Aḥmad (–1899), Mahdist amir, a Ta'ā'ishī by tribe, brother of Aḥmad wad 'Alī wad Aḥmad; a loyal officer of the Khalīfa 'Abdullāhi he served in several big battles of the day and was governor of Kassala, 1888–93; he was killed at Umm Dibaikarāt along with his leader

149. Hamilton, William Richard. ll.6–7, *for Aegyptian Monuments read Aegyptiaca*

150. Hammām (or Hummām) abū Yūsuf. l.1, *name to read* Humām (without variant)

152. Hartmann, Robert. l.2, *after* mountains; *add* in 1859

158. Ḥasan Pasha Rā'fat Asitānlī. l.1, *name and dates to read* Ḥasan Pasha Rā'fat Asitānalī *otherwise* Incirköylü Ḥasan Paşa Refet (1793–1901); l.10, *add* this remarkable Caucasian lived to be a farīq of the Egyptian army and retired from the Ottoman army in 1887 at the age of 94; *See* Incirköylü Hasan Refet Paşa in *Türkiye Ansiklopedisi* Ankara, iii, 1956

159. al-Ḥasan Sa'd al-'Abbādī. l.1, *read* Sa'd; l.10, *delete, add* book by him, popularly called *al-Risālat al-'Abbādī*, a defence of the Mahdi's teaching, was printed in 1888

161. Ḥasīb al-Ṣiddīq. l.1, *add after name* al-Amīn al-Majdhūb

161. Hay, Robert. ll.3–4, *delete* whom . . . England, *add* Kolitza, daughter of Alexander Psarake, a chief magistrate of Apadhulo,

162. Hedenborg, Johan. ll.17–18, *delete* he published . . . 1843, *add* only vol. I of his *Resa i Egypten* (Stockholm, 1843) was published and this contains no account of his journeys in the Sudan; for a life with full bibliography *see* P. F. Wahlberg in *Lefnadsteckningar öfver K. Vet.* akad:s *Ledamöter*, Bd. 1, (Stockholm, 1870)

164. Heuglin, Theodor von. l.13, *after* 1870–1 *add* and the Red Sea hinterland of the Sudan in 1874

166. Hood, Sir Horace Lambert Alexander. l.3, *read Nāṣir*

167-68. Hunt, Leigh S. . . J. . . l.12, *read* Mumtāz

168-69. Ḥusain Ibrāhīm wad al-Zahra. l.1, *read* al-Zahrā' (–1895); l.9, *for* 1892 *read* 1894

171. Ibrāhīm 'Abd al-Dāfi'. ll.10–11, *read* Shaikh Muḥammad al-Amīn al-Ḍarīr; l.11, *add* two variants of the above MS. have been published: *Ta'rīkh mulūk al-Sūdān*, ed. Makkī Shibaika (Khartoum, 1947); *Makhṭūta kātib al-Shūna* [i.e., Aḥmad b. al-Ḥājj 'Alī], ed. Shāṭir Buṣailī 'Abd al-Jalīl (Cairo, 1961); a précis in English is in H. A. MacMichael, *A History of the Arabs in the Sudan*, ii, Cambridge, 1922, pp. 354–430

172. Ibrāhīm wad 'Adlān. l.1, *name and date to read* Ibrāhīm Muḥammad 'Adlān (–1890); l.4, for 1889 *read* 1886

174. Ibrāhīm Bey al-Milīh. l.1, *for* –1904) *read* –1903)

176. Ibrāhīm al-Nūr Ibrāhīm al-Jaraifāwī. l.1 *and passim read* Jiraifāwī; l.3, *after* Omdurman *add* 1890–93

177. Ibrāhīm Bey Rushdī. l.1, *after* Rushdī *add* al-'Atabānī

178. Idrīs 'Adlān Muḥammad abū'l-Kailak. l.1, *date to read* (–1854); l.8, after Dafa' Allāh *add* Aḥmad

180. Ilyās Pasha Aḥmad Umm Birair. l.1, *for* Aḥmad *read* Muḥammad

180-81. Inger, Alexander. l.1, *name and date to read* Inger, Karl (1868–1935); l.32, *add* See G. N. Sanderson, 'Emir Suleyman ibn Inger Abdullah', *Sudan Notes and Records*, Khartoum, xxxv, 1954, pp. 22–74

183. Ismā'il 'Abd Allāhi al-Walī. l.1, *for* –1863) *read* –1864); l.8, *after* al-Saiyid *add* Muḥammad

183. Ismā'il Pasha Aiyūb. l.39, *add* see obit, by O. Abbate, Bull. Soc. Khédiviale Géogr., Cairo, ii, 1885, pp. 614–15

184. Ismā'il al-Azharī. *Delete notice, add* Ismā'il Aḥmad al-Azharī (1868–1947), mufti of the Sudan, 1924–32; by birth a Bidairi of the Dahmashīya branch he was a grandson of Ismā'īl al-Azharī, the great *walī* who lived and taught in al-Ubaiyaḍ; himself a judge of the Islamic law he first served in the provinces and was later appointed an inspector of the Islamic law courts, finally mufti; Ismā'īl al-Azharī the statesman is his grandson and al-Saiyid Muḥammad 'Uthmān al-Mīrghanī, shaikh of the Ismā'īlīya brotherhood (d. 1949) was his nephew.

185. Ismā'īl Ḥaqqī Pasha abū Jabal. ll.20–21, *delete* in which . . . Jabal

185. Ismā'īl Kāmil Pasha. l.1, *for* 1821 read 1822

187. Ismā'īl Pasha Ṣādiq. l.1, *for* Ṣādiq *read* Ṣiddīq

189. al-Jadail Muḥammad Jailī. l.1, *read* al-Jidail

191. Jamāl al-Dīn al-Afghānī. l.5, *read al-'Urwat al-Wuthqā*

194. Junker, Wilhelm. l.1, *after* Junker *add* Johann

196. Kanbal, called al-Malik Kanbal. l.1, *name to read* Kanbāl ibn Sha'ūs, called al-Malik Kanbāl

196. Kanbal Ḥamad. l.1, read Kanbāl Ḥamad

196. Kanfu Adam. ll.1–2, *delete* dajazmach . . . Tana, *add* dajjach of Kwara, Chelga and other frontier districts facing the Sudan

196-7. Karam Allāh Muḥammad Kurkusāwi. l.1 *and passim, read* Kurqusāwī

200. Khalīfa. ll.2–3, *for* Muḥammad . . . Mahdī *read* Muḥammad Sharīf ibn Ḥāmid; l.15, *read* Shukkaba

201. al-Khātim wad Mūsā. l.1, *read* al-Khatīm

203. Kirchner, Matthias. l.1, *add date* (1822– ; l.2, *delete* a member . . . Order; l.3, *read* arch-diocese; l.9, *after* Knoblehar *add* and J. Gostner

205. Klancnik, Jan. l.1, *after* from *add* Wippach in

205-06. Knoblehar (Knoblecher), Iğnaz. l.6, *delete* entering . . . Order; l.28, *for* M. Kirchner *read* J. Gostner

207. Kovalevsky, Eğor Petrovitch. l.1, *date to read* –1868)

209. Lambert Bey, Charles. l.1, *after* Charles *add* Joseph; l.7, *for* Lefèvre *read* Lefebvre

210. Lefèvre. *Delete* l.1, *add* Lefebvre, Louis (1790–1839) French mining engineer; born at Falaise (Calvados) he was educated at the École Polytechnique and in 1810 entered the French service des mines; he was one of the party of

219. Lyons, Sir Henry. l.1, *after* Henry *add* George

222. Madībbū Bey 'Alī. l.11, *read* Kurqusāwī

224. Maḥmūd wad Aḥmad. l.1, *for* nephew *read* cousin; l.3, *for* 1891 *read* 1890

224. Maḥmūd Aḥmad Ḥamdī al-Falakī Pasha. l.8, *add* See Khair al-Dīn al-Zuruklī *al-A'lām*, Cairo, 2nd ed., viii, 1956, pp. 39–40, and plate 1326

226. Maḥmūd wad Khalīl wad 'Abd al-Wāḥid. l.1, *name to read* Maḥmūd wad 'Abd al-Qādir

228. Maillet, Benoît de. l.1, *dates to read* (1656–1738)

228. al-Makkī Ismā'īl al-Walī. l.1, *name to read* Muḥammad al-Makkī Ismā'īl

232. Mark. ll.1–2, *delete* one . . . Christ

233-34. Mason Bey, Alexander McComb. l.27, *add* see an obit. by O. Abbate Pasha, *Bull. Soc. Khédiviale Géogr.*, Cairo, v, 1902, pp. 61–66

234-35. Mather, Sir William. l.1, *delete* cotton spinner, *add* engineer

236. Maxwell, Sir William. l.2, *delete* newspaper, *add* latterly of the *Daily Mail*

238. Miani, Giovanni. l.17, *add* his manuscript diaries of his travels are preserved in the Civico Museo di Storia Naturale, Venice; *see* A. Capellini, *Giovanni Miani, ricordi biografici e note di viaggio* (Rovigo, 1927), and C. Cimegotto, *Giovanno Miani, esploratore* (Padua, 1930)

240. Mitterrützner, Johann Chrysostomus Josef. *Delete notice and add after name* (1818–1903), Austrian theologian and linguist; born at Tils near Bressanone (Brixen) in 1843 he entered the Congregation of the Lateran Canons who follow the rule of St. Augustine, and in Rome in 1856 came under the influence of I. Knoblehar, pro-vicar apostolic of Central Africa; though he never visited the Sudan he compiled grammars of the Bari and Dinka languages; he died at Neustift near Brixen; he wrote *Die Dinka Sprache* (Brixen, 1866), *Die Sprache der Bari* (Brixen, 1867), a life of A. Haller, a missionary who died in Khartoum (Innsbruck, 1855) and of I. Knoblehar (Brixen, 1869)

242. Mosgan, Bartholomäus. l.3, *delete* the first, *add* pro-

243. Muḍawī 'Abd al-Raḥmān. l.1 *and passim read* al-Muḍawwī

244-45. Muḥammad 'Abd al-Mut'āl Aḥmad al-Idrīsī. l.3, *after* al-Idrīs *add* al-Fāsī

245. Muḥammad 'Abduh. l.1, *for* (*c*. 1849– *read* (1850–

245. Muḥammad Bey 'Abūd. ll.3–4, *delete* an officer . . . Force, *add* a retired *farīq* of the Sudanese army who was head of the military government, 1958–64; the family is descended from the hereditary *mulūk* of the Suwārāb branch of the Shā'iqīya tribe

245. Muḥammad Adam Sa'dūn. l.5, *read* Arba'at

246. Muḥammad Bey Aḥmad. l.12, *for* 1911 *read* 1909

247. Muḥammad Aḥmad ibn al-Saiyid 'Abd Allāh, al-Mahdī. l.9, *delete* Ismā'īlīya, *add* Sammānīya; l.40, *delete* Tūrshain; *last line delete*, *add* of his grandson al-Saiyid al-Hādī ibn 'Abd al-Raḥmān al-Mahdī

248-9. Muḥammad Aḥmad Bey abū Sin, called Ḥārdallū. l.1, *for* Sin *read* Sinn; l.16, *add* see al-Mubārak Ibrāhīm and 'Abd al-Majīd 'Abidīn, *al-Ḥārdallū shā'ir al-Buṭāna* (Khartoum, 1957)

251. Muḥammad Bey Almās. l.1, *add date of death*, 1878; l.3, *for* 1834 *read* 1844; l.11, *add* he died in Khartoum; See Umar Ṭūsūn, *Buṭūlat al-urtat al-sūdānīya al-miṣrīya fī ḥarb al-Maksīk*, (Alexandria, 1933)

252. Muḥammad al-Amīn al-Ḍarīr. l.1, *name to read* Amīn Muḥammad al-Ḍarīr; l.5, *delete* about

253. Muḥammad al-Badawī. l.1, *name and dates to read* Muḥammad al-Badawī Nuqud (*c*. 1850–1911); l.9, *delete* where, *add* in 1895 as *qāḍī al-islām* in place of Ḥusain Ibrāhīm wad al-Zahrā'; here

253. Muḥammad Badr al-'Ubaid. l.3, *read* Jailānīya; l.11, *add*: *see* Ibrāhīm 'Abd al-Razzāq, *al-Shaikh al-'Ubaid wad Badr* (Khartoum, 1961)

253-54. Muḥammad Bello Mai Wurno. ll.3–4, *after* sultan *add* semicolon; *delete* who, *add* Attahira

260. Muḥammad al-Khair 'Abd Allāh Khūjalī. *Delete* l. 12, *add* he was governor of Dongola, Berber and the Ja'liyīn until 1886 when he was deprived in turn of Dongola and Berber, and the

261-62. Muḥammad Bey Khālid Zughal. l.1, *for* Zughal *read* Zuqal

262. Muḥammad Khashm al-Mūs Pasha. l.1, *after* commanded *add* the troops on board; *after* steamers *add* under Muḥammad Nuṣḥī Pasha

262. Muḥammad Bey Khusraw al-Daramalī, al-Daftardār. l.28, *for* Sennār *read* Wad Madanī

265-66. Muḥammad Ma'nī Bey. l.1, also rendered Mu'annī

267-68. Muḥammad Nādī Pasha. l.8, *read* 1880–83

268. Muḥammad al-Nūr wad Ḍaif Allāh. l.6, *delete* Ṣādiq, *add* Siddīq Aḥmad; ll.15–16, *delete* deputy . . . 1877; l.17, *read* 1881–3

269. Muḥammad Rāsikh Bey. ll.15–16, *for* 1877 *read* 1877–88 l.17, *read* 1881–3

273. Muḥammad al-Sharīf Khalīfat al-Mahdī. l.1, *name to read* Muḥammad Sharīf ibn Ḥāmid; 1-15, *read* Shukkāba

277-78. Muḥammad ibn 'Umar ibn Sulaimān al-Tūnisī. l.23, *add see* M. Streck, al-Tūnisī [etc.], *Encyclopaedia of Islam*, 2nd ed.

278. Muḥammad 'Uthmān al-Ḥājj Khālid. l.1, *after* Khālid *add* al-'Umarābī

278-79. Muḥammad 'Uthmān al-Mīrghanī II. l.23, *add* Zaghlūl Muḥammad al-Waṭanī, *Abṭāl al- aKhtmīya* (Cairo [ ])

281-82. Munzinger Pasha, Johann Albert Werner. l.43, *add* See F. Wild, in *Von Kairo nach Massaua*, Olten, 1879, pp. VIII–XXI; A. Kitt, *Werner Munzinger Pascha*, Basel, 1912

283-84. Mūsā Pasha Ḥamdī. l.2, *for* mīrlivā *read* farīq

285. Mūsā Madibbū. l.3, *for* al-Nūr . . . 'Anqara *read* Ḥamdān Abū 'Anja

285. Musā'd Jaidūn. l.1, *for* Jaidūn *read* Qaidūm

293. Na'ūm Bey Shuqair. l.25, *add* he died in Cairo; *See* Jamāl al-Dīn al-Shayyāl, *al-Ta'rīkh wa' l-mu'arrikhūn* fī Miṣr (Cairo, 1958), p. 184

294. Neufeld, Karl. l.1, *add date of death* 1918); ll.12–13, *delete* his . . . unknown, *add* he served the Turco-German cause in Syria and Arabia, 1916–17 and probably died in Germany

296-97. al-Nūr al-Jaraifāwī. l.1, *name to read* al-Nūr Ibrāhīm al-Jiraifāwī

297. al-Nūr Bey Muḥammad 'Anqara. l.1, *delete question mark*

297. Nyigilö. l.1, *for* c. 1860) *read* –1862); l.3, *for* 1845 *read* 1854

298. Ohrwalder, Josef. l.1, *dates to read* (1856–1913); l.1, *read* Chincarini

302. Parkyns, Mansfield Harry Isham. l.11, *read* 1845–6; l.18, *add* his manuscripts are preserved in the library of the Royal Geographical Society, London

303. Pearse, Henry Hiram S. . . l.1, *add date of birth* (1845–

304. Pedemonte, Emmanuele. l.1, *dates to read* 1792–1867; l.7, *delete* doubtfully

304. Peney, Alfred. l.1, *add date of birth* (1817–

304. Pennazzi, Luigi, Count. l.1, *for* (1838– *read* (1839–

308. Potagòs, Panayótis. l.13, *delete* he left . . . manuscripts, *add* the character of this work throws doubt on the authenticity of his travels in the Sudan; F. Kontoglu wrote a brief life, in *φημισμένοι αντρες καί λησμονημένοι* (Athens, 1942, pp. 91–128

308. Pourpe, Marc. l.7, *read* McClean

310. Pruyssenaere de la Wostyne, Eugène de. l.10, *for* J. Petherick *read* D. Barthélemy

311. Purdy Bey, Erastus Sparrow. l.17, *add* See obit. by C. P. Stone, *Bull. Soc. Khédiviale Géogr.* ii, 1882, pp. 57–64

312. al-Qurashī wad al-Zain. l.1, *for* –1878) *read* –1880)

312. Rabīḥ Aghā, l.1, *read* Rābiḥ

312. Rabīḥ Faḍl Allāh. l.1, (*twice*) *read* Rābiḥ; l.4, *for* -east *read* -west; ll.10–11, *delete* fled . . . sultanate, *add* took refuge with the Azande

313. Rāfa'i. l.1, *read* Rāf'i (*c.* 1850–*c.* 1900); l.9, *delete* he . . . when, *add* in 1912

316. Reinisch, Leo. l.1, *before* Leo *add* Simon

316. Reinthaler, Johann de Ducla. l.1, *read* (1824–62); l.2, *after* he *add* was born in Burgau in Styria and; l.4, *delete* the Jesuit; l.6, *delete* from the Jesuits

316. Reitz, Konstantin. l.8, *delete* Khartoum, *add* Doka

317-18. Ricci, Alessandro. l.2, *read* Siena

318. Rifā'a Bey Rāf'i. l.1, *after* Rāf'i *add* Badawī

319. Rosellini, Ippolito. l.1, *Christian names to read* Niccolo Francesco Ippolito Baldessare

320-21. Roveggio, Antonio Maria. l.3, *for* Colonia *read* Cologna; l.13, *delete* on, *add* shortly after having been carried from; l.15, *add* G. Barra, *Quando l'Africa chiama, biografia di Mons. Antonio M. Roveggio*, (Bologna, 1959)

323. Ryllo, Maximilien. l.1, *add* (1802–; l.2, *after* born *add* at Podorosko; l.4, *for* Collegio Urbano *read* College of the Propaganda;

l.13, *add* in 1901 his body was exhumed and reburied in the Jesuit compound at Matariya near Cairo

325. Sa'īd Bey Juma'. l.1, read Sayyid Bey Jum'a; l.11, *for* commander *read* second in command; l.13, *for* second in command *read* chief

328-29. Ṣāliḥ Pasha al-Mak. l.1, *for* Mak *read* Makk; l.10, *read* Mikāshfī

329. Salīm I. l.3, *delete words* within *to end* of paragraph, *add*, about 1520 sent a force up the Nile valley, defeated a Funj army at Ḥannik and, according to Evliyā Çelebī, occupied the fortresses of Aswan, Ibrim and Sai whose Bosnian and Hungarian garrisons mingled with the inhabitants and left ethnic traces in Nubia; during the reign of his successor, Sulaimān I, Özdemir Pasha, Ottoman beylerbey of the Yemen, occupied Sawākin and Muṣawwa'

330. Salīm Qapūdān. l.8, *for* south *read* north

332. Santoni, Licurgo Alois. l.1, *delete* (*fl.* 1865–98); *add* (1846–1914); l.7, *after* Society *add* he retired to Italy and died at Pisa; l.9, *add*: *see* a short biography by G. del Guerra in *Scientia Veterum*, Pisa, iv, Sept. 1955, pp. 2–4

337. Shahīn Pasha Kinj. l.2, *for* Turkish *read* Circassian

338. Sha'ūs. l.17, *add* he died before 1827/8; Kanbāl ibn Sha'ūs was his son

338-39. Sienkiewics, Hendryk. l.1, *read* Sienkiewicz; l.2, *read* *Puszczy*

339-40. Slatin Pasha, Sir Rudolf Karl von, Baron. l.1, Christian names to read Rudolf Anton [Carl]; l.3 *to read* near Vienna of a Catholic family; l.7, *for* continue his military career *read* perform his military service; l.36, *before* Austrian *add* prisoners of war division of the; l.38, *for* 1931 *read* 1926; l.40, *add* his papers are preserved in the Sudan Archive, School of Oriental Studies, University of Durham; *see* R. L. Hill, *Slatin Pasha* (1965)

343-44. Stanton Bey, Edward Alexander. l.1, *for* Bey *read* Pasha

344. Stella, Giovanni. l.1, *after* Giovanni *add* Giacinto; l.2, *delete* Piedmontese, *add* Ligurian from Carcare, Savona; ll.15–18, *delete* he is said . . . grief, *add* he resigned his orders and married a lady of the district; his attempts to form an agricultural colony failed and in 1869 he was expelled from Keren by J. A. W. Munzinger Pasha, Egyptian governor of Muṣawwa'

345 Steudner, Herrmann. l.4, *delete* at Wau, *add* probably on the bank of the Getti (Gete) river near Bisellia (Buṣailīya)

348. Sulaimān Bey Amīn abū 'Izz al-Dīn. l.11, *read* *fī Sūriyā*; *for* 1925 *read* 1929

351. Surūr, Daniele Deng. l.1, *add date* (1865–; l.6, *after* Beirut *add* and he studied at the College of the Propaganda in Rome, 1877–83

353. al-Ṭāhir al-Ṭaiyib Qamar al-Dīn al Majdhūb. l.1, *for* –89) *read* –90)

353. al-Tai Sa'īd. l.1, *read* Ṭayi al-Sīd

354. al-Ṭaiyib Aḥmad Hāshim. l.9, *add* Aḥmad al-Bashīr al-Ṭaiyib Hāshim edited a diwan of his poems and prose writings, *al-Azhār al-Shadhilīya fī madḥ khair al-barrīya* (Khartoum, 1963)

357. Terranova, Filippo. ll.1–2, *for* Somacatino *read* Sommatino

359-60. Tinné, Alexandrina Petronella Francina. l.1, *name and dates to read* Tinné, Alexandrine Pieternella Françoise (1835–69)

362-63. Ulivi, Nicola. l.3, *after* Tuscan *add* he came to the Sudan as a *sous-aide pharmacien* in the Egyptian army and was stationed at Khartoum in 1838;

364. 'Umar al-Makāshfī. ll.1–2, *read* Mikāshfī

366. Umm Maryam. l.1 *and passim to read* Umm Maryūm

366. Unsā II wad Nāsir. l.1, *read* Ūnsā

367. 'Uthmān Azraq. l.1, *name to read* 'Uthmān Muḥammad 'Īsā, called 'Uthmān Azraq

367-68. 'Uthmān abū Bakr Diqna. l.1, *for* abū *read* ibn abī

369. 'Uthmān Ḥishmat. l.1, *read* 'Uthmān Bey Ḥishmat

370. 'Uthmān Shaikh al-Dīn 'Abd Allāhi al-Ta'ā'ishī. l.1, *name and dates to read* 'Uthmān ibn al-Khalīfa 'Abd Allāhi (*c.* 1874–1900); l.6, *add* he was given the title Shaikh al-Dīn, 1890, and, after the revolt of the *Ashrāf*, 1891, commanded the newly-augmented body-guard of the Khalīfa 'Abd Allāhi

371. Vaissière, Joseph-Marie-François. l.1, *for* –*c.* 1845) *read* –1841); *delete* ll.23–27, *add* he died in Khartoum leaving a daughter, Judith Rose, born 1837 and christened at the Roman Catholic mission, Khartoum, 1842

372. Vaudey, Alexandre. *Delete* l.8, *add* in 1852 and was the first to hold office there; criticisms of his arbitrary acts led to his resignation in 1854 and the closure of the pro-consulate

373. Venturini, Elisabetta. l.1, *add date* (1857–; l.7, *read* Chincarini

373-74. Vinco, Angelo. l.3, *read* apostolic pro-vicar

375. Wad al-Baṣīr. l.10, *delete second reference*

376-77. Wellcome, Sir Henry Soloman. l.1, *read* Solomon

378. Whitehead, George O. l.1, *Christian names to read* George Offley

379. Wilson, Sir Charles. l.1, *name to read* Wilson, Sir Charles William

380. Wingate, Orde Charles. l.2, *for* R.F. *read* F.R.

382. Wright, Henry Charles Seppings. l.1, *add year* of birth (1849–

386-87. Yūsuf Muḥammad al-Amīn al-Hindī. l.14, *read* Būrrī

387. Yūsuf abu Shara. l.1, *read* Shāra

388. Zain al-'Abidīn. l.1, *name to read* Muḥammad 'Alī Zain al-'Abidīn

389. Zakī Ṭamal. l.1, *read* al-Zākī Ṭamal

389. Zakī 'Uthmān. l.1, *read* Muḥammad al-Zākī 'Uthmān

390. Zubair Dīyāb al-Malik. l.12, *for* shaikh *read* 'umda

391. Zucchinetti, Paolo Virginio. *Delete* ll.1–3 *and add* Zucchinetti, Paolo Virginio (1835–*c.* 1890), Italian adventurer; born at Suna di Pallanza (Novara) he graduated from the university of Turin in law, medicine and veterinary science; a volunteer under Garibaldi he afterwards set up in Rome as an advocate and about 1875 joined the service of the Egyptian Govern-; l.18, *add* he wrote 'Mes voyages au Bahr-el-Gebel, Bahr-el-Ghazal et Nouba', Le Caire, *Bull. Soc. Khédiviale Geogr.*, No. 11, 1881, pp. 19–52; *Souvenirs de mon séjour chez Emin Pasha el Soudani.* Le Caire, Imprimerie de l'auteur, 1890

392. Zughal. *Read* (*twice*) Zuqal

392. Zurbuchen. J. ll.1–7, *delete and add* Zurbuchen, Johannes (1844–82), Swiss physician; born at Berghorf Habkern near Interlaken he graduated in medicine and verterinary science at the university of Berne; he went to Egypt in 1870 when, after a few months in private practice he served as ship's doctor in the Khedivial Line Mediterranean fleet, and as a public health inspector in Cairo; he was principal medical officer to the Sudan Railway at Wadi Halfa, 1876–79, and principal medical officer Kordofan and Dār Fūr, 1879–80 when he was appointed head of the state medical service in the Sudan; he died of typhus in Khartoum. *See Petermanns Mitteilungen*, XXX, 1884, pp. 443–4